Worthless Mysteries

Flat Earth, the Divine Council, & the Search for the Immortal Soul

Serial Essays

Noel J Hadley

"You were in heaven, but all the mysteries of heaven had not been revealed to you, and you knew worthless ones, and these in the hardness of your hearts you have made known to the women, and through these mysteries women and men work much evil on earth."

Enoch

"As for the mysteries of God, they knew them not…"

Wisdom 2:22

"Of all men's miseries the bitterest is this: to know so much and to have control over nothing."

Herodotus, *the Histories*

CONTENTS

For Sarah,

Learning Biblical truth
(and removing the horse blinders
of human tradition)
side-by-side.

For Eric and Ira,

Perceiver to the end

And for so many friends lost along the way,

What could fill my heart with more joy
than to meet again and walk
on this pilgrims journey together?

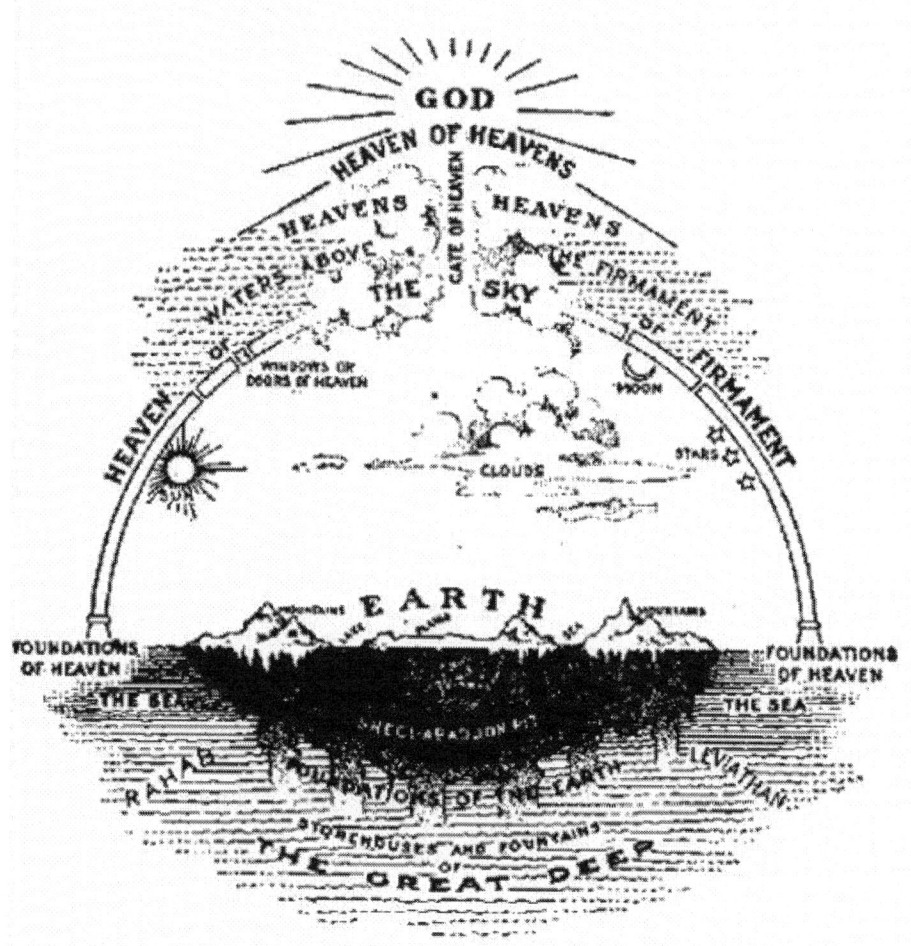

THE ANCIENT HEBREW CONCEPTION
OF THE UNIVERSE

TO ILLUSTRATE THE ACCOUNT OF CREATION AND THE FLOOD

FORWARD: DARK SPEECHES

MOSES HAD MARRIED A BLACK WOMAN. More specifically, she was a Cushite—of Ethiopian descent. For this assault on their intellect, and his father-in-law's constant mingling in Hebrew affairs, Aaron and Miriam succumbed to their pride and took umbrage. "Hath the LORD indeed spoken *only* by Moses?" They groaned with protest. "Hath He not spoken also by us?"

Moses simply records of their discord: "And the LORD heard it (Numbers 12:2)."

God did not delay correction either. He came *suddenly* unto Moses and his quarrelsome siblings, demanding a private conference among them so as not to spread their gangrenous division throughout the ranks of Israel. The pillar of cloud that led them by day and which burned as a pillar of fire by night promptly descended and stood in the door of the tabernacle. But for this particular meeting God had no apparent business or qualms with the lawgiver. It was with Aaron and Miriam, we read, on whom His anger was kindled. Surely, their legs wobbled with the sinewy strength of a wet noddle when He pronounced their names, and feebly resisted the buckling of knees when obediently complying to His demand that they "step forward."

Prophets will receive visions and dream dreams, the LORD explained, but concerning His servant Moses, "with him will I speak mouth to mouth, even apparently, and not in *dark speeches* (Numbers 12:8)."

When Aaron gazed upon Miriam, his sister was "white as snow." She had, rather abruptly, become a leper. But is it true what they say here in the west—is leprosy a thing of the past among God's children today?

Some people want to be the bride at every wedding, others the corpse at every funeral, and ever since the ink was dried on the final pages of *Revelation* our pulpits and pews have been in no short supply of those who personify the protests of Moses' envious siblings. *Hath the LORD indeed spoken only by Moses? Hath He not spoken also by us?*

The church I love—and which I obstinately refuse to give up on—is quite frankly a malodor of Greek philosophy and preconceived notions. I say this at the open risk of being held in *contempt* by the brethren and even more fearfully, in dire hope that the Lord does not call my name, demanding that I "*step forward.*" But the facts remain. Whether it is Plato's globe and the Copernican Revolution which defiantly clothes its intended esoteric purposes with the ordinances of Science; or the Mystery religions modern charismatic uprising by way of a counterfeit Holy Ghost; any one of our cultural or patriotic "high places" which we dare not aggravate; an impending damnation in mythological underworlds flavored with eternal *torment* and *unending* destruction; or the Gnostics we once feverishly hoped to liquidate but have, rather ironically, completely blindsided us with gluttonous hopes of immortality, bodiless souls freed from fleshly shackles, and a heavenly ascension to boot; it seems like everyone wants to be the mouthpiece for God.

For the God-fearing soul, everywhere he turns—be it the congregation he loves or the social media saturation which seeks to inform his beliefs on a minute-by-minute basis—he has little choice but to entangle his soul with the *spiritual* leprous rather than the *bacterial* of old while they seek to enlighten him with horse blinders of the Christian Talmud and *The Gospel According to Plato*. Even now, three millennia's beyond Mount Sanai, and nearly two-thousand years since the last of the Apostles were buried; God's mouth-piece is apparently everywhere.

In short, we have settled for *dark speeches.*

2

I AM EITHER A BRAVE OR VERY STUPID MAN for agreeing to pen these series of articles, as I am still not so old that I shan't have a few blissful decades left, that is, *if* I hadn't done this deed and attached my name to it. I do however see a glaring error in the church—in fact, there are many—and as such do willingly spoil my reputation among the *in-*crowd, even among family and friends, all in hopes that the Lord might bless my efforts and save a few—or one.

This will not be understood by most to be an effort of love, particularly where the Body of Christ is concerned. I also understand *cause and effect* well enough to know what happens when one takes a stick to a wasps nest. I shall be bruised for sure. But I am most willing, giving my very life if it comes to it, all for the sake of the Gospel.

Inevitably everyone has their own agenda. *Worthless Mysteries* has been two, almost three years in the making, and I admit, the three reoccurring topics which perform starring roles in this book, Hebrew Cosmology, Hebrew Mortalism, and the Hebrew Pantheon, is undoubtedly yet one more agenda to crowd the bookshelf. I myself am certainly far from exempt. But let me just be clear from the beginning; I am in no way advocating the gospel of "waking-up," nor do I wish to associate with the logic behind it. Such doctrine demands that we are always swimming in the darkness with an agonizing leg cramp, gasping for a fistful of air, never really knowing which *new* fact is the rightful discernment by which we must truly wake-up to in order to be saved. There are many here in the *truther* community who wish to alert you to the presence of one Luciferian lie only to supplant it immediately with another. The language is often the same. We must *"save ourselves."* And I want nothing to do with it.

Can anybody who is dead save themselves and ascend to heaven on their own? Works-based theology in all their various forms inevitably leads its contributor to the same destination—*the second death*, and it's an eternal one. Salvation only comes through the atoning sacrifice of Jesus our Lord. My fullest and only allegiance is to the cross of Christ and, far more importantly, the empty tomb which immediately precedes it. And I will not be so much as bothered to move an inch to the right or the left of this claim. I bring this up now so that there are no surprises. You can expect ample mention of my Lord throughout, as no discussion in Hebrew history, including death, the shape of creation, and the divine, is complete without its Creator.

If I woke up, and indeed I did, it was an intervention by the Holy Ghost alone—through the pages of God's Word. Not a day goes by that I am not grateful for it. I am often asked what it would take to convince me the earth is a globe or that heaven is brimming with human souls. That's a pretty tall order, since God Himself would have to take it all back. If I adhere to the joyous cosmology, it's because God's true unbroken Revelation and Testimony concerning Himself in His creation says it to be true. Feel free to call me a fool. I'm thoroughly used to it by now. But I stand firmly on the belief that God—in His kingdom, when heaven and earth finally meet and the righteous man receives his inheritance—will not bring His servants to shame.

Besides, science, *true science*, will back the Lord in the end. This I am certain of and am willing to be rebuked by God Almighty if I am falsely prophesying. By prophecy, I mean to imply a "dogmatic tradition" based on the principles of Scripture alone, certainly not the dark speeches of man. Indeed this is the *one* and *only* prophecy I have yet to make, and I hold to it—but on the basis that I am somehow a self-declared prophet. The Lord's Testimony concerning Himself and His creation has already prophesied, and will be rectified in the end. In the meantime, I will attempt to make a case for it.

If its science you're after, you won't find too much of that here. There is no shortage of debate where *that* is concerned. Nor will I hold anybody's hand and attempt to convince him or her of anything, if it's proof you're after. My loyalties lie wholly with the pages of Holy Writ, including all who subscribe to it—and so the purpose of this book is mainly two-fold. It is my intent, knowing the desperate hour in which we live, to expose the terrible Great Delusion of Ball-Earth to as many of my fellow brothers and sisters as possible using the Bible—whoever has been purposed by the Lord to open this book, perhaps out of curiosity—in hopes that their passions for the faith, as well as the joy of their salvation, may be further stoked within this flame.

And secondly, for those who have already subscribed to Hebrew Cosmology and the hope of our resurrection to come, or "*woken-up,*" if you will, I ask now and will continue to do so, that you give the Bible careful consideration, for it gave accurate Testimony all along, despite our frightful rejection of it. The Holy Spirit is calling you. Give Jesus Christ, Creator of the firmament and the heavens above another chance. He alone can cleanse you of all your sins and grant you immortality—eternal life—at the blast of the trumpet

To the rest of you who doubt the severity of my claims based on your high regard for the University and Institutions of men rather than the Inspired Word, I hereby raise my stick and *begin*.

DEATH, THE AFTERLIFE, AND THE SHAPE
OF THE EARTH ACCORDING TO JOB

1

POOR OLD JOB

"Oh that my words were written!
Oh that they were inscribed in a book!"
(Job 19:23)

FOR THE MEDIEVAL COMMENTATOR, HE WAS A LEPER, while some modern scholars' finger scurvy as the culprit. And it has been suggested that no less than fourteen diseases are attributed to him. Poor Job—as the disease laid hold of his body, eating away at his flesh, the elephantiasis twisting him almost unrecognizably into an object of repulsion, those whom he once called *friend* had clearly abandoned him. Perhaps he was simply too gruesome to behold, too offensive a misconstrued thought of moral depravity to wrestle with, and maybe they simply worried the spread of its infection, or all of the above. Regardless, there is no evidence that anything was done to heal him or that any kindness was shown in light of this disease, whatever its final diagnosis.

In the dimension of one solitary day Job lost his oxen and asses to the Sabeans, his camels to the Chaldeans, both of whom murdered his servants with the edge of the sword, and all of his children to a wind from the wilderness—practically everything he'd ever loved, invested in, or owned. Yet when it came to Job's sheep Satan spared no expense. Fire reigned down, one messenger reported, from the *haš-šā-ma-yim* in Hebrew—the third layer and penthouse of heaven. There is only one other instance in Holy Scripture when Satan is budgeted for such a shock-and-awe action among the affairs of men. Such an event will be repeated again by the false prophet of Revelation.

Job is recorded as having found no relief. His boils stood so thick and close together, blanketing him head to foot, that no inch of his flesh was immune. More precisely, Job was infected by one "bad boil." He was deprived of everything but an ash heap and a broken pot, which he used to scrape and saw at the ulcers and the lymph-like fluid which surely discharged like sap—vying for relief. The very Hebrew word *le-hithared*, which is described in Arabic as "pulling off bark from a tree," is a pain so lamentable that it is never mentioned again in the Bible. While Job sat alone in his ash heap, his wife told him to curse God and then go ahead and kill himself while he was at it.

He must have felt helpless and alone, with the meaninglessness of it all the most intolerable agony of all. And yet we shall come to find—like the manger which our Lord was born in, and the cross and the tomb which bookended his life of hardship on earth—that God has a preferred method of speaking to the contrite heart in the puss and ashes of our suffering.

2

"*From Womb to Tomb…*" SHEOL, MY HOME—*and* WORMS ARE ITS INHABITANTS

AFTER DISASTER FELL UPON THE MAN FROM UZ, we quickly read, "Job opened his mouth and cursed the day of his birth (Job 3:1)." Among his few loyal friends, Job wailed:

> 9 "Let the stars of its twilight be darkened;
>
> Let it wait for light but have none,
>
> And let it not see the breaking dawn;
>
> 10 Because it did not shut the opening of my mother's womb,
>
> Or hide trouble from my eyes.
>
> 11 Why did I not die at birth,
>
> Come forth from the womb and expire?
>
> 12 Why did the knees receive me,
>
> And why the breasts, that I should suck?"
>
> 13 "For now I would have lain down and been quiet;

I would have slept then, I would have been at rest,

14 With kings and with counselors of the earth,

Who rebuilt ruins for themselves

(Job 3:9-14)."

It is not merely Job's wish that he had been numbered among the stillborn babes, or adding insult to injury, that he had never been nursed to nutrition upon his mother's breasts. Verses 9-12 should strike our attention. Job had no delusions of grandeur, particularly where heaven was concerned. In Job's worldview, the sum of death amounted to sleep, *not* consciousness. Perhaps we argue against such concepts because we are employing the medieval church and their preference for Platonism as our filter, not the worldview of Job and the Patriarchs to follow. Beginning with verse 13, he transitioned his gaze towards the earth and, speaking nothing of the company of the righteous, longed for rest with the very kings and counselors of the earth who displayed such vanity and contempt for God as to rebuild "ruins for themselves."

A little while later in their discourse, Job returned to thoughts of his mother, particularly the fact that God had willed him to live beyond what he was willing to tolerate. If only he had been "carried from womb to tomb," except perhaps in the memory of his mother, it would have been as though he had never even existed at all.

18 "Why then have You brought me out of the womb?

Would that I had died and no eye had seen me!

19 I should have been as though I had not been,

Carried from womb to tomb."

(Job 10: 18-19)

APPARENTLY, HIS ONLY PROSPECT OF REST WAS DEATH. When he lay down at night, he told his friends, he would ask himself, "When shall I rise?" His flesh was clothed with worms and dirt. *Worms*, he said. Where Scriptural tradition has it, Job framed a recognizable third-person portrait of death. The Prophet Isaiah would later utilize Job's imagery to describe the fate of the wicked when he illustrated a scenario "where the worm dieth not." Jesus would not shy in quoting him. If only his flesh might become a buffet for the worms, then his very self would be at rest. The man from Uz described it again in slightly other terms: "So man wastes away like something rotten, like a moth-eaten garment (Job 13:28)." And yet there was only one obstacle to his ambition. As each night continued, hoping that he might close his eyes and never rise again, he found himself continually tossing until the dawn. The sun set, circled the earth, and rose again, and Sheol rejected his advances while his personal *hell* remained. To his friend he said:

4 When I lie down I say,

"When shall I arise?"

But the night continues,

And I am continually tossing until dawn.

5 My flesh is clothed with worms and a crust of dirt,

My skin hardens and runs.

(Job 7:4-5)

JOB LONGED FOR HOME. IN TIME, THE HOME he would long for was Sheol. It would be a bed, he assured his friends, which could be made in the darkness. It didn't matter if "one dies in his full strength, being wholly at ease and satisfied—his sides filled with fat, and the marrow of his bones moist," or if "another dies with a bitter soul, never even tasting anything good." Their destination was the same. "Together," he said, "they lie down in the dust, and worms cover them." To this effect, he said:

23 "One dies in his full strength,

Being wholly at ease and satisfied;

24 His sides are filled out with fat,

And the marrow of his bones is moist,

25 While another dies with a bitter soul,

Never even tasting anything good.

26 Together they lie down in the dust,

And worms cover them."

(Job 21:23-26)

Likewise, Job would be numbered among them. The pit which had swallowed his bones and the worms which feasted upon his flesh would be his family.

> [13] "If I look for Sheol as my home,
>
> I make my bed in the darkness;
>
> [14] If I call to the pit, *you are my father*;
>
> To the worm, *my mother and my sister*;
>
> [15] Where now is my hope?
>
> And who regards my hope?
>
> [16] "Will it go down with me to Sheol?
>
> Shall we together go down into the dust?"
>
> (Job 17:13-15)

Hope reveals itself as a delectable dish which Job's menu offers us. For the wicked, we shall come to find—their only hope is that they might "breathe their last." But the righteous have another hope, a face-to-face salvation, and it traverses death itself.

Even Sheol has borders.

3

THERE ARE NO NAMES AMONG THE STREET CORNERS OF FIRE *and* BRIMSTONE (JOB 18)

IT WAS BILDAD THE SHUHITE'S TURN TO SPEAK. Fire and brimstone mark the former habitation of the wicked, he told the suffering Job. To this we may *rightly* conclude, where there is fire and brimstone, there are no people. Job and his friends held no persuasion to the doctrine of eternal torment—a necessary component of the immortal soul. To even think a person's soul might reside *eternally* among the brimming smoke of an unquenchable flame was not a topic for conversation. For Bildad, the roots of the wicked man are dried up. His branch is cut off. The light in his tent is darkened, and his lamp goes out above him. He shall not be mentioned in the street, nor maintain a name to be remembered by. More precisely, the very memory of him will perish from the earth. The language of Bildad is purely Biblical.

¹⁵ "There dwells in his tent nothing of his;

      Brimstone is scattered on his habitation.

¹⁶ "His roots are dried below,

      And his branch is cut off above.

¹⁷ "Memory of him perishes from the earth,

      And he has no name abroad.

¹⁸ "He is driven from light into darkness,

      And chased from the inhabited world."

(Job 18:15-18)

Bildad's words gaze forward to unwritten dates and alien landscapes. They perfectly frame the *total* destruction of a wicked people, first at Sodom and Gomorrah, and far more tragically, the expulsion of Israel's ten tribes. In fact, the whole of Scripture falls into alignment with his worldview. "He shall be driven from light into darkness, and chased out of the world," Bildad adds.

It is the first Biblical reference to the *outer* darkness.

Here we might also incorporate another theme of Biblical importance. The inheritance of the righteous was disclosed. The wicked will receive their inheritance in the darkness, in the unknown regions beyond the earth. The righteous however will inherit the earth. Actually, the Saviors own illustrations fell in perfect symmetry with the worldview of Job. Jesus said: "If a man abide not in me, he is cast forth as a branch, and is withered; and men gather them, and cast them into the fire, and they are burned (John 15:6)."

Job was insulted. But it wasn't for want of better allegory. Bildad's *darkened council* relied on his argument that the law of retribution applies to all men, believing Job's suffering to be a result of personal sin.

He answered his friend, "How long will you vex my soul, and shatter me into pieces with words?"

4

THE DUNG PEOPLE... DEVOURED BY THE UNFANNED FLAME (JOB 20)

IT WAS ZOPHAR THE NAAMATHITE'S TURN TO SPEAK. Though the loftiness of the wicked reaches the heavens, he assured his friends, they are at best delusional, for the limits of the Almighty are as *high* as the heavens, His measure *longer* than the earth, and His depths *deeper* than Sheol. Can any man compare with the Creator? The answer is—*No*, he cannot. And besides, "the triumph of the wicked is short." A day is coming when "there will be no escape for them, and their only hope is to breathe their last (Job 11:20)." The Platonist might listen in and argue that what Zophar has actually intended to say is the wicked man can only *hope* to breathe his last. Surely, if man's true self is an eternal soul, completely separate from the shackles of the flesh and therefore incapable of conscious death, then Zophar has dabbled in the doctrine of hell, eternal torment and cognition. But that is not Zophar's intent. For Zophar, the wicked will live out their final hope. Conclusively, they will perish forever like their dung. He says:

> ⁴ Do you know this from of old,
>
>> From the establishment of man on earth,
>
> ⁵ That the triumphing of the wicked is short,
>
>> And the joy of the godless momentary?
>
> ⁶ Though his loftiness reaches the heavens,
>
>> And his head touches the clouds,
>
> ⁷ He perishes forever like his refuse [his own dung];
>
>> Those who have seen him will say, 'Where is he?'
>
> ⁸ He flies away like a dream, and they cannot find him;
>
>> Even like a vision of the night he is chased away.
>
> ⁹ "The eye which saw him sees him no longer,
>
>> And his place no longer beholds him.
>
> (Job 20:4-9)

Here Zophar would also wish to add, for our inspection, that those who survive the *cleansing* of wicked men will consider those whom they once knew, the sort who has "swallowed down riches," and ask: "Where is he?" The wicked, Zophar would have us know, are about as capable of affecting history on that day as the troublesome dream which fails at clutching under the sheets come morning. Everything about his words gleams with Scriptural confessionals. One might even say the Prophets, while moved by the Spirit of God, would only borrow from them. Though Bildad introduced us to *brimstone* and Job to *worms*, Zophar was the first to write of the *unquenchable fire*. He added:

Complete darkness is held in reserve for his treasures,

And **unfanned fire will devour him**;

It will consume the survivor in his tent.

(Job 20:26)

5

"I Know My Redeemer Lives..." THE GOSPEL OF JESUS CHRIST ACCORDING TO JOB

WE ARE GIVEN NO INDICATION THAT JOB DISAGREED with Bildad and Zophar's descriptions of the dead man for the very reason that Job wished to heap such an existence, if we can even define it in such terms, upon himself. Whereas Zophar embossed our minds with imagery of the unfanned flames which shall greet the *whole* man and Bildad with brimstone as his stand-in, Job turned from the circle of life, specifically worms, to the natural laws wedded with water to describe the fate of men's soul. He said:

¹⁰ "But man dies and lies prostrate.

Man expires, and where is he?

¹¹ As water evaporates from the sea,

And a river becomes parched and dried up,

¹² So man lies down and does not rise.

Until the heavens are no longer,

He will not awake nor be aroused out of his sleep."

13 Oh that You would hide me in Sheol,

That You would conceal me until

Your wrath returns to You,

That You would set a limit for me and remember me!

(Job 14:7-13)

This is where Job's doctrine gets particularly good. Job teases the coming apocalypse. Despite the fate of all men lying down, incapable of rising, nor being aroused from sleep "until the heavens are no longer," Job pleaded with God—a likely a familiar request among the children of Abraham. His desire was to remain hidden in Sheol, completely concealed in God's protection until His wrath had met its end. Job's plea, and hope, was that his *unconsciousness*—his introverted being—would be bound with borders. After all was said and done, he kindly asked that Yahweh would remember him. In the entire span of Holy Scripture, Job was the first to say it. The man from Uz hoped for his Redeemer. He knew that the Creator would not forget his beloved children. After all, He longed for the work of His hands. But just as importantly, Job made the connection. To meet the Redeemer would equate the miracle of his own resurrection.

14 "If a man dies, will he live again?

All the days of my struggle I will wait

Until my change comes.

15 "You will call, and I will answer You;

You will long for the work of Your hands.

(Job 14:14-15)

The whole of Scripture concurs. It's almost as if Job's words were lifted into the Apostle Paul's own epistles. From our earliest Biblical doctrine we learn that death has borders. The *change* will come. God will call upon the righteous. Paul later describes the timing of His shout as occurring at "the last trump." And when that happens, Job will answer—but not before.

25 "As for me, I know that my Redeemer lives,

And at the last He will take His stand on the earth.

26 "Even after my skin is destroyed,

> Yet from my flesh I shall see God;
>
> ²⁷ Whom I myself shall behold,
>
> And whom my eyes will see and not another.
>
> My heart faints within me!
>
> (Job 19:25-27)

Finally, Job's doctrine of the afterlife finds its capstone. The Redeemer lives now in heaven, but at the last He will take His stand upon the earth. The wicked, we can assume, have either been forcibly removed from the earth or are begging to breathe their last at the very moment He takes his stand—or immediately thereafter. Job takes no interest in the interim. Heaven is *not* his destination. There are no promised visitation rights as a ghostly, candle flickering wisp of consciousness. For the Hebrew, his inheritance is the earth. But such distributions of eternal prosperity will not happen, Job said, until "after my skin is destroyed." When he adds, "yet from my flesh I shall see God," he is speaking of the resurrection. Meanwhile, death would fill in the gap between his present hope and their meeting. Job would not behold God with his own eyes until the resurrection, and as the whole of Scripture agrees, there is no reason to disagree with this.

Job was the first to proclaim the Gospel.

Strokes of Jesus Christ filled his descriptions of the Redeemer in as little as four lines. Job gazed across the chasm of almost two millennia to grasp in full faith the cross to come.

> ¹⁶ For now You number my steps,
>
> You do not observe my sin.
>
> ¹⁷ My transgression is sealed up in a bag,
>
> And You wrap up my iniquity.
>
> (Job 14:16-17)

But as we have seen, the Gospel according to Job, though brief, is quite different indeed from the gospel of the Platonist. There is no bodily escape to unforeseen realms. The bad news cannot be any more bitter than the final terminal of every man; the conscious man; the *whole* man—a blanket of dirt and worms.

Then again, the good news couldn't be any sweeter.

The coming Messiah wouldn't simply be defined by the physical conquest of a Davidic kingdom. And He wouldn't hand out permission slips for Gnostic ascensions or the ongoing survival of the soul. He was coming to save us from the very sins which Job was accused of committing and which furthermore secured his own doom. Assuredly, Job proclaimed the Gospel which Christ came to fulfill. It is indeed the kiss sweeter than wine. And yet it is also a bittersweet truth.

We today have had the opportunity to fix our whole heart upon the perfect atoning sacrifice of Jesus as he hung upon the tree at Calvary. As I write these very words, Job is a dead man. His situation has not changed. He has yet to resurrect—to meet the Redeemer face-to-face. Then again, neither have we. But unlike the man from Uz, we have savory knowledge of our blessed savior Jesus Christ, and the particular ways in which he satisfied Job's words. Jesus longed so dearly for the works of His hands, that He might call upon them again, that He fulfilled the sort of legal requirement which even Job likely could not imagine, nor wish to fathom.

Jesus *died.*

Imagine then when the cogwheels of time in Sheol click into their final sprockets, daring not to clack even an inch beyond the limits of salvation—when the Creator finally returns to reclaim what's His. And then conceptualize a picture of Job among the dirt and worms of his doctrine. Job—along with every righteous man, woman, and child, who did not live to experience the fulfillments of which they longed for; Job—hearing the shout and trumpet proclamation, perhaps even answering the call of his personal invitation, should the Spirit intimately whispers his name into his ear; Job—opening his eyes to behold the Savior, face-to-face as He takes His stand upon the earth.

Surely, Job and the Patriarchs and everyone who is restored to glorious flesh—and I pray for my own inclusion in the glorious day of His *remembering*—shining even brighter than the stars they had once gazed upon and contemplated in the firmament, will affirm the only *news* worth proclaiming.

But perhaps, in Job's case, he will repeat *verbatim* the very words which fill his book, having contemplated the meeting to come.

"My heart faints within me!"

6

JOB — FLAT EARTHIST AND MORTALIST (*If Job Were Alive, People Would Listen*)

IT IS NO SECRET THAT JOB, LIKELY WRITTEN centuries before the Law of Moses, is a flat earth book. Geocentricism abounds. But there's far more to Job than most contemporary connoisseurs of Scripture are willing to admit. Theologians have long noted that Job ascribed to a peculiar belief regarding the afterlife. Mainly, where consciousness is concerned, there wasn't one. Or more precisely, there wouldn't be—that is, *not* until the resurrection of the dead which, as of the writing of this book, has yet to come. Job was a mortalist. During the reformation, his doctrine would come to be labeled by his Calvinist detractors as *soul sleep*. His position on the soul was akin to his belief in the afterlife. A man lives, he dies, and then he, along with his soul, return to the earth. That's it.

His only hope, Job would add, is in the Redeemer. Let us not fall into despair. *That* is a competent hope to cling to, if ever I've heard one.

If anything, Job sets the stage. It's akin to reading *The Hobbit* before *The Lord of the Rings*. The latter chronicle takes the former publication and stylizes it with a mesmerizing narrative of *epic* (or more precisely, *Biblical*) proportions. The whole of Scripture not only agrees with Job, as I intend to demonstrate, it will seek to expound upon it. Moses and the Law agree, as does John the Revelator, and just as importantly, every writer in-between. Everyone concurs. God revealed heavenly truth to Job, and a little later on He did not change His position. We can rest assured that Yahweh did not simply feed culturally misconstrued assumptions to an ignorant people only to revise doctrine as a method of evolving our cognitive thinking. Rather, the Spirit invited the Prophets and the Psalmists, and later the Apostles, to the pen and parchment in order that they might *expound* upon the only accuracy which God has ever revealed—truth. God's holy revelation is certain on these facts. The earth is flat and immovable and the soul *at present* is mortal. There is no confusion here. So why does the contemporary church refuse to believe it?

If Job were alive today to vouch for the *true* shape of the Earth *and* the condition of the soul—all of which is based upon God's own Testimony to begin with—people would listen. Church congregations would listen. And so would their leaders. They might even choose to follow by his example. I would hope that my readers will too. We have much to learn from him. Among his ash-heap recollections, Job described God's candle as having once shined upon his head. By His light alone he walked through the darkness. And everything he committed himself to was a success. "I washed my steps with butter," he lamented in his anguish, adding: "The rock poured me out rivers of oil." It was because of the life Job lived that he received *everyone's* respect. To this he gives account:

> 7 "When I went out to the gate of the city,
>
> When I took my seat in the square,
>
> 8 The young men saw me and hid themselves,
>
> And the old men arose and stood.
>
> 9 The princes stopped talking
>
> And put their hands on their mouths;
>
> 10 The voice of the nobles was hushed,
>
> And their tongue stuck to their palate."

(Job 29:7-10)

The rulers of the Earth had reason to fear Job. He himself was a bit of a researcher. To this effect he said: "The cause which I knew not I searched out." And if he found evil, wherever it attempted to hide, he exposed it. Job further claimed: "And I brake the jaws of the wicked, and plucked the spoil out of his teeth."

But let us not confuse Job's humble yet entirely honest self-evaluation with a George Thorogood song—or worse, a modern prosperity gospel. The young men did not hide themselves; the aged did not arise; the princes did not lay a hand on their mouth; and the nobles did not cleave their tongue to the roof of their mouth—even when found in disagreement—because the man from Uz washed his steps with butter or knew how to rock a tune. "When the ear heard me, then it blessed me; and when the eye saw me, it gave witness to me," Job confessed, but only—and this is important;

> 11 "For when the ear heard, it called me blessed,
>
> And when the eye saw, it gave witness of me,
>
> 12 Because I delivered the poor who cried for help,

And the orphan who had no helper.

¹³ The blessing of the one ready to perish came upon me,

And I made the widow's heart sing for joy.

¹⁴ I put on righteousness, and it clothed me;

My justice was like a robe and a turban.

¹⁵ I was eyes to the blind

And feet to the lame.

¹⁶ I was a father to the needy,

And I investigated the case which I did not know."

(Job 29:11-16)

If God heaped unto Job earthly riches, they were only as He would upon the four and twenty elders—in heavenly terms—who fall prostrate before Him that sits upon on the throne, and cast their crowns in worship before Him that liveth for ever and ever (Revelation 4:10). God was certainly not speaking presumptuously when he asked of the Satan:

> "Have you considered my servant Job? For there is no one like him on the earth, a blameless and upright man, fearing God and turning away from evil (Job 1:8)."

Job's first action, upon hearing of the calamity that instantaneously dismembered him from his empire of dirt, was to arise, and rent his mantle, and shave his head, and fall down upon the ground, and worship. (Job 1:20). With the words that very well might proceed from the mouths of the kingly co-heirs in heaven, Job immediately confessed: "Naked came I out of my mother's womb, and naked shall I return thither: the Yahweh gave, and Yahweh hath taken away; blessed be *the name* of Yahweh."

There is hardly another man alive like the man from Uz. If Job were counted among our ranks today, people would *listen*. Church congregations would *listen*. And so would their leaders. With Job as our maestro, the God-fearing soul would find little reason to struggle against the otherwise demeaning threats and shallow, often hypocritical, spiritual demands from agenda pushers. The God-fearing soul would first and foremost be delivered savory fruit—action matched with heavenly virtue—before we ever got around to the meat and the delectable dogma. If we as the people who inhabit this joyous cosmology are anything like

Job—a community which bases *much* upon the very book that bears his name—I am a firm believer that the God-fearing soul will not be able to resist the wine we offer them.

7

"Can You Measure the Breadth of the Earth...?"

TO SAY "KANSAS IS AS FLAT AS A PANCAKE" would be to speak an inaccuracy, for Kansas, you see, is *flatter* than a pancake. Actually, according to the meticulous research and findings of Dr. Dobson and Campbell, it's only the ninth flattest state in the continental United States. Minnesota is flatter, as is Louisiana—Illinois too. Even Texas is flatter. And yet the flattest of these—according to *National Geographic*—surrounded almost entirely by sea *level*, is the state of Florida. The Everglades in southern Florida is over 60 miles wide and 100 miles long—all level. Florida receives upwards of 60 inches of rain per year. That water collects into the Kissimmee River and progresses southbound into Lake Okeechobee, eventually flowing over the Everglades massive limestone shelf, which in turn empties into the Florida Bay. It's flat.

Furthermore, the continental United States is approximately 2,800 miles across. If the Earth were a globe, the US would have a terrain with a bulge extending approximately 1,306,666 feet (or 247 miles) above sea level, and yet there is none stretching higher than 2.8 miles. Conclusively, the United States of America is also flatter, *far flatter*, than a pancake. Dobson and Campbell agree. Their conclusions, published in *The Geographical Review*, have never been refuted nor challenged. To do so would be to further expose a false religion. Bad news for globe lovers and flapjacks everywhere, according to Dobson and Campbell, the entire world follows the trend of America. The breadth of the earth is significantly flatter than a pancake.

A God-fearing brother or sister in the faith should find no discouragement in these findings. Though they derive from *true* observation—which the uncorrupted Christian claims to adhere to—that is not the point of this book. They affirm the Testimony of our Lord, who once approached Job in a howling whirlwind, commanding that he "gird up now thy loins like a man," and then promptly demanded that he answer if he knew.

"Have you perceived the breadth of the Earth? Tell me if you know this."

Supposing my reader has experienced an actual tornado, he or she should immediately be hounded with terror at the very thought of God Almighty arriving to their tea party dressed in one. I once was given so little warning of a tornado—in Florida, of all places—hearing no sirens announcing its arrival, and with limited options available outside, clung tightly to a metal pole which dug into a concrete foundation. My only other action was to fight the sharp blade of its wind, which sliced into the pliability of my eyes, and hoped to keep them agonizingly open so as to bear witness to what I would only describe as the cracking of many whirling locomotives tumbling over each other as invisible fingertips lifted the water from a lake and heaved it upon dry ground. And unlike Job's timeless encounter, my tornado wasn't a meeting with God.

The breadth of the Earth and so many other questions which the Lord asked of Job from the raging wind were no doubt rhetorical in nature. So when God demanded that he should answer if he knew, supposing he could muster the breath in his lungs, the response was a clear and resounding, *No!* Job could not possibly have perceived the breadth of the earth. It was immeasurable by Job or any other man. If this were the case, then why do God-fearing Christians assert that Eratosthenes of Cyrene was able to measure the circumference of the earth with nothing more than a friend and a couple of sticks? As we shall come to see, Alexandria was a cesspool of darkened speeches. False teachers surround us everywhere.

Ask any builder who employs a snap or chalk line for his foundation if he would consider doing so on one that was rounded or globular, for the Lord our master-builder "hath stretched the line upon it (Job 38:5)." By the Lord's own Testimony flatness abounds. It was He who laid the foundations of the earth and its cornerstone accordingly, furthermore fastening those foundations and holding the ends of it.

This is Scriptures first creation account—on in which Moses will not take issue with.

The proud man of the faith who gnashes his teeth and stomps his feet at the slightest proof of the Earth's flatness declares the Lord a liar by his obnoxious actions, even if he should in his denial politely brush the thought aside. He would have us all believe that God was writing a syrup-laced holiday card in that storm, sticky to the touch with its abstract yet heart-felt poetry, and specifically directed to the cultural comforts of a primitive un-schooled people, who would not have believed a "globe-revelation" in a tornado had He even bothered to tell them about it, rather than Greek philosophers who, without Holy Writ to guide them, figured it all out on our own. He would rather convince you of his own damnable falsities, that Eratosthenes sidestepped around God's challenge easily enough, as textbooks will surely claim, or perhaps just proved Yahweh facetious. This would seem far more pleasing to him, as would the explanations of the many commentators, rather than confess to his own factual wrongness or let such contradictory matters, what Dr. Dobson and Campbell's findings have fully confirmed and proven, expose his souls condition—that God, being our master-builder as pointedly described, is a dreadful thought to his well-being.

To this we can know for sure. When Yahweh spoke to Job, just as He spoke to the Prophets and the scribes and the poets and the Apostles, He did not converse merely with them, but *through* them He addressed all generations of people, including our own. But in Job's particular case, God wasn't merely speaking. He was dropping a challenge.

Can we, dear reader, measure the breadth of the earth—and if so, will we stubbornly accept the challenge; will we gird up our loins like a man and stand before God Almighty in the roar of a whirlwind; will we stare into the eye of that funnel and claim the contrary? Will we call the Creator a liar?

Our answer waits.

8

THE DARKENED COUNCIL OF JOB'S THREE FRIENDS

IN A WAY, JOB AND HIS THREE FRIENDS were severely handicapped intellectuals. When Eliphaz, Bildad, and Zophar heard of the evil that had befallen him, they made an appointment together to mourn at his side. We quickly read: "When they lifted up their eyes, afar off, and knew him not, they lifted up their voice, and wept (Job 2:12)." Despite the universal application of their tears, they did not have the Major and the Minor Prophets at their disposal for theological guidance. Our blessed Savior would not arrive in the flesh for another thousand years and several added centuries to boot, which would immediately thereafter prompt the warmly welcomed Epistles from the Apostles. They did not even have Moses and the law to contend with. One might think they were fumbling around, slapping the walls while attempting to flip a light switch in the dark.

However, we shan't forget Job's fourth, and dare I call him *mysterious*, friend. We can deduce that Job's friends wrestled with what *truth* was made known to them under the umbrella of Abraham's faith, because Elihu is specifically mentioned as having descended from Buz, likely referencing the Patriarchs own nephew (Genesis 22:20-21).

We see the religion of Abraham coming forward in his promotion of creation. While recognizing God as his maker (32:22), Elihu furthermore declares that the Spirit of God breathed life into him (33:4); that he is formed out of clay (33:6); and chronologically, he is the first in Holy Writ to have described Adam as covering his transgressions (31:33). Job also looked to his mediator between God and man in heaven (Job 16:18). He even went so far as to affirm the seed promised first to Adam and Eve, and then through Abraham, which would surely result with his own bodily resurrection. To this effect he said:

> "For I know that my Redeemer lives, And He shall stand at last on the earth; And after my skin is destroyed, this I know, That in my flesh I shall see God, Whom I shall see for myself, And my eyes shall behold, and not another. How my heart yearns within me! (Job 19:25-27)"

What makes Elihu, Job, and his three friends so fascinating is that they are not quite unlike us today. Ultimately, they were five guys simply trying to *figure it out.*

And yet God reviled Job's three friends and their three arrogant speeches a-piece. They tripped over the booby trap of the ages. They were delusional to believe they could circumnavigate God on their own and figure Him out—or perhaps, by putting their skulls together, they might escape *the eternal gullible* destined for the most enlightened of seamstresses. For all of our wide-eyed bedazzlements of a technocratic, science-blueprinted society today, are we any different—are we any better off in our knowledge than what Eliphaz, Bildad, and Zophar had to contend with? Aside from the revelations found in God's Word as to the nature of the Creator and His divine plan for the sainthood, have we come any closer to circumnavigating God through natural revelation? I think not—far from it, ironically. On these grounds, whatever the height of his ascending stage in enlightened history, no man is without excuse.

In their specific case, they presumed that God presently punishes evil and rewards righteousness on *this side* of glory. Essentially, Job's suffering was due to sin—*his* sin. Eliphaz, who is often thought of as the sensitive friend, accused Job of never really understanding the pain of others while comforting them. Because of Job's sin, he therefore must seek God's favor (Job 4:7, 15:4-6, 22:5). The prophet Isaiah, writing of the suffering servant who would later be *cut off*, may have been directing our attention to the fallacy of Eliphaz, who was the first to critique Job after he cursed the day of his birth and longed for his death. Eliphaz spoke: "Whoever perished, being innocent? Or where were the righteous cut off?" Bildad the logical also accused Job of offending God's justice by committing some evil deed (Job 8:5-6, 18:4). Actually, he surmised that Job's children brought their deaths upon themselves. Zophar, the groups hot-headed member, not only believed Job's anguish was a sign of divine justice, but the punishment he incurred was *not enough* (Job 11:6, 20:29). By robbing God of His sovereignty and His divine plan, Job's three friends spoke ill of Him.

Only Elihu escaped God's impending rebuke. Actually, the two share a common thread. While Job grew increasingly annoyed at his three obstinate friends, he never answered Elihu—just as he wisely kept his mouth shut before the Lord. One might think this is strange, since Elihu—who, much like the unexplained comings and goings of many Old Testament figures, wearing upon his self a cloak of mystery—came to the same conclusions as Job's other three friends. Job had *sinned*. But there is a notable difference. Eliphaz, Bildad, and Zophar held to a judgement that Job was suffering due to a hidden, unknowable digression. Elihu came to a different conclusion entirely. *Since*the time of his present suffering, Job had sinned.

As Christians—we can learn much from Elihu. He was respectful to those whom he disagreed with—and patient. To this he said: "Behold, I waited for your words; I gave ear to your reasons, whilst ye searched out what to say (Job 32:11)." He was passionate but reasonable. "My words shall be of the uprightness of my heart: and my lips shall utter knowledge clearly (Job 33:3)." And what attracts me most to his message is that Elihu was *inclusive*. He implored of Job and those whom sought to counsel him: "Let us choose justice for *ourselves*; Let us know among *ourselves* what is good."

If Elihu were alive today, he would not merely preach about the evils of this world beyond his reach, solely admonishing the Elite or our Luciferian Overlords, and demanding that others *wake up* to the self while keeping himself and his friends at arm's length from the very bed we have made and are expected to lie in. If Elihu called Job a sinner, it's because he also was an acknowledged sinner. Elihu's message is of the inclusive nature—and it is for us. *I* am a sinner. *You* are a sinner. *We* are sinners in need of the Redeemer. If our philosophical quandaries lead us down any other road—as we attempt to figure it all out with friends—then we have wasted our breath. To excuse sin is to defend it, and this Job was guilty of.

Job eventually confessed to God: "Behold, I am vile; what shall I answer thee? I will lay mine hand upon my mouth. Once have I spoken; but I will not answer: yea, twice; but I will proceed no further (Job 40:4-5)."

God cleared Job of all charges, but *only* after he repented.

"Wherefore I abhor *myself*, and repent in dust and ashes (Job 42:6)."

Here we find the true message of Job. It is not a dissection of Job's disease or the ash-heap he lamented in. When properly administered, Job's narrative asks—no, it *requires* that God's people fear Him and His Testimony, even beyond our own intellect. I can't think of a better way to begin the Bible than with a reading of Job. It is with this lens that we can best view Holy Writ—with Godly fear, a penitent heart, and humility. We are in no place to school the Lord at any point in history—lest we succumb to the eternally gullible thinker—as if we have a better understanding of the world around us than His own Testimony concerning Himself, His creation, and the cosmological make-up which He consistently describes throughout the whole of Scripture. It is no secret, and has long been understood, that Job is a Flat Earth book. If God were simply flinging a contextualization of cultural superstition back at Job while crying out for mercy in hellish agony, then the entire point of the book is null and void. We might as well rip it from our Bible's.

Indeed, Job and his friends are very much just like us today. They were five guys faced with wickedness and suffering in light of God's created order. They were simply trying to figure it all out. Though like Eliphaz, Bildad, and Zophar—I ask this first of myself, and then I ask it of you—how often in our own lives, and more importantly in the lives of others, are we guilty of *darkened* counsel?

THE DIVINE COUNCIL: THE ANCIENT HEBREW PENTHEON ACCORDING TO PSALM 82

THE HEBREWS WERE STILL HOPELESSLY CAPTIVE in Babylon when the Prophet Daniel had a rather *hopeful* vision. "As I continued looking," he wrote of heaven, "a multitude of thrones were set up and the Ancient of Days took His seat amongst them." Much earlier on, the Bibles aboriginal writer began the book of Job describing a day when the sons of God came to present themselves before Yahweh, and *Satan* arrived also among them. The prophet Micaiah would have a similar vision involving a lying spirit in the midst of God's council. Likewise, the Bibles final writer saw the thrones of Daniel's earlier vision. The Apostle John described those who sat upon them as "twenty-four elders." The wisdom literature of Job, combined with the visionary books of Daniel and Revelation, and the historical documents of Kings, not overlooking every other Holy Spirit breathed Scripture combined, all agree. *Divine* beings surround the throne of Yahweh. In slightly other terms, they are lower-case "gods." They are the *elohim*.

> "God [*elohim*] standeth in the congregation of the mighty;
>
> He judgeth among the gods [*elohim*]."
>
> Psalm 82:1

The concept of a divine assembly of gods was long held by the Sumerian, Akkadian, Babylonian, Egyptian, Canaanite, Greek, Roman, Celtic, and Nordic religions—and at the threat of shrugging such belief off as mere misguided superstition, the *true* religion of the Hebrew Prophets and Apostles also held to comparable views. There is however a dominant difference between the heavenly pantheon of Israel and every other neighboring countries appraisal of gods. For the Hebrew, there is firstly the God of Israel, and then there is, quite secondly, every other god who is subservient to Him, either real or manufactured, elohim creature or Nephilim demon, imperfect or in rebellion.

"They sacrificed to demons [*lasedim*] who were not God, to gods [*elohim*] whom they have not known, New gods who came lately, Whom your fathers did not dread (Deuteronomy 32:17)."

Human tradition has befuddled us with much. Even among our most well-intended and deeply devoted Bible studies, how often have we glossed right over passages concerning God's immovable and enclosed world and the mortal soul? Likewise, it may surprise most to learn that the divine pantheon of creatures in heaven are deeply embedded in the Hebrew Bible, and just as importantly, command a central role in its cosmological narrative. Unmistakable references to God's royal throne room in heaven and His entourage of *elohim* occur in all three portions of Old Testament Scripture—the Law, Prophets, and Writings; in all major literary genres—narrative, historical, prophetic, poetic, liturgical, wisdom, as well as visionary; and in the earliest to latest dated materials, all of which encompasses the breadth of human history from the earliest moments of creation to the eschatological arrival of the Messiahs Davidic kingdom on earth. The conception of a host of divine, angelic, and other heavenly beings has always been present in Hebrew thinking, even from its very conception, so much so that those who worshiped Yahweh could not conceive of Him in another fashion. In recent decades, historical scholars have noted that the Hebrew position surrounding a pantheon-like council of the divine was immensely popular, a belief which was exercised in widespread practice. New Testament writers would not stray from the Hebrew vision.

This is a lot to unpack.

In order that we might view the assembly of God as the Prophets rightly saw it, and in as simple and clean a manner as possible, we shall therefore employ the pen strokes of Asaph for our guide. As one of the three Levites commissioned by King David to be in charge of singing in the house of Yahweh, he also served in the administration of Solomon his successor. Asaph's contribution to the Bible includes twelve psalms, numbered as 50 and 73–83 in the Masoretic Text, and though it is considered by some that he may not have been the *direct*author of these psalms, it is likewise a valid point, conclusively, that he may have transcribed the very words of David. Regardless, Asaph *the man* is not under interrogation. Psalm 82 is. Asaph perhaps best exemplified the ancient Hebrew worldview—but in a way, he does it *better*. With Psalm 82—and in as little as eight concise and beautifully scripted verses—he managed to capture what many today and Christians throughout the history of sainthood would otherwise assume was a superstitious and wholly disposable belief. Yet Asaph managed to make it Biblical.

> ¹ God [*elohim*] standeth in the congregation of the mighty; He administers judgement in the midst of the gods [*elohim*].
>
> ² How long will you judge unjustly and show favoritism to the wicked? Selah
>
> ³ Judge on behalf of the helpless and the orphan; provide justice to the afflicted and the poor.
>
> ⁴ Rescue the helpless and the needy; deliver them from the hand of the wicked.
>
> ⁵ They do not know or consider. They go about in the darkness, so that all the foundations of the earth are shaken.
>
> ⁶ I have said, You are gods [*elohim*], and sons of the Most High, all of you.
>
> ⁷ However, you will die like men, and you will fall like one of the princes.
>
> ⁸ Rise up, O God, judge the earth, because You shall inherit all the nations.

(Psalm 82)

Psalm 82 thematically falls in line with much of Asaph's work. Judgement is his preliminary concern. The only difference here is that Asaph throws the modern post-enlightenment reader into a dizzying tailspin. One might immediately ask why God needs a council of elohim to exact His judgement. God needs elohim for the same reason the He needs people. He *doesn't*. Regardless, this is *how* the cosmological make-up of God's creation functions. Through the members of His divine council, the Creator maintains order over His creation—especially the affairs of men. Their collective business takes on various aspects. While some recorded acts include the praise and worship of Yahweh or serving as captains and soldiers in the LORD's military unit, among other calls of duty, theirs is often judicial—and always on a cosmic level.

Their first recorded conversation is as follows.

"Let us make man in our image (Genesis 1:26)."

Moses' employment of such phrases as *let us* was not confused by his intended audience. Those who crossed through the red sea and later the banks of the Jordan unquestionably understood this to mean God's consultation with His elohim assembly in heaven. Frank Moore Cross, Professor of Hebrew at Harvard University, has noted: "In both Ugaritic and biblical literature, the use of the first person plural is characteristic of address in the divine council. The familiar *we* has long been recognized as the plural address used by Yahweh in his council." Much later on, it is the early post Apostolic Fathers who altered the intended meanings of the plural to reference the pre-incarnate Messiah Jesus as a person of the Godhead.

My reader will be sorely mistaken to conclude that I do not uphold the Biblical truth that is the Godhead. The Godhead is indeed Biblical. God is one, perfectly embodied by the Father, Son, and Holy Ghost. But the council of *elohim* is not an argument which should be used for it. Actually, as we shall come to find, Psalm 82 and the elohim exemplify the Father and Son relationship of Yahweh in spectacular ways which most of us have never yet imagined. What's more, Psalm 82 is a delightful doorway into the Gospel narrative, which seeks to exact the three-act structure of Israel's messianic story of allotment, judgment and inheritance. This I hope to expound upon.

For the ancient Hebrew, the concept of a divine council did not endanger their unique standing as a monotheistic religion either, nor threaten Yahweh's untouchable position as "God of gods and Lord of lords (Deuteronomy 10:17)." Monotheism is *never* questioned, even if God created others of His kind. Though Yahweh is an Elohim, clearly the elohim are *not* God.

In other words, Yahweh is a unique God, but He is not alone.

PARALYZED UNDER THE GAZE OF THE CREEPING PLANETS *(Hosts of Heaven, Job 38)*

ASKING SUCH INCONSEQUENTIAL QUESTIONS as "How many angels dance on the head of a pin" has long been accredited to the sort of arguments of absurdity, or *reductio ad absurdum* in Latin, which aided and abetted in the crippling of medieval scholasticism while the Turks occupied themselves with more practical matters—mainly, the conquest of Constantinople. For the record, it has been suggested that as many as a million angels or more can dance upon a pins head—and who cares? The mechanical particulars of angelology are of no interest here. I am however pestered with historical and—for the purposes of starry strolls by night—other *natural* quandaries.

That God had managed a former created order, or an undocumented plethora of them—filling an unspecified gap of time between the first and second verses of Genesis—and perhaps more importantly to this discussion, that divine sons of God had looked in upon every previous reality, is not commented upon nor believed by the ancient Hebrew. Moses makes no mention of *when* or *what day* the angels were created, or if they pre-existed at all, except to conclude: "Thus the heavens and the earth were finished, **and all the host of them** (Genesis 2:1)." And if there were any confusion, Yahweh would clarify this when delivering the 10 Commandments: "For in six days the LORD made the heaven*s* [haš-šā-ma-yim] and earth, the sea, and all that is in them *is* [heavens and sky, earth, and sea] and rested the seventh day."

Likewise, Moses furthermore makes no mention of when the divine beings *first* rebelled against their Creator, only that "God saw everything that He had made, and behold, it was very good. And the evening and the morning were the sixth day (Genesis 1:31)."

And yet this we know with assurance. When the LORD laid the foundations of the Earth, marked its measurements, and laid its cornerstone, the *sons of God* were there to witness it. They even shouted for joy. Some will take this to mean that the divine beings, many of whom make up His council, were around before the gun shot sprint of creation.

Then the LORD answered Job out of the whirlwind, and said:

"Where was thou when I laid the foundations of the earth? Declare, if thou hast understanding. Who hath laid the measures thereof, if thou knowest? Or who hath stretched the line upon it? Whereupon are the foundations thereof fastened? Or who laid the corner stone thereof; When the morning stars sang together, and all the sons of God shouted for joy? (Job 38:4-7)"

Far more taboo a subject than the sin of the angels or the date of their origin is something which God Himself testified to. It is an inconvenient truth for men of post-enlightenment, but foundational for the Prophets and the Apostles and Hebrew thinking. Job 38:4-7 has already given it away. The Word of God persistently and consistently identifies the sons of God *with* stars.

"You alone are Yahweh. You created the heavens, the highest heavens with all their host, the earth and all that is on it, the seas and all that is in them. You give life to all of them, and the heavenly host worships You."

(Nehemiah 9:6, HCSB)

Consider if you will the evening of the seventh day, after God rested from the work He had made. It likely occurs to a select few Bible scholars that the *planets* were not among the countless multitude of stars which Adam and Eve first gazed upon from their mountain paradise of Eden. Firstly, Moses makes no mention of them. This is not due to oversight. The word *planet* derives from the Greek, and is intended to mean: *wanderer, vagabond.* Conclusively, the angels who kept not their first estate, as Jude would later remind us, were still within their proper dwelling during the aboriginal week of creation. We know this to be true because "God saw everything that He had made, and behold, it was very good." The wandering stars however had committed a sin so great as to be compared to the transgressions of Sodom and Gomorrah.

The lake of fire was even created for them.

Observing ones pre-directed course was of such gravity for the ancient Hebrew that the writer of Judges even thought to mention the kings who "fought from heaven" and the *stars* who were still capable of defeating Sisera in battle while keeping "**in their courses** (Judges 5:20)." The ancient God-fearing Hebrew would likely read this and understand

44

that the sons of God who remained faithful and obedient to Yahweh can efficiently execute the fate of humanity with authority, but more important to this discussion, they wouldn't employ the astrological apostasies of neighboring Babylon in order to do it. This brings us to our next point.

When the LORD laid the foundations of the earth, the morning stars sang together, and all the sons of God shouted for joy.

And then one night, sometime after Adam and Eve were expelled from God's holy mountain, our human parents—perhaps living among the sons of Cain and Seth, as timelines are concerned—beheld something awe-inspiring in the heavens above.

Quite suddenly a select handful of stars burned a little brighter than they had the previous evening. This was due to the fact that, upon closer inspection, they seemed to dip a little lower in the sky. One pulsated with flashes of bright yellow, while another, large and silver, loomed low on the horizon. There was of course the deeply mesmerizing red planet, and the brightest of these glowed with blazing white intensity throughout the night. One truth remained certain. They had left their constellations behind, so that each night they began to wander a little further, and then a little further, often looping in tiny backwards circles before pulling forwards again, and then a little further from their intended constellations. This was indeed a true mystery. But soon—very soon—these starry vagabonds would seek to make themselves known.

Cities would be built—alters raised. And Ziggurats would house them.

Human history would never be the same.

THEY WALKED WITH GODS: THE "BACKWARDS THINKING" SONS OF SETH AMONG THE "PROGRESSIVE" SONS OF CAIN

THE APPLE HAD FALLEN VERY FAR FROM THE TREE. Unlike his father Adam, who hid from Yahweh in shame and guilt, Cain showed absolutely no remorse for murdering his brother. When Adam's first-born son was confronted by God, he even spun his perjury with a clever pun, as if to spit in the Lord's face, and claim of the deceased second-born (Abel's title being, *the keeper of sheep*): "Am I my brother's keeper?" No, he was nothing like his father. Adam clothed himself appropriately and came clean with his Creator. Contrarily, Cain would not recognize his sin. To God he spoke with an unrepentant passive verb: *"From they face shall I be hid* (Genesis 4:14)." For Cain, more murders were anticipated.

Among the lineage of Seth, Adam's third-born son, little is recorded of their life except for names, years of conception and death. Much however can be said of Cain and his descendants. Despite initial concerns—that Cain would be a "fugitive and a vagabond" on the earth—he did quite well for himself. Perhaps his murderous "Mark," which God placed permanently upon his person, had something to do with it. Cain built a place of refuge—a city, actually—first of its kind. Many cities of refuge can be found throughout tribal history of the world. On the Big Island of Hawaii for example, Puʻuhonua o Hōnaunau provided asylum for lawbreakers, should they survive the frightful journey across the island—or islands—and the pursuing men who wished to avenge the blood of a relative. At any rate, the city named after Cain's son was worthy no doubt of enlightened culture and civil comforts. It is Cain's descendants, we immediately read, who introduced the use of tents, agriculture and pastoral life, invented the elegant art of music with the harp and organ, and became instructors "of every artifices in brass and iron."

The author John Bathurst Deane, in his book *Worship of the Serpent* (1833), says it like this: "...probably in less than three hundred years from the creation of man civilization had arrived at such a degree of perfection, that not only the necessaries, but even the luxuries of life were to be found in the family of the fugitive of Cain."

The Book of Enoch spreads the curtain and reveals the rather unfortunate spiritual truths behind the cultured advancements within Cain's lineage. The Angels, which kept not their first estate (Jude 1:6) taught Cain's sons "to make swords, and knives, and shields and breastplates, and taught them about metals of the earth and the art of working them, and bracelets and ornaments, and the use of antimony, and the beautifying of the eyelids, and all kinds of precious stones, and all coloring of dyes. And there was great impiety; they turned away from God, and committed fornication, and they were led astray, and became corrupt in all their ways (Enoch 8:1-2)"

All Biblical evidence concerning a pre-flood renaissance of man is attributed exclusively to the sons of Cain and the fallen angels. And yet long after these godless events Paul was a tentmaker. Luke was a doctor. Mary washed the feet of Jesus Yeshua with an expensive and exotic fragrance of the Himalayas. The Israelites under the command of Joshua and the Judges even brandished weapons. Never-the-less, we are assured that they, much like Seth's lineage, were "not of this world." Enoch, the son of Cain, had a city named after him, and likely lived in all the luxuries which such a civilization might afford. Nothing of his existence remains. Everything of that city, along with the entire circuit of societies where Cain and his descendants dwelt was washed away in the Great Deluge. Contrarily Enoch, seventh in line of Seth's lineage—not to be confused with Enoch the son of Cain—despite not having a single urban sprawl, city street, or "stroke of genius" attributed to his name, thirsted for something even better. Enoch "walked with God, and was not, for God took him."

This is the tension which we are asked to partake in—to be "not of this world" but to "shine as a light (Matthew 5:16)" in the midst of darkness. With Jesus, so much was his identity based around God His Father, being "not of this world," that we know virtually nothing of His trade except the speculative guesswork that He was a carpenter after his *earthly* father. We are given no insights regarding the skill or accomplishments of his craftsmanship to look for in archeology, be it chairs, roofing, or floorboards, since all we know of Him is what His biography in all four Gospels attests to, that He like Enoch "walked with God," and so much more.

The trade of a Godly man is not often worth mentioning in the Bible, particularly as it pertains to his worth or identity, unless it provides deliverance for God's people and contributes to the redemption of man. The saint who commits himself to this work is not toiling here for the kingdom of Cain, as the godless man believes and likewise glories in, but in the kingdom of the *second* Adam and Enoch to come. Such was the case with Noah. He too, we are told, "walked with God." Noah however was not a ship-builder. We are actually never informed of his pre-flood trade—though he did happen to construct a magnificent vessel. Is it possible that he was not so gifted as we give him credit for? Perhaps, when the waters surged, the barge which he was entrusted to sustain life with barely kept afloat. We'll never know. If he and his cargo were safe, and they most certainly were, it's because God invited Noah into the boat with Him, and at any rate, the blueprints which were first invented in the very mind of our Divine Master Craftsman were nothing short of a technological marvel.

Writes David Wardlaw Scott in his book, *Terra Firma: The Earth Not a Planet* (1901): "The Ark was considered for ages to be a clumsy, strangely-shaped hulk, somewhat like the models sold in toy-shops for children, but, for nearly the last three hundred years, that idea has been entirely changed. In 1609 Peter Jansen, a Dutch shipbuilder, determined to construct a ship on the lines given for the Ark, and, though much ridiculed at the time, he succeeded, and found that his ship would safely carry from thirty to forty per cent, more cargo in proportion to others, and his example was soon followed. In Appleton's Cyclopedia, Vol. XIV., Art. "Ship," we read: 'It is remarkable that its (the Ark's) proportions of length, breadth, and depth are almost precisely the same, considered by our most eminent architects the best for combining the elements of strength, capacity, and stability.' A later writer remarks: 'Ship-building was revolutionized, and the millions that go on the sea owe the change to the Bible. Since that the Cunarders, the Collins, the White Star, and Inman line Companies have built their ocean steamships after the scientific pattern of Him, whose 'way is perfect,' and who designed Noah's Ark.'"

We will most certainly find—though we may perhaps listen to music or strum a tune, read fine literature or attempt ourselves to take up the pen, dress up in fine clothes and make an extra effort to beautify ourselves, even attempt to "discover truth" as our profession permits—if we are to be accredited as "walking with God," then it is increasingly doubtful that we will go down in history as the great maestro of music, the inventor of enlightened thought, the masterful exhibitor of the arts, the exemplar of vain beauty and fashion, or the discoverer of the unknown. At any rate, we will certainly not be seen by our contemporaries as one who has "settled down to it," but as those who are merely "passing through" the cities which Cain and his kindred have built, eyesight always pressed forward upon our certain and eternal meeting with the Creator. And for this disobedience against the "human experience," the rightful renaissance of every man, we shall be perceived as a backwards thinking people.

Mainly, *fools*.

Conclusively, it would be difficult to reckon that any man in Seth's line would continue to be a man of God and walk in His ways if they should have a part in shaping the culture alongside the children of Cain. Our Savior said of those who aspire for Seth's lineage: "Ye are the salt of the earth: but if the salt have lost his savour, wherewith shall it be salted? it is thenceforth good for nothing, but to be cast out, and to be trodden under foot of men (Matthew 5:13)."

An interesting observation is made by Dr. Chuck Missler regarding Adam and the begotten sons of Seth. "The Ten Old Men" proceed in this order of begat: Adam, Seth, Enosh, Kenan, Mahalalel, Jared, Enoch, Methuselah, Lamech, and Noah. Appropriately, each name mean thusly in their exact order of begat: Man, Appointed, Mortal, Sorrow, The Blessed God, Shall come down, Teaching, His death shall bring, The Despairing, Rest.

When spoken in a sentence, Dr. Chuck Missler speaks of the Messianic seed-line accordingly: "Man (is) appointed mortal sorrow; (but) the Blessed God shall come down teaching (that) His death shall bring (the) despairing rest."

The sons of Cain received no such honorary title. They walked with angels rather than God—the Watchers, that is—and as consequence the stain of their seed was forever wiped clean from the Earth. When God asked of Cain concerning "thy brother's blood," he spoke in plural, referring to the many expected descendants of Abel who would never be born, as though also any number of abortions had been committed in the taking of his life. Despite all of their inventions of cultured wealth and comfort, only one sad-sap poem survives the loss of their genetic inheritance. It was written by a descendant of Cain, not to be confused

49

with Noah's father, both of whom were given the name Lamech. I imagine him brandishing the very weapon by which the Watchers wickedly delivered to him—of which his son also fashioned in the fire—as he drunkenly vaunted among the ears of his polygamous household, and in a vainglorious mood that likely paraded along with the seductions of his maestro sons harp and organ wizardry as he boasted of an immunity from vengeance superior even to that of Cain's cursed "Mark." Like Cain before him, murder was on his mind, and plenty of it. Murder records of his song:

> "Adah and Zillah! hear my voice;
>
> Ye wives of Lamech I give ear to my speech:
>
> I will slay men for smiting me,
>
> And for wounding me young men shall die.
>
> If Cain shall be avenged sevenfold,
>
> Lamech seventy and seven!"

"They Imagined In Their Hearts…" THE TOWER OF BABEL: GREATEST ENGINEERING MARVEL IN THE HISTORY OF EARTH?

I PLACE MY FULL UNWAVERING FAITH IN THE WORD OF GOD; even among its grandest of geocentric narratives. I believe Moses when he recounts for us the first and only recorded one-world government, aside now from our prophesied own; specifically the incomplete Tower of Babel which resulted from it (Genesis 11:1-9). That the Chaldeans of Ur set their political ambitions on a marvel of engineering which might ruffle the angelic feathers of the HaShamayim is a worldview only capable of being manifested in a flat stationary realm. Moses did not suppose their superstition necessary for correction, as he had already laid out the Earth's blueprints some eleven chapters earlier, nor did the Lord when He put a thorough end to their wicked schemes.

Let us not forget, Noah was still alive for the duration of this fool's errand. As the sole inheritor of all future generations, he had already instructed his offspring in the ways of the Lord. The Chaldeans were made well aware of the Creation week, of the forbidden tree of knowledge and Adam's disciplinary dismissal from the garden, even the sons of God taking on human wives and the resulting flood to follow, which Noah alone survived by way of godly virtue. This was made well known to them, and they hated God for it.

> *"6 And the Lord said, Behold, the people is one, and they have all one language; and this they begin to do: and now nothing will be restrained from them, which they have imagined to do. 7 Go to, let us go down, and there confound their language, that they may not understand one another's speech."* Genesis 11:6-7

The globular historian dismisses our Creators eye-witness account regarding Babel and its dispersion of tongues. To such an academic—the

Tower is beyond childish—not even worthy of a nursery-rhyme, and yet the furthest corners of ancient anthropology fundamentally disagree with him. Just ask the Bambala tribe of the Congo or the Sangu of Mkulwe and the Kachcha Nagas hill people scattered across Manipur and Nagaland. Ask the Anal Kuki people populating Manipur, India and in Myanmar. Visit the Quiches of Guatemala and the Ashanti tribe of central Ghana or the Mikirs, a Tibetan-Burmese people. Inquire of the Admiralty Islanders of Papua New Guinea, the aborigines of Australia, the people of the great pyramid of Cholula in Mexico, or the Tlingit indigenous peoples of Alaska and the Maidu Indians of California. By their own separate oral histories they mutually agree. Mankind once conspired against the Lord. They sought to murder Him. They even attempted to build a monument devoted to their ambition. It is for this wickedness that God confused their language and scattered them across the breadth of the Earth. Don't believe me? Go find the Lozi people of the upper Zambezi. Ask them.

In his book, *Folk-Lore in the Old Testament,* (1918) Sir James George Frazer writes: "Stories which bear a certain resemblance to the legend of the Tower of Babel are reported among several African tribes. Thus, some of the natives of the Zambesi, apparently in the neighborhood of the Victoria Falls, 'have a tradition which may refer to the building of the Tower of Babel, but it ends in the bold builders getting their crowns cracked by the fall of the scaffolding.' The story thus briefly referred to by Dr. Livingstone has been more fully recorded by a Swiss missionary. The A-Louyi, a tribe of the Upper Zambesi, say that formerly their god Nyambe, whom they identify with the sun, used to dwell on earth, but that he afterwards ascended up to heaven on a spider's web. From his post up aloft he said to men, 'Worship me.' But men said, 'Come, let us kill Nyambe.' Alarmed at this impious threat, the deity fled to the sky, from which it would seem that he had temporarily descended. So men said, 'Come, let us make masts to reach up to heaven.' They set up masts and added more masts, joining them one to the other, and they clambered up them. But when they had climbed far up, the masts fell down, and all the men on the masts were killed by the fall. That was the end of them."

There are variations of course. The Mikirs tell of giants having a part in the towers construction. The Gaikhos even trace their genealogy to Adam, and claim the architecture, which reached halfway to heaven, resembled a pagoda. Certainly, worldwide interviews among the most ancient of anthropological people-groups will produce a handful of modifications to the legend, but the end result is often if not always the same. The mind of every man was cast into confusion. For example, Sir Frazier writes: "The Wa-Sania of British East Africa say that of old all the tribes of the earth knew only one language, but that during a severe famine the people went mad and wandered in all directions, jabbering strange words, and so the different languages arose."

By the end of his life Noah must have felt like the greatest failure that ever was. Essentially, he lived two of them—lives, that is. As a young man, Moses assures us, he "walked with God. (Genesis 6:9)" And yet the world did not. As an old man he continued his walk with God. His descendants, except for the sparse few in his own household, did not. As it was before the Great Deluge, so it remained. Man was darkened by his own humanist thinking. Specifically to the ancient Book of Jasher, Noah lived to see his great-grandson Nimrod reign "in the earth over all the sons of Noah (Jasher 7:45)." Furthermore, "all the earth was under his control (Jasher 9:20)."

But Nimrod did not go in the ways of the Lord. Jasher records, "And he was more wicked than all the men that were before him, from the days of the flood until those days. And he made gods of wood and stone, and bowed down to them, and he rebelled against the Lord, and taught all his subjects and the people of the earth his wicked ways (7:46-47)." That the inhabitants of Nimrod's kingdom, just as it is with the learned citizens of any ruling empire today—including our own, did not perceive themselves as wicked is evident in their desire to "reign upon the whole world," or rather, subdue them, in order that "the evil of (their) enemies may cease (9:21)," rather than first acknowledging their own sin and dealing with it.

The resulting tower was to extend to such great heights that they required a plot of land which could support a wide enough base. Again, according to Jasher, families numbering 600,000 men, not including women and children, sought the whole Earth and found none like "one valley at the east of the land of Shinar (9:23)." As it turned out, the tower became so large that "mortar and bricks did not reach the builders in their accent to it, until those who went up had completed a full year (9:27)." Its circumference was a three days walk (9:38). A man can walk across Manhattan in less than one. And while it is difficult getting a straight answer out of anyone, the true intent of their engineering marvel is made known when "they imagined in their hearts to war against the Lord God of heaven and ascend into heaven (9:25)." Noah's descendants even began to shoot arrows towards the firmament. When each arrow returned, tips dipped with blood, they convinced themselves that God's defeat was assured (Jasher 9:29).

A careful commentator on the grievous conditions of mankind in every age will likely conclude that we needn't build a tower today to transgress or sin wickedly against the Lord. Though admittedly, while Nimrod built one tower, we have entire metropolises of them. Jasher once more records that a third of its builders imagined in their hearts to "ascend to heaven and fight against Him." Another third imagined in their hearts to "smite Him with bows and spears," once arriving, and still another third imagined in their hearts "the placement of their own gods" (Jasher 9:26).

Is it not so terribly uncommon that a man seeks to murder God in his heart? The Psalmist reminds us, "The fool says in his heart, '*There is no God.*' (Psalm 14:1)" Even today tales of heaven, as told by the whimsical inventions of the humanist mind, is filled with the sort of self-enlightenment fitting for a disciple of Rene Descartes rather than Jesus Christ our Lord, each proclaiming, "I think, therefore I am!" rather than identifying his own being by first proclaiming "In the beginning, God...." So too, according to the humanist, is heaven dominated with visions of familiar faces and an ambiance of "love" filling in the centerfold rather than the throne of our living God.

We read throughout Holy Scripture that God's favorite tactic in defeating man is by throwing him into confusion. This is most easily done. A mind turned away from God, firmly pressed upon his own philosophical insight, is always darkened and delusional. Even man's self-declared renaissance of natural revelation and scientific reason cannot possibly rise above his self-enlightened deception. Today we are faced with the Science delusion. Indeed, the act of throwing a people into confusion, be it one soul or a gathering of many, is most easily accomplished. Only in God's light can we see true light (Psalm 36.9). Among the inhabitants of Babel, those who had imagined in their hearts to worship their own gods in heaven became like "apes and elephants" in their cognitive thinking. Those who shot arrows, being morally depraved individuals at best, murdered each other off. Jasher records of this confusion, "When the builder took from the hands of his neighbor lime or stone which he did not order, the builder would cast it away and throw it upon his neighbor, that he would die (Jasher 9:33)." And finally, those who sought to "fight against God," survived the collapse of the Tower, though the tower itself was destroyed among a human casualty beyond number (9:38-39), only to be scattered across the breadth of the Earth.

54

Oral history affirms this.

Reader, be warned. Anyone who attempts to enter into heaven by his own works, be it a magnificent structure such as Babel or by a simple kind word, he is at odds with God.

NATIONS OF INHERITANCE: According to the Sons of God or the Children of Israel?

MY READER IS LIKELY WELL INFORMED REGARDING my desire to honor the *Textus Receptus*, the Greek New Testament by which both the King James Bible stands upon and the Reformation took flight—though I am not beholden to it. The bad blood pitted against the Codex Sinaiticus and the Codex Vaticanus by those indebted to the TR is indeed a divisive one. There is however another sort of fraternal spat between those divided over the scholarship of the Masoretic Text of the Old Testament, which the King James is *also* based upon, and the Greek Septuagint, or LXX. The beautifully preserved Dead Sea Scrolls are a contributor of further historical and textual complications—if one wishes to see it in such light. The wealth of scholarly knowledge available to us, often pitted against each other, will not be discussed at any length here. We have however reached a fork in the road. Therefore a pause is in order. This might get messy.

The ancient Hebrew word *Mesorah* broadly refers to the whole of Jewish tradition, including *oral*, all of which claims to be unchanged and infallible. The Masoretic text is dated to the 7-10th centuries of the modern era, the earliest of which does not contain the Torah. The scholarly work of the Greek Septuagint however, the earliest of which *does* include the Torah, is a thousand years its elder, and matches many New Testament quotations, particularly throughout the Pauline Epistles. In fact, the one time we are told that Jesus read Scripture in the synagogue (Luke 4:14-30), a passage from Isaiah, he borrowed from the LXX.

Ah, but there's more.

Further complications arise whenever Jesus alludes to Scripture in the Gospels. He often does so in a manner which agrees with the Aramaic Targum, not the Greek or Hebrew versions, and when quoting Isaiah 66:24, "where their word does not die, and the fire is no quenched," he clearly favors the Aramaic, because the word *Gehenna* does not appear in the Hebrew or Greek.

Backed with the 1947 discovery of the second temple era Dead Sea Scrolls, *that* and the LXX contain noticeable differences from the Masoretic, both great and small.

Here we arrive at our fork in the road. The Byzantine era Masoretic Text, which informed Reformation thinking and blessed their efforts greatly, takes a clear turn from second temple era Hebrew thinking. According to the King James Bible, Deuteronomy 32:8-9 reads:

8 When the Most High divided to the nations their inheritance, when He separated the sons of Adam, He set the bounds of the people according to the number of **the children of Israel**.

9 For the Lord's portion is His people; Jacob is the lot of His inheritance.

(Deuteronomy 32:8-9)

By this we are to *correctly* understand that Israel alone is Yahweh's portion. The NASB and NIV equally agree with the KJV. The dispute however at hand is the phrase *the children of Israel*. The number seventy, or "the number of the children of Israel," seems rather satisfactory, especially considering that seventy members of Jacob's family went down to Egypt in the days of Joseph. We might therefore read this *accordingly*; When Yahweh portioned out the nations each their own inheritance, He reserved for Israel an inheritance proportioned to its numbers. And yet the far older Greek Septuagint, which indisputable gave insight into Jesus' and Paul's worldview, presents us with an arbitrary departure from the Masoretic Text.

The LXX reads: "according to the number of **the angels of God**."

The difference between *children* and *angels* are undeniably dogmatic. Which is correct? Perhaps the pagan nations surrounding Israel might be of help to us. My reader need also recognize that what I am about to say is not of Biblical origin. Let us turn then to the flip of the coin—the Ugaritic Pantheon of gods. The Semitic speaking Canaanites to the north of ancient Israel tell of El, their chief god, who fathered a total of 70 sons—otherwise known as the 70 sons of El. His wife Asherah is likely recognized among the Biblical literate as one who adulterates the pure religion of Yahweh, though here she is named Athirat. Together with El their sexual union is said to create the dusk and dawn.

Discovered along the Syrian coast in Ras Shamra in 1929, the Ugaritic texts reveal a complicated story—one in which the children of Abraham would have intimately known and—quite tragically for many—become tragically embroiled in. What is not completely understood is Asherah's relationship with Baal. According to the Ugaritic texts, the god of the underworld has not only killed off a number of their children, but even usurped El's throne, thereby taking Asherah as his consort. The evils of Baal run deep into Hebrew thinking, and it should be interesting to note that archeological evidence demonstrates the idolatrous belief on behalf of many Hebrews that Yahweh had likewise taken Asherah as His consort. Kings Jehoshaphat and Hezekiah, among a handful of others, rightfully attempted to eradicate the worship of Asherah in Israel and Judea. And Biblically speaking, the Prophets were dutifully angered when their contemporaries abandoned Yahweh to worship the god of the underworld. Baal may have been a real *god*, and I have no doubt he even attempted to usurp God's throne—particularly where winning over the public opinion is concerned—but as truth would have it he certainly was no Yahweh, nor will he ever have comparable standing with him.

Let us not make the mistake of blending false religion with true religion, a damnable error of so many ancient Hebrews. Though the differences are many, the Semitic similarities among the Canaanites and the Hebrews is in similar point of contact—the human tragedy at the Tower of Babel. It is to the Chaldeans in which we must next turn and by doing so recall how the Ugaritic texts present an unmistakable parallel to the Septuagint. But *ah-ha*, there's more.

The Dead Sea Scrolls introduce an even clearer picture than what the Septuagint hopes to offer. The nations of the world were divvied up among members of God's heavenly entourage. Here the Torah reads:

> [8] When the Most High gave to the nations their inheritance, when He divided mankind, He fixed the borders of the peoples according to the number of **the sons of God**.

> [9] But the Lord's portion is His people, Jacob His allotted heritage.

(Deuteronomy 32:8-9, ESV)

Dogmatic differences indeed. If the second temple-era Dead Sea Scrolls are to be believed, then the long neglected worldview of the ancient Hebrew, as embodied by the Divine Council, changes everything. In a little while we shall see why the papyrus scrolls of Qumran presents us with the *right* interpretation, or rather, the most logical conclusion to make, because elsewhere in Deuteronomy, not even the Masoretic Text can disagree.

The *sons of God* fall in perfect synchronicity.

THE UNTOLD STORY OF BABEL:
CONFUSION OF TONGUES *(and Inheritance of Gods)*

THE EDENIC VISION HAD FAILED, AND THAT IS PUTTING IT lightly. Yahweh's created image and the sons of God who had copulated with the daughters of men had failed so miserably in their commissioned tasks that "it repented Yahweh that He had made man on the earth, and it grieved Him at His heart." We *also* know what became of His sorrow. God destroyed the world with a deluge of water. Afterwards, the family He spared was given the same Edenic responsibility that Adam and Eve had first been tasked with. Noah and his descendants were expected to participate in Yahweh's administrative affairs. They were to make His name known, not only among their own generation, but those to come. But the children of Noah did not wish to spread the commonwealth of Gods kingdom over the face of the earth. Rather, they inverted the very purpose by which they were created. Nimrod and the people of his dominion wanted "heaven as it is on earth," *but never* "earth as it is in heaven." Like most human movements which advertise God as having endorsed them, the generation of Nimrod jointly declared: "Come, let us make a name for *ourselves*."

Scholarly history and the Bible both fall in agreement. Though we do not know *if* or *how* the name of Yahweh was borrowed from, the builders of Babel gladly aligned themselves with the divine members of his pantheon; namely the stars above and the sons of God who seem to embody them; so long as gods helped them achieve their ultimate goals—self-salvation.

Babel was making headlines. It is due to the biggest news story of that generation that the divine council reemerges. Yahweh personally *comes down* from heaven to inspect the city and the tower, perhaps in a similar *physical* fashion as His earthly visit several chapters later with Sodom. Upon returning to his heavenly assembly, He delivers the following report: "Behold, the people are one, and they all have the same language. And this is what they began to do, and now nothing

60

which they purpose to do will be impossible for them." A suggestion is then presented and collectively agreed upon. "Come, let *us* go down and confuse their language, so that they will not understand one another's speech." Though their last documented meeting in Genesis 1:26 discussed the creation of man in their own image, it was God who made it happen. The same is applied here. Moses records: "So Yahweh scattered them abroad from there over the face of the whole earth; and they stopped building the city (Genesis 11:8)."

Thus the genealogy from Shem to Abraham promptly takes flight, and Yahweh's dispersion is deemed such a success that the whereabouts of the plains of Shinar have long been sought, and are still debated to this day. But the historical location of Babel's Tower is not what is important here. Unbeknownst to most of us, the story of Babel does not come to an end—far from it. True, the city itself is no longer built, and if the book of Jasher is to be believed as a historical document, the tower is thrown to disastrous ruin, but that is not to say the *religion* itself has not successfully scattered with her host tongue. It has indeed—*that* and so much more. The various ziggurats which expanded from the plains of Shinar give ample testimony to that fact. With its initial destruction, the celestial mountain of the gods, which once hosted the common language of the day by casting a dominant shadow over the plains of Shinar, simply became a series of mountain ranges. More shadows would be cast.

In fact, the whole world was darkened by what was contained within them.

2

UNDER THE SHADOW OF THE ZIGGURATS — MOUNTAINS OF THE GODS

IT CAN BE SAID OF THE ZIGGURATS SCATTERED ACROSS ancient Mesopotamia that heaven and the underworld *once* met halfway on earth. More precisely, gods and men assembled in counsel, and their astrological significance cannot be overstated. The seven levels of the ziggurat attest to this fact. Their function as temporal dwellings of deity—in essence earthly houses for the very starry beings they studied and served—was made manifest with each name. The ziggurat at Til Barsip was called "the house of the seven directions of heaven and earth." In Babylon it was aptly titled "the house of the foundation of heaven and earth." And its lower Babylonia sibling was "the house of the bond between heaven and earth."

Much like their founding counterpart on the plains of Shinar, the ziggurat represented man's continual attempt at cultivating their own mountainous paradise of Eden apart from the Creator. They personified an Edenic vision grossly perversified. And though few of these muddy ruins of antiquity remain, my reader is likely already advised not to write them off as mere superstition—far from it. The Occult centers of our past, where the Sciences were nurtured from the demonic breast, would have Helena Blavatsky in 1877 asking of her fellow Theosophists: "If modern masters are so much in advance of the old ones, why do they not restore to us the lost arts of our postdiluvian forefathers? The more archaeology and philology advance, the more humiliating to our pride are the discoveries which are daily made, the more glorious testimony do they bear in behalf of those who, perhaps on account of the distance of their remote antiquity, have been until now considered ignorant flounderers in the deepest mire of superstition." In fact, the Mysteries have strengthened since Blavatsky's time—quite considerably. Regardless, Blavatsky wasn't merely grasping for ghosts. So monumental were the intricate inner workings of the Babel religion that the books and epistles of Enoch, Isaiah, Jude, Peter, and John's Revelation would make careful note of its apocalyptic consequence. In other words, their shadows still loom over us today.

The post-enlightenment Christian will have a ghastly time comprehending the reality *behind* Mesopotamia's claimed spiritual experiences, and yet the Bible confirms them as true in so much as the divine sons of Gods, both righteous and wicked, are associated with the heavenly stars of man's unending adoration. That the Sciences of his devotion were also born and nurtured among these Occult monuments must also be confronted. Today the planetary week remains a human institution. It is Noah's grandchildren who we might thank for this. They enlisted the zodiac for their studies, even managing to compute the eclipses of the sun and the moon by means of the saros, and it is Herodotus who credited the Babylonians for having passed the sundial and the division of the day into twelve hours to the Greeks.

The ziggurat builders referred to the planets as Interpreters. "Whereas all the other stars are fixed and follow a single circuit in a regular course," writes Robert Leo Odom in *Sunday in Roman Paganism*, "these alone [Interpreters], by virtue of following each its own course, point out future events, thus interpreting to mankind the design of the gods." The planets have exerted the greatest influence for both good and evil upon the nativity of men. "For sometimes by their risings, sometimes by their settings, and again by their color, the Chaldeans say, they give signs of coming events to such as are willing to observe them closely."

Among their dispensing of hidden knowledge among the *mortal* councils of men, the Interpreters were accredited for advising on eclipses of the sun and the moon as well as earthquakes. When pressed to the predictability of eclipses in modern astronomy as proof of a globular earth, the present patron of a flat, immovable earth needs only remind him of the religion which his entire belief system is derived upon—Babel. Writes Theosophist Grace F. Knoche in *The Mystery Schools*: "...the science of prediction of tremendous cyclic occurrences on earth was mastered not only in India to a fine hair's breath, but also in ancient Chaldea, whose modern representatives of some four and five thousand years ago still held archaic astrology as a major characteristic of their secret Mysteries. The famous ziggurat or high tower of Borsippa in Babylonia is clear testimonial to knowledge of the sevenfold planetary influences on humanity. Called *the stages of the seven spheres*, each of its stories bore a different color, representative of the seven sacred planets."

Each floor of the ziggurat found at Babylon not only celebrated the seven luminaries, or Interpreters, matched with the seven metals and colors associated with them, but the number of heavens they wandered through and, just as importantly, ascending planes of spiritual existence they represented. In *Chaldea from the Earliest Times to the Rise of Assyria* (1886), Zénaïde A. Ragozin describes the Babylon's ziggurat as follows: "The ornamentation of the edifice was chiefly by means of color. The seven Stages represented the Seven Spheres, in which moved, according to ancient Chaldean astronomy, the seven planets. To each planet fancy, partly grounding itself upon fact, had from of old assigned a peculiar tint or hue. The Sun (Shamesh) was golden; the Moon (Sin or Nannar), silver; the distant Saturn (Adar) almost beyond the region of light, was black; Jupiter (Marduk) was orange; the fiery Mars (Nergal) was red; Venus (Ishtar) was a pale yellow; Mercury (Nebo or Nabu, whose shrine stood on the top stage), a deep blue. The seven stages of the tower gave a visible embodiment to these fancies...." Later he writes: "That the ziggurats of Chaldea should have been used not only as pedestals to uphold shrines, but as observatories by the priestly astronomers and astrologers, was quite in accordance with the strong mixture of star-worship grafted on the older religion, and with the power ascribed to the heavenly bodies over the acts and destinies of men."

Furthermore situated among the course of the Interpreters, according to the Chaldeans, were thirty fixed stars, "which they designate as counseling gods," overseers of the regions above and beneath the earth. Odom writes: "Twelve of these gods, they say, hold chief authority, and to each of these the Chaldeans assign a month...and through the midst of these signs [the zodiac], they say, both the Sun and Moon and the five planets make their course, the Sun completing his cycle in a year and the Moon traversing her circuit in a month."

This brings us to the matter of the gods themselves. Each city in Mesopotamia housed its own patron god, and that divine being was usually perceived to be the landowner of its host ziggurat and the area immediately surrounding it. For example, Marduk was the god of Babylon; Enki the god of Eridu; Ishtar the goddess of Nineveh; Nergal for Kuthu; Ninazu for Eshnunna; Ninurta for Lagash; Enlil for Nippur; Nanna for Ur; and Inanna (or the Lady of the Sky and Queen of Heaven) for Uruk, the capital city where Gilgamesh ruled. Though the king served as bailiff, it was the priests alone who were allowed inside each ziggurat, simultaneously tasked with attending to the needs of the gods and giving them absolute power over society.

All of this gives way to a very important point.

The confusion of tongues wasn't *merely* a disbanding of people as an explanation for various population groups—though this, in and of itself, it certainly a true conclusion to make. Yahweh's dispersal of the nations at Babel resulted in a far more peculiar truth—one which is rarely discussed nor understood. The ziggurats are testimony to the immediate aftermath. What ultimately resulted at Babel was the worldwide dispersion of *gods*.

3

THE UNTOLD STORY OF BABEL — CONFUSION OF TONGUES (*and Inheritance of Gods*) ....Continued

THE APOSTLE PAUL WOULD LATER SUM UP the human tragedy that was Babel when he wrote in Romans 1:18-25 that God *gave men over* to their persistent rebellion. God decided that the descendants of

Noah would no longer be in relationship with Him. If they were only interested in "making a name for themselves" then He was not interested in being their God. In dividing the lands to all people, Yahweh exemplified the first half of the parable of the prodigal son. The unthankful nations could now go out and squander their inheritances however it pleased them.

As with the parable of the prodigal son, what remained of God's inheritance would be given to the *elder* child—mainly, a people who had yet to exist; children whom He would personally help to create through Abraham's seed and a woman far too old for conception. And He wouldn't delay either. Though inheritances were divided in Genesis 11, Abraham would receive his call in the following chapter. In this regard, Yahweh generously left room for His own chosen children, a humble sliver of real estate alongside the Mediterranean coast, so that they might cultivate the Edenic vision without any pressure from the surrounding nations.

It is noticeable that the children of Lot and Esau were carefully preserved from disturbing Israel. According to Deuteronomy 2, the LORD instructed the Israelites to venture first northward through the land which had been given unto the children of Esau, and then onward through Moab, which had been given unto the children of Lot. In both instances, they were not to meddle with them, "for I will not give you their land, no, not so much as a foot breadth (Deuteronomy 2:5)."

The Apostle Paul likewise included Babel in his Gospel narrative when addressing the Greek philosophers on Mars Hill. To this effect he said: "And hath made of one blood all nations of men for to dwell on all the face of the earth, and hath determined the times before appointed, and the bounds of their habitation (Acts 17:26)." If Yahweh determined the appointed times and the bounds of their habitation, He would then need to assign *elohim* over the people's so that the laws of the court might be kept. Justice however did not prevail. It is certainly not inconsequential that an endless gauntlet of delirious empires, always ravenous of appetite and salivating at the mouth, would cast their gaze upon the blessed land in order that they might plot and loot it.

A proponent for the Masoretic Text will immediately throw up his arms in protest. If Paul was referencing Deuteronomy 32:8-9, they'll say, Yahweh then "set the bounds of the people according to the number of the *children of Israel*." Such a reading seems straightforward enough. Why must I overcomplicate this? I promised earlier that the Dead Sea

Scrolls rendering of *sons of God* in Deuteronomy 32:8-9, rather than the traditional *children of Israel* reading in the Masoretic Text, not forgetting the Septuagint's decision to describe *angels of God*, would all three find agreement elsewhere.

And they do!

In Deuteronomy 4 the context is the same as chapter 32. The children of Israel are preparing to claim their inheritance in the land which God has kept for them. These are of course instructions on how they are to behave, if they are to be in a relationship with Yahweh. Idolatry is clearly forbidden, "Lest ye corrupt yourselves." The children of Israel are therefore not to make the graven image of any figure, male or female, the likeness of any beast on the earth, fowl in the air, anything the creepeth on the ground of fish in the waters beneath the earth. Yahweh then describes what they are *especially* forbidden to worship.

> [19] And lest thou lift up thine eyes unto heaven, and when thou seest the sun, and the moon, and the stars, even all the host of heaven, shouldest be driven to worship them, and serve them, which the Lord thy God hath divided unto all nations under the whole heaven.

> [20] But the Lord hath taken you, and brought you forth out of the iron furnace, even out of Egypt, to be unto him a people of inheritance, as ye are this day.

(Deuteronomy 4:19-20 KJV)

The hosts of heaven, God says, have been "divided unto all nations under the whole heaven." At an absolute minimal, the Septuagint and Dead Sea Scrolls' rendering of Deuteronomy 32:8-9 which, might I remind you are far older than the Masoretic Text, are at least correct in their worldview. After Babel, Yahweh set the bounds of the people according to the number of the sons of God. But that is not to say that the sons of God are not corruptible. Need we revisit the ziggurats?

Let us rather return to Psalm 82. Once again, it reads:

> [1] God [*elohim*] standeth in the congregation of the mighty; He administers judgement in the midst of the gods [*elohim*].

> [2] How long will you judge unjustly and show favoritism to the wicked? Selah

> [3] Judge on behalf of the helpless and the orphan; provide justice to the afflicted and the poor.

66

⁴ Rescue the helpless and the needy; deliver them from the hand of the wicked.

⁵ They do not know or consider. They go about in the darkness, so that all the foundations of the earth are shaken.

⁶ I have said, You are gods [*elohim*], and sons of the Most High, all of you.

⁷ However, you will die like men, and you will fall like one of the princes.

(Psalm 82)

Asaph neatly describes a meeting of the divine council in heaven. A multitude of thrones are set up, as Daniel might say. When the Ancient of Days stands in the congregation of the elohim, court proceedings begin. As with the case of Psalm 82, God administers judgement over the elohim before Him—why? Asaph informs us they have judged unjustly among the nations, and accepted persons of wickedness into their favored ranks. Among their wealth and storehouses of *hidden knowledge* from heaven, they "know not, neither will they understand;" for "they walk on in darkness," and "all the foundations of the earth are out of course." Their judgement is clear. While the Lake of Fire is not here revealed, the sons of God "shall die like men." And what may be a direct reference to the Prince of Tire (Ezekiel 28), or rather Lucifer, they shall "fall like one of the princes."

With Deuteronomy 4:19-20, Yahweh's warning to the His children is straightforward enough. Those who worship the stars [and the hidden knowledge of the stars, the religion of the stars, and the Sciences of the stars] will receive their inheritance with them.

Even the stars "will die like men."

For this very reason, Jesus became lower than the angels. This is what the eighth Psalmist tells us, anyhow. After considering "the heavens, the work of thy fingers, the moon and the stars, which thou hast ordained," David then turns his attention on the Messiah and a rather peculiar plot point to his ancient Hebrew worldview. "For thou hast made Him a little lower than the angels," he writes. As a result, God "hast crowned him with glory and honor," and "Thou madest him to have dominion over the works of thy hands; thou hast put all things under his feet," including the elohim who rule the nations. By this we are to understand an important component of the Messiahs mission. Jesus, the only begotten Son of God, would descend to the lower parts of the earth in order that He might *inherit* the nations which Yahweh had disavowed.

Psalm 82 therefore ends:

"Rise up, O God, judge the earth, because You shall inherit all the nations."

OUR GOD IS A CONSUMING FIRE

1

STRANGE FIRE: THE IRREVERENT WORSHIP OF NADAB AND ABIHU

SCRIPTURE DOES NOT INTRODUCE US TO NADAB AND ABIHU as malevolent men. Quite contrarily, they were the eldest sons of Aaron—priests of the one true God. Nadab was heir to the office of high priest. Abihu was next in line. Nobody else but their father and Moses their uncle were given a more prestigious standing among God's chosen people. When Moses spoke with God upon Saini, the people of Israel had been instructed not to go "up into the mount, or touch the border of it" on clear instructions that "whosoever toucheth the mount shall be put to death." (Exodus 19:12) Even wild animals were to be put to death, should they dare to wander upon Sinai's skirt. The children of Israel could only watch the fire from afar while the ground jolted their balance and pitch-black smoke clotted the blue sky as it would from a furious furnace—covering their ears "while the sound of the trumpet grew louder and louder..." (Exodus 19:19). And yet Nadab and Abihu were specifically named among the "seventy elders" who were instructed to meet God upon the mountain.

Moses their uncle writes: "Then went up Moses, and Aaron, Nadab, and Abihu, and seventy of the elders of Israel: And they saw the God of Israel...." (Exodus 24:9-10) Aarons two sons, alongside their fellow elders, "saw God, and did eat and drink (Exodus 24:11)."

When the construction of the tabernacle was complete, Aaron and his sons were anointed in a week-long ceremony. On the eighth day Aaron offered the very first sin offering ever made in the tabernacle. As evidence of divine blessing, God miraculously intervened. "And there came a fire out from before the LORD, and consumed upon the altar the burnt offering and the fat: which when all the people saw, they shouted, and fell on their faces" (Leviticus 9:24).

Moses records what happened next. In a stunning turn of events, Nadab and Abihu were struck dead. Specifically, they were completely devoured by a fire from the Lord.

> "And Nadab and Abihu, the sons of Aaron, took either of them his censer, and put fire therein, and put incense thereon, and offered strange fire before the Lord, which he commanded them not. And there went out fire from the Lord, and devoured them, and they died before the Lord. Then Moses said unto Aaron, This is it that the Lord spake, saying, I will be sanctified in them that come nigh me, and before all the people I will be glorified. And Aaron held his peace. (Leviticus 10:1-3)"

How unfortunate for Nadab and Abihu and Aaron who—despite what he may have felt regarding the sentence of his sons—"held his peace." It is a serious crime to dishonor the Lord. And Aaron's sons had clearly offended Him. To this effect John MacArthur writes: "The actual source from which they obtained their fire is not recorded. Nor is it important. The point is they used something other than the fire God Himself had ignited. Their offense may seem trifling to someone accustomed to the type of casual, self-indulgent worship our generation is known for..." This prevailing taste of offhanded-adoration is a humiliation which cannot be over-amplified. Is there no end to the Scripture twisting which might assist the delight of our own extra-Biblical experiences? "Still, what Scripture expressly condemns is the strange fire they offered."

The Apostle of Hebrews would later write: "It is a fearful thing to fall into the hands of the living God" (Hebrews 10:31). Soon thereafter, the same author would direct our attention back upon the Law of Moses, who fearfully wrote: "For the LORD thy God is a consuming fire (Deuteronomy 4:24)."

Likewise, the Apostle of Hebrews would not have us forget: "For our God is a consuming fire (Hebrews 12:29)"

MOUNT SINAI: HOLY MOUNTAIN OF GOD —MORAL DEPRAVITY OF MAN

THE GLORY OF THE LORD UPON THE MOUNTAINTOP was described as *a devouring fire* to the eyes of every man, woman, and child of Israel. Only Moses and Aaron, Nadab and Abihu, and the seventy elders were permitted to gaze upon the God of Israel. However, Moses then instructed everyone involved to tarry where they stood while he alone ascended into the midst of the cloud, where the "LORD spake unto Moses face to face, as a man speaketh unto his friend (Exodus 33:11)." Another forty days would pass. And Israel grew *restless*. What follows is perhaps the most morally depraved narrative in the entire history of the human race. Though the mountaintop itself was *a consuming fire*; though "all the people saw the thunderings, and the lightnings, and the noise of the trumpet, and the mountain smoking," and though, when they "saw it, they removed, and stood afar off (Exodus 20:18)," they also *waited* in the twilight of their cantankerous reverie. When the people saw that Moses delayed to come down from the mount of God, they turned to fiction, to fantasy, and perverse *appetite*. Everyone wants to be a mouth-piece for God. And so they turned to *dark speeches*. Specifically, they turned to Satan—apparently no stranger to the camp of Israel—by making for themselves a golden calf.

Even within eyesight and earshot of God's holy company, mankind chose degradation—how tragic. Moses records, they offered burnt offerings, "and sat down to eat and drink, and rose up to play (Exodus 32:6)." Their total abandonment—their preference in worshiping Yahweh how they wanted to worship Him, preferring the shadows of Sinai rather than the *devouring fire* which crowned the mountaintop, was of such agitation and obnoxiousness that, after Joshua heard the noise of the people, he said unto Moses, "There is a noise of war in the camp."

Moses responded: "It is not the voice of them that shout for mastery, neither is it the voice of them that cry for being overcome: but the noise of them that sing do I hear."

When Moses entered the camp, he "saw that the people were naked; for Aaron had made them naked unto their shame among their enemies (Exodus 32:25)." Though most modern commentators prefer *licentious* or *unruly* when describing the depths of their depravity, the King James translators chose to describe the Israelites as literally naked. This is certainly not outside of the reasonable realm, for the religion of the Mysteries, particularly the Egyptian rites from which they had only recently been delivered from, performed their enchantments in the same orgasmic manner. But either way, it is of no difference. They were stripped not only of their outer ornaments, but the acumen of their mind. Like a naked Adam and Eve hiding from God, they sacrificed the holiness of their Creators image for the pleasures of *another* religious experience. Essentially, they disrobed, and by doing so, they disavowed the only security which protected them from the government of Satan.

About three-thousand men fell that day—not including the women.

"For our God is a consuming fire (Hebrews 12:29)"

By referring us to the Holy Scripture of ages past, the Apostle of Hebrews would have us know there is a lesson to be had. Have we any reason to fear God *less* under this new dispensation as we do under the old? We Christians serve the God of the mountaintop; the very God who rained fire and brimstone down upon Sodom and Gomorrah and who later consumed Elijah's sacrifice on Mount Caramel with fire from heaven after it had been dosed with a wealthy supply of water. The communicable image by which we were created in has not changed— apart from the wrecking ball of our own sin (which has polluted it)—nor has His glorious incommunicable attributes, and the guiding principles of His governance will never be replaced. Writes Albert Barnes in his 1846 commentary on Hebrews: "He was no more the friend of sin now than he was then; and the same perfections of his nature which would then lead him to punish transgression would also lead him to do it now. His anger was really as terrible, and as much to be dreaded as it was at Mount Sinai; and the destruction which he would inflict on his foes would be as terrible now as it was then. The fearfulness with which He would come forth to destroy the wicked might be compared to a fire that consumed all before it."

Christ is truly god, King of kings and Lord of lords, and though He is a dispenser of grace and mercy on all who wish to humble themselves and receive it, His glorious appearing is certain. God is an all-consuming fire, and those who will not have Him to reign over them are sworn to wrath.

Nadab and Abihu were stubble playing with fire.

"Your Breath, As Fire, Shall Devour You..."

IT IS A PORTRAIT OF TOTAL DESTRUCTION. In yet another stunning revelation of the apocalypse to come, the Prophet Isaiah followed the *licentiousness* of Israel at Sinai to its natural and ultimate conclusion. He foresaw such a time of *nakedness* that "the highways lie waste" and "the wayfaring man ceaseth." Moral depravity has run its course. It is the long promised hour of Jesus Christ's return, when His all-consuming fire—once manifested from the mountaintop—resides forevermore with mankind, for he writes:

> "Now will I rise, saith the LORD; now will I be exalted; now will I lift up myself. Ye shall conceive chaff, ye shall bring forth stubble: your breath, as fire, shall devour you (Isaiah 33:10-11)."

Those who will not have the King of kings and Lord of lords to reign over them are dutifully sworn to wrath—it is of their own choosing. They will most certainly attempt to shield themselves, but the security granted them has been abandoned for sandy foundations and the doomed government of Satan. Any attempt at self-preservation will be as pathetic and weak, Isaiah declares, as one who conceives chaff and brings forth stubble. In reading this passage, we shall not overlook one important fact. Their *own sins* will ignite them. "Your breath, as fire, shall devour you." Mankind is doomed.

Isaiah warned that no amount of our righteousness is sufficient in the presence of a holy God. He wrote: "But we are all as an unclean thing, and all our righteousness are as filthy rags; and we all do fade as a leaf; and our iniquities, like the wind, have taken us away (Isaiah 64:6)."

James the brother of our Lord Jesus rerouted our attention to the *sinful breath* when he wrote:

> "And the tongue is a fire, a world of iniquity: so is the tongue among our members, that it defileth the whole body, and setteth on fire the course of nature; and it is set on fire of hell [Gehenna] (James 3:6)."

The Prophet furthermore writes: "And the people shall be as the burnings of lime: as thorns cut up shall they be burned in the fire (Isaiah 33:12)." When the hypocrites witness the despair—a total annihilation of their fellow sinners; while they helplessly stand in line before the unquenchable fires of Gehenna; they will be completely overwhelmed with the very reality they have altogether dismissed, or perhaps simply *put off*. They will quiver with fear after conceding to the terrible fate of what awaits them, for Isaiah writes: "The sinners in Zion are afraid; fearfulness hath surprised the hypocrites." But *eternity* has come, and there can be no escape.

They will even ask each other:

"Who among us shall dwell with the devouring fire? Who among us shall dwell with everlasting burnings? (Isaiah 33:14)"

When God's consuming fire encompasses the entire world rather than the mountaintop, the *moral* man is *finished*. There is no hope for the hypocrite. He shall fade away as a leaf and be swept away with the wind. "They have cast away the law of the LORD of hosts," Isaiah wrote, "and despised the word of the Holy One of Israel." It is for this very reason that they will be devoured in the flames.

"Therefore as the fire devoureth the stubble, and the flame consumeth the chaff, so their root shall be as rottenness, and their blossom shall go up as dust (Isaiah 5:24)."

Only the righteous will survive. Isaiah describes such as person as: "He that walketh righteously, and speaketh uprightly; he that despiseth the gain of oppressions, that shaketh his hands from holding of bribes, that stoppeth his ears from hearing of blood, and shutteth his eyes from seeing evil (Isaiah 33:15)." By this we are assured that some will escape the devouring fire, for Isaiah concludes of the righteous man:

"Thine eyes shall see the king in His beauty: they shall behold the land that is very far off (Isaiah 33:17)."

That day, it seems, cannot come soon enough for the righteous. But let's not get ahead of ourselves, because *God wishes that none shall perish*.

4

OUR GOD IS A CONSUMING FIRE

GOD WISHING THAT NONE SHALL PERISH is the *one thing* which the Apostle Peter would have us not be ignorant of. The Father did not send His Son to die for the *few*. That Jesus said, "For God so loved the *world* that He gave His only begotten Son," is an irrefutable fact of Calvary. The proposition to behold God's consuming fire upon the mountaintop was an invitation open to every child of Israel, just as we are invited to gaze reverently upon Calvary today and believe. But that is not to say that everyone will come to repentance—far from it! God delivered *all* of Israel from Pharaoh's army through the straight gate and narrow way at the Red Sea crossing, but even after their baptism, not everyone chose to remain with Him. At the base of the mountain they chose moral depravity. Many elected the gate which was wide in the wilderness and the path which lead to destruction. They desired God's kingdom come and the land promised to them, but only if Satan was enthroned upon it.

The reality however remains, Jesus Christ is soon returning. If God is a consuming fire, it is because He is holy, and it is for this very reason that everything which is unholy will be completely incinerated. For this reason Jesus died on the cross and it is most certainly why, when considering His Davidic kingdom we long for, "the Lord is *not* slack concerning his promise, as some men count slackness; but is longsuffering to us-ward (2 Peter 3:9)." God wishes that none shall perish; that all would come to repentance; that we would come to comprehend why Christ mitigated God's wrath, becoming sin who knew no sin; exchanging His perfect righteousness for our sin—so that *we* "might become the righteousness of God (2 Corinthians 5:21)" and endure the flames.

The Apostle John stood in agreement with the Prophet Isaiah when he wrote:

> "And the kings of the earth, and the great men, and the rich men, and the chief captains, and the mighty men, and every bondman, and every free man, hid themselves in the dens and in the rocks of the mountains; And said to the mountains and rocks, Fall on us, and hide us from the face of him that sitteth on the throne, and from the wrath of the Lamb: For the great day of his wrath is come; and who shall be able to stand? (Revelation 6:15-17)"

In a somewhat ironic twist, the very world which the ungodly presently covet for their own selves serves a tender box, which will only aide in igniting them.

"But the heavens and the earth, which are now, by the same word are kept in store, reserved unto fire against the day of judgment and perdition of ungodly men (2 Peter 3:7)."

That is not to say God is a consuming fire only for some and not for others. Pass through the fire we *must*. Perhaps this is why the Apostle Paul warned that our works build w upon the foundation of Christ with superior material than wood, hay, and stubble. For though such a man shall suffer loss, Paul writes, he himself shall be saved, "yet so as by fire." To this effect we read:

"For other foundation can no man lay than that is laid, which is Jesus Christ. Now if any man build upon this foundation gold, silver, precious stones, wood, hay, stubble; Every man's work shall be made manifest: for the day shall declare it, because it shall be revealed by fire; and the fire shall try every man's work of what sort it is. If any man's work abide which he hath built thereupon, he shall receive a reward. If any man's work shall be burned, he shall suffer loss: but he himself shall be saved; yet so as by fire (1 Corinthians 3:11-15)."

Unlike Israel under the shadow of Sinai, who chose rather to sing and dance in a naked state before their enemies, we are at a disadvantage. They had a devouring fire to illuminate their thinking and guide their way through the wilderness. We have not yet ascended the mountain, so to speak. We have yet to meet the LORD face to face, as a man speaketh unto his friend, and "not in *dark speeches*." But if we are to be counted among the righteous, it is not because of our filthy rags of self-righteousness and *only* because we are found hidden in Christ.

To put it in slightly different terms, we anticipate the consuming fire, and by doing so, we are living for eternity *now*.

"Go Serve Other Gods..." THE BIBLICAL WORLDVIEW OF KING DAVID *(1 Samuel 26)*

THE KILLING OF THE PHILISTINE GIANT GOLIATH by the shepherd boy David did not go over nearly as well as one might expect. The *initial* twist to the plot is that the King of Israel wanted the child whom the Prophet Samuel had anointed dead. There were of course other complications, but the short of it is that David soon found himself on the run for his life. We pick up years thereafter. David has now fled beyond the borders of Israel. While in pursuit, Saul and his soldiers have fallen into a deep sleep. During the cloak of night, David has snatched the spear which Saul had stuck into the ground near his head, and stands now on the opposite ridge.

It is the dawn of early morning. David confronts Abner, Saul's cousin and the commander-in-chief of his army, and cries out amongst the clayish diffusion of purple light, which has yet to give definition to him, demanding that he is worthy to die for not tending to his master as he ought. Abner initially seems confused by this, particularly his unidentified accuser. Only Saul recognizes the voice of the armor bearer whom he had once so dearly loved.

The king says: "Is this thy voice, my son David?"

In which David replies: "It is my voice, my lord, O king."

He then adds: "Why then is my lord pursuing his servant? What have I done, and what evil is in my hand?" And this is where the underlying message gets rather strange. "Now therefore, please let my lord the king, listen to the words of his servant. If the Lord has stirred you up against me, let Him accept an offering; but if it is men, cursed are they before the Lord, for they have driven me out today **so that I would have no attachment with the inheritance of the Lord,** saying, '**Go, serve other gods.**'"

David is clearly distressed. While pleading the case of his innocence, he is simultaneously reminding the king that he has been unjustly excused beyond the borders of Israel's blessing, and as a result he has "no attachment with the inheritance of the Lord." Furthermore, if there is any confusion on the reader's behalf, the intent of those who wished to chase him out is made known. As an exile, he is mockingly told to go and "serve other gods." David takes this to heart. His confidence in killing the giant Goliath derived from a rooted belief in his own identity as a son of Abraham and Isaac and Jacob. His was an indisputable call to finish what Joshua and the Israelites had started when they sought to annihilate the serpent seed of the Rephaim from the land of God's promise, and which the giants were illegally imposing on.

The children of Israel wandered forty years through the wilderness because of their faithlessness. But David did not share these qualities. He was very much like Joshua, faithful to live according to God's promises. Unfortunately, quite unlike Joshua, he was expelled from God's inheritance. Let us not forget that Asaph, the writer of Psalm 82, was an officer of his court. He was personally commissioned by David the King to lead worship in the house of Yahweh. What is perhaps most important to take away here is that David wholeheartedly believed the gods who had spawned the Nephilim hybrids and their Rephaim descendants, embodied once by the infamous King Og and most recently with Goliath of Gath, not only ruled the lands surrounding Israel—for David, the gods were *real*.

If the surrounding tribes and monarchs were imposing on the commonwealth of Israel, it's because they had already received their inheritance at the table of nations. But for David, the shepherd boy who would become king, there was a greater tragedy afoot. Now even Saul, Israel's first king, had become the thief.

> "For thou, LORD, art high above all the earth: Thou art exalted far above all gods [*elohim*] (Psalm 97:9)."

2

THE WRITER OF FIRST SAMUEL INFORMS US the Philistine Goliath "drew near morning, and evening, and presented himself forty days" without ever finding a challenger brave enough to meet him in combat. With this neatly framed picture we hearken back to the negative report of the twelve men who scouted out the land of Canaan in Numbers 13. After forty days afoot, they brought up an evil report of the land which they had searched, mainly the giants, the sons of Anak, which came, *we are told*, of the giants. Moses further records, "All the congregation lifted up their voice, and cried; and the people wept all night (Numbers 14:1)." Only Joshua and Caleb pleaded with Israel to claim the inheritance which the LORD was freely giving to them.

"Would that we had died in the land of Egypt!" the children of Israel wailed.

For their disobedience, the LORD sentenced Israel to wander through the wilderness for forty years—one year for every day in which the spies searched the land. Here the situation is regurgitated with Goliath of Gath. All the men of Israel, when they saw the giant, fled from him in fear. Upon finally looking about for his challenger and seeing a mere youth, pinkish and of a fair countenance, the giant disdained him.

Goliath scowled: "Am I a dog that you come to me with sticks?"

Here the writer of 1 Samuel notes, "and the Philistine cursed David **by his gods** (1 Samuel 17:43)." Goliath of Gath was not some random intimidator. It is no accident that the report of the spies concerning the giants of Canaan and the Philistine tormentor parallel each other. As one who clearly embodied the seed of the serpent, the giant Goliath was attempting to rob from the LORD's inheritance. The kingdom of Israel, which included the land as well as the people who inhabited it, were His inheritance. And like Joshua and Caleb before him, only David was faithful in his fulfilling the duties of his commission.

David said to the giant: "You come to me with a sword, a spear, and a javelin, but I come to you in the name of the LORD of hosts, the God of the armies of Israel, whom you have taunted!" He then added: "This day the LORD will deliver you up into my hands, that all the earth may know that there is a God in Israel," finally concluded: "the battle is Yahweh's!"

The writer of First Samuel then records, when the Philistine arose, the young lad ran not only towards the Philistine, but the ranks of the army which kept him. After the smooth stone sunk into his forehead, David then stood upon the blasphemer, drew the giants' sword from his sheath, slew him, and then dismembered his head. The writer makes a careful note that David had brought had no sword of his own to the battle.

If the reader concludes this is simply a Sunday school approved underdog story; yet another narrative detailing the prevailing human spirit against tyranny; innocence against corruption; then he has missed an altogether important undercurrent of the Bible—and perhaps the entire point of the ancient Hebrew cosmological worldview. This was not simply a battle pitted between a boy and a rather large individual. It was a show of force between the children of gods. Only Yahweh had a right to the kingdom of Israel and the people of His promise who inhabited it.

The Biblical writer had one important *truth* on his side, which I dare not neglect. The Most High was the God of Israel. There is *none* beside Him. The writer of First Kings would say it like this:

"LORD God of Israel, there is no god [*elohim*] like thee, in heaven above, or on earth beneath (1 Kings 8:23)."

"I Saw Elohim Ascending Out of the Earth!" THE TRAGEDY OF KING SAUL & THE NECROMANCER

"THEN SAMUEL TOOK THE HORN OF OIL, and anointed David in the midst of his brethren, and the Spirit of Yahweh came upon him from that day forward (1 Samuel 16:13)." Though we are not intimately told about the judicial sessions going on behind the scene in heaven, the reader who is well informed on the ancient Hebrew worldview of the divine council can begin to put the pieces together when immediately thereafter he reads: "But the Spirit of Yahweh departed from Saul, and an evil spirit from Yahweh troubled him (16:14)." This even prompted his servants to inform their king, "Behold now, an evil spirit from God troubleth thee." The irony here is that Saul summoned David, the very soul whom the Spirit of Yahweh had chosen in his stead, so that whenever the evil spirit approved in God's council came upon Saul, David played a harp, that the king might be refreshed, and also that the evil spirit might depart from him.

By the end of his life, Saul has become *desperate*. The Prophet Samuel is long dead. He has failed to override the judgement of God's council by *killing* David. Likewise, God has departed from him, answering his cries no more. Quite tragically we even read that Saul has traded in the Prophets of Yahweh for those whom he had once put away—conjurers of the dead. Specifically, he asks for a woman, that he may go and inquire of her. His servants even know where to find one. *There is a woman who has familiar spirits in En-dor*, they inform their king. So Saul disguises himself, being especially vigilant to visit her by night, and with two men at his side asks that she divine unto the familiar spirit, and bring *him* up—that is, Samuel—whom he shall name, if it can be done.

But the witch of En-dor is cleverly on to him.

Her welcoming words are perhaps not quite so dissimilar from a prostitute demanding that an officer of the law reveal himself. "Behold, you know what Saul has done, how he has cut off those who are mediums and spiritists from the land." She likely suspects that her three nighttime visitors are officials from the king's court, if not the king and his bodyguards, and even adds: "Why are you then laying a snare for my life to bring about my death?"

Saul then gives himself away, *if* he hasn't already. "As Yahweh liveth, there shall no punishment happen to thee for this thing." That Saul would evoke the name of the LORD as a down payment of security for necromancy is a strange thing. Saul clearly knows the decision of Yahweh's council in heaven, that God has indeed sent an evil spirit his way, and therefore has no authority to bolster such a claim. Perhaps he is falsely prophesying, or only lying—or both. Or maybe the truth of the matter is that everyone present had become delusional. It is however unlikely that the witch is deceived—at least, where her craft is concerned. The diviner of En-dor clearly has the upper hand, from the moment they enter until she kills the fattened calf and kneads flour into unleavened bread at the end.

The king then falls for a rookie mistake—a knock on the wall, thrown voice, or levitating table sort of parlor trick which gives the séance its gullible allure. We are given no details as to how the witch summons the Prophet except that she suddenly *saw Samuel,* and immediately cries in a loud voice.

And then: "Why hast thou deceived me? Thou art Saul!"

"Be not afraid," the unsuspecting Saul attempts to comfort her. "What sawest thou?"

"I saw gods [elohim] ascending out of the earth."

If the witch is to be believed, she has perceived another sort of divine council. This gathering however is not a vision from the heaven of heavens, but one which derives from the pits of Sheol. The fact that the spirits rise from the ground is consistent with the ancient Near Eastern view of the cosmos and the Bible, and furthermore, that chthonic deities are summoned to assist in retrieving the ghost is attested by Mesopotamian tradition. Saul certainly knows where this is going. If *elohim* are rising from the ground, then their bringing up a member of the dead realm is likely.

The king immediately asks: "What form is he of?"

"An old man cometh up," she says, "and he is covered with a mantle."

The writer of 1 Samuel then adds, "And Saul *perceived* that it was Samuel (1 Samuel 28:14)." Many commentators fail to notice that the gods rising out from the earth and the ghost of Samuel are visible *only* to the professional and not to Saul, though Samuel's ghost can speak to Saul and presumably anyone else in the room. The witch's manipulation has easily won him over. Saul is desperate and emotionally invested. After stooping with his face firmly planted upon the ground, Saul even confesses this much to the voice who soon speaks in their midst.

"I am sore distressed," he cries in good faith to the old man with the mantle, whom only the witch can see, "for the Philistines make war against me, and God is departed from me, and answereth me no more, neither by prophets, nor by dreams: therefore I have called thee, that thou mayest make known unto me what I shall do."

The appearance of Samuel has been explained by conservative theologians as either a clever parlor trick of the séance or a conquest of the séance only so much as a demonic apparition was summoned, while others have concluded that we have before us a genuine appearance of the Prophet. Necromancy involves the use of evil spirits— not *actual* souls or spirits of the dead. For this very reason, many of those commentators do not conclude that God would break His own rules by calling upon one. Still, if it *is* the last option and God has performed a miracle beyond what is humanly natural, then it should be duly noted that Samuel does not arrive from heaven. He has arisen from the underworld with the gods—the *elohim*. Furthermore, Samuel complains that Saul has disturbed him from his rest. He is certainly not breaking habit with the cosmic worldview of the Hebrews.

On the other hand, a fortune has been told—certainly nothing out of the ordinary among the Nephilim spirit of demons. I'll settle with the more likely option. After all, the witch is admittedly demon possessed. If the familiar spirit who bolsters the witch's parlor tricks by *informing* their conversation has inside knowledge of God's council in heaven, we are not told. More than likely, the information provided is nothing beyond the gossip column. It has been long noted that this particular appearance of Samuel in the Bible brings with him his only *falsely* spoken prophecy. Saul is not killed by the Philistines, as Samuel seems to imply. His own servants even refuse to drive him through with the sword. Saul takes his own life. If anything, Samuel's prophecy is a self-fulfilling prophecy. Saul sees to it that he masters his own fate rather than let the God of heaven and of earth do it for him. And that should inform us of one important clue as to Samuel's *true* identity. He or *it* is not Samuel.

It can be said that David, while slinging a stone into the skull of a giant, sought to destroy the seed of the serpent, while Saul was counseled by one.

MICAIAH OVERHEARS A LYING SPIRIT AMONG THE GATEKEEPERS OF THE HEAVENLY VERDICT

A HUNDRED AND FIFTY YEARS AGO KING SAUL took his own life and now the wicked King Ahab of Israel has asked Jehoshaphat king of Judah if he would agree to join him at Ramoth-gilead for battle. Jehoshaphat is legally related through the marriage of his son to Ahab and Jezebel's daughter, which makes Israeli business a Judean family affair. Their alliance seems unorthodox, considering elsewhere we read of Jehoshaphat: "The LORD was with Jehoshaphat, because he walked in the ways of his father David, and sought not unto Baal; But sought to the LORD God of his father, and walked in his commandments, and not after the doings of Israel (2 Chronicles 17:3-4)." Regardless he agrees, so long as they *first* acquire of Yahweh. Ahab promptly gathers four hundred of his finest prophets, and together they prophesy.

"Go up," they tell him, "for the LORD [Adonai] shall deliver it into the hand of the king."

Jehoshaphat looks around perplexed. The king of Judah knows a genuine prophet of Yahweh when he sees one, and the prophets before him are clearly of a counterfeit religion. So he asks: "Is there not a prophet of the LORD [Yahweh], that we might inquire of him?"

"There is one man," Ahab shrugs. "His name is Micaiah son of Imlah, and how I *hate* him. He prophesizes nothing good concerning me—but evil."

Jehoshaphat insists to meet this Micaiah.

So with reluctance the king of Israel calls an officer and says: "Hasten hither Micaiah."

The picture before us is of an earthly council which seeks to model itself in the same vein of the divine council in heaven. The reader who thinks to doubt this ancient Hebrew worldview needs pay careful attention to the event which follows. The king of Israel and the king of

Judah sit each on his throne while the four hundred of Ahab's finest false prophets falsely prophesy in the name of Yahweh. Zedekiah even makes horns of iron for himself. Upon presenting them before his king, he prophesies: "Thus saith Yahweh, 'With these you will gore the Arameans until they are consumed.'" Meanwhile, the messenger who hastens Micaiah pleads with him to declare *good news* unto the king. "As the LORD liveth," Micaiah confesses to the kings messenger, "What Yahweh saith unto me, that will I speak."

When Micaiah appears from within the midst of the kings' counsel, this is what he says: "I saw all Israel scattered upon the hills, as sheep that have not a shepherd."

Ahab sighs to his Judean neighbor. "Did I not tell thee that he would prophesy no good concerning me, but evil?"

But Micaiah isn't finished yet. Micaiah has seen a vision of heaven above. While the false prophets are dogmatically crippled and spiritually impaired from looking beyond the workings of their own delusional earthly council, and certainly incapable of discerning spirits, Micaiah has looked in upon the courtroom of heaven and observed its judicial proceedings—events of such cosmic importance that they are only reserved for the Prophets of God and writers of the Word. To this he says: "I saw the LORD [Yahweh] sitting on His throne, and all the host of heaven standing by Him on His right hand and on His left." By this we are to understand the fate of men and kings are to be decided upon.

In his vision, the LORD [Yahweh] said, "Who shall persuade Ahab that he may go up and fall at Ramoth-gilead?"

There were murmurings among members of the council. We are to understand by this that—though suggestions were given to Yahweh—nothing was yet decided upon. "And one said on this manner, and another on that manner," Micaiah recalls. Still, no agreement was had. This is where Micaiah's vision becomes particularly peculiar. From among the discussion there came forth a *spirit*, who stood before Yahweh, and promptly volunteered his services.

I will persuade him, he said.

We do not know how many suggestions were had, nor the number of services offered and disapproved as a matter of discourse, but according to Micaiah, Yahweh then asked the spirit in His midst: "How so?"

I will go forth, and I will be a lying spirit in the mouth of all his prophets.

To this Yahweh agreed. "You will surely entice him and prevail. Now go and do so."

Upon hearing of the heavenly divine council's decision to deceive the false prophets of Ahab, Zedekiah immediately approaches Micaiah and smites him on the check, scowling: "How did the Spirit of the LORD pass from me to speak to you?" Though jealousy is to be observed here, that God has sought council among His protégés is neither the shock nor insult of Micaiah's vision. The fact that they have taken the bait and spoken in accordance with the council's decision, as Micaiah would rightly have it, thereby tickling the tongue of a lying spirit *is*.

With Micaiah's vision, we are immediately prompted back to our readings of Job, particularly the "day when the sons of God came to present themselves before the LORD, and Satan also came among them. The LORD said to Satan, 'From where do you come?' Then Satan answered the LORD and said, "From roaming about on the earth and walking around on it' (Job 1:6-7)." This would not have been unfamiliar to them. Even Satan is granted power at heavenly assemblies. Likewise, Micaiah's vision of the divine council and the lying spirit in its midst— clearly they are not always of charmed quality—should harken us back to the evil spirit whom Yahweh had sent unto Saul and prompt us to take notes. Was this also a result of heavenly discourse? Ahab's hatred for Yahweh, as embodied through His servant Micaiah, is further bolstered by Saul's complimentary turning against David. Concerning Micaiah, the king immediately orders, "Put this man in prison and feed him sparingly with bread and water until I return safely.'"

To this Micaiah warns as he is led away: "*If* you indeed return safely Yahweh has not spoken by me."

It would be difficult to conclude that Ahab took Micaiah's vision of the divine council lightly. But in actuality, as I have already noted, if he *hated* Micaiah for his counsel, it is only because he first and foremost hated the LORD and His counsel. So he attempted to prove the *both* of them wrong. Ahab attempted to outwit Yahweh and the spirit which had falsely inspired his beloved prophets by betraying Jehoshaphat and disguising himself in battle. If Micaiah proved anything, it was certainly not for the preservation of his own character. Rather, the monologue before Yahweh's throne; the murmurs; the suggestions; the questions and answers; the final verdict; and the council member who is commanded to carry it out, is not a casual matter. The affairs of mortal men are decided upon by a divine council in heaven.

Ahab died in Ramoth-gilead.

TWO MULES & ALL THE DIRT THAT CAN BE CARRIED (FOR NAAMAN'S COSMIC TURF WAR)

ONE CANNOT HELP BUT WONDER, IN THE MIDST of his desperation, if the honorable captain of the kings host in Syria had already gashed himself with knives, perhaps even commissioning others to perform the sacred rites, only to be told by the high-priest that Baal was away on business, or had fallen asleep, or was perhaps occupied with his consort and not to be disturbed, before he succumbed to the far more drastic approach—turning south, into *enemy territory*, for Israel.

Naaman was a leper. And Baal was destitute of help.

The tip-off would arrive through a Hebrew slave girl, we are told, and who had been taken captive by companies of the Syrian guard. As circumstances would have it, she waited now upon Naaman's wife. Despite the conspicuous evil among her aboriginal people—and Joram (son of wicked Ahab), king of their boundless obstinacy—a glimmer of hope remained of the old religion. Though Elijah had been taken away by a whirlwind, and had yet to be seen again, the maiden had heard stories of another man of God, a successor, who had risen up in his stead. "If only my master were with the prophet in Samaria," the little girl explained, "then he would be healed of his leprosy!"

With Naaman's arrival in Samaria, the king of Israel was not pleased, particularly the letter which accompanied him. The king of Syria had authorized Joram to restore his servant Naaman to good health, or *rather*, as Joram saw it, had placed the burden of deliverance upon his government. Israel's king rent his clothes in horror. Leprosy was a death sentence. To heal a man of leprosy was equivalent to raising the dead. Never mind the fact that Elisha had already raised a boy to life. Despite initial appearances, Joram was *not* a man after God's heart. There is not one Israeli king on record who did right in God's sight. Like his father Ahab before him, who had a particular distaste for Elijah, Joram did not think much of his successor either, despite the fact that the LORD had miraculously provided water *through* Elisha for his soldiers and cattle.

Then again, provisions were not granted for Joram, or his ally, the king of Edom. Elisha acted for the king of Judea. Jehoshaphat was a friend of God.

"As Yahweh of hosts lives, before *whom* I stand," he said, "were it not that I regard the presence of Jehoshaphat the king of Judah, I would not look at you nor see you."

Apparently, their feelings were mutual. Joram didn't regard God either.

When Elisha heard that the king of Israel had fallen into despair, he sent word to Joram, saying: "Why have you torn your clothes? Let him come unto me, and *he* shall know that there is a prophet in Israel."

Naaman did not delay his arrival. Horses and chariots almost immediately greeted the very doorway of Elisha's house. But Elisha did not come out to receive him. Perhaps he was away on business—we are not told. Rather, he sent him a message. It simply read: "Go and wash in the Jordan seven times, and your flesh will be restored to you and you will be clean."

To say, with a shrug of indifference, that Naaman was simply offended is to not recognize the sting of a slap across the cheekbone. It must have seemed as proof enough that Israel was another backwater society filled with the stagnate speeches of cultural yokels and hayseeds. "Are not Abanah and Pharpar, the rivers of Damascus, better than all the waters of Israel," he said. "Can I not wash in them and be clean?" For starters, the rivers of Damascus were conveniently closer than the Jordan. They were far more prestigious than the Jordan, sharing no comparative source—and where health was concerned, they were cleaner than the Jordan. Suffice to say, Naaman was not impressed with geographical Israel, its people, or its God.

His story may have ended on quite a different note, had it not been for his wise servants, who pleaded with him, that he might reconsider the prophets' instructions. There was nothing cryptic about his words. No wizardry was involved. There would be no fireside dances, whereas the pleading prophet might work himself into a hypnotic, knife-wielding, drug-induced state; and no orphic ceremonial rites to be shared. His methods were certainly not concealed. And considering what he had already committed to with Baal, had Elisha told him to perform some great deed, would he not have also committed himself to the task? "How much greater then," they insisted, "If Elisha merely instructed him to *wash and be clean.*"

Their logic was sound.

So Naaman went down and dipped himself seven times in the Jordan, as were his instructions, "and his flesh was restored like the flesh of a little child, and he was clean (1 Kings 5:14)."

Upon returning to the home of Elisha with his entire company, the man of God met him. There were two lessons which could immediately be learned here. Firstly, Joram would most certainly have followed through with the news of their meeting, and was once more strained to face the facts, that a true prophet did indeed advocate for the one God of Judea and Israel. And secondly, by not having initial contact with the holy man he sought after, there would be no confusion as to *who* he was healed by—certainly not man! To Elisha he affirmed: "Behold now, I know there is no God in all the earth, but in Israel!"

Despite how Naaman might have initially felt about Israel's suitability, her cultural handicaps, the quality of the Jordan and terrain when comparing the world's great rivers and mountain ranges, his heightened education now relied not only on God, but the land He reigned over. After insisting to monetize Elisha's efforts, yet repeatedly failing to convince him of its benefits (the man of God firmly dismissed his every offering), Naaman then proceeded with what Biblical scholars, preachers, and teachers have long considered a rather peculiar request.

God's gift of salvation was free.

If you will not accept gifts, Naaman said, "then please, let your servant at least be given two mules' load of earth—for your servant will no longer offer burnt offering nor will he sacrifice to other gods [*elohim*], but to Yahweh." He added, "In this matter may Yahweh pardon your servant. When my master the king goes into the house of Rimmon [Baal] to worship there, and he leans on my hand and I bow myself in the house of Rimmon, when I bow myself in the house of Rimmon [Baal], may Yahweh pardon your servant in this matter." ˙

Elisha agreed: "Go in peace."

Naaman was pardoned.

This would indeed present itself as a strange solicitation of his spiritual needs if their theology did not align. *Holy ground* was an important component of Hebrew doctrine. When in the presence of the

Angel of Yahweh at the burning bush, Moses stood on holy ground. Some decades later, Joshua did too. But there's more. Naaman affirmed a belief in the geographical division of land among deities, as Deuteronomy 4:19-20, 32:8-9 and Psalm 82 attest to. The territory of surrounding nations belonged to other *elohim* because God had decreed it. This is why the dirt was so important to Naaman's conversion. His allegiance to the one God of Judea and Israel was correlated to the dirt which He administered. In an ironic twist, the recent convert, given new life from the leprous death which had identified him among his Syrian contemporaries, was now *returning* to enemy territory—the land of Baal. On a spiritual level, Naaman was prepared to wage a cosmic turf war.

Perhaps they were a strange and confused people, Naaman may have contemplated on his return journey. While Israel regurgitated the wretched stench of idolatry, coveting the heirlooms of *other* neighboring gods, each of whom ruled over *disowned* peoples on foreign soil, Naaman delighted in what they forsook—their own birthright. He was adopted by the one God of Judea and Israel. He chose an *eternal* inheritance. However Naaman may have settled into the holy lands cosmic geography, particularly in light of her people who rejected their God, it would be difficult to conclude that he or any other convert—save for a few prophets—would even begin to dream that Israel's days were numbered.

There is one more unexpected twist to this story. While Naaman started northbound for Syria in the company of his servants, Gehazi, Elisha's *only* recorded servant, ran after him. When Naaman saw the servant of the *dear* prophet attempting to pursue him by foot, he halted his caravan and stepped down from his chariot.

"Is all well?" He asked.

Gehazi asked for payment. Elisha, he said, had changed his mind. The joyful convert was pleased to hand it over.

Gehazi became a leper.

"Ashes under the Soles of Their Feet..." THEY SHALL BE AS FROLICKING CALVES RELEASED UPON GEHENNA

ISRAEL'S HUMILIATING DEFEAT IN 722 BC was simply not enough for her captors. The king of Assyria pressed the brunt monarchic weight of his eyesight upon Judah. Within twenty years, 701 to be exact, his successor had conquered every fenced city of the southern kingdom—all but one. Sennacherib wanted Jerusalem. Hoping to appease his unquenchable appetite, Hezekiah king of Judah delivered ransom money—all the silver and the gold found in the temple of the LORD and from his own treasury. He even scraped the gold from every door post. Sennacherib accepted his payment, and then besieged Jerusalem anyhow.

When both parties sent out their negotiators, Hezekiah's representatives pleaded with Rabshakeh, the Assyrian king's chief aide, to converse in the Syrian language so as not to panic Jerusalem's troubled inhabitants. But Rabshakeh was pompous and arrogant. In one of the most blasphemous speeches delivered anywhere within the pages of Holy Writ, Rabshakeh defiantly spoke in the language of the Jews so that everyone within earshot might have a chance to quiver in their boots. Isaiah records that he cried with a loud voice and said:

> "Hear ye the words of the great king, the king of Assyria. Thus saith the king, Let not Hezekiah deceive you: for he shall not be able to deliver you. Neither let Hezekiah make you trust in the LORD, saying, The LORD will surely deliver us: this city shall not be delivered into the hand of the king of Assyria (Isaiah 36:14-15)."

The writer of Kings records of his longwinded speech.

> "Who are they among all the gods of the countries—that have delivered their country out of mine hand, that the LORD should deliver Jerusalem out of mine hand? (2 Kings 18:35)"

According to Rabshakeh, if they would turn away from the LORD God of Israel, they might be carried away to live in a land of corn and wine, of bread and vineyards—basically, the land of his gods. But if they refused, they would eat their own dung and drink their own piss—and die.

Hezekiah was no Hoshea—the last king of neighboring Israel. Upon hearing his words, Judah's king turned not to himself or any other foreign god for protection as his fathers had done, despite the immense pressure to likely do so from those within his fretting ranks. No, no—unlike Hoshea and the people under him, who "obeyed not the voice of the LORD their God…" (2 Kings 17:38), Hezekiah "did that which was right in the sight of the LORD, according to all that David his father did. He removed the high places, and brake the images, and cut down the groves, and brake in pieces the brazen serpent that Moses had made: for unto those days the children of Israel did burn incense to it: and he called it Nehushtan. He trusted in the LORD God of Israel; so that after him was none like him among all the kings of Judah, nor any that were before him (2 Kings 19:4-5)."

Jerusalem was surrounded. But Rabshakeh was delusional. His overconfidence in the vocational superiority and cultural luxury of consciousness and of the prince of the power of the air who governs all manners of the self—essentially, the booby trap of the ages—was his ultimate undoing. In one of the grandest acts ever accomplished in Scripture by His serial line-up of saints, Hezekiah "rent his clothes, and covered himself with sackcloth, and went into the house of the LORD." (Isaiah 37:1) He then sent for the prophet Isaiah. *This*, he told his dear friend, *is a day of blasphemy.*

It was the very night after Hezekiah had devoted himself to prayer that the angel of the Lord went forth and smote the enemies of Judah in their camp. Senncherib king of Assyria fled the slaughter. While worshiping Nishroch in Ninevah, a likely deified rendering of history's first recorded antichrist, Nimrod, and whom the medieval French rabbi Rashi believed to be a literal board from Noah's ark—which, if true, only contributes to the spiritual perversions of this archetypal antichrist figure—his sons usurped his throne, and smote him with the sword. Once more, the spirit of Nimrod had been subdued. When King Hezekiah, Isaiah, and the inhabitants of Jerusalem awoke the following morning after the Lord had *smitten* on their behalf, they saw lying before them "a hundred and four score, and five thousand," or 185,000 dead corpses of the Assyrians. Like Pharaoh's hardened heart against the God of Israel centuries earlier, which prompted the total annihilation of Egypt's army in the Red Sea, what Isaiah the Prophet witnessed was, without a doubt, one of God's greatest interventions in human history.

And according to Isaiah, it will happen again—but on a much grander scale.

It is well noted that the Prophet who once joyously foretold of our Savior's birth: "For unto us a child is born, unto us a son is given... (Isaiah 9:6)" and yet painted His ultimate purpose with the sorrowful strokes of a suffering servant: "He was wounded for our transgressions, He was bruised for our iniquities: the chastisement of our peace was upon him; and with His stripes we are healed... (Isaiah 53:5)"; who artfully penned our future glories when exhorting the wolf dwelling with the lamb, and the calf and the young lion and the fatling together, with a little child to lead them; paused his prophetic fore-longings in order to dabble in the literary genre of history—namely, King Hezekiah and the factual episode which he himself witnessed. He did not forget his monumental morning standing upon the walls of Jerusalem with his friend the king when he once more turned to the ink and pen of *future* prophecy:

> "And they shall go forth, and look upon the carcasses of the men that have transgressed against me, for their worm shall not die, neither shall their fire be quenched, and they shall be an abhorring unto all flesh (Isaiah 66:24)."

Such is a fate, we are told, which awaits all wicked men—whomever has transgressed against the Lord. With this dazzling imagery—the carcasses of men among undying worms and unquenchable flames—the Prophet wet the final line of the scroll (or the 17 sheets of parchment which makes up its Dead Sea scroll counterpart) and concluded his book for the ages. And yet Isaiah 66:24 may be the most ignored Biblical passage concerning the final punishment. That is a rather odd thing considering Jesus quoted from it.

Isaiah has often been called "the evangelical prophet" because he says a great deal more regarding the coming of the Messiah and the redemptive work of Jesus than any other book of the Old Testament. It is certainly not a coincidence that Jesus in turn gazed back upon Isaiah with a—dare I say it—*intimate familiarity*, and conclusively quoted from him more than any other Prophet. He even incited Isaiah 56:7 while turning the tables in the temple. Our Lord said unto the moneychangers: "It is written, 'My house shall be called the house of prayer; but ye have made it a den of thieves (Matthew 21:13).'"

Jesus once again borrowed from Isaiah when warning us that we never "offend one of these little ones that believe in me," specifically claiming: "and if thy hand offend thee, cut it off: it is better for thee to enter into life maimed, than having two hands to go into hell, into the fire that never shall be quenched: where their worm dieth not, and the fire is not quenched (Mark 9:43-44)." When referring us to *the worm that dieth not* and the *fire never quenched*, we are often counseled with dark speeches for Biblical commentary. Indeed, speculative creeds have been placed upon and have even sought to embellish an idealized Greek underworld ever since He spoke these words rather than the Hebrew doctrine which Jesus was actually referencing and directing our attention to. Human tradition has created an unfortunate assembly line of church sermons produced from inferior products and error—namely, the Gospel according to Plato. More precisely, Jesus never actually said *hell*, nor was He directing us to its mythological Germanic origins. He clearly pronounced *Gehenna*. The underworld populated by the immortal soul, first propagated by and invented—for the most part—from the Greek philosopher and wildly imaginative poet Plato, who doubtlessly read a great deal from Homer, is a world removed from the carcasses of men blazing within the Valley of Gehenna.

Hell, as we shall come to find, is globe talk.

Gehenna, or the *Valley of Ben Hinnom*, forms the southwest border of ancient Jerusalem. To this day it is a deep glen, shut in by rugged cliffs, with bleak rocky ridges rising over and above it, and stretches from the foot of Mount Zion rising above Jerusalem's south-side to the Kidron Valley on her east-end, with the valley of the giants, or rather "the plain of Rephaim," named after the ancient giants of the land, terminating its southwest border. Hinnom is generally regarded either as the name of an ancient hero (a giant, perchance?) or perhaps more importantly as an appellative to denote *"groaning"* or *"moaning,"* an appropriate bequeathing due to the fact that the droning cadence of drums could be heard here in Israel's darkest hours, drowned out only by the rising cries from the sons and daughters offered to Moloch. Indeed, the Valley of Ben Hinnom was cursed real estate. A column of smoke endlessly rose above Gehenna during Jesus' own lifetime, which no doubt served as a striking illustration to His ministry. It was reserved as a garbage dump where fires were kept burning, seemingly unquenched, to consume the refuse and, partnered with the maggots which feasted upon the rotting decay, eased the unholy melody of stench. We should not be surprised to learn it is also the location where the bodies of executed criminals, or those denied a proper burial, were dumped.

It is no secret that the Jews were obsessed with cleanliness. In fact, Jesus was even accused of not being clean enough—His crime, not washing His hands before dinner (Luke 11:38). Archeologists have only recently dug up, alongside the slopes of the Kidron Valley, Jerusalem's massive landfill, which dates from early Roman times and may have been the most sophisticated trash collection system in antiquity. It appears to have been put to use for an estimated sum of seventy years, dating from our Saviors infancy until the Jewish revolt in 70 AD. For Jesus, the garbage heap for the ages was appropriated not only for rotting food, but human refuse. It is a literal picture of Jesus' Davidic reign in Jerusalem. While the foolish bridesmaids "went to buy, the bridegroom came; and they that were ready went in with him to the marriage: and the door was shut (Matthew 25:10)."

Regarding the human refuse, Jesus said to the Pharisees:

"There shall be weeping and gnashing of teeth, when ye shall see Abraham, and Isaac, and Jacob, and all the prophets, in the kingdom of God, and you yourselves thrust out (Luke 13:28)."

Twice in Leviticus the Lord forbade the people of His covenant to deliver their children over to the flames of Moloch. In Leviticus 18:21 we read: "And thou shalt not let any of thy seed pass through the fire to Molech, neither shalt thou profane the name of thy God: I am the LORD." The instructions couldn't be any clearer. And yet the Prophet Jeremiah, written a hundred years or so after Isaiah, recorded that seed was indeed passed through the fire to Molech—and as a precise point of reference—in Gehenna. To this effect he writes:

"And they have built the high places of Tophet, which is in the valley of the son of Hinnom, to burn their sons and their daughters in the fire; which I commanded them not, neither came it into my heart (Jeremiah 7:31)."

Actually, Scripture records that Ahaz, Hezekiah's father, being influenced by the very Assyrians who were hell-bent on conquering the world, "burnt incense in the valley of the son of Hinnom, and burn his children in the fire, after the abominations of the heathen (2 Chronicles 28:3)." *This* Isaiah would have personally observed, having received his vision concerning Judah and Jerusalem "in the days of Uzziah, Jotham,

Ahaz, and Hezekiah (Isaiah 1:1)." Quite ironically Hezekiah's son and successor Manasseh hated the God who preserved his kingdom against the Assyrians so much that he reinstated his grandfather's religion and worse—he succeeded in surpassing his wickedness. Isaiah would not live to see it.

"And he made his son pass through the fire, and observed times, and used enchantments, and dealt with familiar spirits and wizards: he wrought much wickedness in the sight of the LORD, to provoke *Him* to anger (2 Kings 21:6)."

Let us not forget when Jesus compared Gehenna, perhaps even referencing a *literal* fulfillment, to Isaiah's vision of a future judgement, which was no doubt based—in part through the inspiration of the Holy Spirit—on his own experiences during the Assyrian's siege of Jerusalem, *He* was there. Our Savior *is* the Angel of the Lord who smote the 185,000 soldiers, laying their corpses for the eyes of Hezekiah and Isaiah to behold. Given further rumination, Isaiah references an actual future event, when the righteous will go out and look upon their enemies corpses, slain by the Lord on their behalf. Isaiah looks forward to the total destruction of their enemies—dead bodies, corpses, rather than *living* bodies in eternal torment.

And we should too.

Is this not what the Apostle John directs our attention to in Revelation? Satan, only recently loosed from prison, "shall go out to deceive the nations which are in the four quarters of the earth, Gog and Magog, to gather them together to battle: the number of whom is as the sand of the sea. And they went up on the breadth of the earth, and compassed the camp of the saints about, and the beloved city (Revelation 20:8-9a)." In Isaiah's own time we can only attempt to imagine what jitters the inhabitants of Jerusalem must have overcome in order to gingerbread their faith with a king who, like David before him, is only a prototype of the Messiah to come. Though the Assyrians had conquered every walled city in Judah, Satan will encompass the entire world. Yet the saints of Jerusalem when Revelation chapter 20 unfolds will have the Messiah, crowned and seated upon David's throne, to guard them when Satan speaks with all the boastful blasphemies of Rabshakeh—or was Rabshakeh really a mouthpiece for Satan?

Imagine the *shock-and-awe* spectacle then when, as John records: "fire came down from God out of heaven, and devoured them (Revelation 20:9b)."

The Prophet Jeremiah likewise records a similar event. He writes:

"...the slain of the Lord shall be at that day from one end of the earth even unto the other end of the earth: they shall not be lamented, neither gathered, nor buried; they shall be dung upon the ground (Jeremiah 25:33)."

Malachi, last of the Old Testaments Prophets, beautifully blended Isaiah's animal parade—the lion and the calf with the wolf and the lamb, and the child leading them—with his and Jeremiah's characterization of the final judgement when describing those, in contrast, who revere God in *this* present age and that hour to come. Expectation swells for the dawning day when God's sons and daughters shall leap from the stall like frolicking calves as they rejoice in the rays of the Sun of righteousness. The minor prophet describes that dawning discovery like this:

"For, behold, the day cometh, that shall burn as an oven; and all the proud, yea, and all that do wickedly, shall be stubble: and the day that cometh shall burn them up, saith the Lord of hosts, that it shall leave them neither root nor branch. But unto you that fear my name shall the Sun of righteousness arise with healing in his wings; and ye shall go forth, and grow up as calves of the stall. And ye shall tread down the wicked; for they shall be ashes under the soles of your feet in the day that I shall do this, saith the Lord of hosts (Malachi 4:1-3)."

We must recognize the stunning difference between what the Prophets have spoken—and which Jesus our Lord referred us to—and the long lineage of darkened speeches which have filled our pulpits from the earliest of centuries until now. I myself have fallen into the web of tradition and taught what is contrary to His Word. The difference between eternal punishment and eternal torment is stunning indeed —an irrevocable destruction or unending destruction. However, our Lord, speaking in terms of destructive *permanence* and decisions *irrevocable*, said it like this:

"And fear not them which kill the body, but are not able to kill the soul: but rather fear him which is able to destroy both soul and body in hell (Matthew 10:28)."

There is a second death. But if Jesus warned of eternal permanence—once justly executed—it is only because the destruction is irrevocable. For this event, we *must* be prepared. We shall all witness its horrors, one way or another. And yet, after the human recluse is removed from His kingdom; after Satan is defeated and thrust with the beast and the false prophet into the Lake of Fire, "tormented day and night for ever and ever"; after the sons and daughters of God look upon the despair and the shame of their loved ones; *corpses eaten by worms*, as Isaiah would say; *burned as stubble*, in Malachi's words; who are, as Jeremiah commands of them, *neither gathered, nor buried*, but remain as *dung upon the ground*; God shall wipe away all tears from the eyes of those who gaze upon their damnation, for death shall *finally* be no more, and the former things, which the righteous have longed to escape from (choosing to live for God's future kingdom, even to the point of death, rather than to live in this present world), have finally passed. To this effect the Apostle John writes:

> "God shall wipe away all tears from their eyes; and there shall be no more death, neither sorrow, nor crying, neither shall there be any more pain: for the former things are passed away (Revelation 21:14)."

The worst, and dare I say *darkest* night—though brilliantly and horrifically illuminated by the burning, tortured flesh of the wicked soul—is still to come. And yet, come morning, a beautiful horizon is promised before us. After the tears are wiped from our eyes, Isaiah's animal parade can finally commence. The sons and daughters of God shall be as frolicking calves released upon the ashes of Gehenna. And just as importantly, Gehenna will be holy again—but this time forever.

Finally, the Prophet Jeremiah has written—and to this I say, *Amen*:

> "And the whole valley of the dead bodies and of the ashes, and all the fields as far as the Brook Kidron, to the corner of the Horse Gate toward the east, shall be holy to the LORD. It shall not be plucked up or thrown down anymore forever (Jeremiah 31:38-40)."

Come Lord Jesus, come.

THE GOSPEL ACCORDING TO PLATO: *aka* "THE SECRET DOCTRINE"

ONCE UPON A TIME THALES WAS OUT TAKING A WALK, counting the crystalline constellations without thinking so much as to observe his footing, when he stumbled headlong into a well. This in itself is not the great tragedy of the tale, as we are quickly informed it wasn't merely the moon-lit terrain whom the absent-minded professor completely overlooked, but a beautiful young woman. We are uncertain whether or not she thought to extend a hand or hoist a rope and help him up as she peered down upon him, apparently still stargazing from the depth of his own doing, but all accounts certainly agree—the Greek mortal wasted no time in teasing his clumsiness.

She said: "You were so eager to know what was going on in heaven that you could not see what was before your feet!" The young girl apparently did not think much of philosophers, for she quickly added: "This is applicable to all philosophers."

Thales, it appears, and those who followed in his footsteps, were walking daydreams.

2

SOCRATES TOOK A VERY LONG TIME TO DIE. One day in 399 BC, having stood before a jury of his peers, the seventy year-old Greek philosopher held a cup of poisoned hemlock in his hand. He was accused and convicted of "refusing to recognize the gods acknowledged by the state" and also of "corrupting the youth" through the "introduction of new deities." But far more importantly, he wanted a Science-hinged totalitarian society with his Socratic friends and students for its iron-fisted monarchs. To do so would dispose of democracy completely. That—or comedy killed him.

Athens had sentenced him to death by suicide, and Socrates was happy to comply. In hindsight there is little bewilderment here. The greatest humanist who-ever was could apparently do nothing without attaching a lesson of his own moral superiority to it. He drank the fully prescribed antidote of poison, but not before conducting a long-winded dialogue of such epic and philosophically perverse proportions that his would become the famous last words for the ages. He expounded on the immortal soul and, in a rather odd twist of the spiritual lemon, introduced the world to spherical earth. With the suicide of Socrates, globe earth was unquestionably born upon the assembly line of existence.

Plato was not there to see his teacher's punishment carried out. Phaedo however was. It is Phaedo who records his famous last words, even going so far as to name the closing dialogue of Socrates life after himself, and immediately we have a problem. While the nagging rumor that Socrates never existed shall not be discussed nor theorized here—particularly because both Socratic schoolmates and contemporary playwrights, as well as his laundry list of political enemies, all lend credibility to his existence—it is the character of Socrates, as delivered to us on Plato's delectable platter, which presents us with another quandary entirely. Diogenes Laertius (180-240 AD), wrote in The Lives and Opinions of Eminent Philosophers:

"They say that, on hearing Plato read the Lysis, Socrates exclaimed, 'By Heracles, what a number of lies this young man is telling about me!' for he has included in the dialogue much that Socrates never said."

Plato had a habit of publishing lies.

It is Plato, in his dialogues Theaetetus, who accredits the story of the astrologer who fell into a well some two-hundred years earlier to Thales (624-546 BC), as opposed to Thales own contemporary, Aesop (620-564), who managed to tell the same parable while failing to identify his source of inspiration. Plato not only had a habit of mocking pre-Socratic philosophers, but as histories great plagiarist, often failed to deliver proper credit to the ideas which he claimed as his own. I am of the opinion that Thales did not write his own teachings down, like Pythagoras after him. To do so would break the code of silence among neophytes and closely guarded secrets of the Mystery schools. It is the very reason why Socrates refused to be initiated into the Eleusinian mysteries. Membership, he said, would seal his tongue. And besides, Plato would have him grin, though her sacred rites were protected even from his ear, her principles were well understood.

Though it is Plato who hoped to give Socrates credit for first dispensing knowledge of the immortal soul, Laertius cautiously delivers the prize to Thales. "Some again...say that he was the first person who affirmed that the souls of men were immortal." To this he added discretion. "But Aristotle and Hippias say he attributed souls also to lifeless things, forming his conjecture from the nature of the magnet and amber."

Aristotle further clarified Thales idea of the soul. "Some think that the soul pervades the whole universe, whence perhaps came Thales's view that everything is full of gods." The some whom Aristotle referred to were Leucippus, Democritus, Diogenes of Apollonia, Heraclitus, and Alcmaeon, later arrivals in the Greek pantheon of philosophers who adopted Thales pantheistic view that the soul was the cause of all motion, thereby permeating and enlivening the entire cosmos.

Once again, Plato would rather direct us to Socrates—a slight of hand trick to promote himself, ultimately—rather than granting credit to Thales, when he had his tutor suggest in Apology that the heavenly luminaries were gods, even painting the soul with such epic strokes that it pervaded the entire universe. Later on in Laws, it is noted that Plato introduced an Athenian stranger who seems to give himself away as a Thales archetypal figure without ever dropping his name, and is quoted to have said: "Everyone...who has not reached the utmost verge of folly is bound to regard the soul as a god. Concerning all the stars and the moon, and concerning the years and months and all seasons, what other account shall we give than this very name—namely, that inasmuch as it has been shown that they are all caused by one or more souls...we shall declare these souls to be gods...? Is there any man that agrees with this view who will stand hearing it denied that all things are full of gods? The response is: No man is so wrong-headed as that."

To conclude that Thales had rejected the old gods by stating that "everything is full of gods" would be a disservice to what the pantheon of gods were ultimately intended for among the Mystery school initiated. This is the big secret, is it not? The Greek gods had hoped to direct their human pupils to their own divine potential. If the soul was immortal, then each of us is divine.

The fact that Phaedo is a fictional character, created by and serving as a convenient stand-in for an otherwise absent Plato, the integrity of his middle period dialogue (his magnum opus, The Republic, was written about the same time) is immediately discredited. Though fictional

Phaedo closes his account by naming Socrates "the best and wisest and most righteous man" whom he or any of his friends had ever known, Phaedo doesn't even attempt to convince us that he himself is in fact anything rising above the pen writer's strokes of imaginative conjuring. Nothing here can be ascertained as moral. Plato lies. In life, we are led to believe, Socrates had a particular affinity for Apollo (or Apollyon), which the Apostle John accredits as being Satan. It was the Oracle at Delphi who reputedly pronounced, through babbling tongue-speak and an interpreter, that nobody but Socrates was wiser in all of Greece (Satan's words, mind you), thereby securing his vocation as a philosopher. Plato used Greece's most highly exalted celebrity, stemming from Satan's own endorsement—backed here with the fictional witness Phaedo—to praise his own ideas.

Oh, but there's more! Much like the long line of Pythagorean mystics before him, Plato may have only organized some rather peculiar instrumental arrangements from the occulting Mystery Religion and passed these ancient pre-deluge Nephilim-operations off as his own. While he lay on his deathbed, and with an advantageous slip of the tongue, Socrates invoked what he called the secret doctrine, which I shall hereafter refer to as the Gospel according to Plato.

And it goes something like this.

In the beginning was God—and the soul; for the soul, you see, is immortal without beginning or end. The soul cannot be murdered. It cannot experience death. Whether rewarded in heaven—the world of ultimate truth and forms—or punished among bubbling pools of mud and oozing rivers of lava within Homer's underworld, not even death itself can destroy it. The soul is immortal. Socrates' student Simmias—a mortalist who believed the soul is inseparable from the flesh and therefore created and destroyed with the flesh—had obviously not yet completed his Socratic training, because even on his teacher's deathbed school awaited him. First there was the Affinity Argument for discussion, which explains how invisible, immortal, and incorporeal things like the soul are different from visible, mortal, and corporeal things, such as flesh. After securing Plato's own tripartite model of the soul through the lips of his master, Satan's very words to Eve in the garden are regurgitated for the consumption of mankind. Indeed, the secret doctrine, first spoken from the gardens tree, is here made known.

Satan asked Eve: "Yea, hath God said, Ye shall not eat of every tree of the garden?" The serpent quickly concluded. "Ye shall not surely die (Genesis 3:4)."

Eve bought it.

Except here Satan, likely disgusted by Moses' lack of elegance in the Holy Books composition, rephrased his one-liner from Socrates own bed in a manner which seemed far more pleasing to his literal intent when the master philosopher is recorded as saying: "Now the doctrine that is taught in secret about this matter, that we men are in a kind of prison and must set ourselves free or run away, seems to me to be weighty and not easy to understand."

He is speaking mainly of two things. Firstly his own impending suicide; which his disciples protested in respect of their own preconceived moral high ground; and far more importantly, Socrates outlined a central tenant of Gnosticism—the fleshly prison. "...so long as we have the body, and the soul is contaminated by such an evil, we shall never attain completely what we desire, that is, the truth."

A Pythagorean philosopher—his name is Cebes—protests: "Socrates, I agree to the other things you say, but in regard to the soul men are very prone to disbelief. They fear that when the soul leaves the body it no longer exists anywhere, and that on the day when the man dies it is destroyed and perishes, and when it leaves the body and departs from it, straightway it flies away and is no longer anywhere, scattering like a breath or smoke."

Please, erase our doubts, Socrates.

Here Socrates expounds on the good news for the humanist religion of all ages, the body and soul who needs no Redeemer to resurrect him— the Gospel according to Plato:

"We believe, do we not, that death is the separation of the soul from the body, and that the state of being dead is the state in which the body is separated from the soul and exists alone by itself? Is death anything other than this?"

"It is this," the room agreed.

"Death," their teacher said, "is a release and separation from the body."

For Socrates, death could not conquer the soul. In this perverse Gospel, the immortal soul of the Platonist would also be born again on his own. Accordingly, if all things that has life dies, or more specifically, if death should remain in that condition, it is inevitable that all things would be dead with nothing alive remaining. Since there is life before us, this is proof for the Platonist that the soul is immortal. Just so that there was no confusion among his friends and students, Socrates supposedly utilized the last moments of his life rephrasing and then rephrasing again his new Gospel for the ages—including, unfortunately, the church age to come, who has had a terrible habit of blending their Gospels with his— an assortment of phrases, all of which outright dismissed the final destruction awaiting the soul.

"If the immortal is also imperishable, it is impossible for the soul to perish when death comes against it," he said. "And so, too, in the case of the immortal; if it is conceded that the immortal is imperishable, the soul would be imperishable as well as immortal." Also, "Then when death comes to a man, his mortal part, it seems, dies, but the immortal part goes away unharmed and undestroyed, withdrawing from death." To the Pythagorean mystic standing before him, Socrates concluded: "Then, Cebes, it is perfectly certain that the soul is immortal and imperishable, and our souls will exist somewhere in another world."

"I cannot doubt your conclusions," said Cebes.

Upon closer reading some will argue that Plato did not necessarily invent the globe. That assignment often falls upon the mystic Pythagoras. However, in all investigations to the original proposition of a spherical Earth, they often begin with Socrates discourse in Phaedo and, while snooping from behind the shadow of Corinthian pillars, barely manage to wander beyond the platforms of various pre-Socratic philosophers like Anaximander, who advertised earth as flat and cylinder-shaped, like a column-drum; or Thales, believing the earth to be a log of wood floating on water; or Anaximenes, theorizing a flat disc held up by air; and never mind the Biblical Hebrews, with their three-part self-enclosed and circular world; before returning henceforth to Socrates again in Phaedo. Who first invented the globe, whether fingering Pythagoras, the mystical son of Apollo; or the helios god's chosen sage, Socrates; is not important. Why split hairs or senselessly argue over the lesser of two evils? This we can most certainly conclude; if Pythagoras made globe earth a speculation for the Mystery neophyte while hiding his face behind the curtain, Plato institutionalized the occult—and ever since has accused men as being delusional for denying it.

After conversing at length about the soul, Socrates proposes that the earth itself—though there are many wonderful regions about it, he says—"is neither in size nor in other respects such as it is supposed to be by those who habitually discourse about it."

Simmias asks: "What do you mean, Socrates? I have heard a good deal about the earth myself, but not what you believe; so I should like to hear it."

We can only speculate if Simmias became globe earth's first Socratic convert. I find it fascinating, considering what we know of his gospel, that Socrates takes an Isaiah 40:22 approach to our first descriptions of a spherical Earth, whereas the Prophet Isaiah, being a mortalist, described the earth from a vantage point which only God is allowed: "It is he that sitteth upon the circle of the earth and the inhabitants thereof are as grasshoppers (Isaiah 40:22)." To this effect Socrates says: "In the first place, the earth, when looked at from above, is in appearance streaked like one of those balls which have leather coverings in twelve pieces, and is decked with various colours, of which the colours used by painters on Earth are in a manner samples."

And yet, while Socrates says there is nothing to prevent him from describing in greater detail what form he believes the earth to trulybe, a poison cup awaits him, and his life will end before he can explain it all. After all, he has to take a bath so as not to trouble the women who tend to his corpse. Oh gee. If only he hadn't wasted so much time blabbing on about the immortal soul.

In another of Plato's dialogues, Timaeus—published 39 years after the death of Socrates in 360 BC and the only of his works available throughout the Middle Ages in Latin—globe earth's provocateur attributed the Demiurge, benign architect of matter, as its creator. How interesting. We read that Plato's idealized Creator "made the world in the form of a globe, round as from a lathe, having its extremes in every direction equidistant from the centre, the most perfect and the most like itself of all figures."

Most stunning of all—for those of us who recognize the Mystery Religions grab at the cosmonaut today, with his astral projections and silver chord journeys into the higher realm by way of televised space walks—Socrates appears to prophesy what is to become our intended reality when he states: "…by reason of feebleness and sluggishness, we are unable to attain to the upper surface of the air; for if anyone should come to the top of the air or should get wings and fly up, he could lift his head above it and see, as fishes lift their heads out of the water and see the things in our world, so he would see things in that upper world; and, if his nature were strong enough to bear the sight, he would recognize that that is the real heaven."

From its very conception Globe Earth, including the unbridled limits of outer space which surrounds it; or as Plato referred to space—the real heaven; is esoteric fecal matter for the minds of Blavatsky and the cosmists. Globe earth holds hands with the immortal soul and, quite tragically, the church's preconceived notion that we shall ascend as bodiless beings into heaven. Wedded together, they are the Secret Doctrine revealed.

The Roman Poet Ennius summed up Thales tumble into the well some two-hundred years earlier, and the blunderous meeting of the two sexes to follow, when writing the obvious: "No one regards what is before his feet when searching out the regions of the sky." Cicero came to the same conclusion. I can't think of a better beginning to the myth of the immortal soul than the philosopher who had his thoughts so fixated upon the heavens that not even his feet had any use for him or any of us here on earth.

There's that, and hemlock.

Socrates drank the cup and then scolded the men around him due to their incessant display of tears. This, he barked, is why he sent the women away. His misty-eyed friends were, he insisted, strange men. And then Satan's chosen master died. Almost two and a half millennia after the concoction was administered into the old man's mouth, one must ponder if that very cup is still being passed around today, because it seems like just about everyone, Christian and non-Christian, has drunk from it.

"Pay No Attention to the Man Behind the Curtain!" PYTHAGORAS AND THE MATHE-MAGIKAL ORIGINS OF GLOBE EARTH

WHY MUST CHRISTIANS WITH ADVANCED DEGREES *persist* in dangling Pythagoras as *"proof!"* for the spherical shape of the world whenever the subject of Flat Earth and the Bible comes up? It's as if I should feel obliged to maneuver my faith in the created order around a mystic rather than God's own account of things. But that's how these conversations often go. Our modern-day pastors and theologians have handed over our spiritual authority to men of another cloth, perhaps because it's dangerous to be *right* when the establishment is *wrong*. Inevitably, as these discussions often go, I am reminded that "all great scholars" who found favor with the Establishment agenda throughout civilized history, from Pythagoras onward, upheld a globular belief over a Biblical one. Never mind three millennia's of *simple folk*; you know, pew boys—Godly men and women who placed their full fledgling faith in Scripture alone. In many ways, Flat Earth is the *untold story*. A multitude of raised hands remain uncounted. Or *squeaky wheels get the grease*, as they say.

These modern-day Christian conversationalists are prepared to fall back upon the position: "But doesn't God's account of creation come to us not only by His Word alone, but also through the halls of Science—mainly, natural revelation?"

So, we return to the subject of Pythagoras again. Flat Earth has come into the discussion, and so must Spherical Earth's first promoter, naturally. Pythagoras (570–495 BC), pagan prophet and priest—or as many of our great globe-trotting scholars would have it; facilitator of God's extra-Biblical scientific enlightenment. It is said among the ancients that Pythagoras was born of a virgin and fathered by Apollo. According to some accounts, Apollo appeared to Pythagoras' *earthly* father with a familiar message. He must not *know* Pythagoras' mother, whom he was betrothed to, until after she gave birth to the child. Other sources claim the babe gleamed with a "supernatural brightness." Even the Oracle of Delphi has a part in the narrative. She prophesied of his great works and wonders, which would benefit all of mankind. This much seems true. And while the globular Christian, sponsored by two-millennia's of "academic backing," will likely discover a sudden flurry of discernment among the bulk of these accounts, enough to wave such nonsense off as another fanciful fabrication by pagan dreamers and wishful-thinkers, I will suppose his rightness to a degree. There is fact and then there is mythology. Still, such textbook folklore might as well be true, should he understand the true identity behind the Mysteries' fingerprints and, quite similarly, what their celebrated—albeit mythological—stage productions are truly pointing to. Satan is the father of lies. He also casts seeds, and plants them. He will have his children, whether they are the children of Cain or of another voluntary nature.

What we can say with a degree of self-assurance is that the man who would "reveal" the once-hidden and long maintained *mystery* of globe Earth was personally discipled by Zarathustra, known as Zoroaster among the Greeks.

Zarathustra also revealed a thing or two regarding the hidden Mysteries in his lifetime. Namely, all mythologies pointed to one Monotheistic belief system. That would be the sun. Sol Invictus. Mithras. It's all the same god really, and relates right back to Pythagoras' father Apollo. Satan goes by many names, and will gladly be worshiped by any one of them. Satan *is* the sun god.

Greece's first great philosopher also received a rather interesting worldly education. He was schooled among the Orphic and Chaldean Mysteries and was even initiated into the Egyptian Mysteries of Isis. Not to be overlooked however was his education from the Jews. No, not the Torah—mind you. Pythagoras doesn't come across as much of a Sabbath "church goer." He became rather well acquainted with the secret *oral* traditions of Moses, or the Jewish Mysteries. For the record, I am of the firm belief in the Biblical narrative—that Moses, who was certainly well educated within the Egyptian Mysteries, left all that behind him when he encountered the true God of creation in the burning bush. Jesus later condemned such perverse traditions (Mark 7:13), which was then orally taught but wouldn't be inscribed until the Babylonian Talmud and Kabbalah texts some several hundred years later. In "*Numbers: Their Occult Power and Mystic Virtues*" (1890), William Wynn Westcott (devoting much of his book to Pythagoras) writes: "Ancient records show...the Jewish Rabbis added to their practical value special peculiar

110

purposes, and looked to them to furnish deeper views of nature, existence, and doctrine.....The Jewish Rabbis discovered so much of interest and importance behind the merely superficial value of numbers, and of words as their representatives, that they gradually developed a complete science of numerical conceptions apart from mathematics. This took the name of the Kabbalah."

Every high-school student, having taken a semester in geometry, has heard of the Pythagorean Theorem. Also known as the 47th Problem of Euclid, it likely hasn't occurred to him that Pythagorean's Theorem has long been an occultist symbol, and highly meaningful among Freemasonry. Which came first, the chicken or the egg is a question which will certainly be proposed by the man who demands Pythagoras is "*proof!*" of the globe. There is no avoiding his blending of magic with numbers. And yet avoiding globe proponents do. The Christian theologian Dr. R.C. Sproul, who as openly advocated redefining Scripture in light of the Copernican revolution, writes: "He had a spiritual and religious interest in mathematics, by which mystical significance was assigned to numbers. He considered the number ten to be the perfect number. In the study of math, the formal (pertaining to form or essence) becomes more important than the material, the intellectual or spiritual more important than the physical. For Pythagoras and his followers, mathematics is a matter of soul" (*The Consequence of Ideas*).

Roman philosopher Porphyry (234-305AD) wrote of him: "The numerals of Pythagoras were hieroglyphic symbols, by means whereof he explained all ideas concerning the nature of things."

And then there's author William Wynn Westcott again: "The principles governing Numbers were supposed to be the principles of all Real Existences; and as Numbers are the primary constituents of Mathematical Quantities, and at the same time present many analogies to various realities, it was further inferred that the elements of Numbers were the elements of Realities."

It is of the utmost importance that the Christian, should he wish to swim against the current of this great delusion without a leg-cramp, understand how theoretical physicists apply the masterful brush strokes of math to *uphold* age-old occultist ideologies. How do we know Earth spins through the gravitational pull of an infinite and boundless universe? Because math proves it so. Writes H.P. Blavatsky in *Isis Unveiled* (1877): "Numbers are a key to the ancient views of cosmogony—in its broad sense, spiritually as well as physically considered and to the evolution of the present human race; all systems of religious mysticism are based upon numerals. The sacredness of numbers begins with the Great First Cause, the One, and ends only with the naught or zero—symbol of the infinite and boundless universe."

Pythagoras would give lectures while standing behind a curtain, thereby denying all access from his students unless they should achieve the higher degrees of learning in their studies. "The philosophical school of Pythagoras was, in a measure, also a series of initiations, for he caused his pupils to pass through a series of degrees and never permitted them personal contact with himself until they had reached the higher grades." Just as it is with the Freemasons today, "his degrees were three in number."

In Protagoras' defense, Dr. R.C. Sproul is quick to add: "That math has served a crucial handmaiden to advances in natural science is documented by history. Advances in mathematical theory have ushered in several revolutions such as the Copernican revolution, the revolution initiated by Isaac Newton with his physics, and the revolution in our day of nuclear science." Lots of fakeness is involved there—on all three counts. And yet his teachings, which derived from the Mysteries, inspired minds well beyond mathematics. The Gnostics owe much to him. In *The Secret Teachings of All Ages,* Manly P. Hall writes: "The God of Pythagoras was the Monad, or the One that is Everything. He described God as the Supreme Mind distributed through all parts of the Universe—the Cause of all things, the Intelligence of all things, and the Power within all things. He further declared the motion of God to be circular, the body of God to be composed of the substance of light, and the nature of God to be composed of the substance of truth."

According to the Christian theologian, Hippolytus of Rome (170 – 235 AD), "Pythagoras, then, declared the originating principle of the universe to be the unbegotten monad, and the generated duad, and the rest of the numbers. And he says that the monad is the father of the duad, and the duad the mother of all things that are being begotten—the begotten one (being mother) of the things that are begotten." In some versions of Christian Gnosticism, especially those deriving from Valentinus, the Demiurge had a role in the creation of the material world separate from his greater contemporary, the Monad. It is important to note that the God of the Old Testament, Yahweh, is often interpreted as the Gnostic's Demiurge, not the Monad.

It is quite ironic that Dr. R.C. Sproul, who rushes to defend the Copernican Universe, despite its opposition to the very Word he claims to uphold, understands that the father of spherical Earth, by his own account of things, taught knowledge, reason, and enlightenment as having come from man—*not* God, just as the serpent promised. "For Protagoras, knowledge begins and ends with man. All human knowledge is limited to our perceptions, and perceptions differ from person to person." When the Greek philosopher spoke such words as, "Knowledge begins and ends with man," and "All human knowledge is limited to our perceptions, which only differ from person to person," he was essentially just summing up what those hieroglyphs of Egypt and Kabbalistic numerology and the worldwide interconnected Mystery Schools proclaim. God is all. He is in everything. More importantly, *we are god.* Or as his father Apollo, the serpent in the garden promised, "You will be like God."

Occultist reasoning drenches the bone of almost all Establishment thinking. The Copernicans and the Newtonians must come to Protagoras' aid. Any pastor who covets the praise of men will align himself—not with God's Testimony concerning creation, but with "all great scholars" who found favor with Establishment thinking throughout civilized history, from Pythagoras onward. What happens when you pull a leg from the table? And Protagoras is most certainly a leg. Why, the whole table falls. Einstein came to his beckoning call. One might even say Einstein was his greatest student. More precisely, Pythagoras was Einstein's first masterpiece, and I am told his most accessible one. From a young age, the great mathematician referred to Pythagoras as the "holy geometry booklet." But Pythagoras was a humbug of spherical Earth. And so was Einstein.

Despite his genius, Einstein was a humbug.

ALEXANDER THE GREAT & THE CITY OF IMMORTALS

1

VISIONS OF HOMER, THE BLIND BARD OF IONIA

HIS OWN PRECIOUS COPY OF HOMER WAS SAFELY LOCKED in a golden casket, which he furthermore clutched between his fingers, when Alexander the Great stood along the Egyptian shore. Alexander had in mind a grand city which would bear his name; a Greek metropolis; a philosophical utopia; the spiritual bread and butter of the ancient world—and indeed, Homer had brought him here. His architects and surveyors had already selected another suitable site, by which digging was to begin, but Alexander was just as assuredly convinced that they had settled on the wrong plot of land. The ancient historian Plutarch writes that, while Alexander was sleeping (likely with his copy of Homer stashed under his pillow), he saw a remarkable vision.

Plutarch writes: "He thought he could see a man with very white hair and of venerable appearance standing beside him and speaking these lines:

"Then there is an island in the stormy sea,

In front of Egypt; they call it Pharos."

To this Plutarch simply adds, "He rose at once and went to Pharos."

The divine figure was quoting Homer. Within Homer, and no doubt a thoughtful nudge from his nighttime informant, Alexander had found a treasure map of sorts. And we shouldn't be surprised by this. In an age enamored with history and beguiled with glory, no single text penetrated the Greek world quite like the poetry of the blind bard from Ionia—modern day Turkey. Even before the child could add logic to their sentences, before he or she could learn to read, their love affair with Homer began. While in school, some of their earliest penmanship lessons would undoubtedly include a pigment on papyri recital: *Homer was not a man, but a god*. Silent reading was an uncommon habit, whether in public or in one's private chambers. Homer was therefore a stage performance for its every orator, spoken with the vigor of a Shakespearean actor. For Homer, one might therefore conclude, the world was his stage. He even gave way to the most powerful art of all—philosophy. "His 15,693 lines provided the moral, political, historical, and religious context, the great deeds and the ruling principles, the intellectual atlas and moral compass," writes Stacy Schiff in *Cleopatra: A Life*. "The educated man cited him, paraphrased him, alluded to him. It was entirely fair to say that children…nursed in their learning by Homer, and swaddled in his verses."

The sculptor Archelaus of Priene, living in the decades surrounding 300 BC, depicted Homer as the divinely-inspired reservoir of all literature. In his surviving masterpiece, Homer is flanked by nine muses and their father Apollo, the god of music and poetry, standing alongside a female figure identified as Mnemosyne, the mother of the muses. Zeus, father of gods, stands above the procession in order to contrast the immortal due his honor, Homer, "father of humankind." Though Canaanite epics and the epic of Gilgamesh stir in our furthest memory, it is Homer and his poems which mark the beginning of our Shakespearian stories.

While the Bible was still being written and compiled in the divided kingdoms of Judea and Israel through the divine inspiration of the Holy Spirit, the blind bard from Ionia, through the divine inspiration of Apollo and his adopted daughter muses, was busy writing his.

2

THE SOUL LIVES ON IN THE FIELDS OF ELEUSIS

"The living are ruled by the dead" — Elysian Neophyte

SHE WAS MINDING HER OWN BUSINESS, PICKING FLOWERS on a spring day, when the young Persephone was brutally raped and abducted by a god. When she didn't return home, her mother went looking for her. She too was a goddess. As she broadened the scope of her search, Demeter found herself wandering about the entire world, neglecting divine duties as she did so—and the earth suffered. Though the rains had assuredly arrived soon before Persephone's carefree jaunt through the country, the advent of summer witnessed no grains or wheat. By this we can quickly conclude, not only was all of creation involuntarily punished for want of nourishment, but the gods were too. They were deprived of their offerings. Someone had to give.

It is for this very reason that, having learned of her daughter's whereabouts in the underworld and imploring her Olympian siblings to demand release, they prevailed over Pluto, its king. There was however a slight complication. The naive Persephone, negligent as to the health of her own soul, had eaten of the forbidden fruit—six pomegranate seeds, in fact. Consequently, Persephone was liberated on one condition; that she must return in Pluto's company every year for six consecutive months. Though Demeter undoubtedly delighted in her daughters' presence throughout the remaining year, her annual sojourn resulted in inconsolable mourning. The harvest was plentiful, but come autumn, the earth once again fell into neglect. That is to say, whenever Persephone is returned to Pluto, winter falls upon us.

The Homeric *Hymn to Demeter*, written in the same heroic verse as the *Iliad* and *Odyssey*, and which was historically accredited to Homer himself, may be one of the most important poems ever written, despite the fact that it is rarely recognized by the educated soul today, and even less discussed. But the story before us, *essentially*, at its most primal level, is the groundwork for the ancient Eleusinian mysteries. Named for the community in Attica where the sacred dramas were first presented, the Eleusinian mysteries captivated not only neighboring Athens, but the entire Greek speaking world for nearly two-thousand years.

The world of Homer consisted of but few men who could hope to attain the sort of godlike stature which his players were attributed to. Likewise, immortality was beyond their grasp—certainly not spoken of the self. It is Homer however, the blind bard from Ionia, who would extend the offer of self-salvation to humanity as an advantage of initiation.

That the soul is *immortal*—that immortality might be *grasped* within each and every neophyte—*this* is the Eleusinian mysteries and the Mystery religion as a whole.

There is an interesting passage in *Hymn to Demeter* where Demeter is prevented from transforming the mortal child Demophoon, a grain god, into an immortal soul—perhaps in hopes of undoing the mess in which the natural world had found itself, due to her haphazard grief. Her inability to perform the deed is relegated upon the fact that the child's mother screams in protest, having witnessed Demeter attempting to immerse her boy into a stew of flames. If Homer's subplot hinted at or

116

sought to provide commentary on the widespread act of passing children through the fire in surrounding Mystery rites, sacrificially speaking, and that it was ultimately a means of immortalization, we are left with an unanswered riddle.

It is frequently commented upon by historians in every generation and rank that the Mysteries today still maintain, rather ironically, a cloak of mystery, despite her widespread practices in practically every human culture, and over multiple millennia on either side of Christ's birth.

Well, let me rephrase that. We *uninitiated* do not know.

Surely, *somebody* knows.

The fact remains, since the Eleusinian mysteries were courted with zipped-lips, with secrecy being held in the highest regard, no initiate openly spoke of them. Her secret rites were enacted with a spacious and rectangular, windowless structure near a cave believed to be the entrance to the underworld. The *telesterion*, as it was called, was designed for the purpose of darkly-lit, perhaps pitch-black showmanship, most likely for the purposes of a spiritual rave, complete with pyrotechnics. Aristotle said of the mysteries that the initiate did not learn anything *academic* during such initiations but rather experienced the mysteries in such a way as to alter their state of mind. The philosopher was no doubt referring to the barley brew exchanged between its participants, called the *kykeon*, and anyone's best guess is that the cup was ramped with psychedelics.

It is probable that the Eleusinian held to third-eye principles—that his or her soul left the body during sleep, or more specifically, was made capable of lifting into the higher plane by the special training they received. Today we know this as astral projection. Many initiates, perhaps while feeling their way through the other side of darkness in the *telesterion*, claimed to have actually seen the living gods themselves.

Rather than acquiring *outright* philosophical knowledge, rites of Eleusis promised to deliver Nature's most mystic and precious secrets— that is, acquiring the free gift of salvation first promised to us through the providence of divine beings. From Demeter we derive Mother Earth. The soul of man, symbolized by Persephone in the Homeric poem, finds "its true home in the higher worlds where, free from the bondage of material form and material concepts, it is said to be truly alive and self-expressive," writes Manly P. Hall in *The Secret Teachings of All Ages*. "The human, or physical, nature of man, according to this doctrine, is a tomb, a quagmire, a false and impermanent thing, the source of all sorrow and suffering." Though perhaps not outright philosophical knowledge of the divine, philosophical it would most certainly become—and more so, an entire world view. The Eleusinian mysteries were later vaulted by Platonism with such indiscretion that her principles, even her *involuntary* initiation, is available to all in modern times.

Besides, Persephone and Demeter can easily be attributed as a retelling of *the Descent of Inanna* in ancient Sumerian literature. "In some way," writes Alan F. Segal in *Life after Death: A History of the Afterlife in Western Religion*, "we keep coming upon the same naked narrative structures, each time newly dressed in the interests of a new culture." Then again, if the Mysteries of Demeter and later Bacchus, her Mysteries competitor, suspiciously compare with the rites of Isis and Osiris in Egypt across the Mediterranean, we shouldn't be surprised. They all relate to the Garden of Eden; the forbidden fruit; the Watchers of *Enoch*. Manly P. Hall assures us, "there is every reason to believe that all so-called secret schools of the ancient world were branches from one philosophic tree which, with its root in heaven and its branches on the earth, is—like the spirit of man—an invisible but ever-present cause of the objectified vehicles that give it expression. The Mysteries were the channels through which this one philosophic light was disseminated; and their initiates, resplendent with intellectual and spiritual understanding, were the perfect fruitage of the divine tree, bearing witness before the material world of the recondite source of all Light and Truth."

Quite contrarily for the unititate however, those who forsook entry into the telesterion and *beyond*, there was no hope. The gods had afforded a way. So when the gates of Hades opened wide for them, if they had put off their neophyte journey for a later date, or altogether rejected the offer, they were on their own.

In *the Hymn to Demeter* Homer wrote:

> "Happy is he among men upon earth who has seen these mysteries; but he who is unititate and who has no part in them never has a lot of good things once he is dead, down in the darkness and gloom."

For the Mystery school initiate, death itself was regulated to a *rebirth*—a rejoining with the gods in the firmament above. Plutarch dipped his pen into the parchment of the Mysteries in order to describe the moment of death when he wrote:

118

"The soul suffers an experience similar to those who celebrate great initiations... Wandering astray in the beginning, tiresome walkings in circles, some frightening paths in darkness that lead nowhere; then immediately before the end all the terrible things, panic and shivering and sweat, and amazement. And then some wonderful light comes to meet you, pure regions and meadows are there to greet you, with sounds and dances and solemn, sacred words and holy views; and there the initiate, perfect by now, set free and loose from all bondage, walks about, crowned with a wreath, celebrating the festival together with the other sacred and pure people, and he looks down on the uninitiated, unpurified crowd in the world in mud and fog beneath his feet."

This is the very crux of the Eleusinian argument and precisely how Plato would later describe the body. Flesh and bones are a sepulcher of the soul. His very being, his physicality and nature, is nothing more than a sarcophagus. To the Eleusinian, birth into the physical world is death in the fullest sense of the world. Divine wisdom contained in the stars is likewise lost to us. If the soul does not rise above ignorance, if he does not acquire the hidden knowledge of his divine self, then he will be delivered over to eternal agony, being incapable of gratifying the desires of his sepulcher-self.

The Gnostics, as well as Dante's *Inferno*, would pick up where the Mysteries left off, and wrap them up with sparkling paper and a bow for the Roman Catholic Church.

3

ALEXANDRIA, SPIRITUAL BREAD AND BUTTER OF THE WORLD

ROME WAS LITTLE MORE THAN A VILLAGE   when Philip II of Macedonia went to war with the Persians. The year was 336 BC. In turn, Darius III had the king of Macedonia assassinated. He would come to regret that decision. At just twenty years of age, his son began the most remarkable military career in human history. Within three years—at the battle of Issus in 333 BC—Darius was defeated. He fled, leaving his mother, wife, and children behind as trophies of Alexander's spoil. It is in the kings golden casket, also abandoned during his plight, in which the Macedonian placed his beloved copy of Homer.

The following year Egypt was liberated. Alexander was welcomed with arms open so wide that, at the age of twenty-three, they crowned him their king. Alexander had inherited a wealth of esoteric knowledge—the very astronomical, mathematical, alchemical, and spell-binding books of spoken verbiage which had attracted Pythagoras and Zoroaster in recent centuries. Some one-hundred years before his arrival, her mysteries had invited Herodotus too. The historian observed of his own visit: "There is no country that possesses so many wonders, nor any that has such a number of works that defy description."

By all accounts, Egypt was a land of mystical wonder and conundrums. The life-giving river Nile, seemingly defying logic by flowing backwards, south to north, and furthermore reversing the known laws of nature by swelling in summer and subsiding in winter, gave testimony to her Mysteries—of her cyclical birth and death and annual re-birth. Consider that the pyramids were as comparatively old to Alexander as the birth of Christ is to us—perhaps even *older*. Even then they were an enigma to the young king. Essentially, like a dreaded crocodile submerged within the Nile, Egypt could effortless leap forth and gorge Greece's library of knowledge and history in one swift swallow. There was no shortage to the wisdom which her gods and goddesses might offer. Herodotus had said that the Egyptians were the most religious of all peoples, and their beliefs imbued every element of their society. Then again, Egypt was a country so backwards, Herodotus added with a flourish of sarcastic salt, that "the women urinate standing up, the men sitting down."

To the Egyptian, divorcing magic from religion was unthinkable, and clearly, Egypt exercised her spells. Perhaps it is true that Alexander *alone* was drawn to her abracadabra—he and very few others. Egypt was populated by an insular and inward looking people. The Mediterranean did not cast her gaze—but the rites of the Nile. Likewise, few were invited in. The Mediterranean however, not the Nile, bound Alexander's world together. He needed a city to supply his army and control the world's first empire. But now, standing along the Egyptian shoreline with the island of Pharos neatly tucked away behind his back, birds descended on his men as they laid barley flour on the sand—perplexing indeed. This may prove a *bad* omen. Alexander's personal soothsayer, Aristander, was not concerned. He said it simply showed that Alexandria would one day feed the whole world. When Alexander consulted the Egyptian gods himself on the matter, they mutually agreed.

"The city you are building," they said, "will be the food-giver and nurse of the whole world."

There is a story told by the Jewish historian Josephus which involves Alexander's arrival in Jerusalem. His visit with Levite priests was clinched with a briefing from the Prophet Daniel, whereas Alexander was shown the scroll and read about himself. "And when the book of Daniel was shewed him," Josephus asserts, "wherein Daniel declared that one of the Greeks should destroy the empire of the Persians, he supposed that himself was the person intended; and as he was then glad, he dismissed the multitude for the present ..." Essentially, Alexander was one of history's foremost prototype antichrist figures, and he approved.

The gods of Egypt did not mince their words. Though Isis—divine goddess, mother earth and queen of heaven—had prospered an inward-gleaning providence, histories great prototype antichrist would wrap Egypt, and her spellbinding charms, not only as a gift to the Greek speaking world, but the whole of human history.

4

PHARAOH, AVATAR OF EGYPT, AND HIS HOUSEHOLD OF ASCENDED MASTERS

THE AGE OF HELLENISM INEVITABLY BROUGHT the cult of Demeter at Eleusis to international fame. The Eleusinian mysteries were so well-financed and world renowned that other religions explicitly rebranded themselves through the efforts of her initiates. This is of course the overarching narrative of Hellenism. Hellenism conquered practically every belief system of the old world. Even the ancient Egyptian cult of Isis caved, and that speaks volumes.

Initially, the sky, Nut, was a woman, while the Earth, Geb, was a man. The Egyptian word for sky is likewise feminine with the earth filling in the masculine. This in itself contrasted practically every religion on earth, most of which depicted the sky with fatherly attributes and the earth as something motherly. But the sky brought too little rainfall. Agriculture was delivered by the annual flooding of the Nile, with its influx of mud, and in a reverse order which simply defied all other seasons on earth. For this reason many early Egyptian myths pictured creation as a big bang event of sorts, a surge of fertility, but accomplished through the masculine and unmistakably magical act of divine masturbation. Such *conjuration* was a particular favorite of Aleister Crowley and Jet Propulsion Laboratory founder Jack Parsons.

The Egyptians held to a watery chaos which existed before material creation. It is Nut, the sky goddess, *outer space*, who holds back the anarchic current of the raging cosmos above, through which its blue waters can be seen by day and the celestial deities she has birthed by night.

Nut's symbol was a water pot.

While wandering through the wilderness, the Hebrews would strip away pantheism and simply call this the *firmament*.

Among her abundance of ancient histories, the Egyptians did not speak in the vocabulary of being *saved* or *damned.* They distinguished between a transfigured person of high pedigree in the afterlife, or the *akh*, and the only available alternative. To be a *mut* was the same as to remain a corpse. *Mut, muth,* or *mooth* is derived from a Semitic root, frequented in both Arabic and Hebrew, and simply intends *death.* Egypt insisted that one simply died forever—that is, unless he was initiated.

The word Pharaoh is actually a Greek word, rather ironically, and though it signifies the ruling king of Egypt, it also denotes *great house.* For thousands of years it was Pharaoh's household, his pantheon of divine beings, the ruling class, who returned to their immortal status in Nut's womb after death. For this reason Egypt's Pharaoh was both Osiris and Horus, serving the role of two different sequential avatars. While on earth he enacted the part of Horus, and upon ascending to the heavens, Osiris. For the great household, life continued. Nut's promise to him and his house was that death has been *denied.*

"Rise up," she says, "for you have *not* died."

It is in the heavens where he was expected to survey the earth each day. His tomb—the *ka*, as they called it—was not simply a tomb. The *ka* could also dwell with him in the sky. Together they interlinked both avatars.

"Open up your place in the sky among the stars of the sky for you are the Lone Stars," says Nut to her princes.

Furthermore, a living pharaoh might proclaim, "My father has not died the death, for my father possesses a spirit in the horizon."

Despite Egypt's multitude of mummies, consider her millions of souls who were not born of pedigree; not of old money; uninitiated; hieroglyph illiterates; without a tomb and the magical rites associated with mummification to preserve them; who simply died and perished. And then consider the Hebrew writers. To say they forbade the magical rites of mummification is an obvious conclusion to make, but in the same token, they were simply uninterested in any notion of the afterlife. Job made this point abundantly clear. The Prophets followed suit. Their covenant initially had nothing to say about the afterlife, certainly nothing of duality, except to warn against believing that another god could supply one. Yahweh alone held the ritual rites to resurrect a righteous people who were not restricted to a ruling household or *hush-hush* initiate. He would perform the miracle in His timing—specifically, at the end of time.

Yahweh's covenant with Israel delivers an absolutely unique signature among the various scripts in the cultures surrounding them, often plagiarized, "and especially strange in the ancient Near East," writes Alan F. Segal, "where elaborate ideas about postmortem existence and even more elaborate rituals were everywhere part of literature, myth, and social life."

But the Egyptians, desperate to throw off the yoke of Persian rule, would recognize the Hellenization which Alexander, their new *welcome* Pharaoh, provided, particularly within the city which he founded. The Ptolemaic dynasty would see to it for another 275 years. Like the darkened *telesterion*and the sunlit Eleusinian fields often discovered within them, the Egyptians would open up the rites of Immortality to all who wished to partake in the Mysteries of Isis.

So also would the Hebrew faith, in time, flounder to Alexander's antichrist religion, to the mysteries of Demeter, to Isis, her Egyptian counterpart, and the human *liberty* her providence promised to bestow upon all mankind, apparently as a natural God given right.

5

DO WE LOOK UPON HISTORY AS HISTORY LOOKS UPON US?

THOUGH IT IS TRUE THAT THERE IS MUCH WE DO NOT KNOW OF THE PAST, the same can be said of the ancients—there is much they did not know of themselves. While the Macedonian king advanced towards ancient Babylon, he couldn't have possibly comprehended that time as we know it *today* was in reverse; that the calendar years were winding down in a backwards fashion, like the upwards compartment of an hourglass or the river Nile, flowing seemingly *against* the laws of nature, while we presently gaze back and trace a finger with an exuberant anticipation of the Jewish Messiah.

He did not have any recollection that the blind barge of his poetic passions was from an *archaic* age, that he was the last born generation of the *classical* philosophers, nor could he have possibly imagined that a nineteenth century German scholar by the name of Johann Gustav Droysen would be the first to designate such terms as the *Hellenized* age in order to describe his sphere of influence. Though it would likely not surprise Alexander in the least, and would surely please him to learn that his world tour was a baton race of sorts, except that he *alone* was handing off the torch of inner enlightenment from one epoch to another.

Still, history—much of history—has recorded its actions for the inquisitive ear, and there are scads which they knew of us but we refuse to know of ourselves. Certainly not to disappoint us, as the great archetypal antichrist figure that he was, Alexander rescued humanity from a Classical age of few Mystery initiates to one in which immortality was freely delivered to all.

Very few of us in the church today have come to acknowledge, or rather *fathom* and equally appreciate a total distaste, more-so *revulsion* for Alexandria's produce. It is in Alexandria where, not surprisingly, the first recorded *atheist* philosopher, Aristarchus of Samos, would put the earth in motion with the heavens above, thus giving birth to heliocentricity. It is likewise in Alexandria, from the forty-story Pharos island lighthouse dedicated to Zeus, where the strange phenomenon of ships disappearing over the horizon was observed and debated. Apparently, the Alexandrians discovered a *globular* horizon. As a successor of Theophrastus at the Academy in Athens, who in turn was

Aristotle's successor, Eratosthenes would follow in the footsteps of Aristarchus by seemingly attempting the impossible. It is there where Eratosthenes *measured* the breadth of the earth using only a stick and a well. Afterwards, he not only measured the depth of the heavens, but flipped the earth on its axis. Some centuries later, through the constantly changing positions of the celestial bodies and Ptolemy's observances of them—mainly his proposal that a continuously fluctuating atmosphere incited a response from and change of fortune for all living creatures—a new and long-enduring brand of astrology was religiously instituted.

Alexander's gift would bring to us the Hellenized rendering of Holy Scripture through the Jewish philosopher and mystic Philo, and not so long thereafter, the first Christian academy—the Catechetical School of Alexandria, under the guidance of Clement and Origen, so that the church today might be masked, unknowingly, with the blinders of Platonic doctrine. Because of Alexandria and her assortment of *initiated* wizards we blindly believe the immortal soul doctrine. It should come as no surprise then that she would nurture the pestilence of Gnosticism; mold the battleground between *hidden knowledge* and Christianity, of which Hypatia, Queen of the Occult, would take the reins—and in doing so attempt once more to advance heliocentricity for the Copernican to come. As the sun finally set on Alexandria, while giving simultaneous rise over Rome, the Egyptian city would antagonize the church with the Arian heresy—thus prompting the council of Nicaea.

But even then, despite her waning hours, men would smell the bouquet of her embalming spices and take delight in her corpse. Time and time again, she would see to it that her body was *exhumed.*

It is in Alexandria where alchemy, in its constant quest for immortality, had been rendered into a communicable, though secret, code. Among her excavations, a person by the name of Hermes—the most mysterious figure in Alexandrian history and the person responsible for her alchemical canon—could once more enlist his age of Enlightenment pupils. There Isaac Newton would dip into his occult studies and, with Jewish mysticism to back him, discover the occulting principles of gravity. For Helena Blavatsky, Alexandria would deliver from her womb Ammonius, father of Theosophy.

Indeed, the Alexandrians knew much about us, our preconceived and eternally gullible notions of reality, that we often fail to recognize ourselves. But despite Alexandria's total disregard for a world propagated solely through Biblical authority, her HTD's were far from through and even now, I suspect, is not short of surprises. Much later on—not so long ago, from our current grasp at the horizon—her ghosts would secure a partnership between Westcott and Hort, a contemptible and unholy pairing who would, quite astonishingly, make a recently discovered Alexandrian Manuscript, the *Codex Sinaiticus*, the standard New Testament text and most cherished reading in modern Christendom; despite the fact that it is, provably, the worst and most disagreeable manuscript in Biblical antiquity. That her sister city was Pergamum, the seat of Satan, is rarely deliberated nor understood. The fruit of Alexandria is rotten indeed.

It is in Alexandria where we may find the most sinister and widespread, though cleverly hidden, offering in our world (or rather, entree of reality) today—the Mysteries of Isis.

An estimated 12 million immigrants entered the United States through Ellis Island, neatly tucked within the Upper New York Bay by the Hudson, from 1892 until 1954—a total span of 60 years. That is, 12 million souls who gazed upon Lady Liberty as they passed, almost ceremoniously, into her providence. If only they knew it is Isis, standing as an emblem for Manhattan, who delivers liberty and enlightenment for the people of her government. 20 million tourists visit Washington DC each and every year. That is, 20 million souls who admire the Washington Monument, almost ceremoniously, for the providence it represents. If only they knew it was a testament to the love and devotion towards Horus, her son. Over 300 million Americans possess a 1-dollar bill in their pockets. Cleanly depicted on the backside of their dollars, *the eye of Horus*, also known as *the eye of Providence*, fills the missing capstone over Giza's great pyramid. If only they knew.

Another 1 billion Catholics celebrate Christmas each year. The Madonna with child whom they worship, *Mother of God* and *Queen of heaven*, is a nothing more or less than a cleverly disguised Isis, *Mother of God* and *Queen of heaven*, holding the artifact of her own immaculate conception—Horus. If only they knew.

Yahweh once commanded of Moses that he stretch out his hand toward the sky, towards Nuit, realm of the divine and the Egyptian immortals, that there may be darkness over the land of Egypt. It would be the sort of darkness, the one God of Israel stressed, which could be *felt*. For the Hebrew, theirs was a *spiritual* slavery, as well as physical—one in which their heartfelt cries reached to Yahweh in heaven, and He remembered them.

Alexandria isn't simply relegated to the dusty boots of archeologists. The Mysteries of Isis are alive. If only my brothers and sisters in the faith could feel the pitch of her providence, the blanket of her darkness, stretched across our land.

"*Against Black Laws of Pagandom*" | QUANTUM MYSTICISM ACCORDING TO SPIRITUAL EGYPT (and the Theory of Everything)

STORYBOOK HIEROGLYPHICS WERE NOT EXCLUSIVELY ON GOD'S MIND when He cautioned of Egypt, commanding His chosen people the Israelites: "Ye shall henceforth return no more that way (Deuteronomy 17:16)." There is more to Egypt than meets the eye. That is my conclusion, anyhow. But for the everyday sort who exhibits a terrible habit of throwing his caution to the wind, the long-forsaken kingdom of the Pharaohs, with its catacombs of dusty tombs and strange illegible markings, is little more than monuments to pagan worship, and worthy perhaps of a museum exhibit. But he alone is not to blame for his candor. Even our Egyptologists seem content to gaze upon these almost-alien engravings and interpret for us a series of ancient polytheistic fables and textbook mythologies without ever so-much as conceiving the broader—though admittedly esoteric—reality by which these deities were once represented to the eclectic fraternities and insiders of higher-learning that they were intended for. As history has proven, the hidden Mysteries have never been a subject for the mainstream-minded—the uninitiated. In this manner they have thrived through the centuries, and *bound* us to them.

Origen Adamantius (184-253AD), an early Christian theologian from Alexandria and mystic in his own right, once confessed of this ancient religion:

> "The Egyptian philosophers have sublime notions with regard
> to the Divine nature, which they kept secret, and never discover
> to the people but under a veil of fables and allegories."

The Mysteries of Isis wasn't exactly a *kiss-and-tell*. Nor are the easygoing societies of secret symbolism which unashamedly surround us in the open halls of academia today. Even among its whispered secrets, just as it is with the various degrees of Freemasons—Egypt's Mystery Schools contained an order of the *lower* and *higher* learning. Occult scholar Lewis Spence (1874-1955) compares the secret society of the Freemasons with initiations into the mystery schools of Ancient Egypt:

"The purpose of initiation is a conventional attempt to realize man's place in the universe and in the divine scheme of things, and for this, I believe, the Egyptian Mystery System achieved for the first time in an orderly and philosophical manner ... Have we no lessons to learn from Egypt? Aye, the greatest in the world, the knowledge of that divine introspection which alone can give man the likeness of the Divine."

Historian Alphonse Mariette has this to say of Egypt's Mysteries:

"To the initiated of the sanctuary, no doubt, was reserved the knowledge of the god in the abstract, the god concealed in the unfathomable depths of his own essence. But for the less refined adoration of the people were presented the endless images of deities sculpted on the walls of temples."

For Plato, the realm of ideas is the haven of *true knowledge*, whereas the realm of material objects is only *mere opinion*. Instruction of the higher divine knowledge might be compared to a form of midwifery, in which the instructor only assists his pupil in giving birth to an idea that has already been conceived. Accordingly, the ultimate objective of Egypt's Mystery Schools, writes author Vashisht Vaid in *The Codified Mysteries*, "were to lead back to the evolutionary principles of the higher realms from which we had descended, causing the true joy and happiness of the soul and spirit, a perfect enjoy-full state of existence."

Today we are faced with the same midwifery. Albert Einstein was clearly in the know when he assured us: "The religion of the future will be a cosmic religion. It should transcend personal God and avoid dogma and theology." Indeed, Quantum Physics is nothing more than a repackaging of the age-old mystical. It swings materialistic science back around full revolution to the ancient occulting Mysteries once embraced by Noah's grandchildren. It is just like Satan and the *gods* to expose one terrible lie—that being paganism—only to turn our head and fix our gaze upon yet another damnation, which ironically is, as it always has been— the *exact same thing*.

With Quantum Physics, what we have come to know as the superstring theory, or the "Theory of Everything," such esoteric knowledge essentially attempts to gather all of the particles and fundamental forces of nature into one *being*, including dark matter and the harmonization of Einstein's general relativity and gravitation as it applies to large-scale structures (such as distant galaxies, black holes, and stars), by modeling them as vibrations of tiny supersymmetric strings. In other words, everything in our universe is interconnected by vibrating strings and membranes of energy. We are only personified as one might detect the sound of a cricket. We find ourselves in a universal field of virtual particles, and therefore we are all part of a single living system. Accordingly, consciousness is nothing more than a biological and wholly physical construct, be it an evolutionary one, and is therefore delegated to a broader ecosystem, a larger universal collective consciousness.

Essentially, all life is fundamentally One. And for Quantum Physicists like Amit Goswami it is a self-saving Gospel. He says, "Consciousness is the ground of all being." Fully realized, mind, body, and spirit create a sacred trinity that allows us to fully experience life on earth. Yoga flourishes off such notions. Austrian theoretical physicist Erwin Schrödinger agrees: "Quantum physics thus reveals a basic oneness of the universe"

If I might be so bold as to try and sum up physicist Fritjof Capra's bestseller, *The Tao of Physics: An Exploration of the Parallels Between Modern Physics and Eastern Mysticism*, into a single comprehensible sentence, then essentially both scientists and secret mystics of ancient and modern times have developed highly sophisticated methods of observing nature which is equal and completely compatible to the other and yet wholly inaccessible to the common lay person. Says Capra:

> "The basic recurring theme in Hindu mythology is the creation of the world by the self-sacrifice of God—'sacrifice' in the original sense of '*making sacred*'—whereby God becomes the world which, in the end, becomes again God."

It is of the highest importance to note that the Judaism of Moses' day and the Christianity which would follow in line with the teachings of Christ has absolutely no notable mention in the construct of esoteric physics— *anywhere*. God's Testimony concerning Himself and His creation is completely absent from any true understanding of the Greek, Babylonian, and Egyptian Mystery Schools. For the righteous man, this is a good thing. Once again, the Word of God compels us with its unique vision of the Divine. He is not His creation, and we are certainly *not* Him. Nor are we the savior of ourselves. God alone is Savior. And yet, despite lifting the veil on spiritual Egypt, we can thank occultist meanderings within the field of quantum mechanics for computers and Smartphones, fiber optic telecommunications and GPS. An entire technological marvel of Babylon has been achieved, and once again, just as it was in the days of Moses and Daniel, we find ourselves indebted to it—in bondage even.

Mind, consciousness, reincarnation, evolution, even the globe and later the heliocentric model, have long been expressed, though most cleverly masked, by Egypt's mystery schools. No wonder why God was absolutely clear on the subject. On no uncertain terms were we to return to Egypt.

> "Yet I am the LORD thy God from the land of Egypt, and thou shalt know no god but me: for there is no savior beside me (Hosea 13:4)."

That Moses received his training among Egypt's most esoteric and sinister of societies was well-known even to the Jews of Jesus' day. Moments before Stephen was cast out of Jerusalem and stoned—being the first Christian martyr of many more to come—he spoke to the Temple priests and to Saul the Pharisee concerning him: "And Moses was learned in all the wisdom of the Egyptians, and was mighty in words and deeds (Acts 7:22)."

Let us now consider Moses' actions. Israel's first redeemer betrayed the scientific establishment of his day—and from what was arguably the greatest, longest lasting Empire in human history. He was even entrusted with it. And yet the esoteric wealth, which built his civilization with the comforts of home, he *completely abandoned*. Moses understood the true spiritual lesson—that God's chosen people were enslaved by a conniving sorcery which bolstered his lavish living in Pharaoh's court. The Egyptian would never divorce magic from his religion. Assuredly, despite the enlightenments which once accompanied him, even molded his thinking, nothing could compare with the burning bush in the wilderness, who called unto Moses: "I AM THAT I AM."

Contrarily, Moses had *likely* been educated with what would later come to be known as the Hermetic Axiom, which is: "The All is in All, and All is in The All." Roughly translated, "God is in All and All is in God." Everything that Moses had at one time intimately embraced for four decades of his life was most easily debunked as a sad pathetic and damnable imitation in light of what that voice in the burning bush would offer. And it was all cast aside the moment he stood before Pharaoh, aptly demanding: "Thus saith the LORD God of Israel, *Let my people go.*"

The LORD brought His people out of spiritual Egypt. Yet ever since their Red Sea crossing we've desired to go back. Those indebted to their slaveholders need only look to the Kabbalist, Hermeticists, Gnostic, Buddhist, and Alchemist and thank them, not only for their private preservation of the higher learning—far from the reckoning of gullible man—but constructing western society from the foundation and ground floor on up, with its plush comforts of living, and blindfolding us Christians into actually believing that the God of the Bible was behind it all.

For those of us whom the Spirit has woken—*woken* from this present darkness, that is—what are we to do with this knowledge, particularly our continued involvement in the technological fruits of mysticism? Take it to God. I am but a man. Always take it to God. But might I suggest, if we are to model ourselves after Enoch, who walked with God, then let us walk right on through Egypt for the Red Sea and Promised Land beyond. Let us never look back again.

In the meantime, I invoke the 8th-century prayer of the missionary to the Irish, Saint Patrick. He knew darkness where he saw it. The secret societies were certainly not hidden from him. Mainly, the "black laws of pagandom" and its magical crafts which sought to "corrupt man's body and soul." If only the everyday Christian of the last few centuries—even the saints of today, prayed as our great spiritual fathers once did. Would that the Mysteries of ancient Egypt blind us as they now do?

"I summon to-day all these powers between me and those evils,

Against every cruel merciless power that may oppose my body and my soul,

Against incantation of false prophets,

Against black laws of pagandom,

Against false laws of heretics,

Against craft of idolatry,

Against spells of women and smiths and wizards,

Against every knowledge that corrupts man's body and soul."

"Crist with me, Christ before me, Christ behind me,

Christ in me, Christ beneath me, Christ above me,

Christ on my right, Christ on my left,

Christ when I lie down, Christ when I sit down, Christ when I arise...."

"*Worthless Mysteries...*" THE FATAL SILENCE: MYSTERY BABYLON, LAKE OF FIRE, AND THE OUTER DARKNESS ACCORDING TO 1 ENOCH

LONG AGO TWO HUNDRED ANGELS DESCENDED upon Mount Hermon in order that humanity might learn the *mysteries* of heaven, and then one day, while Azazel, Semjaza, and the lot of their fellow transgressors were sitting around weeping, the Prophet Enoch met them. He had been asked to write a petition on their behalf, that they might be forgiven of their sins. They were forbidden audience with the Lord and condemned from lifting their eyes up and beholding heaven. On the night prior, Enoch had fallen asleep by the waters of Dan and dreamt of beautiful places. He had visions of the very heaven which they longed to survey, and of a far worse place which awaited them. It was at the very ends of heaven and earth itself, the Prophet wrote, where he saw *something horrible*. There, in the chaos and the void, he witnessed neither a heaven above nor a firmly founded earth below, but a desert numbered with seven stars. These stars, Enoch wrote, had the appearance of "great burning mountains," for as he stood there watching them, paralyzed with a trembling fear, they rolled about in the fire. And nothing could quench their torment.

The Prophet asked the angel standing next to him: "For what sin are they bound, and on why have they been cast in here?"

Uriel responded: "These are some of the stars of heaven, which have transgressed the commandment of the Lord. This has become a prison for the stars and the host of heaven. And the stars which roll over the fire are they which have transgressed the commandment of the Lord in the beginning of their rising, because they did not come out at their proper times."

Among these terrible revelations the Prophet would write: "And I, Enoch, alone saw the vision, the ends of all things, and no man shall see as I have seen (Enoch 19:3)."

Despite the fact that Azazel and Semjaza and their confederacy of Occult fathers threw the host of humanity into delusion by revealing the *hidden knowledge* of heaven, even now we see at best "through a mirror, darkly (1 Corinthians 13:12)." Unlike Enoch, we can only gaze heavenwards through the eye of a telescope and wonder. And yet if the book of Enoch is to be believed, the Prophet who "walked with God" was given the greater truth altogether. He was delivered the greater mysteries of heaven "face to face." His revelation was a legitimate reality, for he was shown the *consequence* behind the delusion of astrology and its Science counterpart—astronomy. Beyond the firmament, in a desert place nestled among the chaos and the void, Enoch saw what no other man has seen nor shall see. No telescope nor Scientific contraption can ever show us the angels we know today as the planets Mercury, Venus, Mars, Neptune, Jupiter, Uranus, and Saturn, who were reeling in torment before him.

For this reason, Enoch was instructed to tell the Watchers: "You were in heaven, but all the mysteries of heaven had not been revealed to you, and you knew worthless ones, and these in the hardness of your hearts you have made known to the women, and through these mysteries women and men work much evil on earth."

And so, returning to Azazel, this is what Enoch told him: "Azazel, you shall have no peace."

The Biblical Scholar who *insists* John the Revelator introduced the world to the Lake of Fire has overlooked two irrefutable facts; that Plato spoke of a burning lake within his esoteric *globe* myth, a place where the *immortal* souls of the wicked are tormented until the moment they are reborn, via reincarnation, and also the Prophet Enoch, who sought to correct the *worthless* mysteries of heaven as revealed in *Phaedo* and other bestsellers. Four times John brings Enoch's Lake of Fire to our attention—in Revelation 19:20; 20:10; 20:14-15; and 21:8—and if we refer back to the Gospels the message is irrefutably consistent. According to Jesus, the eternal fire was "prepared for the devil and his angels."

Jesus furthermore named this geographical landmark the "outer darkness." Enoch would surely agree with this unknowable zip code. In His parable of the wedding crasher, the king said of his unwelcome guest: "Bind him hand and foot, and take him away, and cast him into outer darkness; there shall be weeping and gnashing of teeth (Matthew 22:13)." But here is our *direct* connection. Jude would later concur with his brother Jesus when he identified the deceived soul—those who do not contend earnestly for the faith but "have gone in the way of Cain, and ran greedily after the error of Balaam for reward"—by cleverly and perhaps sarcastically comparing them to *planets*, rather ironically, and the *blackness of darkness* which await them. "Wandering stars," Jude writes, "to whom is reserved the blackness of darkness forever (Jude 1:13)."

The Apostle Peter likewise understood the correction of a Hellenistic myth when he himself accepted the premise of Plato's fiery underworld only so much as it was a prison prepared for angels by God and *not* the immortal human soul doctrine. This is no doubt why he accredited Enoch's fiery place of torment with the name *Tartarus*.

With this in mind, I have little doubt that the Book of Enoch was written, at minimal, as a knee-jerk reaction to the cancer of Platonism. The Greeks had prepared enough poisoned hemlock from Socrates deathbed for the whole of humanity to drink and with adequate leftovers to pass around again. The transcendentalist Ralph Waldo Emmerson would later write of him: "Plato is philosophy, and philosophy, Plato—at once the glory and the shame of mankind, since neither Saxon nor Roman have availed to add any idea to his categories." This was very much true for the Hellenistic Jew. With *Phaedo*, Plato introduced the uninitiated public to the neophyte's globe earth, which outwardly consisted of seven ascending spires and the eighth heaven of heavens encapsulating it. In response to Plato's cosmological *halo,* Enoch is taken on a grand tour of a flat, enclosed earth, beyond the earth and under the earth, even beyond the firmament to the chaos and the void and the prison of the angels, and finally to heaven above. We learn of the courses of the luminaries, of the sun and the moon in their ceaseless rising. We learn of that and so much more. With Enoch's rebuttal against the fashionable incursion of Platonism, the loyal literalist is beckoned to a sense of Biblical nationalism. While waking up to the reality of Eratosthenes' globe measurements, the child of God was once more challenged to gaze back upon Job 38, when the LORD spoke to Job from out of the storm and rhetorically asked if he could calculate the breadth of the earth.

To this effect, Enoch asks of his reader:

"And who is there of all men that could know what is the breadth and the length of the earth, and to whom has the measurement been shown of all of them? Or is there anyone who could discern the length of the heaven and how great is its height, and on what it is founded, and how great is the number of stars, and where all the luminaries rest (Enoch 93:13-14)?"

So also Plato popularized another worthless *hidden knowledge* from the Mystery religion—the immortal soul doctrine. Once again, Enoch clung to the belief of his Hebrew contemporaries—that the soul is mortal; that the *spirit* must return to God and wait upon the day when "the congregation of the righteous shall appear, and sinners shall be judged for their sins, and shall be driven from the face of the earth (Enoch 38:1)."

This is to concur with the resurrection of the dead according to Daniel.

"And at that time shall Michael stand up, the great prince which standeth for the children of thy people: and there shall be a time of trouble, such as never was since there was a nation even to that same time: and at that time thy people shall be delivered, every one that shall be found written in the book. And many of them that sleep in the dust of the earth shall awake, some to everlasting life, and some to shame and everlasting contempt. And they that be wise shall shine as the brightness of the firmament; and they that turn many to righteousness as the stars for ever and ever (Daniel 12: 1-3)."

With the physical shape, quality and character of the soul always in debate between the Platonist and Aristotelian, Enoch attempts to pull the child of God away from the philosophical discourse of imagination and delusion by asking his reader: "And how should there be one who could behold heaven, and who is there that could understand the things of heaven and see a soul or a spirit and could tell of it, or ascend and see all their ends and think them or do like them (Enoch 93:12)?"

There is of course the perpetual onslaught of the Babylonian Mysteries to consider. Of particular interest is the apkallu incursion of Mesopotamian literature which Moses first sought to correct in Genesis 6. So did Enoch. The book which bears his name completely dismissed the transmission of divine knowledge from the Watchers of Mount Hermon as a nightmarish knowledge altogether. In his book *Reversing Hermon*, Dr. Michael S. Heiser writes: "A well-known tablet from Uruk dating to the Seleucid period plots out this transmission of divine knowledge on both sides of the Flood. It lists [seven] pre-diluvian kings, each of them accompanied by an assisting apkallu, the divine sage who gave the king the knowledge necessary for civilization." According to Dr. Heiser, the point of the Jewish writers behind the Enochian literature "was to turn the Mesopotamian belief system on its head, to make sure that Israelites and Jewish readers would know that what happened between the sons of God and the daughters of humankind was not something that bettered humanity. It was the opposite—a transgression of heaven and earth that would corrupt humankind and produce a lineage that would later be a threat to the very existence of Israel, Yahweh's *portion* and *people.*"

Enoch's underlining doctrine stands in accordance with Moses. The Lawgiver wrote: "When the Most High divided to the nations their inheritance, when he separated the sons of Adam, he set the bounds of the people according to the number of the children of Israel. For the LORD's portion is His people; Jacob is the lot of his inheritance (Deuteronomy 32:8-9)."

A day is coming when everyone will receive *his portion*. A man will either receive his portion with "the angels which kept not their first estate, but left their own habitation (Jude 1:6)," or with the King of kings and Lord of lords. Our Savior hoped to wet our appetite while simultaneously prompting us to action: "And, behold, I come quickly; and my reward is with me, to give every man according as his work shall be (Revelation 22:12)." John's Revelation equally warns his reader by returning their attention to Enoch's Lake of Fire, particularly "the cowardly, the faithless, the detestable." John writes: "as for murderers, the sexually immoral, sorcerers, idolaters, and all liars, **their portion** will be in the lake that burns with fire and sulfur, which is *the second death* (Revelation 21:8)."

Though the angel's prison is eternal, and their sentence irreversible, Enoch seems to keep in line with the Hebrew mortalist position, because even the angels will be "burnt up with the condemned" and ultimately "destroyed." To this effect, the LORD told His angel Gabriel: "In those days they shall be led off to the abyss of fire and to the torment and the prison in which they shall be confined forever. Then Semjaza shall be burnt up with the condemned and they will be destroyed (Enoch 10:13-14)."

This is the final judgement, the darkest hour before the endless light of eternity dawns upon us. "In those days, Sheol will return all the deposits which she had received and hell will give back all that which it owes (Enoch 51:1)." John the Revelator once more mirrored Enoch when he wrote: "And the sea gave up the dead that were in it, Death and Hades gave up the dead that were in them, and all were judged according to what they had done (Revelation 20:13)."

There is however another rarely discussed feature of Enoch's Lake of Fire, perhaps because confusion has long been a pestilence here. In his vision, Uriel told Enoch: "The angels who have had sex with women shall stand here." The Prophet then made special mention of "the women also of the angels who went astray," specifically, that they "shall become *sirens* (Enoch 19:2)."

Sirens, he says.

In his notebooks, Leonardo da Vinci wrote of the siren: "The siren sings so sweetly that she lulls the mariner to sleep, then she climbs upon the ships and kills the sleeping marines." Enoch could not stand to look at that "fearful place [prison of the angels] because of the spectacle of the pain (Enoch 21:10)," and yet we are expected to believe the wives of angels are comparable to the coquettish bare-bosomed women of Greek mythology who lured sexually malnourished sailors to a rocky and shipwrecked doom with their enchanting instrumental arrangements and singing voices.

Perhaps John the Revelator can be of help again. The Apostle John appropriately understood the *corrected* vision of Enoch. The sirens, he suggested, might best be looked upon as a *whore*.

"This calls for a mind that has wisdom: **the seven heads are seven mountains on which the woman is seated** (Revelation 17:9)."

Those intimate with Enoch would have immediately understood *the seven mountains* on which the woman is seated. Once again correcting a misguided faith in the Occult, John dismisses any supposed enlightenment which may have derived from the Watchers and, only partially comparable here, the seven pre-diluvian kings of Mesopotamian literature when he adds: "also, there are seven kings."

This calls for a mind that has wisdom.

By this we are to understand John furthermore aims to direct our attention to Isaiah's conspiratorial penmanship. With the spell casting of Babylon on his mind, the Major Prophet wrote concerning Satan's great and awful secret religion:

"And thou saidst, I shall be a lady forever: so that thou didst not lay these things to thy heart, neither didst remember the latter end of it. Therefore hear now this, thou that art given to pleasures, that dwellest carelessly, that sayest in thine heart, **I am, and none else beside me**; I shall not sit as a widow, neither shall I know the loss of children: But these two things shall come to thee in a moment in one day, the loss of children, and widowhood: they shall come upon thee in their perfection for the multitude of they sorceries, and for the great abundance of thine enchantments. For thou hast trusted in they wickedness: thou hast said, **None seeth me**. Thy wisdom and they knowledge, it hath perverted thee; and thou hast said in thine heart, I am, and none else beside me. Therefore shall evil come upon thee; thou shalt not be able to put it off: and desolation shall come upon thee suddenly, which thou shalt not know (Isaiah 47:7-11)."

According to Isaiah, the soothsayer of Babylon thinks she is clever enough to remain hidden while luring mankind with her perverted wisdom and knowledge. If Enoch and John can be inserted here, she conclusively is reeling them into the lake of destruction. And yet her ultimate goal is always the same—to ascend to heaven and dethrone God, or perhaps convince us *she can—we* can—by way of evolutionary doctrine and heavenly know-how entangled with enchantment. More-so, she wants to be God, for she deliriously says in her heart: "**I am**, and none else beside me."

Those who go whoring after her attend another sort of church altogether. It is one in which adulterous relationships and alliances have been entered with the leaders and the kings of the world—in this *current* election year and every other; past, present, and future—so that the inhabitants of the earth are made drunk by the very false realities which give credibility to her teachings.

The Apostle Paul wrote of the *true* church: "For I am jealous over you with godly jealousy: for I have espoused you to one husband, that I may present you as a chaste virgin to Christ (2 Corinthians 11:1-2)."

John further tips us off to the Babylon whore religion as dealing in Mysteries. "And upon her forehead was a name written, MYSTERY, BABYLON THE GREAT, THE MOTHER OF HARLOTS AND ABOMINATION OF THE EARTH (Revelation 17:5)."

140

Knowing this *now,* the planets which Enoch observed and their very prison which Jude and the Apostles Peter and John concluded were true, one thing is certain.

We have been duped.

"The second angel blew his trumpet, and something like a great mountain, burning with fire, was thrown into the sea (Revelation 8:8)."

The woman who sits upon the seven mountains of Enoch's vision is *space.* She is atomic theory. She is the *other* dimension just beyond our reach. She is evolution and transhumanism, artificial intelligence and the promise of singularity. She is the immortal soul doctrine. She is the flickering television—the life-giving idol which is granted permission to speak. She is music—the song which mesmerizes and beckons the soul to sing and the voice which slowly lulls us to sleep. She is alchemy and astrology and their Science counterparts in the Neophyte's modern halls of initiation. She is Hollywood, Nashville, New York City, London, Mecca, Alexandria and Rome. She is hidden knowledge from heaven above, revealed unto us through religion and philosophy. She is self-salvation. She is that and more—so much more. She is the great delusion which the western and eastern world is built upon. She is the Mother of Harlots and Abomination of the earth. She is the Copernican Revolution.

The Apostle John laid out the great deception of the ages.

No wonder why *they* had the book of Enoch buried.

THAT HIDDEN DARKNESS: SCIENCE & ITS UNION WITH FALLEN ANGELS (DID JESUS ENDORSE 1 ENOCH AS SCRIPTURE?)

IT IS NO SECRET THAT ENOCH WAS IMMENSELY POPULAR within Orthodox Judaism during the centuries leading up to Jesus' ministry—a trend which would undoubtedly change hands into Christian circles for the following two or three centuries. Second century Apostolic fathers such as Justin Martyr and Irenaeus, Polycarp's successor, hailed it as Scripture. So right there I'm in good company. Seminary students today are not taught the many New Testament phrases and theological teachings which finds first precedence in 1 Enoch. There are well over a hundred such cross-references. As I have already noted, the Gospel writers and Apostles basically took Enoch textually and ran with it. Enoch is the perfect puzzle-piece that seamlessly locks the Old and New Testaments together into a colorful tapestry. Even more tragic of an oversight by today's teachers of the Word is the surmounting evidence that Jesus Himself used the book as a springboard for many of His sermons, including perhaps dozens of theological quotes which mirror or match that of Enoch's.

In Luke 20:27-40 we read an account of the Sadducees, who did not believe in a resurrection from the dead, coming to Jesus with a question concerning which of seven brothers would be married to a woman in eternity if each in successive turn inherited her as a wife during their life on earth.

This is how Jesus responded.

[34] And Jesus answering said unto them, "The children of this world marry, and are given in marriage: [35] But they which shall be accounted worthy to obtain that world, and the resurrection from the dead, neither marry, nor are given in marriage: [36] Neither can they die any more: for they are equal unto the angels; and are the children of God, being the children of the resurrection (Luke 20:34-36)."

Let us now mirror this with Enoch.

> [1]And He answered and said to me, and I heard His voice: "Fear not, Enoch, thou righteous man and scribe of righteousness: approach hither and hear my voice. [2]And go, say to the Watchers of heaven, who have sent thee to intercede for them: 'You should intercede for men, and not men for you: [3]Wherefore have ye left the high, holy, and eternal heaven, and lain with women, and defiled yourselves with the daughters of men and taken to yourselves wives, and done like the children of earth, and begotten giants as your sons? [4]And though ye were holy, spiritual, living the eternal life, you have defiled yourselves with the blood of women, and have begotten children with the blood of flesh, and, as the children of men, have lusted after flesh and blood as those also do who die and perish. [5]Therefore have I given them wives also that they might impregnate them, and beget children by them, that thus nothing might be wanting to them on earth. **[6]But you were formerly spiritual, living the eternal life, and immortal for all generations of the world. [7]And therefore I have not appointed wives for you; for as for the spiritual ones of the heaven, in heaven is their dwelling** (Enoch 15:1-7).'"

Jesus wasn't saying that angels *cannot* marry. He was saying wives were not appointed to angels. Such was the wickedness in the hearts of men when the inhabitants of Sodom had hoped to have intercourse with the visiting angels. This is why Jesus' brother Jude found little effort in comparing the sins of the Watchers with Lot's neighbors in Jude 1:6-7. We have already rehearsed this scene of horror. The angel Uriel has taken Enoch to the very edge of the earth and beyond, in "a place which had no firmament of heaven above, and no firmly founded earth beneath it." It is there where he witnessed the fate of those angels who left their own habitation. Let us therefore once again mirror Enoch 15:1-7 with Jesus, but rather than depending on Luke 20, let us compare the very same account in the Gospel of Mark.

> [24]And Jesus answering said unto them, "Do ye not therefore err, because **ye know not the scriptures**, neither the power of God? [25]For when they shall rise from the dead, **they neither marry, nor are given in marriage; but are as the angels which are in heaven** (Mark 12:24-25)."

Jesus said: "Ye know not the scriptures."

Wait, what scriptures?

Jesus answers our questions. While Enoch certainly taught the resurrection of the righteous, we can be assured that Jesus referred his audience to Moses. But there is another ingredient to the conversation beyond Moses. Of the angels in heaven (for *"ye know not the scriptures"*), there is no other source available to us but Enoch.

2

I HAVE OFTEN HEARD IT STATED HOW THIS GRAND-SCHEMED heliocentric lie could not have been made possible without the angels who kept not their first estate, forsaking their prescribed courses in the heavens to become the seven wandering stars we know today, or planets in Greek. This is only a partial truth at best. The luminaries did in fact forsake their first estate, and when Jesus walked the Earth, this was well regarded by the elect. Not only did the Savior authorize Enoch as Scripture, but his disciple Peter and half-brother Jude each devoted a book thematically to it. Yet what is the good of a deception if everyone is in the know? In order for the globe delusion to be made possible, Enoch not only had to be removed from canon entirely—far more devilishly, he had to be buried so far deep into the ground that it wouldn't be rediscovered for an entire millennia.

Finally, having a grand scope of things, we can now see the true brilliance of Satan who, unlike a chess battle with the child prodigy Bobby Fischer, was plotting his strategy several dozen moves—no, centuries—no, even millennia's before him—even from the very beginning. So too is Satan a patient fellow, seeking not the philosophical oversight with one solitary generation, where sound doctrine is concerned, but with careful groundwork and the slow build-up of grand engineering—an entire metropolis of lies rather than suburban housing—room enough for the total overthrow of many. We may simply take note of his handiwork in the generations following our founding church fathers, having once hailed Enoch as sound doctrine, now hear whispered in their ear, "You don't really believe this silly interchange of business between celestial angels and humans, do you? If you truly are a God-fearing fellow, you must denounce such nonsense as untrue."

How embarrassing for Enoch's antagonists, once he was rediscovered among the Ethiopians and under the sands of Qumran, included with his original Hebrew and Aramaic texts, that we would confirm over 100 New Testament phrases and theological teachings which first find precedence in Enoch, not the other way around—that Gospel writers and the Apostles basically took Enoch textually and ran with it, including Peter, including Jude, including John the Revelator—that Enoch is the perfect puzzle-piece which seamlessly locks the Old and New Testaments together into a colorful tapestry—and even more tragically, and a glaring oversight by its staunchest rejecters, that Jesus Christ Himself used the book as a springboard for many of His sermons, including perhaps dozens of theological quotes which mirror or match that of Enoch's.

No, not only embarrassing—it is truly tragic for generations of the gullible that we bothered listening to Satan at all, casting aside sound doctrine which would have spared many, only to have him turn the very lie used in the expulsion of Enoch to elevate the great globe delusion, *and worse*, write into astronomy the very testimony of Enoch into his own warped gospel for the masses, "The aliens are soon arriving for an interchange of business with man—and they're coming from the stars!"

Imagine the God-fearing woman who might look up at the planets—named so-much as gods demanding the worship of past ages and the occultist practices of present—and with Enoch opened in her hands, and with Peter and Jude and John to back them, say to the luminaries, "You have transgressed the commandment of the Lord in the beginning of your rising, because you did not come out at your proper times!"

What might the god-fearing child have to say to her godless government-sponsored teacher and class, when asked to make a "scale" model of the planets around the sun in defiance of Hebrew Cosmogony and Enoch, and with Peter and Jude and Jesus Christ to stand in her defense, but: "And the angels, keeping not their first estate, but left their own habitation, He the Lord hath reserved in everlasting chains under darkness unto the judgment of the great day."

The Copernican delusion would certainly have sidestepped around us—those of us who fear the Lord, and likely would not have happened at all if the church had the courage to stand against it. But his rediscovery under the sands of time arrived too late in the narrative of human history. Entire empires had risen and fallen, two World Wars had already been fought and, without even inventing an airplane or a tower so high, which might check to see if there truly was a curve—as was so eagerly anticipated by all—everyone had agreed upon it, including the Christian.

The lie was embedded, decided upon and celebrated, and the long sought-after book, no matter how truthful it proved, with wisdom that defies the ages, was no longer the knowledge they sought after. That ship had sailed.

No worries, Enoch was not written for them anyways.

In his opening dialogue, the wise and knowledgeable Enoch states: "But it (his revelation) was not for this generation to know, but for a remote one which is to come."

That generation is *us*. We are the remote one first spoken of, which rediscovered his words and cherished them as fact, not as silly-superstitious fact but as heavenly manna for the poor in spirit who recognizes the angelic oppression of Scientism and Academia upon this Earth and desperately need words to cling to. We are the generation, which Enoch takes careful note of in his very opening remark, "....the elect and righteous, who will be living in the day of tribulation, when all the wicked and godless people are to be removed from the Earth."

When we open the pages of Enoch, for those of us who embrace the complete Testimony of God through Moses and the Prophets and the Apostles—we call this the joyous cosmology—it is as if he speaks *only* and *directly* to us (beyond the first few generations which were needed to establish its credentials), and I most certainly believe this to be the case. It was lost and found that it might confirm our observations as true, to this generation only, and thereby commission us to turn to Jesus as our Lord and Savior, because when we begin to understand these things—the great globe delusion that is, *as in the days of Noah*—we can know the end is near.

> "And Enoch also, the seventh from Adam, prophesied of these, saying, Behold, the Lord cometh with ten thousands of his saints, To execute judgment upon all, and to convince all that are ungodly among them of all their ungodly deeds which they have ungodly committed, and of all their hard speeches which ungodly sinners have spoken against him (Jude 1:14-16)."

3

NOWHERE IN THE BIBLE DO WE FIND "TECHNOLOGY" and "scientific understanding" portrayed as a means by which God pours out his grace upon the world. Nor are there described in Scripture invisible laws imbued upon creation which our Lord purposed us to seek out, to swoop up with a philosophical butterfly net, to quantify or formulate secret mysteries as a way to seek Him and get to know Him better—and in the end harness that power for our own advancement or pleasure. False teaching has taken the church captive. If the Holy Spirit is waking up a remnant of His church to the truth of creation, and I certainly believe this to be the case, then the murky tomb by which He pulled us up and out of—this terrible idolatrous slumber—quickly becomes exposed. It wasn't God who commissioned mankind to bring to light the mystery knowledge, but Satan's angels—the fallen ones.

A spiritual subscriber to the Book of Enoch simply would not veer to the right or left of his message to support any government's quest for scientific or technological superiority over their enemies, because Enoch made it clear that our communion with the angels, not God, made "cultured civilization" as we know it possible. No wonder the "Holy" Roman Church, when acquisitioning the traditions and culture of the very spiritual kingdom that it had for centuries attempted to mutilate in the arena, the same Christianity it now crowned itself the rightful heirs and caretakers of, not only stripped Enoch's rights as an inspired Book from the Bible, but had it buried deep underground—the simplest of readings will attest to this.

> "And Azazel taught men to make swords, and knives, and shields, and breastplates, and taught them about metals of the Earth and the art of working them, and bracelets, and ornaments, and the use of antimony, and the beautifying of the eyelids, and all kinds of precious stones, and all coloring and dyes. And there was great impiety; they turned away from God, and committed fornication, and they were led astray, and became corrupt in all their ways (Enoch 8:1-2)."

Enoch further describes in verse 3 how the angels taught "the casting of spells," "counter-spells," "astrology," "constellation portents," and "knowledge of the clouds, signs of the earth, sun, and course of the moon." Contrast needs to be made here between this false-scientific delusion that was once hidden in darkness and brought to light accordingly by the fallen angels compared to the Hebrew belief in a self-enclosed cosmological order, revealed by God's own testimony in the Holy Scripture and further upheld by Enoch throughout his continued narrative. As a result of these teachings, not Enoch's but the angels, the writer notes: "And as men perished, they cried, and their cry went up to heaven."

While I seek to employ The Book of Enoch for consideration, which stands as a lasting testimony to the truth of an enclosed cosmology, to be fair it's the Flat Earth revelation itself, when contained within the boundaries of our existing Bible, which reveals in no uncertain terms that the contemporary church has succumbed to a gross misconception of science. If we're honest I think we all bought into this idea—I certainly know I did—that it was our own "Christian worldview" which made modern science possible and that "Scientism" took a wrong turn only recently in history when several loose cannons within its ranks invented Darwinism, allowing for the terrible conclusions which naturally skew from its preconceptions. It's all a part of the same lie.

Rather than embracing what God testifies of Himself in the Bible and all that the joyous cosmology broadly implies, I hear this rebuttal constantly by those in the church who reject that doctrine merely on the basis of: "But what of all the scientists? The Christian scientists! You can't group all scientists into one basket!"

Despite the technological nightmare that encapsulated our last century, led by our Masters of Ceremony in the cult of Scientism, and which further promises to define ours beyond any comparable measure, those of us who have come out of the globular lie must acknowledge that we were blinded to the false teaching of the Kabbalistic texts which inspired such great men as Sir Isaac Newton, with his discovery of "gravity," and the simultaneous embracing of Hermeticism, with its invisible forces which can be understood and manipulated and turned into a formula. We were lost unknowingly in the fog by this entire notion that it was God's desire all along to reveal Himself through the natural philosophy that originated with the Greeks and mystery schools and the Babylonians and the Egyptians and not merely through the Hebrew writers of the Holy Scriptures who forsook such teachings as devotions to sorcery, and the Rephaim voices lifting from Sheol, which imbued its practitioner with worthless mysteries.

This debate isn't just about ball earth verses flat earth. What the Flat Earth awakening brings to light is not the secret mysteries of science as the Globe Earth does, but western civilization itself, fully exposed in its wretched nakedness—again, and I can't repeat this enough, not God's instrument for the continual-expansion of His kingdom, as Globe Earth proposes. Rather, it's rooted in the very Luciferian lie by which the globe chains its disciples to. Plato's globe, and all that pertains to it, is an end-times instrument for the kingdom of darkness.

THE GOSPELS AFFIRM 1 ENOCH'S ACCOUNT OF DEMONS (*and* THEY'RE NOT FALLEN ANGELS)

THE TRAGEDY CONCERNING THE BOOK OF ENOCH is not its dismissal from fourth-century canon, but the mere fact that it was almost lost for the entirety of Christendom's two-millennium history. In a theological game of connect the dots, Scripturally speaking—let's just say some of those dots were misplaced in time—because once a genuine document was finally rediscovered, it's clear that bits and pieces of the picture, as we know them now, didn't look quite right. As it turns out, when it comes to demonic possession, as recorded throughout the Gospels, we've been wrongly blaming fallen angels all along.

Upon finally rediscovering the long lost and often sought after Book of Enoch, some scholars hastily concluded that Enoch had to have been written *after* the New Testament and not the other way around, despite evidence to the contrary, because if so, the Gospel writers and Apostles didn't simply reference *Enoch* once or twice, as is still often claimed to this day, but well over a hundred times! Even more concerning to its dismissal is the accumulating evidence that Jesus was an authentic student and teacher of the book, which makes the Gospels various accounts of demonic possession and their role in His ministry all that much more intriguing, especially considering it was Enoch which gave license to them.

There's an account in Matthew where Jesus crosses over the Sea of Galilee and is immediately approached by two demon possessed men.

> [28]And when he was come to the other side into the country of the Gergesenes, there met him two possessed with devils, coming out of the tombs, exceeding fierce, so that no man might pass by that way. [29]And, behold, they cried out, saying, **What have we to do with thee, Jesus, thou Son of God? art thou come hither to torment us before the time?**

(Matthew 8:28-29)

150

In Luke's account of the same occurrence, he writes:

> [30] And Jesus asked him, saying, What is thy name? And he said, Legion: because many devils were entered into him. [31] **And they besought him that he would not command them to go out into the deep** [abyss].

(Luke 8:30-31)

My reader will likely recall that in both accounts Jesus, at the demons request, sends them seemingly with reckless ease into a heard of unclean swine, thereby allowing those evil spirits to continue committing their acts of evil rather than face judgement before their appointed time—and killing pigs in the process. Similarly, anyone acquainted with both the Old and New Testaments will easily find, in the simplest of surface reading through *Enoch*, numerous familiar visuals, albeit some unexpected ones, which not only mirror and affirm what we already know of first century Judeo-Christian thought, but in some cases gives sharper clarity—if not altogether redefining what we previously thought we knew.

In Enoch we read.

> And at the death of the giants, spirits will go out and shall destroy **without incurring judgement**, coming from their bodies their flesh shall be destroyed **until the day of the consummation, the great judgement in which the age shall be consummated**, over the Watchers and the godless, and shall be wholly consummated.

(Enoch 16:1)

The demons who encountered Jesus knew there was an appointed time of judgement, and it is because they were referencing *Enoch*! They gave signature to it much as one might with their own biography. When *Enoch* declares: "And at the death of the giants, spirits will go out," the demons themselves identified with the disembodied spirits of the giants who once roamed the earth before and again *after* the flood.

Moses had this to say of the Nephilim.

> [6]And it came to pass, when men began to multiply on the face of the earth, and daughters were born unto them, [2] That the sons of God saw the daughters of men that they were fair; and they took them wives of all which they chose. [3] And the Lord said, My spirit shall not always strive with man, for that he also is

flesh: yet his days shall be an hundred and twenty years. ⁴There were giants in the earth in those days; and also after that, when the sons of God came in unto the daughters of men, and they bare children to them, the same became mighty men which were of old, men of renown.

(Genesis 6: 1-4)

When Moses sent Hebrew spies into the Promised Land, he writes this of their report:

And there we saw the giants [Nephilim], the sons of Anak, which come of the giants: and we were in our own sight as grasshoppers, and so we were in their sight.

(Numbers 13:33)

We are pressed to consider ghastly accounts of giants throughout all major world cultures. Scripture would have us believe those very giants, whom once inhabited the earth and invoked God's judgement with the flood, as recorded in Genesis 6: 1-4, Jubilees 7:21-25, and Jasher 4:18-20, later possessed the land during Jesus' time, according to *Enoch* and the Gospels, and conclusively, still do.

Consider there is not one passage in all of Holy Scripture which accredits demons to angelic entities. Rather, they are the children of angels—or put in slightly different terms, sons of the elohim. While one might argue that Moses wrote of the giants long before the publication of *Enoch*, the later however clearly introduced the evil spirits wandering the earth in such a manner that the New Testament writers enthusiastically ran with. When one considers the immense popularity of Enoch at the time of Jesus' ministry, specifically with its Gospel writers, the connection becomes immediately clear. They were simply continuing a narrative that Enoch introduced.

⁸And now, the giants, who are produced from the spirits and flesh, shall be called evil spirits on the earth, ⁹And shall live on the earth. Evil spirits have come out from their bodies because they are born from men and from the holy Watchers; their beginning is of primal origin; ¹⁰They shall be evil spirits on earth, and evil spirits shall they be called spirits of the evil ones. (As for the spirits of heaven, in heaven shall be their dwelling, but as for the spirits of the earth which were born on the earth, on the earth shall be their dwelling.) And the spirits of the giants afflict, oppress, destroy, attack, war, destroy, and cause

152

trouble on the earth. [11]They take no food, but do not hunger or thirst. They cause offenses but are not observed. [12]And these spirits shall rise up against the children of men and against the women, because they have proceeded from them in the days of the slaughter and destruction.

Enoch 15:8-12

THE *Long* DIVORCE

1

A HOUSE DIVIDED CANNOT STAND

THE BOOKS OF MOSES ENDED WITH A CURSE. If the children of Abraham did not hearken unto the voice of Yahweh, if they did not observe His commandments, then *curses* would be their lot. Moses writes:

> But it shall come about, if you do not obey the Lord [*Yahweh*] your God [*eloheka*], to observe to do all His commandments and His statutes with which I charge you today, that all these curses will come upon you and overtake you.
>
> Deuteronomy 28:15

For a relatively short time, all twelve tribes were ruled by three kings. Saul was a failure. Only David obeyed the Lord because, despite his successor's wealth of wisdom, Solomon loved *foreign* women. He bedded with the daughter of Pharaoh and also those from his surrounding nations, Moabite, Ammonite, Edomite, Sidonian, and Hittite women, all of whom the Lord had said to the sons of Israel: "You shall not associate with them, nor shall they associate with you, for they will surely turn your heart away after their gods." Solomon's gluttony was unmatched. Seven hundred wives, many of them princesses, and another three hundred concubines assembled into the arsenal of his affections. In the end, his heart was turned. Though Yahweh had twice appeared to him, Solomon whored after the promises of other gods. The writer of *Kings* simply writes, Solomon "held fast to these in love."

> [11] So the Lord said to Solomon, "Because you have done this, and you have not kept My covenant and My statutes, which I have commanded you, I will surely tear the kingdom from you, and will give it to your servant. [12] Nevertheless I will not do it in your days for the sake of your father David, but I will tear it out of the hand of your son. [13] However, I will not tear away all the kingdom, but I will give one tribe to your son for the sake

154

of My servant David and for the sake of Jerusalem which I have chosen."

1 Kings 11: 11-13

Thus Solomon's reign over the united kingdom of Israel amounted to a total sum of *forty* years. But he would be the last to do so. He then *slept* with his fathers, we are told, and was buried in the city of David. The writer of *Kings* simply records that Israel persisted in rebellion against the house of David. When Jeroboam received word that Rehoboam was to be crowned as Solomon's successor, he returned from Egypt and, with the assembly of Israel to back him, demanded that Solomon had coupled his people with an unnecessary burden.

"Lighten the hard service of your father and his heavy yoke which he put on us, and we will serve you," he said.

King Rehoboam consulted with the elders who had served his father Solomon while he was still alive. *Lighten their load*, they insisted. But Rehoboam forsook their advice for the young men whom he had grown up with.

Their advice: "Tell the people, 'My little finger is thicker than my father's loins!'"

And that is just what he told them.

His edict was not well received. It is at this moment when the kingdom definitively split in two, just as Yahweh had said. The northern kingdom became the House of Israel, with the two southern tribes, Judah and Benjamin, remained in the House of Judah, because Judah had received the firstborn blessing. Jerusalem remained under Judah's jurisdiction.

The northern kingdom of Israel, founded in 930 BC, would host a succession of 18 kings over the span of two centuries. The student of Biblical history will likewise note that not one single king of Israel devoted himself to Yahweh—No, not one. The kings of Israel were *wicked* through and through. They repeatedly *did evil* in the sight of the Lord, and their final demise did not come without admonishment. Yahweh commanded the voice of the Prophets to be heard—Abijah, Jehu, Micaiah, Elijah, Elisha, Amos, Hosea, and Jonah, in that order. But their pleas, it seems, were of little to no effect.

Yahweh not only defined what the curse was, but in no uncertain terms, simultaneously summed up precisely why they would prefer it. Moses wrote:

> And the LORD [*Yahweh*] shall scatter thee among all people,
> from the one end of the earth even unto the other; and there
> thou shalt serve other gods [*elohim*], which neither thou nor thy
> fathers have known, even wood and stone.

Deuteronomy 28: 64

Like Solomon before them, the norther kingdom of Israel went whoring after a pantheon of gods. They forsook Yahweh's inheritance for an alien providence. And in doing so, God finally delivered them to the desires of their heart. In 722 BC the house of Israel was taken captive by Assyria. Those ten tribes would never return. Israel not only assimilated into the surrounding nations, they became *Gentiles*.

In short, they chose the *curse*.

2

AN EXCERPT FROM *"THE ANIMAL APOCALYPSE"* (1 ENOCH & THE 70 SHEPHERDS OF PSALM 82)

BY CLAIMING THAT HE HAD KILLED A LION and a bear, the shepherd boy David was making an astonishing connection. The giant Goliath, he told King Saul, might as well have been a wolf, a bear, a lion, a desert jackal, tiger, a Congolese ape, or an east African hyena—because Israel had a shepherd. The boy who had arisen from the quiet sheepcotes of Bethlehem knew what it was to lie his father's sheep down in green pastures, to lead them beside still water, and to guide them on the right path, for his names sake. He knew the value of his father's sheep, and what it was to forsake his very life in order to defend them rather than run. Likewise, Israel's shepherd was no hireling. His sheep knew His voice. If they huddled around Him when the wolves arrived, even clung to Him as if their very lives depended upon it, He would not abandon them. It would be *His life* before theirs. And yet here is another hungry beast emerging from the malevolent shadow—a foreign invader. The uncircumcised Philistine had come, not only to round up the sheep of their shepherd's providence and scatter them, but to spit upon the shepherd. Why should they fear?

Then again, David was one of the few who truly understood what it was, as a matter of life or death, to cling to Israel's shepherd. Of his twenty successors, nineteen of which were kings of the southern kingdom, only a select handful followed Yahweh in a likewise manner. The same cannot be said for the northern kingdom of Israel. They desired the providence of any shepherd other than their own. In fact, they welcomed them into the paddocks. And so Yahweh delivered them into their hands.

There is an interesting account in Enoch's "*Animal Apocalypse*" (1 Enoch chapters 85-90) that sheds further light on the Hebrews understanding of Psalm 82—*which*, I remind you, was David's worldview. Enoch's vision involves a dazzling display of various colored bulls and heifers, elephants, camels and donkeys, lions, tigers and eagles, rams and sheep, bears and the sort—an animal parade, if you will. It begins with Eden and ends with Eden. But in chapter 89, somewhere about three quarters of the way through humanities redemption narrative, Enoch tells of the many sheep whom Yahweh sent to His flock in order that they might testify of Him and lament over their incessant lostness. He writes:

> And many other sheep He sent to those sheep He sent to those
> sheep to testify to them and lament over them (Enoch 89:51).

In turn, his flock turned on those sheep and slayed them. Enoch is no doubt speaking of the prophets—a familiar Hebrew narrative. Only one sheep among all of them was saved. We will immediately recognize him as the prophet Elijah. Enoch writes:

> They sought to slay it, but the Lord of the sheep saved it from
> the sheep, and brought it up to me, and caused it to live there
> (Enoch 89:50).

We will also recall that four more prophets followed in his steps—Elisha, Jonah, Amos, and Hosea. Regardless, the northern kingdom of Israel forsook the house of Yahweh, and to the point, Enoch assures us, that they *invited slaughter*. And so, "He gave them over into the hands of the lions and tigers, and wolves and hyenas, and into the hand of the foxes, and to all the wild beasts, and those wild beasts began to tear in pieces those sheep (Enoch 89:53)."

Enoch mourned the butchery.

It is here where the narrative takes a familiar turn for those of us who are acquainted with Psalm 82 and Yahweh's divine council.

157

Yahweh calls upon the angelic princes of the Gentile nations—they tally seventy in number—to let them in on His plans. We must also recall that Yahweh disinherited humanity after the tower of Babel, further entrusting them to the care of the *elohim*. Yahweh essentially tells them, *I am now disinheriting the ten tribes of Israel*, further commanding that they commit themselves to the moral responsibilities and obligations required of their regal calling. It should be further noted that those seventy shepherds had *companions* with them. We can therefore surmise that this is indeed a diverse pantheon of divine beings. The children of divided Israel desired the inheritance which the divine shepherds offered, and their variety of angelic companions, not Yahweh's. It was as if Yahweh said: *You seduced them, and so you can have them. Now take them into your care and uphold your campaign promises.* We are given no knowledge of their initial reaction.

Enoch writes:

[57] And He called seventy shepherds, and gave those sheep to them that they might pasture them, and He spoke to the shepherds and their companions: "Let each individual of you pasture the sheep from now on, and everything that I shall command you that do you.

[58] And I will deliver them over to you duly numbered, and tell you which of them are to be destroyed-and them you will destroy." And He gave over to them those sheep.

We can now assume that the council meeting is adjourned, its members dispersed, because Yahweh calls upon another divine being, perhaps he is the court stenographer, and asks that he follow them out the door. In fact, Yahweh *knows* they will disobey His ordinances and do as they please. For this reason, He asks that His servant take a tally of their wrongdoings. Yahweh has no interest in tapping his divine princes on the shoulder whenever they willfully transgress against the Law. They are well aware of the eternal Law, and would clearly not have justifiable reason to dispute the Psalmist David when writing of God's Law being pure, eternal, and just—mainly:

[10] The statutes of the Lord are true,

all of them just;

[11] More desirable than gold,

than a hoard of purest gold,

Sweeter also than honey

or drippings from the comb.

Psalm 19:10b-11

For this reason, the court reporter is not to inform the seventy shepherds regarding his findings, not to mention the mere fact that an investigation is underway. Perhaps they are not taking their sin seriously, or the fact that they will be brought into judgement. Their full measure of their breezy attitude is of course all speculation, but this we do know, Yahweh's detective is only to report back to Him. In time, they will be held into account. This is Psalm 82 all over again.

> 59 And He called another and spoke to him: "Observe and mark everything that the shepherds will do to those sheep; for they will destroy more of them than I have commanded them.

> 60 And every excess and the destruction which will be done through the shepherds, record how many they destroy according to my command, and how many according to their own caprice; record against every individual shepherd all the destruction he effects.

> 61 And read out before me by numbers how many they destroy, and how many they deliver over for destruction, that I may have this as a testimony against them, and know every deed of the shepherds, that I may comprehend and see what they do, whether or not they abide by my command which I have commanded them.

> 62 But they shall not know it, and you shall not declare it to them, now admonish them, but only record against each individual all the destruction which the shepherds effect each in his time and lay it all before me."

The seventy shepherds, we read, immediately began to slay and destroy, gleefully delivering the former sheep of Yahweh's flock into the jaws of ravenous animals. Enoch began to weep and lament on account of those sheep, for each shepherd "slew and destroyed many more than was prescribed." But that is not to say that Yahweh did not have his detective on the case. Heaven's commissioned officer kept careful record of every perished soul.

> 66 And the shepherds and their associates delivered over those sheep to all the wild beasts, to devour them, and each one of

them received in his time a definite number, it was written by the other in a book how many each one of them destroyed of them.

We further read that, after the investigation came to a close, the book which contained his findings (and tallied their transgressions) was read before the Lord of the sheep, "and He took the book from his hand and read it and sealed it and laid it down (Enoch 89:69)." Yahweh has a habit of *sealing* books.

Early on in 1 Enoch, we learn that it is the angels Michael, Uriel, Raphael, and Gabriel who look down from heaven and witness the unprecedented bloodshed upon the earth, and all the lawless deeds stemming from men and the giants and the fallen Watchers who had begat them. After initially authorizing that the cries from the destruction of the earth below reach the very gates of heaven, they then approached the throne of Yahweh and said: "You know all things before they come to pass, and you see these things and you have permitted them, and say nothing to us about these things. What are we to do with them about these things? (Enoch 9:11)"

This is stunning insight into the life of a divine being. They were rigorous in their work. They paid attention to detail. The angels despised injustices. They were certainly aware regarding the activities of men in the earth below them, and could keep a tally on each lawless dead. Furthermore, they not only understood that Yahweh knew all things before they came to pass, they also concluded that nothing could transpire unless He permitted it. Yet they were left clueless. It appears as though, for this very reason, they were frustrated. Evil had been wrought upon the earth—and in such a manner that their former colleagues had committed themselves to the task. They had only now become aware of its extent as to open up the gates and let all of heaven in on the news. Yahweh knew this calamity would happen, but he didn't let anyone in on it. This prompted the question on their end, "What are we to do...?"

The seventy shepherds who received the northern ten tribes of Israel knew full well that Yahweh could not remarry His bride, once she was divorced. He was through with them—so to speak. And so they treated them as playthings. But that is not to say that Yahweh was finished with them, or that He hadn't thought this through. He had plans. In fact, He had *big* plans. Israel's story was far from over. Then again, the Gentiles whom He had disinherited at Babel, He had an arrangement in mind for them too. We are dealing with a divine program so clandestine that members of Yahweh's council were left unaware. His prophets could only receive them as jigsaw pieces, and even when assembled—if properly assembled—they might be best read as illegible *codes*. Only *after* the fact, when the perfect works of Jesus Christ was through, could anyone make sense of them. Once revealed, it was undoubtedly the most brilliant maneuver in all of human history. But by then it would be too late.

The *elohim* never saw it coming.

3

"And Jezebel Looked Out the Window..." ISRAEL — A HOUSE OF PAINTED FACES and WHOREDOMS

THE SEVENTY SHEPHERDS WERE LIKELY REJOICING from the frosty, windswept slopes of the Golan Heights, hungry and salivating for a scattered flock, the very day when the last prophet of Israel took unto himself a wife of whoredoms. The word of Yahweh had come unto Hosea. He said: "Go, take to yourself a wife of harlotry and have children of harlotry; for the land commits flagrant harlotry, forsaking Yahweh (Hosea 1:2)." Hosea's sentiments are not made known to us. All we are given is that he did what he was told. The wife whom he chose, her name was Gomer, was likely morally pure at the hour of their vows—a virgin. She soon thereafter conceived and bore him a son. At Yahweh's instructions, Hosea named him Jezreel, which means *God sows*. "For yet a little while for yet a little while, and I will punish the house of [king] Jehu for the bloodshed of Jezreel, and I will put an end to the kingdom of the house of Israel."

It was at the royal palace in Jezreel, slightly more than a century earlier, where Jehu was determined to overcome the last formal obstacle to his kingship, and triumphantly entered. Every descendant of Ahab had to go. Only one remained. Upon hearing of his arrival, Ahab's widow painted her eyes and adorned her head. The wicked queen Jezebel then looked out the window.

Jehu was not seduced.

"Throw her down," he said.

Two or three of her own trusted officials did as Jehu commanded. The horrors of her scream was perhaps bested only by a crackling thud and the striking silence to follow, when a splattering of blood painted her palace wall and adorned her horses. As Jehu trampled her underfoot in order that he might enter into the palace to eat and drink from the table that was now his, one would think the binding was closed on one of the wickedest dynasties in Hebrew history. But there was still one final paragraph which needed filling. When his attendants went to bury her, as soon as his appetite was quenched, they found nothing more of her than a skull and the feet and the palms of her hands. Even her own dogs, apparently, had turned on her.

Jehu was apparently not dazed. This was to fulfill the word of Yahweh, he insisted, which He had spoken through His servant Elijah the Tishbite, saying, "In the property of Jezreel the dogs shall eat the flesh of Jezebel, and the corpse of Jezebel will be as dung on the face of the field in the property of Jezreel, so that nobody can say, '*This is Jezebel.*'"

Hosea's firstborn son was named Jezreel after the very soil which was fertilized by Jezebel an entire century earlier. Jezreel however would remain the only child of Hosea's seed. But that is not to say that he would be Gomer's last.

His wife then conceived and bore a daughter.

Said Yahweh, "Call her Lo-ruhamah, for I will no longer have compassion on the house of Israel, that I would ever forgive them."

She then conceived and bore another son.

Said Yahweh, "Call him Lo-ammi, for you are not My people and I am not your God."

Though the full measure of Gomer's discontentment, particularly the number of lovers she bedded with, is not known, our imagination is not to be undermined. When Hosea finally succeeded in tracking down his wife, Gomer had sunk to such wretched undesirable depths, likely indebted into the service of a cult prostitute, that she wasn't even valued at 30 pieces of silver—the going rate for a slave (Exodus 21:32). He redeemed her anyways. He purchased his own wife for fifteen pieces of silver and a helping of barley, food fit only for barn animals.

Like Gomer, the northern kingdom of Israel had gone to lovers who supplied her with the bread and water, the wool and flax, the oil and drink which she desired. Even Yahweh's good gifts, she claimed in her willful ignorance, were attributed to the bounty of her extra-marital providers. She had bedded with so many *divine spirits* that there was no longer any truth, not even knowledge of their Elohim, in the land. They wanted His consort instead. Israel preferred the queen of heaven. For this reason, her children were to plead with her as a sort of last ditch effort, because the prophets had been ignored. Unless she put away her whoredoms, her adulteries from between her breast, Yahweh would "strip her naked in public, while all her lovers look on. And no one will be able to rescue her from [His] hands." Furthermore, Yahweh would expose her "as in the day that she was born, and make her as a wilderness, and set her like a dry land, and slay her with thirst." Yahweh would build a wall so large that she would never find her way through the thickets home.

In this manner, He would put an end to her gaiety, her feasts, her new moons, her Sabbaths, and all her solemn feasts, adding "and I will destroy her vines and fig trees." Essentially, Israel's very identity would become *strange* to her.

722 BC. That was the year that Yahweh divorced Israel. Hosea barely had time to let the pigment dry on papyrus. Over a century later the Judean prophet Jeremiah would write:

And I saw that for all the adulteries of faithless Israel, I had sent her away and given her a writ of divorce

Jeremiah 3:8a

Attention must be called to the Mosaic Law, namely Deuteronomy 24:1-4. By law, a husband is not permitted to remarry a wife whom he has divorced due to immorality.

[1]When a man takes a wife and marries her, and it happens that she finds no favor in his eyes because he has found some indecency in her, and he writes her a certificate of divorce and puts it in her hand and sends her out from his house, [2]and she leaves his house and goes and becomes another man's wife, [3]and if the latter husband turns against her and writes her a certificate of divorce and puts it in her hand and sends her out of his house, or if the latter husband dies who took her to be his wife, [4]then her former husband who sent her away is not allowed to take her again to be his wife, since she has been defiled; for that is an abomination before the Lord, and you shall not bring sin on the land which the Lord your God gives you as an inheritance.

Deuteronomy 24:1-4

Israel was through. Had the divine princes of the surrounding Gentile nations tired of them, or should they be usurped from the throne of their providence, or conquered, by other members of the diverse pantheon, Yahweh still had no legal rights to restore them. Jeremiah wrote, "They say, if a man put away his wife, and she go from him, and become another man's shall she return unto her again? Shall not that land be greatly polluted?" And by the way, this is not to say that Judah did not also play the part of the harlot. Jeremiah would add:

> ...yet her treacherous sister Judah did not fear; but she went and was a harlot also.

> Jeremiah 3:8b

Her harlotry challenged Yahweh to take similar action as with her sister Israel. This was accompanied by an invitation to repent—an additional 136 years' worth. Meanwhile in Gehenna, they sacrificed their children to the flames while the Temple of Yahweh looked on. Under the shadow of the Temple, idols filled households. Like Israel before them, they also went whoring after Yahweh's *supposed* consort, Asherah, the queen of heaven. And then one day, the prophet Ezekiel observed with his own eyes as the Shekinah glory, accompanied by members of His heavenly host, left the Temple behind. If they did not want him as their Elohim, then He would not have them as his people.

Elijah wrote:

> [18] Then the glory of Yahweh departed from the threshold of the temple and stood over the cherubim. [19] When the cherubim departed, they lifted their wings and rose up from the earth in my sight with the wheels beside them; and they stood still at the entrance of the east gate of Yahweh's house, and the glory of the God of Israel hovered over them.

> Ezekiel 10:18-19

In turn, the Temple was free to *burn*. The year was 586 AD when the southern kingdom of Judah was utterly humiliated by their Babylonian captors. The prophet Jeremiah lived to see it. Much of his ministry was defined with the wet of papyrus, no doubt attributed to the sogginess of his tears rather than the stain of pigment. Concerning Israel and Judah's demise he wrote: "Israel is a scattered flock, the lions have driven them away. The first one who devoured him was the king of Assyria, and this last one who has broken his bones is Nebuchadnezzar king of Babylon (Jeremiah 50:17)." Among those taken into captivity was the young prophet Daniel. Neither he nor Jeremiah and Ezekiel would live to see Judah restored. But unlike Judah, who served a 70 year sentence, the northern kingdom of Israel would make no such return.

That mystery would not be resolved before the Old Testament came to an end.

4

"Feed My Sheep…" JUDAH & THE SCATTERED SHEEP OF ISRAEL

THE ANSWER TO ISRAEL'S PROBLEM RELIES ON THE SIMPLE FACT that Jesus Christ, Yeshua HaMashiach, *is* the good shepherd whom King David and the Prophets spoke of. He *is* the angel of Yahweh who stood before Moses in the burning bush—the pillar of cloud who led Israel by day and the pillar of fire who led them by night. Though the Word became flesh and dwelt among us, in many ways little changed. Jesus had *always* been the guiding light of salvation, the pathway to the Promised Land. But very few desired the good Shepherd. They wanted *any* elohim but their own. They wanted a sacrifice of their design. If Judah believed Him not, Jesus said, it's simply "because ye are not my sheep." In other words, not everyone who alleges Judah as their heritage, or cries "Lord, Lord!" for that matter, can rightfully claim spiritual kinship with Abraham.

Though it is true that the books of Moses ended with a curse, the bad blood pitted between Yahweh and the adulterous house of Israel, which included now the seventy people groups He disinherited at Babel, would not always remain. A day was coming, Yahweh promised, when He would gather His children from every nation, indeed, from the very ends of the earth, by which they had been scattered.

> [1] So it shall be when all of these things have come upon you, the blessing and the curse which I have set before you, and you call them to mind in all nations where the Lord your God has banished you,

> [2] and you return to the Lord your God and obey Him with all your heart and soul according to all that I command you today, you and your sons,

³ then the Lord your God will restore you from captivity, and have compassion on you, **and will gather you again from all the peoples where the Lord your God has scattered you**.

⁴ If your outcasts are at the ends of the earth, from there the Lord your God will gather you, and from there He will bring you back.

⁵ The Lord your God will bring you into the land which your fathers possessed, and you shall possess it; and He will prosper you and multiply you more than your fathers.

⁶ Moreover the Lord your God will circumcise your heart and the heart of your descendants, to love the Lord your God with all your heart and with all your soul, so that you may live.

Deuteronomy 30:1-6

In a likewise manner, Jesus actually spoke of *two* folds. On the night He was betrayed, the Shepherd sat around a table with his friends, breaking bread, washing feet, and outlining a rather peculiar plan for the congregation of His coming kingdom. He said it like this:

"¹⁴ I am the good shepherd, and know My sheep, and am known of mine. ¹⁵ As the Father knoweth Me, even so know I the Father: and I lay down My life for the sheep.¹⁶ **And other sheep I have, which are not of this fold: them also I must bring**, and they shall hear my voice; and there shall be one fold, and one shepherd."

John 10:14-16

The sheep whom He spoke of were undoubtedly the northern ten tribes. They had been *lost* to the Gentile nations for nearly an entire millennium. When Jesus had earlier announced His imminent departure, the Jews quickly inquired among themselves, "Whither will He go that we shall not find him—will He go unto *the dispersed* among the Gentiles and teach the Gentiles?" In a way He would do just that, but first and foremost through the Apostles. By announcing His intent to bring the sheep back into the fold, Jesus was directing their attention to the prophet Micah:

> I will surely assemble all of you, Jacob,
>
> I will surely gather the remnant of Israel.
>
> I will put them together like sheep in the fold;

> Like a flock in the midst of its pasture
>
> They will be noisy with men.
>
> Micah 2:12

The prophet Amos said it like this:

> For behold, I am commanding,
>
> And I will shake the house of Israel among all nations
>
> As grain is shaken in a sieve,
>
> But not a kernel will fall to the ground.
>
> Amos 9:9

Ezekiel spoke of it too.

> 16 Therefore say, "Thus says the Lord God [Yahweh], 'Though I had removed them far away among the nations and though I had scattered them among the countries, yet I was a sanctuary for them a little while in the countries where they had gone.'"
>
> 17 Therefore say, 'Thus says the Lord God [Yahweh], "I will gather you from the peoples and assemble you out of the countries among which you have been scattered, and I will give you the land of Israel.'"
>
> Ezekiel 11:16-17

The prophet would further add:

> As a shepherd cares for his herd in the day when he is among his scattered sheep, so I will care for My sheep and will deliver them from all the places to which they were scattered on a cloudy and gloomy day.
>
> Ezekiel 34:12

Such promises fill the pages of the prophets. Isaiah's position was that Yahweh would raise a sign for the nations and would assemble banished Israel, gathering them and Judah from the four corners of the earth (Isaiah 11:12). This is what Amos meant when he said the very nations would be shaken as grain in a sieve, that Israel might be separated—further insisting, not a single "kernel will fall to the ground." That is, none of whom the Father has given can be snatched from His hand. But these promises in and of themselves do not resolve the mystery. Despite best intentions, one must ask, how could the Messiah possibly regather Israel? Specifically, what gave Him the legal authority to remarry a divorce bride when His very law openly opposed it?

Why—He would make her a widow, of course. Jesus *died* for the sins of the world.

To this effect Paul writes:

¹ Know ye not, brethren, (for I speak to them that know the law,) how that the law hath dominion over a man as long as he liveth?

² For the woman which hath an husband is bound by the law to her husband so long as he liveth; but if the husband be dead, she is loosed from the law of her husband.

³ So then if, while her husband liveth, she be married to another man, she shall be called an adulteress: but if her husband be dead, she is free from that law; so that she is no adulteress, though she be married to another man.

⁴ Wherefore, my brethren, ye also are become dead to the law by the body of Christ; that ye should be married to another, even to him who is raised from the dead, that we should bring forth fruit unto God.

Romans 7:1-4

The Apostle Paul was undoubtedly a brilliant orator of the Law—and widely misunderstood. He has already made his intended audience known, that he is speaking "to them that *know* the law (Romans 7:1)." And the law was clear. It unequivocally stated that a husband can never remarry his bride once she has been given the bill of divorce—particularly once she has become another man's wife. This is the law. It is eternal. Yahweh will not break it. However, by saying we are *loosed from the law of her husband,* or rather, *dead to the law,* he is directing our attention to Deuteronomy 24. The woman is only free from the law of adultery once her original husband dies. To this Paul adds the glorious fact—she is now free to marry "him who is raised from the dead."

Finally, *this* is the mystery revealed—the good news so rarely spoken about or known among the brethren. The scattered northern kingdom of Israel can now *legally* return to the Father through the death and resurrection of His son, the bridegroom. Unbeknownst to the spiritual princes of the nations, His master plan was indeed brilliantly executed. Yahweh disinherited the nations at Babel. He then scattered the assembly of Israel into all the nations so that they in turn *became* the Gentiles. And then He re-

168

inherited not only all the peoples of the world, but the very earth which had once been given to the princes to govern. Then again, that is not to say everyone chooses Him as their shepherd. In fact, few will. But should they do so, there have only ever been two houses to discover. In all of Scripture, we are hard pressed to find a *third* option. Yahweh did not make a covenant with a Gentile church that is distinct from Israel. Israel is not sitting around waiting for our imminent rapture so that Yahweh may continue with his scheme. This is *false* advertising. There has never been a break in the story. If Jesus is our bridegroom, then we have no choice but to find our identity in one of those two houses—Judah or Israel.

Jesus instructed Peter to "feed My sheep," and though it is true that Peter, James, and John initially agreed to spread the Gospel among the circumcised—that being the house of Judah—while Paul labored with the uncircumcised, Peter did not always shy from the scattered sheep. Paul's first epistle to the Galatians, an assembly which Peter frequented, was in itself a prophetic fulfillment that Israel would begin to draw back to Yahweh in the latter days. The Galatians *were* Israelites. But getting back to Peter, the first line of his own epistle reads: "Peter, an apostle of Jesus Christ, to the strangers scattered (1 Peter 1:1)." James likewise addressed his book "to the twelve tribes scattered abroad..." In both cases, the Apostles were writing to the scattered sheep of Israel.

If we are not *Jews* but claim Jesus as our Messiah, then we are the children of painted faces and whoredoms, finally freed by law of her former adulteries, and brought back into the fold. Like the parable of the prodigal son, we are the foolish younger child who claimed his father's inheritance in order that he may live with the pigs in a foreign land. The fact that we have been welcomed back with open arms is proof enough that the grace of God is awe-inspiring. Jesus said: "My sheep hear my voice, and I know them, and they follow me. And I give unto them eternal life; and they shall never perish, neither shall any man pluck them out of my hand (John 10:27-28)."

For this very reason, we must be careful of Christ's warning:

"[1] Verily, verily, I say unto you, he that entereth not by the door into the sheepfold, but climbeth up some other way, the same is a thief and a robber.

[2] But he that entereth in by the door is the shepherd of the sheep.

[3] To him the porter openeth; and the sheep hear his voice: and he calleth his own sheep by name, and leadeth them out.

⁴ And when he putteth forth his own sheep, he goeth before them, and the sheep follow him: for they know his voice.

⁵ And a stranger will they not follow, but will flee from him: for they know not the voice of strangers.

John 10:1-5

This parable Jesus spoke unto the Pharisees *but*, John writes, they did not understand. Regardless, He spoke unto them again: "Verily, verily, I say unto you, I am the door of the sheep (John 10:7)." He would quickly add: "I am the good shepherd. The good shepherd giveth his life for the sheep." Blessed are those *today* who do understand. There are at present two divided houses, but if the Word of Yahweh through the prophets is to be fulfilled, then we are faced with a singular option. There is only one sheep gate. Conclusively, Judah and Israel will be reunited into one fold. By this we are to understand that all of the good Shepherd's sheep will be regathered to the Promised Land. But that day has not *yet* happened. We have yet to be sifted out of the land—from the furthest ends of the earth. We have not, as Deuteronomy 30 foretold, been brought into the inheritance which our fathers possessed, in order that we too may possess it.

The final trumpet has not yet alerted us to heavens rallying cry. The good Shepherd has not yet descended with a shout, commanding the eyes of the dead, with the blessed voice that is only legible among His dearest friends, to be woken and behold Him. We have yet to be gathered as one flock, with Psalm 23 eternally constituting our rule of faith.

Or as Jesus told the Jews in Jerusalem, while confronted with charges of blasphemy: "My sheep hear my voice, and I know them, and they follow me. And I give unto them eternal life; and they shall never perish, neither shall any man pluck them out of my hand (John 10:27-28)."

Upon hearing this, the Jews, John wrote, took up stones *again* to stone him. They wanted a shepherd—*any* shepherd but their own.

"*Jesus Wept...*" TRAPPED IN THE TOMB OF THE SLEEPING DEATH

"For in death there is no remembrance of thee: in the grave who shall give thee thanks?" (Psalm 6:5)

LAZARUS WAS NOT WELL. BUT THAT'S SOMEWHAT of an understatement. Fact is, Lazarus was dying, and everybody knew it. His sisters Mary and Martha sent a currier from their town of Bethany east across the Jordan to find Jesus. How long he sought for the Savior is unknown, but the return trip would prove a two days journey. *Lord, behold, he whom You love is sick,* the sisters had said, and their message was clear. If He wanted to say goodbye to His dear friend, let alone *save* him from his ills, it had better be *now*. But it was too late. By the time Jesus received the news, Lazarus was already dead. At that very hour he had likely been ceremoniously washed and anointed with myrrh, aloes, and nard, before being elaborately wrapped in a shroud, and then paraded to his tomb among the wails of both loved ones and paid professionals, all of whom threw dust in their hair as a demonstration of their sorrow, and flutists played doleful arrangements. Within eight hours of his death, all of this would have been accomplished. And Jesus knew it.

Regardless, Jesus had another message for Mary and Martha. He told their courier: "This sickness is not to end in death, but for the glory of God, so that the Son of God may be glorified by it." So began the messengers return journey to Bethany without the man he had been sent to retrieve. Jesus would tarry another two days.

The Apostle John records that Jesus then told His disciples: "Our friend Lazarus sleeps, but I go that I may wake him up."

His disciples seemed puzzled by this. They said, "Lord, if he sleeps he will get well."

Then Jesus spoke to them plainly, "Lazarus is dead."

If they had confused Jesus' message to the sisters—specifically, that Lazarus was *not* expected to die—it is understandable. However, describing the dead as a *sleeping* patron was also not out of line with

Biblical revelation. David had written of making his bed in Sheol (Psalm 138:9), and much earlier in ancient Hebrew history, a lamenting Job had confessed he wished he died *before* childbirth. To this effect he cried: "Why did I not die at birth? Why did I not perish when I came from the womb?...For now I would have lain still and been quiet, I would have been asleep; then I would have been at rest...There the wicked cease from troubling, and there the weary are at rest (Job 3:11-17)."

Upon finally arriving at Bethany, Jesus and His disciples found that Lazarus had already been laid in the grave for four days. The stench had even set in. When Martha heard that Jesus was coming, she immediately went to meet Him in order that she might protest the couriers' response, and more importantly, His delayed arrival. But Mary *stayed* at the house.

"Lord, if You had been here, my brother would not have died," Martha said. After considering *who* it was that she was speaking to, it is possible that she reflected upon the message her courier had returned two days earlier, and added: "Even now I know that whatever You ask of God, God will give You."

Jesus said to her, "Your brother will rise again."

Martha then spoke the most telling doctrine of the Hebrew faith and the plain teaching of the Bible. She confessed, "I know that he will rise again in the resurrection on the last day."

Jesus certainly did not disagree with her. The dead *would* resurrect on the last day. Her theology was sound. Furthermore, the dead are unconscious, waiting in the grave for the day of their resurrection. If He added anything to her doctrine, it was not to inform her or the reader of John's Gospel that Lazarus had ascended to heaven or some spiritual holding cell while he consciously waited for the fulfillment of that day. No, Lazarus *was* dead. Rather, Jesus was the living Redeemer who would one day stand upon the earth, and whom the troubled Job had longed to see, "after my skin is destroyed, yet from my flesh I shall see God."

Jesus said unto her, "I am the resurrection and the life. He that believeth on Me, though he were dead, yet shall he live. And everyone who lives and believes in Me will never die. Do you believe this?"

Martha believed. "Yes, Lord; I *have* believed that You are the Christ, the Son of God, even He who comes into the world."

When Mary rushed to where Jesus was, and saw Him, she fell down at His feet and wept, saying: "Lord, if You had been here, my brother would not have died."

Jesus asked, "Where have you laid him?"

"Lord, come and see," they said.

John simply records of the Savior's response, "Jesus wept."

I am often told that the Bible's purposeful reference to *sleep* is only a metaphor for the *illusion* of death—particularly those who are left behind and cannot see the immortal soul leave the body behind. It is all poetic, they say. There is however no allusion to the contrary immortal soul, poetic or otherwise. As one will find with the whole of inspired Scripture, the Gospel of John complies, and presents us with no conscious knowledge of the afterlife. Lazarus has not *ascended* to heaven and then—after Jesus beckoned and called his name—*descended* again to tell of it. If Lazarus slept—and he most certainly did sleep—he was not an exception to the rule. Lazarus was dead.

Mary and Martha and his gathering of loved ones, not forgetting Jesus, were mutually weeping in accordance with the ancient Hebrew worldview—one which ascribed to the revelation given to them through the Prophets and the Psalmists and the whole of inspired Scripture. Solomon described death as a *lack of memory*. "For the living know that they shall die: but the dead know not anything, neither have they any more a reward; for the memory of them is forgotten (Ecclesiastes 9:5)." Furthermore, "Whatsoever thy hand findeth to do, do it with thy might; for there is no work, nor device, nor knowledge, nor wisdom, in the grave, whither thou goest (Ecclesiastes 9:10)."

Psalm 115:17-18 declares: "The dead do not praise the LORD, nor do any that go down into silence, but we [*the living*] will bless the LORD."

Quite similarly, Isaiah wrote: "For the grave [Sheol] cannot praise thee, death cannot celebrate thee: they that go down into the pit cannot hope for thy truth (Isaiah 38:18)."

From Job to Isaiah, including Solomon and the Psalmists in-between, the message was understood. Though Lazarus had lived in such a time as to befriend the very Redeemer whom Job longed to behold with his own eyes, he had succumbed to the tomb before the Davidic Kingdom could be ushered in. As consequence, his dwelling place was Sheol. He could no longer *praise* nor *celebrate* the Lord. His only

173

contributions were *silence*. For Lazarus, there was no knowledge, no wisdom, nor memory of life. Only the living, Isaiah would conclude, could praise the Lord. "The living, he shall praise thee, as I do this day: the father to the children shall make known thy truth." But not the dead.

So Jesus, again being deeply moved within, came to the tomb.

"Take away the stone," He said.

Once more, Martha protested. "Lord, by this time there will be a stench, for he has been *dead* four days."

Jesus reminded her of the courier's message. "Did I not say to you that if you believe, you will see the glory of God?"

The time had come for Jesus to act. They obeyed Him, and rolled away the stone, and Jesus, after praying to the Father in heaven, cried with a loud voice: "Lazarus, come forth~"

John records, "And he that was dead came forth, bound hand and foot with grave clothes: and his face was bound about with a cloth (John 11:43)." If the Apostle neglected to speak of the soul of Lazarus adjoining into his flesh, having only returned from *beyond* the grave, it's because such a notion was not even considered in ancient Hebrew thinking—nor the Scriptures which informed them.

Jesus said to them, "Unbind him, and let him go."

According to the Apostle John, it was Jesus' final miracle before His own death. Soon, His followers would behold the greatest miracle in the history of the world.

THE COMPLETE DEATH AND TOTAL DESTRUCTION OF JESUS CHRIST: He Died Two Times, or "*Dying, He Died*"

1

THE DAY LIGHT AND DARKNESS EXPLAINED THEMSELVES TO EACH OTHER

PONTIUS PILATE WASHED HIS HANDS of the entire affair. The trial of Jesus had likely been conceived by all parties involved, both His accusers *and* authorities, as a kangaroo court. Jesus was a noncitizen of Rome, which entitled him to no rights before the law to speak of. This no doubt encouraged his accusers. They were emboldened with the hope that their Passover trial, what we might call "the State vs the Son of God," would prove a swift and standard affair. And yet when it came to convicting Jesus, Pilate found no evil, nor cause of death in him. The apostle John has the prefect of Judea standing alone and face to face with the Son of God in the inner-cave, his *praetorium*. Here we see a man swimming in the unexpected tide of truth, completely enveloped by the light of this world, while outside stand the Jews willfully clinging to the darkness of their ignorance, refusing to enter.

It is there in the praetorium where light and darkness explained themselves to each other. That Pilate should repeatedly travel back and forth between the two, Jews to Jesus, darkness to light, ignorance to truth, struggling with a leg cramp of indecision among the two clashing kingdom currents, is unexpected protocol for any Roman trial. Truth or beauty—*would* he, *could* he forsake the fragrance of power and the momentary wisp of glory in which the secular power of the state, the material world, and the ever-persistent darkness of ignorance offered him, if it meant bowing to the holy and unsettling embrace of God? In his Gospel, Mark employed the Greek word *thaumazein* to describe Pilate. Essentially, the governor was surprised and awestruck with wonder, plagued with fear and respect. It was as if Pilate had awoken to, and must contend with, the presence of a heavenly angel.

When he sat down upon the judgement seat, his wife sent unto him, saying, "Have nothing to do with that just man, for I have suffered many things this day in a dream because of him."

"I will therefore chastise him," he told the crowd, "and let him go."

But the darkness which put the light of the world on trial spoke with insistent voices. They wanted Him crucified. More precisely, the Gospel of Matthew records, "But the chief priests and elders persuaded the multitude that they should ask Barabbas, and *destroy* Jesus (Matthew 27:20)."

In the end Pilate became all men in every age who look upon the sacrificial Lamb of God, deliberated the pros and cons in his mind, and ultimately seared his conscious of Truth. The Gospel of Mark documents the exact time of the Saviors crucifixion—about 9 o'clock—the very hour of the Passover sacrifice. A sin offering dealt with sin in the manner of its death. For this reason the sacrificial animal had to be destroyed in order that the sin which it embodied, the sin of the offeror, might be equally destroyed. In this manner, Christ became nothing. The Gospel of Luke records: "And Pilate gave sentence that it should be as they required. And he released unto them him that for sedition and murder was cast into prison, whom they had desired; but he delivered Jesus to their will (Matthew 23:24-25)."

Jesus was *destroyed*.

2

HE DIED TWO TIMES OR "DYING, HE DIED…"

NOW FROM THE SIXTH HOUR UNTIL THE NINTH HOUR, precisely 12 noon until 3pm in Roman time, Matthew records darkness over the whole land while Jesus hung on the device of His crucifixion. It was about the ninth hour, he wrote, when Jesus cried in a loud voice: *"Eli, Eli, lama sabachtani?"* That is to say, "My God, my God, why hast thou forsaken me?" The syllables which proceeded from His mouth contain within them perhaps the most difficult words in all of Holy Scripture to comprehend. The perfect union which had bonded Yahweh with the Angel of Yahweh, Father and Son, since before creation or time even began—the very divine Person who once stood before Moses in the burning bush; who before that broke bread and ate meat with butter and bread before his friend Abraham; who wrestled with Jacob; and who later led the Israelites across the wilderness—was *severed*.

Jesus had not yet succumbed to physical death. That moment would soon arrive. But that is not to say He hadn't yet already tasted death, because at present, Jesus experienced another sort of death altogether. It was the *immediate* death of Adam and Eve after they ate the forbidden fruit which He Himself tasted. Like Adam before Him, He died two times.

The Apostle Peter would later claim: "He Himself bore our sins in His body on the tree (1 Peter 2:24)." The prop which would serve as a Roman crucifixion device, and as a symbol for atonement, was no accident, for it is a tree which equally served as the prop and symbol of sin itself for all humanity. Genesis records of this tree.

> "And Yahweh God [*elohim*] commanded the man, saying, Of every tree of the garden thou mayest freely eat: But of the tree of the knowledge of good and evil, thou shalt not eat of it: for in the day that thou eatest thereof thou shalt surely die (Genesis 2:16-17)."

The Hebrew word *muwth* (pronounced "*mooth*") indicates that something either already has died or will die, or that an act of *killing* is being committed. There is no preference here between man and animal. As we shall come to learn, the soul (*nephesh*) resides in everything that has a spirit (*ruah*), the breath of life. Both man *and* animal die the same death.

Consider the following.

> "The fish in the Nile will die (*muwth*), and the river will stink; and the Egyptians shall lothe to drink of the water of the river (Exodus 7:18)."

> "But Nadab and Abihu died (*muwth*) before the LORD when they offered strange fire before the LORD in the wilderness of Sinai (Numbers 3:4)."

In Genesis 2:17 *muwth* is employed twice. One might therefore phrase it as:

> "…for in the day that you eat of it you shall **die die**."

Rather that translating *muwth* twice, the 1611 King James translators understood this to mean an extra emphasis on that promise of death was needed, and therefore stressed that Adam would "*surely* die."

177

Half a century earlier, the Geneva Bible had translated the double usage of *muwth* in Genesis 2:17 as:

"...for in the day that thou eatest thereof, thou shalt **die** the **death**."

The emphasis here is that his death would be promised future-tense, not immediate. And yet it also seems understood by all involved that Adam was on an irrevocable path of certainty. *Surely*, as the King James translators had implied it, he had *begun* the journey towards death. Immediately afterwards, Yahweh told Adam: "By the sweat of your face you will eat bread, till you return to the ground, because from it you were taken; for you are dust, and to dust you shall return." This is not however to be confused merely with a spiritual *separation*, as many claim. If God had intended to warn Adam that He would separate, He would have employed the Hebrew word *badal (baw-dal')*. There is another, and I think many to most will agree, far more literal way of reading *muwth* into Genesis 2:17.

The Young's Literal Translation, first published in 1862, some two decades before Westcott and Hort first translated the New Testament Greek from the Codex Sinaiticus and Codex Vaticanus, most clearly indicates the process of dying with the words, "*dying* thou dost *die*."

"...for in the day of thine eating of it—dying thou dost die."

Adam *did* die that very day. He lost his immortal nature—which is to say the death of his immortal nature was merely the consequence of a much deeper death—spiritual death. The spirit (*ruah*), first breathed into his nostrils, was *dead* to God. Tragically, Adam had fallen out of relationship with Yahweh. Despite the wealth of hidden knowledge which his descendant would later claim, it was of no use to them. They were spiritually dead.

This is why Jesus told the woman at Jacob's Well, "God is a Spirit: and they that worship Him must worship Him in spirit and in truth (John 4:24)."

He died two *deaths* that day on the tree. He died a spiritual death, and then, only moments later, a physical one. He died so that we might live.

For Jesus, it would be His last parable.

HE GAVE UP THE GHOST (*and Returned to God*)

CONFUSION OFTEN SURROUNDS THE DISSIMILARITIES between *soul* and *spirit*, and yet the Bible gives us a clear distinction. If the theologian has his way, Christ's *conscious* ghost immediately left His body at the cross. Whether He ascended or descended to heaven in the interval between His bodily death and resurrection—or moved, independent of the body, to the left or the right of the cross—is therefore the subject of much debate. This is due to the fact that the Bible makes no assertion whatsoever that He even had consciousness to contend with. Confusion assuredly arises whenever Greek and Alexandrian wisdom holds hand with straightforward doctrine. The Platonist diligently seeks the slightest suggestion of the immortal soul and yet, if the Gospel and Epistle writers did not think the extracurricular whereabouts of his soul important, it is simply because such a concept was not even within the grasp of their reasoning. For the first-century Christian, the Savior had only one destination.

Jesus was laid in a tomb.

The Hebrew word *ruach* is translated "spirit," "breath," "spirit," "ghost," or "wind." This is consistent with the idea that the spirit [*ruach*] is a wind or a breath from God. The Greek word [*pneuma*] is equivalent to the Hebrew word [*ruach*], and can be traced over four-hundred times in the Old Testament. Already by the second verse of Genesis we read that "the earth was without form, and void; and darkness was upon the face of the deep. And the Spirit [*Ruach*] of God [*Elohim*] moved upon the face of the waters."

Man's *spirit* and *soul* are both described in Genesis 2:7, and cleverly wedded together, when Yahweh "formed man of the dust of the ground, and breathed into his nostrils the breath [*ruach*] of life; and man became a living soul [*nephesh*]." Just consider this prodigious fact. The very breath we breathe, lungs to nostrils, originated from the divine—the one God of Israel. Should that not cause us to stumble over our own breath and gasp in exaltation? It is for this reason *alone* that we owe Him our fullest allegiance. For the Hebrew, this was an explicit truth, which Moses later rephrased when he affirmed that Yahweh was "the God of the spirits of all flesh (Numbers 27:16)." And yet the anthologies of human history, as we well know, are an ominous read—filled with dark speeches. The men and women who were intended to represent themselves as God's *imagers* on earth did not consider their very breath to be a moral obligation. It would take floodwaters "to destroy all flesh, wherein is the breath [*ruach*] of life, from under heaven" so that "everything that is in the earth shall die (Genesis 6:17)." Afterwards, God remembered Noah and his family, "and God made a wind [*ruach*] to pass over the earth, and the waters aswaged (Genesis 8:1)."

The children of Abraham, at least, those who subscribed to the true saving faith, likewise understood the exhilarating fact that the very breath in their nostrils was an inheritance from Adam, ultimately from God, and was therefore on loan. We need only look back once more upon Job, who declared:

"You have granted me life and lovingkindness;

And Your care has preserved my spirit."

(Job 10:12)

Job's spirit was preserved by God. He would further add:

"All the while my breath is in me,

and the spirit [*ruah*] of God is in my nostrils..."

(Job 27:3)

The book of Job aims to educate the reader of Scripture in elementary knowledge. Job's godly friend Elihu would likewise add:

"The Spirit [*ruah*] of God has made me; the breath of the Almighty gives me life (Job 33:4)."

Though it is true that the Creator has faithfully preserved our spirit, if God should set His heart upon the matter, Elihu made known, He could gather to Himself His spirit and breath, and all flesh would perish. Man, he said, *his very being*, would return to dust.

14 If He should determine to do so,

If He should gather to Himself His spirit and His breath,

15 All flesh would perish together,

And man would return to dust."

(Job 34:14-15)

180

So when the Gospel according to Matthew records that Jesus, while hung upon the cross, "yielded up the ghost," he is keeping in line with Hebrew tradition while making an astonishing claim—which I shall turn to in a moment. To allege however that His spirit returned to God is *proof*—or rather, the only argument one needs—that we consciously ascend to heaven after we die is also to divorce ourselves from the consciousness of Scripture which preceded the cross.

David understood our separation of spirit from flesh in completely separate terms. He gazed back upon the writer of Job, and agreed with him. The Psalmist wrote:

3 Do not trust in princes,

In mortal man, in whom there is no salvation.

4 His spirit [ruach] departs, he returns to the earth;

In that very day his thoughts perish.

(Psalm 146:3-4)

The worldview of Israel's greatest king would have us believe that the spirit is *not* the man. His identity remains with his body, even after his spirit has departed. There is consequently no salvation in mortal man to be had. He returns to the earth, and rather than transferring his consciousness—with a flickering candle among the chilling wisp of the haunted being—into the spirit realm, his very thoughts *perish*. Why do our Scriptural lecturers persist in telling us the Hebrew writers never aspired to rise above poetic jargon? We can learn *much* from the shepherd boy. If we allow God's Word to speak for itself, we will indeed encounter good doctrine.

David's worldview is rephrased in Psalm 115 with even greater resounding clarity.

16 The heavens are the heavens of the LORD,

But the earth He has given to the sons of men.

17 The dead do not praise the LORD,

Nor do any who go down into silence;

18 But as for us, we will bless the LORD

From this time forth and forever.

Praise the LORD!

(Psalm 115:16-18)

In these three brief poetic verses we learn much of Hebrew thinking—and more earsplitting propositions. It is here, quite astonishingly, where we read that "the heaven—even the heavens—are Yahweh's." Rather, it is the earth which He has given to the sons of men. Heaven above is not a prize to be won, nor ours to claim, in this present life or death, because: "the dead do not praise the LORD."

Rather than buckling to accusations of vernacular metaphors, I take his intentional phrasing to mean, in a straightforward attitude, that "the dead do not praise the LORD."

His son Solomon would carry on these very Scriptural traditions. He rather famously carved into papyrus the following ink:

"And the dust returns to the ground it came from, and the spirit [*ruach*] returns to God who gave it (Ecclesiastes 12:7)."

Admittedly, from these few words alone, one might easily conclude that Solomon was swayed by a dualistic education in Greek philosophy. Perhaps this is the reason he is so often quoted by the Platonist (and the Occultist), as though Solomon confessed the hidden knowledge of the Mystery religion hundreds of years before the loose lips of Plato. And yet, had dualism been his intent, when we stop to consider the whole of his Ecclesiastic view, and the theological forefathers which informed his doctrine, he would have employed his own words against himself. Though it is true that the spirit returns to God, Solomon's intent has long been noted by the scholar. *Every* spirit returns to God—*both* righteous and wicked. If, by returning the spirit to God, we are inciting breathtaking flavors of heaven above, then everyone it seems is intended for it. Rather, the breath of life, first exacted into Adam, is on loan to everyone. And besides, Solomon has already instructed us to an inexplicable parallel. Concerning the wind he writes:

"As you do not know the path of the wind [ruah], or how the bones grow in the womb of a woman who is pregnant, so you cannot understand the work of God, the Maker of all things (Ecclesiastes 11:5)."

Furthermore, like David and Job and the whole of Hebrew thinking, the dualism of man is never recognized. When our breath returns to God, who lovingly gifted it for our praise and admiration of Him, our consciousness is not carried with the gale. Solomon further writes:

"For the living know they will die; but the dead do not know anything, nor have they any longer a reward, for their memory is forgotten. Indeed their love, their hate and their zeal have already perished, and they will no longer have a share in all that is done under the sun (Ecclesiastes 9:5-6)."

Reading such confessionals, it would be difficult to calibrate how Scriptural lectures on the afterlife could be made any clearer. This is not ambiguous thinking. The dead know *nothing*. If the very accomplishments of their life have forsaken them, it is because memory itself is forgotten. With these words, Solomon has taken a dagger to the shroud of Platonism. He literally chokes any hope of posthumous consciousness at the throat. Even the emotions which relate to our sense of self, how we see ourselves and how we think others perceive us, or how we perceive others, are extinguished. These are the biological and metaphysical truths what Solomon intends to relay to his reader when describing our return to the dust of the ground, and it should be noted that Genesis 2:7 mirrors Ecclesiastes 12:7 with astonishing clarity. The former speaks of the creation of man—the first Adam; while the latter describes the de-creation of man. Adam had no consciousness to speak of before his creation. The same can be said of his de-creation.

Adam *died*. He died—he died—he died. And since we have yet to witness a resurrected Adam once again walking the earth in our lifetime, we can safely assume that our aboriginal forefather is still *dead*.

There is of course the second Adam to consider. He also died. Suffice to say—when the breath [*pneuma*] left Jesus' lungs, the second Adam experienced the de-creation of man.

All four Gospels astonishing concur.

He "yielded up the ghost (Matthew 27:50)."

"And Jesus cried with a loud voice, and gave up the ghost (Mark 15:37)."

"And when Jesus had cried with a loud voice, he said: Father, into thy hand I commend my spirit: and having said thus, he gave up the ghost (Luke 23:46)."

"When Jesus therefore had received the vinegar, he said: *It is finished*: and He bowed His head, and gave up the ghost (John 19:30)."

The most obvious conclusion to make, Jesus *gave up the ghost*. To say He "breathed His last" would place a very different emphasis on the fact that, though Jesus surrendered Himself to the cross, the security of His life was always in His hands.

On the night He was betrayed, Peter drew his sword upon the servant of the high priest and slivered off the ear. Jesus rebuked him. He said: "Thinkest thou that I cannot now pray to my Father, and He shall presently give me more than twelve legions of angels?"

Even now as I attempt to picture Jesus on the cross; tormented, broken, bleeding, mocked, spat upon; to even try and grasp the Savior wrestling with the anguish of *my sins* thrust upon Him by the Father—I shudder to imagine another scenario altogether. That Jesus might simply change His mind and expire of His intended mission, and command His father to dispatch more than 72,000 angels to His immediate aide—that they might pull Him from the cross, restore Him to good health and, right then and there, thrust all of humanity into the fires of Gehenna—is a scenario which Jesus Himself declassified to Peter.

But rather, crying with another loud voice, He gave up the ghost by His own free will—and died. "No man taketh my life from me, but I lay it down of myself," He said.

The earth itself, apparently, could not contain itself. If Satan and other divine beings who ruled over the earth had grasped for victory by putting the angel of Yahweh into the tomb, they must have been extremely nervous when, almost just as immediately, "the veil of the temple was rent in twain from the top to the bottom," as Matthew records. This in itself is proof that the mission of Jesus Christ was an instantaneous success. But there mere fact that the earth did quake, and the rocks were split, "and the graves were opened; and many bodies of the saints which slept arose, and came out of the graves after His resurrection, and went into the holy city, and appeared unto many," must have caused the powers of darkness to tremble with fever.

The gig was up.

Their immortal soul doctrine was a lie, and death itself had begun to reverse itself.

184

HE RECEIVED OUR PUNISHMENT IN FULL MEASURE (An Insult to the Sinner *and* the Saved)

IF THE TRUE SACRIFICIAL DEATH OF JESUS IS UNTHINKABLE, it is only because human religion has made it permissible to find dogmatic detours and attain the alternative. That the only begotten Son of God should become flesh, grow and mature as a man, suffer as a man, and die as a man, is stiff doctrine enough. It is often believed however only because *it must* in order that we participate under the umbrella of the Christian faith. We must therefore not negate the purpose of His death nor underwhelm the spectacular importance of the resurrection to come. To say that Christ's eternal life began at His death or that He was liberated from the cross immediately after *giving up the ghost* would be a Gnostic conclusion to make. Without His resurrection to come, there would be no hope—no life after death. And yet, despite a treasure-trove of Scriptural evidence to the contrary, it is the ascension into heaven which most souls are after.

It is the Prophet Isaiah who looked forward to the day when the Savior would "pour out His life unto death," and in doing so would be "numbered among the transgressors (Isaiah 53:12)." By saying Jesus died, we can rightfully conclude He was *destroyed*. The Bible exhausts such vocabulary, and it shouldn't surprise us. Jesus compared His own death to the dissolution of a kernel of wheat (John 12:23-26).

In his book *The Fire That Consumes*, Edward Fudge writes: "We naturally recoil from such a thought, that the Son of God could truly have perished—even for a moment. Yet is this not the same difficultly we face in accepting Jesus' true kenosis and humiliation in becoming a man? (Philemon 2:5-10). In the first century the Docetics tried to avoid the implications of saying the incarnate God truly died, but the apostolic witnesses refused to yield an inch (1 John 5:6-10)."

To this day, the true implications of Jesus' death are not willingly understood nor embraced. The Apostle Paul saw the death of the sacrificial animal as the death of the sinner, that is, the destruction of both the sacrifice and his sin. This is why God "made him to be sin for us, who knew no sin." Our sin was destroyed with Christ "that we might be made the righteousness of God in him (2 Corinthians 5:21)." Christ Jesus "gave Himself as a ransom for all men," he wrote to Timothy (1

Timothy 2:5). And to Titus he penned, he "gave himself for us, that he might redeem us from all iniquity, and purify unto himself a peculiar people, zealous of good works (Titus 2:4)." To the Colossians he said: "And you, that were sometime alienated and enemies in your mind by wicked works," the Apostle Paul wrote, "yet now hath he reconciled in the body of his flesh through death, to present you holy and unblameable and unreproveable in his sight (Colossians 1:21-22)." In slightly other terms, "Christ hath redeemed us from the curse of the law, being made a curse for us: for it is written, Cursed is every one that hangeth on a tree (Galatians 3:13)."

Jesus "was made a little lower than the angels for the suffering of death," the writer of Hebrews insists, "that he by the grace of God should taste death for every man (Hebrews 2:9)." Likewise, "Christ was sacrificed once to take away the sins of many people (Hebrews 9:28)."

We simply *cannot* separate Jesus from the complete death and total destruction of the sacrificial lamb. "Christ died for sins once for all, the righteous for the unrighteous, to bring you to God (1 Peter 3:18)." Jesus Christ "is the atoning sacrifice for our sins," the Apostle John wrote (1 John 2:2). He "laid down his life for us (1 John 3:16)." By doing so, He lost His life rather than loving it so much as to deny the resurrection to come from those who longed for the day of His arrival—from those who loved Him and to this day long for His return.

"Greater love hath no man than this," Jesus told His loved ones on the night He was betrayed, "that a man lay down his life for his friends." Jesus died for His friends. It is true that He died for Peter, James, and John, and for Mary and Martha, but He died also for Adam and Enoch, Noah and Abraham, Job and Moses, David and Isaiah. He died for Eve and Sarah, Rahab and Deborah, Ruth and Esther, Bathsheba and Hannah. He died for His friends. He died for them and so many others. He died for those whom He prayed for on the night of His betrayal—the faces that must have swam through His head. "Neither pray I for these alone," He told the Father, "but for them also which shall believe on me through their word." He died for those whom He had conversed with and dined with, but also for those whom He longed to converse with and dine with *face-to-face*, in the church age to follow and the ultimate inheritance of His kingdom to come. Specifically, Israel's greatest king and high priest who ever lived became the sacrifice for me—and *you*.

Jesus died because of sin. He died in the place of sinners. But more so—He died the sinner's death. He died the death *required* by sin. God "demonstrated His own love for us in this: While we were still sinners, Christ died for us (Romans 5:8)."

The true death of Jesus is an insult to the sinner, and when the totality of his demise is presented, more often than not it is a suggestion for scorn also from among the Christian. The total destruction of Jesus Christ is a notion which John Calvin vehemently objected. For Calvin, it was unthinkable that Jesus' soul truly died or even slept. And yet the eternal torment of John Calvin makes a gross error. It is without a doubt one of the greatest miscalculations in the history of the church, short of blundering over salvation. For the sinner, the consequence of sin is death—or rather, eternal punishment, *not* eternal torment. If finite sinners require conscious punishment infinitely—eternally, without end—for justice to be exacted, then Christ did not die the sinners' death.

In hindsight, the cross is a perfect picture of the consequence for sin—the first and the second death exacted in one grandiose swoop, whereas its agent, our Lord, became the very incarnation of the judgement of God. Jesus drank from the cup of God's wrath, and in like manner, our rightful end—one in which we will face if we are not found hidden in Christ. For the saved soul, Jesus reversed the order. His sacrifice—His punishment, was sufficient.

5

WHO RAISED JESUS FROM THE DEAD?

UPON HIS OWN DEATH A MILLENNIA EARLIER, King David would, as he himself wrote, "go down into silence." It is David who once penned: "for there is no mention of you in death. In Sheol who will give you thanks? (Psalm 6:5)." The writer of 1 Kings records: "So David slept with his fathers, and was buried in the city of David." Exactly fifty days after the feast of first fruits—on the day of Pentecost to be exact, and while standing before David's sepulcher—the Apostle Peter confirmed the reality of David's worldview when he proclaimed: "Men and brethren, let me freely speak unto you of the patriarch David, that he is both dead and buried, and his sepulcher is with us unto this day (Acts 2:29)." Peter would take a knife to the fabric of our cognitive dissonance, which separates us from the blunt reality before us (should we employ Platonism as a shroud for our soul), when adding:

"For David is not ascended into the heavens: but he saith himself, 'The LORD said unto my Lord, Sit thou on my right hand, until I make thy foes thy footstool (Acts 2:34)."

JESUS EXPOSED THE MONEY CHANGERS. AND THEY HATED HIM for it. After fashioning for Himself a scourge of chords, he drove them out of the temple, jangled the coins from their pockets, overturned their tables, and shepherded the sheep and the oxen out with them.

The Jews fumed.

They demanded, "What sign do you show us as your authority for doing these things?"

"Destroy this temple," He answered them, "and in three days I will raise it up."

The Jews were naturally confused by this. The construction of Herod's temple, they said, had taken forty-six years from beginning to end. How could Jesus possibly gift them with a new one in as little as three days? To this inquiry the Apostle John adds as commentary: "But He spake of the temple of His body (John 2:21)."

While it is certainly true that God raised Jesus from the dead, as Peter confessed to the crowd (Acts 2:32), it is also a fact that Jesus Himself was acting to bring about His own resurrection. It is God the Father, Yahweh, who gave Jesus the authority to do so. Jesus said: "For not even the Father judges anyone, but He has given all judgment to the Son, For just as the Father raises the dead and gives them life, even so the Son also gives life to whom He wishes. For not even the Father judges anyone, but He has given all judgment to the Son (John 5:20-22)."

At a later date there was a division among the Jews. Many of them said He was mad, and had a devil in Him. "No man taketh my life from me, but I lay it down of myself," He told them. "I have power to lay it down, and I have power to take it again. This commandment have I received of my Father." Others in the crowd insisted, *these are **not** the words of one possessed by devils.* Some would add: *Can a devil open the eyes of the blind?*

During His earthly ministry, Jesus raised four *known* people from the dead. He raised the widow's son and the daughter of Jairus. He raised his good friend Lazarus too—after he had been buried four days. But he saved His greatest two miracles for the last.

Jesus raised Himself.

"No man hath ascended up to heaven," He once told a crowd, "but He that came down from heaven." And that's just what He did.

Jesus ascended into heaven and sat at the right hand of God.

6

WHEN WILL WE SEE HIM AGAIN?

"SO CHRIST WAS ONCE OFFERED TO BEAR THE SINS of many," the writer of Hebrews says. Pay attention, because where our *next* meeting with the Messiah is concerned, this is solid Scriptural thinking—and good doctrine. "And unto them that look for Him shall He appear the second time without sin unto salvation."

"Who Alone Hath Immortality..." SONS OF ADAM, DAUGHTERS OF EVE, AND WHAT IT MEANS TO BE CREATED IN THE IMAGE OF GOD

ON THE SIXTH DAY OF CREATION THE LORD GOD FORMED man from the dust of the ground, and breathed into his nostrils the breath of life, and man became a *living soul*. God later caused the man to fall into a deep sleep. Upon opening his eyes, he beheld a woman near his side. The Hebrew word *nephesh* can be translated as "living being" or "soul," and is aptly applied in the King James as "living creature." A careful reader will likely observe that Adam, not overlooking his wife thereafter, were in fact the last recorded souls to be made in relation to the creation week. Before Adam was formed from the dust of the ground and Eve from his rib, the waters and the air and the whole face of the earth had already brought forth abundantly a host of living creatures—each after their own kind. And yet, the man and his wife were not simply *living souls*. Unquestionably, they were God's crowning achievement. They were the result of a conversation. *Let us make man in our image*. Ever since Moses penned these words mankind has sought a definition as to what it exactly means—and yet the Bible never explicitly gives one. But let us not overlook the forest for the trees, because God's image *is* the story of the Bible.

I am often reminded that proof of our immortality is the fact that we're created in God's image. And yet this attribute is clearly incommunicable. *Why?*—because the Bible plainly tells me so. There is quite a difference between recognizing a Scriptural truth, that we are created in God's image, and equating ourselves with God. Let us not confuse the two. We *are* created in His image, but we are *not* the Creator. To equate ourselves with God in this way is a direct teaching of the Mystery Religion. Quite ironically, its founder and master architect, that crafty serpent of old, woke Eve with forbidden fruit by asking: "Hast God truly said...?" Satan led Eve to believe, if she ate of the fruit, she would *become like* God.

190

Many of our church fathers bought it, hook, line, and sinker—for the most part. To let a Christian brother in on the truth *today,* that we are indeed a mortal soul, is to speak against God's Word—at least, in their rationale. Regardless, God "only hath immortality," and the Bible is not mistaken when declaring it. The Apostle Paul, clearly forsaking his Hellenistic education, wrote to Timothy:

> "Which in his times he shall shew, who is the blessed and only Potentate, the King of kings, and Lord of lords; **Who only hath immortality**, dwelling in the light which no man can approach unto; whom no man hath seen, nor can see: to whom be honour and power everlasting. Amen (1 Timothy 6:15-16)."

God *alone* is immortal—Amen. Adam and Eve *were not.*

And neither are we.

In the whole of Scripture, there is not one exception to the rule—at least, not at present. And why should we be surprised? God's Word tells us not all of His attributes are communicable to man. For example, God is self-existent. Adam and Eve were not. In Jesus' epistle to the church we read: "I am Alpha and Omega, the beginning and the ending, saith the Lord, which is, and which was, and which is to come, the Almighty (Revelation 1:8)." Secondly, God is omniscient. In 1 John 3:20 we read: "For God is greater than our heart and knows all things." *This* also we cannot attribute to Adam and Eve. Thirdly, God is omnipotent. Job once spoke to the LORD, "I know that thou canst do everything, and that no thought can be witholden from thee (Job 42:2)." Adam and Eve were clearly not all-powerful. Furthermore, God is infinite. Upon building Israel's first temple, Solomon is recorded as praying: "But will God indeed dwell on the earth? Behold, the heaven and heaven of heavens cannot contain thee; how much less this house that I have builded? (1 Kings 8:27)" Adam and Eve were not infinite, nor were they incorporeal, transcendent, triune, indivisible, and they certainly did not attain incomprehensibility, as Isaiah attributed of the LORD: "There is no searching of His understanding (Isaiah 40:28)." There is more of God—so *much more*—that we are not.

Rather, Adam and Eve were created to reflect a *perfect* character which was communicable to no other *living soul* on earth but them. Firstly, they were self-aware. Scripture says: "Examine yourselves, whether ye be in the faith; prove your own selves. Know ye not your own selves, how that Jesus Christ is in you, except ye be reprobates? (2 Corinthians 13:5)" Therefore, *we* also are self-aware. And much like our creation week parents, we are to be merciful and keepers of justice. To this effect, Hosea 12:6 reads: "Therefore turn thou to thy God: keep mercy and judgment, and wait on thy God continually." We are furthermore to be dispensers of grace. Concerning grace, the Apostle Paul wrote to the church at Ephesus: "But unto every one of us is given grace according to the measure of the gift of Christ (Ephesians 4:7)." And I shan't overlook this central tenant of the human experience—we are to love one another (John 13:5). In these ways—and more—we are very much created in God's image.

And yet in these communicable attributes, which Adam and Eve at one moment in time *perfectly* exhibited, sin has disrupted. Quite tragically, it has twisted, contorted, and perverted the image of God to no end. Even our self-awareness has been thrust into the arms of humanist lovers. Accordingly, what we perceive of reality is more often than not a bath house of pagan perversities. Moral depravity is a sad state of affairs filling the reality of our lives, a truth which the pages of the Bible unbiasedly exhumes. It is the gangrenous story of avarice and lust, gluttony and sloth, envy, pride, lies, idolatry, and murderous ambition, all of which we have genetically inherited through our forefather Adam. Essentially it is paradise *lost* and, in a dazzling plot twist—this cannot be overstated—paradise *restored*. The Apostle Paul neatly fleshed out this stunning new act in the Adamic drama to the Church of Corinth when he wrote:

> "And so it is written, The first man Adam was made a *living soul*; the last Adam was made a quickening spirit. Howbeit that was not first which is spiritual, but that which is natural; and afterward that which is spiritual. The first man is of the earth, earthy: the second man is the Lord from heaven. As is the earthy, such are they also that are earthy: and as is the heavenly, such are they also that are heavenly. And as we have borne the image of the earthy, we shall also bear the image of the heavenly (1 Corinthians 15:45-50)."

The Apostle Paul once again defied Hellenistic Judaism's insistence in the pre-existence of souls, particularly the Platonic influence found in the Jews highly influential *Book of Wisdom*. He is saying to the Corinthian that our blessed Savior, who existed *before* Adam, did not originate from the dust of the earth like every other mortal soul when taking on Adamic flesh. The Second Adam is from heaven, and because He is found without blemish, Jesus is a life-giving Spirit; the first-fruit who promises that "we shall also bear the image of the heavenly" at the resurrection.

192

This much is *future* tense. And yet, we are commanded at present to put on the *new man*—that is, the spiritual genetics, if you will, of the Second Adam. Let us not confuse our present command and future promise.

To the saints at Ephesus, Paul wrote:

"And that ye put on the new man [*second* Adam], which after God is created in righteousness and true holiness (Ephesians 4:24)."

Just as consistently, Paul reminded the saints at Colossae:

"...And have put on the new man [*second* Adam], which is renewed in knowledge after the image of Him that created him (Colossians 3:10)."

To the church at Philippi, Paul's message remained undeniably consistent with the rest. We are presently in the image of the first Adam. And yet one day our LORD Jesus "will transform our lowly [earthy] body to be like His glorious [heavenly] body, by the power that enables Him even to subject all things to Himself (Philippians 3:21)."

There is a lot of confusion as to why we are still the *earthy;* the natural body; and yet we are also expected to be a *new creature*, or as Paul would write: "Therefore if any man be in Christ, he is a new creature: old things are passed away; behold, all things are become new (2 Corinthians 5:17)."

I have often heard it spoken from the Calvinist, *If I'm born again, how can I be unborn?* To him I ask, if we are *born again* now, will we be born *again-again* at the resurrection? I believe the *new creature* teaching should be quite separate from the *born again* doctrine. One is present, a shadow of what is to come; the later still future tense, a fulfillment of all that was formerly promised. The *new creature* is born of baptism. Our participation with Christ's crucifixion is a death to the old *earthy* man. More precisely, because we have died to the earthy man, we have been given the Holy Spirit as an assurance of our down payment, and may therefore set our eyesight upon a *kingdom come* eternity in new spirit bodies. Specifically, we must live now for the heavenly man. To be *born again* into our new spiritual bodies—I think both Jesus and His servant Paul were clear of its ultimate fulfillment—we must be patient and await the resurrection. *And as we have borne the image of the earthy*, the Apostle wrote, *we shall also bear the image of the heavenly* (1 Corinthians 15:50).

> "So also is the resurrection of the dead. It is sown in corruption; it is raised in incorruption: It is sown in dishonor; it is raised in glory: it is sown in weakness; it is raised in power: It is sown a natural body; it is raised a spiritual body. There is a natural body, and there is a spiritual body (1 Corinthians 15:42-44)."

So let us become the *new man* then! No, no—by stating that we are a *new creation*, the Christian is not hoping to achieve the impossible. His lofty goals are not *earthy* ambitions, which liken to Satan's own hopes of self-ascendancy to the heights of heaven. The true saint has died to the mystery religion. His hopes are therefore not impossible works-based undertakings. He is not the Superman of Friedrich Nietzsche lore, nor the *practically-perfect* Mary Poppins of P.L. Travers' witchcraft and Theosophy. Let us not be confused any longer. In order to put on the new man, the sinner understands he must be *found in* Christ. Or as Paul would instruct Colossae, we must be *hid* with Christ in God. To this effect he wrote:

> "For ye are dead, and your life is hid with Christ in God (Colossians 3:3)."

If we are dead to our earthy selves, then we cannot keep to our former ambitions and still expect to enter into the presence of a holy God. Scripture is clear on this. As earthy men, we were enemies of God (Romans 5:10). In order to be *born again* at the resurrection, we must die to the self and be hidden in the righteousness of Christ. Paul wrote: "For as many of you as have been baptized into Christ have put on Christ (Galatians 3:27)." Here we discover our new self—not clothed with a cape or a parrot-face umbrella, but in the arms of our Savior. It is not because *we* are the second Adam. It is only because our Father in heaven, when He looks upon us, sees Christ the Savior—the second Adam; the lamb who takes away the sins of the world—standing in our place.

Paul wrote to Corinth:

> "For He hath mad Him to be sin for us, who knew no sin; that we might be made the righteousness of God in Him (2 Corinthians 5:21)."

And quite similarly, to Ephesus he wrote:

> "But now in Christ Jesus ye who sometimes were far off are made nigh by the blood of Christ (Ephesians 2:13)."

The untarnished *image of God* is one which bears the righteousness and holiness of our Creator because Christ Himself bears it in our place. This is the very image which Adam and Eve were constituted to bear before their decision for sin. In other words, for those of us found in Christ Jesus, God "will be merciful to their unrighteousness, and their sins and their iniquities will I remember no more (Hebrews 8:12)." So let His *kingdom come* be restored unto us in the only way achievable; let us be hid with Christ, in His righteousness and holiness, and therefore be found *created in the image of God* on the day of resurrection. As new creatures, we must willfully live for our resurrected bodies by forsaking our earthy selves, for it is written: "they that are Christ's have crucified the flesh with the affections and lusts (Galatians 5:24)."

The Christian must see to it that holiness is restored. The Apostle Peter wrote: "But as he which hath called you is holy, so be ye holy in all manner of conversation (1 Peter 1:15)." He furthermore must see to it that humility is restored, for Jesus "made Himself of no reputation, and took upon Him the form of a servant, and was made in the likeness of men (Philippians 2:8)." The second Adam became nothing, even becoming "obedient unto death, even the death of the cross." This also we are to become—*nothing*. To this point, concerning the self-conscious man's natural inclination for humanism, Galatians would remind us: "For if a man think himself to be something, when he is nothing, he deceiveth himself (Galatians 6:3)." We are expected to be curators of justice and mercy and dispensers of grace, like our Savior, but love also must be restored. As further evaluation that the *new man* exhibits the very image of God, which he claims to be hidden in, Jesus gave this strict command: "By this shall all men know that ye are my disciples, if ye have love one to another (John 13:5)."

These are communicable attributes of God's image. "For we are His workmanship," Paul wrote to Ephesus, "*created* in Christ Jesus unto good works, which God hath before ordained that we should walk in them (Ephesians 2:10)." The path of the *new creature* is the narrow way. To the church of Galatia Paul accredited the saintly man as the "many as walk according to this rule."

> "For in Christ Jesus neither circumcision availeth anything, nor uncircumcision, but a *new creature*. And as many as walk according to this rule, peace be on them, and mercy, and upon the Israel of God (Galatians 6:15-16)."

Elsewhere, Paul writes of the *new creature* as one who "also should walk in newness of life" while awaiting the resurrection.

"What shall we say then? Shall we continue in sin, that grace may abound? God forbid. How shall we, that are dead to sin, live any longer therein? Know ye not, that so many of us as were baptized into Jesus Christ were baptized into his death? Therefore we are buried with him, by baptism into death: that like as Christ was raised up from the dead by the glory of the Father, even so we also should walk in newness of life. For if we have been planted together in the likeness of his death, we shall be also in the likness of his resurrection (Romans 6:1-5)."

Becoming a *new creature* doesn't make us immortal any more than it makes us omnipotent, omnipresent, transcendent, or triune. But dare I forget our blessed hope! Our *becoming* like the second Adam will not merely secure a return of what once *was*. Adam was of the earth. But Jesus was of heaven. With Christ serving as a witness and first fruit of our own resurrection to come, our spiritual bodies will dramatically expound upon and ultimately fulfill what it means to be called *sons of God*. The Apostle John wrote concerning the sainthood: "But as many as received Him, to them gave He power to become the sons of God, *even* to them that believe on His name (John 1:12)." Though we shall never become omnipotent, omnipresent, transcendent or triune at the resurrection, nor beyond (Scripture makes no mention of these attributes), we will finally secure what the self-conscious human hopes to achieve on his own—by way of persuasive argument. We will be given an unconditional *immortality*. After all, the Apostle Paul wrote of the resurrection: "this mortal must put on immortality (1 Corinthians 15:53)."

The self-proclaiming *immortal* man, desiring to be *like God* rather than *made in His image*, wishes for nothing else but to climb over the wall of heaven or hop the back fence into eternity and sit upon the throne of its King rather than wait in the grave for the LORD to wake him with a trumpet blast, followed with the radiating starry-light of resurrected *immortality*. But know this, the sainthood of all ages wait upon His glorious appearing. Even the dear Apostle John understood of his youthful friend, the Savior whom he longed to be with; they would not be reunited again (on this side of curtain or the other) until He returned to establish His Davidic kingdom, *"for we shall see Him as He is."* But not before.

"Dear friends, now we are children of God, and what we will be has not yet been made known. But we know that when He appears, we shall be like Him, for we shall see Him as He is (1 John 3:2)."

The quick and the dead wait upon the LORD.

THE ANATOMY OF A WHITE-WASHED TOMB: THIS SIDE OF GEHENNA (*The Hellenistic Jew, Immortal Soul & Reincarnation*)

WHILE PREGNANT WITH A SECOND CHILD, the 35 year-old Empress Poppaea Sabina was kicked to death by Nero, her third and final husband. Yet another antichrist in a succession of many reigned from Rome. Only one year earlier, on a muggy July night in 64 AD, over half of the city was leveled by fire. Rome's citizens immediately suspected their beloved Emperor of wicked intent. The historian Tacitus is even accredited with first suggesting that Nero had sung about the destruction of Troy while watching it smolder. The rest of history is aptly reminded that he *played the fiddle*. Regardless, its hot ashes were likely still raining down over Italy when the Emperor contrived another devilish smoke screen of his own. The Christians, he claimed, were responsible for its wreckage.

About this time, and as a likely consequence, the Apostle Paul was beheaded. Nero then built his Golden Palace and its surrounding pleasure gardens, complete with pastures, an artificial lake, and a 114 foot-tall bronze statue prizing himself as the sun god Sol, on the land so conveniently cleared by his Christian tormentors. When the massive project was completed Nero—who rode about town in a sun-chariot embroidered with golden stars and ostentatiously publicized himself as Apollo incarnate—simply shrugged.

"At last I have begun to live like a human being," the *immortal* said.

"As for the mysteries of God, they knew them not..."

(Wisdom 2:22)

Within the maddening gale the young Hebrew ambassador Josephus set out for the Imperial capitol. His was a diplomatic mission to free the 12 Jewish priests whom Judean procurator Felix had sent to Nero for trial. While in Rome he met with Empress Poppaea and fell in good terms with her. His mission was deemed a success, but his journey wouldn't come without tragedy. While initially bound for Rome, he narrowly survived shipwreck on a charter. Of its 600 passengers, only 80 survived. And yet such senseless tragedy would go down as an inconvenient footnote to his life and to the impoverished world around him, because it was his return to Judea which secured the *true* nightmare to come.

In Jerusalem the mood had spoiled. Revolt was firmly fixed upon the minds of the Jews and nothing could convince them otherwise. Though the Jewish people had long been fractured into three political fringes—the Essenes, the Sadducees, and the Pharisees—there was one commonality which they could all seemingly agree upon. They were sick of Rome; sick of the Occult which manipulated and gave muscular tenacity to it; sick of the pagan gods and Apollo and Plato's globe and the Mithraic globe-cult which Plato inspired and which mutually perverted the firmament above. They wanted their Davidic kingdom, and they were sick of waiting for it. In short, they were *sick*. History will testify to their fever. Of particular note, they didn't actually want their *David*. Rather, they wanted *his kingdom*, and they wanted it *now*. And yet this was a war, Josephus pleaded, which they surely could not win.

It can be said that the first century of our modern era was one propagated and prepared for in advance by architects who lapped up dreams enlivened with apocalyptic strokes—encircled with visions of hellfire and brimstone; and yet one which fell on deaf ears by almost everyone involved, particularly those who gaily kept in cadence with the drumbeats of war in order that the kingdom of heaven might finally prosper on Earth. A psychopath managed the world's day-to-day culinary menu from Rome while zealots in Jerusalem provided his cake with the icing and whipped cream and a cherry to crown it. Sanity was not the spoken dialect of the day. Mental illness was a delectable recipe, and as evidence, Socrates cup of poisoned hemlock was distributed to the public for mass consumption. For the first time in history, the Jew needn't *truly* die. The Jew was *immortal*.

Before Plato and Pythagoras, belief in the continuous life of the soul was represented as a fraudulent doctrine of the surrounding Mystery religions, upheld for the purposes of ancestor worship, self-salvation, and the rites of necromancy, and—despite widespread and persistent mishandling of the soul among Christians today (and likely of every Christian generation since the Apostolic end)—such vocabulary is found nowhere in the pages of Holy Writ, including its New Testament writers. With Alexander the Great's conquest of the world some four-hundred years earlier—at the end of which he *wept*—the Greeks were finally free to export their prized product. An antichrist in his own right, Alexander brought with him a doctrine of the devil. For Aristotle, you see, was his personal tutor. In turn, Aristotle was personally schooled by Plato. After Antiochus IV Ephiphianes—a man whom all scholars agree is perhaps the most significant antichrist archetype in the whole of Biblical history—committed the Abomination of Desolation by offering a sacrificed pig on the altar of Zeus in the Temple; Plato endured.

Though *the Secret Doctrine*, which had strictly remained a *hush-hush* subject for the neophyte, was finally available for public consumption, not every *enlightened* soul was pleased. Occultist Manley P. Hall once remarked: "Plato, an initiate of one of these sacred orders, was severely criticized because in his writings he revealed to the public many of the secret philosophic principles of the Mysteries." The Medieval Italian-Jewish writer Immanuel be Solomon has also stated, Plato "was led to it [*the immortal soul*] through Orphic and Eleusinian mysteries in which Babylonian and Egyptian views were strangely blended."

Regardless, Israel was undeniably Hellenized, and in the first century, immortality was their swan song. The immortal soul became in and of itself a literary genre. With *4 Maccabees*, the immortal soul found its conversation piece with the teachings of Philo—a first-century Jewish philosopher who harkened from the Occults fuselage in Alexandria and where the Mystery religion would, by no coincidence, take its final stand—by completely suppressing the resurrection of the dead. For Philo, the blessed hope of the resurrection was no longer fashionable. More precisely, the resurrection became a subservient to that of the soul. Righteous souls were suddenly released from their imprisoned bodies here on earth, transported to heaven, transformed into a holy sainthood, and lived eternally in bliss with the patriarchs and God while souls of the wicked continued on in eternal torment. *Wisdom of Solomon*, also penned in Philo's own hometown of Alexandria, offered a wrench to the loose screws of the creation account by declaring; "for God created man to be immortal, and made him to be an image of his own eternity (Wisdom 2:23)." According to *IV Esdras*, immortals are kept in *soul cages* before entering their earthly existence. Likewise, the *Slavonic Enoch* concurred with the Platonic doctrine and conclusively taught: "every soul was created for eternity before the foundation of the world."

With the *Testament of Abraham,* the familiar Patriarch fell in with his usual stereotypical self; he was typecast as a querulous meddler in divine affairs, particularly through the medium of God's angelic emissary, Michael. Abraham bartered for a prolonged life, and though his impending death brought Michael sorrow—the calendar date, we come to learn, could not be moved to the left or the right—God warmed his angelic heart with glad tidings, and a new revelation. Quite suddenly, the orthodoxy had changed. For the first century Hellenist, Father Abraham was given the assurance that "at this time you are going to depart this vain world and leave the body, and you shall go to your own Master among the good." Abraham was no longer born for an inheritance in this present creation, because another and far better world awaited him. *Wisdom* says it like this:

> "But the souls of the righteous are in the hand of God, and there shall no torment touch them. In the sight of the unwise they seemed to die: and their departure is taken for misery, and their going from us to be utter destruction: but they are in peace. For though they be punished in the sight of men, yet is their hope full of immortality (Wisdom of Solomon 3:1-4)."

Though the first-centuries widespread and misguided faith in immortality is certain, there are some things—dare I say, *natural conclusions* of the Pythagorean and Platonism—which remain somewhat ambiguous. Immanuel ben Solomon clung to the same questions when he wrote: "It is not quite clear whether the Sadducees, in denying resurrection, denied also the immortality of the soul. Certain it is that the Pharisaic belief in resurrection had not even a name for the immortality of the soul. For them, man was made for two worlds, the world that now is, and the world to come, where life does not end in death."

This we know of the Essenes. They were in effect sprouts of the Pythagorean seed. The transmigration of the soul is of particular interest, and was not taken lightly for the Essene. They most assuredly believed souls discarded the broken body after its pronounced death in order that it may soon occupy another. Then again, for the Pythagorean, possession of a *human* is not necessarily assured for the wanderer. Rather, it may occupy a plant or a tree or any other form of living being, particularly the animal food chain. How a soul preforms in its previous occupancy will determine his future identity. And he needn't possess a weaning baby either! This will seem strange at first, but consider the Gospel of Matthew.

> "When Jesus came into the coasts of Caesarea Philippi, He asked his disciples, saying, Whom do men say that I the Son of man am? And they said, Some say that thou art John the

Baptist: some, Elias; and others, Jeremias, or one of the prophets (Matthew 15:13-14)."

Assuming this is merely addressing Essene-inquiry, it would be a strange belief indeed to posture that Jesus, a man beyond thirty, could be the resulting experiment of a reincarnated Baptist, who had only recently been beheaded, unless the transmigration of souls became intimately involved. Scripture is often testimony to the ideas of the common people, as well as the self-proclaiming moral, the celibate, the learned, and the religious, most of whom often succumb to eternally gullible thinking. For the Pythagorean as well as the Essene, it was not outside his realm of belief to consider or conclude that our Savior was possessed by the Baptist.

There is another Gospel account involving reincarnation—or rather, a potential belief therein—which deserves mentioning. After Jesus narrowly escaped a public stoning at the hands of the Pharisees, he left the temple and passed a man who had been pronounced blind since birth. We read in John:

"And his disciples asked him, saying, Master, who did sin, this man, or his parents, that he was born blind? (John 9:2)"

The mere fact that his own disciples would even consider a possibility in which a man could be *born* blind due to an *earlier* sin could only come from Essene influence—but what of the Pharisee?

The Pharisee undoubtedly believed in immortality. And yet, when Nicodemus secretly approached Jesus in the night, our Savior challenged his misguided belief. He said: "Verily, verily, I say unto thee, except a man be *born again*, he cannot see the kingdom of God (John 3:3)." Nicodemus was naturally confused by this. His preconceived notions had hit a theological wall. If the Christian today is a well-watered sprout of Platonism, he will likely think Jesus was agreeing with Nicodemus on his position of the immortal soul. He will therefore refer to his self or any other soul who has made a decision for Christ as being "born again." If however the Christian shuns Hellenistic thinking and clings to Hebrew doctrine—a banner which refers us to the words of the Prophet: "*The soul who sins shall die...* (Ezekiel 18:4)"—he will likely understand that Jesus was correcting the Pharisees erroneous faith. Our Savior was redirecting the Pharisees attention to the blessed hope of resurrection which He would secure as its very first fruit. Three chapters later, Jesus informed a group of murmuring Jews as to our *true* hope— our *born again* moment. To this effect He said:

"Murmur not among yourselves. No one can come to me unless the Father who sent me draws him, and I will raise him up at the last day (John 6:3-4)."

There is more which needs said of the Pharisee—*much more*. The problem however is that the Pharisees followed an imaginary set of principles which they claimed was handed down to them quite separately from what is written. Apparently an esoteric on the side, or so the claim goes, Moses delivered hidden wisdom to Joshua from the mountaintop—and so on and so on. What we might today call a game of *Chinese Whispers*, they called the Oral Law, and though it would not be published for another 300 years in the Talmud, post-temple rabbi Simeon bar Yochai is believed by many to be the author of the Zohar, the chief work of Kabbalah—with the help of the Prophet Elias, no less. Reincarnation is an undeniable part of his doctrine. While the full spectrum of the Pharisees positions have been endlessly argued, historians will at least agree; they were the leaning liberals of their day.

Like any typical leftist party, their audience was enormous. Rather than blindly following the letter of the Law as the conservative Sadducee might, even if it conflicted with reason or conscience, the Pharisees harmonized the teachings of the Torah with their own ideals or, more precisely, conveniently found their own ideas implied in it. Essentially, they interpreted the Law according to its spirit, not its letter. By doing so, they provided a long-winded resilience to scriptural interpretation among the turmoil of changing circumstances. The Pharisee was *progressive.*

I can't help but wonder if Philo held any sway over their *hidden wisdom*. According to Josephus in *The War of the Jews*, the Pharisee taught "that every soul is imperishable, but that only those of the righteous pass into another body, while those of the wicked are, on the contrary, punished with eternal torment." In *Antiquities of the Jews*, he further elaborated: "they hold the belief that an immortal strength belongs to souls, and that there are beneath the earth punishments and rewards for those who in life devoted themselves to virtue or vileness, and that eternal imprisonment is appointed for the latter, but the possibility of returning to life for the former." If Josephus is to be believed, they also followed Plato's soul to its natural conclusions and hearkened a belief in reincarnation—perhaps even transmigration.

The last Apostle may be of some help to us. Paul was, at one time or another, a "Hebrew of Hebrews" and Pharisee of Pharisees; reared with enough notoriety as to be groomed under the highly respected Pharisee

Gamaliel. It is evidently clear that *Wisdom of Solomon* was an inspirational source of his education. In his own writings Paul referred to it. I only wish to bring it up, but shall touch upon the specifics another time. His inclusion of *Wisdom* into the epistles is critical, because Paul as an Apostle of the Lord renounced many of his former educational conclusions, including *Wisdom*—for *Wisdom*, you see, advocates the preexistence of souls. Clearly, Paul did not.

> "As a child I was by nature well endowed, and a good soul fell to my lot; or rather, being good, I entered an undefiled body (Wisdom of Solomon 8:19)."

After Jesus healed the blind man, the Pharisees told the blind persons parents: "We are Moses' disciples. We know that God spoke to Moses." And yet Jesus broke the *hidden wisdom* of their Talmud repeatedly. He referred to them as nothing more or less than "human traditions." God may have spoken to Moses "mouth to mouth," but the Pharisees spoke with *dark speeches*.

When Josephus returned to Judea from Rome, he was unable to restrain his people. This is the political environment which fractured Judea. Likely fearful that he would be accused of treachery if he did not comply, the 30 year-old accepted an appointment as commander of Jewish troops among the lush hills of Galilee where, less than three decades earlier, Jesus the Messiah had once focused His ministry. While Nero relished in paranoia, executing the ringleaders who plotted his assassination in Rome—most of them his own courtiers—Josephus trained his rebellion and secured provisions in preparation for battle against overwhelming odds. Like the Essenes, and very likely the Pharisees, Josephus was an unapologetic Platonist. By following Satan's *immortal soul* doctrine through to its natural conclusions, Josephus led his own men into the eternal gullible. The cat was out of the bag. Josephus believed in reincarnation. His men likely did too. Having already rejected their Messiah—hence the *true*Davidic kingdom, unlike the counterfeit they sought after—this was the strange idolatrous god whom Abraham's children willingly passed through the fires of Gehenna for.

With these *immortal* words, Josephus rallied his men to a final fight. He cited, not from Moses or the Prophets, but from Plato's Gospel. He said: "Do ye not remember that all pure Spirits when they depart out of this life obtain a most holy place in heaven, from whence, in the revolutions of ages, they are again sent into pure bodies?"

After a 47-day siege, in July of 67 AD, the Jewish stronghold at Yodfat fell to Vespasian's army. The defeat was purely one-sided. Thousands of Jews were killed in the slaughter. The remainders committed suicide. Josephus, who was soon cornered in a cave, was one of only two survivors.

And yet the worst was yet to come.

Roman legions under Syrian governor Cestius Gallus pitched camp around Jerusalem in hopes of quelling the Jewish rebellion. From the safety of their walled city, the Jews fought back—but to no avail. Cestius' army overlapped their shields, as though claiming a carefree asylum under the shell of a tortoise—it was a favorite mobilized tactic known as *testudo*—and boldly advanced forward. Josephus recounts: "The darts that were thrown fell, and slided off without doing them any harm; so the soldiers undermined the wall, without being themselves hurt, and got all things ready for setting fire to the gate of the temple."

Jerusalem was lost. Except it wasn't—because what followed could only be described as an intervention attributed to God. "It then happened," wrote Josephus inquisitively, "that Cestius recalled his soldiers from the place," adding, "He retired from the city, without any reason in the world." In actuality, one of Jesus' most stunning prophecies was already unfolding. It was their *final* warning. Few listened.

In a rather odd plot twist, the ambassador who became general and then slave soon found himself—in just as quick of a succession—a devoted family friend of his captors, General Vespasian and Titus his son. Across the Mediterranean, on June 9, 68 AD, having learned that he had been tried in absentia and condemned to death as an enemy of the public, Nero drove a dagger into his throat. Following Nero's suicide, his three successors would each meet a similar violent end, and in as little as 18 months. Though Galba immediately seized the throne, he was assassinated by Otho, one of his earliest followers and a trusted companion to Nero, after the Emperor dressed himself in a linen corset. A soldier cut off his head and, thrusting his thumb into the mouth, carried the horrid trophy about. With Otho, the Empire teetered on the brink of civil war. His reigned lasted but three months before digging a dagger into his breast. As 69 AD came to a close, Vitellius fell prey to a military coup. He was tortured and then dragged by a hook into the Tiber. Here the plot thickens. His usurper was none other than Josephus' Roman captor, Vespasian—*strange* indeed.

How Josephus is *not* accused of espionage, considering the lack of witnesses to his survival at Yodfat, his easing into the Flavian dynasty, or why his meeting with Nero's wife some years earlier in Rome is not closely scrutinized, considering the outcome, is beyond me. Josephus is simply *too much* of an underdog success story. The man who lost every last soul to Vespasian's army soon re-emerged among his peers as Titus Flavius Josephus, having adopted the name of his captor. Returning once more to the war in Judea, Josephus would become eye-witness to the fulfillment of Jesus' most stunning prophecy by serving as a negotiator alongside the Emperor's son, General Titus, during the final siege and complete destruction of Jerusalem. It is recorded that General Titus offered peace and amnesty if the city surrendered its rebellion, but sanity was not the spoken dialect of the day. They chose *immortality*.

One day, some 37 years earlier, Jesus left the temple. Certain disciples remarked how beautiful it was. Matthew records:

> "And Jesus said unto them, See ye not all these things? Verily I say unto you, there shall not be left here one stone upon another, that shall not be thrown down (Matthew 24:2)."

Naturally, His disciples wanted to know when these things would come to pass. Luke records His answer.

> "And when ye shall see Jerusalem compassed with armies, then know that the desolation thereof is nigh. Then let them which are in Judaea flee to the mountains; and let them which are in the midst of it depart out; and let not them that are in the countries enter there into. For these be the days of vengeance, that all things which are written may be fulfilled (Luke 21:20-22)."

Our Master added: "Verily I say unto you, This generation shall not pass, till all these things be fulfilled (Matthew 24:34)." James the brother of Jesus, former leader of the Jerusalem church, was of *that* generation. But he would not live to see the words of his earthly sibling fulfilled. In 62 AD James met martyrdom. Clement of Alexandria relates that he was thrown from the pinnacle of the temple and then beaten to death with a club. The Apostle Peter, who served as a co-elder with James, was also of that generation. But he was also was martyred—crucified actually— under Nero. Paul also. After Cestius simply walked away from his siege of the city three years earlier, whoever remained of Jerusalem's church likely heeded the words of their Master—and fled to the mountains.

Josephus and his closest family did not heed to the words of the Savior. Over a million souls were killed during the siege, mostly Jews, according to the historian. His wife and parents were among them. Horrifying atrocities followed, some too scandalous even for blood-sporting Romans. Hearing reports that fleeing refuges were swallowing coins to hide them from robbers, besieging troops disemboweled two thousand Jews in one night. Once inside the city, bloated corpses lay open-faced in the street and the discovery of cannibalism—a woman serving up her child—curdled the nerves of Roman soldiers. Seditious robbers had already destroyed property and murdered men of noted importance, fighting "against each other, while they trod upon the dead bodies as they lay heaped one upon another." There could be no doubting it now, the city of God was a white-washed tomb of wickedness. Some "were in such distress by their internal calamities that they wished for the Romans." But they too would die—men, woman, and children were trampled underfoot. Blood literally flowed in the streets until Titus' men were simply "tired of killing." Round the Altar of the temple, Josephus records, "the heaps of corpses grew higher and higher, while down the Sanctuary steps poured a river of blood and the bodies of those killed at the top slithered to the bottom." Of the 97,000 survivors, thousands were forced to become gladiators in the arena. The feeble were murdered. The underage were sold into slavery, probably to pedophiles. The rest were shipped off to Egypt.

They wanted a kingdom without its king.

They perhaps best exemplified a salvation found in wisdom, which is quite impossible, mind you, rather than a free gift of salvation found only in faith. Their own beloved text, *Wisdom of Solomon*, says:

> "And thus the paths of those on earth were set right, and people were taught what pleases you, and were saved by wisdom (Wisdom of Solomon 9:18)."

Among Jesus' warnings of this coming destruction, He said to the Pharisees: "Wherefore ye be witness unto youselves, that ye are the children of them which killed the prophets. Fill ye up then the measure of your fathers. Ye serpents, ye generation of vipers, how can ye escape the damnation of hell?"

The *damnation of hell* which He spoke of can best be translated as: "being judged worthy of Gehenna." The generation to which these words were addressed represented the climax of the whole sinful history of the nation, beginning with the murder of Abel, and would be judged accordingly. "That upon you may come all the righteous blood shed upon the earth, from the blood of righteous Abel unto the blood of Zacharias son of Barachias, whom ye slew between the temple and the altar. Verily I say unto you, All these things shall come upon this generation." With the date of Jerusalem's destruction finally upon them, the Apostle Paul had already made clear, in no uncertain terms; the *true kingdom* was grafted into the story (Romans 11). The church lived on. But after *that* generation, Jesus promised, Israel was over.

The first century was a dizzying carousel of paradoxes. The distance by which the Jewish faith had strayed is cringe-worthy. They had succumbed to the very Zarathustrian occult practices which they—on the outset, at least—had hoped to suppress. In short, Platonism *inspired* them, and as a result of the Great Revolt, millions of Jewish souls were likely killed. It is a sum so abstractly vast and incalculable as to never be known on this side of eternity. By adopting Occult practices, even if in secret, they followed Plato's *immortal soul* doctrine to its natural conclusions. The Hellenistic Jews forsook the *blessed hope* of resurrection for a counterfeit reincarnation, despite the fact that Jesus had proved to them that His promises could and would be kept.

It is finished.

I am reminded of the Confederate Freemason and Occultist Albert Pike, who wrote so breathlessly of the immortal soul. He accredited it not to a belief in the Biblical, but rather gave praise where praise is due. The immortal soul arose from his "ancient brethren" who strove to "return to the bosom of the Deity." The immortal soul, he insisted, must attempt to "pass through the darkness to reach the light."

For Manly P. Hall, this is the *very reason* for the Mystery religion. He wrote: "The Mysteries were organized for the purpose of assisting the struggling human creature to reawaken the spiritual powers which lay asleep within his soul. In other words, man was offered a way by which he could regain his lost estate."

Our Savior mourned for the preconceived notions and willful disorientation of an obstinate people without a shepherd to guide them while they fumbled around, slapping at the walls in hopes of flipping a light switch in the dark, despite the light of the world, who stood right before them, arms wide open. His own creation knew Him not. How tragic. "O Jerusalem, Jerusalem, thou that killest the prophets, and stonest them which are sent unto thee," He mourned the Pharisee, "how often would I have gathered thy children together, even as a hen gathereth her chickens under her wings, and ye would not! (Matthew 23:37)"

Indeed, counterfeit spirits and *dark speeches* swept the Hellenistic world. Even today the church is still imprisoned by them and worse, unwilling to unshackle the chains. Nobody is binding us to them but our rapacious appetites. Jesus looked upon the engineers and self-promoters of immortality and saw what they could not—nor would not: white-washed sepulchers filled with an anatomy *bones*. Before pronouncing the temple's destruction, He said to them:

> "Hypocrites! for ye are like unto whited sepulchres, which indeed appear beautiful outward, but are within full of dead men's bones, and of all uncleanness (Matthew 23:27)."

Quite literally, bodies were thrown into Gehenna. Their souls would die with them.

"*Strange Doctrines...*" THE RESURRECTION ON TRIAL BY THE RACONTEURS OF MARS HILL & THE ARCHITECTS OF ATOMISM

IT IS OFTEN ASSUMED BY THE CLERIC that Paul the Apostle *agreed* with Saul the Pharisee, his fleshly counterpart, on any number of extra-Biblical doctrines, particularly the *immortal* soul; that the road to Damascus did little to reform his erstwhile faith in the celebrated *oral* dogma of Hellenistic Judaism—despite an intervention by the *written* Prophets, whom I have no doubt rehabilitated him; nor abolish his wealth of worldly education, particularly a diploma in Platonism. When Ananias found the last Apostle shortly after his arrival in Damascus, he met the authenticated Saul—a blind man. "And immediately there fell from his eyes as it had been scales: and he received sight forthwith, and arose, and was baptized (Acts 9:18)." Straightway he preached Christ in the synagogues, and as he did so, "increased the more in strength, and confounded the Jews which dwelt at Damascus." By this we are to understand that his conviction of the truth of the *bona fide* religion strengthened tenaciously every day as he made obsolete the dark speeches of his former companions and acquaintances by thoroughly stifling their perversities at the throat. Paul's life was a courtroom—and quite ironically, still is. The jury today *must* deliberate on the most elementary of Christian doctrines, because Paul's *good news* for both the Jew and the Gentile was *not* the immortal soul. No, no—quite contrarily, it was the resurrection of the dead.

Paul's second missionary journey would prove no exception to the judiciary drama. Likely arriving at Athens in 50 AD, the Apostle found himself in a pagan realm cankered with the most peculiar of ideals. Today their perverse appeals have become the very asphalt and pavement of Science by which we are expected to commute upon. And yet Paul, we shall come to learn, was to the intellectuals who shaped the rebar, mortar, and brick of the world around him a senile *babbler*, for he opposed everything which their philosophies deemed as true. Paul's "spirit was stirred in him, when he saw the city wholly given to idolatry." He therefore disputed first "in the synagogue with the Jews," as was his proper custom, "and with the devout persons, and in the market daily with them that met with him (Acts 17:17)."It is there in the marketplace where Paul confronted the fathers of *modern* cosmology, for we read: "Then certain philosophers of the Epicureans, and of the Stoicks, encountered him." As atomic materialists stemming from the pre-Socratic schools of Democritus and Epicures, the Epicureans were originally a challenge to Hellenistic society and harsh debaters of Stoic living. While the Platonists dreamt of heaven, the imaginative conjuring of atomism advertised a reality consisting of invisible, indivisible bits of randomly colliding matter. Essentially, atomists developed their theory of matter to support a pantheistic worldview in which everything was divinely interwoven together. If one atom affects another it is conclusively because they are collectively of one and the same mind. The pre-Socratic philosopher Heraclitus equated fire and Zeus as the divine ruling order by referring to "the thunderbolt that stirs all things." With Zeus, the atom came to form. Later Epicurus, who was better known for his emphasis on pleasure as the greatest achievable good, stapled to atomism the comic book notion that an infinite number of worlds or parallel universes could be adjacent or even wholly contained within each other so that one might occasionally overlap another.

Seth Shostak, lead astronomer at SETI—an institute founded by Carl Sagan in partnership with the NASA Ames Research Center and which hopes to discover extraterrestrial life in space—has perhaps best phrased Epicurean doctrine by stating: "The next time you check your moves in the mirror and reflect on how special you are, consider that somewhere in this universe or in another parallel universe, your double might be doing the same. This would be the ultimate Copernican Revolution. Not only are we not special, we could be infinitely ordinary."

In her book, *The Mystery School*, occultist Grace F. Knoche exhibits inside knowledge of the atoms esoteric ancestry, particularly its Mystery School origin: "The physicist cannot point to the physical atom, yet he knows it exists as the basis, the foundation, of all matter; the student of theosophy cannot show you a Mystery school, yet he knows it exists as the heart or atomic center of the spiritual and intellectual life of the planet. Who then would dare assert the non-existence of the Mysteries, of this potent atom of esotericism, when luminous traces of spiritual power are seen scattered all over the world? If our physical bodies are rooted in invisible fiery lives, why should not our human spiritual, intellectual, and moral bodies likewise have their origin in the spiritual and intellectual fire-mist of the planet?"

Atomism eventually won British chemist John Dalton a Royal Medal in 1826 for its prolonged discovery. Dalton maintained that chemicals always contain whole-number ratios of atoms—the very reason we say H20 rather than H2.40. He furthermore suggested that we cannot have half an atom or the fraction of an atom, only whole atoms. Belief in the atom is faithfully subscribed to and yet it has never been seen with an optical microscope or the naked eye due to the fact that visible light is thousands of times larger. As further perspective, a single sheet of paper is roughly half a million atoms thick. In other words, one atom is as small to an apple as that very apple is to the proposed size of *globe* earth. For this very reason chemists employ x-rays—first developed in the 1890's by German scientist Wilhelm Rontgen, who aptly realized that photographs taken with x-rays allowed him to see through objects—and bounce them off crystals. Let me be clear, we are all made of *smaller* parts. I would be a fool to deny it. And yet, need I remind my reader that Occultists are aficionados at maintaining their purported cosmogony where it cannot be seen by the naked eye nor otherwise perceived? Deception abounds at the micro and the macro level. I also recognize that atoms are thus far from being a mere theoretical concept anymore. The development of a scanning tunneling microscope in 1981—an instrument for imaging surfaces at the atomic level—won its inventors, Gerd Binnig and Heinrich Rohrer, the Nobel Prize in physics in 1986. Scientists have seen them. They have toyed with them. And they have also sought to manipulate them.

Perhaps the atomists of Athens thought Plato's allegory of the shadowy cave and his immortal soul, which might escape the illusion of death by ascending to his heavenly world of Forms, too simple minded. Platonism held a dualist model of the soul, preferring an immortal soul which can exist independently of the body and maintain its consciousness, whereas Epicurus was a true materialist and balked at the assertion of a soul's ascension into the spiritual realm. The Stoic at least in part argued for Aristotle's position. Blending dualist and materialist qualities into a sort of spiritual alchemy, Aristotle held that the soul is "the form (or actuality) of a natural body which has life potentiality," whereas the Stoic maintained that the soul is not immortal but could and would survive the destruction of the body. In short, the ancient atomists did not subscribe to Plato. For these reasons the Greek philosopher Aristoxenus of Tarentum—a pupil of Aristotle—recorded that

Plato *hated* Epicurean-thinking and had wished all of Democritus' books to be burned.

Quite contrarily, the Stoics represented the new philosophical movement of Hellenistic thinking and elitist society, and vainly hoped to maintain a lifetime's pursuit of philosophical virtues within the framework of Greek ethics, all of which had been handed down to them from Plato and Aristotle. As a father of metaphysical logic, Zeno was the administrator of the Stoic school of philosophy, which he taught in Athens. So if his disciples and the Epicureans gathered together, it was likely to *argue*—and argue they did. The Epicureans quibbled for the atomistic void hypothesis while the Stoics sought to discredit them with the paradoxes of Parmenides according to Zeno, and it should be noted that Isaac Newton and Albert Einstein later came to the defense of Democritus and the Epicureans in their own revised editions when explaining the theory of absolute space and the theory of relativity, in that order.

Luke further explains of their centuries-long tiff: "all the Athenians and strangers which were there spent their time in nothing else, but either to tell or to hear some new thing (Acts 17:21)." From stage right, Paul enters in. Among this tug-of-war of Occultism in the halls of Science the once-Pharisee from Jerusalem thrust upon their laps the *truest*science which ever was—and will soon again prove to be. Finally, those who vehemently opposed each other could at least in part mutually agree upon one thing. Paul had arrived in Greece and had become a promoter of *strange doctrines*.

The raconteurs of Mars Hill said to their opposing party (like opposing atoms attempting to dance through the void): "What will this *babbler* say?" And yet for others: "He seemeth to be a setter forth of strange gods: because he preached unto them Jesus, and the resurrection (Acts 17:18)."

The world was wrangled by Hellenistic Platonism and—always eager for fresh produce of intellectual curiosity—Paul was cordially invited to Mars Hill, its soapbox. Of this historical event we read:

> "And they took him, and brought him unto Areopagus, saying, May we know what this new doctrine, whereof thou speakest, is? For thou bringest certain strange things to our ears: we would know therefore what these things mean (Acts 17:19-20)."

One might wonder why the Jews of Athens, whom Paul first met with—especially his Pharisee contemporaries—hadn't thought to school the Epicurean or the Stoic on the matter of the resurrection. Perhaps this is not simply so because the resurrection was a unique Christian doctrine; perhaps more-so because the oral teachings of the Jews had already blended mystical concoctions with the pure faith of Moses. Their preference for the dark speeches of Pythagoras and Platonism is already established. This is precisely what Saul the Pharisee had turned away from. For the first-century Jew, the road to the Kabbalah was already paved before them. Pantheistic to its core, the Kabbalah states: "In the flow of the holy spirit, one feels the divine life force coursing the pathways of existence, through all desires, all worlds, all thoughts, all nations, all creatures." And according to Jewish mystic Moses ben Jacob Cordovero, the Kabbalah regrettably adds:

> "The essence of divinity is found in every single thing—nothing but it exists. Since it causes everything to be, nothing can live by anything else. It enlivens them; its existence exists in each existent. Do not attribute duality to God. Let God be solely God. If you suppose that Ein Sof [the Eternal, literally *"without end"*] emanates until a certain point, and that from that point on is outside of it, you have dualized. God forbid! Realize, rather, that Ein Sof exists in each existent. Do not say, "This is a stone and not God." God forbid! Rather, all existence is God, and the stone is a thing pervaded by divinity."

By the time Paul was taken to the prominent rock outcropping in Athens known as the Areopagus, the very plot—located northwest and within eyesight of the idolatrous Acropolis (which the Apostle likely toured)—had already functioned as an ancient court for the trying of homicides, violent crimes, and religious matters. How appropriate. In his passionate address to the Athenians, Paul famously chastised their gluttonous superstitions. Concerning their vast collection of marble busts and incense-fragranced idols, specifically one in particular, he said: "For as I passed by, and beheld your devotions, I found an altar with this inscription, TO THE UNKNOWN GOD. Whom therefore ye ignorantly worship, Him declare I unto you (Acts 17:23)."

The Apostle was essentially saying, "You can have your lifeless gods and sciences falsely-so called, but that unknown god over there, he's not a Platonist, nor is he an atomist. He is actually quite different from anything a man might naturally imagine."

214

To the mistaken atomist he said: "For in Him we live, and move, and have our being."

Creation was not some random cataclysmic smashing of atoms, as Democritus would have us believe. Life did not begin in a primordial void, nor had man evolved from a fish, both of which Anaximander of Miletus had poetically proposed. "God that made the world and all things therein, seeing that He is Lord of heaven and death, dwelleth not in temples made with hands;" particularly the Mystery schools; "Neither is worshiped with men's hands;" especially their perverse doctrines which hopes to shape Him; "as though He needed anything, seeing He giveth to all life, and breath, and all things."

By stating that God "hath determined the times before appointed, and the bounds of their habitation" the Apostle did not incite the Stoic with visions of Platonism. Paul did not assure the Stoic of the immortal soul, nor did he convince the Epicurean that there was one. He certainly did not affirm Hellenistic Judaism's insistence that we escape the illusion of death and ascend to heaven after we die. Rather, Paul took them to Holy Scripture, and by doing so, enlightened them to a central tenant of the Christian faith—the resurrection.

We further read: "And when they heard of the resurrection of the dead, some mocked; and others said, We will hear thee again of this matter (Acts 17:32)."

"Howbeit certain men clave unto him, and believed," we are told, among the which was Dionysius the Areopagite, a member of the Athenian high council and likely a Stoic, "and a woman named Damaris, and others with them (Acts 17:34)." Most, *however*, remained. On Mars Hill the Nephilim spirits, issuing forth from the marble nostrils of their gods, clave unto the tongues of esoterists so that the hidden things might be conjured and manipulated by them; specifically so that the very church which the Apostle sought to build upon might be fooled. Even today—*especially* today in the Apostle's absence—the discourse of demons continues.

Quantum physics has lit a match to the fuses of Zeus' thunderbolts so that we today may haphazardly climb the Areopagus and snoop into the religious and mystical artistry of the peculiar, and dare I say it, *spiritual* realm of the renaissance alchemist. Pantheism is wedded with Science. On an atomic level, Scientists affirm that particles do not appear until they are directly observed. The Nobel Prize-winning physicist Erwin Schrödinger has devoted himself to the idiosyncratic.

215

When not directly observed, he maintains, electrons and other subatomic particles diffract as waves of light, only to behave like particles when a human measurement is attempted. "It's as if somebody were playing a trick on us," he says. "Imagine for example that you have a relay system. We know that the trains cannot go faster than light, but you might by studying the timetable very carefully discover that during the night trains have to be returned to their starting point faster than light, so behind the scenes extraordinary things are happening..." Essentially, it's as if these particles exist in multiple places simultaneously until directly observed.

"I'm also obliged to admit," Schrodinger shrugs, "that there's nothing I can do with these." Presently, as *always*, there are human limitations to the observable study of the esoteric. "I cannot use these long-range effects to send messages faster than light....there's this strange dichotomy between what I can do. Human actions are limited by locality..."

In the last Apostle's absence, we find ourselves waking up once more in Egypt, the idolatrous land of ritual and dark magic which the Lord had commanded that we "henceforth return no more that way (Deuteronomy 17:16). Rather than living in a world where science seeks out all that is natural to the works of our Creator, I Am that I Am; we are expected to live by the Hermetic maxim of pantheism; "All is in The All." In her book, *9 Life Altering Lessons: Secrets of the Mystery Schools Unveiled*, Kala Ambrose writes: "....some things do travel faster than the speed of light. This work has begun to be explored, as evidenced by a Paris research team in the 1980's which discovered that under certain conditions and circumstances, subatomic particles such as electrons are able to simultaneously communicate with each other. It was found that distance was not a factor in their ability to communicate, which revealed the understanding that the particles were aware of what the other particles were doing, regardless of how far away they were from each other. Fascinating isn't it? Mystics have taught a similar concept for eons, that We Are All One, and that as part of the Whole, the Energy/God/Spirit whatever you wish to call it, is always aware of you on some level."

Pantheism is an *edict* of this great delusion. We must therefore rise each morning recognizing the hour in which we were purposed to live and face a world bedded with *strange doctrines*, whereas one thing can suddenly be in two separate places. We must contend with the fact that "the laws of the subatomic world and the laws of the human mind parallel each other precisely, exquisitely, and elegantly, down to minute details," as American futurist author and self-described agnostic mystic Anton Wilson has wishfully stated. We must be brave and courageous while inhaling a supposed reality of ever-deepening mysteries promoted by the Occult and endorsed by its wicked slave master, whereas the practitioner deals in the sort of Ouija board and tarot card Sciences which begs for a response and yet believes he is not being fooled by the manifested guidance of a demonic entity conjured from *beyond* the looking-glass. We must rise each day understanding advertised reality doesn't *really* exist until it is perceived and measured from the wizard's purse. We must recognize that they have indeed broken through to the other side. This is the midnight hour—an existence which Indian guru Paramahansa Yogananda once pronounced as *a dream within a dream*. Or as he further put it: "From science then, if it must be so, let man learn the philosophic truth that there is no material universe; its warp and woof is *maya*, illusion." We must therefore boldly swim upstream against the terrible current of this great delusion, and with a sarcastic sigh, we sip our coffee and say *hello* to quantum entanglement.

Occultist Brendan D. Murphy, who emphasizes DNA activation and "the forces and energies produced by our consciousness that act on the world around us," writes in *wake up world*: "Previously, it was believed that once things got to the level of atoms and molecules, the universe started acting strictly deterministically again, according to predictable Newtonian laws. This is no longer a scientifically viable view. A review of developments on entanglement research in March 2004 by New Scientist writer Michael Brooks concluded that 'Physicists now believe that entanglement between particles exists everywhere, all the time.'"

It was these hidden Mysteries which Paul openly shrugged, despite likely being educated in them, just as Moses once was. To the atomist of Epicurean-thinking, Paul quipped: "And the times of this ignorance God winked at; but now commandeth all men everywhere to repent (Acts 17:30)." To put this in a slightly different way, God is done *winking*. "Because He hath appointed a day, in which He will judge the world in righteousness by that man whom He hath ordained." It is Jesus *alone* who is worthy to righteously judge, for God "hath given assurance unto all men, in that He hath raised Him from the dead." This is good news. This is the resurrection.

Whether speaking on behalf of the unknown God from Mars Hill or scribbling on papyri to faraway lands by dim candlelight, for Paul the resurrection was *everything*—and rightly so. Had Saul the Pharisee written in Paul's place, the message would undoubtedly be Hellenistic.

But for Paul the Apostle, his message fell in perfect cadence with the Prophets. From the church in Corinth, perhaps the very year he argued from Mars Hill, Paul wrote to the church of Thessalonica the precise message which the idolatrous atomist and the Platonist had heard:

> "...and how ye turned to God from idols to serve the living and true God; and to wait for His Son from heaven, whom He raised from the dead, even Jesus, which delivered us from the wrath to come (I Thessalonians 1:9-10)."

Paul the Apostle did not attempt to convince Christ believers that they might circumnavigate the long wait for His return by simply dying and meeting him in heaven. No, sir; wait they *must*. If not for Christ, then those which are *fallen asleep*—Paul's own words, not mine—awaiting their resurrection from the dead, have *perished*. How can this be so if the soul is immortal and enjoying His fellowship unspoiled in heaven? While staying in Ephesus sometime in 54-55 AD, Paul instructed this to the Corinthians:

> "And if Christ be not raised, your faith is vain; ye are yet in your sins. Then they also which are fallen asleep in Christ are perished. If in this life only we have hope in Christ, we are of all men most miserable. But now is Christ risen from the dead, and become the firstfruits of them that slept (1 Corinthians 15: 17-20)."

Being ever so consistent and always in step with the whole of Scripture, Paul wrote to the church at Philippi:

> "For our conversation is in heaven; from whence also we look for the Saviour, the Lord Jesus Christ: Who shall change our vile body, that it may be fashioned like unto His glorious body, according to the working whereby he is able even to subdue all things unto himself (Philippians 3:20)."

Our meeting with the Lord however is mutually scheduled so that no man may receive his reward without the other. To Corinth he wrote: "so that ye come behind in no gift; waiting for the coming of our Lord Jesus Christ (1 Corinthians 1:7)." He was no doubt addressing the Stoic and the Platonist when he affirmed our *mortal* souls. But there is hope for the righteous. To this effect he wrote:

> "So when this corruptible shall have put on incorruption, and this mortal shall have put on immortality, then shall be brought

to pass the saying that is written, Death is swallowed up in victory (1 Corinthians 15:54)."

Today the resurrection is on trial, and the Christian-Platonist of every Mars Hill on earth has no doubt already protested with a shaking fist: "I don't care what you say, Paul said to be absent from the body *is* to be present with the Lord! That line trumps them all!" This is truly the speech of a *babbler*—and I am constantly reminded of it—for Paul never once said to be absent from the body *is* to be present with the Lord. Rather, the tentmaker is stating what would otherwise be a terrible sales pitch. It is better to be absent from this body—tent of destruction—and clothed with our heavenly body. And those are two completely different things.

> "For we know that if our earthly house, this tent, is destroyed, we have a building from God, a house not made with hands, eternal in the heavens. For in this we groan, earnestly desiring to be clothed with our habitation which is from heaven, if indeed, having been clothed, we shall not be found naked. For we who are in this tent groan, being burdened, not because we want to be unclothed, but further clothed, that mortality may be swallowed up by life. Now He who has prepared us for this very thing is God, who also has given us the Spirit as a guarantee. So we are always confident, knowing that while we are at home in the body we are absent from the Lord. For we walk by faith, not by sight. We are confident, yes, well pleased rather to be absent from the body and to be present with the Lord (2 Corinthians 5:1–8)."

The tentmaker likens our present mortal bodies with an earthly tent, and should we have the Spirit as a purchased insurance of our salvation, we needn't worry if it is destroyed because a building from God awaits us. There is no context here which presents a meeting with God as a disembodied spirit, as the Platonists would have it. Rather, we will not enjoy God's presence in *this* body. By stating that "we shall not be found naked," Paul repeatedly referred his audience away from the immortal soul and to Job, who set the standard of *true* religious thinking when he lamented (in his most deplorable state):

> "For I know that my redeemer liveth, and that he shall stand at the latter day upon the earth: And though after my skin worms destroy this body, yet in my flesh shall I see God: Whom I shall

see for myself, and mine eyes shall behold, and not another; though my reins be consumed within me (Job 19:25-27)."

Job would certainly agree with Paul, that his "conversation is in heaven; from whence also we look for the Savior, the Lord Jesus Christ." But Job also clearly understood that his eyes would not behold Him until "he be fashioned like unto His glorious body (Philippians 3:20)." When we compare this language to 1 Corinthians 15:51–54, also written by Paul, it becomes even clearer. This mortal body shall be clothed with immortality. This is our *blessed hope* of salvation. The passage reads:

"Behold, I tell you a mystery: We shall not all sleep, but we shall all be changed—in a moment, in the twinkling of an eye, at the last trumpet. For the trumpet will sound, and the dead will be raised incorruptible, and we shall be changed. For this corruptible must put on incorruption, and this mortal must put on immortality. So when this corruptible has put on incorruption, and this mortal has put on immortality, then shall be brought to pass the saying that is written: 'Death is swallowed up in victory' (15:51-54)."

Saul the Pharisee would certainly not have agreed with the Apostle Peter when pronouncing the good news of the resurrection to the crowd on the day of Pentecost: "Men and brethren, let me freely speak unto you of the patriarch David, that he is both dead and buried, and his sepulcher is with us unto this day (Acts 2:29)." For Paul the Apostle, however, there would be *no* disagreement. "It is hard for thee to kick against the pricks," God told Saul on the road to Damascus. Saul surrendered. David was dead and buried, just as Adam and Even were dead and buried. Abraham was dead and buried. Isaac and Jacob were too. And in only a few years, the last of the Apostles, even those blessed witnesses who had seen the resurrected Christ with their own eyes, they would join them. To this very hour their souls lie in waiting.

They wait…

…for the sound of a trump…

Paul's entire life was a courtroom. He stood before Felix. He stood before Agrippa. And his meeting with Nero did not end so well. This is because the true religion of the Prophets and the Apostles defied every sensibility of the Hellenistic world. It was the resurrection of the dead which stood on trial—truly, a *strange doctrine*. And for the Platonist-Christian *today*, it still is.

Perceiving "that one part were Sadducees and the other Pharisees, he cried out in the council, "Men and brethren, I am a Pharisee, the son of a Pharisee; concerning the hope and resurrection of the dead I am being judged! (Acts 23:6)"

THE RUNAWAY AND THE APOSTLE (Paul Sent Philemon a Letter)

AS THE WEEKS CRAWLED INTO THE AGONY OF MONTHS, loyal friends began to trickle into the Apostle Paul's hellhole with fragile hopes of shining a light upon the dark days of imprisonment. His resolve however would ultimately be strengthened in the unlikeliest of accomplices. Sometime in 55 or early 56 AD, Onesimus paid him a visit. Onesimus was a slave. More precisely, he was a *runaway*. Paul's jail cell in Ephesus was some 150 miles away from Colossae, the whereabouts of his plight, and it is no large leap of imagination to speculate, or rather conclude, that Onesimus had either stolen his owner's purse before beginning his journey or had similarly funded himself along the way. Such offenses were not easily forgiven.

Under Roman law, slaves had no rights; no recognized personhood. The decision *for* morality was not even an attribution of his authority. Accordingly, Onesimus was a piece of furniture with autonomous legs. He came to the right man, because Paul dealt in a new way of thinking. He administered a new covenant which financed a spiritual sort of currency and bankrolled people of circumcised hearts. The outbreak of God's long-promised kingdom on earth was unparalleled. The old way of thinking had begun to unravel at its seams. Not surprisingly for the pagan world, the scattered pockets of new creations which arose in Paul's wake as he zigzagged across the map was nothing more or less than a trail of wreckage. No wonder he found himself rotting in a cell. Onesimus had likely heard that Paul sought to abolish all such discriminations in this bizarre new kingdom he advocated; ruled oddly enough by a crucified Christ. In his very first Epistle, the Apostle had made it known to the church in Galatia, and in turn Jerusalem, that "there is neither Jew nor Greek, there is neither slave nor free man, there is neither male nor female; for you are all one in Christ Jesus (Galatians 3:26)." Perhaps Onesimus wanted *out*.

There was however an added complication to the mere fact that he had entertained a runaway—thereby committing another serious crime. Paul personally knew his slave master. While on a previous mission's

222

trip to Ephesus, his master had been led to Christ. Paul found himself in a multiplex of morality.

One might wonder if Paul considered, even for an isolated moment, setting him free. Had the crucified Christ not overthrown every god; every administration—even the very gates of Hades? He might instruct his friends to aid his plight beyond the Black Sea or the Balkans, the destination of other successful plights. It was worth a thought. Contrarily, if he sent him back, a slave under such circumstances might have an iron collar strapped to his neck, for starters—and alternatively, runaways were often crucified. Then again, where mortal wounds are concerned, there are some things far worse than death.

As his first action, Paul did neither. Paul did what Paul does best. He simply told his unexpected visitor about the crucified Christ. Onesimus was captivated. That the Son of God would descend to the lower parts of the earth, as Paul wrote to the church of Ephesus, in order that He might become a servant—and, ascending on high, lead captive a host of captives—the runaway convert undoubtedly knew now what Paul meant in his letter to Galatia: "there is neither slave nor free man…" Paul was a willing prisoner for Christ, and now, in not so dissimilar a term, so was he. Onesimus had joined the revolution. He was a new creation. Paul saw to it that he had circumcised his heart.

Paul next brilliantly followed through with his second course of action. It is in the Ephesian prison where Paul most likely first wrote to the church at Philippi, and afterwards, where Onesimus is concerned, he wrote his slave master a tender letter. We know the book which ascribes his name today as *The Epistle of Paul to Philemon*.

The unbelieving Onesimus, he wrote, was formerly "useless to you, but now is useful both to you and to me." He was "not now a servant, but *above* a servant," and more, "a brother beloved." Paul further pleaded, "If then you regard me a partner, accept him as you would me. But if he has wronged you in any way or owes you anything, charge that to my account."

Paul then sent him back.

By doing so, essentially, he delivered unto Philemon his *very heart*. "For perhaps he was for this reason separated from you for a while," Paul added, "that you would have him back forever."

Though the author of Acts makes no mention of Paul's imprisonment in Ephesus, Luke carefully describes the very establishment which the Apostle obstinately offended head on. The early Christian would aptly call them *pagan*, but today, his plaintiff would be best identified as stemming from the Occult. Such were the hinges, applicably *now* as then, which the world was and *is* still very much hung upon.

The magistrates of *curious arts*, Luke explains in Acts 19, willingly exposed themselves. In a rather shocking twist, they brought their books of spells into the light and burned them publicly before men. Such news did not sit so well with most, particularly the idol makers. Ephesus housed the temple of Artemis and a statue of which—in the likeness of the goddess—had been sent from heaven, or so went the claim; a gift from Zeus himself.

After quieting the rowdy crowd, idol crafters mostly, the town clerk begged this very claim upon his countrymen: "Men of Ephesus, what man is there after all who does not know that the city of the Ephesians is guardian of the temple of the great Artemis and of the image which fell down from Jupiter?" Apparently, one man's Gospel is another man's bad news. If Paul was to be believed, the crucified Christ had ascended on high, carrying with Him a host of captives. The pantheon of Zeus had mismanaged the affairs of men. He and his kind were stripped of their authority. But that is not to say that the powers of darkness were carefree in plotting their revenge. The town clerk insisted: "these things cannot be spoken against." Paul was learning firsthand that human authorities were merely playthings for the powers which sought to execute their affairs.

Were the rules any different for Paul and Onesimus, or Philemon for that matter; was the One God of Israel not at work through them also? There is a power far greater than any self-will or human revolution—both ironically engendered and willed by the illegitimate gods. Onesimus' 150-mile return journey of pacifism to his slave master proved that point. One might even say he tilled the ground and planted the seeds of another sort of Eden paradise altogether. By picking up his cross and following after the crucified Messiah, as were the Savior's instructions, he became the image bearer—Christ in us.

Jesus was on the move.

We might never know the fate of Onesimus the slave had it not been for a gratuitous mention by Ignatius of Antioch (35-108AD). Fifty years after his conversion at Paul's side in prison, the man named Onesimus became the bishop of Ephesus.

"Though I Speak with the Tongues of Men and of Angles...." THE CHARISMATIC MYSTERY RELIGION ARRIVES AT CORINTH

WE MUST NOT FALL UNDER THE FALSE ASSUMPTION that the followers of religions extrinsic to Christianity, once surrendering to the saving faith, were immediately dissatisfied with paganism. The Mystery religions, which dominated practically every Mediterranean neighborhood where the church sought residency, lacked any serious attempts at doctrine and, just as it is with irrational post-modernists today, paid little attention when consolidating their antithetical deluge of beliefs. They were free to worship other deities, *even* Jesus. No sooner had the Apostle Paul left Corinth than the Dionysian mysteries and devotion to Apollo hemorrhaged into the very church culture he was attempting to spread. So we should not be surprised to find in Corinth "the resounding gong or a clanging cymbal," women who *refused* worshipful silence, and the self-centered praise of ecstasy. Could the love of Christ be found in its pews? Essentially, the Dionysian mysteries had brought with it the charismatic practice of *glossolalia*—or what we know today among Pentecostalism as speaking in tongues. Paul received word of it, and *naturally* he wrote them a letter.

Dionysus, the god of wine and religious ecstasy (being also the Greek counterpart of the Roman Bacchus), was often pictured in the nude, though *womanly* or "man-womanish" facial recognition is attributed, despite his unmistakable masculine organ, and his procession—made up of wild female followers and bearded satyrs with erect penises—would likewise fit the description of any David Bowie rock concert. In his book *Delphi* (1967), Peter Hoyle describes the sort of disciples who later converted to the Corinthian church: "Following the torches as they dipped and swayed in the darkness, they climbed mountain paths with head thrown back and eyes glazed, dancing to the beat of the drum which stirred their blood.... In the state of *ekstasis* or *enqousiasmos*, they abandoned themselves, dancing wildly.... and calling *'Euoi!'* At that moment of intense rapture they became identified with the god himself.... They became filled with his spirit and acquired divine powers."

Ecstasy and the act of speaking in tongues which accompanied it were not merely limited to the cult of Dionysus, but a trivial experience among all mystery religions. The Canaanites spoke in tongues. No surprise, the Egyptians spoke in tongues. In three of Plato's dialogues the Greek philosopher makes references to the ecstatic speech associated with tongues. He calls it "prophetic madness." Its immense popularity is best explained in the fact that here the prophets and priests alone did not hold a private cartel. As possessed by the god—or partaking of the Divine *pneuma* or "breath of life," in Stoic terms—the common neophyte might burst forth into mysterious ejaculations and rapt utterances. In his book *A History of Greek Religion*, Martin Nilsson explains:

> "Not every man can be a miracle-worker and a seer, but most are susceptible to ecstasy, especially as members of a great crowd, which draws the individual along with it and generates in him the sense of being filled with a higher, divine power. This is the literal meaning of the Greek word '*enthusiasm*,' the state in which 'god is in man.' The rising tide of religious feeling seeks to surmount the barrier which separates man from god, it strives to enter into the divine, and it finds ultimate satisfaction only in that quenching of the consciousness in enthusiasm which is the goal of all mysticism."

New Testament scholar Grant R. Osborne writes:

> "In the ancient world, pagan prophets were commonly associated with ecstatic utterances, trances, and frenzied behavior ... In the Hellenistic (ancient Greek) world the prophetess of Delphi and the Sibylline priestess spoke in an unknown or unintelligible speech. Moreover, the Dionysian rites contained a trancelike state as well as *glossolalia* (unintelligible tongue utterances)."

New Testament scholar J.D.G. Dunn also relates:

> "What Celsus (and Lucian) understood as the nonsense [speech] born of madness was accepted at the level of *Volksreligion* [popular religion] as the sure sign that a prophet was genuinely inspired by the god for whom he spoke. By lifting the prophet to this high level of ecstasy, the deity

thereby authenticated the message delivered previously in understandable language. Put simply, among the common people *'tongues'* was recognized as the divine legitimation of prophecy in the Hellenistic age."

Likewise, there is the Cybele-Attis mystery religion to consider. Known among her followers as the Mother of all gods, Mother Nature, or the mistress of life, Cybele's priests and priestesses would become stirred to a dancing frenzy through the clashing of cymbals, beat of drums, and screeching of flutes. Her converts to Christianity would have already been comfortably familiar with picturesque portions of the Gospel account because Attis, her youngest of consorts, was said to be born of a virgin on December 25th. But of greater importance, Emperor Claudius (AD 41-54) introduced a festival of Cybele-Attis, which focused on his self-mutilating death, burial, and springtime resurrection from the grave. Once again, in the century following Paul's first and second letter to the Corinthians, it is no surprise that Montanus, the tongue-speaking heretic, began his career as a priest of Cybele.

After his conversion from the Occult to Christianity, Montanus believed he was a prophet sent by God in the last days immediately before Christ's return. His purpose was to reform Christianity through asceticism, the practice of *glossolalia*, and added revelation from the Holy Spirit, which supplemented the Word. As such, he believed God's kingdom would be set up within his own lifetime, and from the ground floor in his own home village of Pepua. Two so-called prophetesses, Priscilla and Maximilla, were instrumental in the spread of Montanism from Asia-Minor to North Africa. One of Christianities first spin-off cults was a colossal success, because it survived the collapse of Rome, finally struggling for its last breath sometime in the ninth century. While the prophetic movement at first expected an imminent transformation of the Christian world, Montanism soon evolved into sectarianism claiming a "new revelation"—thereby leading the council of Constantinople to reject it as paganism.

The church father Hippolytus (170-235) wrote of the Montanism:

"They have been deceived by two females, Priscilla and Maximilla by name, whom they hold to be prophetesses, asserting that into them the Paraclete sprit entered...They magnify these females above the Apostles and every gift of Grace, so that some of them go so far as to say that there is in them something more than Christ. These people agree with the

Church in acknowledging the Father of the universe to be God and Creator of all things, and they also acknowledge all that the Gospel testifies of Christ. But they introduce novelties in the form of fasts and feasts, abstinences and diets of radishes, giving these females as their authority...."

Likewise, Eusebius (263-339) wrote:

"...In a certain village in that part of Mysia over against Phrygia, Montanus, they say, first exposed himself to the assaults of the adversary through his unbounded lust for leadership. He was one of the recent converts, and he became possessed of a spirit, and suddenly began to rave in a kind of ecstatic trance, and to babble in a jargon, prophesying in a manner contrary to the custom of the Church which had been handed down by tradition from the earliest times.

And he also stirred up two women and filled them with the bastard spirit so that they uttered demented, absurd and irresponsible sayings... And these people blasphemed the whole Catholic Church under heaven, under the influence of their presumptuous spirit, because the Church granted to the spirit of false prophecy neither honor nor admission. For the faithful in Asia met often and in many places throughout Asia upon this matter... and rejected the heresy, and thus these people were expelled from the Church and debarred from communion....

...In his lust for leadership, he became obsessed and would suddenly fall into frenzy and convulsions. He began to be ecstatic and speak and talk strangely, and prophesied contrary to that which was the custom from the beginning of the church. Those who heard him were convinced that he was possessed. They rebuked him and forbade him to speak, remembering the warning of the Lord Jesus to be watchful because false prophets would come"

Sadly, the church father Tertullian (160-220), a prolific early Christian author from Carthage in the Roman province of Africa, instrumental in shaping the vocabulary of Christian theology, ultimately abandoned the faith. Later in his life, possibly after a dispute with Roman bishops, Tertullian marked himself as an unrepentant heretic by adopting Montanism. His awe-inspired portrait of the cult might easily describe any charismatic church today.

"We have among us now a sister who has been granted gifts of revelations, which she experiences in church during the Sunday services through ecstatic vision in the Spirit... And after these people have been dismissed at the end of the service it is her custom to relate to us what she has seen ... 'Among other things,' says she, 'there was shown to me a soul in bodily form, and it appeared like a spirit; but it was no mere something, void of qualities, but rather a thing which could be grasped, soft and translucent and ethereal colour, in form at all points human.'"

Speaking in tongues, I am told, brings with it feelings of euphoria, and love and goodness and power of spirit and all that might be attributed to *experiencing*God. While proclaiming these Mystery religion *origins* as merely coincidental, and furthermore irrelevant to their lives, I have heard many charismatics proudly proclaim: "The Baptists read the Gospels but skip right over Acts!" Perhaps it is the Pentecostals who are not reading Acts with the proper monocle, particularly the second chapter, where-as Luke records the birthday of the church:

"And when the day of Pentecost was fully come, they were all with one accord in one place. And suddenly there came a sound from heaven as of a rushing mighty wind, and it filled all the house where they were sitting. And there appeared unto them cloven tongues like as of fire, and it sat upon each of them. And they were all filled with the Holy Ghost, and began to speak with other tongues, as the Spirit gave them utterance. (Acts 2:1-4)"

Modern-day Pentecostals would have us believe the Apostles were participating in the babbling absurdities of the raving mad men found within their own congregation and personal devotions today. And yet I have *never*heard a single "Spirit-filled" individual in my lifetime unexpectedly bursting out in the unlearned dialect of an ethnic foreigner so that the Gospel of Jesus Christ might be preached to them. The miraculous event recorded in Acts was a unique wonder; a feast fulfillment of prophecy centralized in Jerusalem and one-time event for all; a pronunciation of judgement on the Jews who rejected their Messiah as the Gentile age of grace began—in other words, the first and final Pentecost of human history. What we discover here is the *true* Biblical gift of tongues. It involves *actual* linguistics. No unintelligible babbling—just real words. Everything else is a counterfeit. So let us read on:

"And there were dwelling at Jerusalem Jews, devout men, out of every nation under heaven. Now when this was noised abroad, the multitude came together, and were confounded, because that every man heard them speak in his own language. And they were all amazed and marvelled, saying one to another, Behold, are not all these which speak Galilaeans? And how hear we every man in our own tongue, wherein we were born? (Acts 2:5-8)."

Paul clearly did not have the ecstatic ravings of a charismatic in mind when *insisting* that an interpreter be present to translate the *unknown* tongue (1 Corinthians 14:13). In actuality, the Apostle criticized the Corinthians for employing their tongue-gifts as communication with God rather than men. "For he that speaketh in an unknown tongue speaketh not unto men, but unto God: for no man understandeth him; howbeit in the spirit he speaketh mysteries (2 Corinthians 14:2)." Nothing about the authors comment suggests that the tongues of their former religion should be utilized as a prayer language. Paul wrote with irony. Speaking in tongues without an interpreter is a futile practice, because only God could possibly know if anything was said. Esctatic babbling shouldn't even be considered a spiritual gift! (1 Corinthians 14:1).

"But he that prophesieth speaketh unto men to edification, and exhortation, and comfort. He that speaketh in an unknown tongue edifieth himself; but he that prophesieth edifieth the church (1 Corinthians 14:3-4)."

Quite contrarily, spiritual gifts were never intended for tickling God's ear, nor for personal gratification. In the *true* Biblical speaking of tongues, others were edified by the message. The Apostle Peter made that certain when he wrote:

"As every man hath received the gift, even so minister the same one to another, as good stewards of the manifold grace of God (1 Peter 4:10)."

When the Apostle Paul first arrived to Corinth, he came "not with *excellency of speech* or of *wisdom*, declaring unto [them] the testimony of God. For [he] determined not to know anything among [them], save Jesus Christ, and Him crucified. (1 Corinthians 2:1-2)" Here Paul apparently pleads some ignorance as to their occult perversions. The Apostle was not a neophyte. He was never initiated, and therefore knew as little of their secrets and heavily guarded rites as historians do today.

We know of the widespread usage of *tongues* because it was not hidden knowledge utilized only by the learned. However, always butting heads with the pitfalls of human philosophy and the willful ignorance it produces; Paul rarely wastes an opportunity. The Apostle contrasts the hidden nature of their wisdom with another mystery altogether. Dr. H.W. House explains:

"In heathen religions this word (*mystery*) referred to the hidden secrets of the gods which only the initiated could know. Those initiated into such mysteries claimed to have contact with the spirit world through emotional excitement, revelations, the working of miracles and the speaking of unknown words revealed by the spirits."

Dr. House further writes:

"The term *mystery* is used in the New Testament but with a difference force ... In the New Testament it refers to the things of God that could not be known by man except through revelation from God. The revelation given of these things by the Holy Spirit is not obscure but clear and given to be communication to God's people (1 Corinthians 2:1-16). It is not given privately in unknown words."

Most charismatics believe the ambiguous gifting of tongues is a private prayer language belonging to the heavenly realm of angels and with God. There is no evidence in Scripture that angels use a heavenly language—*nada*. And God certainly never spoke to His prophets, psalmists, Gospel writers or Apostles in this proposed heavenly language. So why do charismatics participate in the deception—so that they might experience the illusion of love? When writing of the tongues of angels, Paul was making a hypothetical case. He couldn't possibly understand all mysteries and all knowledge, which the Corinthian Christians—former neophytes—were spewing. The counterfeit tongues at Corinth was a self-serving lust of the flesh, and in no way loving. Their pagan spirituality—the Kundalini spirit they spewed from their mouths—wasn't even on par with the rhythm band in a kindergarten concert.

"Though I speak with the tongues of men and of angels, and have not charity, I am become as sounding brass, or a tinkling cymbal. And though I have the gift of prophecy, and understand all mysteries, and all knowledge; and though I have all faith, so that I could remove mountains, and have not charity, I am nothing. And though I bestow all my goods to feed the poor, and though I give my body to be burned, and have not charity, it profiteth me nothing. (1 Corinthians 13:1-3)"

William Samarin, professor of linguistics at the University of Toronto, is one of many men who have conducted studies on *glossolalia*. His conclusions agree with the multitude. What we are hearing today in private prayer and worship services is *not* language—and therefore cannot be the Biblical language of tongues. In *Tongues of Men and Angels*, he summarized:

"Over a period of five years I have taken part in meetings in Italy, Holland, Jamaica, Canada, and the United States. I have observed old-fashioned Pentecostals and neo-Pentecostals; I have been in small meets at private homes as well as in mammoth public meetings; I have seen such different cultural settings as are found among the Puerto Ricans of the Bronx, the snake handlers of the Appalachians [and] Russian Molakans in Los Angeles... Glossolalia is indeed like language in some ways, but this is only because the speaker (unconsciously) wants it to be like language. Yet in spite of superficial similarities, glossolalia is fundamentally *not* language."

Love never fails. Yet *"if* there are tongues, they will be done away with. (1 Corinthians 13:8)" Indeed, *true* tongues have been done away with. Love however never will. The supernatural pronunciation of any given language at a whim, as was miraculously accomplished and recorded in Jerusalem, is no more. The church is once-born. The Gospel has gone forth. Augustine was certainly not speaking of the counterfeit tongues found in the Mystery religion of Corinth and later Montanism when he concluded—once and for all:

"How then, brethren, because he that is baptized in Christ, and believes on Him, does not now speak in the tongues of all nations, are we not to believe that he has received the Holy Ghost? God forbid that our heart should be tempted by this faithlessness... Why is it that no man speaks in the tongues of all nations? Because the Church itself now speaks in the tongues of all nations. Before, the Church was in one nation, where it spoke in the tongues of all. By speaking then in the tongues of all, it signified what was to come to pass; that by growing among the nations, it would speak in the tongues of all."

And yet, the counterfeit Kundalini spirit *lives on*.

"This Is My Body..." | MITHRAS, MUSHROOMS, AND OUTER SPACE (Also Sprach Zarathustra)

WE COME NOW TO THE UNTOLD STORY OF EARLY CHRISTENDOM. The Roman cult known as Mithras didn't always function in the belly-crawling muck and mire of a secret society. No sooner had the religion of Jesus the Christ expanded from Jerusalem into Antioch, Ephesus, Corinth, and the political center of Rome when so too the myth of Mithra, that ancient sun god identified with Sol Invictus, and whose foretold virgin birth was celebrated on the 25th of December, found its own captivated audience. Resistance was everywhere. No matter what neighborhood marketplace or back ally residence the Christians sought recluse to worship in—the Mithrians seemed to meet them there, and in superior numbers. Something had to give. Indeed, it did. And in the centuries to follow, there would be no shortage of human sacrifices. Blood flowed in the coliseum.

Throughout this nightmarish assault on Christ's followers, similarities between the two opposing faiths were at times so striking that our spiritual fathers had no choice but to claim Satan's plagiarized-part in the penmanship of the Mithrian doctrines. Much like Christianity, the god Mithras—known affectionately by his followers as the "Light of the World"—became an intermediary with the one god of the Greco-Roman world, much like Christ with the Father. Even they, the worshipers of Helios, partook in a sacramental meal—not common bread or drink, mind you, but something of the symbolic nature which, when ingested, promoted communion with their inner-divinity. To this Justin Martyr confirms:

> "And this food is called among us the Eucharist...which the wicked devils have imitated in the mysteries of Mithras, commanding that the same thing be done. Bread and cup of water are made flesh and blood with certain incantations of the one who is being initiated (*First Apology*)."

All things considered, Satan is long-suffering in his scheming. See, over a millennium before the first advent of Christ, the Prophet Moses not only had an adversary in Pharaoh, but a sparring-partner of another theological nature entirely with Zarathustra. While Moses pointed the children of Israel to YAHWEH, who was not in any means whatsoever to be mistaken *as* His creation, the man who would come to be known by the Greeks as Zoroaster entrusted his followers with yet another branding of monotheism—namely creation itself, the sun god. In 1896, Richard Strauss would compose a symphonic poem, Also sprach Zarathustra, Opus 30, based on the writings of Nihilist philosopher Friedrich Nietzsche. It also involved an epic opening musical number which would ironically be craftily utilized as a central theme in the space-time indoctrination and Hollywood masterpiece, writer Arthur C. Clarke and director Stanley Kubrick's 1968 film, *2001: A Space Odyssey*. Wrote Nietzsche in his parable, *Thus Spake Zarathustra*:

> "Thou great star! What would be they happiness if thou hadst not those for whom thou shinest!"

In their book, *Mushrooms, Myth, & Mithras: The Drug Cult that Civilized Europe*, Authors Carl A.P. Ruck, Mark A. Hoffman, and Jose Alfredo Gonzalez Celdran disclose, or perhaps naively confess, that the three great early antichrists of Christendom would arise from Zoroastrianism influence, which had now developed into the cult of Mithras. Together all three authors wrote:

> "Augustus [Caesar] styled himself as the putative son of Apollo and once officiated at a sacramental meal dressed as the Sun with twelve of his colleagues costumed as the signs of the zodiac." Similarly, "Nero was depicted in a sun-chariot surrounded by golden stars. He also installed an enormous stature of himself in his Golden House as the Sun God." And finally, "Julian the Apostate (361-363), in his attempt to reverse the Conversion to Christianity and revive the old pagan religions....He had a Mithraeum erected in his place in Constantinople. Like Nero, he saw himself as the incarnation of the god Mithras."

It was actually during the short reign of Julian the Apostate that "adherents of the briefly restored pan religions lynched George the Arian, bishop of Alexandria (later to become Saint George) when he attempted to build a Christian church above one of their underground sanctuaries. According to the legend, the Mithracists tied him to a camel, tore him to pieces, and then burnt him with the beast (Mushrooms, Myth, & Mithras)."

At any rate, with the cult of Mithras, Satan, whom we shall also refer to here and other places as Apollo, had his first great competing counter-religion in the age of grace. But when the two finally bled together through order of Emperor Constantine, the devil had the best of both worlds. Now his agents saturated the church within every rank and file, and rather than simply persecuting an enemy that seemed to defy logic by thriving on their own martyrdom, Apollo could finally act as the man behind the curtain and pull the strings with the carefree ease of a humbug. Satan is a loser.

It is believed by many and just as often quoted that the cult of Mithras found the core of its doctrines some four-hundred years before Christ with the Greek philosopher Plato. Unlike the Hebrews, Plato believed the Earth was not established upon the waters (Psalm 24:2), but rather was shaped as a spherical globe. Such a concept was not strange to the nature worshiping occult. Even the esoteric knowledge found within Egypt's Mystery Schools might very well have taught—and I'm inclined to believe this is true as a sort of insiders knowledge—that the shape of their master's Earth was not a flat one. But at any rate, Plato worshiped creation. This was evident by the seven celestial spheres—eight really— which he described in great detail as part of *Timaeus* and *The Republic* dialogues, and the very model which would later be developed by Ptolemy and Copernicus. Essentially, the astronomical realms surrounding us, which spins around a fixed central axis aptly named the Spindle, was intrinsically associated with and specifically served the transmigration of souls. For Plato, each planet was divine. And furthermore every human soul was given assignment to a particular star, which they would travel to but eventually return from when duties demanded their reincarnation on Earth. Spiritually then, every man was capable of travelling through the realm of the gods, and ultimately to the realm of the Demiurge himself. Have we not heard this tall-tale before— that we all originated from stardust?

The space race, it seems, was born with Plato.

"Mithraism initiated its members through seven stages of transcendence, culminating with an ecstatic vision in which one journeyed into a sacred realm where one experienced the entire pattern of the Universe, an experience that was expressed in the prevalent Roman philosophical system known as Stoicism (*Mushrooms, Myth, & Mithras*)."

What separated the Eucharist of the Mithream with the Christian church was the item of digestion. Mainly, mushrooms. Humphry Osmond, who in the 1960's coined the term 'psychedelic,' described such a divine and forbidden fruit as the ability "to fathom Hell or soar angelic." Or as Socrates is quoted, "Our greatest blessings come to us by way of madness, provided madness is given us by way of divine gift."

The Nicodemites of this thriving occult, many of whom would twiddle their thumbs in weekly mass, perhaps even give the benediction, would then secretly meet in underground cave-like dwellings resembling tombs, all of which were lined with tubs rather than crypts. Many such ceremonial chambers have been discovered across Europe. Even the Vatican—and this should come as no surprise—was built upon one. In such a place they would eat the body of Mithras, lie down in the water-filled tubs, and very soon ascend through holes in the ceiling to the stars above. If they were especially lucky, astral beings, aka the Watchers, would communicate with them on their astral journeys, perhaps even give a nickel and dime tour. The fruit of the Copernican deception was already secured.

I have made it known that the Egyptians, being worshipers of nature, likely saw the Earth as a sphere. Not surprising, since their fallen gods would have revealed it to them as such. In the Egyptian Book of the Dead, mushrooms were also employed. They were aptly labeled "the food of the gods," or "celestial food," and in communion terms, "the flesh of the gods." James Arthur, in his book, *Mushrooms and Mankind,* confirms Mithras ties to the Mystery Schools of ancient Egypt:

> "The religion of Mithra centered around the initiate's ability to communally, astral-travel. Of course the out-of-body experience was facilitated through the eating of the sacred meal. After consumption, the initiates could traverse the galaxies, witnessing, as the ancient Egyptians, first hand, the reality that the spirit of the human being is not restricted to the physical universe, or the physical body for that matter. This is the true revelation of the immortality of the soul, or at least the realization of such. This concept is so similar to the Egyptian initiatory rites that it is solid evidence some of the hidden traditions of the ancients did migrate into later incarnations of various religious orders......There are a number of hieroglyphic

depictions of plants (many of which are psychedelic) on walls and within texts throughout Egypt. This is to be expected, yet this goes undetected or dismissed by most who are studying Egypt and its religious writings ... The pillars that are at every temple in Egypt are shaped like giant mushrooms. These are shaped like the Amanita, some are shaped like Psilocybe. Others look like tree fungus and are decorated with pictures of an incredible variety of plants."

Cicero (106 BC–43 BC), a Roman politician and lawyer, gives such an account in *Dream of Scipio*. It not only describes the Platonic experience and Mithrian excursion into the outer spheres, but oddly mirrors NASA's own testimony to the satellite imagery which God has made otherwise impossible—and forbidden—to see with the naked eye today.

"And I looked on every side I saw other things transcendently glorious and wonderful. There were stars which we never see from here below, and all the stars were vast far beyond what we have ever imagined. The earth itself indeed looked to me so small as to make me ashamed of our Empire, which was a mere point on its surface."

Shroom or no shroom, we call this practice astral-projection. No action of leaving one's body behind in the bathtub or bed is complete without an accommodating silver cord, assuring each astral-projector a safe return to his or her physical body, just as an unborn child is bound to an umbilical cord. It is a symbolic gesture also shared by the astronaut. For the disciple of Mithras, his salvation was assured through a personal relationship with the cosmos as perceived through his pineal gland—the third-eye. By mastering spiritual ascension through the seven planetary spheres—the eighth being heaven—a Mithrian could guarantee his souls passage after he died. I guess faith in Jesus Christ, particularly His atoning sacrifice for our sins, is not worth considering for such an apostate.

There is an entire cryptozoology catalog of inter-dimensional beings to be discovered in the practice of astral-projection; astral citizens so bizarre in character and description—creatures with fish lips, bulging eyes, and leathery bat-like ears but long as rabbits, for starters—as to make Dr. Seuss either jealous or raving mad for competition. I have read enough firsthand accounts of audacious explorers to know these fallen angels and demons—though they are rarely recognized by the practitioner as such—have agreed to hold hands with them on their cosmic voyage through the clay-like canyons of Mars, even daring to go so far as Neptune's atmosphere of blueish hydrogen, helium, and methane. Such spiritual enthusiasts worship only nature. And wherever nature is worshiped, as the Egyptians have proven, there Satan and his fallen spirits can and will be found. The entire Helios-model, by which the Earth forms a spherical shape and revolves around Apollo, is an act of worship with the created, not the Creator.

God was not being suggestive when He spoke unto Israel:

"If there be found among you, within any of thy gates which the Lord thy God giveth thee, man or woman, that hath wrought wickedness in the sight of the Lord thy God, in transgressing his covenant, And hath gone and served other gods, and worshipped them, either the sun, or moon, or any of the host of heaven, which I have not commanded; And it be told thee, and thou hast heard of it, and enquired diligently, and, behold, it be true, and the thing certain, that such abomination is wrought in Israel: Then shalt thou bring forth that man or that woman, which have committed that wicked thing, unto thy gates, even that man or that woman, and shalt stone them with stones, till they die (Deuteronomy 17:2-5)."

Israel's King Josiah, who later sought to restore true worship with God, dismantled the high places among his own people—where idolatrous priests, burning incense to Baal, sought relationship with the sun and moon, the constellations, and all the starry hosts (2 Kings 23:5). It is indeed perplexing to discern the cult of Mithras out in the open of a so-called "Christian nation"—the United States of America, in case you were wondering—fully illuminated by the counterfeit "Light of the World" their descendants worshiped, yet we have seen no such king here in the United States willing to take up Josiah's task. NASA has beguiled us. In the most crafty and serpentine fashion, a malevolent priesthood has set our sights on the high places which godly men of old once so nobly dismantled.

We stand here at the crossroads where the ancient Helios-worshiper meets the priests of Scientism, awaiting the return of Augustus, Nero, or Julian the Apostate—mainly, Apollo or the son of Apollo—the final antichrist. All of society which inhabits the fictitious globe, revealed by way of mushrooms and fallen angelic beings, and the very beast government which defies the Spirit's own Testimony concerning Himself and His creation by wickedly governing over the globe, already revolve around him—Apollo that is, so that his coming, or his offspring's coming, will in no way defy what we already perceive as natural.

A swift conclusion to this heliocentric lie has already been promised. Its fate is sealed. We know what will happen to its wide-swath of prophets, priests, and ruling principals, all of whom lord their so-called cosmic knowledge over us simple Bible-believing folk from the lecture halls of academia, just as it has been since the Mysteries were fermented within the temples and among the hieroglyphs of Egypt. Unless they should repent, and indeed there is still time, their destruction is bound to the coming antichrist and his confederacy of conspirators. Jeremiah prophesies:

> "At that time, saith the Lord, they shall bring out the bones of the kings of Judah, and the bones of his princes, and the bones of the priests, and the bones of the prophets, and the bones of the inhabitants of Jerusalem, out of their graves: And they shall spread them before the sun, and the moon, and all the host of heaven, whom they have loved, and whom they have served, and after whom they have walked, and whom they have sought, and whom they have worshipped: they shall not be gathered, nor be buried; they shall be for dung upon the face of the earth (Jeremiah 8:1-2)."

They choose death rather than life.

"The Contagious Superstition..." THE GOSPEL OF PLATO ACCORDING TO THE APOSTOLIC FATHERS

1

IT IS A LITTLE KNOWN FACT THAT THE CELESTIAL HALO, which has adorned the portraits of so many *heavenly-residing* saints, did not originate with the Christian religion. For this we must first look to the Egyptian Mysteries; to the hidden knowledge of Zarathustra; to the heroes of Homer's literature; as far-east as ancient India and Buddhism; to the worship of Apollo in Rome, and perhaps most importantly of all, Apollo's counterpart—to the religion of Mithras. By garnishing one's skull with the coveted *halo* we are expected to believe the venerated saint has ascended through the seven luminaries to the eighth and final layer of heaven itself. If the artists' rendition is spiritually accurate, the saint of his devotion now resides *beyond* the orb of Plato's universe.

I am often reminded that the convictions of the educated—and not to be overlooked, the *initiated*—were groomed with a globe and the literature of Plato to guide them. With this understanding of history I must concur—for the most part. Plato has dictated much. But there is another story rarely considered. It is the untold account of the pew parishioner, the often illiterate and competently *uninitiated* soul; essentially those without a voice for public discourse and the necessary education to accommodate it. The belief in a mortal soul and a flat, stationary earth—though perhaps not simultaneously held together—is of interest here; a thorn which has pestered the skulls and splintered the brightest minds of university alumni for several dozen generations.

Despite its occultist origin, the Christian storyteller sought to add one unique contribution to the haloed saint. This should be of particular interest here, because the portrait of a living saint—while his soul still animated the body—had not yet become intimately familiar with the orb of the universe. The shape of the earth was still his concern.

For this reason, the living Christian was crowned with a *square* halo.

2

PETER WAS DEAD. PAUL WAS DEAD. JOHN WAS DEAD. With the advent of the second-century the last of the Apostles—sanctioned mouth-pieces of God—were unquestionably buried and dead. In their absence, Christianity would expand into Egypt and Greece, to every sea port across the Mediterranean, but not everything of the Hebrew faith remained. For this reason, scouring through the writings of the early church is a fluorescent though somewhat jarring exercise. Those who immediately followed in the second centuries dawning hours, particularly apostolic fathers Ignatius and Polycarp, best functioned by pointing their congregations to the traditions of the Apostles, begging that they strive to live in light of Jesus' teachings. And yet, despite the destruction of the Temple in Jerusalem and Judea's violent end, the promise of Christ's return had not been fulfilled. The occult still reigned supreme from Rome. Actually, the worst was still to come. And the pressing question on everyone's mind seemed to be: "*What now?*"

Philosophers would answer that call.

As the road to Rome was slowly lighted with the saving Gospel, the learned men who bore the torches did not give up philosophy. Rather, it is said they became *better* philosophers. When we attempt to estimate the wide-ranging scope of Christianity today in its dizzying plethora of genres, it is easy for us to assume that it has always been this way—that the true narrative of the Bible has won over easily enough. We might even begin to think this version of Christianity had to have prevailed— how could it not? And yet in hindsight, a careful examination of their unapologetic affair with Plato is nothing short of criminal.

The Greek-speaking Gentile Justin Martyr (110-165) was born in Judea, not far from Jacob's Well, where Jesus had offered the Samaritan woman "living water" some 80 years earlier. Martyr was a seeker of *philosophical* truth. Naturally, he became a Platonist. Then one day he was out walking along the seashore when an old man introduced him to Jesus of Nazareth. Martyr was convinced. Like the Apostles before him, Martyr devoted the rest of his life in defense of the Gospel. But quite unlike the Apostles, Martyr did not disrobe of his philosopher's cloak. In order to win converts, the Platonist from Samaria advertised Christianity as the "true philosophy." Perhaps more brazenly, he embraced the ancient bread crumbs of Greek wisdom long before Christ's incarnation as the "seeds of Christianity." His conversion was indeed a strange one, because for Justin Martyr, Socrates and Plato were *unknowing* Christians.

To this day historians tend to promote the Protestant point of view, particularly church historian Adolph von Harnack (1851-1930), who emphasized a new beginning with the fathers of the second century. While the church still remained in its infant stages, the simple Gospel of Jesus Christ was overwhelmed with Greek philosophy. Despite widespread use of the phrase *immortal soul*, this terminology, along with *globe* earth, is found nowhere in the Bible. One must read Holy Writ through the lensing of Plato, its principal exponent, who was led to them through Orphic and Eleusinian mysteries in which Babylonian and Egyptian views were strangely blended, in order to nurture these conclusions. For Harnack, the post-Apostolic church embraced Hellenization. With the rare exception of John of Damascus and Gregory Palamas, who were ostensibly Aristotelians, and the untold Christians who embraced the Bible's *mortal* narrative, Plato ruled supreme.

3

IRENAEUS HAD HEARD THE PREACHING OF POLYCARP, who in turn had personally known John the Revelator. Only twice removed from the Apostles, **Irenaeus (140-202)** clung to the Hebrew position of the soul, which was in no way affected by the Hellenizers. This should be duly noted. If Irenaeus is to be believed, the early church held Platonism to be an ignorant and heretical doctrine which went "beyond the prearranged plan for the exaltation of the just," and whose members, "some who are reckoned among the orthodox...affirm that immediately upon their death they shall pass above the heavens and the Demiurge, and go to the Mother or to the Father whom they have feigned," and by doing so, "disallow a resurrection affecting the whole man." For Irenaeus, the elementary doctrine of the resurrection, which the Apostle Paul once affirmed, seemed to be slipping from the faith. It is for these very reasons that Irenaeus laboriously argued for an apostolic succession.

In *Against Heresies* he wrote:

"Some who are reckoned among the orthodox go beyond the prearranged plan for the exaltation of the just, and are ignorant of the methods by which they are disciplined beforehand for

242

incorruption, they thus entertain heretical opinions. For the heretics, despising the handiwork of God, and not admitting the salvation of their flesh, while they also treat the promise of god contemptuously, and pass beyond God altogether in the sentiments they form, affirm that immediately upon their death they shall pass above the heavens and the Demiurge, and go to the Mother or to the Father whom they have feigned. Those persons, therefore, who disallow a resurrection affecting the whole man, and as far as in them lies remove it from the midst [of the Christian scheme], how can they be wondered at, if again they know nothing as to the plan of the resurrection? For they do not choose to understand, that if these things are as they say, the Lord Himself, in whom they profess to believe, did not rise again upon the third day; but immediately upon His expiring on the cross, undoubtedly departed on high, leaving His body to the earth. But the case was that for three days He dwelt in the place where the dead were…as Jonas remained three days and three nights in the whale belly."

Historians have long noted the mortalist doctrine in the early church. The humble opinion held by the less educated and *uninitiated* constituted what we might refer to today as the *silent majority*, and for this belief Plato cannot be held responsible. When Justin Martyr met the old man along the seashore, the philosopher understood that becoming a Christian meant castrating his Hellenized faith in the immortal soul, so as not to jeopardize the good news of the resurrection. That Martyr understood the majority Christian position held by those who personally knew and were handed the saving Gospel by the Apostles is also duly noted by historians. The mortal soul awaiting the resurrection "in the place where the dead were," as Irenaeus would say, further elaborating, "as Jonas remained three days and three nights in the whale belly," is a Biblically grounded position untainted by the dark speeches of Hellenization.

Martyr did not have his wires crossed when he understood the immortal soul doctrine to be in conflict with the Gospel message of the resurrection, nor when he wrote of the Platonists: "They who maintain the wrong opinion say that there is no resurrection of the flesh." As in the case of a yoke of oxen, he further explained; if one or the other is loosed from the yoke, neither of them can plough alone. "So neither can the soul or body alone effect anything, if they be unyoked from their communion. The soul can have no separate, active existence." For what is man, Martyr pondered, but the reasonable animal composed of body and soul?

243

"Is the soul by itself man? No; but the soul of man. Would the body be called man? No; but it is called the body of man. If then neither of these is by itself man, but that which is made up of the two together is called man, and God has called man to life and resurrection, He has called not a part, but the whole, which is the soul *and* body."

The early defender of the faith concluded: "Why do we any longer endure those unbelieving arguments and fail to see that we are retrograding when we listen to such an argument as this: that the soul is immortal, but the body mortal, and incapable of being revived. For this we used to hear from Plato, even before we learned the truth." Martyr seemed to grasp what very few others care to address. "If then the Saviour said this and proclaimed salvation to the soul alone, what new thing beyond what we heard from Plato, did He bring us?"

Justin Martyr's indiscrete alliance with the Platonists proved an odd choice. Eventually, Martyr would be silenced and oppressed by the very philosophy-pushers he sought to promote. In as little as a few short centuries after the last of the Apostles had died, the Greek and Alexandrian teachers whom Irenaeus and Martyr had branded as heretics turned the tables on them so that the apostolic commentators were now the heretics.

4

TO EVEN BEGIN AND LIST EVERY THEOLOGIAN WHO SUBSCRIBES to the immortal soul doctrine would fill an entire book. I confess I began to do it—list them on paper, that is—but I shan't for a shortage of trees. One truth however is certain. From its very conception, other doctrinal complications arose. If the soul was truly immortal, then it could neither die nor be destroyed. The *anguish* of hell apparently was eternal. Well—not necessarily. From its outset, the introduction of the immortal soul doctrine aroused another Scriptural perversion. We know it today as Universalism. But for the throngs of Christians today who embrace the immortal soul doctrine and yet shy away from the heretical, very few come to realize that their extra-biblical belief and Universalism, as well as reincarnation, were all three betrothed together.

For this we must first look to Alexandra, the epicenter of learning, intellectual discourse, and most importantly of all the adulterous Mystery Schools, all of which served as a theological nurturing ground for the early church before the rise of the Roman Church. Its great library contained upwards of 700,000 volumes, and it is speculated that at one time 14,000 students were assembled. **Pantaenus the Philosopher (120-216)** can be found there among a plethora of Christian successors. Like Justin Martyr in Judea and later Rome, Pantaenus was another such convert, a brilliant scholar, who attempted to reconcile his new faith with Greek philosophy. According to one ancient source, Pantaenus had begun his career as a Stoic philosopher and, after his conversion, found it necessary to apply such teachings to his newfound faith. Though not nearly so widely known today as Martyr, he is a significant figure for his role in the Catechetical School of Alexandra. His learning center, the Didascalia, would go down in history as the first school of Christian religion anywhere in the world, and its influence in the development of Christian theology cannot be overstated. For starters, the first translation of the New Testament from Aramaic and Greek into Coptic, the language of the Christian Egyptians, can be claimed here. Though here it must be noted that the Didascalia was not exclusive to Christian learning; rather, it was open to everyone who sought Greek wisdom. As such, instruction did not rely on Scripture alone, but the classics, including all manner of scientific inquiry, probably even Occult learning. .

Truly, Alexandria was Christianity's cradle.

In his book, *Universalism*, author J. W. Hanson wrote: "Those who are truly called the fathers and founders of the Christian church were not the simpleminded fishermen of Galilee, but men who had received the highest education which could be obtained at the time—that is Greek education. In Alexandria, at the time the very center of the world, it had either to vanquish the world or to vanish. Christianity came no doubt from the small room in the house of Mary, where many were gathered together praying, but as early as the Second Century it became a very different Christianity in the Catechetical school of Alexandria. What Clement had most at heart was not the letter but the spirit, not the historical events, but their deeper meaning in universal history."

After a missions trip to India, Pantaenus eventually returned bearing a copy of the Gospel of Matthew in Hebrew, which had originally been carried there a century earlier by Bartholomew—this according to Clement. It is however at his departure in 189 that Clement of Alexandria (150-215) was selected as the second dean of the

Like Martyr and his teacher Pantaenus before him, **Clement of Alexandria (150-215)** believed that Greek philosophy was the handmaiden of *saving* theology. This should not surprise anyone concerning his upbringing and education in Athens. Actually, Clement was influenced by Hellenistic philosophy to a greater extent than any Christian theologian of his time. "Before the advent of the Lord, philosophy was necessary to the Greeks for righteousness," he wrote in *Stromata*. "For God is the cause of all good things, but of some primarily, as of the Old and New Testaments; and of others by consequence, as philosophy. Perchance, too, philosophy was given to the Greeks directly and primarily, till the Lord should call the Greeks. For this was a schoolmaster to bring the Hellenic mind, as the law the Hebrews to Christ. Philosophy, therefore, was a preparation, paving the way for him who is perfected in Christ."

While the common unlearned and *uninitiated* man heard gladly the simple story of the Gospel, the scholar and the philosopher were attracted by the genius of Clement and more importantly, Origen after him. Writes Hanson: "The materialistic philosophy of Epicureanism, that happiness is the highest good and can best be procured in a well-regulated enjoyment of the pleasures of life; the Pantheistic system of Stoicism, that one should live within himself, superior to the accidents of time; the logical Aristotelianism, and the Platonism that regarded the universe as the work of a Supreme Spirit, in which man is a permanent individuality possessing a spark of the divinity that would ultimately purify him and elevate him to a higher life; and that virtue would accelerate and sin retard his upward progress--these different systems all had their devotees, but the noblest of all, the Platonic, was most influential with the Alexandrine fathers, though, like Clement, they exercised a wise and rational variety, in adopting the best features of each system."

To this effect, Clement once quipped: "And by philosophy I mean not the Stoic, nor the Platonic, nor the Epicurean, nor that of Aristotle; but whatever any of these sects had said that was fit and just, that taught righteousness with a divine and religious knowledge, this I call mixed philosophy."

Clement was not willing to accept punishment if it endangered his immortal soul doctrine. He saw no other way around eternity than to embrace Universalism. Clement insisted that punishment in Hades was remedial and restorative, and that punished souls were cleansed by a spiritual fire, which acted as an agent to purify the immortal soul and beckon its gaze once again to the Creator. "God's punishments are saving and disciplinary (in Hades) leading to conversion, and choosing rather the repentance than the death of the sinner," he wrote. Elsewhere he

246

concluded: "We can set no limits to the agency of the Redeemer to redeem, to rescue, to discipline in his work, and so will he continue to operate after this life."

It is evident that Clement had confused and compromised the saving faith with elements of the Mystery religion which likely clothed him. Scholars have had little effort equating his doctrine with the three degrees of the Neoplatonic mysteries: purification, initiation, and vision. Perhaps this is why even pagans were aroused by this new teaching and willing to answer their invitation. The students who roamed the halls of the Didascalia would have come to learn the "new song" of the Logos, the Word of God, as personified by Christ, so that they might awaken all that is good in the human soul and lead it off leash to the boundless possibilities of immortality.

Clement furthermore argued for an equality of sexes on the basis that Jesus Christ is neither male nor female, and that God the Father has both male and female aspects. Then again, he advanced Gnosticism. His *Miscellanies* was a disciplined instruction for "Christian Gnostics." Among his works he gladly confessed that Plato and Pythagoras were taught by the Egyptians, and though this seems a rather obvious conclusion to make today, Clement likely had an inside knowledge of it.

But that is not all of his extra-Biblical teaching which derived from Alexandrian influence. Clement was a true Platonist. In *the Paedagogus*, or *the Instructor*, the theologian wrote concerning the shape of the earth:

> "Out of a confused heap who didst create
>
> This ordered sphere, and from the shapeless mass
>
> Of matter didst the universe adorn."

Like the immortal soul doctrine, it can be said that *globe* earth entered into the pantheon of Christian thinking soon after the simple fishermen from Galilee were dead and buried. The Universalism of Clement and Origen after him, as well as "their successors, must, beyond question, have been taught by their great predecessor, Pantaenus," Hanson assures us, "and there is every reason to believe that the Alexandrine school had never known any contrary teaching, from its foundation."

Even today, at least to some degree, the Didascalia's lectures are still in session.

AMONG THE MANY DECORATIVE ACCUSATIONS heaved upon the infant Christian faith, one particular claim was presented, rather early on, which can be deemed as true. Christians refused to worship the gods. As early as 111 AD, Pliny the Younger, governor of Bithynia along the Black Sea, wrote Emperor Trajan a letter. He accused Christians of endangering the whole of the empire on the basis that they were a *superstitious* people. Pliny's implications fell in perfect synchronicity with the Roman historian Tacitus and Suetonius, both contemporaries of his, who wrote of Nero's decision to persecute Christianity on the grounds of being a "pernicious superstition."

This is not to say that the Roman did not take religion seriously. On the contrary, they were expected to uphold religion as a personal and public devotion—a responsibility of each citizen in order that the social, economic, and political structure of the Roman Empire might be stabilized. This is what their prosecutors meant when Christians were indicted of being *atheists* and a *superstitious* people. They did not fall in line with their expected errands. Such charges would undoubtedly invert their public image as one who lived in contempt for the welfare of their neighbor. No wonder they were equally accused of being a people-group who exhibited a "hatred of mankind." For the most part, Rome had finally secured peace with the gods. It is for this very reason that the new religion of the divine man Jesus, who was declared by His people as exhibiting a Name above all names, had become a threat to the security of the Empire.

In his dialogue *Octavius*, one of Christianity's earliest apologists, Marcus Minucius Felix (he died, 250 AD—in Rome), presented the pagan Caecilius Natalis's disdain for the faith when he told the Christian Octavius Januarius: "You do not attend the shows; you take no part in the processions; fight shy of public banquets; abhor the sacred games, meats from the victims, drinks poured in libation on the altars. So frightened are you of the gods you deny!" Caecilius was undoubtedly expressing the concerns of Pliny the Younger before him.

The public life was in disorder. Christianity was not rejected by a *secular* government. Rome was as religious as they come.

"This contagious superstition," Pliny wrote to Trajan, "is not confined to the cities only, but has spread through the villages and rural districts." He further boasted that he had, during his investigation of the growing threat, forced the hand of many Christians. Under torture or threat of death, they would recant, "asserting that they had been but had ceased to be." They not only cursed Christ, he wrote, but "repeated after me an invocation to the gods."

Among those Christians whom Pliny was successful in hounding down, they each confessed in turn, he further wrote, "to meet on a fixed day before dawn and sing responsively a hymn to Christ as to a god, and to bind themselves by oath, not to some crime, but not to commit fraud, theft, or adultery, not falsify their trust, nor to refuse to return a trust when called upon to do so. When this was over, it was their custom to depart and to assemble again to partake of food—but ordinary and innocent food." After torturing two female slaves who identified themselves as church deaconesses, Pliny finally concluded of his investigation that he had "discovered nothing else but depraved, excessive *superstition*."

That isn't to say that pagan society was without hope. "It seems possible to check and cure it," Pliny surmised. While the extent of Pliny's persecution against the contagious superstition is not known, perhaps pretentiousness blinded even his paranoia, because: "It is certainly quite clear," he boasted of his efforts, "that the temples, which had been almost deserted, begin now to be frequented; and the sacred festivals, after a long intermission, are again revived; while there is a general demand for sacrificial animals, which for some time past have met with but few purchasers."

Pliny ended his depressing letter on a rather hopeful note.

> "Hence it is easy to imagine what a multitude of people can be reformed if an opportunity for repentance is afforded."

Trajan responded.

> "If they are denounced and proved guilty, they are to be punished, with this reservation, that whoever denies that he is a Christian and really proves it—that is, by worshiping our gods—even though he was under suspicion in the past, shall obtain pardon through repentance."

The horror, it appears—that is, the cure-all against the contagious superstition which had, by the first decade of the second century, filled every city of the Empire, even though the villages and rural districts— had only begun. The Christian was to curse Christ and denounce his inheritance with Him, or *die*. And he was to do it for the sake of humanity.

6

MORE BAD NEWS FOR CHRISTIANS EVERYWHERE—the year was 175 or perhaps 180, when along came a man, and his name was Celsus. Christianity's first noted intellectual tormenter had likely been raised in a Jewish home, possibly even Christian. He had been on the inside. He had listened in to dinner table conversations. He speculated on their simple equations, leaving no stone unturned. And then one day he set off on a covetous career in Greek philosophy. In turn, he would write a hit piece against the people of his upbringing. This was a century when Christians were plagued with blatantly false rumors. It was one thing to refute silly claims, such as partaking in cannibalism and eating the flesh of their children during secret meetings, but quite another to respond intellectually and even philosophically to a Roman orator, particularly one who had the ear of Marcus Aurelius.

His long-winded critique against the early Christian faith was nothing short of sarcastic, jocular, and endlessly biting. And just so there was no confusion, he titled his hit-piece, *The True Doctrine: A Discourse Against the Christians.* By this, his readers were to understand that the true doctrine was a reference to Greek philosophy—Neoplatonism mainly. During Marcus Aurelius' generation, one might venture to think Stoicism was the state religion. And for all intents and purposes, it was. For the following century, Celsus' dissertation would remain a bestseller. His accusations did not shy away from debasing adjectives when describing the Christian as:

> "Only foolish and low individuals, and person devoid of perception, and slaves, and women and children of whom teachers of the divine word wish to make converts... For why is it an evil to be educated and to have studied the best opinions, and to have both the reality and the appearance of wisdom? Why should it not rather be an assistance, and a means by which one might be better to arrive at the truth?"

For Celsus, Christianity was a superstition embodied mostly by women and children, and also slaves, uninterested in learning the truth of the world through higher education. Christians, he said, were uneducated, deluded, unpatriotic, close-minded towards reason, and too accepting of

250

sinners. He was sick and tired of their arrogant separatism; that they dared to claim a special relationship with God, a chosen Sonship, which imbued them with a supposed heightened superiority over the rest of society. Such assurances were blatantly false, Celsus asserted. Platonism had already demonstrated humanities shared relationship with the divine. If anything, the Christians had not only failed to add anything to the wisdom of the ancients, they had in fact distorted, or rather perverted, the minds of the great classical philosophers. Jesus had simply learned magic from the Egyptians. And their very assertion that Christ was born of a virgin was a copyright infringement, seeing as how the Greeks had already published their own accounts of divine insemination. If anything, the fact that the Christians were a persecuted people and that the Jews had been driven from their homeland was proof that God was actually prejudiced against them. His refutations however did not come without an appeal to Christians to renounce their faith and return to the pagan fold of the True Word, or Logos. Such appeals however seemed to come with little personal hope, as Christianity did not require the wisdom of philosophical inquiry from its adherents for attaining salvation, but simple faith. This Celsus could simply not understand. As things stood, *Christians*, he said in no uncertain terms, *were a stupid people.*

> "The following are the rules laid down by [the Christians]. '*Let no one come to us who has been instructed, or who is wise or prudent (for such qualifications are deemed evil by us); but if there be any ignorant, or unintelligent, or uninstructed, or foolish persons, let them come with confidence.*' By which words, acknowledging that such individuals are worthy of their God, they manifestly show that they desire and are able to gain over only the silly, and the mean, and the stupid, with women and children."

As if to add insult to injury, his claims would go unchallenged for another generation.

7

THE DAWN OF YET ANOTHER CENTURY WAS ALREADY AFOOT, and what better way to celebrate it than with a high tide of persecutions against the *superstitious* faith? The year was 202 when Emperor Severus' orders found their way to the doorstep of Origen's childhood home. The young Origen (184-253) insisted on accompanying his father, Leonides, after he was dragged from their house by Roman soldiers. His mother apparently hid both his shoes and his clothes in an effort to dissuade him. How Origen still managed to follow the heels of his father is best left to the imagination. It was at the Caesaareum, that very night, where Origen witnessed his father's head thrown into a mound of heads, his body disposed of in another such pile-up.

The very persecution which had claimed Leonides' life, and countless others, led Bishop Clement of Alexandria to abandon the catechetical school in Alexandria and seek refuge in neighboring Palestine. But that is not to say that Origen had not already been schooled by the master. Origen's father was Greek, his mother Jewish. From the earliest age she taught him to sing the psalms in Hebrew. In his formative years he attended both the lectures of Clement at the catechetical school and Ammonius in his school of philosophy, and in the months leading up to Leonides' beheading, the young pupils excellence was so widely regarded that his father simply became known as "Leonides, father of Origen." It seemed only apparent to Bishop Demetrius, and perhaps necessary among those who survived the horror, that Origen would be appointed as the new dean of the Didascalia.

The brilliant scholar was only eighteen years of age.

In hindsight, it seems abundantly clear that Origen of Alexandria had, like his two predecessors, been initiated into the Eleusinian mysteries. It is a shame then that Origen's contributions to church history cannot be overstated. He Hellenized the Christian church in a likewise and dramatic manner as Philo of Alexandria radically transformed Judaism. For Origen, an unapologetic Platonist and Pythagorean, the immortal soul and Plato's globe reigned supreme, and like Plato, the pre-existence of human souls, the reincarnation of the wicked, and the purifications of souls bolstered his doctrine. Actually, Origen took Universalism to its ultimate conclusion—the devil would be saved at the end of time.

It is Origen who is first accredited with teaching the intercession of saints. He wrote: "But not the high priest [Christ] alone prays for those who pray sincerely, but also the angels...as also the souls of the saints who have already fallen asleep." His lavish and rather self-indulgent interpretations no doubt derived from a familiarity with Hellenistic literature, which is ironic, since these very readings—abreasted with his Platonic and Pythagorean pupilage, as well as his Eleusinian advisers— aptly informed him that the entire Bible was not to be interpreted literally. Concerning the Genesis account of creation, he wrote: "Who is so silly as to believe that God…planted a paradise eastward in Eden, and set in it a visible and palpable tree of life… and anyone who tasted its fruit with his bodily teeth would gain life?" Rather, Origen employed his instructions in philosophy as an ancillary—at least, in his own mind—to the exposition and harmonization of Scripture. He also believed that such hermeneutics should be enforced in the Gospels.

Rather than employing the Lord's eye-witness Testimony to apply his cosmology, he is among the first to prefer the Science of his day when embracing it. To this he writes: "Certainly what some say of this world, that it is corruptible because it was made, and yet does not go to corruption because the will of God, who made it and preserves it from being mastered by corruption, is stronger and more powerful than corruption, may more rightly be believed of that world which we have above called a *fixed sphere*, because by the will of God it is in no way subject to corruption, for the reason that it has not admitted the causes of corruption."

Among his philosophical propositions, Origen claimed that the body and the spirit are on opposite ends of the moral spectrum so that the arms of the soul are tugged by both in either direction. That the body and the spirit held the soul at a conflict of interest is an understanding which derives directly from Platonism. For Plato, the immortal soul was cleft into three parts: reason, instinct, and desire. Furthermore, its divisions promised two alternative motives: rational concerns which aimed at the virtuous and secondly, mere desire. Origen agreed.

Jerome would later confirm that Origen "clearly supports the doctrine of transmigration taught by Pythagoras and Plato." Perhaps Origen's best-known quip on the matter can be summed up in *De Principiis* when he writes: "The soul has neither beginning nor end [They] come into this world strengthened by the victories or weakened by the defeats of their previous lives."

In his *Commentary on John*, Origen referenced the *Apocryphal Gospel of Hebrews* to garnish his Pythagorean doctrine when writing of the Patriarch, Jacob: "I am an angel of God; one of the first order of spirits. Men call me Jacob, but my true name, which God has given me, is Israel." To this Origen added: "Many of the Jewish doctors have believed that the souls of Adam, Abraham, and Phineas, have successively animated the great men of their nation." The point here is that Origen believed John the Baptist was embodied by an angel who had previously animated the prophet Elijah, just as the Essenes likely concluded in his own day. He further bolstered his claims by summoning the great Alexandrian theologian of Judaism, Philo. Here he writes: "Philo says that the air is full of spirits, and that some, through their natural propensity, join themselves to bodies; and that others have an aversion from such a union."

Origen taught that God had created matter, his *globe earth*, only to accommodate the throngs of fallen souls so that they could be restored to their proper spiritual state. It is here where the various loose-ends of his philosophical ponderings are neatly adjoined. For Origen, redemption required the active application of free will tin order that the agent might reunite with God in heavenly bliss. The only problem with free will is that it allows the fallen soul, embodied in the shackles of dirty flesh, to reject his maker. This would necessitate an elongated interim whereas stubborn souls could go whirl round and round on carousel of life, occupying human bodies until the salvation of every last child was grasped. In his foundational book, *On First Principles*, Origen further expounded on this cyclic-like samsara. Evil souls come into bodies, first of men. However their association with irrational passions would secure the existence of a beast, after their allotted span of human life, until finally they sunk to the level of plants. He wrote: "From this condition they rise again through the same stages and are restored to their heavenly place." Origen has given himself away. Origen was a Gnostic clothed as a professor.

This likely explains why Origen took Matthew 19:12 to the letter and castrated himself. Flesh was *dirty*, and passions, even of procreation, were to be avoided. Later in life the eunuch regretted his decision. It was an extreme act, he admitted, and probably beyond the call of his faith.

Origen's school was open to all—not just Christian doctrine. One of his pupils, Gregory—later known as Thaumaturges—recalled that "they were given complete freedom to find their way around the entire world of knowledge, and to investigate anything which took their interest, enjoying any mode of teaching and savoring the sweet pleasure of the intellect." He further wrote:

> "To be under the intellectual change of Origen was like living in a garden where fruits of the mind sprang up without toil to be happy with gladness by the happy occupants... He truly was a paradise to us, after the likeness of the paradise of God... and to leave him was to renascent the experience of Adam and the Fall."

Considering what we know of Origen's teachings, there is much to be pulled from Gregory's nostalgic recollections. It is evident that the theologian from Alexandria did not receive his knowledge of the soul nor creation from the Prophets or the Apostles, but from beyond Pythagoras closed curtain and Socrates deathbed confessions in *Phaedo* and Plato's *Republic*. Origen, Clement, and Pantaenus—and in fact, the whole of Alexandria—was filled with *dark speeches*. An entire generation after the death of Christianity's first great intellectual tormentor, it is Origen who would finally accept Celsus' challenge—at the request of his contemporary, Saint Ambrose, bishop of Milan—and debate him. By the time the first great defender of the faith was through with his theological tinkering, the bold face of Christianity would be thoroughly Alexandrian.

8

NOT A SINGLE COPY OF CELSUS' BOOK SURVIVES. This is due to the astonishing fact that Christian emperor Valentinian III, tag-teaming with Archbishop Theodosius, ordered in 448, and successfully saw to it, that every copy of *The True Doctrine* was destroyed. Then again, such aspirations were not unheard of. In fact *many* books were destroyed in the cockcrow hours of the Christian empire. Some monks and scribes, unwilling that their forbidden volumes should be brought to ruin, simply buried them in hopes that future decades or generations might once again favor them. It is unlikely however that they would threaten their own careers by needlessly refusing to hand Celsus over. And besides, there is an irony here. Origen's rebuttal in *Contra Celsum* quoted so much of *True Doctrine* that nineteenth century scholars have been successful in reconstructing 90 percent of the original.

Contra Celsum was deemed an immediate masterpiece, particularly because Origen's work was arguably the first Christian apology to hold its own against paganism. An entire generation or two later the church historian Eusebius, born in Palestine and had come into contact with the teachings of Origen there through his student Pamphilus, lauded *Against Celsus* as an adequate rebuttal to all criticisms the church would ever face. It was however written exactly as one ought to expect from a Neoplatonic philosopher. And let us not forget, Celsus had the ear of the Stoic Emperor at his disposal. Though it is true that Origen set out to refute many of Celsus' claims, he essentially agreed with him on much, including a rejection of religious literalism. Rather than simply attempting to win him over by presenting the simple Gospel, "foolishness to the self-professed wise," Origen clothed his religion in the embalming fragrance of Greek philosophy.

The fact that Origen had already derided any endorsement that God *literally* planted a garden in the east to be a childish and simple understanding is here expounded upon when Origen wrote to the dead Celsus of the pre-existing souls losing their wings and being cast down to earth. He wrote:

> "And the expulsion of the man and woman from paradise, and their being clothed with tunics of skins (which God, because of the transgression of men, made for those who had sinned), contain a certain secret and mystical doctrine (far transcending that of Plato) of the souls losing its wings, and being borne downwards to Earth, until it can lay hold of some stable resting-place."

This in itself raises other concerns. If the flesh is *dirty*, if material creation—embodied for the Platonist by a globe earth—was *necessary* only so that fallen souls, expelled from a mystical paradise, might have a chance to reclaim their wings (like something out of a Frank Capra movie), then the physical resurrection of the righteous is a decrepit conclusion to the redemption story. Celsus mocked the Christian for their widespread belief that the body would be given over to the worms, as Job would say, but that the corruptible would put on incorruptible on that last day. Such a thought was unthinkable to the Neoplatonist—and apparently *also* for Origen.

The dean from Alexandria often sought to affirm his allegiance to the philosophical brotherhood, and likely the Eleusinian mysteries. "I speak now according to the opinion of Pythagoras and Plato and Empedocles, whom Celsus frequently names," he wrote. "Is it not more in conformity with reason that every soul for certain mysterious reasons are introduced into a body, and introduced according to its deserts and former actions?" He then added: "The soul, which is immaterial and invisible in its nature, exists in no material place without having a body suited to the nature of that place; accordingly, it at one time puts off one body, which was necessary before, but which is no longer adequate in its changed state, and it exchanges it for a second." Origen spoke here of the resurrection, but in doing so has mistaken the Apostle Paul, not only for a Platonist, but as an initiate into the brotherhood of the occulting mystery religion. What we are to conclude here, if the Alexandrian is correct in his assumptions, is that Paul could not have possibly believed nor advocated a restoration of *this* created order and *this* flesh, especially if, in our immortal nature, we have been clothed in a successive legion of bodies. "Our hope, then," Origen assured Celsus, "is not the hope of worms, nor does our soul long for a body that has seen corruption."

Accordingly, the apostle Paul had hoped to conceal the secret meaning of his message to the church in 1 Corinthians chapter 15, "which was not adapted to the simpler class of believers, and to the understanding of the common people, who are led by their faith to enter on a better course of life." It is not only Celsus who fails to understand the meaning of Scripture on these matters, Origin insists, but also the Christian simpleton. Essentially, Origen confirmed that the back porch majority of Christians were *stupid*, if they actually believed that the hope of the Gospel was our physical resurrection from the dead. Paul's magnum opus was a secret and mystical message. For this reason, Celsus has not "the capacity of judging that the meaning of our wise men is not to be determined by those individuals who make no profession of anything more than of a simple faith in the Christian system."

If Christians are not *initiated*—then they have no say on the matter.

But regarding all these hidden truths, Origen surmised that it is good to closely guard the secrets of a king. The doctrine of transmigration of souls into various bodies and how that plays into our eventual resurrection in another sort of body should not be lightly "thrown before the common understanding, nor what is holy given to the dogs, nor pearls be cast before swine. For such a procedure would be impious, being equivalent to a betrayal of the mysterious declaration of God's Wisdom."

In 250 Origen Adamantiuswas, 69-years of age, was captured during yet another wave of persecution, this time by Emperor Decius. Bound head and foot for days on end, Origen was met with repeated torture. He survived, but only because Decius died before him. Though the old man was released, he couldn't lick his wounds. The Alexandrian dean of the Didascalia died shortly thereafter.

Kenneth R. Calvert, writing for *Christianity Today*, summed up Origen's life when he wrote: "Origen of Alexandria, a third-century Christian scholar, loved Jesus, the Scriptures, and Neo-Platonic philosophy—a combination that Christians since have viewed as either the height of faithful theology or the depth of horrendous error." Though it is true that Origen was initially praised by his contemporaries as a champion of the faith, in time successive Roman theologians, eager to snatch the reigns of Christianity away from Alexandria, would gaze back upon the man and call him a devil. The Second Council of Constantinople in 553 accursed many of his teachings—but that is not to say all of them. Though Pythagoras was expelled, essential components of Plato remained. By the time of his death, Origen had done a thoroughly Alexandrian job on Christianity.

9

THE CHRISTIAN FACELIFT THAT WAS ALEXANDRIA was not a driverless carriage in the passing of Origen. Those reigns were simply handed over to Athanasius the Great of Alexandria (296-373), who bore traces of Origen before him, and then to a succession of others. Among his earliest work, *Against the Heathen—On the Incarnation*, written before 319, Athanasius repeatedly quoted Plato while borrowing from Aristotle, and later in life he would become a repeat offender of citing Homer. "Since the soul moves itself," he wrote, "it follows that, after putting aside the body, it should continue to move itself, for it is not the soul that dies, but the body, which dies after the departure of the soul." Athanasius appears to be speaking the very words rising from the lips of Socrates on his deathbed. Death is but an illusion. And one shouldn't be surprised to learn that C.S. Lewis described his work a masterpiece. Athanasius was practically dripping with wet and seemingly logical pen strokes of Lewis when he wrote: "The soul considers and thinks of things that are eternal and immortal because it is immortal."

An added emphasis should be placed upon Athanasius' relationship with Anthony the Great (251-356), the Egyptian monk who helped to found and orchestrate the Christian monastic movement. The father of the monastery was educated into the Hellenism of his Alexandrian forefathers, and his steady flow of letters reveals him to be a theologian in the tradition of Origen and Didymus the Stoic. Among his correspondences he wrote: "A true man is one who understands that the body is corruptible and short-lived. Such a man also understands what the soul is: divine and immortal." Quite similarly, "As regards the body, man is mortal; however, as regards the mind and reason, he is immortal."

Macarius the Egyptian (300-391) was a direct inheritor of Anthony the Great. He seemed to elevate Aristotle's concept of the human soul to the sons of God in the heavens above when he wrote: "The soul has a form similar to that of the Angel. For, as the Angels have form, and the outer man has form, so also the inner man has a form resembling that of the Angels and the outer man." For Macarius, like the lot of them, death was an illusion only perceptible with the body. "If He [God] was moved to such compassion over bodies that were to be dissolved and die, and did with eager kindness for each supplicant the thing that he desired, how much more will He do for an immortal, imperishable, incorruptible soul, laboring under the disease of ignorance, wickedness, unbelief, unconcern, and all the other maladies of sin."

The charges brought against Athanasius the Great of Alexandria included the illegal taxation of the Egyptian people, supporting rebels to the Imperial throne, murdering a bishop and keeping his severed hand for use in magical rites, and other immoral conducts. It was Eusebius of Caesarea (263-339) who presided over the First Council of Tyre in 335, where Athanasius was convicted. His fate was then determined before Emperor Constantine. In Constantinople the Emperor cleared him of all charges but one: threatening to cut off the grain supply to Constantinople from Egypt. Athanasius was promptly excommunication from the Holy Roman Empire, and as Constantine's personal counselor, Eusebius saw to it that his opponent was polemicized against.

The man who was trusted as an officiate to Biblical canon and instrumental at the Council of Nicaea was also an admirer of Origen, much like his Alexandrian opponent, and therefore diligently sought to harmonize Platonism with Christianity. Eusebius famously said of Plato that he was "the only Greek who attained the porch of [Christian] truth." It is my personal conviction that the book of Enoch stands as a defiant enemy of Hellenization and consequently the Holy Roman Empire which would soon inherit the mantle. Unsurprisingly, the book which bore Enoch's name was not a friend of Eusebius. It wasn't even considered for a place within the binding. The canonical historian furthermore questioned the authenticity of Jude, 2 Peter, and Revelation, and though Eusebius grudgingly conceded in the end, it should be duly noted that any book which dared to associate with Enoch were deemed unworthy or heavily contested for their inclusion from canon.

"Platonism is part of the vital structure of Christian theology," Dean Inge (1860-1954), professor of divinity at Cambridge confirmed. According to Inge, if the congregation could truly comprehend the Platonic invasion into Christian doctrine, "they would understand better the real continuity between the old culture and the new religion, and they might realize the utter impossibility of excising Platonism from Christianity without tearing Christianity to pieces." This is important.

Inge stresses: "The Galilean Gospel, as it proceeded from the lips of Jesus, was doubtless unaffected by Greek philosophy." Here he adds: "but from its very beginning [Christianity] was formed by a confluence of Jewish and Hellenic religious ideas."

For the Christian today, *this* is the rarely contemplated elephant in the room. Much of what we believe is *not* what the earliest Christians, hearing the Gospel from the mouths of the Apostles, believed—and dare I say it, is *not* Biblical.

The Holy Roman Empire had yet to be introduced to Saint Augustine of Hippo.

HE FOUND THE ORACLE OF TOMORROW | COPERNICUS, MEET HYPATIA [QUEEN OF THE OCCULT—MOTHER OF HELIOCENTRICISM]

SOME SAY THE DARK AGES BEGAN THAT VERY DAY. On the streets of Alexandria a mob of Christian zealots led by Peter the Lector apprehended a woman as she boarded her chariot—having only finished the days lecture at the University—and dragged her into a nearby church, where they stripped her naked and barbarically murdered her with roofing tiles. Though parts of her flesh were reportedly scattered across the city, the rest was burned. The woman was described by her students as exceptionally exquisite to behold. Her name was Hypatia, and men gazed from afar. The year was 414, and at the time of her death—being perhaps sixty years mature—she was Egypt's trophy intellectual. Hypatia's crime, *they say*, she clung to occultism in a generation when Christianity sought to purge Luciferian doctrine from its Empire. If it is true, that the murder of Hypatia swept humanity into the medieval cauldron, then it is hardly a stretch of fantasy to imagine that it was her very ghost, once excavated, which certified our arrival into this modern age of Science. Hypatia had enemies. And one day she'd return to haunt them all.

"They could not argue with her, so they murdered her."

The Roman Empire may have once ruled the *known* world, but by the end of the fourth century it was apparent that the world had grown far too large for one central government to manage. And so in 395—almost a century after the edict of Milan (which legalized Christianity under Emperor Constantine)—the Empire itself was historically split in two. Hypatia was roughly 40 years young at the time, and though Rome would continue its management of Western Europe for the remainder of her life, she and the rest of Alexandria suddenly found themselves under the sanction of Constantinople.

Founded by Alexander the Great some 750 years earlier—in 331 BC to be exact—the city soon swelled into a metropolis of Occult Sciences.

At its heart was the Museum. An estimated collection of some 700,000 scrolls were housed at one time in its library. The Alexandria of Hypatia's day may not have been a seat of power, as was Rome or Constantinople, but it remained the heart of the ancient world; a hotbed of intellectual activity, with the roots of Paganism and the exploding Gospel of Jesus Christ acting as competing rivals for the salvation of the soul and mind—depending on whom you spoke with. As such, Alexandria was the last refuge of humanism. If the dark ages dawned in Alexandria, then so too would the entire ancient world darken.

There was a time before Emperor Constantine when Occult Science embellished Rome with its muscular physique, even supplying the very air it breathed. Hypatia did not live under this umbrella. With Emperor Theodosius I, last to rule over both the eastern and western halves of the Roman Empire, the ancient Mystery Schools perished. Few were strong enough to resist his hand. A decree promulgated in 391 that "no one is to go to the sanctuaries, or walk through the temples" resulted in the abandonment of many pagan institutions throughout the Empire. The Roman state gave free reign to Christian extremists to destroy pagan shrines and commit violence against its priests. Arson was a favorite tactic. Monks stand out as primary aggressors. Some were not above murder. The pagan Eunapius remarked that these monks looked like men but behaved as pigs, "and openly did and allowed countless unspeakable crimes." He added bitterly, "For among them, every man is given the power of a tyrant who has a black robe and is prepared to behave badly in public." In 396 Christian monks—the Occultists referred to them as "black shirts"—led Visigoth barbarians towards the School of the Eleusinian Mysteries near Athens. It too was decimated. The Sanctuary of Eleusis, one of the grandest buildings in the ancient world (the outer courts of which could reportedly hold 300,000 worshipers) was reduced to ruins—another striking blow to the Occult. So too did Theodosius I turn his thoughts upon Alexandria.

Starting in 390 the Emperor had the obelisk of Pharaoh Thutmose III transported from Alexandria to Constantinople. Though the Museum had already been under the control of Catholic priests since the time of Constantine, the vast group of buildings known as the Serpeum remained within the clutches of Paganism. So too was the Temple of Serapis—employed now as a University—and the Library of the Serapion still housed a vast collection of books. It was at the University where Hypatia taught the "old religions and sciences." Here the Mysteries as a public institution would make their final stand.

Bishops were called to exercise the immense powers conferred upon them by the Emperor. Charges of political corruption, ill-will, evil-nature, and irreverent abuse of their leadership are overwhelming against Theodosius I and the church leaders of that generation. As the Archbishop of Alexandria, Theophilus was no exception. The English historian Edward Gibbon has labeled him "the perpetual enemy of peace and virtue; a bold, bad man whose hands were alternately polluted with gold and with blood." Colorful descriptions within modern scholarship continue to bedevil him. He is said to have "bribed the slaves of the Serapion to steal some of the books, which he sold to foreigners at exorbitant prices." Theophilus went to work confiscating abandoned Temples and restructuring them into churches. Naturally, Pagans objected to the desecration of their sacred places and symbols. Riots ensued. The philosopher Olympus, a contemporary of Hypatia, attempted to defend the Temple of Serapis. Under orders of Emperor Theodosius, men "sacked the Temple, broke the statue of Serapis in pieces, dragged it ignominiously through the streets of the city, and finally burned it." The year was 398. When a Christian Church was later erected upon its ruins, the "martyrs" who had suffered in the riot were honored there.

So too was the Serapion Library eliminated from use. While some historians frame its destruction against a long-term backdrop of frequent mob violence in the city, particularly a four-hundred year conflict between the Greeks and Jews who inhabited those quarters, most agree its final demise came with the Christians rejection of Paganism. Only the Neoplatonic School remained.

Hypatia's father Theon may have been the last man whose name is recorded as a professor at the Alexandrian Museum, but she herself sat in the chair of philosophy, and throughout the city she wore the cloak of the Philosopher. Though an astronomer and mathematician, Theon was devoted to divination, astrology, and the Mysteries. He wrote a commentary on Ptolemy's *Syntaxis*, and acknowledged his daughter in its composition. Suidas claims Hypatia wrote commentaries on *Diophantus*, on the *Astronomical Canon of Ptolemy*, and on the *Conics of Apollonius of Perga*. Like most of Alexandria's once-rich literary collection, none now survive. He furthermore penned commentaries on the books of Orpheus and Hermes Trismegistus and poems relegating the planets as forces of Moira—*destiny*. Nothing indicates that Hypatia departed from her upbringing. In actuality, Hypatia carried them *further*. The Chaldean Oracles and Pythagorean numerological mysticism figured in her teachings, as the letters of

Synesius indicate. Like her father, she saw astronomy as the highest science, opening up knowledge of the divine.

Of the little that is known about Hypatia, biographically speaking, the following account by Socrates Scholasticus, which was completed sometime in the decade before the death of Theodosius II in AD 450, is the best and most substantial. Socrates wrote:

> "There was a woman at Alexandria named Hypatia, daughter of the philosopher Theon, who made such attainments in literature and science, as to far surpass all the philosophers of her own time. Having succeeded to the school of Plato and Plotinus, she explained the principles of philosophy to her auditors, many of whom came from a distance to receive her instructions. On account of the self-possession and ease of manner, which she had acquired in consequence of the cultivation of her mind, she not infrequently appeared in public in presence of the magistrates. Neither did she feel abashed in coming to an assembly of men. For all men on account of her extraordinary dignity and virtue admired her the more."

As a devoted Neoplatonist Hypatia never married—despite the astonishing beauty which cast men's gaze from afar. Plato's suggestion in *The Republic* to abolish the family-unit in favor of Government-accredited "Guardians" derived from a desire to create the Utopian society. In such a world inequitable ownership of private property no longer exists. This dream—more precisely, *nightmarish reality*—persists even today at the UN. In Hypatia's own words, she justified her non-commitment to any one man—her virginity is likely a mystical metaphor, by the way—as "already being married with the truth..." According to the Greek historian Damascius, two different and potential responses were delivered after one of Hypatia's students professed his unreserved love for her. The more polite version, which he sighs as the less likely, is that she told him that music was the antidote for love. The less polite version is that she handed him a bloody menstrual rag and said "this is what you really love—my young man but you do not love beauty for its own sake." How Platonic of her.

The March 1937 edition of THOSOPHY states: "The Neoplatonic School reached its greatest heights in the days that immediately preceded its destruction. Hypatia brought Egypt nearer to an understanding of its ancient Mysteries than it had been for thousands of years. Her knowledge of Theurgy restored the practical value of the Mysteries and completed the work commenced by Iamblichus over a hundred years before."

With theurgy—a system of white magic practiced by the early Neoplatonists—its practitioner could reach God through spiritual magic and ascend up the scale of creation through rigorous prayer, fasting, and devotional preparation, particularly with the goal of achieving *henosis* (uniting with the divine) and perfecting oneself. According to A. Wilder, "the problem of life is man. Magic—or rather Wisdom—is the evolved knowledge of the potencies of man's interior being..." Pierre A. Riffard, a French philosopher and esoterists, says of the practice: "Theurgy is a type of magic. It consists of a set of magical practices performed to evoke beneficent spirits in order to see them or know them or in order to influence them, for instance by forcing them to animate a statue, to inhabit a human being (such as a medium), or to disclose mysteries."

THOSOPHY further adds:

"Following in the footsteps of Plotinus and Porphyry, she demonstrated the possibility of the union of the individual Self with the SELF of all. Continuing the work of Ammonius Saccas, she showed the similarity between all religions and the identity of their source."

Occultist Manley P. Hall holds Hypatia in the highest regard. Alexandria's trophy intellectual "eclipsed in argument and public esteem every proponent of the Christian doctrines in Northern Egypt." As part of her Neoplatonic School curriculum, Hypatia employed the inductive method of reasoning first sponsored by Aristotle to pull the rug out from under the foundations of Christian dogma. She was so well versed in the accumulated belief systems of ancient times, it is said that one of her books was about a "compendium of comparative religion," and may have resembled something of Hall's very own *The Secret Teachings of All Ages*. She further mocked the religion of Christ by openly exposing metaphysical allegories from which Christianity had borrowed its dogmas. According to Hall, "Hypatia not only proved conclusively the pagan origin of the Christian faith but also exposed the purported miracles then advanced by the Christians as tokens of divine preference by demonstrating the natural laws controlling the phenomena."

Hypatia sought to dispel the belief that the doctrines of Plato and Plotinus and the Mysteries from whence their philosophies had arisen were in any way dangerous. She was particularly gifted—by way of reasoning—at turning the tables on the Church of Rome. Now the ancient Mysteries would be flung into the open and, by treating the old Pagan view and Christianity as one and the same, Jesus would be treated as pagan and *esoteric*. In other words, what was the sin in peering into the ancient Mysteries, which was not only built upon the Serpents damnable promise to Eve in the garden, but expounded on his lie?

"A number of writers," Hall adds, "have credited the teachings of Hypatia with being Christian *in spirit*." Perhaps because she attempted to bleed Platonism and the teachings of Christ together into one ecumenical stewpot, and in fact, many new converts to the Christian faith deserted their first love to become one of her disciples.

One such convert from Christianity to Occult Science, perchance Hypatia's most adoring pupil, was Synesius of Cyrene—a bishop ironically consecrated by Theophilus himself. Seven letters addressed to Hypatia still survive, though he refers to her in several more. He laments not hearing from her, for she is "the only good thing that remains inviolate, along with virtue. You always have power," he writes, "and long may you have it and make a good use of that power." About the time of his death (a year or two before her own), he dictated a letter calling her "mother, sister, teacher, and withal benefactress, and whatsoever is honored in name and deed." She is the one "who legitimately presides over the mysteries of philosophy" and "my most revered teacher." More than just a philosopher, mathematician, astronomer, and scientist, Hypatia was clearly regarded in the light of a spiritual leader. For Synesius the Cyrene, she was "the most holy and revered philosopher," "a blessed lady," and "divine spirit" with "oracular utterances." His teacher, Synesius contemplated, was "beloved by the gods."

Despite these confessional heresies, many modern historians paint Synesius in the light of a persistent Christian—too academic perhaps for his unintelligible contemporaries—and yet because of her influences he obstinately held to the Platonic belief in an eternity of the cosmos and worse, the Luciferian divinity of the soul which—unlike the Judeo-Christian insistence in an unsustainable existence apart from the flesh, returning to dust due to sin and demanding *physical* resurrection— stressed a separate but distinct and sustainable substance, eternally speaking.

Essentially, Orthodox Christians in Alexandria were abandoning their faith to follow Hypatia's esoteric branding—which the Gnostics were already succeeding at anyhow. Egypt had a way of perverting *true* religion. In a broader picture, Synesius and his brethren, though perhaps clinging to a Christian title, were in direct conflict with the Cappadocian Fathers—Basil the Great (330–379), who was bishop of Caesarea; Basil's younger brother Gregory of Nyssa (335–395), who was bishop of Nyssa; and a close friend, Gregory of Nazianzus (329–389), who became Patriarch of Constantinople.

In *Synesius of Cyrene, Philosopher-bishop*, Jay Bregman writes: "The Cappadocians' approach was diametrically opposed to Synesius'. They believed the Scriptures, not philosophy or the Platonized Chaldean Oracles, were the Gnosis and Christian Oracles (logia) of God. This Gnosis is in the Old and New Testaments. They were revealed by the Holy Spirit through the theologoi or mouthpieces of God. For Synesius there were also a few autodidacts instructed by God, but these were to be found in all religious traditions. As a syncretist, Synesius had no trouble including Zoroaster and other pagan and Christian figures."

Surviving fragments of letters and affectionate correspondences indicate a mystical orientation. Glimpses of her spiritual views describe and assign "the eye buried within us" as a "divine guide." Furthermore, as the soul journeys toward divinity, this "hidden spark which loves to conceal itself" *grows into a flame of knowing.* True to her theurgy tutelage under the Aristotelian philosopher and magician, Plutarch of Athens, Hypatia's philosophy circumnavigated the "mystery of being," an elevator approach to consciousness, and "union with the divine," or the One.

Truly, Hypatia was adored by many, "but the admiration was not quite universal," writes Will Durant in *The Age of Faith: The Story of Civilization.* "The Christians of Alexandria must have looked upon her askance, for she was not only a seductive unbeliever, but an intimate friend of Orestes, the pagan perfect of the city." Alexandria was a populace, says Socrates, which "is more delighted with tumult than any other people: and if at any time it should find a pretext, breaks forth into the most intolerable excesses; for it never ceases from its turbulence without bloodshed."

In 412, Cyril, the nephew of Theophilus, succeeded him as patriarch of Alexandria. Upon taking his uncle's place, Cyril needed his own conquest against paganism. In time, he would set his gaze upon Hypatia. Orestes resisted ecclesiastical encroachment upon his civil jurisdiction. The two clashed. Meanwhile, riots between Christians and Jews persisted. After a brawl in the theater, the Perfect had one of Cyril's followers arrested and tortured. When Christians were killed in yet another riot, the archbishop led a mob which resulted in the expulsion of Jews from Alexandra. Even their possessions were looted. No sooner had Orestes objected when he himself was assaulted by monks "of a very fiery disposition." One such assailant was tortured to death. Cyril made a martyr of him.

The 7th-century Egyptian Coptic bishop John of Nikiu, who served as a general administrator of Egypt's upper monasteries around 696, chronicled a historical narrative which extended from Adam to the end of the Muslim conquest in Egypt. He described Hypatia as a pagan philosopher "devoted at all times to magic, astrolabes and instruments of music" who "beguiled many people through Satanic wiles." Orestes, the Imperial Perfect of Egypt and Alexandria's governor: "honored her exceedingly, for she had beguiled him through her magic."

Prefect Orestes enjoyed the political backing of Hypatia. Though an Occultist in an ever-widening Christian Empire, her political influence cannot be denied. Indeed, many students from wealthy and influential families came to Alexandria, purposely forsaking the newly endorsed religion of the land to study privately with Hypatia, and many of these later, quite ironically, attained high posts in government and the Church. Not only would the Imperial Perfects customary church attendance cease, "but he drew many believers to her…" Cyril's supporters charged Hypatia with being Orestes' chief instigator, "for as she had frequent interviews with Orestes, it was calumniously reported among the Christian populace," wrote Socrates, "that it was she who prevented Orestes from being reconciled to the bishop." The Christians of Alexandria had no weapon against her—none but violence.

"She was torn to pieces by a mob of incensed Christians not because she was a woman," wrote Iain Pears in *The Dream of Scipio*, "but because her learning was so profound, her skill at dialectic so extensive that she reduced all who queried her to embarrassed silence. They could not argue with her, so they murdered her." It should be noted that the Neoplatonist historian Damascius, likely sympathetic of Hypatia's Occultism, was "anxious to exploit the scandal" that was her death. His account is the sole historical source attributing direct responsibility to Bishop Cyril. The church of Rome insists he had nothing to do with it.

Despite the scattering abroad—and ultimate survival—of neoplatonists, Saint Cyril of Alexandria held onto few friends, even in the church. Nestorian bishops at the Council of Ephesus declared the man who became a saint a heretic, labeling him a "monster, born and educated for the destruction of the church." The Bishop Theodoret of Cyrus wrote to Domnus, Bishop of Antioch, after learning of Cyril's death: "At last and with difficulty the villain has gone. The good and the gentle pass away all too soon; the bad prolong their life for years..."

While Cyril's direct involvement in Peter's lynching of Hypatia is still debated to this day, it is clear that no punishment was exacted on anyone. It was "an act so inhuman," recalled Socrates, and yet "this affair brought not the least opprobrium, not only upon Cyril but also upon the whole Alexandrian church. And nothing can be further from the spirit of Christianity than the allowance of massacres, fights, and transactions of that sort." Emperor Theodosius II merely restricted the freedom of the monks to appear in public, and excluded pagans from all public office. Cyril had managed the tightrope balancing act of his uncles legacy. As a public institution, the Mysteries were no more. Together, their victory was complete. "All the people surrounded the patriarch Cyril and named him 'the new Theophilus'," wrote John of Niku, "for he had destroyed the last remains of idolatry in the city."

Very few will remember Cyril as being the man responsible for promoting Mary from the Mother of Jesus to the "Mother of God," and even less know he introduced the image of Isis—pictured nursing the infant Horus at her breast—into the Christian Church under the guise of Mary. Here in America the eye of Horus is printed upon our one dollar bill. We even have an obelisk erected to him in Washington D.C. For the Occult, which is healthier now than it was in Hypatia's generation, Horus is cleverly hidden with the Lady Madonna and double-downs as the coming anti-Christ. Oddly enough—and perhaps there is a piece of the puzzle missing here, where the archbishop and Hypatia's ambitions come together... and conflict—Saint Cyril helped integrate into the Catholic Church the very hieroglyphic penmanship which he himself was publicly suppressing. When Christianity overthrew Rome, many clergymen simply exchanged one cloak for another and remained within the same breach of mysticism.

There is a reason why God said regarding Egypt: "Ye shall henceforth return no more that way (Deuteronomy 17:16)." Egypt had a way of perverting *true* religion. Here before us is a case study. In the outer-rim of the Christian Byzantine Empire, the Occult—albeit Occult Science—was infiltrating, compromising, and perverting the *truth*. "And then you can cast her story—as generations of allegorists, from Voltaire to Gibbon to Charles Kingsley have done," writes an embittered Harvard University Press; "as a battle between the waning light of the ancient pagan world, with its amassed wisdom, and the encroaching darkness of Christian dogmatism."

So we commence with the dawn of the dark ages. It is a marathon length funeral procession which the Theosophists, the Occultists, and members of secret societies have long-since agonized over. Freemason Albert Pike would resort to name-calling, specifically the "dunces who led primitive Christianity astray" and "succeeded in shrouding in darkness the ancient discoveries of the human mind—so that we now grope in the dark to find again the key of the phenomena of nature....." The details of Hypatia's so-called brilliance would die with her, for the most part—though some delectable thoughts remained. And while the Mysteries which she championed would trudge on among the goop of crypts and catacombs, it would not, as history has proven, slither among the snakes and the roaches forever. *Clergymen have a way of exchanging one cloak for another.*

Nicolaus Copernicus, it seems, was there for the momentous occasion. Before his new conception of the universe was published posthumously in 1543, Copernicus was but a pupil under Domenico Maria de Novara, an astronomy professor in Bologna. While in Florence, it is extremely likely that Copernicus read the *Almagest,* complete with Theon and his daughter Hypatia's comments scribbled within; given that the only copy of Ptolemy's work was in the Medici library of that city, a library which Copernicus visited for his research. Hypatia never accepted the earth-centered model. Her notes in Ptolemy's *Almagest* prove that she clearly rejected the geocentric Ptolemaic theory in favor of the heliocentric model. Copernicus was enthralled by the thought of it– possessed even. The Mystery Religion, it seems, struck back.

Hypatia once said: "All formal dogmatic religions are fallacious and must never be accepted by self-respecting persons as final." Indeed, the ghost of Hypatia was exhumed in Florence, Italy. By overturning the cosmological-belief of a sacred Word which had overseen her own undoing, the Copernican Revolution was the perfect revenge.

> "Fables should be taught as fables, myths as myths, and miracles as poetic fantasies. To teach superstitions as truths is a most terrible thing. The child mind accepts and believes them, and only through great pain and perhaps tragedy can he be in after years relieved of them"

—Hypatia

Truth or Beauty…? SAINT JEROME: SACRED SOULS SEVERED BY THE PAGAN AND PROFANE

1

HEINRICH HEINE WAS NOT WELL. In May of 1848, the German-Jewish writer, known for his lyric poetry set to music by such composers as Schumann and Schubert, suddenly fell paralyzed. Heine would not recover. Further musings were confined to bed, a sickly pulpit for the pen which he dubbed his "mattress-grave," where a cruel malady of the spine plagued him for the remaining eight years of his life.

During this final tenor—and even long before—the author confessed to his all-consuming love affair with marble statues and dead women. His greatest love was discovered in 1820, some three decades earlier, on the Greek island of Melos in the Aegean. It was Olivier Voutier, a 23-year-old ensign in the French navy, who witnessed the unexpected unearthing of Aphrodite by a farmer attempting to remove rocks from his field. The farmer apparently found absolutely no beauty in the goddess, either in classical or contemporary terms. Voutier had to pay him not to rebury her.

Aphrodite's statue, known as Venus of Milo, quickly fell into the hands of Marquis de Rivière, French ambassador to the Sublime Porte of the Ottoman Empire, who presented it to Louis XVIII. In turn, the king of France donated the marble goddess to the Louvre the following year. This masterwork of the late Hellenistic-era, once adorned with succulent jewelry, won instant fame. Standing before her in the Louvre, one couldn't help but speculate at her missing arms, which may have at one time held an apple, a crown, or a mirror by which she admired her reflection, and be all the more drawn to her. Perhaps it was *that*, her divine mystery, counterbalanced by her association with eroticism and beauty, as her half-nakedness testified to—her sensual, feminine curves, and inviting drapery—which effortlessly clapped the eyes of countless souls upon her. Or as Gregory Curtis, author of *Disarmed: The Story of Venus de Milo* put it: "The statue is beautiful in a way that even an untrained eye immediately understands."

It was there in the Louvre where Heinrich Heine, so enraptured with her beauty, held private talks with the divine being. For Heine, Venus was the most blessed of goddesses arising from the ancient pantheon. She could promise the erotic pleasures as a radiant seductress or the domesticated charms of a loving and caring housewife. In other words, he saw her *everywhere*—first and foremost through his many loves, dead and living, and was without question his literary muse. "As the butterfly flutters round a flower," he wrote, "So my soul always fluttered round her rosy lips."

Despite the ongoing conflict between the ancient pagan and the Christian world, Homer, Virgil, and Ovid were largely unharmed by the church—perhaps because Rome itself was Hellenized. In Heine's writings however, the Pope of Rome would grant no forgiveness of sin for his unrepentant adoration of Venus. She was the devil, adorned with beautiful claws.

It was in the Louvre where—upon visiting Venus one final and momentous time—Heine burst into tears.

2

ON THE FORTNIGHT OF HIS OWN DEATH, the troubled words which spilled from Heine's pen recounted a rather recent dream. Heine described a dead man. Specific to his disturbances, *he* was the man. The poet saw himself lying in an open sarcophagus, the kind one might find in a museum, associated with Egypt, Greece, or Rome, and surrounded by shards of broken sculpture. This particular funeral receptacle however was clearly Hellenized, like the statue of his devotion, as it was decorated with scenes depicting both classical mythology and the Hebrew Old Testament. Suddenly, and perhaps not so quite out of the ordinary (when one stops to ponder his frequented conversations with stone), bitter and quarrelsome voices broke his silence of rest. To this effect Heinrich wrote:

"Oh, the argument will never end.

Always will Truth quarrel with Beauty.

The human host will always split

In two halves: Greeks and the Barbarians."

His poem, titled *"For Mouche,"* would prove his last.

28 years later, after Madame Heine's own passing, his *dear friend* Camille Selden recounted another troublesome irregularity surrounding his death. "On that Sunday – February 17th 1856," she wrote, "I had a strange waking." As the eight o' clock hour dawned, she heard a noise in her room, "a sort of fluttering, such as that produced on summer evenings by the wings of nocturnal butterflies which come in through the open window and search desperately for an exit." She then opened her eyes, but just as suddenly closed them, for "in the first glimmerings of day, a black form was writhing, like a gigantic insect and seeking some way of escape."

Despite the winter cold, Madame Selden hastened through Parisian streets to his home. But the poet who had intimately named her *Mouche* was already dead. He had passed, she said, recounting her terrible waking vision of the tormented spirit, somewhere between 5 and 8 o'clock in the morning.

3

THE MAN RESPONSIBLE FOR TRANSLATING the bulk of Hebrew Scripture into the Latin text we know today as the Vulgate never could erase the guilt of his lifelong love affair with Virgil, Plato, Cicero, and Homer. Like the sarcophagus of Heine's dream some fifteen-hundred years later, Jerome was unquestionably Hellenized. The church father was simply unwilling to abandon his great library in Rome, which he had slavishly collected book-by-book "with great care and toil." His guilt would bring on dedicated fasts, but *only*, he confessed to a friend, "that I might afterwards read Cicero. After many nights spent in vigil, after floods of tears called from my inmost heart, after the recollection of my past sins, I would once more take up Plautus." He quickly added, "And when at times I returned to my right mind, and began to read the prophets, their style seemed rude and repellent." He was offended by the stylistic rudeness of the early Christian writings, the way the Hebrew language rolled off the tongue and—had it not been for the encouragement of his teacher, he would have abandoned his study of the book of Daniel completely, as the Bible's greatest prophetic offerings simply paled in comparison to Quintilian and Cicero. In short, *truth* could never compete with the *beauty* of the pagan.

One might say Jerome was a human host split in two halves. And *yet*, he pondered of himself: "What agreement have Christ and Belial? What has Horace in common with the Psalter? Virgil with the Gospels? Cicero with the Apostle?"

According to his same letter, Jerome was on the eastward path for Jerusalem when, quite suddenly, he was caught up in the spirit and dragged before the judgement seat of the God. The light surrounding him was so bright, and those who stood around him so radiant, that he cast himself upon the ground, daring never to look up.

A voice then asked him who he was.

To this Jerome replied: "I am a Christian."

"Thou liest!" cried the voice. "Thou art a follower of Cicero, not of Christ. For where your treasure is, there will your heart be also."

It was his Saul on the road to Damascus moment. As one would expect of such comparisons, his life would likewise never be the same— or so he promised the Judge at the time. "If ever again I possess worldly books," he vowed, "or if ever again I read such, I have denied thee."

Jerome assured his reader as to the graveness of his encounter. "This was no sleep nor idle dream." His friends would hold him to it. Regardless, his was a promise impossible to keep. The images of his former lovers had remained as furniture pieces neatly arranged in his mind. Those memories would prod at him, knock upon his better senses, muddle clarity, and ultimately reel him in. Ultimately, powers beyond him beckoned, and Jerome, weary of the fight, would change his oath before God within fifteen years of the vision. Rather than *denying the Lord* by settling into a pagan page turner, as he had once surmised, he agreed "to read the books of God with a zeal greater than [he] had previously given to the books of men." For Jerome, it became a necessary compromise.

So legendary were Jerome's insistences to bleed pagan verse into Christian literature that his one-time friend Tyrannius Rufinus of Aquileia—the two had studied together in Rome—not merely satisfied as his strongest intellectual and confrontational opponent, became intent rather on persecuting him. Jerome was not only accused of instructing a monk in Bethlehem to copy dialogues of Cicero, but of teaching the classics to his pupils. And in a letter to the monk Pammachius, Jerome openly insisted that one could study *secular wisdom* provided the reprehensible was met with discretion. The Roman orator Magnus sought to inquire why Jerome insisted in making use of ancient pagans in his ecclesiastic work; thereby "contaminating the sacred with the profane." Though Jerome insisted to his critics that he had not read the profane authors since his school days, he did admit to reading them with an air of enjoyment, adding with the spice rack of nostalgia: "Must I then drink the waters of Lethe that I may forget?" In defending himself, rather ironically, the first figure which occurred to him was not taken from the *truth* of Scripture, but the *beauty* of mythology. For Jerome, profane literature was a captive of Christ, and could therefore be enjoyed—but to what end?

Well, for starters, *that dream*, he insisted, was probably misinterpreted for overzealousness, and was after all a dream—and only a dream.

His was a generation which pronounced such severe blows against paganism, notably the destruction of the temple of Sarapis and the murder of Hypatia in Alexandria, including the worldwide prohibition of pagan worship in 392, that his willful abstinence from works directed against the occult-faith is telling. Perhaps, to be fair, he was unwilling to go along with the mob; unafraid to cross a picket line. Lack of team spirit would certainly arouse suspicion.

Or perhaps he was simply more honest about his hypocrisy—even *if* lame intellect attempted to distract from the compromise. Despite the surface level turning of tables across the Mediterranean, from the Senate floor in Rome to the streets of Alexandria, compromises were had—dire compromises. The pagan religion simply exchanged the image of a mother *goddess* with child for a *blessed* mother with child. The illustrious world of Homer remained and the ideals embodied by Plato reigned supreme. Finally hidden in plain sight, the beauty of paganism could and would thrive. To target the few loud mouth compromisers like Jerome, willing to publicize his own love of beauty over truth, would be unfair to the universal hush of the human heart in his generation and our own.

Today we are faced with the same charges. Are we not also charmed by Apollos muses? If we were the protagonist of Jerome's dream, what name might the voice accuse us of following? If our extra-curricular lovers were to blanket our souls in death, what illustrations might engrave the sarcophagus of our intended rest? If our minds were a museum—the Louvre, if you will, what sort of furniture, artifacts of antiquity, human masterpieces, marble gods; more precisely, how much barren *truth* would fill its floors and ceiling in proportion to *beauty*? Whose eternal inheritance would they give testimony to—the tomb of the crucified Christ or the all-consuming fire prepared for Satan and his angels?

"For where your treasure is, there will your heart be also..." Perhaps Jerome's vision (or was it simply a dream) was not for him alone.

GODS OF DISNEY: THE LION KING IN LIGHT OF PLATONISM & THE MYSTERY RITES OF ISIS AND MITHRAS

THERE IS A SCENE IN DISNEY'S *THE LION KING* in which Simba, Timon, and Pumbaa are lying on their backs, having nestled into a soft bed of grass, and presently gazing, with philosophically wonder, at the stars in the firmament above.

The warthog, they call him *Mister Pig*, asks Timon: "Timon, ever wonder what those sparkly dots are up there?"

The meerkat coolly responds: "Pumbaa, I don't wonder. I know."

Pumbaa shrugs: "*Oh*. What are they?"

"They're fireflies," says Timon. "Fireflies that, *uh*…got stuck up on that big bluish-black thing."

Pumbaa shrugs, "*Oh, gee*. I always thought they were balls of gas burning billions of miles away."

I seem to recall, being thirteen years of age when *The Lion King* was first released in June of 1994, that Pumbaa's declaration garnished one of the audience's largest howls of approval. Even I laughed along because, in a way, the logic was inverted. Though the warthog was apparently *ignorant* in the scope of his imaginative prowess, as globe earth Copernicans, we knew him to be *right*.

For added comic relief, Timon then exchanges one laugh for another.

"Pumbaa," he sighs, "with you, everything's gas."

Insert laugh track….

"Simba, what do you think?" The warthog wants to know.

Simba sighs, "Well, I don't know…"

His *sigh* is important. Simba does in fact have a varying opinion on the matter, and should we have been paying close attention, astrology fills in those gaps. Early on in the narrative, the cub has already been instructed by his father Mufasa regarding the legitimate identity and divine personhood of the stars.

"Simba," Mufasa instructed his son, "Let me tell you something that my father told me. *Look at the stars. The great kings of the past look down on us from those stars.*"

His cub was intrigued, "Really?"

"Yes. So whenever you feel alone, just remember that those kings will always be there to guide you, and so will I."

In 1994, Simba's *sigh* immediately abreasted us with the need to clench our gut. As royalty, we know he has been taught hidden mysteries which the little people, the uninitiated, are not aware of. We know what *he knows* on the matter, but the question is, does he still *believe*? Culpability is a necessary recipe for his sigh. Simba is filled with guilt. He holds himself responsible for the death of his father. And rather than claiming accountability in such a way as to deal with the trauma, he has chosen to stump his own emotional maturity, despite taking on the biological markings of an adult. He has forsaken his moral obligation in favor of a carefree life. *Hakuna Matata.* That's his philosophy, we are told. In Swahili, it means *no worries.* But you probably already knew that.

Still, Pumbaa wants to know. "*Aw* come on. Give, give, give..." he pleads. "Well, come on, Simba, we told you ours... *pleeeease?*"

Timon joins in with the plea.

Rather reluctantly, Simba says: "Well, somebody once told me that the great kings of the past are up there, watching over us."

Pumbaa says, "Really?"

And then Timon, apparently trying to keep his composure, asks: "You mean a bunch of royal dead guys are watching us?" Timon immediately collapses into side-splitting laughter. Pumbaa joins in.

Simba does so too, but only half-heartedly.

"Who told you something like that? What mook made that up?"

Simba shrugs: "Yeah, pretty dumb, *huh?*"

But we recognize cinematic *conflict* when it is feed to us. This is 1994, and as audience members seated in that darkened theater, we share a common optimism. The applause solely belongs to Simba, even it he hasn't earned it yet. If only Simba would not forget his *true self*. In typical Hollywood fashion, the reality truly is inverted. Pumbaa's laughable agreement with the elementary-age textbook is in fact the punishable ignorance. If we cling to a single faith, it is in whimpered hopes that Mufasa's worldview will conquer the east African dark—how can it not? Despite Simba's *sigh*; despite his slumping off into the night; orthodoxy is about to be manifested. It is through a witch doctor named Rafiki—the word means *friend* in Swahili—in which Simba will receive a vision from the stars itself.

Simba beholds a god.

"Simba," calls a familiar voice, "you have forgotten me."

The blazing eyes... the fiery hair and crystalline complexion... And yet Simba does not stop to question the identity of the divine being in the stars.

"No, how could I?"

Mufasa explains: "You have forgotten who you are, and so forgotten me. Look inside yourself Simba, you are more than what you have become. You must take your place in the Circle of Life."

"How can I go back? I'm not who I used to be."

"Remember who you *are*. You are my son, and the one true King."

Peculiar weather, the baboon quips.

Another joke. *Insert laugh track*. If the audience cackles, its likely because they know what the baboon has already long known—that Simba also is now in the *know*. In slightly other terms, he has been granted *hidden knowledge*. But more importantly to the turn of the tide, he has not disposed of nor fumbled it this time. Gnosis prompts action. And no king, whatever his lineage, may assert his claim to the throne without it. What the audience likely doesn't realize however is that Simba's initiation eerily depicts the very sort of vision which filled crypt-like catacombs throughout the Mysteries of Mithras. His father, in a way, personifies Mithras himself.

It is a scene directly out of Plato's *Timaeus*.

For Plato, individual adepts could find immortality through initiation and transformation. Essential to this were the stars. Specifically to *Timaeus*, each soul was connected with its own star, one which he or she would return to after death. This is why Plato believed all knowledge was nothing more than a recollection of our previous existence in the spiritual realm of *perfect* forms, critical truths which are aptly forgotten and likely corrupted in this present world of matter. A century later, the Turkish-born Greek philosopher Heraclides Ponticus (387-312) identified the Milky Way as the path on which the souls ascended and descended—hence the thick concentration of stars. He wrote, "The great Plato had comparatively recently insisted that while our fallen, corruptible world may be analyzable using rationality, the really pure, uncontaminated cosmic bodies were to be found in the skies, or rather the heavens. Here were the seats of pure spirituality, divine beings if you like." The early twentieth-century scholar Franz Cumont would refer to this religion as "celestial immortality," or "sidereal eschatology."

Platonism, and the Mysteries which the Patriarch of Greek philosophy derived his intellectual inquiry from, as well, rather ironically, as the clockwork occulting wisdom which emerged from his water well, monopolizes *The Lion King*'s entire weltanschauung. If Pumbaa's imaginative conclusions *were* accurate, then the entire script would be capsized.

Consider that Simba had braved his own demise by entering into the confines of death itself; the only land void of light—the elephant graveyard. Surely, he would have been killed by its inhabitants, the hyenas, had it not been for the intervention of his father. Every episode of Simba's life lacked responsibility. While ignoring his moral obligations on the *Hakuna Matata* parade, death itself swallowed up his kingdom. Simba was no neophyte—at least, up to this point. His father however was. Clearly, Mufasa has been initiated several degrees into the Mystery cult of celestial immortality. And now, with the ascended master's *appearing* in the heavens, everything has changed. Simba, finally a true initiate of the Mysteries, must now master himself by gazing so intently at the heavens above that he ultimately punctures and penetrates deep within his very being and remembers *who he is*, and by doing so, journey into the sunless realm of death itself. Mortality must be hurdled back to the hyena's realm.

And so, by closing credits, it is done.

In yet other terms, *The Lion King* is simply another retelling of the Mysteries of Isis. Simba's parents, their names are Mufasa and Sarabi, are stand-ins for the paternal gods of Egypt, Osiris and Isis. Twins from conception, Mufasa and Sarabi, or rather, Osiris and Isis, were such perfect lovers that they conjugated within their mother's womb. And as a pointed feature in the transmigration of souls, Osiris inherited his kingship form a divine lineage which he could trace back to Ra, creator of the world. A fellow initiate would likely hear Mufasa and Sarabi's religious devotion to *the Circle of Life* and understand what they were inferring. After all, the ruling king and queen were children of the earth god Geb and the sky goddess Nut. Though it is true, upon dying, that their corpse would return to the earth god Geb, essentially becoming leaves of grass for the antelope's consumption, it is also assured that their souls would simultaneously return to Nut, their mother goddess, and so, like the cyclical deposition and condensation of rain, the soul continues on in the Circle of Life.

But there was only one problem, Mufasa's brother Scar—or rather, Osiris' brother, Set.

Set was jealous. Osiris held his kingdom in perfect balance. And Set wanted it.

There is very little information provided in Egyptian literature regarding the specifics of Osiris' reign. Within the Mysteries of Isis, it is his murder at the hands of Set and the devastating aftermath which grips the interest of her devotees. Osiris, you see, was not only a righteous king; his precedent materialized the rule of *maat*. For the Egyptian, the goddess Maat personified the ideal natural order—truth, balance, harmony, law, morality, and justice. Maat not only regulated the stars in the womb of their mother Nut and the seasons emanating from their father Geb, but managed both mortals and deities alike. Essentially, *maat* is best exemplified in The Lion King's opening ceremony, when mortals pay homage to the cub born in the cave, like Mithras before him, and with the aid of the baboon shaman, is metaphorically ascended for the praise and reverence of all. However, with Set upon the throne of Osiris, the goddess Maat has apparently lost her authority. Order is therefore ruled by disorder—balance by imbalance. In *her* place the rule of *Isfet* materialized. In Egyptian terms, this simply meant injustice, chaos, violence and evil reigned supreme.

It is through Simba, or in this case Horus, child of Osiris and Isis and nephew of Set, in which the usurper might be defeated and Maat restored to the throne. Only through Horus might his father Osiris still live.

And so, you see, the Circle continues.

But do understand. *The Lion King* isn't simply an outdated story highlighting our mythological superstitions of old. The esoteric, in one ear and out the other for most, is as far from lazy storytelling as one can get. For the initiate of every age, Isis and Horus is a parable embellishing divine providence. Though it is true, at present, that the Mysteries of Isis prompts us to gaze so intently into the firmament above that we are expected to discover the divine within; it also directs us towards what is expected to come.

Or as Rafiki, the witch doctor baboon, concluded for the Occulting hopeful:

"The king has returned."

Roll end credits.

"MYSTERY, BABYLON THE GREAT, THE MOTHER OF HARLOTS AND ABOMINATIONS OF THE EARTH (*Globe Earth, That Is*)"

THE PROTESTANT REFORMERS WERE CERTAINLY NOT SHY when promoting the Roman Catholic Church as "the Whore of Babylon." Indeed, Greco-Roman culture had infiltrated its every rank of papacy, despite Roman Catholicism's claim to the contrary. The church was Hellenized. Pagan ceremonies, many of which funneled through Pergamum, were cleverly masked with Christian symmetry, once Emperor Constantine successfully merged the two together. As such, heathen festivals were converted into 'Holy Days' so that deities of solar monism such as Mithras and Saturnalia or the Spring Equinox and Esther could be upheld by its devotees. Saints stood in for the pantheon of mingling gods, just as Isis, Queen of Heaven, and mother of Horus, easily disguised herself as Mary, Queen of Heaven and mother of Christ. Transubstantiation seemed to originate with the rest of them, not only with the reemergence of Aristotle, but in the various hidden mystery schools of Greece and ancient Egypt and Babylon, and in such a way that a devotee to that serpent of old could pass his practices off to the uninitiated as Christian while worshiping him in plain sight.

Even the pope's title, which he proudly wears on his crown, is VICARIUS FILII DEI, or *Vicar of Christ*. Strange indeed, since he is making a blasphemous and totally unashamed statement that he is publically taking the office of our High Priest, Jesus Christ. Martin Luther and the Reformers were certainly not shy of this either, rightly labeling him his Greek-language counterpart rather than the Latin, *Anti-Christ*. For this is what he is, by his own disclosure. And the number of his name is 666.

In 1 John 2:18 John writes: "Little children, it is the last time: and as ye have heard that antichrist shall come, even now are there many antichrists; whereby we know that it is the last time."

Yes, it certainly is strange in light of this, should modern Christians consider the Jesuit a friend of his—he is certainly no companion with the authority of Scripture. Indeed, the Reformation must be an unpleasant feculence in the pages of church history for that obtuse Christian who eagerly attempts harmony with the very totalitarian institution, and the Jesuit Pope they've recently put into power, which formed only out of a perverse necessity to sever and destroy Luther, Sattler, Zwingli, Knox, and their band of rebels with a counter-reformation of the their own.

It is said of the Spanish noble Ignatius Loyola that, while lying wounded with fits of fever in a hospital bed, a vision of the Virgin Mary encouraged him to found the Society of Jesus in 1534. The Protestant historian Wylie writes, "He who lay down on his bed the fiery soldier of the emperor rose from it the yet more fiery soldier of the pope."

Loyola developed homespun *"spiritual exercises"* in order to bring his devotees to godly perfection. In their own words, Jesuits were to be "corpse or cadaver" in order to "unhesitatingly obey" the will of their superiors. Through systematic meditation, prayer, contemplation, visualization, and illumination, Loyola and his followers would mystically slink and slither into trances of ecstasy, where they might encounter the face of God or Christ in person. He was even seen to levitate off the floor, as have many Jesuits completely under satanic power, and reportedly even worked himself to such enlightenment as to ascend to the heights of heaven. All Loyola truly succeeded in doing is refitting witchcraft with a Christian mask over it—more Mystery religion delusion.. And it worked.

"And it must be confessed," writes Wylie, "that these new soldiers did more than all the armies of France and Spain to stem the tide of Protestant success, and bind victory once more to the banners of Rome."

While pushing the Protestant ranks back on all fronts, the Jesuits would succeed in administering a strict coherence to Roman Catholicism, particularly at the Council of Trent, which was fully predicated on ecclesiastical tradition. During Trent's final session, the arch bishop of Reggio awarded church tradition as authority over Scripture. Among the evidence he cited was the change of Sabbath from the last to first day of the week, which even the Reformers admittedly kept. Indeed, in their insistence on *Scripture Alone*, the Reformers had succeeded in stirring the pot, and the result was *thus*: the Roman Catholic Church, having sold its soul to the Devil himself, mustered the motivation to grasp supreme dominance over the world.

This cannot be overstated. The Catholic Church was the motivating force behind Copernicus, persistently urging their reluctant cleric to spread the heliocentric model which openly contradicted and ridiculed Scripture. With Copernicus' deathbed publication made open to the public, *On the Revolutions of the Heavenly Spheres*, the apostates now had an army to back them. Jesuits were the perfect instruments to effect a clandestine operation, amending the publics' opinion in the authority of Scripture, the creation, and ultimately its Creator as they saw fit.

Together they planned an evil which not one collected generation of human souls could dream of aspiring to or accomplishing on its own. Work of supernatural influence was manifest in their renowned prowess, succeeding at everything the Order of Jesus attempted, by infiltrating all levels of world government and institutions of learning, from the lowest education to the highest form, deceiving even protestant congregations where they could. For the first time in church history it's leaders, whom our Master Shepherd had once entrusted his keys to, were now under demonic influence.

If the Platonists were responsible for originating the globe religion and the Kabbalists the big bang which created it, the Jesuits surely had their part in sponsoring and spreading the forgery. Their lie could easily travel halfway around the world before a Reformer tied his boots. Father Andrew Pinsent serves on the Faculty of Theology at Oxford University. He holds advanced degrees in theology from the Pontifical Gregorian University in Rome as well as a doctorate in philosophy, and a doctorate in particle physics from Oxford. In 2015 he stated: "Being both a priest and a former particle physicist at CERN, I am often asked to give talks on faith and science. Quite often young people ask me the following question, 'How can you be a priest and believe in the Big Bang?' To which I am delighted to respond, 'We invented it! Or more precisely, Fr Georges Lemaître invented the theory that is today called the 'Big Bang' and everyone should know about him.'"

The author of the Big Bang theory was none other than a Jesuit-trained priest, Father Georges Lemaître. After once hearing his presentation on the matter, Einstein famously applauded and said, "This is the most beautiful and satisfactory explanation of creation to which I have ever listened!"

Was it not our very own Jesuit Pope Francis who said, "The Big Bang, that today is considered to be the origin of the world, does not contradict the creative intervention of God; on the contrary, it *requires it.*"

For a church that wickedly denies the authority of Scripture, placing its trust wholly on priestly institutions, it should turn the head of any God-fearing Christian to learn that the religious Jesuits have produced more star-gazing astronomers than any other group of men. That the Vatican operates an observatory in Arizona, manned by Jesuits, which happens to be configure LUCIFER, a large binocular telescope, into its ownership, should keep the God-fearing Christian's full attention (despite the Vatican's insistence that they didn't name it that).

Lucifer was named by fiver German scientists, who were apparently tossing around names, when they thought of *the devil.* So they made the Latin word for "morning star" into an acronym. "Large Binocular Telescope Near-infrared Utility with Camera and Integral Field Unit for Extragalactic Research,"

"In Germany, they wouldn't have the same hesitation that Americans would have, since it's a very secular country," said Daniel Stolte, a spokesperson for the University of Arizona. "I may be completely off, but that's just my hunch— for us Germans, Lucifer just sounds cool. It's more historical than emotional."

Follow from cause to effect: it was the Catholic Church which pushed the agenda of their hesitant cleric to the forefront, thereby dismissing the very Biblical cosmology of a geocentric earth which they had been entrusted with protecting. It was the Catholic Church, undeniably under the guide of the Jesuits, who altered the entire calendar into the Gregorian we honor today, so that we wouldn't know the times, let alone the true week or day, in which we live. With a globe earth circling the sun now in place, and with billions of other planets equally adhering to distant suns, the path was paved for Gap Theorists, Darwin, and the Big Bang. We are now insignificant to the order of God's thoughts, as *clearly* He has business elsewhere to attend to. Indeed, the apostate may attempt to merge the two, evolution with creation—all under the Pope's orders—but such a thought does not flow from the mind of innocence, nor does it spring from God Almighty, for it does a far superior job of driving men away from Him rather than bringing them into the fold.

We are now expected to live in a reality where John Lennon's words ring true:

"Imagine there's no heaven

It's easy if you try

No hell below us

Above us, only sky

Imagine all the people living for today."

It's ironic really—by adhering to *Scripture Alone* as their bedrock of authority, and rightly so, the Protestant Reformers seemingly managed to whip the devil into submission, at least by their reckoning. But far from it! Certainly, by her mere association with alchemy and the hidden mystery schools which dominated her worship, the Roman Catholic Church was exposed as an HTD to the Gospel—Revelation's Whore of Babylon—just as the Pope made himself known as the Anti-Christ, to anyone with ears of discretion, who seeks no other purpose but to drive men away from God.

If Pope Francis is claiming that Luther's Reformation is over, it's only because he has the inside information which so few of us are willing to take into our own private council. Satan, being not so threatened by the measly whipping of a few, simply turned his tormentors gaze from those lies they found so appalling, seemingly small in retrospect, to a far greater conspiracy in which they could all mutually agree upon—being wholly beautiful to them. The church fled from one City of Destruction into the Metropolis of another.

Listen to me carefully, fellow brother and sister in the faith. We will *never*—NO NEVER!—escape our adulterous bondage with Mystery Babylon until we cast down every human institution and governing authority, not by physical means but in our own spiritual willpower, which seeks to supplant the Lord's Testimony concerning Himself and fully conform, to the best of our spiritual know-how and ability, to the simplistic freedoms which we find in *Scripture Alone*.

"And upon her forehead was a name written, **Mystery, Babylon the Great, The Mother of Harlots and Abominations of the Earth.** *" Revelation 17:5 (KJV)*

"*Ye Shall Not Add nor Take Away....*" ORAL TRADITION INSERTED INTO THE WRITTEN WORD IS REBELLION AGAINST THE LORD

THE JEW HOLDS NOT TO THE TORAH, as some of us have been led to believe, but to the Kabbalah and the Talmud. It is said that Moses, descending from the Mountain, wrote down the Torah but presented the Talmud in oral form, which was faithfully passed down to each generation in succession—until it was, of course, finally put to print. Where conflict arises with the Torah, oral traditions often if not always take precedence.

The Apostle Paul warned us of this when he wrote:

"Beware lest any man spoil you through philosophy and vain deceit, after the tradition of men, after the rudiments of the world, and not after Christ (Colossians 2:8)."

Perhaps Rabbi Ben Zion Bokser, author of "*The Wisdom of the Talmud,*" correctly addressed this conflict when he said, "Much of what exists in Judaism is absent in the Bible, and much of what is in the Bible cannot be found in Judaism...."

The Christian should pay attention, if such realization has yet to occur to him. Judaism *is not* the religion of the Bible, nor has it ever been since before Jesus Christ walked the earth.

Jesus Christ condemned such oral nonsense when he spoke, "*Making the Word of God of none effect through your tradition....*" (Mark 7:13). Perhaps we must conclude that Jesus, as a standing first-century Jewish Rabbi, missed out on the higher education, because He only seemed to study the written tradition afforded to Him by His Father as opposed to the academic oral, and clearly had Deuteronomy 4:2 in mind. "*Ye shall not add unto the word which I command you, neither shall ye diminish ought from it, that ye may keep the commandments of the Lord your God which I command you.*"

How odd—hundreds of years ago, relying on ancient Jewish teachings, the kabbalists described what modern physicists are discovering and describing today. How do two theories that seem so far apart come together? They both start from the same observation—Jewish mysticism.

Long before Charles Darwin, 13th century Rabbi Isaac ben Samuel of Acre made *this* following insight. Since Sabbatical cycles existed before man was created, time before Adam and Eve must be measured in divine years. Rabbi Isaac of Akko, who held that we are in the seventh Sabbatical cycle, concluded our Universe to be 15 billion years old.

The Higgs Boson "God particle," which CERN discovered in 2012, needs only trace its origins back to kabbalist Moshe ben Nachman, known as Nachmanides or Ramban (1194-1270), and Isaac Luria (1534-72). Ramban, who refers to his discoveries as coming from "hidden knowledge," expressed the kabbalist view that the universe at its creation was immaterial and not bigger than a mustard seed, while "Divine Rabbi Luria," who remains this day undisputedly the greatest kabbalist in history, expounded on the Universe's origins to such a degree that astrophysics owe a great debt of gratitude, mainly because their concept-for-concept theory of the Big Bang is rooted directly through him. Accordingly, ten vessels were originally meant to contain the emanation of God's light, but were unable to withstand that light and were hence shattered. As a result of this cosmic catastrophe, the *Sefirot*, the archetypal values through which the cosmos was created, are shattered and out of place. The world within which we reside is composed of the shards of these broken values.

Though many Copernican Christians recognize the obvious and long-standing kabbalist affair with our present science delusion, their wisdom falls short where the globe is concerned—perhaps out of wishful thinking. And yet the two are inseparable. It is all the same delusion. Plato's globe can also be traced to the Babylonian Talmud. For this reason, Jews were prohibited from having images, if indeed that image "is holding an orb," because it would imply that the idol "grasps the whole world as if it were a globe."

It is in the Zohar in which we read: "….all the world rolls in a circle like a ball, these down and these up, and all the creatures in six lands (our continents) are different in their appearances in accordance with the differences of air in each place…..Therefore there are places in the world that when it is light for those on one side of the sphere it dark for those on the other side of the sphere, for these it is day while for those it is night; and there is a place in the world where it is always day and there is no night, except for a few moments." (Zohar vol.3, on the portion of Vayikra, fol. 9b-10a)

The Jerusalem Talmud, or *Talmud Yerushalmi*, Avoda Zara 3:1, states: "R' Yonah said: When Alexander the Macedonian wanted to go back, he flew [on the back of an eagle] higher and higher until he saw the earth as a ball and the sea as a plate."

Jesus wisely advised His disciples, "Take heed and beware of the leaven of the Pharisees and of the Sadducees (Matthew 16:6)."

We are further told that His disciples reasoned among themselves, saying, "It is because we have taken no bread."

Perhaps our present congregation is also confused as to the meaning of this passage, because though bread we may lack (or have plenty of), oral tradition and the wisdom of the Greeks have infiltrated the church to such a degree that our entire belief in the created order has capsized. Just look what has happened to the world and our church and the apostasy of so many and then consider Galatians 5:9, which reads: "a little leaven leaveneth the whole lump." These are not idle words. Bread we may or may not be in need of, but we are certainly in desperate need of another reformation without the leaven.

THE SCARECROW AND JOHN CALVIN:
"Astronomy Loves Me... It Loves Me Not..."

THE MERE MENTION OF HIS NAME can break the moral sweat of the most law-abiding churchgoers. One might say he can even yank their knickers in a twist—*especially* during a Sunday school discussion. I've personally witnessed these unpleasantries unfold, but I can't blame them. How one *reads* the Bible changes everything, including the shape of the world. John Calvin's employment of such celebrated Scripture as "For God so loved the *world*," and wrenching it to signify, "For God so loved the *elect*," in order to corroborate with his Augustine doctrine, exhumes a rather pungent odor for the Biblical literalist, who'd prefer the Spirit mean what He says rather than spoon-feeding Him like a magic bunny in-route to the cooing babies mouth. The French theologian had a habit of that—*contorting*. For example, Calvin admittedly trusted science, which is odd for an individual on the outs with Rome. Or perhaps not so odd, since Calvin and Ignatius of Loyola, who founded the Society of Jesus, were classmates at the University of Paris. Calvin even referred to astronomy as "an art" which unfolded "the admirable wisdom of God." For John Calvin of Geneva, a terrible sin was committed. He placed Science in higher standing than God's own Testimony. And like any wicked dog, which he so lovingly and obediently fed, it would cruelly turn around and bite him.

It is true that many acknowledged and accomplished men believed the earth to be a globe long before Nicolas Copernicus. We need travel back to the Greeks, as far as the third-century BC, to observe its spherical status fundamentally recognized among the powerful Elite. There is little doubt in my mind that the globe has been the favored narrative by esteemed scholars, despite the jargon of *we* common folk, pew-boys and peasants who—throughout ages past—admire God's own account of creation over the imaginative conjuring of philosophers. The silent majority have not always been documented as they ought. And yet how many recorded men, I wonder—especially those in high-standing positions of the worldly institutes—wholeheartedly regarded the earth to be flat and yet chose to remain silent by adopting the only alternative anecdote? I believe there are a good number throughout recorded history, including our own, who have kept it at a *mum*. Calvin, one might argue, was not among them. Unlike many of his Reformer contemporaries, let us therefore consider, for sake of argument, that he considered the earth as spherical.

We shall henceforth deny Calvin of his own conclusions and speak hypothetically—for sake of academic argument—while pressing forward. It is here in *Institutes of the Christian Religion* that John Calvin writes:

> "...every one appropriates to himself some peculiar error; but we are all alike in this, that we substitute monstrous fictions for the one living and true God—a disease not confined to obtuse and vulgar minds, but affecting the noblest, and those who, in other respects, are singularly acute. How lavishly in this respect have the whole body of philosophers betrayed their stupidity and want of sense? To say nothing of the others whose absurdities are of a still grosser description, how completely does Plato, the soberest and most religious of them all, lose himself in his round globe?"

We shall overlook Calvin's rightful denial of the globe and turn to his commentary on Genesis, because the Reformer placed sincere trust in natural revelation. Here he contemplates the following oddities on astronomy: "...this study is not to be reprobated, nor this science to be condemned, because some frantic persons are wont boldly to reject whatever is unknown to them." He is speaking of those, in his own day as well as ours, who would hold up the words of Moses in protest, should the *supposed* honesty advertised from the halls of Science lead them to different—dare I say, *opposing*—realizations. Concerning the penmanship of Moses, Calvin is quick to enlighten us (much as he would his own understanding of John 3:16): "...because he was ordained a teacher as well of the unlearned and rude as of the learned, he could not otherwise fulfill his office than by descending to this grosser method of instruction. Had he spoken of things generally unknown, the uneducated might have pleaded in excuse that such subjects were beyond their capacity. Lastly since the Spirit of God here opens a common school for all, it is not surprising that he should chiefly choose those subjects which would be intelligible to all."

That Science was always intended to one day *interpret* our understanding of Holy Writ, once we had properly acquainted and educated ourselves through the education which Moses—being himself wise in Egypt's eyes—properly received, Calvin claims: "Moses wrote in a popular style things which without instruction, all ordinary persons, endued with common sense, are able to understand; but astronomers investigate with great labor whatever the sagacity of the human mind can comprehend." Where in Scripture this prophecy is foretold, I cannot say. A reference has yet to be found.

At any rate, this is where Calvin gets *practical* in his high-regard for Science as a superior magistrate to the Bible. He writes: "Moses makes two great luminaries; but astronomers prove, by conclusive reasons that the star of Saturn, which on account of its great distance, appears the least of all, is *greater* than the moon." In other words, Moses' declaration is *incorrect*, but is acceptable in its error, because his message was intended for "common usage." He further writes: "If the astronomer inquires respecting the actual dimensions of the stars, he will find the moon to be less than Saturn; but this is something abstruse, for to the sight it appears differently. Moses, therefore, rather adapts his discourse to *common usage*," and, "There is therefore no reason why janglers should deride the unskilfulness of Moses in making the moon the second luminary; for he does not call us up into heaven, he only proposes things which lie open before our eyes."

If Moses did not bother to "call us up to heaven," it's because the Lord had reserved a time when men of a "more exalted knowledge," as Calvin put it, would pull the curtains back for us. The problem is, according to this logic, once astronomers committed themselves to the task—revealing the heavenly stage behind the curtain, so to speak, the firmament (that solid glassy dome of Biblical mythology) did not exist as advertised; nor the waters above it. Or so the claim goes. In the eternal gullible we must go. Writes Calvin: "Moses describes the special use of this expanse, to divide the waters from the waters from which word arises a great difficulty. For it appears opposed to common sense, and *quite incredible*, that there should be waters above the heaven."

It has already been established by this point that the Prophet, according to his post-enlightenment spokesperson, wrote for the common knowing the more exalted knowledge was still to come. Unfortunately, a problem arises. Mainly, the faith-sharers. As such, "The assertion of some, that they embrace by faith what they have read concerning the waters above the heavens, notwithstanding their ignorance respecting them, is not in accordance with the design of Moses." *Tell us of Science again, Mr. Calvin.* He continues, "And truly a longer inquiry into a matter open and manifest is superfluous."

Despite Calvin's arrogant embrace of a Scientism, which apparently acts as the overriding mouth of God, there came a point in history where even he drew a line in the sand. The Copernican who smugly reminds us that "the globe has been long believed," and "it is proof that God is a Copernican," is presenting us with a strawman argument. He will give the impression that he has refuted the disagreement while actually refuting an argument which was never once presented.

Regarding the overriding truth of cosmology, our long lineage of spiritual fathers all agreed upon one thing. The earth is stationary, with a sun which revolves around us—*not* the other way around. Though many—and I stress many—were also devoted citizens of flat earth. But that is beside the point at the moment, because we are dealing with a strawman, and the longstanding church doctrine, by which no one thought reasonable to part from, was that of geocentricism. Ambrose, Anatolius of Alexandria, Athanasius, Augustine of Hippo, Basil, Chrysostom, Clement of Rome, Cyril of Jerusalem, Gregory of Nyssa, Hippolytus, Irenaeus, Jerome, Justin Martyr, Tertullian—and I am only naming a few—though might I even add John Calvin as well as Luther—were all geocentrists. Calvin was a geocentrist. There was simply no debate where the intent of the Holy Ghost was concerned. The Bible presents us with no other authoritative view. And as far as our line-up of spiritual fathers was concerned, anyone who disagreed with this undeniable Testimony was a *compromiser.*

Still, John Calvin was a compromiser. Indeed many, including some names mentioned above, very well may have been compromisers—if they employed Science as an informant for their Biblical beliefs, and not the other way around. Saint Augustine was a clear violator. But that is also to be expected. Spurgeon once quipped: "Perhaps Calvin himself derived it [Calvinism] mainly from the writings of Augustine." Calvin himself wrote: "Augustine is so wholly with me, that if I wished to write a confession of my faith, I could do so with all fullness and satisfaction to myself out of his writings."

It is not easy seeing someone get hustled. But Calvin, caught with his grimy fingers in the jar of Scientism, was certainly hustled. His exasperated reaction is to be expected. The men who "call us up to heaven" with a "more exalted knowledge" through "an art" which "unfolds the admirable wisdom of God" were committing themselves instead to a terrible deception—one which even Calvin himself would come to terms with. A number of scholars, ranging from Bertrand Russell to Thomas Kuhn, attributed Calvin as having challenged: "Who will venture to place the authority of Copernicus above that of the Holy Spirit?"

Whether or not such a question was ever asked, the following we know is true. Spoke Calvin from his pulpit: "The Christian is not to compromise so as to obscure the distinction between good and evil, and is to avoid the errors of] those dreamers who have a spirit of bitterness and contradiction, who reprove everything and prevent the order of nature. We will see some who are so deranged, not only in religion but who in all things reveal their monstrous nature that they will say that the sun does not move, and that it is the earth which shifts and turns. When we see such minds we must indeed confess that the devil possess them, and that God sets them before us as mirrors, in order to keep us in his fear!"

So the next time a Copernican berates you for your flat earth beliefs in the face of all the men who blindly went along with the globe parade, remember the strawman and John Calvin. Even John Calvin was a geocentrist. Though admittedly, John Calvin mocked Plato's globe. He believed in Flat Earth. But I'm getting off point, because Calvin was a geocentrist. In fact, *they all were.*

SCIENCE AND THE SPIRIT MIRROR—OUR UNENDING HONEYMOON WITH ANGELS

KING ARTHUR HAD MERLIN AND QUEEN ELIZABETH did too, only we know him today as Dr. John Dee (1527-1608)—or the gift which keeps on giving. Not only was he a mover and shaker behind Britain's Empirical rule, he was the inspiration for the character Doctor Faustus, Shakespeare's Prospero, and being a spy for His Majesty, Ian Fleming even borrowed Dee's signature, "007." His students included Francis Bacon, promoter of the "scientific method," and the astronomer Thomas Diggs, who believed the universe to be infinite. As the Queen's "science" adviser, his duties included astronomer, mathematician, navigator, spy, cabalist, alchemist, and perhaps most important of all, celestial necromancer.

Dee once explained to the Holy Roman Emperor Rudolf II during a visit to Prague that he found no book which could teach him the truths he so longed for. Dee hoped communion with the angels would help him solve the mysteries of the heavens—certainly not as they were revealed by the Holy Ghost in the Bible, and therefore accepted everywhere by God-fearing men and women of the faith. My discerning reader should immediately take note of *which* angels formed the opinions of the modern day universe then—certainly not those who are obedient to the Lord Almighty. True servants of God, even our modern day scientists, which I am accused of dishonoring, will not willingly contradict the Spirit. And yet they do—openly, knowing the Christian is gullible in these matters. I know. I myself used to be one of them.

England could and would not partake as a contributor to modern Science without John Dee. Yet it is no secret that he was a mystic. As Dee read the Talmud, the heavens were *opened*. Dee organized this new transcendence of knowledge, mathematics, optics, astrology, science, and navigation, through the only available avenue to him, a polished obsidian mirror by which the angels would in turn appear.

Occultist Edward Kelley and he were friends. Together they conversed in what they referred to as the Enochian language, which was taught to them directly through their stones of obsidian. It was while on tour in Poland, giving lectures on magic and alchemy to the aristocratic Elite, Kelley was told by his celestial informants that the two were to swap wives—which they did for a night. Nine months later, Dee would raise Kelley's son as his own.

My reader will take note that Western Science derives from Hermetic thought and natural philosophy, a banner which it proudly waves to this day. John Dee was influenced by the two, as were the lot of them. He believed numbers formed the basis of all phenomena. The numerical value of his name, which he freely boasted in his writings, was 666. Bacon too was involved with the occult, but unlike Queen Elizabeth, who openly confided in it, her successor King James was not so appreciative. As such, mathematics could cypher a number and geometry could present symbols for truth. Using them repeatedly in cryptic ways was important ritually for the occults survival.

From Hermeticism, Dee drew the belief that man had the potential for divine power, which could be exercised through mathematics. His ultimate goal was to help bring forth—pay attention, discerning Christian—a unified world religion. The recent breach of the Protestants from the Catholics was not exactly smiled upon by many, and recapturing "pure theology" of the ancients in Hermeticism could and would be accomplished through the iron fist of Scientism.

And yet this is not the story which we who grew up in the church were told. We have been cleverly diverted in thought by our own leaders. We have been sacked and blindfolded by the modern Creationist, who employs the very understanding of an infinite cosmos which magicians once conceived through angels and stones of obsidian. He proudly justifies his cause by pointing fingers at the Darwinist as the great corrupter of "God's perfect gifting" to humanity, while obstinately overlooking the fact that what he knows first arrived to him through the Occultist.

"A Doctrine of Demons" | JOHANNES KEPLER'S JOURNEY TO THE DARK SIDE OF THE MOON

AT THE TURN OF THE 17TH CENTURY THE REFORMATION was still waging its theological war over the will of the humanist mind in every corner of Europe, and Johannes Kepler, a German mathematician, astronomer, astrologer, and alchemist, chose his side. He aligned himself with what he aptly christened 'New Astronomy.' It was a position that openly opposed the firm foundation by which men like Tyndale, Melanchthon, and Luther and anyone else who proclaimed the principles of *Scripture Alone* stood upon. Kepler was no stranger to theology either. Both sides of the feud held hands with Biblical doctrine, or in the very least some form of it—selectively. And yet Kepler, along with his contemporaries, believed God had created the world according to an intelligible plan which could not be accessed through a reading of His Word, but only through the natural light of human reason.

Kepler described his Copernican-based 'New Astronomy' as "celestial physics," being "an excursion into Aristotle's *Metaphysics*," and "a supplement to Aristotle's *On the Heavens*." The recovery of Aristotle into Latin texts from its Greek and Arabic counterparts no doubt fueled the Big Bang explosion of apostasy and humanism in the Enlightenment church, despite the reformers best efforts, and is conclusively a radical departure from the teachings of early Christianity. It is somewhat strange that the first serious treatise on lunar astronomy, as told in Kepler's 1608 novel *Somnium* (Latin for *The Dream*), and only published by his son after his death, also happened to be what Carl Sagan referred to as the first real work of science-fiction. Then again, the truth is stranger than fiction. *Somnium* gives dark insight inside the mind of a man who gifted the world with *"Kepler's Laws of Planetary Motion,"* works which would later provide one of the foundations for Isaac Newton's theory of universal gravitation. In short, according to Kepler's novel (strange ruminations for a recognized figure of science), knowledge of the Universe, particularly its scope and motion, came not to us from the observant eye of an astronomer pressed firmly against his telescope, but through communion with demons.

The story, which centers around Kepler's own dream about himself reading a book, involves Duracotus, a 14 year-old Icelandic boy with a witch for a mother, who makes a living selling bags of herbs and cloth with strange markings on them. *This*, after Kepler first reads from another book about Libussa, a historical sorceress and prophetess in her own time, before falling asleep—and who may have evoked the story within the dream. On a side note, her habit of summoning demons—the boy's mother, that is—comes well rewarded. She has learned all she knows about astronomy from them, even knowledge concerning great unobservant distances. It is the demons, we come to learn, who not only help their human counterparts travel around the world, but through their own technological *sorcery*, to the moon and back. I'm looking at you, *Apollo*.

Yahweh commanded His congregation in the wilderness:

"Do not turn to mediums or spiritists; do not seek them out to be defiled by them. I am the LORD your God (Leviticus 19:31)."

And again in Leviticus 20:6

"As for the person who turns to mediums and to spiritists, to play the harlot after them, I will also set My face against that person and will cut him off from among his people."

The moon is of particular interest to the boy and his mother. So upon summoning her favorite demon, they are told in elaborate detail about it. Levania is its demon-given name, and is referred to as an island in the Aether. Levania is divided into two hemispheres, Privolva and Subvolva. Privolva, being the dark side of the moon, never has visual contact with the earth, but planets appear bigger. The residents of Subvolva on the other hand, oddly mirroring Einstein's own up-and-coming *theory of relativity*, can observe the rotation of Earth without ever feeling any movement themselves.

As it turns out, there's a pathway between Levania and the Earth which, when opened, some humans are said to have traveled, so long as the demons are there to escort them. The journey, spanning fifty-thousand miles and taking as little as four hours, is such a shock to a person's fragile physicality (especially when the Aether and extreme temperatures are taken into consideration), that the demons sedate their mortal travelers, much as aliens might their abductee, even propelling them notably forward with magnificent force, all in order to sustain human life and overcome the otherwise impossible hurdles of lunar travel. Here we are exposed to the wealth of their devilish sorcery.

Perhaps the most menacing presence among *Somnium's* many celestial inhabitants is in the specifics of the narrative itself, some of them being awkwardly true details concerning Kepler's scientific theories, all of which also seem to invoke a biographical recollection of his own life. For example, Kepler and the boy share the same mentor, Tycho Brahe. He and the boy also share the same mother. And when the dream is cut short, we should not be surprised to read of a spiritual confession. Kepler wakes with his head covered, and he is wrapped in blankets just like the character in his story.

This is precisely what Knox and Zwingli, alongside their reformer contemporaries, were fighting against. They called the Copernicans out, and as history has proven, very few listened! They clearly understood the Apostle Paul's warning that "*a little leaven leaveneth the whole lump* (Galatians 5:9), and also to young Timothy when he spake, "*Now the Spirit speaketh expressly, that in the latter times some shall depart from the faith, giving heed to seducing spirits, and doctrines of devils* (1 Timothy 4:1)."

There is not a modern Christian astronomer alive who would in his right mind disagree with this—*giving heed to seducing spirits, and doctrines of devils*, that is—and yet it is difficult, if not entirely impossible, to discern the doctrine of demons from truth when the natural light of human reason has pushed the Infallibility of Scripture from the forefront of his mind.

"Holding the Mystery of Faith in Pure Conscience" — JOHN LOCKE & THE HUMANIST OVERTHROW OF THE CHURCH

HEBREW COSMOLOGY IS THE SIMPLEST OF LITMUS TESTS. The writers of the Bible were not shy in this. And so the Christian, who is presented with facts yet still manages to reject what the Scripture proclaims as truth—should it not adhere to his intellectual preferences— is a humanist. The doctrine is sound. An ignored doctrine does not make it any less sound. For this we can thank the self-rationalizing humanists and great apostates such as John Locke. He has poisoned the well, so to speak. He has contaminated even the waters from which the Christian bends down to drink. And suddenly, yes quite suddenly, the man who thirsts only for and nothing else but the Written Word begins to see his face, Locke's that is—balancing among the necks and shoulders of those he only a moment ago recognized as lifelong church friends and colleagues.

This, the true Christian will surely come to find, having also learned of his own glaring error—a lifelong oversight regarding the joyous cosmology—and now, repentantly adhering to God's Word as a lamp unto his feet and light unto his path, will be immediately apprehended by his contemporaries, should they come to find out about it. They will only wish to spare him of his foolishness, as though he is easily detoured, and speaking as an Obstinate unto the Christian Pilgrim, who is fleeing from the City of Destruction, feverishly proclaim (as it was told in John Bunyan's dream): "There is a company of these crazy-headed coxcombs, that when they take a fancy by the end are wiser in their own eyes than seven men that can render a reason!"

See, the Latitudinarian will not conform to such doctrines which fail to please him, unlike those silly-stitious Puritans of old, who rightly kept to their Biblical beliefs. To such an admirer of the self, human intellect decides what is necessary and what is not. Human reason, he believes, when combined with the Holy Spirit, is a sufficient guide for determining doctrine, including what he may throw out or simply choose to ignore. Special instructions from God make individuals less amenable to human reason, whereas compromise is preferable. This is broad-based Protestantism. Under such leadership, the congregation has forsaken its birthright, Holy Writ, and in a vile adulterous act, has replaced sound doctrine with the autonomous reasoning of its choosing, casting aside dependence on God in hopes of raising human wisdom metaphysically above Him.

John Locke (1632-1704) was a true Latitudinarian, and his influence cannot be overstated. Locke's *"tabula rasa,"* an idea which first appeared with *"An Essay Concerning Human Understanding,"* cleverly understood the human to be born knowing nothing, without original sin that is, and thus through reason and education may soon himself be improved upon. He wanted nothing to do with theological mysteries, even though the Bible is filled with them. The Old Testament, he concluded, was far too irrational for civilized thinking. If it cannot be fully explained, he has a right in his "latitude thinking" to reject it.

And besides, what God ultimately cares about, according to Richard Hooker (1554-1600) in his book, *"Of the Laws of Ecclesiastical Polity"*—he was a precursor for the Latitudinarian—is the moral state of the individual soul. This is still the calling card of the modern-day Latitudinarian. And they're everywhere, in every religion of man.

The man who has repented of his glaring error holds up the pages of Holy Writ for all to see. He runs his finger across any number of scripture passages, there's over a hundred of them, which give in great length the nature of the Lord's created cosmology.

He shows them that the Earth is indeed a circle (Isaiah 40:22), made with a compass (Proverbs 8:27), laid upon a face (Genesis 1:2). It is bound (Job 26:10) at its ends (Job 38:13), established on pillars (Job 38:4) over the Great Deep (Psalm 104:6), and is fixed forever in place, immovable (Psalm 93:1), with a sun which moves in our stead, complete with a circuit to run (Psalm 19:4-6). It is covered by a solid firmament (Genesis 1:6-8), spread out as molten glass (Job 37:18), containing the sun, moon, and stars (Genesis 1:14-18), with waters above it (Genesis 7:11), which once drowned the entire world in a great deluge but still remains there (Psalm 148:4), and a heaven which establishes God's throne upon it (Psalm 104:3).

He shows his fellow Christian this most basic Hebrew understanding of the world around them, which for thousands of years

303

has otherwise not been confused. But the humanist mind is darkened, and even the special revelation in which he receives from God is mishandled in order to fit his worldview. Such are the times we live in, that a man who adheres to the complete written Testimony of God is considered a degenerate. After guiding him through all of these things the humanist cries out to him, as one would a fool, proclaiming the very line which likely resounds from the highest-sounding prayer towers of a person's own hell, "God is lost in the translation!"

"And the Sun Stood Still" | HOW FAITHLESS MEN IN A GODLESS AGE DISMISS THE MIRACLES OF GOD'S WORD

SO QUICKLY IT HAPPENS, REVERED MEN OF THE CONGREGATION expose their own faithless heart whenever the theory of *Scriptural Poetry* is promptly applied—that is, as soon as the Holy Ghost does not please their appetite for academic conformity. All Biblical spouts of the poetic, it is argued, are allowed some wiggle room in their exaggeration of historical facts. Such men permit themselves to bend facts quite frivolously into clever sounding figments—also known to our spiritual fathers as deceptions—and this is somehow a good thing. Nowadays everybody is afforded the privilege of being a poet to their own liking. Perhaps this would also explain why there is such a lack of discernment, such tireless confusion, when the fabrications of our hearts are improperly weighed among the virtues of true poetic integrity.

As the Israelites defended the Gibeonites in Canaan, we are pressed with a rather inconvenient truth.

> So the sun stood still, and the moon stopped,
> Until the nation avenged themselves of their enemies.

> Is it not written in the book of Jashar? And the sun stopped in the middle of the sky and did not hasten to go down for about a whole day.

Joshua 10:13

A miraculous claim is made by this writer of history, and backed no less than by the authority of the Holy Ghost—that the Israelite's victory over their enemies was due to a promptly answered prayer made by Joshua, in which the sun stood "in the midst of heaven, and hasted not to go down about a whole day." It would seem strange, knowing the likelihood that there is seemingly always and without fail a revered man of the faith in the room who will undoubtedly subscribe to the theory of *Scriptural Poetry* upon hearing such claims; how a straight reading seems just as historical from one verse to the next. Such a man makes assertions which have the charm of both intelligence and sincerity, but also the vice of willful inaccuracy.

The humanist claims: "We know now that couldn't possibly be true!"

To wrest the Scriptures, to twist and torture its language until it is created in our own image is neither honest nor *truly* scientific—though I must admit, it is certainly keeping to all that applies of Scientism!

Please, expert on poetry in the room, explain to me where the poetry begins and where it ends. *Oh*, that's right, sirs, you're displeased with the fact that heliocentric materialism has no place to roam, nor freely rest its head, anywhere in your personal translation of the Bible. God Himself, by His own testimony, is conclusively not a Copernican, and does not seek to conform science to the academia of Scientism, which Creationists apparently desire to rub the feet of.

The belief that it was the Earth which held fast and not the sun is not only in disobedience with the entire canon of Scripture, but is not even kept within the facts of "nature," as the Darwinian or Copernican model would demand. The very attempt to explain it in another light just goes to show the injurious effect—if even a subconscious trauma on the brain—a blind faith in the ability of educated men to grasp at the truth of God has had on the otherwise good intention of such searches, if there is such a thing as good intent. I believe Isaiah the Prophet when he said, "*To the Law and to the Testimony; if they speak not according to this Word, it is because there is no light in them (Isaiah 8:20).*" However "educated" the humanist mind may be, it is clear that they are not searching for the truth of God in science or any other hallway of academia, if the Holy Spirit and what He has revealed to us in God's Testimony is not there to guide them. Why we should be so deathly afraid of looking like fools before them is beyond me.

The verb **Shemesh**, "sun" in Hebrew, means: *to run hastily, to move very fast.* If I am to take Peter at his word, that "*prophecy came not in old time by the will of man: but holy men of God spake as they were moved by the Holy Ghost (2 Peter 1:21),*" then I am to take the pages of Holy Writ at its word. Are not its very words inspired by God? Paul reminds us, "*Which things also we speak, not in the words which man's* *wisdom teacheth, but which the Holy Ghost teacheth; comparing spiritual things with spiritual (1 Corinthians 2:13)."*

So when the Holy Ghost employs the word *Shemesh*, I take it to mean He wanted us to understand the sun as something that runs hastily and moves very fast. Therefore, Joshua 10:13 should be understood as thus: "And the hastily running, very fast moving sun stood still!"

We have no record of Joshua praying to Heaven that the Earth, fixed *"immovable and firm (Psalm 96:10),"* stand still. This is an assertion, not of the Holy Ghost, but of the "expositor." What this miraculous account in Joshua instantly reveals is that God hears prayer, and answers it. But when doing so, He never presents obvious falsities or prods men with erroneous interpretations that might lead them out of harmony with the cosmogony so unashamedly revealed, and without a single lick of contradiction, among the many authors of the Word.

Every other imaginative explanation as to the true meaning of this passage in recent church history, and there's been several, has so far fallen to the wayside, with the expositor in question fading from the spotlight into obscurity of namesake, as hell itself would have it. There is one sacred narrative and only one straightforward view that will never fade from heavens light, and that is the obvious one, for we are told that "there was no day like that, before it or after it, that the Lord hearkened unto the voice of a man, for the Lord fought for Israel."

The sun stood still in the sky.

THE LAST MAGICIAN | ISAAC NEWTON AND THE QUEST FOR IMMORTALITY

THE SCENE WAS SOTHEBY'S AUCTION HOUSE IN LONDON. It was just after luncheon on July 13, 1936. The clock struck one. Bidding began. If appetites were not yet assuaged by the food and drink presently settling in their bellies, it is simply because the item before them was a truly remarkable find. From the bidding room floor attendees beheld a metal chest containing Sir Isaac Newton's private, hand-written papers and lab books. Newton's own alma mater, Cambridge University, had acquired the treasure chest from the Earl of Portsmouth in 1872. Soon thereafter, a dedicated team of scholars set out to catalogue its contents. "This was Newton, after all," writes Sam Kean in *Humanities*, "and they were hungry for any insight into how he'd developed his theories of motion, gravity, light, and color." They were, Kean enforces, "work that defines the very Newtonian universe we inhabit." And yet, upon completing their studies sixteen years later, those papers were never published—strange indeed. Cambridge simply returned the bundle they had acquired, practically all of it, to its original owner, on the basis that they had "no scientific value." In turn, the hidden compartments of Newton's mind were soon forgotten, as *intended*, and barely survived a house fire some three years later. But Newton's *secret knowledge* would not remain *hidden* for long.

At Sotheby's in London, Newton's metal chest fell into the hands of the highest bidder—an amateur collector. Economist John Maynard Keynes sought papers on any topic of his, but after July 13, 1936, all of that would change. The father of modern science, Keynes would soon learn, was an alchemist. Cambridge had simply decided that alchemy was a disfigurement to the very paradigm which Newton had helped us to own. Keynes then set about acquiring anything of Newton's that might give insight into Newton the hobbyist. But as his alchemical papers continually filled his mailbox, Keynes finally acknowledged the inevitable. Alchemy wasn't simply a secret avocation. Alchemy was Newton's life work. In 1942, some six years after his initial discovery, Keynes concluded before distinguished members of the Royal Society,

Newton "was not the first of the age of reason. He was the last of the magicians."

> "Newton was not the first of the age of reason. He was the last of the magicians, the last of the Babylonians and Sumerians, the last great mind which looked out on the visible and intellectual world with the same eyes as those who began to build our intellectual inheritance rather less than 10,000 years ago. Isaac Newton, a posthumous child born with no father on Christmas Day, 1642, was the last wonder-child to whom the Magic could do sincere and appropriate homage."

His choice words are important here. Keynes does not shy from anointing Newton with messianic oil, comparatively with Jesus Christ, and most ironically born not on the night of Christ's historical birth, but a date deeply embedded with Occultism. It is Newton, Keynes stresses, who stands as a legitimate priest of the Babylonian whore religion. It is through Newton in which we are delivered our *inheritance* apart from divine revelation, and purposed for the sort of soul, Jesus once identified, as a son demanding his father's inheritance so that he might live among the pigs in a foreign land; the sort of soul, John further affirms, who claims his or her inheritance with Satan and his angels in the Lake of Fire.

The roots of alchemy derive from metallurgy. Essentially, by applying intense heat to specific rocks they can be purified and transformed into metal. In *The Rise and Fall of Alexandria: Birthplace of the Modern Mind*, authors Justin Pollard and Howard Reid write: "From the very start this process acquired occult or secret status, and the objects produced by this sacred craft—ornaments, jewelry, and currency from gold and silver; weapons and tools from copper, its alloys, and iron—were always given high prestige and value." We are once more directed to *Song of the Sword* in Genesis 4:23-24, proudly recited by Lamech (the lineage of Cain), and choreographed no doubt by the murderous weapon he presently brandished, and then the Watchers of Enoch who had helped him to it. Pollard and Reid continue: "It's clear from ancient texts that iron especially had divine qualities: The Egyptians called it the 'metal from heaven'; the Babylonians, 'celestial fire.' These and other sources make it seem likely that people first encountered iron as meteorites which had fallen from heaven to earth. When they later discovered the same metal underground, inside the womb of Mother Earth, it must have seemed like confirmation of the metal's divine status."

For hundreds of years alchemists toiled to produce a mythical substance known as the philosopher's stone. The supposedly dense, waxy red material was a thing of legend—an alchemical substance capable of turning base metals such as lead or mercury into gold. "There are close parallels between Egyptian beliefs and practices concerning death and the afterlife and the theory and practice of alchemy that developed in the medieval world," writes Pollard and Reid. "More specifically, the Egyptian Book of the Dead offers precise prescriptions for the transfer of the human soul from life to death and then to rebirth in immortal form which are extremely close to the prescriptions adopted by alchemists."

Cleary, Newton was in the *know*. The philosopher's stone was also called the elixir of life. It's goal, rejuvenation of the soul. It is the promise of immortality which attracted Newton. And Alexandria, as it often did, had the hieroglyphs, *apparently*, to back it. "He knew perfectly well that all this talk of transforming metals was just a façade, even a cover, for a far more profound spiritual awakening," Pollard and Reid again. In Keynes collection of papers, Newton himself wrote: "For alchemy does not trade with metals as ignorant vulgars think, which error has made them distress that noble science, but she has also material veins of whose nature God created handmaidens to conceive and bring forth its creatures."

It would be difficult indeed to track down a phone book of researchers which contained even one scholar who had read the entirety of Isaac Newton's work. No such directory exists. With an estimated 10 million written words having survived the centuries, half of which is of the religious nature and another one million devoted to alchemical material, his is a behemoth collection. Even Sarah Dry, author of *"The Newton Papers: The Strange and True Odyssey of Isaac Newton's Manuscripts,"* laughs at the very notion. Though, concerning its contents, she warns, "And one of the messages of the book is that getting too involved in the papers can be hazardous to your health. One of the first editors of (Newton's) papers said an older man should take up the task, because he'd have less to lose than a younger man."

But this we know. Isaac Newton was a disciple of "Jewish philosophy, the mysticism of Kabbalah and the Talmud;" *This,* according to Aron Heller at the *Times of Israel*. What most Christians fail to recognize or know—or rather, the cat which has remained for the most part in the bag—is that Isaac Newton was a mystic and occultist. When nobody else was looking, he exhumed rotting flesh from Alexandria, and that corpse was Hermes Trismegistus.

Pollard and Reid further write: "Few realize that his occult work, his alchemical studies, gave him the keys to the biggest breakthrough in his life. Alchemy insists that there are unseen, invisible forces at work in the universe, capable of acting on objects at a distance. An apple may (or may not) have dropped on Newton's head, but beyond a shadow of a doubt, it was alchemy which prompted Newton to formulate the notion of gravity—alchemy which had been rendered into a coherent and communicable, if secret, code in Alexandria."

S. Pancoast, author of *Kabbala: Or True Science of Light* (1883) celebrates Newton's *discovery* of gravity when he writes: "Indeed, so much of the Newtonian Philosophy do we find in the ancient, that we cannot doubt he had been exploring the old mines of Kabbalistic lore, and had arrived at his great discoveries by following up clues gained therefrom." Again he writes: "He (Pythagoras) was never permitted to declare publicly what he knew and believed, but taught his immediate pupils all the wonders of his philosophy, under the most binding obligation of secrecy. Pythagoras was forbidden to divulge this knowledge because it would reveal the law of attraction and repulsion, which constituted one of the great secrets of the sanctuary. Over a millennium later, Newton was led to the discovery of these forces by his studies of the Kabbalah."

It is of no coincide then that Abraham Yahuda, a Zionist Jew and contemporary of Albert Einstein, scoured the world collecting Newton's religious writings. According to Sarah Dry, Yahuda "set about trying to purchase the Newton papers and wrote to (his wife) Ethel on July 28, 'I am thrilled with the thought of acquiring them. He wrote a lot about the Bible and the Jews, about Cabbala and all sorts of Jewish questions."

Einstein took an immediate interest in his work. According to Dry, Einstein had hoped that Newton's papers would never get published. "Einstein considered Newton's private papers with an eye toward gleaning as much as possible of his method of discovery, what he refers to here in 'the formative development' of his work in physics. Einstein implicitly links the process by which Newton developed his physics and his theology; by studying the one, we might gain insight into the other."

Gravity simply cannot be proven. No apple can do that. What's worse, it cannot even be *tested* except by the measure of a man's faith. Neil DeGrasse Tyson might phrase it like this, "the Universe doesn't have to make sense to you." *Just believe*. Despite what Carl Sagan and his contemporaries might demand of adherers to the scientific method, the entire heliocentric religion is often explained with the familiar flag colors of pseudo-science. Make no mistake about it; the theory of gravity is Kabbalah through-and-through. According to Migene Gonzalez-Wippler, author of The *Kabbalah & Magic of Angels*, gravity "is equated with *Tiphareth*, the sixth sphere of the Tree of Life."

Author Edward Hendrie sums it up like this: "Gravity is not only an attribute of the Jewish god, *Ein Sof*, it is actually one of the god's of the Kabbalah, in its own right."

I guess I just want to know why our so-called understanding of modern astronomy and the most basic ideas in string theory today, as well as astrophysics, not forgetting Newton's gravity, all seem to concur with Babylonian mysticism in so-much as they're mirrored astonishingly with the Zohar and Kabbalistic texts of old. They're certainly advertised as such. Specifically, in my pursuit of understanding Jewish mysticism and its necessary visage behind today's establishment of Copernican and Darwinian Scientism, a deception which the Lord has gladly delivered me out of, I want to know why modern Christians, who are so hasty in dismissing God's revelation of creation in the Bible, mocking the very notion that its intended as *literal*, are so eager to back up the Zohar's *literal* account of it

If, according to the big bang theory; matter, space, and time all instantaneously collaborated in their formation, or "10" is the number for space-time in string theory, with "26" standing out as a requirement for mathematics in bosonic string theory, with both numbers agreeably forming the building blocks of the universe through "magic dimensions," as modern theorists claim, in Kabbalah and modern science, how it is that medieval Jewish writers so splendidly divided truth from fantasy without knowing today's mathematics or physics then, well, I guess I'm stumped—if modern scientists are truly "rediscovering" it, that is. And that's the thing. How one perceives this, be it a fantastical retelling in the department of wishful thinking or coincidental and completely innocent discovery in the pursuit of truth—well, one's personal conclusion changes everything.

I'm especially intrigued by Kabbalah's teaching regarding "God's retreat," or emptying Himself from the cosmos by retracting infinite light, so as to make room for big-bang creation, and how the new spirituality of Scientism can match this to portray everything before us as a potential vessel for the enlightenment of divinity. After a while, Darwinian Evolution and the Babylonian religion and the Copernican globe, each apparently backed with these Kabbalah texts, all bleed into the same agenda—the Luciferian lie.

Isaac Newton, priest and wizard.

I realize now that talking about Kabbalah and Babylonian mysticism wasn't my actual intent when sitting down to write this, nor was it the secret papers of Newton. So far as my reevaluation into astronomy and astrophysics has gone, now that I've decided to take my stand with a Holy Word which outright opposes such beliefs, all of this, particularly my previous indoctrination into the very system by which I claimed to oppose, has produced more of a culture shock, if anything. If I never realized the extent to which Creationists fooled me into believing their pursuit of Science was a Biblical one, it's simply because never in all my life could I nor did I wish to believe that my own church leaders would pull the wool over my eyes in either stance, be it a purposefully deceitful or subconscious decision on their part. I certainly didn't set out on this quest considering either two as an option, not even in the back of my inner-skull, and yet here we are.

Now we peel the curtain of the great hypocrisy. I was instructed to align myself with creationists who willingly apply cosmic evolution into their teachings of Biblical astronomy, among other disciplines. I'd hear them talking about stars and planets being formed by the coalescing of cosmic gases or starlight traveling from quadrillions of miles away and somehow incorporating that belief-system into Genesis while simultaneously adding a *young-earth* time stamp for our approval, and convince myself that the very "Science" by which they were rationalizing was somehow a Biblical one. Quite frankly, it's not.

This all goes back to my original question. I guess I just want to know why modern Christians, who are so hasty in dismissing God's revelation of creation in the Bible, mocking the very notion that it's intended as *literal*, are so eager to back up the Zohar's *literal* account of it. Are we so arrogant as to claim we know more or better than God's own testimony of Himself through creation, described by Moses, the prophets, scribes, poets, and Apostles, as to oppose it, or is it at all possible that, by skewing off the straight and narrow path in our solitary pursuit of quantifying what was once-hidden in creation, disclosures perhaps never intended to be found at all, it isn't a better understanding of "God" that we're actually discovering?

In a 1991 issue of Christianity Today, "*Women in the Medieval Church*," Charles E. Hummel dedicated the sort of lovey-dovey propaganda-piece to Isaac Newton, dripping with all the springtime sap and the patriotic fluff and gloop of a tender-hearted eulogy, which a proponent of gravity or Scientism delusionist, as well as Newton's own descendants could be proud of. Hummel writes, "A member of the Anglican church, Newton attended services and participated in special projects, such as praying for the distribution of Bibles among the poor." In the same article, he douses an extra coating of sugar-coated frosting with: "Newton's understanding of God came primarily from the Bible, which he studied for days and weeks at a time."

Strange indeed that *Christianity Today* thought it unimportant to divulge the fruit of Newton's laborious studies—mainly, what his "understanding of God" entailed. Despite the fact that, during his own lifetime, Newton was a master of the mint, mathematics professor at Cambridge University, President of the Royal Society, and a knight of the realm; despite the fact that he barely even had time to breath his dying last before Westminster Abbey made a monument of him— privately, Newton denied the *divine* Jesus. The positions which he lavished upon himself were wholly conditional upon public manifestations of a certain religious devotion, and so he hid his true self under a bushel while letting the hypocrisy shine as a beacon of light. Essentially, he was a Nicodemite. Newton wore the clothes well. He masterfully fooled the church into thinking he was devoted to the cause of Christ while secretly he gazed into the dark abyss of his own humanist mind. Though in a way, as a believer in the *literal* interpretations of Holy Writ, I admit I am not so different than Sir Isaac Newton. I too am a proponent of pseudoscience. And yet there can only be *one* truth, where the shape of creation is concerned. All other roads, apparently, lead to *Planet* Earth.

GIORDANO BRUNO: *Perceiver of Many Worlds* | DISTANT SUNS... RATIONAL BEINGS... EVERLASTING PERDITION... PERVERTED IMAGINATIONS

BELIEF IN A PLURALITY OF WORLDS was as instinctive a conclusion to make as the "natural revelation" which fermented mankind's very foundation of erroneous thinking apart from God's Testimony. That those distant earths were furthermore *inhabited* spread rapidly during the dawning hours of the Copernican Revolution—though some might argue the Italian astronomer is not to blame. While Copernicus declared the earth to revolve around the sun, he otherwise did not alter the accepted framework of Aristotelian cosmology. For Copernicus, the fixed crystalline stars were still bounded by the outermost sphere of the created order. Copernicus was mainly concerned with the arrangement of the earth and wandering stars in relationship to the sun, and in doing so—rejecting the Bible's belief in an immovable earth—he opened up the floodgates of perverted imaginations. One contorted tinkerer of the mind hatches yet another. Astronomy needed new management, and Giordano Bruno was eager to volunteer for the part.

Giordano Bruno's book, *On the Infinite Universe and Worlds,* was first published in 1584 while living in London as the secretary of the French ambassador to England, and stands as a champion-feat of intellectual freedom. Queen Elizabeth granted a flexibility of opinion among foreign refugees, and though the first telescope would not be turned on a heavenly body for another twenty-five years, nor would the first wandering star, which was otherwise invisible to the naked eye, be discovered for another two-hundred, and though Bruno had certainly never taken up the discipline of astronomy, not even as a hobby, he was free to open up the heavens and fantasize. Perhaps that is why popular histories of astronomy often do not think to mention him. Bruno was not a scientist. He was a mind-tinkerer.

"In the first place, Bruno was not an astronomer," writes Sylvia Engdahl in her book, *The Planet-Girded Suns: The Long History of*

Belief in Exoplanets. "He was a philosopher. To be sure, all scientists were called philosophers in his day, since what is now 'science' was then known as 'natural philosophy.'" But Bruno was a philosopher even by the modern definition. He did not watch the stars systematically; he simply thought about them. His theories were based not on observation, but on what he had read and what he was able to imagine."

Bruno's blind-belief in a myriad of planets is no longer opposed by the church; his vision of a universe infinite is now adopted by scientists everywhere; and finding a Biblical literalist who contests his insistence that a large number of suns inhabits those infinite spaces is far and few between. "That was the revolutionary concept Bruno originated," writes Engdahl. "Others before him had suggested that there might be an infinite number of stars. But Bruno taught that stars are suns—or, more significantly in the implications both for his own fate and for the history of human thought, that the sun is only a star."

In as little as a century later, Bernard Fontenelle would carry Bruno's apocryphal aptitude even further. His book, *Conversations on the Plurality of Worlds*, first published in 1686, successfully snatched Bruno's plurality of worlds out of the philosopher's hand and delivered it to the public. Finally, the average parishioner could open up the heavens, without their Bibles to guide or advise them otherwise, and dream of alternate possibilities on their own. More specifically, Fontenelle garnished the adoration of women across Europe and America. In her essay, *Becoming a Scientist: Gender and Knowledge in 18th c. Italy*, Paula Findlen writes: "No longer a man of the university, a scholastic master surrounded by male disciples, Fontenelle's philosopher was a charming seducer of women, a wit who made science comprehensible by cultural analogy. His knowledge was no social liability that removed him from ordinary conversation, but the very reason that he held the attention of an aristocratic Marquise for several days and nights, as he educated her in the mysteries of the post-Copernican, Cartesian universe."

During one starlit stroll, as Fontenelle's narrative unfolds, the countess confesses to her courter: "You have made the Universe so large," *says she*, "that I know not where I am, or what will become of me."

Here the philosopher replies: "I think it is very pleasant, when the Heavens were a little blue Arch, stuck with Stars, me-thought the Universe was too strait and close, I was almost stifled for want of Air; but now… I begin to breathe with more freedom."

316

The philosopher commissions the countess with these words: "I find the fix'd Stars to be like our Sun, therefore I attribute to them what is proper to that: You are now gone too far to be able to retreat, therefore you must go forward with a good grace." Fontenelle's readers did just that—and never looked back. *Conversations on the Plurality of Worlds* made such an impression on cultural flights of fantasy that, according to one source, "Not long after, at the time of the death of Newton, vast amounts of sentimental poetry about other solar systems appeared in literary magazines, much of it by women and some based on the theme of Newton's soul viewing other solar systems on the way to heaven."

The poet Robert Gambol, in *Beauties of the Universe*, first published in 1732, presented a somewhat playful banter with this carefully disguised esoteric view of spiritual ascension into the cosmos when he quipped:

"Unbounded in its ken, from prison free

Will clearly view what here we darkly see:

Those planetary worlds, and thousands more."

Meanwhile, across the Atlantic, Cotton Mather of Salem witch trial fame devoted many pages in his book, *The Christian Philosopher*, to a plurality of worlds, and with as much willful vigor as any Christian who promotes and ultimately confuses Darwinism with a truly Biblical worldview today:

"Great GOD, what a Variety of Worlds hast thou created! How astonishing are the Dimensions of them! How stupendous are the Displays of thy Greatness, and of thy Glory, in the Creatures with which thou hast replenished those Worlds! . . . Who can tell what Uses those marvelous Globes may be designed for?"

In actuality, the sinful state of those creatures "with which thou has replenished those Worlds" was of much debate. Indeed, it was a perplexing puzzle. In *Paradise Lost*, which was first published in 1667, almost two decades before Fontenelle's classic, the poet John Milton wrote: "Solicit not thy thoughts with matters hid...Dream not of other Worlds, what creatures there Live, in what state, condition, or degree."

Regardless, men dreamt of other worlds. And philosophical questions, as well as theological, plagued them. Scottish Astronomer James Ferguson wrote a book for children, *Easy Introduction to Astronomy for Young Gentlemen and Ladies*, first published in 1768 in

London, whereas a conversation is held between a brother and sister. "I cannot imagine the inhabitants of our earth to be better than those of other planets," his sister protested. "On the contrary, I would fain hope they have not acted so absurdly, with respect to him, as we have done."

Unlike Mather's wishful thinking, typical of the religious sort who embeds a charitable and wholly contradictory spin of apocryphal-tinkering into God's Word—like today's so-called Christian Darwinists—Benjamin Franklin exhumed the tragic, despairing words of a true humanist when he wrote:

> "I believe that Man is not the most perfect Being but One, rather, that as there are many Degrees of Beings his Inferiors, so there are many Degrees of Beings superior to him. Also, when I stetch my Imagination thro' and beyond our System of Planets, beyond the visible fix'd Stars themselves, into that Space that is every Way infinite, and conceive it fill'd with Suns like ours, each with a Chorus of Worlds forever moving round him, then this little Ball on which we move seems, even in my narrow Imagination, to be almost Nothing."

Later in *Poor Richard's Almanac*, dated September 1749, Franklin wrote: "It is the opinion of all the modern philosophers and mathematicians that the planets are habitable worlds." In a letter to a friend, he confessed the natural conclusions to such beliefs: "Superior beings smile at our theories, and at our presumption in making them." To another friend he expressed the wish that his idea of happy conduct might "grow and increase till it becomes the governing philosophy of the human species, as it must be that of superior beings in better worlds."

On the 24th of April, 1756, John Adams confessed to his diary: "Astronomers tell us, with good Reason, that...all the unnumbered Worlds that revolve around the fixt Starrs are inhabited, as well as this Globe of Earth." Sylvia Engdahl writes: "That day and the next, he went on to reflect upon whether all the 'different Ranks of Rational Beings' in those worlds had committed moral wickedness, and if so, whether any church leaders would think they must be 'consigned to everlasting Perdition.' It is evident that he himself did not think so."

Indeed, a Copernican or Darwinian worldview are two sides of the same coin. One can further see the very attitude which would grip and later define the Darwinian Revolution in as little as a century when English astronomer and mathematician Thomas Wright (1711-1786), having calculated that there must be "within the whole celestial Area 60,000,000 planetary Worlds like ours," likewise said:

> "In this great Celestial Creation, the Catastrophy of a World such as ours, or even the total Dissolution of a System of Worlds, may possibly be no more to the great Author of Nature, than the most common Accident in Life with us, and in all Probability such final and general Doom-Days may be as frequent there as even Birthdays, or Mortality with us upon the Earth. This Idea has something so cheerful in it, that I own I can never look upon the Stars without wondering why the whole World does not become Astronomers."

An 1825 textbook for use in girls' schools stated that to reject the idea of plurality of worlds would be "to narrow our conceptions of God's character." So popular was the alien mythology among the learned that in 1854 William Whewell, a prominent scholar of the history and philosophy of science and Master of Trinity College at Cambridge, published a book anonymously for fear that merely suggesting earth might be unique in housing intelligent beings, which was completely unorthodox in academia, might damage his reputation. Indeed, critics took notice. Whewell's identity was soon divulged, despite not appearing on the cover or anywhere in print. And they were not pleased.

The London Daily News wrote in sharp criticism of Whewell: "We scarcely expected that in the middle of the nineteenth century a serious attempt would have been made to restore the exploded idea of man's supremacy over all other creatures in the universe... Nevertheless, a champion has actually appeared who boldly dares to combat against all the rational inhabitants of other spheres."

Isaac Watts, best known for writing 750 hymns, including "When I Survey the Wondrous Cross" and "Joy to the World," perhaps best sums up the squandering tolerance and bleeding compromise of an apostate worldview, which is insinuated among the so-called "Christian" Darwinists of our day, by improperly force-feeding a narrative where it doesn't belong. In *The Knowledge of the HEAVENS and the EARTH Made Easy*, first published in 1726, Watts writes:

> "It may be manifested here also that several of the Planets have their Revolutions round their own Axis in certain Periods of Time, as the Earth has in 24 hours; and that they are vast bulky dark Bodies, some of them much bigger than our Earth, and consequently fitted for the dwelling of some Creatures; so that

'tis probable they are all Habitable Worlds furnished with rich Variety of Inhabitants to the Praise of their great Creator. Nor is there wanting some Proof of this from the Scripture itself. For when the Prophet Isaiah tells us, that God who formed the Earth created it not in vain because he formed it to be inhabited, Isa. XLV.18. He thereby insinuates that had such a Globe as the Earth never been inhabited, it had been created in vain. Now the same Way of Reasoning may be applied to the other Planetary Worlds, some of which are so much bigger than the Earth is, and their Situations and Motions seem to render them as convenient Dwellings for Creatures of some Animal and Intellectual Kind."

In twisting the Prophet Isaiah for his purposes, as the Copernican *must* do, Isaac Watts, along with Cotton Mather and the lot of them, have disregarded Biblical fact for fancy. God never thinks to mention the imaginative planets of Giordano Bruno or the inhabitants resulting from them in His Word—mainly, because it took Bruno to perversely imagine them on his own. God had no part in that. Indeed, He did not create in vain. The entire lot of stars, and let us not forget the Copernican's pile-up of purported planets—10^{24} in number, or when written out, 1,000,000,000,000,000,000,000,000—all of which are reportedly nestled within 200 billion galaxies, could only have been spoken into being on the fourth day of the creation week. It would only make logical sense that our master builder should first lay down the foundations and the ground floor of our house—mainly all of creation— before constructing its ceiling, as Moses attests to. The Earth was created in six days, and anything else brought into being on any other day of the week was done so in order that the joyous cosmology might be fully appreciated by its only inhabitants.

> "For thus saith the Lord that created the heavens; God himself that formed the earth and made it; He hath established it, He created it not in vain, He formed it to be inhabited: I am the Lord; and there is none else (Isaiah 45:18)."

What Watts and Mather and U.S. President John Adams have overlooked in their compromise with the world is the Apostle Paul's letter to the Romans, where-as the *whole creation*—all six days of it—*groans*.

> "For we know that the whole creation groaneth and travaileth in pain together until now. And not only they, but ourselves also, which have the first fruits of the Spirit, even we ourselves groan

within ourselves, waiting for the adoption, to wit, the redemption of our body (Romans 8:22-23)."

Accordingly, Jesus our Great Atoner, once completing His task here on earth, would need to descend upon each additional inhabited world throughout the created cosmos so that they too may have the chance to taste of his saving graces. One might further speculate if he would require the use of a virgin for every visit within every world, including a death, burial, and resurrection. But that is not what Jesus did. He returned to our Father in heaven and sat enthroned at His right hand. Here the Apostle assures us:

> "Which he wrought in Christ, when he raised him from the dead, and set him at his own right hand in the heavenly places.... (Ephesians 1:20)"

If there is any doubt in our minds as to the territories of His dominion, the Apostle here makes mention of only two worlds—not a multitude of them.

> "Far above all principality, and power, and might, and dominion, and every name that is named, not only in this world, but also in that which is to come...."

There is our present world to consider, and then the next to come. Meanwhile, humanity is stumbling around intoxicated while attempting to conjure up the alternative possibilities. But if God doesn't think to imagine another, then neither should we.

A PLURALITY OF WORLDS | THOMAS PAINE (*the Celebrated Infidel*) AND THE RELIGION OF GLOBE EARTH

THERE IS NO REASON WHY MOST CHRISTIANS SHOULD BE BOTHERED to read the enlightenment humanist Thomas Paine except to validate what they have already sanctioned and celebrated of heathen society in their own minds. They have accepted perjury as truth, and in turn have placated that lie by committing an even worse offense against the self. They look to Moses and the Prophets and our Master Jesus, whom rightly upheld the completeness of their testimony, and wickedly take the surgical knife to the Holy Spirit wherever and whenever He disagrees with our modern day prophets of Mount Sinai—namely, the priests of astronomy. I will concur with Thomas Paine only so much in *The Age of Reason* that he recognized: "The two opposing beliefs (astronomy and the Bible) cannot be held together in the same mind; he who thinks he can believe both has thought very little of either." But such an observation is obvious to make. Anything beyond recognition of this glaring contradiction in the church is where the celebrated infidel and I part ways.

The humanist mind is darkened, and even the special revelation in which he receives from God is mishandled in order to fit his heathen worldview. We must dutifully remind him anyways, so long as he calls himself *Christian*—though the two should never be yoked together in one mind—that the earth is a circle (Isaiah 40:22), made with a compass (Proverbs 8:27), laid upon a face (Genesis 1:2). It is bound (Job 26:10) at its ends (Job 38:13), established on pillars (Job 38:4) over the Great Deep (Psalm 104:6), and is fixed forever in place, immovable (Psalm 93:1), with a sun which journeys in our stead, complete with a circuit to run (Psalm 19:4-6). It is covered by a solid firmament (Genesis 1:6-8), spread out as molten glass (Job 37:18), containing the sun, moon, and stars (Genesis 1:14-18), with waters above (Genesis 7:11), which once drowned the entire world in a great deluge but still remains there (Psalm 148:4), and a heaven which establishes God's throne upon it (Psalm 104:3). By doing so, we must be prepared. We shall most certainly receive a barrage of mockery and scorn, if not a more severe bruising, wherever these truths are spoken—even among those whom we once broke bread with. Our only crime, of course, is confiding in God's intellect over our own. Just know this and take courage; some will, as a result of our witness, lean upon the Holy Ghost and believe. For them, dear Christian, we willingly expel our reputation and take the beating.

Soon any personal injury which may result from their conscientious dismissal of truth will wear off. I have become quite accustomed to the humanist's outright rejection of Holy Writ, namely the Lord's own Created order; but certainly not calloused. My heart still aches. I am deeply burdened, so long as church pastors advocate Satan's globe deception over the Lord's creation. I can't help but wonder if the "temple of God" they so often speak of is none other than the humanists motto— what Thomas Paine defiantly referred to when he advanced his dogma: "I do not believe in the creed professed by the Jewish church, by the Roman church, by the Greek church, by the Turkish church, by the Protestant church, nor by any church that I know of. My own mind is my own church." Jesus Christ is the head, Thomas Paine. Pastors, take note of this. If our body is a temple, then we are His appendages. The Bible is written. Its pages are filled. There is not room for the insertion of natural revelation in a single sentence—should they conflict—even where the created order is concerned.

The Copernican likely agrees with Paine, or has little choice to (should he maintain an air of consistency), when the philosopher writes of the Creation account, "Why it has been called the Mosaic account of the Creation, I am at a loss to conceive." Indeed, Science with an upper-case "S" has followed the dark path, and therefore contradicts it. I do once again find myself concuring with Paine only so much that—before his encounter with the burning bush—Moses had been educated into the higher platforms of the Mysteries, by which modern enlightened society finds its cornerstone of knowledge and so many earthly pleasures. Paine has little problems connecting the dots. Why must the Christian err? Very quickly however, we part ways. For Moses, Paine assures us, is not to blame. "Moses, I believe, was too good a judge of such subjects to put his name to that account. He had been educated among the Egyptians, who were a people as well skilled in science, and particularly in astronomy, as any people of their day."

At any rate, the Copernican has little choice but to believe that the Israelites were not only uninformed, but *stupid* in their defiance against the world around them, despite instruction from the Most High: Thus saith the LORD, *Learn not the way of the heathen* (Jeremiah 10:2). "The

323

case is," Paine adds, "that every nation of people has been world-makers, and the Israelites had as much right to set up the trade of world-making as any of the rest; and as Moses was not an Israelite, he might not choose to contradict the tradition." That God would not think so highly of his own people at Mount Sinai, and that Moses, Israel's great leader, as well as Jesus, who later upheld the Prophet's every written word, would knowingly guide them into erroneous consequences is, if true, a terrible tragedy, and should henceforth not deserve our devotion.

The doctrine of the shape of the earth is without blemish, and the Spirits Testimony concerning it is not in error. The earth stands eternally fast. And our Lord Jesus Christ, upon His return, will set this straight. To this I unashamedly stand firm upon. Anyone who subscribes to God and yet claims otherwise, in his support of a globe—spinning and whirling through infinite space—is dishonest, and where such application is concerned, the truth is not in him.

The Copernican has no choice but to agree with the snarky humanist Thomas Paine. Living by the standards of "*Sola Scriptura!*" is to the enlightenment humanist the equivalent of cutting "learning down to a size less dangerous to their project," and worse, "restricting the idea of learning to the dead study of dead languages." God's Word is living, and its creation account is not excluded from the life which the Spirit breaths with each reading of it. At any rate, he should at least conclusively flex his muscular rationale to question God's foreknowledge, as Paine did. It is only logical. "The setters-up, therefore, and the advocates of the Christian system of faith could not but foresee that the continually progressive knowledge that man would gain, by the aid of science, of the power and wisdom of God, manifested in the structure of the universe and in all the works of Creation, would militate against, and call into question, the truth of their system of faith."

For Paine, God speaks to us not through dead languages, but through Science. "It is a fraud of the Christian system to call the sciences human invention; it is only the application of them that is human. Every science has for its basis a system of principles as fixed and unalterable as those by which the universe is regulated and governed. Man cannot make principles, he can only discover them." Quite conclusively, for the sad-soul who believes his mind to be his godly temple and which may discern truth from fiction apart from God's written Testimony, he must dutifully agree with Paine, who writes of God's spoken revelations in Science: "That the Creation we behold is the real and ever-existing word of God, in which we *cannot* be deceived. It proclaims his power, it demonstrates his wisdom; it manifests his goodness and beneficence." This, oh man, is the Great Delusion.

Most notably, Paine champions the Copernican deception to its fullest measure. In such cosmogony, the Bible has no final authority. The philosopher cleverly inserts, "Neither does the knowledge stop here." Remember, it is fallacious of the Copernican to recognize, should he understand that "two opposing beliefs (astronomy and the Bible) cannot be held together in the same mind," how Moses and the Prophets, even Jesus Christ and the Apostles, spoke in anything other than *dead languages* when they described and upheld the created order. The Science of Copernicus and Kepler lead us to the most natural conclusion of all, *universal* in its application. There is a plurality of worlds to be discovered. "The system of worlds next to us exhibits, in its revolutions, the same principles and school of science to the inhabitants of their system, as our system does to us, and in like manner throughout the immensity of space."

Thomas Paine had no love for the God of the Bible, but that is not to say that he didn't have a good logical head to him. While Paine admits with a sigh, there was at one time "no moral ill in believing the earth was flat like a trencher," the so-called Christian who claims the same of himself, that there is no moral outrage in his decision to believe the Copernican Universe if it proves to please him and yet claims contrary to what God actually Testified to creating, should actually put some thought into this. Moral rightness and wrongness does exist. According to Paine, the man who upholds God's Testimony is provably obscene and immoral. "When a system of religion is made to grow out of a supposed system of creation that is not true, and to unite itself therewith in a manner almost inseparable therefrom, the case assumes an entirely different ground. It is then that errors not morally bad become fraught with the same mischiefs as if they were."

I wonder if the Copernican finds the time, or is at least honest enough, to thank the Lord for the age of reason and the temple of his mind which might dutifully enlighten and guide him through the darkness, unlike the Israelite's, who had no age of reason to counsel them. If he cannot see that the globular theory, with its mountainous waste of perverse entertainment to support its agenda (as agencies of brainwashing) is the mainspring of modern infidelity, then he is mentally shortsighted. The Christian who attempts to rape and plunder Scripture of its true Divine wealth by substituting and forcibly wedging inferior human products into its blessed account of Cosmogony, namely the

Copernican and Darwinian faiths—among other HTDs of Scientism, would be more logical to end their religious profession altogether. They have collaborated with darkness. And besides, should they at least fess up to this much, the humanists will gladly have them.

THE DEVIL IS IN THE DETAIL—IN OTHER WORDS, SCRIPTURE INTERPRETS SCRIPTURE (*Except For When Science Interprets It*)

FLAT EARTH FAULT-FINDERS WILL LIKELY BREATHE a sigh of relief to note the PhD thesis submitted by a young Tunisian Muslim woman, and which caused a worldwide uproarious scandal in 2017 for exhibiting such chutzpah as to dismiss the physics of Newton, the math of Einstein, the astronomy of Copernicus and Kepler, and big bang cosmology, as well as Darwinian biology, has been soundly *rejected*.

I'll wait for the applause to end.

By doing so, declaring the earth to be immovable, young of age, and at the center—Or perhaps more precisely, *floor*—of the universe, as both the Quran and Bible boldly proclaim, she is unforgivably chastened for taking the meanings of religious texts *literally* and *blindly*, at the "irresponsible cost of rejecting sanctioned knowledge." Her worldwide critics, suddenly taking an interest in the thoughts of a professional and independent-minded woman of North Africa, are morally outraged *merely* on the sleepless understanding that somewhere in the world a doctorate student has defected from the religion of Scientism. Examples *must* be made of sinners.

After immediately reassuring his readers that the young woman's arguments are riddled with moon-sized potholes, Nidhal Guessom, writer for *Gulf News* in Dubai, conclusively hints at the treasure-trove of comfort and wealth to be found in the compromised religious-morals of Western Civilization by stating: "The Arab world will continue to suffer educational and cultural crises until it properly digests the different methodologies of science and religion."

What I think Nidhal Guessom is *trying* to say here, is a deal must struck with the devil! *Er*, I mean—the west! Not *devil*. West! And by *deal*, I mean antichrist spirit! Strike that. Not antichrist spirit. I meant *comprise*. A compromise must be made! Western civilization has committed itself to such a task centuries ago, recognizing the different

327

methodologies of science and religion, choosing *science* where religion fails, and just look at our wealth!

In an article titled, *"When Science and Scripture Conflict—A Reformed Approach to Science and Scripture,"* Keith Mathison reported on a then-recent Q&A session at Ligonier's 2012 National Conference, in which Dr. R.C. Sproul—some might consider him the greatest Christian theologian of our generation—addressed a series of questions concerning the age of the Universe. Essentially, Scripture interprets Scripture—*sort of.* He phrased it like this: "However, if something can be shown to be definitively taught in the Bible without questioning, and somebody gives me a theory from *natural revelation*—that they think is based off of natural revelation—that contradicts the Word of God, I'm going to stand with the Word of God a hundred times out of a hundred." Sproul then adds, "But again I have to repeat, I could have been a *mistaken* interpreter of the Word of God."

Apparently that *"hundred times out of a hundred rule"* didn't work out so well. And let me just state here that I have immense respect for Dr. Sproul. I have no desire to quarrel with his immense accomplishments as a minister of the Gospel, nor paw senselessly at his reputation. But please, Sir, let us not take a surgical knife to the Holy Spirit. By dismissing the *"Scripture interprets Scripture"* principle almost as suddenly as he *seemingly* acknowledges it, he has opened the floodgates of humanist interpretation. This is most apparent when he takes to the popular opinion by addressing the glaring disagreement between the Copernican theory and the entire Biblical canon in the following way. Sproul says, "Here the advances of science helped the church to correct an earlier misinterpretation of Scripture. To say that science cannot overturn the teaching of Scripture is not to say that science cannot aid the church in understanding Scripture, or even correct false inferences drawn from Scripture or actual misinterpretations of Scripture."

Dr. Sproul is of the opinion that Martin Luther and the Reformers were incorrect in lining up their understanding of Scripture as a *literal* interpretation. There *must* be some other explainable meaning, and which the religion of Scientism will surely enlighten us to. John Calvin was not overlooked either by Dr. Sproul, who is historically documented as having spoken in a sermon that those who believe "the sun does not move and that it is the earth that moves" are "stark raving mad" and "possessed by the devil!" John Calvin, it seems—according to Dr. Sproul—was too irrationally tempered and hastily set upon lining his own views with clear Biblical doctrine when not allowing our Scientism overlords to bend the rules of *"Sola Scriptura!"* and pronounce themselves as our self-assigned theological superiors.

Again, just so that he's not mistaken, Dr. Sproul rephrases his point: "But historically, the church's understanding of special revelation of the Bible has been corrected by students of natural revelation with the Copernican revolution."

Such illogical nonsense tires me to no end. I am regularly directed to the dark catacombs of the humanist mind and asked to surrender any understanding of literal intent to the physicist, mathematician, and the astronomer. But what of the geologist, the biologist, and professor of metaphysics—must I also surrender to them? Everybody wants a turn at reshaping the Bible, from the paleontologist and the historian to the geographer, script writer, and onscreen actor. There will never be an end to it. Science and the scientific method is a human invention. The Scripture comes from God. How can the two be compatible, if and when such obvious human invention as the scientific method disagrees with God? Indeed, they are two opposing faiths intermingled.

For Dr. Sproul, should he or any of his inside-circle admirers read this, my opinion shall likely pronounce the feathered weight of a passing burp. And I'm fine with that. I am certainly not seeking attention or special audience with the doctor. My Christian reader however needs to understand, and I can't stress this enough—our church has been taken hostage by false doctrine. We've compromised our faith. Essentially, we made a deal with the devil. We have tasked ourselves with preforming the devils work in his stead. And western comfort, which we gladly exchange for the centuries-old compromise, shows for it.

Spiritually we are a naked people (Revelation 3:17).

By abandoning a far superior theological professorship, which teaches the only principle ensuring the light of God, that is: *"Scripture interprets Scripture;"* he and every other theologian who bends to the will of the humanist in the higher chairs of academia by allowing outside affluence to interpret Scripture, even if ever so slightly (perhaps nobody will take notice—*or care*), has willingly opened up the floodgates. The Darwinists may commence with their invasion of the church.

To this point Dr. Sproul, who seems terribly trusting with the *goodness* of men for a man who teaches the need for repentance in a swamp of sin, readily concludes, "When people ask me how old the earth is I tell them, 'I don't know,' because I don't. And I'll tell you why I don't. In the first place, the Bible does not give us a date of creation. Now it gives us hints and inclinations that would indicate in many cases a young earth. And at the same time you get all this expanding universe and all this astronomical dating, and triangulation and all that stuff coming from outside the church that makes me wonder."

BEATEN & BRUISED BETWEEN THE APPLAUDING HANDS OF THE HIGHER CRITIC: "GAP THEORY," A FATAL COMPROMISE

GIVEN ENOUGH TIME, ALMOST ANYTHING IS POSSIBLE. It was 1785, and the Enlightenment was not yet through, because Englishman James Hutton had one more treatise to contribute to its garbage heap of humanism. With *Theory of the Earth*, the age of creation became an issue of antiquity. History would no longer exemplify a six-thousand years old narrative—*oh no*. Quite suddenly, there were millions of years which needed accounting for. We should not be surprised to find that the high critics of academia met Hutton's treatise with thunderous applaud. Hutton disfavored the Bible. And like most behemoth lies, he had peppered his theory in such a way as to make his observations seem strictly based on scientific knowledge rather than philosophical speculation. From the pulpit to the pews, panic ensued. The church had only recently forsaken the pleas of Martin Luther and settled into the Copernican Revolution—which he outright opposed—in hopes of harmonizing faith with higher criticism. Once again, Christianity was no longer immutable. Something else had to give. You know what they say. "The road to hell is paved with good intention." Good intention and *compromises*.

Less than a decade earlier, French cosmologist and naturalist Comte de Buffon had already attempted to lift Science from the hinges of Biblical authority with his publication of *Les époques de la nature* in 1778. Before the 19th-century, Christians universally ascribed to a 6,000 year-old creation and a catastrophic flood, which not only gave the earth's features its observable contour, but preserved the totality of God's created order. Buffon's theory of extinction fell on deaf ears. So too did his imaginative storytelling, which employed the new physics of Newton as his springboard and sought to hypothesis how matter in motion might have formed the earth. "The father of all thought in natural history" accredited the planets of the Copernican Universe as having been created by a comet's catastrophic collision with the sun.

The snubbing he received—one might conjecture—can best be attributed to the fact that a war was presently being waged over the New World. And besides, Buffon was not loved by Americans. After propounding a theory that the New World and its inhabitants—including plants and animals—were inferior to Eurasia in all facets, going so far as to accredit its inferiority to "marsh odors," an incensed Thomas Jefferson dispatched twenty soldiers to New Hampshire with explicit orders to capture a bull moose as proof of the "stature and majesty of American quadrupeds." Buffon later admitted his error. Unfortunately, an even grosser transgression was committed. His comet theory, which posited the age of the earth to be 75,000 years old, was based on calculated figures which projected the cooling rate of iron. His attempt was a success—*somewhat*. Though the comet theory itself was not admitted, the age-old Universe which accommodated the error remained. Science was determined to come up with something—prove anything—which might give credence to their undeveloped religion.

French naturalist and zoologist George Cuvier came to Buffon's rescue. As the "founding father of paleontology," Cuvier was praised for his capability to work with a few bone fragments and reconstruct the complete anatomy of previously unknown species "with uncanny accuracy"—a practice which paleontologists would quickly make a habit of. While studying elephant fossils discovered near Paris, Cuvier demonstrated that their bones could not be paired up with their living African and Asian counterparts. They were provably distinct even from fossils in Siberia. In 1789 Cuvier published a treatise detailing the differences between the lower jaws of a mammoth and an Indian elephant. When a counter theory was proposed—that living members of these fossils still lurked somewhere on Earth, unrecognized—Cuvier scoffed. Extinction *happened*. For the Christian, this was a nagging problem which seemed to plague God of His divine plan. The saving faith may still have held the higher ground, culturally speaking, but its gates were being battered down. If Science was winning the war, it's only because most combatants wanted favor with the mob. And besides, compromise is the cheapest lawyer.

Christianity's *unfulfilled* need, particularly acknowledgement from higher criticism, is indeed unfortunate. In the most merciful of death blows, Cuvier threw them a bone. He suggested that there may have been a series of great floods throughout the undocumented and ever-elongated epochs of antiquity which wiped out any possible number of civilizations and species—all of which happened before the creation described in

Genesis 1:1. In part, the church could keep to their 6,000-year theology, while simultaneously new doctrines were born.

Before Cuvier there is no historical record of a Christian anywhere advocating an age-old approach to creation. Famed theologian Thomas Chalmers, founder of the Free Church of Scotland, took it upon himself to save the church from spectacle. "One has only to read the writings of this man to understand how acutely he felt the attacks of science, and geology in particular, upon the Scriptures," writes Weston Fields in *Unformed and Unfilled* (1976). He was "part of the age during which men were breaking loose from and thrusting aside what they felt had been the shackles of the Scriptures, and were placing all their hopes in the new science and its "assured" results. It is not without significance that Chalmers deemed it necessary to harmonize the Scriptures and science in order to save Christianity from the onslaught of atheism!"

During a sermon to his congregation in 1804, Thomas Chalmers brought the Gap Theory into being. According to Chalmers—the world existing between Genesis 1:1 and 1:2 was destroyed before its recreation in the six literal days described by Moses. With Science as their framework, they bought it. His views reached an even wider audience ten years later when in 1814 he wrote a review of Cuvier's theory. Between Genesis 1:1 and 1:2, the Christian now had any number of years— billions if need be—in which he could agree to the fantastical pre-recorded fantasies of the Science religion. God apparently had more savory dishes to offer humanity through Natural Revelation.

Chalmers later wrote of Genesis 1:1: "My own opinion, as published in 1814, is that it forms no part of the first day— but refers to a period of indefinite antiquity when God created the worlds out of nothing. The commencement of the first day's work I hold to be the moving of God's Spirit upon the face of the waters. We can allow geology the amplest time . . . without infringing even on the literalities of the Mosaic record. . . ."

With *Earth's Earliest Ages,* first published in 1884, G. H. Pember perhaps best outlined Gap thinking, and certainly attempted to qualify it, when he wrote: "It is thus clear that the second verse of Genesis describes the earth as a ruin; but there is no hint of the time which elapsed between creation and this ruin. Age after age may have rolled away, and it was probably during their course that the strata of the earth's crust were gradually developed. Hence we see that geological attacks upon the Scriptures are altogether wide of the mark, are a mere beating of the air. There is room for any length of time between the first and second verses of the Bible. And again; since we have no inspired account of the geological formations, we are at liberty to believe that they were developed just in the order in which we find them. The whole process took place in preadamite times, in connection, perhaps, with another race of beings, and, consequently, does not at present concern us."

It was a happy ending—sort of—well, not really.

One compromise gave way to another accommodation, and yet another... and another... and another. By the 1820s, Reverend John Fleming argued for a Noachian deluge which was perhaps not quite so catastrophic as Moses records, and in the decade to follow the evangelical Congregationalist theologian John Pye Smith advocated a local creation account and quite similarly a local flood, both of which occurred in Mesopotamia. Anglican clergyman and Oxford geometry professor Baden Powell went even further. He argued that Genesis was a myth simply intended to convey theological and moral truths. Hugh Miller, a prominent Scottish geologist and evangelical friend of Chalmers, abandoned his friend's gap theory in favor of the day-age theory, which dismissed a week-long creation for days which represented entire ages. Miller came to this conclusion and shortly thereafter committed suicide.

Charles Lyell made Hutton's contempt for the Bible look elementary in comparison. As a contemporary of Thomas Chalmers and a man "of superior talent who thought" *for himself* and was "not blinded by (Scriptural) authority," Lyell's soaring ambition was to "free the sciences from Moses." With *Principles of Geology*, first published in 1830, he did just that. Throughout its indignant pages Lyell refers to Scripture as "false conclusions... futile reasoning... founded on religious prejudices... ancient doctrines sanctioned by the implicit faith of many generations, and supposed to rest on scriptural authority." Basing his work in part on Hutton, Buffon, and Cuvier, Lyell imagined other possibilities. He suggested the best way to account for the age of the Earth was through present observable processes in topography, a process which, he said, had been building *very gradually at the same rate over vast amounts of time.* He then divided stratum into layers and assigned each one an increasingly-deepening age. The ever-expanding chapters of pre-recorded history finally had names, so that on top of the Paleozoic and Mesozoic Ages is the Cenozoic—the spinning, whirling globe we currently stand upon.

Charles Lyell invented the geologic column.

Lyell's creative storytelling became Scientific doctrine in 1830, long before carbon dating, potassium argon dating, and rubidium strontium dating could account for it. Then again, when carbon dating, potassium argon dating, and rubidium strontium dating were finally invented, Lyell not only dethroned Moses, as was his claim, but stood in the lawgivers place. How Lyell's imaginations could be *so precise*, down to the fine print—we must conclude—could only come from Divine inspiration. But Lyell didn't believe in that sort of thing.

Martin Luther was right. He once implored the brethren:

"We Christians must be different from the philosophers (scientists) in the way we think about the causes of these things. And if some are beyond our comprehension (like those before us concerning the waters above the heavens), we must believe them and admit our lack of knowledge rather than either wickedly deny them or presumptuously interpret them in conformity with our understanding."

Little did Scottish theologian Thomas Chalmers suspect that harmonization with *Natural Revelation* was about as complimentary with Christianity as the roof of a house is on fire. Ultimately, Chalmers served the very evil which he supposed to prevent. Indeed unfortunate—it was a wholly avoidable disaster. And yet in hindsight Weston Fields sympathetically writes: "he could not have realized the full implications of his position" when Chalmers wrote:

"Should, in particular, the explanation that we now offer be sustained, this would permit an indefinite scope to the conjectures of geology—and without any undue liberty with the first chapter of Genesis."

As it is with all great deceptions, man needs time—and more time. He needs time a-plenty if his perverse imaginations can coax his contemporaries away from the guiding light which only Scripture can provide in hopes of delivering *counter* promises. First the church knelt down to the astronomer—then the geologist—and finally the biologist. The set-up was perfectly executed. Charles Swindoll once said, "The swift wind of compromise is a lot more devastating than the sudden jolt of misfortune." In actuality, all hell broke loose.

The church was ill-prepared for Mr. Charles Darwin.

INERRANCY IN ERROR: THERE'S THE TEXTUS RECEPTUS (*and Then, Quite Tragically, There's the Rest of Them*)

IT IS A MATTER OF PUBLIC RECORD THAT MANY GOOD MEN were either cooked alive or drained of blood in order to get the Greek text known as "*Textus Receptus*," or the Received Text—we call it the King James Version in its English equivalent—into our hands today. Only Martin Luther's German translation, as well as his English counterpart William Tyndale, along with the 54 scholars who produced the King James Bible based on Tyndale's work, translated their Bibles from the *Textus Receptus*. Nobody else, of the hundreds of English translations in existence, have thought to make it worth their while, for you see, the *Received Text* is not, nor has it ever been, Catholic approved. One might even conclude in light of this that the Great Reformation, culturally speaking, has failed.

The original autographs of the men moved by the Holy Spirit to pen His Word in the decades immediately following Jesus Christ's resurrection are all gone. No one admittedly has a copy in their possession. There are however over 5,300 extant Greek manuscripts of the New Testament available. The founding Koine Greek gospels and letters, which the Apostles wrote, were copied and recopied again throughout the surmounting centuries in what is referred to as the Byzantine textual tradition, and vastly distributed throughout the world. Today they are collectively called the "*Majority Text*," and from what has been gathered, about 95-97% of them textually agree with one another. Indisputably, the best solitary representation of the Byzantine Majority Text, be it a printed one, comes from the *Textus Receptus*, which is the rewarding result of various Greek Majority Text revisions by a Dutch priest of the Renaissance, Erasmus.

The two primary manuscripts employed for the New International Version (NIV), which envelops almost half of all Bible sales, and *every other* English version available is the "Codex Sinaiticus" matched with the "Codex Vaticanus" texts. In 1859, the fourth-century *Sinaiticus* was allegedly discovered by Constantine Tischendorf (1815-1874) in a waste basket at St. Catherine's Monastery on Mount Saini. Though a protestant, he clothed himself with close and uncomfortably-fitted ties to the Roman Catholic hierarchy, including a recorded private meeting with the Pope. That was his account of it, at least—the texts discovery—being a heroic rescuer of antiquity. It is noted that the monks of Sinai vehemently denied his wastebasket story.

When the true author of *Sinaiticus* discovered that his manuscript written at Catherine's was being promoted as a fourth-century discovery, Constantine Simonides (1820-1867) made this discrepancy known. He even challenged Tischendorf to a duel of sorts, a debate actually, where he would demonstrate for the public eye *proof* that he had indeed authored it, specifically by identifying markings that only its author would authenticate. Tischendorf initially agreed to an appointment, but never showed. While his retreat is easily overlooked and forgiven by academia, to this day it has never been explained.

A Greek Archimandrite named Kallinkos, being a resident of St. Catherine's, verified that he witnessed firsthand Simonides writing *Sinaiticus*. He furthermore saw Tischendorf at the Monastery with Simonides' document, and knew duplicity when he saw it. Kallinkos accused Tischendorf of ill-will, specifically washing Simonides' handwritten document with lemon juice and herbs to lighten the text and make it appear as though it were of antiquity. Indeed *Sinaiticus* was mutilated, both in its codex and destruction of some leaves, likely so as to conceal acrostics that would otherwise identify the author of the codex—hence the fabricated wastebasket story. Alterations disfigure every page, systematically defaced by at least ten separate revisers.

The manuscript *Vaticanus* fares no better, worse actually—only because it originated in the Vatican library, hence the name. Its *true* origins, if there is indeed another, are unknown. It should be of interest among my readers to note that Tischendorf held meetings in Rome with the Vatican Librarian, Cardinal Angelo Mai (1782-1854), who wrote an 1838 edition of the *Vaticanus*. Collaboration, perhaps even conspiracy, seems likely. In the *Vaticanus*, Christian doctrines is suspiciously absent like it's nobody's business. Genesis 1:1-46:28 is missing, as is Psalms 106-138, Matthew 16:2-3, Romans 16:24, the Pauline Epistles, everything in Hebrews beyond 9:14, and no surprise, considering its parentage, the entire book of Revelation.

It is tragic indeed that academia praises the *Vaticanus* and the *Sinaiticus* as a trustworthy offering—and a superior one at that. Together they are often referred to by the scholar as the "Critical Text." This coalition is a scrutinized and wholly-noble attempt, I am told, resulting in the "critical" preservation of the most accurate wording possible, and yet how can this be? Both documents don't even come close to comparing with the *Textus Receptus*. Missing from the *Vaticanus* is at least 2,877 words, with an additional 536 words added and another 953 substituted. It furthermore modifies 1,132 words and transposes 2,098. *Sinaiticus* is a far worse agitator, with 9,000 divergences from the Received Text.

Indeed, the Received Text, which is supported by the overwhelming collection that makes up the Byzantine Majority Text, holds hands in agreement. Together, the Written Testimony of God is forever preserved. The King James Bible originates from the *most* perfect documentation in existence. It is unequivocally strange to hear my Christian brethren dismiss any notion of Martin Luther and William Tyndale's separate German and English translations of the New Testament *Textus Receptus*, along with the 54 scholars who produced the KJV, on the basis that it is "cult-like" to declare *"King James Only"* or, in my case, *"Textus Receptus only,"* as one's slogan when in fact they are, by committing to any other English version in the world, shackling themselves down to the far inferior *"Westcott and Hort Alone"* principle.

The Westcott-Hort partnership survived 28 years, a result of which established their hotly praised "Critical Text"—replacing the universality of the Byzantine Majority with the locality of an Egyptian wastebasket and the basement of the Vatican—as the standard Greek used for all modern interpretations of the Bible. And yet by their own testimony through a correspondence of letters, which my reader shall be satisfied in knowing can be accessed at least in parts and read-through, the infallibility of Holy Scripture was denied by the both of them. Believing that the ancient philosophers should garnish equal merit with the Prophets and the Apostles, Hort wrote: "For ourselves, we dare not introduce considerations which could not reasonably be applied to other ancient texts, supposing them to have documentary attestation of equal amount, variety and antiquity." This is an unfortunate truth which agitates our so-called God-fearing modern scholars to no end, who wish to bury any such spiritual criminality between the two, furthermore criticizing anyone who takes issue with their godless indiscretion. But it gets worse.

Fenton John Anthony Hort (1828–1892) not only denied infallibility of Holy Writ, thinking Shakespeare and Plato of equal importance, he shunned any notion of Satan, and most tragically, Christ's atonement. He wrote: "The fact is, I do not see how God's justice can be satisfied without every man's suffering in his own person the full penalty for his sins." By this he implied our place in purgatory. The true heresy, Hort insisted, was believed by those who held that Christ bore our sins on the cross. To this effect, he wrote: "Certainly nothing can be more unscriptural than the modern limiting of Christ's bearing our sins and sufferings to His death; but indeed that is only one aspect of an almost universal heresy." By calling the doctrine of the substitutionary atonement "immoral," Hort sided with the normal doctrine of the High Church Party of the Church of England, which taught salvation by good works, including baptism and church membership.

Hort was a *true* 19th-century Apostate in that he was a proud first-generation Darwinist. To his longtime friend and correspondence Reverend John Ellerton he confessed Darwin's *Origin of the Species* was "the most engaging book" he'd read. "It is a book that one is proud to be contemporary with...." furthermore stating, "....it opens up a new period."

It should be of no surprise—his love for Darwin—being also a devout Communist. In his letters to Ellerton, he confessed, "I have pretty well made up my mind to devote my three or four years up here to the study of this subject of Communism," *and*, "I can only say that it was through the region of pure politics that I myself approach Communism." As such, his hatred for the United States is legendary, and to such a degree that he hoped for its *total* destruction during the American Civil War. To Ellerton in 1862, again he wrote: "I care more for England and for Europe than for America, how much more than for all the niggers in the world!"

Brooke Foss Westcott (1825–1901) was a political Socialist, and therefore had similar distastes for Scripture. By his own testimony, infallibility was not considered. Genesis and the six-day creation account it totted was merely an allegory. Jesus committed Himself to nothing resembling a miracle. Even Moses and David were literary characters, and not to be taken historically, as one would expect of a character in a Shakespearean play. Heaven itself was not a physical place, only a state of mind. Evangelical Christians were, according to his own correspondence, dangerous, perverted, unsound, and confused. And considering his admiration and devotion for John Newman, who defected from the Church of England for Roman Catholicism, pulling a great many disciples with him, it should not be a surprise that he worshiped Mary and participated in communion with the dead.

Westcott's own son writes, "The Communion of Saints seems particularly associated with Peterborough. He had an extraordinary power of realizing this Communion. It was his delight to be alone at night in the great Cathedral, for there he could meditate and pray in full sympathy with all that was good and great in the past. . . There he always had abundant company."

One night, while returning from his customary meditations in the solitary darkness of the chapel at Auckland castle, his daughter asked him, "I expect you do not feel alone?"

"Oh, no," he said. "It is *full*."

Despite these unfortunate blemishes, and that's putting it kindly, my beloved brethren who adhere to the principle of "Hort and Westcott Alone," *not* "Majority *or* Received Texts Alone," will aptly argue that both men's youthful participation as members in "The Ghostly Guild," which sought to gather information and knowledge for contacting spirits, is of no consequence to their future lives. Westcott was a serial participant in secret societies and occultist clubs well beyond the Ghostly Guild. The Eranus Club included Arthur Balfour, the future prime minister of England, who was renowned for his séances and practice of spiritualism. Westcott even founded "Hermes." Much can be said of Hermes, but contemporary H.P. Blavatsky said of *Hermes* that he and Satan were the same. What am I missing here? This information is mocked by our most respected scholarly adherents to "Hort and Westcott Alone," as if their participation with the occult is only a mere burp or speed bump to the spiritual state of their souls, and yet Westcott admittedly and *often*—throughout the entirety of his life—found solace by filling his *emptied* church with the dead, so that he alone might commune with them.

Included in the Westcott-Hort "Critical Text" assembly line was Dr. G. Vance, a Unitarian who denied Christ's deity, Holy Scripture, and the very God-head which the entire Bible is based upon. Even the Jesuits had their part to play in it. Roman Catholic Cardinal Carlo Maria Martini served as their editor. He believed in the enlightened divinity of humanity. These are the men who were entrusted with the Bible, and whom our pastors and church leaders demand that we continue placing our faith in. Together this all-star ensemble interpreted the corrupted

Vatican and Egyptian wastebasket texts using a free-form translation method known as "dynamic equivalence." Consider that the NIV has 64,098 fewer words than the KJV, a natural out-flowing considering they each derive from very different sources, and then recall how *every* Word of God is important, not just a selection of them which the Holy Roman Church might grudgingly agree upon.

Not only is God's Word important, according to Psalm 138:2, the truth of His Testimony is even magnified *above*, according to the King James translators, or *according* to His Holy Name, as a straightforward reading of the Hebrew Masoretic Text seems to imply.

The Psalmist writes:

"I will bow down toward Your holy temple

And give thanks to Your name for Your lovingkindness and Your truth;

For You have magnified Your word according to all Your name."

(Psalm 138:2, NASB)

When our Protestant Reformers cried, "*Sola Scriptura!*" resulting in a bloody body count of martyrdom which will in this life never be fully known, they weren't simply giving us the option of succumbing to corrupted texts out of some malnourished need for Roman approval. For centuries the King James Bible *alone* was the Bible of Presbyterians, the Congregationalists, and the Quakers. It was the exclusive Bible of the Puritans and the Anabaptists—renowned soul sleepers. In England, Wales, Scotland, and Ireland, it was the Bible of the Evangelicals, and across the Ocean, where the Pilgrims fled in hopes of worshiping God without the continual disruption of Rome; it too was the recognized Bible of the New World. It has produced more fruit and more revivals and preserved the salvation of more souls than any other translation in the history of the world.

It could be said that for almost three-hundred years, until a "wastebasket discovery" and the ghostly Westcott-Hort partnership, all God-fearing men and women were "*King James Only*" people. Through them and their efforts alone has the Word of God been preserved, even magnified *above* His Name, accordingly, in the desire to faithfully keep to it. And if these facts were dispensed by our current church leadership to the congregation in which they weekly campaign to shepherd, such identification would undoubtedly ring true by anyone who loves the Lord today.

"Say Among the Heathen…. The World Shall Not Be Moved"

THE WRITERS OF THE BIBLE EXPECTED A STANDARD OF FAITH which is no longer upheld. The heathen, we are told in Psalm 96, has difficulty believing that the world stands still. More importantly, he must be informed of his wrongness. *The world shall not be moved.* And who shall remind him but the man who fears God? It is painfully transparent however that the Christian and the Jew has failed the simplest aptitude test, where an essential knowledge of God is concerned. The heathen has not only done a far superior job of converting the Christian to his position, but has even gone so far as to convince the so-called man and woman of the faith that they are truly indebted to him for it.

> [9]O worship the Lord in the beauty of holiness: fear before him, all the earth.
>
> [10]Say among the heathen that the Lord reigneth: the world also shall be established that it shall not be moved: he shall judge the people righteously."
>
> Psalm 96:9-10

God is not an "exchange of ideas" for the imaginative soul. He has already made Himself known. And yet I think back over the last couple of decades, to the various churches my wife and I would attend, always employing the use of the tippy-toe around the Darwinist. You know, the "Christian Darwinist"—we all know one or two of them—the man and woman, shiny around the blushing cheek-bone and squeaky in the ears, who robe themselves for the Sunday choir, bowing their heads reverently in prayer. The "Christian Darwinist," who believes that nothing in the Bible is true should it contradict our tedious, seemingly eternal crawl beyond the primordial soup, which raises opposition to almost all of it, front flap of leather to the back (except for the geographical maps, if a Bible happens to contain them). If Evolution were true, as the heathen claims, and God made man in His image, to borrow from Ken Ham, then the Lord Himself evolved from the ape.

"Noel, you didn't get a doctorate in Biology or Geology as we did," the Darwinist in sheep's clothing has informed this author, "So don't even think you know better of the Bible than we!"

To them I say: "The Holy Ghost must not have received a doctorate in Biology either, let alone a masters, bachelor, or associate."

The Scientific community rejects Stationary Earth, not because true science contradicts it, but because it has become the religion of the land—the humanist religion. Many attempts have been made to establish heliocentricity as true and geocentric Earth as false. Every snark endeavor by the heathen to disprove what God has created and revealed provides yet another pathetic glance into their fraudulent faith. God has granted them use of the chalkboard. He has given us the entire field of vision.

I am expected to believe the Earth is spinning faster than the speed of sound, orbiting the sun approximately 80 times faster than the speed of a bullet, while the sun is hurtling an additional 500 times faster than the speed of a bullet, with the Milky Way moving another additional 1000 times faster than the speed of the bullet. And yet I am expected to visit an amusement park for a thrill. The religion of man is truly tragic. It contains not a single scientific experiment which grants rhyme to reason.

The heathen has likely never heard of *true* science. True science is kept out of the textbooks just as God's Testimony is kept out of the textbooks, because both are trustworthy.

He has likely never heard of the James Bradley experiment, which in 1729 proved the ether—the clear sky, or upper region of air beyond the clouds, is not carried along by the Earth. He has little choice but to learn of Einstein's theory of relativity, which claims ether is a work of fiction, while likely never once hearing of the Sagnac experiment, which in 1913 proved that there was in fact ether. He has no knowledge of Airy's experiment, which in 1871 proved that the stars move, carried by the ether, while the earth remains stationary. He has likely not learned of the Michelson-Morley experiment, which in 1887, using an interferometer to measure light rays, established that the earth is undeniably stationary. Nor has he heard of the Michelson-Gale experiment, which in 1925 proved once and for all that the ether passes over the Earth once every 24 hours, not the other way around.

He has been kept in the dark regarding all of these honest men along with the meticulous work documented and detailed in every experiment because the high priests of Globe Earth, with their many mathematical equations and chalk board theories, are disproven by all experimental evidence, just as it was with Pharaoh's priests standing before Moses and Aaron. God frustrated Egypt's greatest graduates of its Mystery School then, and He still does today. He even hardened Pharaoh's heart. Apparently, much of history is repeated. They are in error before true science. But far more importantly, they stand in error before God Almighty. His Testimony takes issue with them.

The heathen has little choice but to believe everything is relative. Perhaps this explains why he opens up the pages of Holy Writ and believes God's Testimony concerning His own creation is also relative, because he is expected not to accept common sense in regards to his own observations.

"But Noel," protests the Copernican in sheep's clothing, "You didn't get a doctorate in Astronomy or physics as we did, so don't even think you know better of the Bible than we! You're no Einstein!"

To them I say: "Neither is God, apparently."

"He Walked With God"—THE DARWINIAN LIE IN CONFLICT WITH OUR TRUE COMMON ANCESTRY

SATAN IS BY NATURE A FLATTERER AND A KNEE-KNOCKER. There are few who can withstand the cajolery of his sparkling eyes and blushing smile. That one cannot object to evolution while holding almost any position of prominence, particularly in the fields of science and academia, is evidence of his totalitarian grip. That we have so many persons, who counsel in whispers from the sidelines and confess secretly that they are in opposition to Darwin's assertions while loyally keeping to his narrative in the forefront of their career, if even by their well-tempered silence, reveals in the most simplest terms it's effectual power and what men will do for a paycheck. The Holy Bible is our God-given birthright. And for a few measly dollars, mankind will publicly forsake it.

The great institution of Darwin demands that we set our gaze well-beyond the cradle of civilization. Any temptation to rightly consider or settle-upon the *Ten Old Men* promised upon the not-so distant boundary of our birthright must be forsaken for an ongoing horizon never once recorded but in the gluttonous imagination of human perversity. We *must* set our sights, we are told, upon the ape.

I have held dialogue with enough so-called "Christian" Darwinists to observe some very disconcerted issues with their personal life. Admittedly, they gaze fondly upon the ape. And God, according to the testimony of those whom I've conversed with, does not speak to them— as if this is simply a coincidence. It is peculiar to a man of such reason, perplexing even—as strange a spiritual concept as any other—that God would make His Will clearly known to a multitude of "lesser-informed" individuals who rely only on Scripture as their final authority, this author included, rather than he who employs the full muscle of his "better common sense," believing the Spirit will support his enterprises.

Having once politely listened in to a team of husband and wife "Christian" Darwinist's as they explained how my infant twin sons were exhibiting "evolutionary ape-like behaviors," I sat a little longer through their sad-sap story, particularly the man, who had devoted his life to the ministry—only so much as the Bible did not conflict with his devotion to Darwin. He was an ordained pastor, and simply did not know nor understand what it was like to hear the Lord speak and to have His will pronounced upon him. To have such an authoritative church leader smile unapologetically upon my infant sons for exhibiting "evolutionary ape-like behavior" while still holding to the belief that we were made in the image of his god, certainly not mine, and then ask what it was like to hear the Spirit's voice, is nothing short of tragic. Such men, befuddled in the darkness of their own enlightened mind, are terrible at connecting the dots.

God has made our common ancestors known. They are the *Ten Old Men*. And each one of us—stemming from every tribe and nation on this earth—share lineage with the first to the last of them. Let this be an encouragement to us all. We who dine at the table of God's future kingdom will know nothing of racial bigotry. We shall eat and drink as one completed family. Even Yeshua Hamashiach, Jesus Christ our Lord, has eagerly grafted Himself into it.

The Ten Old Men are as follows:

Adam

Seth

Enos

Cainan

Mahaleleel

Jared

Enoch

Methuselah

Lamech

Noah

The person who loves the Lord understands his birthright. It is his constitution. He upholds his oath of office in support of it. Contrarily, a man who thinks himself worthy of taking up the pastorate or any position of church leadership while adhering to his own enlightened thinking, believing the Holy Spirit will honor him for it, should think twice of ascribing what Satan has already given allowance for: *metaphors*. What he and his ambassadors cannot tolerate, why we *must* indoctrinate every child to set their gaze upon the ape—certainly not as metaphorical—is because of one small but incredible biographical detail regarding *everyone's* common ancestor.

Let us consider the last man on that list—particularly, *why* he was worthy of inheriting the entire world, being the sole survivor (with his wife and children) of the Great Deluge, and therefore grandfathering every person who has since been given the opportunity to live rightly and contribute to it.

Noah, we are told, *"walked with God."*

WHAT ALICE FOUND THERE | (*This Side of the Science Delusion*) LEWIS CARROLL'S ADVENTURES IN A WONDERLAND OF IMAGINARY NUMBERS

1

WHAT MIGHT CAUSE THE CHESHIRE CAT TO VANISH of everything but its grin? An increasing abstraction in mathematical discipline would surely be to blame, *naturally*. To claim that each of us inhabit Wonderland will come as no surprise to some of you. Perhaps the far more practical question is; are we trying to make sense of ourselves in proportion to the nonsensical world surrounding us, as Alice might— or like the creatures which tormented her tutoring; have we settled in as one of Wonderland's *curiouser* and *curiouser* residents? Hold off on your response, because author Lewis Carroll drew a line of the mathematical nature in the sand, and which side we find ourselves on, based of course on the author's own account of the Science delusion— particularly the math which makes its fabrications entirely possible—will conveniently answer the question as to where we should stand.

Charles Dodgson, pen name Lewis Carroll, was a stubbornly conservative mathematical lecturer and tutor at Christ Church College in the University of Oxford, tasked with preparing its students to pass examinations in the numbers department. For the record, it was the 19th century. His was a generation of swirling tempests, when new controversial concepts in mathematics, such as imaginary numbers (like the square root of a negative number), symbolic algebra, and projective geometry—characteristic expressions only found in allegorical formalism—were explored and ultimately exploited as groundwork to expand whatever perceived realities its master magicians could conjure.

In earlier centuries—for more than two-thousand years, in fact, Euclid's *Elements* had been the personification of rationality. The very adjective "Euclidean" was unnecessary on the mere basis that no other sort of geometry had been conceived. His was grounded in a physical reality and backed by rigorous reasoning. Theorems which might fall under his axioms, once proven, were deemed an absolute truth. In such a world, mathematical objects were conceived as the ideal representation of their physical counterparts, both in universal applicability and the objects themselves. Masterfully applying the geometry of circles, quadrilaterals, parallel lines and trigonometry, Euclid could settle complex arguments using simple, logical steps. And it worked.

These were principles however which Dodgson's contemporaries were openly straying from. The Euclidean presentation was worn fashion; old news; a tired code of moral conduct—because after all, it was the 19th century, and humanism reigned supreme. Rene Descartes was leading the charge of abstraction within the darkened catacombs of his skull. He introduced geometry of an analytical nature. Post-Cartesian mathematics gave its artists freedom to explore new *unseen* ideas, so long as these manipulated concepts found a consistent framework of operations. Such calculated techniques of modern mathematics weren't simply the favored tool for esotericism. New Science had found its art too. Russian Nikolai Lobachevsky (1792-1856), Hungarian János Bolyai (1802-1860), Germans Bernhard Riemann (1826-1866) and Carl Friedrich Gauss (1777-1855) further advanced the post Euclidean abstractions once explored by Descartes, and in the intervening years, an entire fairyland of geometric worlds would explode to consciousness beyond that which Euclidean logic had been intended, mainly in N-dimensions, projective geometry, affine geometry, and finite geometry. And yet all of this would seemingly culminate with Albert Einstein's theory of general relativity. Space itself, according to Einstein, is not Euclidean.

In short, Wonderland inhabited both inner-space and the fourth-dimension of time. Over a decade after Alice's famous adventures—1879 to be exact, Dodgson would publish his mathematical treatise, "*Euclid and his Modern Rivals*," where-as thirteen contemporary geometry textbooks were exhibited and shown to be of inferior quality or equally—if not better explained—by Euclid. According to Dodgson, post-Cartesian mathematics was a nonsensical land of the delusional mind, where his students were being guided to perversion and led away from an arithmetic which actually described the real world. For a true Euclidean, planes are flat and parallel lines never meet. Yet this is simply not so on a globe. The earth has multiple longitude lines that all meet at the North and South Poles, despite being parallel. *Alice's Adventures in Wonderland* was written with an ink-dipped dagger, mocking such reckless concepts which opened up a slippery slope between what one could fathom through the language of algebra and that of geometry at the cost of concrete existence. Wonderland was a warning for the 20th century, particularly what it might become. Depending on what side of the line you're standing on, you'll agree with me. Mad results followed.

> "I wonder if I shall fall right through the earth! How funny it'll seem to come out among the people that walk with their heads downward!"   Alice

Indeed, we all inhabit Wonderland. And like Alice, falling down the rabbit hole means leaving the world of Euclidean geometry behind. Goodbye plane Earth. Hello globe logic.

2

IF WONDERLAND HAD A MAXIM, IT MIGHT READ: *reductio ad absurdum*, which, when translated from the Latin, means "reduction to absurdity." In philosophical logic as well as mathematics, it is a form of argument quite familiar with Euclid's proofs and which attempts to discredit a statement by establishing contention between both parties and showing the absurdity of its denial, which will—if its course is not properly redirected—inevitably lead all participating members to a ridiculous and most impractical conclusion. With that in mind, let me now introduce to you one of Wonderland's most esteemed residents; the caterpillar whom Alice, being only 3-inches tall at the time, had the displeasure of taking advice from.

He is a 19th-century London math professor, and his name, according to Oxford PhD graduate Melanie Bayley, is none other than Augustus De Morgan. De Morgan was the first British mathematician to lay out a consistent set of rules for symbolic algebra. Morgan's book, *Trigonometry and Double Algebra*, first published in 1849, "explained the departure from universal arithmetic," wrote Bayley, "where algebraic symbols stand for specific numbers rooted in a physical quantity–to that of symbolic algebra, where any "absurd" operations involving negative and impossible solutions are allowed, provided they follow an internal logic." Bayley added, "De Morgan wanted to lose even this loose association with measurement, and proposed instead that symbolic algebra should be considered as a system of grammar. '*Reduce* algebra from a universal arithmetic to a series of logical but purely symbolic operations,' he said, 'and you will eventually be able to *restore* a more profound meaning to the system.'" Much like the hookah-pipe which the caterpillar smoked, De Morgan employed algebra's original Arabic translation in his footnotes, *"al jebr e al mokabala,"* which means, "restoration and reduction"—but more on that in a moment.

If Dodgson, aka Lewis Carroll, took personal displeasure with symbolic algebra, it's partly because of the added aggravation he saw in his own students, who had to *unlearn* a perfectly logical system of real world practicality for something which might easily become perverse in application, as Alice would soon come to find out.

Firstly, consider Alice's baffling stabs at reality. Already she had grown far too behemoth in size to enter through the Lilliputian door, which in turn led directly into the rose garden. To quote Alice, "Now I'm opening out like the largest telescope that ever was! Good-bye, feet!" After indiscreetly indulging in a mysterious bottle which read: "DRINK ME," she then became too small to reach the key on the table. An oddly placed cake on the floor made her enormous, while the White Rabbit's fan shrunk her down to size again. After nearly drowning in her own tears and surviving the political campaign-trail of a Dodo-based Caucus race, another unmarked bottle caused her to swell up again in the Rabbit's house while, quite conveniently, pebbles thrown in the window turned to cakes and, upon ingestion, was thoroughly waned again.

"Being so many different sizes in a day is very confusing," she confessed to the caterpillar, having been asked, rather impolitely, *who* she was, "...at least I know who I was when I got up this morning, but I think I must have been changed several times since then."

Certainly she has changed—quite inconsolably too; fluctuating anywhere between 9 feet and now 3 inches. Alice functioned best in a rational world, where her multiplication tables and something as simple as poetic grammar might be rightfully recited. Not so here. "Alice," writes Bayley, "bound by conventional arithmetic where a quantity such as size should be constant, finds this troubling." The post-Cartesian rules which regulated Wonderland were very confusing indeed, *especially* for the traditional Euclidean sort such as Carroll. But the caterpillar, who behaves as erratically as the imaginatively skewed world he inhabits— for you see, he has seemingly mushroomed up from nowhere—responds with the very apathy which might lend someone to believe the little girl, and her mocking narrator, are both siding with the wrong side of history.

Regarding any concluding notion that Alice is dutifully confused or ebbed of mind, he quips, "It isn't."

Lewis Carroll's views on the madness of this new symbolic algebra might best be explained—*reductio ad absurdum*—by the mushroom which the hookah-smoking caterpillar instructed her to partake of, seeing as how "one side will make you grow taller, and the other side will make you grow shorter." Esoteric references aside, this advice was dreadfully confusing for Alice, "trying to make out which were the two sides of it; and as it was perfectly round, she found this a very difficult question." Perhaps this perplexing circle of rationality relates to Dodgson's many tutoring sessions. Unfortunately for Alice, she calculated the wrong balance between *tall* and *short*, because within a moment her chin collided with her foot.

What happens when Alice eats the other side of the mushroom? Carroll writes: "...she found that her shoulders were nowhere to be found: all she could see, when she looked down, was an immense length of neck, which seemed to rise like a stalk out of a sea of green leaves that lay far below her."

Suffice to say, Alice might have interpreted the Caterpillars further promulgation of apathy, particularly his advice, to "Keep your temper," quite differently than Lewis Carroll's own contemporaries. Among Oxford's educated, the word "temper" still retained its original definition, essentially meaning: "the proportion in which qualities are mingled." One might consider *tempered metal*. And here, when faced with Alice's difficulty formulating a tempered resolve with the mushroom, we can once more discern Carroll's own frustration with symbolic algebra. It is a dreadfully poor substitute to the grounded realities of Euclidean geometry.

3

WHAT HAPPENS WHEN A TERRIBLE COOK DOUSES HER STEW with too much pepper? Well, if it has anything to do with projected geometry, particularly Lewis Carroll's distrust of it, and the narrative unfolds in Wonderland, we follow such action to its logical conclusion. Let's observe. Everyone in the room sneezes, except for the Cheshire Cat. But more importantly, the baby turns into a pig, *naturally*. This certainly doesn't seem to surprise the Cheshire Cat at all. As Master of Ceremonies to the unfolding madness, his simple and conclusively apathetic reply to a perturbed Alice, we might assume, leads us to the very voice of Carroll himself when he speaks from behind his crescent-shaped grin. Carroll, *I mean*, the Cheshire Cat concludes:

"I thought it would."

French mathematician Jean-Victor Poncelet (1788-1867) served as an army lieutenant in the Corps of Military Engineers. Actually, Poncelet took part in Napoleon's invasion of Russia. That was in 1812 when, at the Battle of Krasnoi, he was left for dead. Despite interrogation by General Mikhail Andreyevich Miloradovich, the mathematician disclosed no private information. It was during his imprisonment over the next two years when he wrote his most notable work, *"Traité des propriétés projectives des figures,"* which outlined the foundations of projective geometry.

Projective geometry examines the properties of figures that stay the same even when that figure is projected onto another surface. A basic precept is that projective space has more points than Euclidean space for any given dimension. Therefore, geometric transformations are permitted which *mutate* Euclidean points to its counterpart "extra" points, and vice versa. Accordingly, it is possible to assign meanings to the terms "point" and "line" in such a way that they satisfy the first four postulates but not the parallel postulate. Poncelet describes his theory as follows: "Let a figure be conceived to undergo a certain continuous variation, and let some general property concerning it be granted as true, so long as the variation is confined within certain limits; then the same property will belong to all the successive states of the figure." At any rate, if Wonderland is a series of ridiculous notions and academic grudges, then Poncelet's geometry made Carroll's hit list. It's a notion that the Euclidean math tutor found ridiculous.

The scene in question plays out like this. Alice enters the house of a Duchess who is doing a terrible job of nursing a baby. It howls inconsolably. The cook is doing a terrible job too. Smoke fills the kitchen. The pepper is causing everyone but the Cheshire Cat to sneeze. Frustrated beyond her own limitations, the Duchess violently tosses the baby through the air so that Alice must catch it, which causes the seven year-old Euclidean to ruminate silently among herself: 'If I don't take this child away with me, they're sure to kill it in a day or two: wouldn't it be murder to leave it behind?' This of course comes after the cook begins throwing everything within arm's reach at the Duchess and her baby. "The fire-irons came first; then followed a shower of saucepans, plates, and dishes." If Alice were to conclude that everyone in the house is preforming terribly, which she most certainly does, then she would be correct.

It has already been established by this point that Alice has left the world of plane Euclidean geometry behind. Here Projective Geometry is free to perform its theatrics. With Euclid, railroad tracks will never meet. But with projective, at some point in the infinity of our horizon they will. With infinity there is no distance. Parallel lines may be free to wander—so to speak; just as an imaginative mind has room to wander. "The case of two intersecting circles is perhaps the simplest example to consider," writes Melanie Bayley. "Solve their equations, and you will find that they intersect at two distinct points. According to the principle of continuity, any continuous transformation to these circles— moving their centres away from one another, for example—will preserve the basic property that they intersect at two points. It's just that when their centres are far enough apart the solution will involve an imaginary number that can't be understood physically."

"The principle of continuity," Melanie Bayley continues, is "a bizarre concept from projective geometry, which was introduced in the mid-19th century from France." That would be mathematician Jean-Victor Poncelet. "This principle (now an important aspect of modern topology) involves the idea that one shape can bend and stretch into another, provided it retains the same basic properties — a circle is the same as an ellipse or a parabola (the curve of the Cheshire cat's grin). Taking the notion to its extreme, what works for a circle should also work for a baby. So, when Alice takes the Duchess's baby outside, it turns into a pig."

The reader of Carroll's work will immediately notice that the baby and the pig essentially keeps its same basic original features, as any theoretical object going through a continuous transformation must. Carroll writes: "Alice caught the baby with some difficulty, as it was a queer-shaped little creature, and held out its arms and legs in all directions, *just like a star-fish*,' thought Alice." Like the Duchess herself, a caricature likely based off of sixteenth-century Flemish artist Quentin Matsys painting of the fourteenth-century Duchess Margaret of Carinthia and Tyrol—she had the reputation of being the ugliest woman in history, and Matsys' portrait is titled "The Ugly Duchess," appropriately—Alice notes that the baby is somewhat homely in and of itself. It has a queer shape, turned-up nose and small eyes. Alice only realizes the transformation when its howling sneezes turn to grunts.

355

What follows between Alice and the Cheshire Cat is perhaps one of the most popular exchanges in the entire history of literature. Wonderland's Master of Ceremony has witnessed the baby's untidy transformation into a pig from the branch of a tree, *naturally*, and the short transaction of words to follow may best describe Carroll's personal frustration towards the maddening rush of his academic contemporaries away from a solid reality-based Euclidean construct to the abstraction of Post-Cartesian mathematics.

Cat: "Where are you going?"

Alice: "Which way should I go?"

Cat: "That depends on where you are going."

Alice: "I don't know."

Cat: "Then it doesn't matter which way you go."

4

WILLIAM HAMILTON WAS MAD AS A HATTER. Of course, so was a certain Theophilus Carter. The later was a furniture dealer residing near the Oxford of Carroll's time. The fact that he was actually known by locals as the Mad Hatter, partly due to an obsession with his top hat and because eccentricities became his order of business, is not a coincidence. Carter's invention of an "alarm clock bed," for example, which promised to wake the sleeper by tossing him upon the cold, hard floor, was exhibited at the Crystal Palace in 1851. No surprise though, it didn't catch on. Critics have long explained Theophilus Carter as the reason why Alice's Hatter is so concerned with time and arousing a sleepy dormouse, not to forget his gratuitous mentions of furniture. Then again, Lewis Carroll didn't have a bone to pick with Theophilus Carter.

All things considered, it would most certainly be a mistake to overlook the Irish physicist, astronomer, and mathematician William Hamilton. The fourth dimension had become quite the craze in the 19th-century, and Hamilton played his part. Hamilton was looking for ways of extending complex numbers to higher spatial dimensions. The third-dimension failed him. But in working with four dimensions he created 'quaternions.' As early as 1843, quaternions had been hailed as an important milestone in abstract algebra, since rotations could be calculated algebraically, and would later be employed within the Kepler

Problem and the study of celestial mechanics. Makiko Minow-Pinkney writes, Hinton "believed that with enlarged imaginative powers gained by the practice of visualizing the four-dimensional cubes which he called 'tesseracts,' individuals would gain access to true reality (*The Question of the Fourth Dimension*)."

Hamilton, it seems, was driven by the notion that algebra was the science of time. Specifically, Melanie Bayley writes, he believed "algebra allowed the investigation of 'pure time,' a rather esoteric concept he had derived from Immanuel Kant that was meant to be a kind of Platonic ideal of time, distinct from the real time we humans experience." As a result, he "discovered a four-dimensional manifold of numbers, the 'quaternions'—usually called hyper complex numbers today," writes David Booth in the introduction to Rudolf Steiner's *The Fourth Dimension: Sacred Geometry, Alchemy, and Mathematics* (1905). "Hamilton did explore the fourth dimension, but still refused to actually accept the notion of a four dimensional space. He carried out his research at a time in which—according to our hypothetically accepted view of Cultural Revolution—man's consciousness had descended to the greatest degree into matter. Hamilton used three dimensions (the vectors), along with a fourth (the tensor), that were kept separate so that they did not combine into a single four dimensional manifold."

The fourth dimension certainly wasn't loved by all. In his critique of Charles Howard Hinton's book *The Fourth Dimension*, Bertrand Russell wrote that such impropriety would "stimulate the imagination, and free the intellect from the shackles of the actual," and that by claiming "our three-dimension world is superficial," Hinton came across as a "conscientious bigamist." Carroll also took an offensive position. For the author of Wonderland, "the fourth-dimension," says Ana Teixeira Pinto, a lecturer at Berlin University of the Arts, "was a case of the hypostatization of language: abstraction taken literally, and set phrases, metaphors, and figures of speech given concrete reality."

At any rate, Alice finds herself at a tea party, or perhaps it should read "t-party," with three curious inhabitants of Wonderland: the Hatter, the March Hare, and the Dormouse. Notice that the character Time is absent from the t-party. Actually, the Mad Hatter has had a falling out with Time, and is stuck at 6 o'clock accordingly—and perhaps even eternally. Says the Hatter to Alice: "If you knew Time as well as I do, you wouldn't talk about wasting it. It's HIM."

Writes Melanie Bayley: "The members of the Hatter's tea party represent three terms of a quaternion, in which the all-important fourth term, time, is missing. Without Time, we are told, the characters are stuck at the tea table, constantly moving round to find clean cups and saucers." The movement around the table can be seen as Hamilton's unsuccessful attempts at calculating motion, which was limited to rotations on a plane until he added time to the equation. Bayley continues, "Alice's ensuing attempt to solve the riddle pokes fun at another aspect of quaternions: their multiplication is non-commutative, meaning that x × y is not the same as y × x. Alice's answers are equally non-commutative."

There is an exchange between the Hatter, March Hare, and Alice that goes like this.

"Then you should say what you mean," the March Hare went on.

"I do," Alice hastily replied; "at least–at least I mean what I say–that's the same thing, you know."

"Not the same thing a bit!" says the Hatter. "Why, you might just as well say that 'I see what I eat' is the same thing as 'I eat what I see'!"

Hamilton's stimulation of the imagination, specifically his freeing "the intellect from the shackles of the actual," as Russell would say of Hinton, found its fullest realization in the establishment of Globe Earth—or rather, it's only *proof* of existence. And it's a mathematical one. "The development of abstract mathematical formalisms, notably that of tensor calculus," writes the astrophysicist John Barrow. "A deep physical insight orchestrated the mathematics of general relativity, but in the years that followed the balance tipped the other way. Einstein's search for a unified theory was characterized by a fascination with the abstract fomalisms themselves."

Gerrard Hickson put the general theory of relativity, backed in part by the fourth dimension, to rest in his book, *Kings Dethroned*. He wrote: "While claiming 'time' as a fourth dimension, Einstein explains that 'by dimension we must understand merely one of four independent quantities which locate an event in space.' . . . This is to imply that the other three dimensions which are in common use are independent quantities, which is not the case; for length, breadth and thickness are essentially found in combination; they co-exist in each and every physical thing, so that they are related—hence they are not independent quantities. . . . On the contrary, time IS an independent quantity. It is independent of any one, or all, the three proportions of material things, it is not in any way related; and therefore cannot be used as a fourth dimension."

"When the scene ends," Bayley adds, "the Hatter and the Hare are trying to put the Dormouse into the teapot....If they could only lose him, they could exist independently, as a complex number with two terms. Still mad, according to Dodgson, but free from an endless rotation around the table." Quite unlike *pure* time, for a conservative mathematician like Lewis Carroll, the non-Euclidean world of Wonderland was *pure* madness. Non-commutative algebras contradicted the basic laws of arithmetic, and as we've come to see, opened up strange new worlds, where the imagination and abstraction roams free. But as always, Alice said it best.

> "Let me think. Was I the same when I got up this morning?
> ...But if I'm not the same, the next question is, who in the
> world am I? Ah, that's the great puzzle!"

"There Is a Fourth Dimension….."
MISADVENTURES THROUGH MIND OVER MATTER IN A GEOMETERS FAIRYLAND

THERE IS A NEIGHBORHOOD OF THE MATHEMATICAL MIND which seeks to exercise the rights of the unsatisfied entrepreneur who finds our created order too confining for his imaginative prowess, as if the infinity of Kepler's "New Astronomy" were not enough for his limitless gaze beyond a flat, enclosed, and stationary Earth. With a wizardly muscleman at his side, he is able to dazzle the non-mathematical thinker by invoking an invisible astral-universe through various displays of equations and which is advantageous to his every intellectual and artistic purpose. For this reason, the fourth-dimension is something its critics once labeled *the geometers fairyland*. That the "Hyperspace Theory" was inconceivable by any human means beyond Nth-dimensional geometry and linear algebra proved of little concern to the nineteenth-century fantasizer. There is hardly a science to be "discovered," let alone adequately nurtured to maturity, should it not afford the legitimacy of an E-ticket attraction. Philosophers, spiritualists, esotericists, and sexual provocateurs, anyone clinging to the legacy of the ancient Mysteries, needed an invention to back their growing market, and indeed, as one might expect, the Theosophical Society provided one.

Naturally, Christian culture—as they so often do, put their stamp of approval on contradictory concepts; detrimental ideals to the age-old faith in which they couldn't possibly have thought through. Pantheism was on the rebound in the nineteenth century. Reinforced by a Victorian surge of interest in Eastern mysticism, mainly Buddhism and Hinduism, the fourth-dimension myth was further bolstered by a renewed belief in the "world soul." Occultist Isaac Newton himself proposed the idea that "space" is God's *sensorium*, what might be described as the organ which God makes use of to perceive things. *Oh well*. Out with the old, in with the new; Euclidean geometry was yesterday's mathematics. Modernists had physics.

With the fourth dimension, the occultist unveiled a hidden compartment by which their pixies and ghostly apparitions might be conveniently stored, and where the laws of physics needn't apply— that is, until their insatiable appetite for the next séance should summon them to Newtonian conducts; and where shadowy specters for the trans-humanist mind might freely roam—Christians also wanted their fair share of the baggage. Besides, heaven no longer fit within the Copernican's latest-greatest Apollo-centered cosmology. God was left homeless by Newtonian physics. The Newtonians had declared the very notion of "up" or "down" to be fashionably outdated wherever there is a globe and gravity retrofitted to it, which meant the Bible's account of heaven's "up-ness" could not possibly be taken at face value, if they— the Christian—should be allowed to play along. The Christians put their stamp of approval on that too—at least some of them, if only to be picked last on the team. And now, where the fourth dimension was involved, they too had a "plane"—ironically enough—an entire unexplored Universe of the mind to store their angels and demons and Platonic heavenly *forms* within.

And while they were at it, God could reside there too.

The fourth-dimension found its initial calling with French mathematician Henri Poincare (1854-1912). For Poincare, the realm went beyond its geometric nature to penetrate perceptual "inner space." His original 1880 article: *What is the Fourth Dimension?* would be subsequently reprinted another nine times. Poincare's insight not only inspired Albert Einstein's *Theory of Relativity*, but presented Pablo Picasso with such a quandary as to whip up his lifetime devotion to Cubism. Not surprising, since the fourth-dimension is perceived as the realm of the psyche. Art acts as a receiver to the *higher realm*—so to speak, achieving telekinesis where science cannot. Its career strengthened through Charles H. Hinton (1853-1907), an untenured mathematics instructor at Princeton. For Hinton, the fourth dimension was a mathematical concept represented by the cube, which essentially entailed our higher and immortal self. In his book, *Mystery School in Hyperspace*, author Graham St. John writes:

> "Hinton developed his views on the mystical and evolutionary significance of four-dimensional space. The fourth dimension was perceived to be the source of alternative modes of consciousness like those experienced by mystics, psychics, mediums, and others with evolved means of perception. For Hinton, the fourth dimension was not a mathematical

abstraction, but a mode of perception integral to the development of human consciousness."

Russian theosophist Petr Ouspensky (1878-1947) found reason for lasting disappointment with Hinton, whose work he personally translated into his own native tongue. Albert Einstein mutually agreed, albeit *indirectly*. Hinton's exercises, which hoped of deducing fourth-dimensional awareness for himself and his fellow observers, were restricted to mathematical parlor games and landlocked lab experiments, and therefore severely handicapped what may have otherwise been an advantageous outcome. Wrote Ouspensky: "In art it is necessary to study occultism—the hidden side of life. The artist must be a clairvoyant: he must see that which others do not see; he must be a magician; must possess the power to make others see that which they do not themselves see, but which he does."

Theosophists Annie Besant and Charles Leadbeater, co-authors of *Thought-Forms* (1901), neatly summed up the hallmark of Victorian theory. For the Victorian, wildly in pursuit of new ideas and hidden gods of the mind, his psychological *was* the transcendental. Or as the two put it, "thoughts are things." More precisely, visitation to the astral-plane was akin to a form of four-dimensional sight. Leadbeater writes: "We must beware of falling into the fatally common error of supposing that what we see is all there is to see."

Perhaps not so dissimilar *theologically* from Nikolai Kibalchich—a fellow Russian and revolutionary rocket pioneer who believed humanities ultimate self-salvation would be triumphed through a technological and spiritual blending of transhumanism—Petr Ouspensky believed: "the evolution in consciousness was to be achieved through the development of a culture that augments the new consciousness and causes it to flourish." In *The Occult in Russian and Soviet Culture*, Bernice Glatzer Rosenthal writes: "That astronomy grew out of astrology and chemistry out of alchemy is well known, but the links between the occult and modern psychology are yet to be generally recognized. Occult doctrines appealed to people who were interested in what was then called the "inner man," the soul of the psyche, which rationalists and empiricists neglected or even disdained." Ouspensky regarded the fourth dimension as a way to escape from death into the *real world* of the spirit. As an occultist, Ouspensky not only wrote about the mystical potentials of yoga, breathing exercises, dreams, prayer, fasting, and tarot card reading, he even held private conversations with the devil. Through experiments in modified states of consciousness combined with nitrous

362

oxide and hashish, he once had a vision of *Linga Sharira*. Again, Graham St. John writes:

> "A theme lifted from Blavatsky's *The Secret Doctrine*—itself adopting Hindu philosophy, where this idea infers *the form on which our physical body molded*—this referred to a four-dimensional "temporal body."

Helena Blavatsky defined *Linga Sharira* in *The Key to Theosophy*. Here she says: "This term designates the doppelganger or the "astral body" of man or animal. It is the eidolon of the Greeks, the vital and prototypal body; the reflection of the men of flesh. It is born before and dies or fades out, with the disappearance of the last atom of the body." Blavatsky believed everything in the Universe was conscious—endowed with a consciousness of its own kind and on its own plane of perception. The Universe was the periodical manifestation of this unknown Absolute Essence. Conclusively, the Absolute was "beyond the range and reach of thought." The key to attaining higher consciousness lay in one's own ability to change their perception of time, mainly escaping the limitations of the present moment. Blavatsky looked to the fourth-dimension.

While the Victorians and the late nineteenth-century Russians perfected the ideal fourth-dimension, oddly enough it was philosopher Immanuel Kant who first gave notice to the concept. In *Thoughts on the True Estimation of Living Forces* (1747), he wrote: "if it is possible that there are extensions with other dimensions, it is also very probable that God has somewhere brought them into being; for His works have all the magnitude and manifoldness of which they are capable." Three decades later, while penning *The Prolegomena to Any Future Metaphysics* (1783), Kant would inquire:

> "If all space were empty but for a single human hand, would it make sense to ask whether that hand was specifically a right hand?"

In a four-dimensional space the notion of a distinct gender becomes obscured, to say the least. Like Kent's hand, it may appear as a *right* hand or a *left* hand, depending on the observer's position. So too might a male appear as female, or a female as male. Accordingly, if our astral-plane doppelganger, our true fourth-dimensional self, cannot be identified, then we as Christians have serious theological problems. French author Jean Clair, in *Sur Marcel Duchamp et la Fin de l'Art*, sums up why:

"We are sometimes given a vagina—and that designates a "woman"—virgin, bride, etc.—and sometimes a penis—and that indicates a "man"—bachelor, groom, etc. This physiological accident was never anything more than the effect of an assuredly ironic causality: the laws of Euclidian geometry. In a four-dimensional study … vagina and penis, like an anamorphic illusion, would immediately lose all distinctive character. It is the same object that we would sometimes see as "male" and sometimes as "female," in this perfect mirror-like reversal of the body that presupposes, because it takes place, the existence of a fourth dimension."

Yet again, we find ourselves fumbling miserably through a dark room, slapping at the wall for a light switch. What if the fourth-dimension was nothing more or less than another humanist invention, a furniture piece for his temple—that is, the delusional catacomb of the mind? For the truest humanist, there is no *absolute* except for what he might ascertain in the warped perversions of his imaginations. Like evolution; like the theory of relativity used to support the globe itself; the so-called fourth-dimension is yet one more dizzying piece to the behemoth puzzle. It's nothing more than a walk-in closet for the esoterists, and we must—we *simply must* climb out of it.

Almost as though this were a scene from *The Matrix*, Russian theosophist Petr Ouspensky invokes a picturesque moment in the life of the self-enlightened soul who "wakes up" from the *superficial* created order that supposedly, like a well-oiled machine, binds us as slaves: He writes: "Attaining consciousness is connected with the gradual liberation from mechanicalness, for man is fully and completely under mechanical laws." If we as Christians should possess a lick of discernment within us, we can see where this originated, and where this is *going*.

French existentialist Simone de Beauvoir cleans the platter up nicely, as one who has transcended from the higher realm, when famously claiming:

"One is not born a woman. One becomes one."

DARK MATTER... ARCANE SOUL... [INVISIBLE FIRMAMENTS... HIDDEN WORLDS...]

THERE IS BUT ONE FIRMAMENT. THE BIBLE TELLS ME SO. Yet this is "*simply not true*," according to the esoteric and the Copernican. The apostate doctrine, auspiciously milked at the succulent tit of occultism and then parented within the congregation of Scientism, postulates there are a minimal of 100 billion planets in the Milky Way Galaxy *alone*, each with a firmament all its own. Theosophist Helena Blavatsky said it like this: "There are millions and millions of worlds and firmaments visible to us; there are still greater numbers beyond those visible to the telescopes, and many of the latter kind do not belong to our objective sphere of existence." As if Biblical cosmogony was not expanded upon enough by the Copernican—in fact totally erased and rewritten; I direct your attention once again to the unseen realm—the space between spaces—to that which lies just beyond the twilight of our humanist thinking, yet another tenant of the Secret Doctrine. Science has a name for it—Dark Matter.

The longstanding feud between Newtonian physics and the observable pull of "galaxies," which the Bible never thinks to make mention of and can only be observed, at any rate, through augmented reality—is not my concern. Dark matter is. Everything that science can currently give account for, *matter* that is, which includes Earth and its human inhabitants—everything below the Bible's *only*recorded firmament—apparently consists of less than 5 percent of the entire universe. This dark "energy," which populates the remaining 95 percent, cannot be tested, measured, nor quantified, and yet what is observably known of gravity is that there is not enough of it for the Copernican Universe and Newtonian physics to properly function. We've been fooled by the drop of an apple. Gravity is simply too impossibly weak to form the galaxies and complex structures necessary for the Copernican revolution. Scientists need something which interacts with gravity—something which doesn't reflect or emit light—-something *dark*. In other words, they desperately need a failed experiment to work. And what better than another unseen, undetected, untestable, and unmeasurable force?

Dr. Rick Strassman writes of dark matter: "The only way we know it is there is by its gravitational effects. It *must* exist by virtue of the fact that the visible universe maintains its particular shape. Without this mass, there would not be enough gravity to hold the universe together—it would fly apart."

Scientists have no clue how dark matter and dark energy works. Never-the-less, because galaxies are tightly bound clusters of mass held together by gravity, the insertion of dark matter is what makes it possible for galaxies, spread out over a large pallet, to exist. If dark energy is growing, it's because outer space is continuously expanding—thank you Kabbalah and the Big Bang. This "dark" is therefore advertised as energy intrinsic to empty space—energy that not only fills in the gaps— energy which not only writes its own rules of physics—but is stronger than anything else known to man.

Put it slightly in other terms, everything that we experience is only a tiny fraction of reality. Ironically, if the occultist is correct—our sunlit existence is non-other than the shadow world of Plato's cave. The mystic has long pointed his spiritual dog-tail away from the physical self, preferring to travel in the direction of light *beyond* form, and even more specifically, if one should find himself so thoroughly flagellated in his self-renaissance of enlightenment—to the darkness *behind* light. What is important to note about the esoteric tradition is that light and darkness are both interchangeable. If the word *absolute* can be defined as: "something beyond our knowing," then Absolute Light is conclusively darkness to us. Helena Blavatsky herself writes: "In the sense of the Unmanifested and the Unknown as the opposite pole to manifestation, and that which falls under the possibility of speculation....it is not Darkness as absence of Light, but as one incomprehensible primordial Principle, which, being Absoluteness itself, has for our intellectual perceptions neither form, color, substantiality, nor anything that could be expressed by words" (*Transactions of the Blavatsky Lodge*).

In *The Secret Doctrine* Helena Blavatsky further elaborates:

"According to the tenets of Eastern Occultism, DARKNESS is the one true actuality, the basis and root of light, without which the latter could never manifest itself, nor even exist. Light is matter, and DARKNESS pure Spirit. Darkness, in its radical metaphysical basis, is subjective and absolute light; while the latter in all its seeming effulgence and glory, is merely a mass of shadows, as it can never be eternal, and is simply an illusion, or Maya."

Should the inventions of Science penetrate the mysterious dark matter of esoteric tradition, they will surely arrive into the higher etheric planes of the theosophist's wet-dream, a twilight realm of pure consciousness without ego which has at its correspondence the penetration into the higher ethers of the cosmic physical plane. The doorway into darkness is quite contrarily the darkness simultaneously entering our consciousness, and more importantly, is the occultist's covetous contact with the Monad.

Consciousness is a universe too. And the brain is a receiver, *apparently*. If the Copernican is correct, should there really be another 100 billion planets in our minuscule back-alley Milky Way Galaxy, then stop to consider the occultist implications, and what the next generation Columbus is determined to discover—another countless New World landscapes available for the Psychonaut to explore within the realms of dark matter—a universe amply multiplied. Writes Dr. Strassman: "The strangest realms to which DMT might lead are those that exist within the mysterious realms of dark matter. There, which may indeed be here, no one knows what we will find."

Once again Helena Blavatsky explains:

"Although as invisible as if they were millions of miles beyond our solar system, they are yet with us, near us, within our own world, as objective and material to their respective inhabitants as ours is to us....Each is entirely under its own special laws and conditions, having no direct relation to our sphere. The inhabitants of these, as already said, may be, for all we know, or feel, passing through and around us as if through empty space, their very habitations and countries being interblended with ours, though not disturbing our vision, because we have not yet the faculties necessary for discerning them. Yet by their spiritual sight the Adepts, and even some seers and sensitives, are always able to discern, whether in a greater or smaller degree, the presence and close proximity to us of Beings pertaining to other spheres of life. Those of the (spiritually) higher worlds, communicate only with those terrestrial mortals who ascend to them, through individual efforts, on to the higher place they are occupying...."

Science has the oddest habit of conforming to the sure-promises of esoteric tradition. Perhaps more than any other discipline, they have manifested the Mysteries and made the "Light-Bearer" known. Even more extraordinarily, "Modern science has validated Magikal theory," claims D. Lawrence Meredith, author of *Modern Alchemy and Occult Psychology*, "except with a bit more power and substance tautologically. This thin line, the twilight state where neither consciousness nor unconsciousness is dominant, it is both. As one becomes more skilled at Magik and the creative progress, the regressive process, this will become more evident."

On the importance of dark matter and energy, Meredith adds:

"Another aspect to this paradigm is that large portions are hidden, DNA. Surely, we can make the obvious parallel between the universe's being made mostly of invisible material, the mind being controlled largely by unconscious psychic forces, and most human DNA being inaccessible and having an unknown use. The result of making such a connection is the realization that this TRINITY (i.e., dark matter, junk DNA, the unconsciousness) is the part of the universe that interfaces with the sublime, the eternal, the non-d*ual, the non-local, what is called Heaven."*

Blavatsky paid no lip-service to the Bible. "And now it stands proven that Satan, or the Red Fiery Dragon, the 'Lord of Phosphorus,' and Lucifer, or 'Light-Bearer,' is in us: it is our Mind," she wrote. Her largest imposing threat was the Christian who planted his gaze within the uncompromising light of Holy Writ. In order for the occultist's plans of human transcendence into "the non-dual, the non-local," as Meredith described it, specifically the eternal Overmind—in order for such a scheme to ultimately succeed, she could only hope the collective consciousness of the non-ego, which makes up the higher realm of dark matter, could outmatch her opponents by tickling their novel love of gullibility.

Tickling she did.

"Darkness is absolute light," she wrote, "a fact now neglected if not entirely forgotten in theology."

THE GOLDEN BRICK ROAD OF THEOSOPHY: L. FRANK BAUM'S TRANSMISSIONS FROM OZ

1

OCCULTISM SELLS—NOW MORE THAN EVER. Not that it's ever been out of print, *per say*. After all, occultism is a provable cockroach, and can thrive not only in the chilling darkness—once it is rightfully swatted away from the daylight—but could and most certainly *would* survive a nuclear holocaust, except the LORD Himself finally put an end to it. Perhaps no other empire in the history of western civilization has achieved such financial success at marketing the esoteric, branding it as *entertainment*, and then repackaging it as *childhood nostalgia*, than the current country where this author resides. Like the globe itself, and the "American" mythology of space which accompanies it, occultism is best served to children. Indeed, the mystic author who convinces his reader that he is simply wetting their appetites beyond what God has permitted, or rather divulging in the imagination that God rightfully gave to them, flourishes here. Being a member of the Theosophists Society, author L. Frank Baum was no exception.

First published in 1900, *The Wonderful Wizard of Oz* has yet to fall out of print. In the following nineteen years before his death, Baum would add a total of fourteen titles to his Oz series. It is a stunning legacy, a marathon of endurance matched only by the MGM color-spectacular staring Judy Garland. Writing for the Aberdeen Saturday Pioneer in 1890, an editorial position which he held for fourteen months—and an entire decade before premiering Oz, Baum described America's Occult fascination.

"There is a strong tendency in modern novelists towards introducing some vein of mysticism or occultism into their writings. Books of this character are eagerly bought and read by the people, both in Europe and America. It shows the innate longing in our natures to unravel the mysterious: to seek some explanation, however fictitious, of the unexplainable in nature and in our daily existence. For, as we advance in education, our desire for knowledge increases, and we are less satisfied to remain in ignorance of that mysterious fountain-head from which emanates all that is sublime and grand and incomprehensible in nature."

"The appetite of our age for occultism demands to be satisfied, and while with the mediocrity of people will result in mere sensationalism, it will lead in many to higher and nobler and bolder thought; and who can tell what mysteries these braver and abler intellects may unravel in future ages?"

February 22, 1890

Baum was never one who accredited himself with originality. Quite contrarily, he saw himself as a "receiver." Much like the radio, which the Italian inventor Guglielmo Marconi would first send and receive in 1895, Baum claimed that his most popular stories were unequivocally transmitted to him, perhaps from Oz itself. As of 1890, it was the longstanding influence of his mother-in-law who had formulated his religious ideals. Matilda Joslyn Gage was a noted supporter of woman suffrage, and though she became a member of the Theosophical Society in 1885, Gage had already been sharing its magazine, *the Path*, among family and friends. By Matilda's own account in 1887, her daughter (and Baum's wife) Maud was busy reading H.P. Blavatsky's *Isis Unveiled* (1877) and other texts on Esoteric Buddhism. The Baum family, Matilda claimed, was eagerly anticipating Blavatsky's forthcoming book, *The Secret Doctrine: The Synthesis of Science, Religion, and Philosophy* (1888), which would prove to be Blavatsky's—as well as the entire movements—magnum opus. In 1896 or 1897, Gage, who was living then with the Baum's in Chicago, recorded that Frank had acquired the book, *The Astral Plane*, by C. W. Leadbeater.

Blavatsky perhaps best lays out the Theosophists doctrine in *The Secret Doctrine*, when she writes:

"But it is perhaps desirable to state unequivocally that the teachings, however fragmentary and incomplete, contained in these volumes, belong neither to the Hindu, the Zoroastrian, the Chaldean, nor the Egyptian religion, neither to Buddhism, Islam, Judaism nor Christianity exclusively. The Secret Doctrine is the essence of all these. Sprung from it in their origins, the various religious schemes are now made to merge back into their original element, out of which every mystery and dogma has grown, developed, and become materialized."

In the *Pioneer*, Baum eagerly directed his readers' attention to the occult fiction of Edward Bulwer-Lytton, H. Rider Haggard, and Mabel Collins. Other spiritualist needs filled his column, but his devotion to the Theosophist Society—he would finally become a member of Chicago's branch of the Theosophical Society on September 4, 1892—only proved to alienate his Aberdeen weekly readers. On January 25, 1890, Baum wrote:

"Amongst the various sects so numerous in America today who find their fundamental basis in occultism, the Theosophist stands pre-eminent both in intelligence and point of numbers.

The recent erection of their new temple in New York City has called forth the curiosity of the many, the uneasiness of the few. Theosophy is not a religion. Its followers are simply "searchers after Truth." Not for the ignorant are the tenets they hold, neither for the worldly in any sense. Enrolled within their ranks are some of the grandest intellects of the Eastern and Western worlds.

Purity in all things, even to asceticism is absolutely required to fit them to enter the avenues of knowledge, and the only inducement they offer to neophytes is the privilege of "searching for the Truth" in their company.

As interpreted by themselves they accept the teachings of Christ, Budda [sic], and Mohammed, acknowledging them Masters or Mahatmas, true prophets each in his generation, and well versed in the secrets of nature. But the truth so earnestly sought is not yet found in its entirety, or if it be, is known only to the privileged few.

The Theosophists, in fact, are the dissatisfied of the world, the dissenters from all creeds. They owe their origin to the wise men of India, and are numerous, not only in the far famed mystic east, but in England, France, Germany and Russia. They admit the existence of a God–not necessarily a personal God. To them God is Nature and Nature God.

We have mentioned their high morality: they are also quiet and unobtrusive, seeking no notoriety, yet daily growing so numerous that even in America they may be counted by thousands. But, despite this, if Christianity is Truth, as our education has taught us to believe, there can be no menace to it in Theosophy."

The Aberdeen columnists claim that "there can be no menace to it [Christianity] in Theosophy" garnishes my irritable gaze. For the person who believes the Word of God is true, Spirit-breathed and inspired—and for good reason, Baum makes a terrible salesman. Either Baum himself is eternally gullible, or he is a bold-faced liar. Either way, it is the darling prophet of his Society, H.P. Blavatsky, who shamelessly wrote: "And now it stands proven that Satan, or the Red Fiery Dragon, the 'Lord of Phosphorus,' and Lucifer, or 'Light-Bearer,' is in us: it is our Mind." As part of "The Secret Doctrine," she would also write, "Holy Satan! Lucifer represents Life Thought Progress Civilization Liberty Independence Lucifer is the Logos the Serpent, the Saviour," and, "It is Satan who is the God of our planet and the only God."

Or perhaps his nonchalant claim, which goes something like this: that "the Theosophists open-armed embrace of Lucifer isn't quite as menacing as we overzealous minds might otherwise perceive," is a better pitch than I give him credit for. The author of Oz has enthralled many with his otherworldly transmissions, which I shall turn to in a moment. As successive generations of television viewers have shown, the Christian will entertain himself with the notion that he might freely visit a world where there are good witches right alongside the bad; that he might furthermore participate in the tenants of their magic and think nothing of it. The adherer to the Word of God however should recognize that Satan comes disguised as an angel of light and want nothing of him. And besides, we Christians need not worry of being whisked away over the rainbow and to a magical plane against our will. The only tornado of such enlightening capabilities is an esoteric one.

2

A DREARY KANSAS LANDSCAPE, MYSTICAL CYCLONE, and conscious-driven journey down the yellow brick road. It all adds up. L. Frank Baum's *The Wonderful Wizard of Oz* is an allegorical tale—albeit a subconscious one, *arguably*—outlining the soul's path beyond the material plane to spiritual illumination. It has all the added spicy American ingredients to a far older tale of the occulting Mysteries. The Theosophical Society agrees. In 1986, The *American*

Theosophist magazine recognized Baum as a "notable Theosophist," a devoted ambassador for their philosophical and religious causes. As the 20th century neared its end, with decades of annual televised reruns of the MGM classic loyally garnishing the attention of nostalgic households, the cat was out of the bag. Dorothy was a neophyte.

> "Although readers have not looked at his fairy tales for their Theosophical content, it is significant that Baum became a famous writer of children's books after he came into contact with Theosophy. Theosophical ideas permeate his work and provided inspiration for it. Indeed, The Wizard can be regarded as Theosophical allegory, pervaded by Theosophical ideas from beginning to end. The story came to Baum as an inspiration, and he accepted it with a certain awe as a gift from outside, or perhaps from deep within himself."

American Theosophist no 74, 1986

Baum's son Frank later admitted the author's devotion to Theosophy, but also maintained that his father "could not accept all its teachings. He firmly believed in reincarnation; he had faith in the immortality of the soul and believed that he and his wife had been together in many past states and would be together in future reincarnations, but he did not accept the possibility of the transmigration of souls from human beings to animals or vice versa, as in Hinduism. He was in agreement with the Theosophical belief that man on Earth was only one step on a great ladder that passed through many states of consciousness, through many universes, to a final state of Enlightenment. He did believe in Karma, that whatever good or evil one does in his lifetime returns to him as reward or punishment in future incarnations. He believed that all the great religious teachers of history had found their inspiration from the same source, a common Creator."

The royal historian of Oz was well aware that his accomplishments as a storyteller was achieved through his ability to serve as a "medium," or what the *American Theosophist* referred to as a *gift from outside*. "It was pure imagination," Baum once told a reporter concerning Oz. "It came to me right out of the blue. I think that sometimes the Great Author has a message to get across and He has to use the instrument at hand. I happened to be that medium, and I believe the magic key was given me to open the doors to sympathy and understanding, joy, peace and happiness."

Consider if you will, though somewhat lengthy, the Prologue to *The Patchwork Girl of Oz*, in which Baum writes:

"Through the kindness of Dorothy Gale of Kansas, afterward Princess Dorothy of Oz, a humble writer in the United States of America was once appointed Royal Historian of Oz, with the privilege of writing the chronicle of that wonderful fairyland. But after making six books about the adventures of those interesting but queer people who live in the Land of Oz, the Historian learned with sorrow that by an edict of the Supreme Ruler, Ozma of Oz, her country would thereafter be rendered invisible to all who lived outside its borders and that all communication with Oz would, in the future, be cut off.

The children who had learned to look for the books about Oz and who loved the stories about the gay and happy people inhabiting that favored country, were as sorry as their Historian that there would be no more books of Oz stories. They wrote many letters asking if the Historian did not know of some adventures to write about that had happened before the Land of Oz was shut out from all the rest of the world. But he did not know of any. Finally one of the children inquired why we couldn't hear from Princess Dorothy by wireless telegraph, which would enable her to communicate to the Historian whatever happened in the far-off Land of Oz without his seeing her, or even knowing just where Oz is.

That seemed a good idea; so the Historian rigged up a high tower in his back yard, and took lessons in wireless telegraphy until he understood it, and then began to call "Princess Dorothy of Oz" by sending messages into the air.

Now, it wasn't likely that Dorothy would be looking for wireless messages or would heed the call; but one thing the Historian was sure of, and that was that the powerful Sorceress, Glinda, would know what he was doing and that he desired to communicate with Dorothy. For Glinda has a big book in which is recorded every event that takes place anywhere in the world, just the moment that it happens, and so of course the book would tell her about the wireless message.

And that was the way Dorothy heard that the Historian wanted to speak with her, and there was a Shaggy Man in the Land of Oz who knew how to telegraph a wireless reply. The result was that the Historian begged so hard to be told the latest news of Oz, so that he could write it down for the children to read, that Dorothy asked permission of Ozma and Ozma graciously consented.

That is why, after two long years of waiting, another Oz story is now presented to the children of America. This would not have been possible had not some clever man invented the "wireless" and an equally clever child suggested the idea of reaching the mysterious Land of Oz by its means."

L. Frank Baum

"OZCOT" at Hollywood in California

For the occultist, his mind and the brain are not to be confused as one and the same. The brain is only an organ. It is a material mechanism which operates as a receiver on the physical plane. The mind however needs no use of the brain when it functions on other non-physical planes of existence. The brain itself is only required for the mortal, for his mind continues on into the metaphysical. Manas, what is known as "the Mind Principle," is that connecting link between our pure, eternal, spiritual nature and our mortal, physical, material, personal nature. Writes Blavatsky: "Matter is spirit at its lowest level. Spirit is matter at its highest level."

Dorothy Gale lives in Kansas. She's an orphan. Kuthumi Lal Singh, one of Theosophies early teachers and which Baum would have likely been made well aware of, referred to humanity as "the great Orphan." At any rate, Kansas is a stand in for our plane of existence—the material world. While *Over the Rainbow*" is the MGM brainchild of composer Harold Arlen and lyricist Yip Harbur, most will agree that it is a faithful adaptation of Baum's vision—conceptually speaking, despite the movie's overarching depression-era message. Dorothy's aspirations are to reach the ethereal realm. She is seeking a higher truth. And it is the cyclone who will grant her conscious wish. Over the rainbow, into a far more colorful tapestry of reality, she will go.

The Vigilant Citizen states: "Dorothy is then brought to Oz by a giant cyclone spiraling upward, representing the cycles of karma, the cycle of errors and lessons learned. It also represents the Theosophical belief in reincarnation, the round of physical births and deaths of a soul until it is fit to become divine. It is also interesting to note that the Yellow Brick Road of Oz begins as an outwardly expanding spiral. In occult symbolism, this spiral represents the evolving self, the soul ascending from matter into the spirit world."

In his book, "*Secrets of the Yellow Brick Road: A Map for the Modern Spiritual Journey Based on The Wizard of Oz*," author Jesse Stewart notes that the unwinding spiral complements the cyclone by reversing the path of her involution. In fact, the Encyclopedic Theosophical Glossary defines **spiral**:

"The path of a point (generally plane) which moves round an axis while continually approaching it or receding from it; also often used for a helix, which is generated by compounding a circular motion with one in a straight line. The spiral form is an apt illustration of the course of evolution, which brings motion round towards the same point, yet without repetition.

The serpent, and the figures 8 and sideways eight, denoting the ogdoad and infinity, stand for spiral cyclic motion. The course of fohat in space is spiral, and spirit descends into matter in spiral courses. Repeating the process by which a helix is derived form a circle produces a vortex. The complicated spirals of cosmic evolution bring the motion back to the point from which it started at the birth of a great cosmic age."

According to Buddhism, which plays an important part of Theosophical teachings, the yellow brick road mirrors the "Golden Path," or the "Middle Way." Such a concept refers to Buddha's view of life and describes the path that transcends and reconciles the duality characterized by cognitive thinking. One might consider it a universal pursuit of all Buddhist traditions—the quest for a way of life that would give the greatest value to human existence and help relieve the world of suffering. To this Stewart adds: "Her three companions represent both three aspects of the human personality (thinking, feeling, and will) and the three paths of Yoga: knowledge, devotion, and action....Dorothy and her companions wander off the Path, however, and come to a broad river; they try to cross to the other side (shades of Buddhist metaphor), but find themselves in deep water, drifting out of control. Eventually they get to land and enter a field of soporific poppies; the flowers are like those in the Hall of Learning of The Voice of the Silence: 'the blossoms of life, but under every flower a serpent coiled.'"

From here on out—and perhaps I should have mentioned this earlier—we must forget all about Dorothy's ruby slippers. MGM's *The Wizard of Oz* was a product of Technicolor, and they needed their price of admission. The slippers of Baum's transmission have a higher esoteric wealth, for they are silver. It is of no coincide that Dorothy receives her shoes upon arrival in Oz, and that they alone hold the power to ensure her trip home. The silver shoes represent the "silver cord" of the Mystery Schools; a vital lifeline between our material and spiritual selves which the Neophyte must learn to master. Dorothy's enlightenment is begun by defeating the wicked witch of the East, whom the shoes once belonged to, and is certainly heightened of her refinement by killing the wicked witch of the West. Together they formed an "evil horizontal axis: the material world." Dorothy's ultimate illumination likely results from her association with the good witches of the north and south: "the vertical axis" *or* "the spiritual dimension." In his book, *"Finding OZ: How L. Frank Baum Discovered the Great America Story,"* author Evan I. Schwarz writes:

> "In Theosophy, one's physical body and one's Astral body are connected through a "silver cord," a mythical link inspired by a passage in the Bible that speaks of a return from a spiritual quest. 'Or ever the silver cord be loosed, says the book of Ecclesiastes, 'then shall the dust return to the earth as it was and the spirit shall return unto God who gave it'. In Frank Baum's own writing, the silver cord of Astral travel would inspire the silver shoes that bestow special powers upon the one who wears them"

God shows up in Dorothy's journey as well, and with unexpected though "enlightening" consequences. But *He* is not the "common creator" of occultist lore. No, this God is oppressively cruel. The Creator of the Bible is an enemy of Theosophy. By convincing everyone to wear glasses with "emerald shades," so as not to succumb to blindness when staring at his glorious city, the Wizard has cast the wickedest of spells— spiritual ignorance. For you see, the Emerald City is not so glamorous after all, should the glasses chance to come off. Despite his bag full of special effects, the Wizard is a humbug. He is incapable of fulfilling any task except to scare the ignorant into worshiping him.

But thank the "common creator" for Toto. Concerning the most popular Cairn terrier who ever was, the Theosophical Society's website writes:

> "Toto represents the inner, intuitive, instinctual, most animal-like part of us. Throughout the movie, Dorothy has conversations with Toto, or her inner intuitive self. The lesson

here is to listen to the Toto within. In this movie, Toto was never wrong. When he barks at the scarecrow, Dorothy tries to ignore him: "Don't be silly, Toto. Scarecrows don't talk." But scarecrows do talk in Oz. Toto also barks at the little man behind the curtain. It is he who realizes the Wizard is a fraud. At the Gale Farm and again at the castle, the Witch tries to put Toto into a basket. What is shadow will try to block or contain the intuitive. In both cases, Toto jumps out of the basket and escapes. Our intuitive voice can be ignored, but not contained.

In the last scene, Toto chases after a cat, causing Dorothy to chase after him and hence miss her balloon ride. This is what leads to Dorothy's ultimate transformation, to the discovery of her inner powers. The balloon ride is representative of traditional religion, with a skinny-legged wizard promising a trip to the Divine. Toto was right to force Dorothy out of the balloon, otherwise she might never have found her magic. This is a call for us to listen to our intuition, our gut feelings, those momentary bits of imagination that appear seemingly out of nowhere."

It is a sad but likely scenario: Christianity's gradual demise in western civilization is resulted in part from its numbing down to the very mystics who flagrantly oppose the God they claim to serve. A willing partnership, all for the sake of entertainment—even in its most playful and child-like distribution—is hardly arguable here. "In God we trust" is imprinted on the US dollar and the esoteric supermarket will have it. Occultism sells. The results show. Yet there will be few still remaining in the pews that'll read this and find the moral outrage—that is, unless their allocation of justice is directed away from the obvious perpetrators and against my audacity to strike a match and flick the flame towards their conscious. How do I know this? I've already been told with the raised nose of a passive-aggressor—in fact, *many*—and will surely be reminded again (I have little to no doubt about it):

"It's clear that imaginative storytelling is not for everyone."

No, I suppose not.

Can you believe it? I was once a collector of first and early-edition Oz books. But that was back in the days when I could look Christianity's perpetrators in the face and think little to nothing of it. After all, it was only storytelling.

COUNTERFEIT PENTECOST | CHARLES PARHAM LEARNS HIS SPIRITUAL "A, B, C'S" & AGNES OZMAN "THE CHINESE"

IN THE EARLY MORNING HOURS OF NEW YEAR'S DAY, 1901, *something* extraordinary happened. Or rather, an extraordinary—and dare I say supernatural—*claim* was made. The 40 students at Bethel Bible College in Topeka, Kansas, along with their teacher, 27 year-old Methodist Holiness minister Charles Fox Parham, were desperate to experience the presence and power of the Holy Spirit. True to their background in the Wesleyan Holiness movement, which emerged from 19th-century Methodism, they collectively agreed that the baptism of the Holy Spirit took place subsequent to conversion. After weeks of study in the book of Acts, they took their conclusions one step further—speaking in a foreign tongue *was* the sign of Spirit baptism.

A young woman named Agnes Ozman was desperate to receive her own Spirit baptism. With the sun still dawning upon the 20th century, Ozman asked Parham to lay hands upon her while she prayed a benediction which might be found in Hebrews 13:20-21. Parham agreed. What happened next would alter the course of church history. Parham and his 40 students rediscovered—lost to the church since the apostolic age, *evidently*—the gift of speaking in Biblical tongues.

In his book, *With Signs Following—The Latter Day Pentecostal Revival*, Stanley Frodsham quotes Miss Ozman as having testified: "…it was as if hands were laid upon my head that the Holy Spirit fell upon me and I began to speak in tongues, glorifying God. I talked several languages, and it was clearly manifest when a new dialect was spoken. I had the added joy and glory my heart longed for, and a depth of the presence of the Lord within that I had never known before. It was as if rivers of living water were proceeding from my innermost being."

Parham later recounted: "I laid my hands upon her and prayed. I had scarcely completed three dozen sentences when a glory fell upon her, a halo seemed to surround her head and face, and she began speaking the Chinese language and was unable to speak English for three days. When she tried to write in English to tell us of her experience she wrote the Chinese." Her colleagues also reported a halo surrounding her head, with the Chinese language, and *only* Chinese, exploding from her lips.

Not long after Ozman's halo story, Parham and thirty-four other students began speaking in unknown tongues. More than twenty languages were reportedly spoken—including Russian, Japanese, Bulgarian, French, Bohemian, Norwegian, Hungarian, Italian, and Spanish. Charles Parham himself claimed to speak in Swedish "as well as other languages." Word of this new Pentecost spread. Not long thereafter African-American holiness pastor Lucy Farrow (1851–1911) received the gift of tongues. African-American holiness pastor William J. Seymour (May 2, 1870 – September 28, 1922) did too. In 1906 an estimated 13,000 people began speaking in tongues on Bonnie Brae Street in Los Angeles, California under the ministry of Farrow, and by 1909, another 50,000 had experienced their Spirit baptism under Seymour's Azusa Street revival. The modern Pentecostal movement was born.

Pentecostal historian Vinson Synan writes, "Ozman's experience thus became the prototype experience for all the millions of Pentecostals who were to follow." In short, Charles Parham had lit a match and set a forest ablaze. He christened this *holy fire* the "Apostolic Faith Movement."

History will note that Jonathan Edwards, Charles Hodge, Charles Spurgeon, and B.B. Warfield all believed the gift of speaking in Biblical tongues involved another human language. In fact, the universal church as a whole has rightly believed as much. Charles F. Parham did as well. This would most certainly line up with the opinion of our church fathers. Gregory of Nazianzus (c. 329–390) wrote of it: "They spoke with foreign tongues, and not those of their native land; and the wonder was great, a language spoken by those who had not learned it. And the sign is to them that believe not, and not to them that believe…" Parham and company would attempt to follow the natural conclusions of Gregory's belief.

On January 7, 1901, a rather confident Charles Parham promised the *Topeka State Journal:* "The Lord will give us the power of speech to talk to the people of the various nations without having to study them in schools."

To the *Kansas City Times*, dated January 27, 1901, Parham claimed: "A part of our labor will be to teach the church the uselessness of spending years of time preparing missionaries for work in foreign lands when all they have to do is ask God for power."

And then on May 31, 1901, Parham told *the Hawaiian Gazette*: "There is no doubt that at this time they will have conferred on them the 'gift of tongues,' if they are worthy and seek it in faith, believing they will thus be made able to talk to the people whom they choose to work among in their own language, which will, of course, be an inestimable advantage. The students of Bethel College do not need to study in the old way to learn the languages. They have them conferred on them miraculously... [being] able to converse with Spaniards, Italians, Bohemians, Hungarians, Germans, and French in their own language. I have no doubt various dialects of the people of India and even the language of the savages of Africa will be received during our meeting in the same way. I expect this gathering to be the greatest since the days of Pentecost."

The Hawaiian Gazette reports the following:

Envoys to the Heathen Should Have Gift of Tongues

TOPEKA, May 20.—Rev. Charles F. Parham, of the "College of Bethel," at Topeka, and his followers are preparing to give the people of the churches some new work along the line of missionary endeavor.

His plan is to send among the heathen, persons who have been blessed with the "gift of tongues"—a gift which, he says, no others have ever had conferred upon them since apostolic times. His missionaries, as he points out, will have the great advantages of having the languages of the various peoples among whom they work miraculously conferred upon them and will not be put to the trouble of learning them in laborious way by which they are acquired by other prospective missionaries.

"Our summer Bible school will begin in Topeka June 10," said Rev. Mr. Parham last night. "It will be held on the campus of the college. We are expecting thousands of ministers, evangelists and other people from all parts of the United States who desire to become missionaries to attend. There is no doubt that at this time they will have conferred on them the 'gift of tongues,' if they are worthy and seek it in faith, believing. They will thus be made able to talk to people whom they choose to work among in their own language, which will, of course, be an inestimable advantage.

"The students of Bethel College do not need to study in the old way to learn the languages. They have them conferred upon them miraculously. Different ones have already been enabled to converse with Spaniards, Italians, Bohemians, Hungarians, Germans, and French in their own language. I have no doubt that knowledge of Chinese, Japanese, the various dialects of the people of India and even the language of the savages of Africa will be received during our meeting in the same way. I expect this gathering to be the greatest since the days of Pentecost."

Here *the Hawaiian Gazette* concludes:

There is always a great deal about hell and damnation, the gift of the tongues, divine healing, etc., in his sermons. He claims that he and his disciples have received all the gifts that Christ conferred upon His earliest disciples. Last night's sermon was of the usual order. Rev. Mr. Parham is very optimistic concerning the future prospects of his sect. He says it is growing rapidly. He calls his followers "Believers."

"There are 500 Believers in Topeka," he said, "and there are already thousands in other parts of the United States and the world. I receive letters every day from people inquiring whether it is true that the gifts of tongues and healing have been conferred again. Many are skeptical at first, but are convinced when the evidence is presented to them. The conferring of the gift of tongues upon us is, I am sure, the first step in the evangelization of the world."

What followed is a historical embarrassment of Biblical proportions, not only for the immediate players involved within Charles Parham's Apostolic Faith Movement, but their legions of followers baptized with the same counterfeit spirit today. For starters, Charles Parham, Agnes Ozman, and their contemporaries at Bethel Bible College in Topeka, Kansas never actually experienced the supernatural sign they were seeking. Parham's promise failed miserably. That embarrassing fact became painfully obvious as missionaries willfully evaded language schools and arrived at their "tongue-gifted" countries. Nobody understood them—*nobody*—not a lick. The miraculous ability to speak in authentic foreign languages, just as the Apostles did on the day of Pentecost, was never repeated by anyone involved. Rather—and very much *unlike* the explosive birth of the church in Acts—the natives of those foreign countries listened in to the ravings of lunatics and mad men.

Charismatic authors Jack Hayford and David Moore confess this awkward miscalculation when they write: "Sadly, the idea of xenoglossalalic tongues [i.e. foreign languages] would later prove an embarrassing failure as Pentecostal workers went off to mission fields with their gift of tongues and found their hearers did not understand them."

Parham's Apostolic Faith missionaries soon returned, bitterly shipwrecked. Alfred G. Garr and his wife's expedition to the Far East, both of whom were dead set on preaching the gospel in 'the Indian and Chinese languages,' failed miserably, and Lucy Farrow returned from Africa after a seven month trip. Her alleged claim that she preached to the natives in their own 'Kru language' went unchecked. In his book, *Vision of the Disinherited: The Making of American Pentecostalism*, Robert Mapes Anderson writes: "S.C. Todd of the Bible Missionary Society investigated eighteen Pentecostals who went to Japan, China, and India 'expecting to preach to the natives in those countries in their own tongue,' and found that by their own admission 'in no single instance have [they] been able to do so.' As these and other missionaries returned in disappointment and failure, Pentecostals were compelled to rethink their original view of speaking in tongues."

This should come as no surprise, but *"The Topeka Daily Capital* reported that not everyone at the school embraced the new experience. In an interview with the newspaper, S.J. Riggins said of Parham and his fellow students, 'I believe the whole of them are crazy.'"

In *Strange Fire,* John MacArthur writes, further investigation "calls the legitimacy of Parham's claims into serious question on at least three fronts.....Parham stated that Ozman did not speak in English for three days after her experience, but Ozman reported praying in English after only one day." Parham took credit for directing his students to the book of Acts before their history-making. Ozman however contradicted that claim, asserting "she had no part of any bible study assignment by Parham prior to her tongues speaking experience. In fact she says she pointed students to Acts 2 in answer to their questions about her glossolalic experience."

Furthermore, Historian Martin E. Marty writes: "Like all such mythically cast stories, these had certain features that remain open to question. In an earlier stratum of testimony Miss Ozman referred to having spoken in tongues three weeks before New Year's Day, a less neat date, but one which others corroborated. She also claimed that she realized the significance of her speaking only later, but it is known that Parham had instructed her in advance to look for precisely that sign."

There is another regrettable error which I must not fail in mentioning. The Chinese lettering from Ozman's halo story was released to various newspapers, including the *Los Angeles Daily Times*, fully confident it would prove their conviction. The fruit of Ozman's Spirit baptism is completely unintelligible, resembling no known language— nor is it a cryptic alien or angelic language which might be deciphered by the brighter mind.

Though Ozman never recanted of her halo and Chinese story, an alien tongue certainly swept the world—not quite unlike the plot to *Invasion of the Body Snatchers*—and *this* she felt a tinge of responsibility for. The confession from the woman who had already awakened the halo in tens of thousands fell on deaf ears. She could not find anyone so much as willing to publish her words. Writing in *The Latter Rain Evangel* of January 1909 she lamented: "Some time ago I tried but failed to have an article printed which I wrote calling attention to what I am sure God showed me was error. The article maintained that tongues was not the only evidence of the Spirit's Baptism." Ozman added: "For a while after the baptism I got into spiritual darkness, because I did as I see so many others are doing these days, rested and reveled in tongues and other demonstrations instead of resting alone in God."

The father of American Pentecostalism, Charles Fox Parham, began his career as a Freemason. For the remainder of his life he endorsed the Ku Klux Klan, and did so as late as 1927, two years before his death. Within those intervening years Parham would be stricken with scandal, including accusations of sodomy, which he was even arrested for. In 1904 Nettie Smith, a nine-year-old girl, died because her father refused medical treatment in favor of Parham's healing. As a result, he was forced to leave Kansas for Texas. Parham was further riddled with doctrinal illiteracy. For example, he taught that those who received the spirit baptism by speaking in tongues would make up the bride of Christ, with a partial rapture composed of tongue speakers. Those tongue speakers, by the way, would uphold a special place of eternal authority.

It is inconceivable to imagine the twelve Apostles present in Jerusalem's upper room falling into such salacious scandal—and I have only so far spoken of Pentecostalism's father, Parham. What we have before us is an unfolding drama. There are more players to come Believe me when I say it gets worse. It is strange indeed to contrast a Holy Spirit in the first century and now who, when seeking the Lord's kingdom vessels, would choose Freemasons and Klan members for the later. A healthy dosage of discretion is required if a Christian is to face this terrible deception head-on, and it is very clear that few, I am afraid, who fall for the sort of experiences which a counterfeit may give—having perhaps never tasted of the real thing, the third member of the Trinity—exhibit the discretion to shake off their error and run. Finally, the Pentecostal no longer needs Scripture as their final authority. This counterfeit spirit gives witness not only of himself, but they have their own experiences to guide them.

In the little upper room where the Apostles first experienced the gift of tongues, ten days after the ascension of Christ, the church was gloriously born. That birth was a one-time event. Almost two-thousand years later, in a tiny classroom at Bethel Bible College in Topeka, Kansas, the oldest *religion* of all, the Mystery religion, was finally distributed to a new class of the initiated.

WILLIAM SEYMOUR & THE "SENSATIONAL HOLY ROLLERS" | THE DEVIL LIVES ON AZUSA STREET

WHILE ON HIS WAY TO LOS ANGELES in the spring of 1906, thirty-six year-old African-American holiness preacher William J. Seymour walked into Alma White's Bible School in Denver, Colorado hoping to win new converts for his *glossolalia* doctrine. "Oh, the feeling that came over us!" recounted White. "We thought of demons, snakes and other slimy creatures before he had finished praying. After he had left the room a number of the students told that they felt that he was possessed with evil spirits." Alma Bridwell White (June 16, 1862 – June 26, 1946) was the founder of the Pillar of Fire Church, and later in 1918—being a staunch feminist—would become America's first female bishop. By the time of her death at age 84, she had as many as 61 churches, seven schools, 4,000 followers, ten periodicals and two broadcasting stations under her care. In the months to follow, White would take a keen interest in Seymour. Charles Fox Parham, the founder of Pentecostalism, would too. And like Parham, White was noted for her devotion to the Ku Klux Klan.

As one might imagine under such historical pretenses, their meeting failed to inspire the other. Actually, Seymour had only just exited Charles Fox Parham's Bible Training School in Houston, Texas, with similar results. In the summer of 1905 Seymour had served as the temporary replacement pastor for Lucy Farrow, a Holiness minister and niece of black abolitionist Frederick Douglass. It was through Farrow that Seymour met the founder of Pentecostalism. Seymour was eager to learn the gift of "speaking in tongues," or *glossolalia*, from the man who had reportedly brought about the second Pentecost into being. Parham agreed to take him in that December—perhaps grudgingly. Because he was a segregationist and supporter of Jim Crow laws, Seymour was obstinately refused a seat in class. Rather, Parham allowed Seymour to listen to instruction through an open door or window. No surprise— Seymour's attendance did not last very long. According to various sources, he tolerated the Bible Training School anywhere from a few days to a few weeks. Seymour had his sights on California.

On February 22, 1906, Seymour had already landed another gig preaching in a Los Angeles church established by Julia M. Hutchins, who had herself only recently been expelled from the Second Baptist Church due to her Holiness doctrines. Hutchins would in turn lock Seymour out of her church—quite literally—for including *glossolalia* in the Holiness doctrine, particularly as a sign of Spirit baptism. Mr. and Mrs. Richard Asberry however were sympathetic to Seymour's beliefs. They offered their home as a meeting place. Once again, William J. Seymour found himself with another preaching gig.

It was the evening of Monday, April 9, 1906 when the first spark was ignited. Before arriving at the Asberry home, Seymour stopped to pray with Edward Lee for a healing. In direct violation of Leviticus 19:31; 20:27; and Deuteronomy 18:10-13, Lee had become involved with "familiar spirits." Specifically—as he related—Lee was visited by the twelve apostles, who consulted him on the matter of speaking in tongues. Lee eagerly asked Seymour to pray with him to receive the baptism of the Holy Spirit. Though Seymour himself had yet to receive the gift, Lee immediately began speaking in *other* tongues. This may have been Seymour's first favorable outcome, but before the evening was yet over it certainly wouldn't be his last.

From the Asberry's living room, filled with a small but loyal group that had broken away from a nearby church after the elders rejected his teaching, Seymour held his meeting. It is recognized that his knowledge of Scripture and grasp of essential gospel truth seemed marginal at best. Even the Holiness Church Association considered his teaching dangerously unbiblical. But the naysayers were all behind him now because—before he finished preaching from Acts chapter 2—Bonnie Brae began speaking in tongues.

Once again, just as it was with Ozman's account in Topeka, Kansas several years earlier, "embellished reports later claimed that tongues of fire swirled above the heads of the band of 'prayer warriors.'" Jennie Evans Moore was the first woman to reportedly "speak in tongues—Spanish, French, Latin, Greek, Hebrea, and Hindustani—none of which she knew prior to that evening." She even "reportedly played the piano under the divine inspiration...." Pandemonium ensued. In the words of one observer, "They shouted three days and three nights. It was Easter season. The people came from everywhere. By the next morning there was no way of getting near the house." It was on April 12, three days later, when Seymour finally received his Holy Spirit baptism.

News of Seymour's great revival breaking out in a dilapidated section of downtown Los Angeles quickly reached Alma White. "It was said that God had raised up a colored man to bring Pentecost back to the earth again, and that people through his ministry were receiving the baptism of the Holy Ghost and speaking in tongues." Many reliable persons, "some of whom are with us to-day," writes White, told of things they saw in the so-called Azusa Street Mission. "They declared that what they saw and heard from those who were under the spell of demons far exceeded anything they could have imagined or that ever had been told them."

On Azusa Street a monster was born.

For three and a half years there was never a time, day or night, when a service or some other curious happening couldn't be overheard at 312 Azusa Street.

Meetings began in the mornings and continued for at least 12 hours. Often no could be found to lead. People sang at the same time but "with completely different syllables, rhythms, and melodies," writes Ted Olsen in *American Pentecost*. Seymour rarely preached. When he did he simply uttered a few words of Scripture before challenging people to "let the tongues come forth." The tongues most certainly came. In the words of Paul Fahy, "All the phenomena associated with the Toronto Experience took place repeatedly: shaking, slaying in the Spirit, tongues, various physical gestures, gibberish, contortions, sexual impropriety, jerking, shrieking, barking, hooting, crawling etc. Women often lay on the floor for hours; blankets were kept ready to cover their nakedness (common in early Pentecostalism). Men would jump, women would dance. In the midst there were people attacking the abuses, while everyone sang different melodies, rhythms and words. It was utter chaos. In the cacophony, Seymour put his head in a shoebox to pray; others like Frank Bartleman put their heads under benches. Many times people fell off the platform onto benches and chairs. But there was worse to come. Worship was based on African traditions: expressive praise, shouting & dancing; most were poor, uneducated people; women wailed and screamed while men would fall or rush in crowds to the front."

Charismatic writer and missionary Frank Bartleman, who had participated in prayer meetings with Seymour before the opening sparks of Azusa Street, quickly became disenchanted with the fruit of his labor.

"It was also reported that the 'jerks' and 'treeing the devil' (that is, crawling on all fours and barking up a tree like a dog) were in evidence in the (Azusa) mission."

In *Demons and Tongues*, Alma White reports an eyewitness account:

"When I visited the Azusa Street Mission the first person that attracted my attention was a woman ... who stood shaking from head to foot...a man in front of her slid down out of his chair and became unconscious...the man...was...under high nerve pressure...He arose, staggered to them and began to shake his hand in front of their faces and wave his arms over their heads and moan...Then he put his hands on the heads of the women and began to shake their hair. Some of them lost control of themselves and went under an hypnotic spell. He rubbed a man's jaw until the victim tumbled over on the floor and lay for half an hour, then suddenly began to jabber. Those who had received their 'Pentecost' cried out, 'He has the baptism, he has the baptism!'

"A young colored woman, doing her best to get the gibberish, went through all kinds of contortions in her effort to get her tongue to work.

While work at the altar was going on a colored woman had her arms around a white man's neck, praying for him. One man of mature years leaped up out of his chair and began to stutter. He did not utter a distinct syllable, but as fast as he could make his tongue work he said *tut-tut-tut-tut-tut-tut'*. This, of course, they claimed was evidence that he had the baptism. The woman with the silk wait on appeared again, this time singing a far-away tune that sounded very unnatural and repulsive There were others who mingled their voices with hers in the production of these strange notes.

While the altar call was being made a woman walked up to the front and kissed a man. It was evident that the man, who was one of the prominent workers in the mission, was not her husband or even a relative. Kissing between the sexes is a common occurrence in the 'Tongues' meetings."

One missionary leader spoke with horror about what happened at Azusa Street, declaring—according to White—that "it would be impossible to publish the things that have occurred there. The familiarity between sexes in the public meetings has been shocking, to say the least. Hell has reaped an awful harvest and infidelity has become more strongly rooted...than ever before."

And yet another of White's eyewitnesses reported: "...I found men and women lying on the floor in all shapes...(they were) jabbering all at one time in what they called unknown tongues. While I was praying, one of the workers took hold of me and said, 'Holy Ghost, we command Thee to go into this soul'. The workers were jabbering and shaking their hands over me, and a demonic power (as I now know) took possession of me, and I fell among the people on the floor and knew nothing for ten hours. When I came to my senses I was weak and my jaws were so tired they ached. I believed then that this power was of God. They said I was wonderfully blessed, and the leader sent me from one place to another so that I could jabber in tongues."

Azusa Street developed other troubling problems.

It is said the spiritual atmosphere emanating from the mission could be felt for several blocks. Conclusively, it opened the door for witches, mediums, and other spiritualists. More specifically, it *attracted* them. In *The Holiness Pentecostal Movement in the United States* (1971), Vinson Synan writes: "Spiritualists and mediums from the numerous occult societies of Los Angeles began to attend and to contribute their séances and trances to the services." To this effect, loyal Pentecostal Bartleman would confess: "...spiritualists, hypnotists...all the religious soreheads and crooks and cranks came...We had the most to fear from these...This condition cast a fear over many which was hard to overcome. It hindered the spirit so much. Many were afraid to seek God for fear the devil might get them."

Seymour, "ultimately repudiated the initial evidence teaching (speaking in tongues) as providing an open door for witches and spiritualists and free lovism (*Dictionary of P & C Movements*)." In a fit of fright, the Azusa Street missions founder frantically wrote to his mentor Charles Fox Parham, begging that he come out to Los Angeles and clean up the mess. When Parham arrived at the mission, he was not pleased.

Parham condemned the Azusa Street meetings. He described them as "a seduction of the devil... the work of hypnotists and evil spirits... all kinds of spells... men and women falling on one another in a morally compromising manner... chattering, jabbering and sputtering, speaking no language at all." He encountered Occultists. Two-thirds of the people professing Pentecostalism in his day, he confessed, "are either hypnotized or spook driven." In *The Life of Charles F. Parham: Founder of the Apostolic Faith Movement*, first published in 1930, Sarah Parham wrote: "He testified that the Azusa Street meetings were largely characterized by manifestations of the flesh, spiritualistic controls, and the practice of hypnotism." He he saw "hypnotic influences, familiar spirit influences, spiritualistic influences, mesmeric influences and all kinds of spells and spasms, falling in trances etc...." He refuted them as being of God, as his own wife testified. Quite conclusively for Parham, "God is sick at His stomach" because of the "animalism going on there."

He even coined the term "sensational Holy Rollers."

Once again—just as it was with Topeka, Kansas on New Year's Day, 1901—the much desired Biblical gift of speaking in tongues, or *glossolalia*, was never spoken on Azusa Street. Charles Parham was clear on this teaching; tongues were a God-given ability to speak a human language—never succumbing to incoherent jabber. As a result, "Parham and others were quick to criticize Seymour's teaching and practices as counterfeit," writes Gaston Espinosa in *William J. Seymour and the Origins of Global Pentecostalism,* "since he believed that true tongues must always evidence real human languages." The father of Pentecostalism never wavered from his view. Seymour however *did.* Tongues did not always have to be a real human language, his student rationalized; but could, quite contrarily, be a divine language known only to God.

> "Men and women, whites and blacks, knelt together or fell across one another," said Parham. "Frequently, a white woman, perhaps of wealth and culture, could be seen thrown back in the arms of a big 'buck nigger', and held tightly thus as she shivered and shook in freak imitation of Pentecost—horrible awful shame! (*Fields White unto Harvest*, James Goff)"

When the father of Pentecostalism attempted to clean up the mess—as he was commissioned in Texas to do—Seymour and his followers excused him from leadership. In yet another twist to the plot, one of Azusa's elders was a hypnotist. Quite suddenly, it would seem that Parham's role in the Pentecostal movement was over, but not before he openly opposed the evil which he was inadvertently responsible for unleashing by holding parallel meetings of his own. What followed is nothing short of an embarrassment for every tongue-speaking Charismatic. Under

Parham, people were delivered of Seymour's *tongue* spirits and filled quite as efficiently with another. The man who began his adult career as a Freemason and ended it with the Klan quipped: "between two and three hundred who had been possessed of awful fits and spasms and controls in the Azusa Street work were delivered, and received the real Pentecost teachings and many spake with other tongues."

In His book, *The Toronto Blessing and Slaying in the Spirit*, Nader Mikhaiel would have us ask of Azusa Street: "How could an outpouring of the Spirit of God attract the witches, the mediums and the spiritualists?" Quite simply, because "fragrance does not attract flies. A decomposing carcass does." The first Pentecost, as recorded in Acts chapter 2—which consisted of the 12 Apostles and another 120 unsuspecting persons in the upper room—attracted no such necromancers or Occultists to participate with and share in the Spirit's outpouring. Mikhaiel is correct in concluding what all of us already know. I myself couldn't state it better. He writes:

> "Mediums and spiritualists are attracted to the spirit that is at work in them, that is, the Devil."

THE EARTH IS NOT A SPINNING BALL, CHARLIE BROWN!

1

CHARLES M. SHULZ REMEMBERED A TIME when the Earth was flat. Perhaps not very fondly—and I'll explain why in a moment—but in the early decades of his monumental fifty-year run drawing *Peanuts* for the funnies, its memory certainly hadn't escaped him. The Evangelist Wilbur Glenn Voliva and his religious band of rebel-rouser Flat Earthers likely had a part to play. So successful were Voliva's attacks on the space ball mythos, using the Testimony of the Holy Ghost as his platform, that he even got critical-thinking writers like George Orwell, in his own newspaper column, to openly *suggest* the possibility. But that was *another* generation. They were not Schulz's spokespersons. Wack jobs like Voliva and the last remaining Biblical literalists who gave him a podium had already faded into the oblivion of America's Great Depression. Schulz was a veteran of the War. Under the flag of victory, the entire world's landscape had been changed—including its outlook. His was the "space age." And like so many of his generation, born into households of Christendom—including the baby-boomers whom they raised—Charles M. Schulz would die a secular humanist.

At the turn of the twentieth-century the gloves came off. Scientism went to Total War. For men like Voliva and William Jennings Bryan, theirs was a last ditch effort—and for anyone who decided to join them in the trenches by clinging to a literal interpretation of God's Word, the bombardments were nothing short of shock-and-awe. Western philosophy and secular humanism were pulverizing them. Bryan was unfairly beaten down by the main stream media simply for daring to oppose academia's *evolving* narrative in the Scopes Monkey Trial and taking the witness stand. Not long after, Voliva and his ministry succumbed to financial bankruptcy and controversy. By the 1950's, Bryan and Voliva were dead, and their last remaining loyal followers, who had dominated dinner-table conversations only two decades earlier, were few enough in number to be forgotten—or too old to be remembered.

On Sunday, June 4, 1922, from a *Washington Times* column titled: "HEARD AND SEEN: A Column FOR and FROM Everybody," the following question is asked of columnist Bill Price.

IS THE EARTH FLAT?

Dear Bill:

We are taught that the earth is round. We have no way of knowing except to follow what the scientists say. So far as my mundane affairs are concerned it makes no difference. But I'm getting all balled up about the whole thing. Between reading the declarations of WILBUR VOLIVA, of Zion City, that the earth is positively flat, and W. J. BRYAN that we are not descended from apes, I don't know where I stand. Voliva quotes the Bible to show that the Earth is flat and Bryan relies upon it to prove that Darwin was imbued with imagination.

Can't we settle this thing in the Old Column, the only real forum the people have? Just suppose the earth is flat after all. What are we going to do about it? The thing ought to be settled.

There are thousands of cake-eaters and flappers all over the World who are living their sweet lives under the impression that the earth is round. If they are being deceived it's terrible, that's all. They should know the real truth. Are there not among your contributors many bright minds who will tell us just what the flappers do think on this subject?

PROF X.

Earlier that year, *The Washington Times* ran a far less flattering story. On Friday, January 27, 1922, columnist Arthur Brisbane, clearly not a fan of Flat Earth, Voliva, or the Bible, wrote:

"Mr. Voliva, the "prophet" of Zion City, says the earth is not round, but flat. Thus Zion City's children are taught.

There is more in that than mere stupidity, refusing plain truth that patience might make dear to a chimpanzee. Mr. Voliva knows his people, knows that they accept his mental trash because it is more easily swallowed than hard fact. Kroger, of the Transvaal, also said the earth was flat. That's one reason why the English got him and his land. Superstition loses its fights in these days.

From Voliva you learn how strongly men cling to old falsehood, how they hate new truth.

Every really great inventor, statesman, and thinker has known how men cling to original error end even invent new brands of "error" to escape unpleasant thought Thinking, to the average man, is like standing on its hind legs to a dog—possible, but unpleasant. Both become impossible as dog and man get old."

Even George Orwell, author of *Animal Farm* and *1984*, chimed in on the conversation. On the 27th of December 1946, as part of his *"As I Please"* column, the author wrote a piece titled: *"How Do You Know the Earth is Round?"* He began his article by stating:

"Bernard Shaw remarks that we are more gullible and superstitious today than we were in the Middle Ages, and as an example of modern credulity he cites the widespread belief that the earth is round. The average man, says Shaw, can advance not a single reason for thinking that the earth is round. He merely swallows this theory because there is something about it that appeals to the twentieth-century mentality."

The battle for Flat Earth was *real*. This was the world which parented Schulz and his generation. Schulz however would father another. By the time Linus, Lucy, Schroeder, Charlie Brown, Peppermint Patty, Marcie, Franklin, Pig-Pen, Snoopy and their fellow baby-boomers were born, the outcome was almost certain. Within twenty years of their conception, the space race would achieve its ultimate mission. Not only was the Soviet Union to be humiliated—the Bible was too. The appeal of "twentieth-century mentality," as Orwell put it, won over. The Bible's "mental trash," to quote Brisbane, particularly from those clinging to its "old falsehood," did *not*.

2

CHARLIE BROWN FIRST LEARNED ABOUT *planet* Earth as most of us did—in the classroom. The date was October 27, 1950, only three weeks after *Peanuts* first premiered, and Shermy's claim that a globe is "proof" of its spherical nature did not pass by Brown without an initial air of skepticism. By May 11, 1957, some seven years later, Brown was thoroughly indoctrinated—though apparently glum about it, as one would expect of America's favorite block-head. Lucy however had not passed the exam, because the thought of an Earth "spinning through space" was laughable at best—and reserved for one's wildest imaginations.

"People come and people go, but the Earth keeps on spinning," says Charlie Brown.

"Spinning?" Lucy asks from behind a stone wall. "What do you mean, spinning?"

"Spinning through space...." Charlie brown explains. "The Earth keeps on spinning through space."

Lucy explodes into laughter: "Oh, my, Charlie Brown! You may not be the brightest person in the world, but you sure have some imagination!"

"Good grief!"

There's a reason why *Peanuts* reverberated so well with the adult crowd, especially college students—beatniks, hipsters, and eventually, as the sixties progressed, with hippies. In 1957, adults would have *gotten* the joke. But perhaps more importantly, they would have had a sort-of first-hand appreciation for it. They were laughing at their superstitious grandparents, and maybe even their crazy uncles. Schulz said it like this: "I feel that Peanuts reflects certain attitudes of life in our country today and perhaps some basic fears." For most Cold War-era Americans, the very idea of a flat stationary Earth exhumed all the bad tastes associated with the food poisoning from a past memory—proof of religious zealotry gone tragically wrong. Lucy Van Pelt came with a fist, and she could even pound it into the creative gut of Schulz himself. She was crabby, for one—or in her case, a fuss budget—authoritatively bossy, judgmental, at times sadistic (when a football was involved), and for all her attempts at leading Charlie Brown through psychological therapy (which may have also included a football—now that I think on it), stunningly arrogant.

Consider one of Schulz's most enduring strips. On September 19, 1966, Snoopy's house burned to the ground. Lucy's response can best be summed up in *everything* that Schulz likely saw wrong with Christian fundamentalism. While the cause of the fire was never revealed, for Lucy, the conclusion came easy. Snoopy, she said, had *sinned*.

To blindly call Schulz a "Christian apologist" or evangelical spokesman is to brown-nose his strip with *wishful thinking*. In part, he curbed his own contemplations with the changing moralities of his time. Schulz's most morbid view of religion comes, I believe, with Lucy's younger brother—the serial Scripture-memorizer, Linus Van Pelt. His undying devotion to the Great Pumpkin is nearly as unbearable to watch for the agnostic after humanist Thomas Payne's own heart as Charlie Brown's blind faith in Lucy, who is completely incompetent in her promises to hold his football in place.

And yet here is another account of *Peanuts* lasting power—Schulz's clever ability to pander to *everyone*. In June of 1963, the Supreme Court ruled 8–1 in favor of Edward Schempp, thereby declaring school-sponsored Bible reading in public schools in the United States to be unconstitutional. Schulz followed that decision on November 3rd, 1963 with one of *Peanuts* most nostalgic and hotly-debated moments.

After making sure the *coast is clear*, Sally beckons her brother Charlie Brown to follow her behind the couch so that she can whisper into his ear: "We prayed in school today."

Charlie brown is aghast.

Sally's confession masterfully played to the emotions of both sides, and not only proved a rallying cry for Christian groups across America, who cried *foul* at the Supreme Court's decision; it doubled-down as a banner for atheist groups too. *Everyone* concurred with Sally.

Some will claim I am being unfair. And yet, despite his Christian upbringing, it is clear—by his own testimony—that the creator of *Peanuts* had changed. The man who once fought CBS Executives to keep Linus' speech intact at the end of *A Charlie Brown Christmas*; which first aired in 1965—had changed. The man who once berated Hank Ketchum's use of shallow spirituality in *Dennis the Menace*, as well as Bil Keane's *The Family Circus*—had changed. The very man who once taught Sunday school and quipped: "I preach in these cartoons, and I reserve the same rights to say what I want to say as the ministers in the pulpit," simply shriveled up inside and died. Perhaps he had been punched in the creative gut too many times by Lucy Van Pelt, because Charles Schulz gave up on church. But far worse, he gave up on Jesus, because in the sunset of his life Schulz unashamedly referred to himself as a "secular humanist." Not only had the Bible lost its credibility as the final authority on philosophical matters, including a salvation which could only come through Jesus's blood, but other religions now filled the void—all of which provided the hope of legitimate paths to God.

Schulz confessed: "I do not go to church anymore. I guess you could say I've come around to secular humanism, an obligation I believe all humans have to others and the world we live in."

As Schulz faith slipped through the very fingertips which so devoutly held his creative pen and outlined his sketches for five-consecutive decades, he asked his readers to do the same. In a January 1986 strip, Sally asked Charlie Brown: "When we die, will we go to Heaven?"

Charlie Brown's response was: "I'd like to *think* so."

At any rate, in October of 1950, the mere fact that a classroom globe could be used as proof of a proposed spherical Earth—and made to be a joke—was a confessional in and of itself that Schulz had at least been in on the table-talk. By 1957, he'd passed it off as a gross and arrogant error of fundamentalism. In March of 1969, Snoopy beat not only Apollo 11 and the Russians to the moon, but "the stupid cat next door." During the 1980's, Schulz was clearly all in. Who needed the globe for indoctrination? With *"This Is America, Charlie Brown!"* a series of made-for-TV episodes which gave aide to American patriotism, the *Peanuts* journeyed aboard the International Space Station. And during the last decade of his life, the very notion of Evangelist Wilbur Glenn Voliva's claim—that the Bible was *literally* true and the Earth was flat—was a disposable joke.

Woodstock, we come to find out, is a Flat Earthist—*this* according to Snoopy's brother, Andy. It is October 17th, 1997, and Schulz casts the same grin of mockery that so many seem to possess the moment they find out that the golden canary and Biblical literalists have something in common. You know, "Why don't you do us all a favor and jump off the edge of the Earth?"

Olaf, being Snoopy's fat, dopey, and rather gullible brother, does *just that*.

"E-MC2" *or* MASTERS OF THE UNIVERSE: MATHEMATICS IN THE MINDS OF MANIACS

KISS! KISS! BANG! BANG!

R.I.P. Biblical FLAT EARTH

Creation Week – 1915

I guess what I'm trying to say is, *the theory of relativity* thoroughly succeeded in holding a gun to Stationary Earth's head and pulling the trigger. Einstein's theory, which I shan't here pretend to understand—nor do I even care to—has the most brilliant of modern physicists throwing up their hands in confusion in order to blindly follow the script, allowing for no exceptions. An entire century later nobody *truly* understands it. And yet relativity is a *necessary* component of globular Earth. Without the chalk board, *true science,* such as the Michelson-Morley experiment, among dozens of others, rings undeniably true. Relativity wasn't only the weapon which sent geocentric earth to the coffin; it was the *first* nail, the *last* nail and every single nail in-between. Knowing this, one can begin to understand the world-wide festivities. Even in the pews of the church, it seems, there was cause for celebration. Lady Blount and the New Zetetics, you see, would not—no, they most certainly *could not*—bother them again. With one fail swoop, God's Biblical creation was finally dead and buried, or so they thought.

> *"If the facts don't fit the theory, change the facts"* — Albert Einstein.

If anybody truly understood relativity, it was Professor Herbert Dingle. From the very decade of its conception Dingle was the premiere expert on Einstein's theory, and as his staunchest apologist, he labored tirelessly to explain it. So renowned was his expertise that when Einstein died in 1955 the BBC asked Dingle to broadcast his tribute. He wrote multiple books on the subject, starting in 1922 with his publication of *"Relativity for All,"* and then its follow-up two-decades later, *"The Special Theory of Relativity."* As such, he was conferred by scientists all over the world, and in 1959, after successfully promoting the theory for decades, Dingle found a *slight* problem. Perhaps *slight* isn't the best word. It was a paradox, actually—one in which he devoted an additional 13 years of his life attempting to solve—even employing his spreadsheet of colleagues to back him.

But none was found.

When he attempted to go forward with his findings, being an honest man, and finally recognizing the taste of a baloney sandwich when he chewed on it, Dingle was blocked all access by the science journals which might otherwise inform the world of Einstein's error. Without the help of the Scientism Establishment which once supported him, he had no choice but to go at it alone.

I am content knowing Dingle's book, *"Science at the Crossroads,"* published in 1972, is readily available for my reader, and may therefore be dissected at length. Much of what I have to say here is paraphrased only as a result of Mr. Dingle's own wealth of knowledge. In it he shall surely find that the premier expert on Einstein's *theory of relativity* has one somber truth to prove.

Albert Einstein is a humbug.

Einstein's *theory of relativity* is held to be true, not because it is true, but because mathematical formulae is devised and held up as a silhouette of truth. The good in a mathematical formula is to prove that it is somehow real in hopes that it corresponds beyond the imaginary, thereby marrying itself to the natural world it attempts to prop up. Mathematical symbols *may* correspond with that which is observable. Then again, they may only prove the formula-makers rich imagination. Math symbolizes truth in the hand of its masters, and when amplified it is given the ringing endorsement of symbolized truth despite the impossibility of such an equation evolving legs and lungs and emerging from the primordial soup of the chalkboard. Such a stroke of genius is only a "great discovery" to the man who is too afraid to sound stupid by questioning it. If we start there—with the mathematical, in the *realm* of imagination that is—then the master of that equation, who presses us to confide in his artistry, is no different than a chronic liar believing the world around him will blindly give allowance and eventually conform to his perversions.

Perhaps the most brilliant scientist of the 20th century was non-other than Nikola Tesla, who's findings and discoveries were apparently so temperamental to the truth of the world we live in that the FBI, at the request of the U.S. War Department, seized his research papers and made it top secret upon his death in 1943. It was Tesla who said of his contemporaries, "Today's scientists have substituted mathematics for experiments, and they wander off through equation after equation, and eventually build a structure which has no relation to reality."

Similarly, Professor Herbert Dingle had this to say, not only of mathematics as a whole, but the very theory which he once upheld as the supreme truth: "In the language of mathematics we can tell lies as well as truths, and within the scope of mathematics itself there is no possible way of telling one from the other."

The only way to know if a mathematical formula holds any merit to truth is to test it beyond "thought experiments," specifically in the wild, where there is ether. I bring up *ether* because relativity's sole purpose is to disregard the Michelson-Morley experiment, which *proved* that the sun is moving, *not* the Earth. As Einstein would say, "Science without religion is lame. Religion without science is blind." With mathematical formulae, the religion of Globe Earth finally has a "science" to back it.

This is what Einstein asks of us, to ignore measured reality where God's creation declares itself—that the Earth is in fact flat and stationary—and in its place prop up the existence of the globe religion with the masterful stroke of a mathematician's brush. That moon Martians should believe their world is stationary, with the Earth and the sun revolving around them, is what we are expected to believe of relativity. That the track is moving and not the train is also to be believed. That the sidewalk rises to slap us in the face rather than we falling down to meet it is also a possibility we must put our faith in, if relativity is true and the Earth is a globe. This is the superstitious religion which all Copernicans *must* adhere to, that motion is all relative to the reference of the observer. True science proves otherwise.

Anyone who's thoroughly read the Bible and therefore subjects himself to it will rightfully conclude that Albert Einstein is a relativist (as the theory dutifully implies), while God, according to His own Testimony, is *not*. And yet virtually no one who is taught relativity, even from an intellectual distance, and therefore adheres to the theory of relativity, continues to believe the Bible.

In his own words, Einstein had this to say of his life's work: "What we mean by relative motion in a general sense is perfectly plain to everyone. If we think of a wagon moving along a street we know that it is possible to peak of the wagon at rest, and the street in motion, just as well as it is to speak of the wagon in motion and the street at rest. That, however, is a very special part of the ideas involved in the principle of Relativity."

This is likely why, when one looks up inspirational quotes on imagination, Einstein is regularly regurgitated as the crowning achievement of them. Quotes such as, "The true sign of intelligence is not knowledge but imagination," come to mind, and, "Imagination is more important than knowledge. Knowledge is limited. Imagination encircles the world." Einstein was a true magician of the imagination, using equations as his wand, but a scientist he was not.

Yet the religion of Scientism and its worldwide assembly of worshipers willingly lap up the stench of relativism, every bit of it. If TIME Magazine would name Einstein "Person of the Century" in its December 31, 1999 issue—I remember it well, having just turned 19 three days earlier—it shows how serious the issue of Globe Earth truly is, particularly among those who desperately need the lie upheld.

In that issue, Frederic Golden said, "He was the embodiment of pure intellect…he was unfathomably profound---the genius among geniuses who discovered, merely by thinking about it, that the universe was not as it seemed….his ideas, like Darwin's, reverberated beyond science, influencing modern culture."

When it comes to supporting the globe with science, *true* science, and not merely the chalk board equations which seek to prove it, we can all learn from Albert Einstein when he said, "Insanity is doing the same thing over and over again and expecting different results."

THE THIRD REICH, THE USSR, & NOW THE USA—A MODERN CASE OF HISTORICAL NEGATIONISM

"IT IS THE ABSOLUTE RIGHT OF THE STATE to supervise the formation of public opinion." Josef Goebbels words, *not* mine. Goebbels was Adolf Hitler's Reich Minister of Propaganda, serving his office faithfully from 1933 until 1945, when several conflicting accounts accredit his final undoing to any number of possible murder and assisted suicide scenarios. At any rate, most patriotic Americans will readily admit, when faced with the reality of Nazi Germany and the Soviet Union, the rewriting of history *literally* became institutionalized during the 20th century. It is a feat not entirely impossible, given absolute control over the media to overwrite the memories of hundreds of millions of people. All one needs is the collaborative efforts of the few powerful and a single generation to accomplish it in. History has proven this much. Almost always such malicious tampering is done to secure the monopolized hold which the conglomerate of power has over the very people they vow to shepherd. And yet in light of this, the average American will faint with horror, *oh the horror*, at the mere suggestion—the audacity—that anyone would dare suggest our world governing Empire has in any way supervised or shaped our own understanding of history.

Soon after Stalin achieved power, rival Leon Trotsky, founder of the Red Army and a monumental force behind the Bolshevik Revolution, simply *disappeared* from the public eye. He was of course assassinated with an ice ax to the brain, but with his political removal, so too was every portrait that had once hung in public squares and private households stripped from public consciousness. For the everyday Labour Party Soviet, Stalin and Lenin were inserted into the very role which Trotsky had once held, standing together as the imperial leaders of the Bolshevik. History was re-written, and every media outlet east of Berlin—from museums and building-sized posters to postage stamps passed between hands—had a part to play in it.

While younger generations of Soviets believed this illegitimate distortion of the historical records was a true linear portrayal of political events, and likely saw no reason to question it, older generations—who had once personally familiarized themselves with the works and portraits of Trotsky in real time (perhaps rationalizing it all as but a dream in the face of relentless indoctrination)—notably struggled with false-memory syndromes.

George Orwell took notice. Said Orwell, "The most effective way to destroy people is to deny and obliterate their own understanding of their history." In his dystopian novel "Nineteen Eighty-Four," such a condition: knowing what is otherwise true and yet cognitively finding no contradiction in simultaneously believing what the Establishment demands is true, is called *doublethink*. In "Nineteen Eighty-Four," *doublethink* is a central contributor of Big Brother's formal brainwashing programs. People voluntarily learn doublethink due to peer pressure, mainly the desire to fit in, thereby gaining status within the Party. Anyone who recognizes, let alone mentions, any contradiction within the Party's policy is deemed a "blasphemer." He will likely receive harsh disciplinary action and immediate disownership from patriotic party members.

Doublethink is the cognitive language of the modern Christian. By no mere coincidence, it is Big Brother approved. My serial reader will immediately note that I am not so concerned with the unbelieving. Flat Earth is not for everyone—clearly. My issue is with the *true* believer. Doublethink is his intellectual language too, and he—the Christian, once being presented with such Biblical facts that he has likely grown intimately knowledgeable of on his own—is without excuse.

By its very definition, *doublethink* demands that such an adherer holds two conflicting views at the same time. Because its subscriber is plagued with a total lack of cognitive dissonance, he is completely suspended with disbelief when he is faced with his own contradiction. While claiming Infallibility of the Word—if indeed he is a Christian—he also simultaneously believes what the Copernican astronomer says of distant neighborhoods or the Platonist of the soul, despite the Bible's claim to the contrary—that God's creation is immovable and stationary and that He alone is immortal. If he remains completely untroubled by the contradiction, it's because *doublethink* can only thrive in a society that is Big Brother approved. Globe Earth is Big Brother approved. The Christian who snubs God's Testimony expresses his contrary opinion precisely with the rank and file which Academia and Scientism requires that he falls in line with.

I am simply perplexed by the sheer overwhelming number of Americans who truly believe the rewriting of history, or historical negationism, would not—*No*, it simply *could not* happen to them. And yet it clearly has. It's happened to all of us. The American Government gave us something the Soviets could only wish to invent in their grandest of wet dreams—the television. It is predictably in every household across our nation, and likely all of western civilization, if not the world. And it is owned—the media, that is—maintained, and produced from its very ground-floor conceptions, even in its most imaginative Hollywood grandeur, from a stunning conglomerate of six corporations, every single one of them Zionist run. Collectively, they can dictate whatever narrative they want.

It was the Jew, my serial reader will likely recall, who first took the knife to the Torah in favor of his Kabbalistic texts and the Babylonian Talmud, pronouncing God's flat stationary Earth to be a spinning globular one—always spinning. At any rate, parents have lost their authority. They've handed the raising of their children over to the government. It's a terrifying thought. When did we as a society mutually agree upon this? I can't even stomach plopping my children down in front of the Public Broadcasting Service anymore. PBS produces shows where, for an entire thirty minutes, children can stare at cartoon images of the globe—never a single real image, mind you—and for no other purpose but to let Carl Sagan's words ring true: "Who are we? We find that we live on an insignificant planet of a humdrum star lost in a galaxy tucked away in some forgotten corner of a universe in which there are far more galaxies than people."

Today, *doublethink* surrounds us. A Christian reads of a stationary Earth in Holy Writ and likely never stops to contemplate why the only commentary that can be found which might otherwise grant geocentricism the courtesy of a passing nod regards a heliocentric globe. And while the ink-stains of historical negationism have been finely dried in every mainstream and government endorsed publication for two or three generations now, real history is still available to the student who wishes for nothing less than truth over the writing of fiction—meaning, not every book on the matter has been cooked.

I look to the resident astronomer at *Answers in Genesis*—Danny Faulkner—who aspire to scrub *true* history from the minds of every believer by openly campaigning on the platform that 19th century atheists invented the Flat Earth domed-cosmology model as a way to make mockery of the Bible. Since when have astronomers usurped theologians, anyhow? Naturally, according to Faulkner, we few who stand boldly against the entire weight and scorn of academia are the poor ignoramus souls so easily deceived. It is his only position, if he wishes to impose the illusion of truth on the subservient, to scrub and scrub and scrub the floor until the stain of Godly men and women who've come long before him are not even dared to be read or mentioned for fear of ridicule. I can't help but wonder; how many page scrubbers are merely hoping to polish the diploma on their wall, having been caught picking and choosing what he will take *literally* of God's Testimony concerning His creation; or are they gatekeepers?

Danny Faulkner, dear friend in the faith, great Christian men and women like Samuel Rowbotham confront you. William Carpenter confronts you. Alexander Gleason and Thomas Winship confront you. David Wardlaw Scott confronts you, as does Lady Blount, F.E. Pasche, Albert Smith, and Gabrielle Henriet. These Godly men and women pleaded with the church not to give in to the Copernican apostasy. Even Martin Luther and John Calvin, Philipp Melanchthon and A.W. Pink— all of whom boldly stood against the Copernican—confront you. Generations of our spiritual forefathers confront you.

History has been re-written. Much like Stalin and Lenin with Trotsky, the modern day Copernican Creationist has overthrown these men. In every public square their portraits are erased. And they would have us think the God-fearing Christian paraded the theory of Copernicus—and the so-called Christian astronomers still to come—as something that finally—Yes, thank the Lord, FINALLY! — made Biblical sense. Yet in 1856 Dr. Valentine Ernest Loescher wrote: "No sooner was the very uncertain doctrine brought up that the sun is at rest and our globe revolves around him, than the contempt of Holy Writ and infidelity notably increased. On the other hand, vanity was rampant, and the desire to accept and circulate absurd opinions." (His Life, by Engelhardt, 1856, p. 283.)

Danny Faulkner, dear friend in the faith, *real* history, *church* history, confronts you.

HISTORY IS WRITTEN BY THE VICTORS,
and RAY BRADBURY

TO THE VICTOR BELONGS THE EMPTY PAPER AND THE PEN. The author of such a notebook writes not merely in the realm of history, as Winston Churchill once so brazenly yet truthfully proclaimed; he writes *future* fantasy as well. Yet what might happen if, as a result of our indiscretion—tossing aside the long-standing belief in Biblical cosmology, an act which the writers of history convinced us to commit— just what if our long-promised transcendence into the infinite cosmos simply proved to be another imaginative flight of fancy? According to Ray Bradbury, that writer would fake it, *naturally*. And what makes a better agent of indoctrination for any governing body than the television.

Such was the case for poor Fiorello Bodoni, small-time junkyard owner, big time dreamer. Star gazing hobbyist mainly, particularly where his admiration for distant planets was concerned. He so desperately wanted to visit them, and so he needed a flying contraption to transport him there. What does such a schemer do? He spends his life-savings on a mock-up rocket rather than contributing to the well-fare of his family. He secretly spends his nights constructing a theater for its interior, complete with color film, mirrors, and screens. And having convinced his children that this is *indeed* a very real space vehicle capable of transporting them to another planet, they excitedly take part in it, much to their mother's initial disdain for such an idea. Her opinion changes however once her children return from the deception that carried them across the galaxy and back, what ended up being a two-day journey to nowhere—having never once actually left the ground. It is a deception, Bradbury assures us, in which they will happily "*remember for always.*"

First published in 1950, Ray Bradbury's "*The Rocket*" arrived during the dawn of television, the computer, modern media, the Cold War, United Nations, Rothschild's Israel, the Antarctica Treaty, and NASA. I was in a library, kind of just meandering around, and looking. You know, seeking my next read. That's when I first discovered "*The Illustrated Man*," the collection of short stories where-in "*The Rocket*" was first contained; the year Bradbury died—2012, for the record. It was buried in some obscure aisle, a well-preserved first copy—hardbound. How it wasn't *stolen*, I cannot say. I only stumbled upon it having fumbled my scissor-fingers recklessly across the binding of random books until they tripped over the spine which aspired to suite my tastes.

If I fondly recall sliding *"The Illustrated Man"* out from its contemporaries—specifically now that I inhabit a completely different shape to the Earth—it's because the thought first occurred to me, after scouring through each and every word which Bradbury thought necessary to clap upon paper, that science and science-fiction are intermingled. There is no severing the two apart. Some will believe a lie by the will of our administrators, if only so that science can be lived out. Ray Bradbury taught me that.

What we are left with, mainly two separate compartments of thought that bleed into one single complex of cabinetry; is satisfactual only to the warped mindset of humanism. The liberal humanist believes in the superiority of his own agency over the acceptance of dogma or creed, and so sees little reason why he cannot pick apart and choose truth to his own fancy.

A Christian humanist, as if the two titles should or can in any way go together, will similarly give praise to the independent intellect. He will gladly advertise his distant cerebral gazes as something in which God *prefers* of His children rather than easily admit to the reality of his sinful nature and the imaginative perversions which derives from free-ranging logic. Suddenly I am expected to believe with every so-called Christian humanist that I meet: imagination is innocent—*no*, virtuous, if they're being honest—in its transcendent desire to *reach for the stars*, metaphysically speaking. He believes the Holy Spirit supports his cognitive decisions, weighing truth and lies at the expense of traditional doctrine, which he has willingly tossed to the side of the road so as not to have his intelligence bogged down by it.

Science-fiction is indeed a messy business. We are saturated with its religious message of transcendence at every turn of the day. Wishful thinking, I call it. In Bradbury's case, we'll label it a Freudian slip of the pen. If such a spiritual principle is unachievable, physically speaking (it most certainly is *unachievable*; the Bible taught me that), then our administrators will go about controlling our destinies in a slightly different *achievable* way. If the rocket itself is a worthless heap of bolts then they shall easily enough employ its scraps. They will convince us of its good use through the manipulation of a free-ranging mind, and worse, they'll make us think, like any thoughtful session with a psychologist, that it was our idea to go along with it in the first place.

> *"What the space age was seeking all along was not so much an expansion of physical space as an expansion of the mind"* – Marina Benjamin

"*We Choose to Go to the Moon!*" SAYS THE NEW RELIGION OF KENNEDY | OR AS ROBERT FROST PUT IT: "*Must God Allow the Firm Firmament to Soften?*"

A MANIFEST DESTINY OF THE COPERNICAN NATURE was finally pressed upon and dutifully commissioned by President John F. Kennedy when he inspired his nation with the following decree: "We set sail on this new sea because there is new knowledge to be gained, and new rights to be won, and they must be won and used for the progress of all people!"

This was 1962. Though most cleverly masked with the modernity of 20th-century Scientism, an undeniable religious fervor had been set ablaze in the hearts of every man, woman, and child. Kennedy had a way of doing that. This was 1962, and the Great Delusion promised by the Apostles Paul and Peter—but up until now was only prescribed to abstractly—was finally becoming realized in its incarnation. Gone was the Biblical cosmology of earlier centuries. This was 1962, and America, being the good Christian nation, was determined to dispose of it. "*Good-bye and good riddance!*" Before the decade came to a close, television would redefine God's Word by ceremoniously imprinting a couple of Freemason's shoes on the moon. But neither President John F. Kennedy nor poet laureate of Vermont Robert Frost, who happened to speak at Kennedy's inauguration, would live to see it.

Throughout the Second World War, Frost refused any contribution of his words should they fuel allied propaganda, despite insistence from colleagues and friends that his poetry help in the effort. And yet in the closing months of his life, having already celebrated Kennedy at the podium, Frost finally took up the commentators task with his pen. The winds had changed. Not even Frost could deny it. But rather than finding praise in Cold War espionage, the old farmer aptly and altogether dismissed its politics. "*In the Clearing,*" which consisted of somewhere around forty of his lesser known poems, would prove his final publication before his death. To his colleagues, America's beloved poet

410

simply came across as an old fuddy-duddy. By rejecting Scientism, thereby preferring the road less trodden upon, Robert Frost had become a dissenter—even against the American dream, which relished now in the conquest of heaven.

Or perhaps more precisely—to be fair; the very readership which had once given praise to his metaphysical and cosmological simplicity had, almost overnight, suddenly *outgrown* him.

In *"A Concept Self-Conceived,"* the old farmer from Vermont did not shy when he wrote:

"The latest creed that has to be believed

And entered in our childish catechism

Is that the All's a concept self-conceived,

Which is no more than good old Pantheism."

Accordingly, if traditional thoughts should hinder the progress of man, then the religion of Scientism will see to it that God is nothing more than an evolutionary construct of our poorer imaginations. How unfortunate. And what's worse, this "latest creed" has "entered our childish catechism." For Frost, there is human "fact," and then there is "divine" fact. Should the first pounce upon the second, or God forbid, indoctrinate and endanger the minds of children, then the conclusion is simple. Frost retorts:

"The rule is, never give a child a choice."

Harsh words for a space racer. Elsewhere, *"Lines Written in Dejection on the Eve of Great Success,"* hearkens back thematically to one of his earlier poems, *"Birches."* The former was originally released during the outbreak of the First World War, and recalls the poet wishing he might climb a tree as he once managed in his childhood, all so that the rational world might be left behind. But now with *Lines Written in Dejection*, Frost is a tired old man, having first survived one World War and then another. Though the New World Order presses onward without him, he has yet to see their new man-made religion outmatch the beauty of untarnished imagination planted firmly in the soil and gazing skyward, a worldview which can only be gifted by the Divine. While Science may claim to land man on the moon, it will never *catch the cow's tail*. After all, did Frost not once witness a cow jump over the moon? Indeed he did. To this realization he sighs:

"That was back in the days of my Grandmother Goose."

Might I be so bold to suggest his pupilage under Grandmother Goose included a cosmological view quite unfamiliar with ours. Even today the sun and the moon still rise while the Earth stands still. Polaris remains permanently fixed in place while the luminaries play their part in the merry-go-round parade—endlessly carousing around our central point of light. The constellations within, which gave picturesque realities to the ancient man of "less fortunate times," as the Copernican blindly believes—apparently "not knowing better" for lack of telescopes and television—*refuse* to change even now for the modern man. How odd. Water remains level. And quite similarly, the horizon *always* rises; no matter how high we climb—as if to mock the very notion of a globe.

We are told of course by our television—and also today by the World Wide Web—that everything we experience with our own eyes is an illusion. To this I firmly plant my foot down in the soil. The old faith, which was based on God's own Testimony and further counseled through our common senses, must be cast down to make way for the new religion. So says the Copernican. For this incursion—the *out with the old in with the new* attitude, Frost retorts:

> "Once I was fool enough to think
>
> That brains and sweetbreads were the same,
>
> Till I was caught and put to shame,
>
> First by a butcher, then a cook,
>
> Then by a scientific book.
>
> But 'twas by making sweetbreads do
>
> I passed with such a high I.Q."
>
> (*Quandary*)

The pervasive nature of Scientism, being ultimately materialistic and technologically driven, is at best an artificial vision. It is nothing more than a shadow Universe, sentenced to isolation and loneliness. Because we can only experience the Copernican revolution by the chalk equations of a few academic Gnostic's, or perhaps more practically for us simple-minded folk, through the government's own programming services—Google and the television; it is therefore impossible to partake in the fundamentals of Scientism without first turning our gaze away from the realities with which God has chosen to surround us with. The man who agrees to go along with an augmented reality must do so through a self-effacing, materialistic-driven, and quantitative standard of truth. He must therefore alienate himself. Technology thrives on weaning a man off reality. And worse, he endangers estranging himself from God.

Need I repeat myself? The sun rises in the east and sets in the west. The very notion that the world turns in place of the sun goes against our every real human experience. What sort of couple sit on a bench, holding hands, watching the sun set and proclaim: "Woah! We're leaning backwards!" To reject the reality of a moving sunset drives the evil even deeper. Despite reported black holes, satellites, distant nebula's, and an unmentionable number of uninhabitable planets, the old world view is still present and accounted for in abundance, if only we should shut off the technological means which seek to callous and pervert the human experience. The old world reality is all around us.

Frost mourns this augmented experience in "[*Four-Room Shack...*]," yet another cranky old man poem describing Sciences contempt of those real God-given experiences in favor of a television (as in, the "four-room shack"), complete with "visions in the sky" and bunny-eared antennae serving for its "scrawny mast."

"Four-room shack aspiring high

With an arm of scrawny mast

For the visions in the sky

That go blindly pouring past.

In the ear and in the eye

What you get is what to buy.

Hope you're satisfied to last."

Society's trust in another reality, conveniently hid behind a curtain—as the Copernicans would have it, and which only a ticker-tape machine can reveal—is troublesome in the least. Indeed, by the end of his life, Robert Frost was a dissenter. In yet another cranky old man poem, he even scoffs at the notion of participating in a contradictory worldview beyond our own day-to-day functions. Appropriately titled *"Some Science Fiction,"* Frost quips:

"They may end by banishing me

To the penal colony

They are thinking of pretty soon

Establishing on the moon."

413

He even goes so far as to mock man's gullibility, if he should actually believe a scenario might arise where the poor farmer from Vermont might be banished to an up-and-coming colony on the moon, claiming:

"With a can of condensed air

I could go almost anywhere,

Or rather submit to be sent

As a noble experiment."

Frost's criticism trudges on with "*Wishing Well.*" Mankind continuously showcases a rather obstinate treatment towards the Divine Creator. This was particularly made known in his own life with the space race. Here the poet revels in picturesque Biblical cosmology by invoking the firmament (raqia in Hebrew)—that solid dome boldly acting as a barrier between Earth and the so-called "space" which both NASA and the Soviets were purporting to explore. He says:

"It merely would entail the purge

That the just-pausing Demiurge

Asks of himself once in so often

So the firm firmament won't soften."

Frost apparently knew the function of the firmament better than almost anyone living today, even if he did settle on mythological origins. After all, the poet made no claim to Christendom. At any rate, the firmament of Noah's day even now withholds the waters which once drowned Godless revelers in a worldwide flood. Noting the firmaments ties to this account, he most naturally adds:

"There's always been an Ararat

Where someone someone else begat

To start the world all over at."

Robert Frost certainly was not in on the deception, nor do we find any reason to doubt his allegiance towards Spherical Earth, and yet being born only nine years after Abraham Lincoln's assassination, his was a generation which ought to have known better. The space race likely conflicted with his own memories, and his full catalog of poetry certainly shows it. Indeed, conflicts of opinion—where the shape of the Earth is concerned—was publicly aroused in Frost's younger years. This is a documented fact, even in the mainstream media. And despite the new

414

Copernican "morality," which tugged dutifully at the heart of almost every American, there were some who adhered to their better senses. Not everyone succumbed to the demands of the Scientific religious, even if they died alone in their thinking. This was 1962, and being first and foremost a simple farmer, the poet laureate from Vermont kept to his.

Presently, we are those whom Frost frightfully spoke of when he wrote: "The latest creed that has to be believed entered in our childish catechism." That is us. We are the generation which has—well, a select few of us at least—turned our gaze from the repulsive "four-room shack" with an "arm of scrawny mast" that has attempted to bewitch us with "visions in the sky." Those few of us have been so fortunate to see the moon as the cranky old farmer from Vermont once perceived it; a luminary more likely to sponsor a cow leaping over its dish-like rim rather than a couple of televised Freemasons bobbing in slow-motion across its face.

Whatever his cosmological conclusions, Frost's disdain for any further exploration within the perceived realities of the Copernican Universe, and the devastating personal alienation which belief in such a technocratic society would cause, couldn't have become any more transparent than the 19 words which made up one of his life's closing poems, "[*But Outer Space...*]" in which he writes:

> "But outer Space,
>
> At least this far,
>
> For all the fuss
>
> Of the populace
>
> Stays more popular
>
> Than populous."

"The Earth Standing out of the Water and in the Water..." CHURCH BELLS RANG THE DAY JOHN GLENN CONQUERED HEAVEN

COLONEL JOHN GLENN RECEIVED LETTERS, and *oh,* how I wish I could get my hand on them. My interest lies particularly with those postmarked in the months leading up to his momentous—though often delayed—flight of passage *beyond* Earth. It is as they say, *one man's trash is another man's treasure*, and I fully believe there is something of value for a guy like me buried within them.

Glenn himself was not capable of answering the "mountain of mail that was piling up..." He told the March 9, 1962 issue of LIFE Magazine that there were among them "some letters which informed me that the postponements were God's way of letting us know that we should not be tampering with the heavens." Glenn addressed those very concerns just as promptly as he'd confessed them by relieving LIFE Magazines readership of any potential doubt in his own spiritual motivations. Glenn was just as morally consciousnesses, clean-cut, and all-around American as the rest of them. Specifically, he was given leave of his quarters in Cape Canaveral now and then, he wrote, either for a haircut or on Sundays a church service in Cocoa Beach. In other words, we should expect no shenanigans, either from ground control or beyond.

Regardless of his assurances, in as little as 8 years a poll conducted by Knight Newspapers found that 30% of Americans were "suspicious of NASA's trips to the Moon," with the number rising to 54% in some Afro-American areas. But the up-and-coming moon landing deception, I suspect, was not the mere focus of those unanswered letters. They are a narrative of the cosmological nature—religious as well as scientifically inclined—stemming from a then-dying generation. It is a narrative lost now to the ages; erased from public discourse; a conscientious worldview which no doubt lines up with Robert Frosts own words in 1962 when the farmer from Vermont thoughtfully contemplated such puzzling notions as a *firm firmament softening.* John Glenn kept to church and a proper schedule of haircuts.

416

In *We Seven*, a collection of essays written by the seven pioneering Astronauts themselves and published following his return to Earth in 1962, Glenn further addressed his religious critics in *A Past to Draw On*. Here the tone of those phantom letters, I suspect, are hinted at when he writes: "There is nothing superhuman, however, about being an Astronaut. There is nothing spooky or supernatural about flying in space. I have talked to people, both before and after my orbital flight, who seemed to think that both of these propositions were true and that an Astronaut must have to be some sort of Yogi and put himself into a trance of some kind to go through such an experience." Within a few sentences Glenn adds: "Space flight, like any other kind of flying, is simply the product of normal human skill and technical proficiency. Both of these have to be of the highest order, but there is nothing mysterious or esoteric about either one of them."

"There were a lot of unknowns in the early days of spaceflight," former astronaut Scott Carpenter, who followed Glenn's flight with an *orbital* mission of his own in May of that year, later reminisced. "We were considered guilty of being unable to fly in space and required to prove our innocence, counter to the American custom."

Prove they most certainly did. Perhaps this was NASA's true intended purpose. As many critics of the Apollo program have noted, very little of their achievements were scientific. With Glenn, the firm firmament was softened. Mission: accomplished.

That same March 9, 1962 issue of LIFE Magazine, which depicted the Astronaut and his wife overshadowing even the all-familiar caricature of vice president Lyndon Johnson in a police-line motorcade, reported of Glenn's Earthly homecoming: "As though swirling down from conquered space itself, a splendor of ticker tape and shredded paper almost blots out the view of Manhattan throngs straining for a glimpse of Colonel John Glenn. Along the traditional Route of Heroes through the canyons of skyscrapers, Glenn and his fellow Astronauts received New York's greatest acclaim. Despite the windy cold, the crowds all but overwhelmed Glenn by the weight of their numbers and enthusiasm. Bands played and church bells rang, but they were drowned out by cheering that approached the decibel force of a rocket at liftoff. At the end of the parade, the man who had known the utter loneliness of space could only say of the welcome that he had *'never seen anything like it.'*"

LIFE Magazine aptly concluded: "...Nor had anyone else."

Whoever the unidentified authors of these letters, I also suspect they were not numbered among those who had "stirred the national pride." Glenn observed, "As the focus of that pride, I have been almost overwhelmed. I felt this way when I was honored by President Kennedy and by the Congress. But I have felt it even more strongly when I was honored by so many other people. Riding along parade routes in Florida, Washington, New York, and New Concord, my home town, I have looked at all those faces and waved and smiled when I really felt much more."

Indeed, those letter-writers were of a generation who, for the most part, did not understand nor comprehend *true* Biblical cosmology—by way of argument—but the Spirit of God had not yet been quenched within them that He should fail to whisper:

"Fear before him, all the earth: the world also shall be stable, that it be not moved (1 Chronicles 16:30)."

Knowing how something was not right with this historical turn of events, they likely did not feel the American spirit surging within them, nor gladly participate when church bells heralded Glenn's conquest of space. There is indeed a contrary spirit at work to that of the Holy Ghost. It *or* he is most certainly American, and more—so much more. He is as old as Babylon itself—and older. There were those in the years leading up to America's conquest of space—and in the months surrounding it— who perhaps did not connect all the end-times dots, particularly where the coming of the lawless one according to the working of Satan is concerned—*"with all power and signs and lying wonders...* (2 Thessalonians 2:9)" Even now it is impossible to connect them all. Yet I have personally interviewed a handful of such men who lived the Cold-War propaganda, listened to their better discretion and refused to bow to this patriotic spirit at work, despite not being able to place a finger on the specifics.

To be fair, perhaps those who held their breath under the suffocating downpours of paper confetti—which surely lined each parade route in Florida, Washington, New York, and New Concord—did not scoff at the Lord, and God forbid, ask: "Where is the promise of His coming?" Certainly not. But yet, with Glenn's presidential caravan through America's grand avenues of hero-worship, the age of scoffers had undeniably begun.

The Apostle Peter prophesied such a time when he wrote:

"For this they willingly are ignorant of, that by the Word of God the heavens were of old, and the earth standing out of the water and in the water: Whereby the world that then was, being overflowed with water, perished... (2 Peter 3:5-6)"

Glenn wrote in *We Seven*: "We Astronauts have a mission, an extremely serious and important one. We are helping to break the bonds that have kept the human race pinned to the earth..." As for the throngs of Americans who line the streets, Glenn quipped: "Here they were, identifying with me, and I was identifying with them—right back."

Colonel and four-term senator John Glenn was an unrepentant Freemason. Who better to pull off the "all power" of Satan, his "signs and lying wonders" which seeks to destroy any notion of an earth "standing out of the water and in the water" but the Freemasons—and others who will go unmentioned here. By 1962, the age of deceit—though perhaps not in today's mature formation—was finally fluttering its wings. With Glenn, the deceivers had their man. And I ask myself: Would I have ranked among the gullible jubilant? I hope not. Perhaps one of the overriding themes of this end-times narrative—and I myself am guilty of it—is that all too easy we as a human species revel in the parade routes of our own funeral. Quite tragically, it wasn't for the conquest of space that those church bells rang.

The war for heaven was finally here. And the public was invited to watch.

"The Russian Soul..." EXOTERIC THAUMATURGY: HOW THE COSMISTS FORGED THE SPACE RACE FOR AMERICA

1

WE KNEW THEM THEN AS THE MERCURY SEVEN. April 9, 1959—at a conference in Washington, seven pioneering Americans were asked by a reporter if there were any brave men in the rank who were ready to launch into space right then and there. Everyone raised their hands. Wally Schirra and John Glenn doubled their vote by raising both of them. Yet John Glenn's historic spaceflight, which commenced on board *Friendship 7* three years later, was no sure thing. "Delays for weather and for technical difficulties were facts I could accept," he wrote afterwards to LIFE Magazine, "but a postponement or a possible replacement while the Astronaut recovered from a childhood disease seemed a bit silly. It would make quite a headline: GLENN HAS MUMPS." While Glenn "was especially careful to steer clear of anyone who had even the slightest sign of a cold," NASA's engineers had other obstacles. Before completing three successful laps of the Earth, no American had spent more than 15 minutes *in space*.

"Earth is the cradle of humanity, but one cannot remain in the cradle forever."

With Glenn's final *GO* on February 20, 1962, the Soviet Union had already successfully launched two manned orbital missions and a dog named Laika. Yuri Gagarin circled the Earth once in April 1961, and Gherman Titov outperformed his fellow countryman that following August by orbiting the Earth seventeen times in a period outlasting 24-hours. American astronauts Alan Shepard and Gus Grissom had only managed a 15-minute jump into orbit. Doctors were concerned with how Glenn's body would hold up during nearly five hours in Earth orbit and whether or not his eyes would function properly in micro-gravity. NASA engineers also worried that spaceflight might cause fluid to move around randomly in Glenn's inner ear, perhaps resulting in nausea and vertigo. Nobody was even sure if he would be able to swallow properly.

Glenn recounted years later: "Some of the ophthalmologists were literally concerned at that time that your eyes might change shape and your vision might change enough you couldn't even see the instrument panel enough to make an emergency re-entry if you had to." He also added: "They were enough concerned about it, we actually put a little miniaturized eye chart at the top of the instrument panel. And that's still in *Friendship 7*—up in the Smithsonian."

The October 21, 1957 issue of LIFE Magazine seemed intent to plague its readers with anxiety. Space was a headache. Such questions were asked: "How heavy is cosmic ray bombardment at these altitudes? How will it affect pilots? What will happen to the skin of an aircraft when it runs into clouds of tiny micrometeorites, the dust of outer space? What about the less numerous but larger meteorites that might conceivably strike a plane with explosive force? How do the earth's magnetic and gravitational fields change, and how will these changes affect electronic guidance systems?" The space race was raging between two world empires; the future of humanity was at stake; and yet one thing seemed certain—the U.S. was intent on sending men *beyond* the Earth, and they hadn't a clue what space actually was.

The following month, on November 18, 1957, LIFE published an article titled *The Seer of Space*, which focused on the father of rocket technology and science in the U.S. himself, Wernher von Braun. The former Nazi, who posed on the cover with a moon rocket he designed for Disney's film, *Man in Space*, attempted to alleviate America's apprehensions. "It's been said there are so many unknowns in space, we cannot proceed. The Russians have demonstrated clearly that this is untrue. A rocket-propulsion expert will tell you there's no sweat in solving propulsion problems but the medical problem is the barrier. A doctor will tell you space flight is medically possible but he doesn't think propulsion can be licked. Many of these obstacles will fade away...." The Soviets, he said, had already been integrating space flight with their missile program since 1946. *For America*, Von Braun seemed to sigh, their lack of interest after the War were some terrible years lost. "One fine day we suddenly decided we had to have an ICBM. It was like telling the Wright Brothers to build a B-29."

Von Braun reminded the reader of LIFE on the need for 100% secrecy while they developed the necessary technology for space flight—

and more money. They needed *more* money, but "congressmen must believe in what we're doing, and they won't until the public believes in us..."

Sputnik I made America believe in space travel, and better—it conveniently provided a necessary threat.

"RUSSIA'S SATELLITE, A DAZZLING NEW SIGHT IN THE HEAVENS: THE FEAT THAT SHOOK THE EARTH"

"A glittering metallic pinpoint of light streaking across the predawn sky last week gave the U.S. its first look at Soviet Russia's great feat, the artificial moon Sputnik. After the satellite's first hundred or so orbital trips across the earth, Americans were settling into uneasy familiarity with the unarguable fact that Russia's moon was passing over them four to six time a day"

—LIFE Magazine, October 21, 1957

Sputnik I struck terror in the west. "A colossal panic was underway," wrote Tom Wolfe in *The Right Stuff*, "with congressmen and newspapermen leading a huge pack that was baying at the sky where the hundred-pound Soviet satellite kept beeping around the world... Sputnik I took on a magical dimension... It gave birth to a modern, techno logical astrology. Nothing less than control of the heavens was at stake. It was Armageddon, the final and decisive battle of the forces of good and evil. Lyndon Johnson, who was the Senate majority leader, said that whoever controlled 'the high ground' of space would control the world."

In actuality, U.S. reaction to *Sputnik I* took on many forms. Bartenders concocted *Sputnik* cocktails with vodka as the base. Rather than popping out of a cake in the traditional *Earthly* fashion, pretty models were reported to burst from a balloon gondola during a Chicago sales meeting. For fashion, space-themed skirts, jackets, hats, and quite ironically, balloons with satellite motif were rushed onto the market. Even the under-aged wanted a part of the Cold War madness. To cash in on the *Sputnik* craze, toy manufacturers released a variety of desirable play things. Employees at Macy's in New York even dressed the part of space men in order to fill the cash drawers. But not everyone was in a pleasant mood. A young rocketeer named G. Harry Stine was fired by the Martin Company for too volubly belittling the U.S. missile program, specifically in regards to his sharp remark made after Sputnik. "This is really and truly the shot heard round the world," said Stine. "I wonder what the dead veterans of Lexington and of Korea are thinking."

Despite the toys and the cocktails and the pretty models bursting out from balloon gondolas, America needed reassurance—and fast. The media spun the *Sputnik* narrative with a series of articles which basically read: "WE TOLD YOU SO"—In so many words. *It should have been America up there first, and it was the voters fault for not pressing Capitol Hill.* LIFE Magazine wasn't shy in taking this approach. As a tireless vocal advocate of tying the U.S. space flight program to its military missile effort, Von Braun had urged in a 1952 speech that the U.S. needed to build a "manned satellite to curb Russia's military ambitions." But despite Von Braun's scientific achievements, some of which, LIFE rather awkwardly sums up, included building "the V-2 missiles that plagued England toward the end of the war," remarks like this "were usually dismissed as if made by a tiresome crackpot." For most Americans, space was still a marketing ploy of of science-fiction—not taxpayer dollars.

But no worries—the story of the United States was that of the underdog. It would bounce back. President Eisenhower promised as much. His U.S. satellite would be scientifically superior to the *beep-beeping* tin-can that was *Sputnik*. America's armed forces agreed. *Sputnik* served no practical purpose—none that anyone knew. Theirs would be "the launching of a reconnaissance vehicle which would circle the globe much as *Sputnik* is doing now, observing every point in the world at least once a day. Such periodic inspection of the earth will soon be possible." According to one estimate, the U.S. Air Force would launch a "true reconnaissance satellite" by 1960, which had already been christened "Big Brother," because "it will see everything, as did the fictional Big Brother in George Orwell's book, 1984."

When asked about trips to the moon, Von Braun estimated it would happen within 25 years—perhaps 1982—but only by "a few selected people who could withstand the trip." Freemasons, likely. Oddly enough, he compared the upcoming moon landing as a challenge akin to Admiral Byrd's recent expedition to Antarctica. "People went there [Antarctica] because they thought it would be fun, and found uses for it they hadn't dreamed of." To wet the reader's appetite, he even compared Antarctica's potential—which has yet to be explained to this day—in the tone reminiscent of the New World. "Columbus couldn't have predicted what the United States would be like today."

LIFE neatly summed up America's mission into space. It was "to make this world more habitable even while we explore others..." But as of 1957—even John Glenn's flight in 1962—one thing remained certain; world peace was being threatened by another world power. It had become "all too apparent Russian scientists are as good as any in the world—or better."

> "There is that in the Russian soul which corresponds to the immensity, the vagueness, the infinitude of the Russian land, spiritual geography corresponds with physical... Two contradictory principles lay at the foundation of the structure of the Russian soul, the one a natural, Dionysian, elemental paganism and the other monastic Orthodoxy."—Nikolai Berdyaev, *The Russian Idea.*

2

IF NIKOLAI FYODOROVICH FYODOROV WENT BY ANY OTHER NAME, *Socrates* would suffice. From a library in Moscow he lived out his peaceful days (1828-1903) committing himself to esoteric studies—dreaming of transhumanism, resurrection from the dead, and space travel. Here in the west very few people have heard of Fyodorov and the Russian Cosmists he inspired. Theirs is not a frequented tale. Perhaps because Fyodorov published very little work in his own lifetime, though he wrote much, and the Cosmists themselves went quietly into the miserably long winter night that was the Bolshevik Revolution. Men like Valerian Muravyov were sentenced to the camps in 1929. Alexander Svyatogor was sent to the camps in 1937, where he died. Father Pavel Florensky was shot that very year—though others were more fortunate. Because of his overzealous credentials in rocket science, Tsiolkovsky lived out his days in a manner of peace. Vladimir Vernadsky was afforded teaching and researching rights until his death in 1945. And though a minor privilege was granted to him, Alexander Chizhevsky was allowed research of his own—in the camps.

Decades thereafter, once the Berlin Wall—which President Kennedy had referred to as "a hell of a lot better than a war"—had been reduced to heaps of rebar, wire, and graffiti-stained mortar, trunks of cars were unlocked and drawers were opened, and the books of the Russian Cosmists were returned to shelves next to Dostoyevsky, Tolstoy, and others. Odd thing though—despite the glaring fact that his writings were repressed by Stalin, Fyoderov was highly influential to the Soviet space program. One of his students was the astrophysicist Konstantin Tsiolkovsky—the father of spaceflight due to the groundbreaking equations he developed. With the collapse of the U.S.S.R., the return of cosmism-consciousness brought with it a new magnifying glass of sorts, affording a deeper transparency and keen sense of intuition among the headlines of antiquity. One thing is now *certain*. Despite the Cosmists massacre in the bloodbath of Marxism, the space race couldn't have happened in this manner—and likely wouldn't have happened at all—without them.

Konstantin Tsiolkovsky (1857-1935) arrived in Moscow in 1873 from a provincial village with no money, no friends, and barely a lick of education. Nearly deaf from a childhood bout with scarlet fever, there was very little school could do with such an extraordinarily gifted mind. Only 16 years old at the time, Tsiolkovsky was met and personally befriended by the father of Cosmism, Nikolai Fyodorovm at the library which served him. Tsiolkovsky said he joined with an "enchanted group" of young people who visited Fyodorov daily, and gladly succumbed to Fyodorov's spell. Each day the master brought his young scientist a fresh stack of books, and together they dreamed of possibilities. Under Fyodorov's personal guidance, Tsiolkovsky began a course of self-education and esoteric embodiment that eventually led to him becoming the honored grandfather of Soviet rocket science and space exploration. Tsiolkovsky calculated the first mathematical formulas for orbiting the satellite which author Arthur C. Clarke had imagined in a science-fiction novel. Without Tsiolkovsky, *Sputnik* wouldn't have happened.

Tsiolkovsky would go on to write science fiction of his own—fantasies which salted his readers with "theosophical treatises on panpsychism, and humanity's future in a cosmos in which every atom is not only alive, but sentient (Hagemeister 2007)." Fyodorov taught his library students that all matter was the dust of our ancestors. Panpsychism was the heart of Tsiolkovsky's writing—the belief that the "atom spirit" is "inherent in every particle of matter in the cosmos."

All that Nikolai Fyodorov's philosophical energy was concentrated upon can be best summed up with the "One Idea." Every problem is centrally rooted in the certainty of death. Everyone and everything *must* die. For Fyodorov, no solution to any social, economic, political, or philosophical quandary would prove sufficient until immortality was solved. If death could be conquered, then all other solutions—the kingdom of heaven itself (in his words)—would flow from the water-well of victory. It is indeed strange that Fyodorov was nurtured under Russian Orthodoxy. He apparently even considered himself "Christian," as so many apostates do. And yet nothing of Fyodorov's learnings conclude that Jesus Christ conquered death and that—because of His perfect atoning sacrifice on the cross through His precious blood—we can evade the second death and partake in the resurrection and restoration of all things. Contrary to the mythology of space travel, Utopia will be fully functional in the final settlement of New Jerusalem. *Oh no*—for Fyodorov, it was the task of humanity to restore to wholeness and life everything that nature drove to death. By *everything* he meant every living person who had ever lived. Science, he assured us, would bring them back.

Fyodorov advocated "immortality for all."

According to *The Russian Cosmists: The Esoteric Futurism of Nikolai Fedorov and His Followers,* author George M. Young describes Russian Cosmism as "a highly controversial and oxymoronic blend of activist speculation, futuristic traditionalism, religious science, exoteric esotericism, utopian pragmatism, idealistic materialism—higher magic partnered to higher mathematics." Michael Hagemeister, a leading western scholar of Russian intellectual history, adds the following "genetic marks" to the definition:

"Russian cosmism and Russian cosmic thinking…is based on a holistic and anthropocentric view of the universe which presupposes a teleologically determined—and thus meaningful—evolution; its adherents strive to redefine the role of humankind in a universe that lacks a divine plan for salvation, thus acknowledging the threat of self-destruction….Cosmic evolution is thus dependent on human action to reach its goal, which is perfection or wholeness. By failing to act, or failing to act correctly, humankind dooms the world to catastrophe. According to cosmism, the world is in a phase of transition from the biosphere (the sphere of living matter) to the "noosphere" (the sphere of reason). During this phase the active unification and organization of the whole of humankind… into a single organism is said to result in a higher *'Planetarian consciousness'* capable of guiding further development reasonably and ethically… changing and perfecting the universe, overcoming disease and death, and finally bringing forth an immortal human race."

This cannot be stressed enough. Everything Fedorov inspired towards throughout his multi-tasking of scattered projects—everything in evolution's grandiose Gnostic tale pointed towards the final resurrection of the dead which, first and foremost, included the conquest of space. The necessity of annexation with the heavenly realms and the Soviets part in the race arose directly from Fyodorov's grand ambitions. Since there is clearly not enough real estate on Earth for all resurrected fathers, a certain measurement of infinity would first be settled. Fedorov and the Cosmists needed as part of their grand project of resurrection the gathering of all nations into one political unit governed by a single autocrat—preferably Russian. In their own twisted thinking, the Cosmists had humanities best interest at heart, particularly humanities starring role in cosmic evolution. Such concentrated efforts harken right back to Tsiolkovsky's novels. Brave international teams of unified scientists—often French, German, Chinese, and American descent, though led most importantly by a Russian—served as a launching pad for his fantasies.

Cosmists were expansive thinkers. If they were to accomplish this, they'd need everything at their disposal—not only centralized religion and world government, but the sociological and the economic, the illusion best mastered in every medium of entertainment—like television, and the magic which art afforded. Science-fiction, the Occult, and esoteric mysticism would appoint us to destiny. George M. Young refers to their philosophy as "exoteric thaumaturgy" which, in so many words, is essentially the capability of a magician or a saint to work magic or miracles in a way that can be understood by the general public. Young refers to Fyodorov as a "man with a twenty-first-century mind and a medieval heart."

The Cosmists were attempting to transform esoteric knowledge into exoteric, to raise the curtain on traditional occult wisdom, thereby treading new directions within philosophy, theology, literature, art, and science. Some critics have dismissed Cosmism as *mere* pseudoscience. Certainly, they may have delivered a pseudo approach to the halls of academia, but they were notably successful at it—brilliantly so. Moreover, they would prove to a worldwide audience through cunning feats of trickery that space was possible, despite being "a borderland, a crossover area between science and magic," a wave of the wand, "a back-and-forth process in which thaumaturgy finds academic legitimacy, and academic knowledge becomes thaumaturgical." Theirs is a tale as old as Genesis chapter 3. *Each of us*, according to the Serpent, *is truly divine*. Only here in the case of the space mythos, it is gravity which binds us and keeps us grounded in this material world.

In order to mold all humanity, all time, all space, all science, religion and art into their Occult paradigm, a totalitarian fist must be applied to all without exception. The proper totalitarian regime requires complete subservience to the state, and because Cosmists were interested in universal solutions, they most certainly held to a totalitarian mindset. With the space race came the total—and *seemingly* final—deconstruction of Biblical cosmology through the sleight of hand. The good of the whole community was placed "above the freedom of the individual to go his or her own independent way." In this case, Geocentricism—or Flat Earth—was sacrificed on the cutting room floor of necromancy. The mythology of space, with its wealth of esoteric value, would once and for all be elevated above the throne of God. For Cosmists such as Chaadaev, the one virtue was to "captivate our being whether we wish it to do so or not." Chaadaev seems to whisper *pantheism* when he writes:

"There is no reason which is not obedient reason. But that is not all. Does man do anything his lifelong but seek to submit to something? ... What would happen if man could make himself so submissive that he wholly rid himself of freedom? Clearly, according to what we have said, this would be the highest degree of human perfection. Every movement of his soul would then be produced by the principle which produced all other movements of the world. Thus, instead of being separated from nature, as he now is, man would fuse with it. Instead of the feeling of his own will, which separates him from the general order of things, which makes him a being apart, he would find the feeling of universal will, or, what is the same thing, the intimate feeling, the profound awareness of his real relation to the whole creation."

One only becomes truly free by forsaking his personal freedom and becoming part of a greater evolutionary and conscious whole, so long as he allows the few but fully enlightened to lead. For the Cosmist, it mattered little if their broadly esoteric ambitions were not immediately workable or realizable. Despite their oppression under Stalin, Marxists believed in **thought as action**—as did the Cosmists. This best represents Berdyaev's characterization of *"the Russian soul."* It is facing and overcoming "a multitude of apparent contradictions" in action. It is no accident that the Russians adopted Marxist ideas more immediately and thoroughly than westerners. Both philosophical approaches wed together like a hand and glove.

428

Writes Young: "...the focus has characteristically been not on the theoretical nature of *this* or *that* concept but on the actions required by *this* or *that* ideal—not the nature of reality but the consequences of any given model of reality." For example, in the Russian tradition, it is not enough to ask: *What is true?* The true Russian must go on to ask: *What must we do about it?* Young continues: "Thus, long embedded in Russian philosophy, as we have seen in Fedorov's view of science, is a tendency to view every ology as an opportunity for an urgy, every discussion of *what is* as an invitation to consider *how to accomplish what ought to be.* And this insistence on not merely observing and defining, but radically transforming the given world is a further example of Cosmisms' thaumaturgical tendencies, of an eschatological historiosophy that links Russian Cosmism of the nineteenth and twentieth centuries to the age-old practice of magic and alchemy."

Freemasonry would have a most significant impact in Russia, "with its emphasis on the craft of constructing a better man and better world." With Freemasonry arose resurgences in alchemy—particularly through Peter the Great and his closeted Masonic friendships. As the forerunner of modern-day chemistry, alchemy is an attempt not only to create gold from base metals but to forge higher men from common mortals. Such doctrines seemed to speak explicitly to *the Russian soul.* In fact, Nikolai Fedorov's grandfather, Prince Ivan Alekseevich Gagarin, was a leading figure in Russia's Masonic movement.

Actually, many of western histories leading figures in esotericism invested their budding years in Russia. Theosophist H.P. Blavatsky is one of them. Names like George Gurdijieff, P.D. Ouspensky, Nicholas and Helena Roerich, and Rasputin will ring the chimes of familiarity for some. The Cosmists however separated themselves from the western Theosophists only so much as Blavatsky and her kind were devoted to Hindu and Buddhists esotericism, whereas the Soviets had not forgotten their Orthodox background. For them, esoteric Christianity would do— like Gnosticism. Ironically though, while the Theosophists made names for themselves glorifying a Luciferian future in their literature, the lesser known Cosmists climbed *beyond* the staircase of speculation. Writes Young: "The all but unnoticed Cosmists were devoting serious philosophical, theological, and scientific attention to matters usually considered topics for esoteric speculation, such as self-directed evolution toward higher levels of humanity; human attainment of virtual omniscience, omnipotence, and immortality; the restoration of life to the dead; the influence of astral forces on human affairs; the human attainment of superhuman powers; the radical alteration and spiritualization of the material world."

Unlike western esotericists, Soviets put *thought to action*. The Occultists gave the Americans assurance that such esoteric concepts could be nurtured beyond the tit of the mind. While much may be drawn from the space race, the myth of space itself—animated with a wave of the hand and academic thaumaturgy—has ultimately served one purpose; unify the world into one last beast-government under the UN banner for the final showdown, but not with the Soviet Union. We call this the battle of Armageddon. And there is a threat far greater than every conceivable asteroid, advancing black hole, or doomsday planet which a science-fiction writer might hurl at us, and it lives behind the *dark water* we call space. Diviners will continue their sleight of hand, much as they've always done, until the kings of the Earth muster men into battle for one common purpose—to stop the long-promised and inevitable return of our Lord.

Fyodorov said: "At the present time everything serves war; there is not one discovery which the military does not study with the aim of applying it to warfare, not one invention which they do not attempt to turn to military use." In order to achieve the goal of a new world order, which in turn would lead to man's crowning achievement in spiritual and physical evolution, they *needed* war—though a Cold War might suffice.

With *Sputnik I* the conjurer had exercised his rights—to a degree. The board was set and the pieces were moving. Henry Cabot Lodge proposed to the U.N. immediate discussions for keeping deadly weapons out of the ionosphere, "so that this vast new realm will be used for the "exclusively peaceful and scientific purposes" of the human race. Even Commander George Hoover of the United States Navy, a veteran of Project Vanguard, remarked confidently of *Sputnik*: "I think this is the first step toward the unification of the peoples of the world, whether they know it or not."

As of 1962, American scientist had science-fiction at their disposal—not forgetting Nazi scientists. With *Operation Paperclip*, the U.S. had Nazi's too. The Soviets, however—the Soviets had the Cosmists. But unlike the United States, Soviets could only take the propaganda so far. They may have succeeded in casting the technological gold of another alchemical nature, but even their mastery over art was limited. The western powers could carry it further—in fact, to the moon and back. America had something they lacked. For nearly seventy years

430

they'd been plugging away at perfecting the animated idols of Babylon. Americans had Hollywood.

In 1957 Wernher Von Braun confessed to LIFE: "We could put a man into orbit in a year...but don't ask me how we'd get him back. If a man would be ready to sacrifice his life by being fired into orbit it would answer some of the questions about space flight, but even if one volunteered we probably couldn't find anybody willing to shoot him up there."

Two years later, John Glenn volunteered with both hands. On his momentous orbit around Earth, the man who'd flown 59 combat missions during the War and another 90 in Korea was able to flip his space capsule around, mid-orbit, so that the heat-shield faced forward while Glenn rode backward. "I started having my troubles with the automatic control system late in the first orbit," Glenn told LIFE in March 9, 1962. "Something was obviously wrong with the system and it became necessary for me to control the capsule's movements by hand." He added: "The idea that I was flying this thing myself and proving on our first orbital test that a man's capabilities are needed in space was one of the high spots of the day."

Upon re-entering Earth's fiery atmosphere over the Hawaiian isles at an orbital velocity of approximately 17,500 miles per hour—he would safely land in the Atlantic, just north of the Grand Turk Islands—Colonel John Glenn continued piloting *Friendship 7* backwards. Because three rocket boosters "were firing backwards against the direction of the flight, I had the sensation of accelerating back toward Hawaii. Actually the rockets were only slowing me down." It is a feat which he had never once attempted during the War, in Korea, or any time thereafter, and no daredevil has yet attempted to revisit his legacy. How he gained such mastery of a wingless space capsule, using only boosters to find his landing zone, no reporter has ever dared to ask.

IMMORTALITY FOR ALL—OUR COPERNICAN UNIVERSE & THE WORSHIP OF PANTHEISM

THE GULLIBLE CHRISTIAN WILL SIT WIDE-EYED AND CROSS-LEGGED, intently hinged upon every word of the astronomer, who has seemingly grown confused between his telescope and recent readings in Eastern mysticism as he amazes his hearers with tall-tales from the furthest reaches of our cosmic flea market. That poor gullible soul—I myself used to be one of them, not recognizing a bold faced lie when I saw it—convinces himself that the God of the Bible is somehow behind all of this, if only we can grasp the right verbiage, when in fact the astronomer has not confused the *two*—the telescope with his library. The Copernican model, with its promise of ascension to heaven, most certainly does arise from cosmological books, just not the Bible. And it leads us not to the true Creator, as we blindly convince ourselves of, but the oldest religion in the world, which as you likely already guessed began in the Garden—the humanists dream.

God is not the infinite cosmos, nor is His creation a manifestation of Him. Yet we are told by astrophysicists to "marvel at the remarkable symmetry and wonder" of our universe when observing the clusters of galaxies and invisible dark matter which supposedly fills the bulk of its open gaps—all of which proves nothing but collected data on a computer screen—and when stretching billions of light-years across from end-to-end, incredibly match the neurons in a mouse's brain.

Similarly, NASA's Spritzer space telescope informs us there is a stellar system made up of two intertwined chains just like a double helix in a DNA molecule, and stretching 80 lightyears in length. These most clever of deceptions, both the neurons of a mouse's brain and the strand of our own DNA, effectively wrap themselves around an element of God's truth and then distort them into a humanistic worship of the self.

We are expected to believe a black hole, which is nothing more than the fantastical ponderings self-created in a storytellers head, resembles the cell nucleus. Furthermore, a black hole's event horizon—a sort of point of no return where the gravitational pull sucks objects into the black hole—also resembles the nuclear membrane, or so we are expected to believe. Physics will remind us that a cell is made up of molecules, and molecules made up of atoms, and atoms composed of a nucleus and electrons, which in turn revolve around the nucleus. Planets, we are conclusively led to believe, are electrons and the sun the nucleus, the atom being our solar system, with the galaxy being a molecule, and the entire universe a cell. The multitude of solar systems, so they conclude, makes up the remaining cells.

The universe as a whole, or so the greatest deception of this age goes, can grow just like a gigantic brain, with the firing of brain cells mirroring the expanding galaxies around us. The gullible Christian forsakes his Bible to embrace this, convincing himself that the mystical message of astronomy is somehow confused in the verbiage—that we couldn't possibly be embracing what its bold-faced conclusions demand—that we are gods, every one of us.

Basically, as astrophysicists and astronomers seek to prove; our universe is one singular cell of many inside a gigantic living organism, all of which gives birth and then dies again. Everything small and large is interrelated as a whole, says both the gurus of Eastern Mysticism and our priests of Scientism. THE COSMOS IS ALIVE! And looking into the face of the Supreme Being—pay attention, dear brother and sister— should and when he decide to reveal him or her or itself to us, is to see the Living Universe. He is us, our embodiment of light—and we are he— his vessels.

Let this be known to the man with discernment; God is not the universe, nor is the universe a manifestation of Him. And somewhere along the line, when the Word of God lost its Divine merit, our parents— as did their parents and grandparents before them—volunteered their children through a societal mush pot of delusional thinking, that we be handed a globe and led by the hands of strangers into the apostasy of pantheism.

A discerning Christian should find it strange indeed to learn that this laughable "space race" began in Russia during the adolescent years of Darwinism, years before the Wright Brothers even flew, and its dancing partner was trans-humanism. So it began with trans-humanism, and there it shall end as the capstone of Luciferian wisdom.

I introduce you to a man by the name of Konstantin Tsiolkovsky, father of astronautic theory. Tsiolkovsky was also a mystic. His mentor was Nikolai Fedoror, a so-called Christian who openly advocated "immortality for all." This would be accomplished, he claimed, through the pursuit of trans-humanism, whereas the crowning achievement of Evolution would be man's union in his biological human condition with the technology which would ultimately seek to surpass him, thereby becoming one and the same, whereas intellect and physiology may increase until their end-means are met. Accordingly, where Fedoror's vision was concerned, while achieving immortality through his biological and physiological union with technology was a worthy cause, that and the resurrection of all people who ever lived would prove two inseparable goals.

Is this not Plato's Gospel of Ascension?

Eugenics, the same doctrine which embraced the holocaust and abortion clinics of many, has not been so easily forgotten. That and transhumanism flourish together and must remain together. Darwinism must have its supreme race, Lucifer must have his sacrifice, and our biological union with the mark is assuredly the long-awaited answer to both. If biology alone cannot perform the task, then the mark must.

It is here where we can recognize, if we have the eyes and ears for discernment, the promised Great Delusion of this age. We can see where it fermented, where it is soon arriving, and how it has so easily enveloped us with its illustrious promises and Hollywood narrative. Perhaps the greater deception still is the mark to come. There's this longstanding belief in the faith community that it will seem repulsive to the Elect when in fact the lie may be beautiful as any before us, as this globe delusion already proves to those of us who embrace the full unbroken Testimony of God concerning Himself—the joyous cosmology. If they cannot deny the lie now, why will they deny it then?

What is this space race, my fellow discerning Christian, but a transfiguration of the soul through death, the cheating of sins' consequence, a back-door approach to heaven if you will, apart from the necessary repentance which assuredly leads to God's forgiveness through the atoning sacrifice of our Lord? Indeed, man has a longstanding history to desire the conquest of heaven by his own strength of mind rather than accepting the free gift of salvation through Jesus Christ our Creator and Lord. Surely, a discerning Christian must see that we've been lied to.

We have been lied to again and again and again and again. In fact there is no end to it—the lies. Yet in the midst of confusion—really, there is no end to it—some of us have been woken by the Words of the Spirit, like Lot and his family in Sodom before destruction, as a means to escape. And so also we must face the graver possibility, that not everyone will be rescued. Just as many of our brethren in Christ have been deceived from the beginning, and even now choose to continue not the first lie seeded centuries ago, but the lie within the lie within the lie into tomorrow's lie and well into next week's lie to the following lie until the very last lie is told, so too will many willingly take the mark, if only because the lie seems beautiful and innocent to them or otherwise not worth looking the fool for refuting.

Perhaps Mark Twain said it best. "It's easier to fool people than to convince them that they have been fooled."

THE FLICKER INDUCED HYPNOTIC STATE: FOCAULT'S PENDULUM & THE EFFECTIVE FREQUENCY OF COLD WAR ESPIONAGE

THE WORLD IS A PEEP SHOW OF THE UNKNOWN. There is an E-Ticket attraction for everything that is unseen by the common practitioner but which might be imaginably conjured with the mind. The mystics of Scientism and the philosophers of academia, as well as the prophets of Churchianity, all of whom promise to lift the curtain on his stage and dazzle the curious sort with exotica incarnate—should their inquisitor purchase a ticket—have much to profit here. There is no shortage of master magicians on Planet Earth. And yet should a man situate himself center stage on a stool and read out loud from his Bible—the Spirit gives illuminating Testimony to many curiosities of life within its pages—he would have a difficult time selling enough tickets to fill the first few rows.

Perhaps he is only reading from 1 Chronicles 16:30—a history book, where genre is concerned—which boldly states: "Fear before Him, all the earth: the world also shall be stable, that it be not moved!" Fascinating exposition of truth for some, just not for most, it seems.

Globe Earth and everything that can be found within its supposed 25,000-mile circumference has made a name for itself among its own endless line-up of Vaudevillians and humbugs. Verification of the Copernican model is no exception. In 1851 French physicist Leon Foucault suspended a 61-pound weight from a 200-foot-long wire at the Pantheon in Paris and set it swinging. *Oohs* and *ahhs* were reported to have followed. For the Copernican, it was the first real proof of a rotating Earth. But more importantly, for the patron of "New Astronomy," the Bible had finally been disproven. Celebrations were in order. For astronomer Selim H. Peabody it was a "beautiful experiment" and a marvelous success. Yet it was nothing more than a parlor trick for the wide-eyed masses. And for the following century, at carnivals across the western world, Foucault's pendulum would prove a star attraction.

Never-the-less, despite the mainstream media's typical ear-tickling narrative, honest men were present as eye-witness to Foucault's premier experiment. Dr. Shoepffer served as one of them, and he wasn't impressed. According to author F.E. Pasche in his book, *50 Reasons: Copernicus or the Bible* (1915), Shoepffer had this to say of Foucault's sleight of hand:

> "In an introductory speech Dr. Menzzer at Quedlinburg showed that until then there had been no proof for the Copernican hypothesis, the so-called proofs being, after close investigation, just as many confutations, until the Foucault pendulum showed the rotation of the earth uncontrovertibly. The pendulum was tied, the string was burnt, the swingings began, but the pendulum deviated to the left, instead of to the right. It was hastily brought to rest. New burning of the string. This time the deviation was the one desired, and we were invited again to be present in the church the next morning at eight o'clock, to be convinced that the deviation agrees with the theory. On the following morning, however, we saw that the pendulum during the night had changed its mind, and had from the deviation to the right again returned to the left. To me this new proof did not seem to be quite in order. My belief in the Copernican doctrine was shaken by the speech of Dr. Menzzer, and I concluded to go to Berlin for an explanation. After seeing the pendulum-experiment here also and strangely again with a deviation to the left, I went to Alexander v. Humboldt, who was indeed ever the first refuge of those seeking information. He received me very friendly and spoke the memorable words: 'I have known too for a long time that as yet we have no proof for the Copernican system, but I shall never dare to be the first to attack it. Don't rush into the wasps' nest. You will but bring upon yourself the scorn of the thoughtless multitude.'"

Foucault's pendulum is best served as pigeon glitter for the typical rank and file—those preferring platform magic and susceptibility over their own God-given right to common sense. In other words, why fall prey to a humbug showman's sleight of hand when El Shaddai is being revealed by the man sitting mostly alone and reading his Bible from the stool? Yet it is still to this day preformed—Foucault's pendulum, that is—as champion-evidence of the globe, and in highly regarded museums across the world. Ironically, such lapses in judgement are as Paul McCartney once sang:

> "But the fool on the hill
>
> Sees the sun going down
>
> And the eyes in his head
>
> See the world spinning round."

Released as part of the Beatles *Magical Mystery Tour* in 1967, *The Fool on the Hill* arrived in perfect historic timing—where soundtracks are concerned. The Copernican Maestro's next great stage performance, seeing as how Foucault's pendulum had lost its thrill, was about to be unveiled in their latest Vaudevillian platform—the television. Specifically, the Apollo 11 moon landing. The gentlemanly adventures behind Cold War espionage were already well regarded and fantasized over, all thanks to spy author Ian Fleming and filmmaking producer Albert R. Broccoli. While admittedly fictional, razor-edged bowling hats, ejecting convertibles and Maxwell Smarts shoes helped to quench the nuances for the unseen and plausibly unknowable until our government could come up with something better. They gave their American audience and the world a glimpse—or rather, a show—of the hidden war between the western allies and the Eastern Bloc which, as President Kennedy promised, they could finally follow.

Some three decades earlier Freemason H.G. Wells wrote in an unpublished memo:

> "The Universities and the associated intellectual organizations throughout the world should function as a police of the mind."

Well's police of the mind would very soon arrive in the glorious medium of television. In their book, *The Ascendancy of Scientific Dictatorship,* authors Phillip Darrell Collins and Paul David Collins had this to say:

> "The TV 'world' becomes a self-fulfilling prophecy: the mass mind takes shape, its participants acting according to media-derived impulses and believing them to be their own personal volition arising out of their own desires and needs. In such a situation, whoever controls the screen controls the future, the past, and the present (Nelson)."

Effective frequency refers to the number of times a person must be exposed to an advertising message before it is deemed effective. In 1969, same year as the moon landing, Herbert Krugman conducted a series of

438

experiments regarding the effect television had on a person's brainwaves. He worked for General Electric, by the way—which currently owns and operates NBC. Accordingly, there are only three levels of exposure—never a fourth or a fifth.

They are:

1. Curiosity

2. Recognition

3. Decision.

4. Rinse and repeat.

"Krugman monitored a person through many trials and found that in less than one minute of television viewing, the person's brainwaves switched from Beta waves — brainwaves associated with active, logical thought — to primarily Alpha waves. When the subject stopped watching television and began reading a magazine, the brainwaves reverted to Beta waves."

In Krugman's report, his findings particularly note: "the mode of response to television is more or less constant and very different from the response to print. That is, the basic electrical response of the brain is clearly to the medium and not to content difference.... [Television is] a communication medium that effortlessly transmits huge quantities of information not thought about at the time of exposure."

With a remote in hand, the viewer convinces himself that he is in control of his TV programming when in fact the TV is programming him; effective frequency or police of the mind. Within seconds of turning on his television, his mind has already slipped into the hypnotic state. That remote, if he should ever convince himself that it were a wand obeying his every command, has now turned the spell back upon him. His brain waves have entered into the "Alpha state." This is the realm of witches—the trance, the enclosed space of meditation and relaxation; where magic meets our altered state of consciousness. He has convinced himself that his susceptibilities to gathering information, particularly on a subconscious level, only affect his memory pool, when in fact he has overlooked the far more grim reality: our very beliefs are formed by our memories.

Writes Laurie Cabot in her book, *Power of the Witch: The Earth, the Moon, and the Magical Path to Enlightenment* (1989):

> "Alpha is the springboard for all psychic and magical workings. It is the heart of witchcraft."

Elsewhere, Cabot adds:

> "The science of witchcraft is based upon our ability to enter altered states of consciousness we call "alpha"....This is a state associated with relaxation, meditation, and dreaming....In alpha the minds open up to non-ordinary forms of communication....Here we also experience out-of-body sensations and psychokinesis and receive mystical, visionary information."

If the connoisseur of God's written Word, sitting alone on his stool center stage, has a difficult time assembling the crowd while Foucault's pendulum—or particular to our own stage performances, the television—keeps the masses away, it is because humanity has chosen the realm of mysticism and meditation over the God-given powers of critical thinking.

"But!" my critics often demand, "Haven't you seen proof of the globe? It's on TV!"

Did God not warn His elect that a strong delusion would come our way? Indeed He did. And why would it come but that we might follow the desires of our heart and obey the lie (2 Thessalonians 2:11)? And perhaps, by delivering the wondrous world of television into our daily lives—as many as three in the average household—God knew, by His own divine wisdom, what would nurture those delusional desires. Meanwhile, the man of God knows the Creator has exclusively chosen to reveal Himself through the Beta waves which emanate from in His Word, and has neglected any appearances on television or in the media.

Apparently, President Richard M. Nixon did too. He once famously stated, "The American people don't believe anything until they see it on television."

So it should come as no surprise that the man who prefers a remote control and the alpha state of mind should gaze rather dreamily into the flickering glow of the NWO's mind police and convince himself that, somehow, President Nixon could dial up Neil Armstrong on the moon and converse with him from a landline telephone.

440

"And Aaron Cast down His Rod..." HOW THE TWO WITNESSES ARE COMING TO EXPOSE THE MAGIK OF GLOBE EARTH

1

THIS FACT IS WELL REGARDED BY ANYONE in the know; the United States of America, according to NASA's own account of things, suddenly grew several times larger in the year 2012. I am of course referring to that year's release of the Blue Marble. So behemoth was North America's proportions that Los Angeles and New York almost enveloped the whole of the globe. While one might suspiciously finger GMO and late night binge eating as the culprit behind this unsettling turn of events, coming to the knowledge that we have not one single real photograph of the Earth in our possession should settle any otherwise irrational fears. In fact, Globe Earth is created. More precisely, the so-called planet that sends us hurdling through infinite space at thousands of miles per hour is only data interpreted and reimagined, not by God—but artists entrusted with a spreadsheet.

God's own Testimony concerning His Creation, according to His Word, has me content knowing that Globe Earth is nothing more than a figment of our more perverse imaginations. Conclusively, many in the know will see to it—they will demand of it—that NASA has committed itself to a series of preposterous blunders. Though treasonous these actions may be—mismanagement it is not. This is precisely how Globe Earth's pimps and handlers have always wanted it.

Same goes for the July 20, 1969 Apollo moon landing. That also is not a poorly construed product of American Cold War mishandlings. In short, fifty years of good and dedicated detective work have upended any such notion that Armstrong and Aldrin's space romp should be taken factually. It was an elaborate hoax. The photography is sloppy. More precisely, they are some of the worst fabrications in all of human history. My readers have likely all seen what cannot be unseen by the thoughtful eye; mainly, Ball Earth. It's literally cropped into the background. Need I mention multiple contradictory angles of light, the flag which flaps gaily in windless flight, and not to be overlooked—the lack of burn marks or imprints from the lunar lander when contrasted with the imprints of Armstrong's boot. Then of course there is the "Earth rise" to contend with. I could go on. There's as many holes in this as there are craters on the moon. NASA's manipulation and deceit has become legendary in its shamelessness.

What happens when we pull the leg from a table? Surely, the whole table, and everything upon it, will topple.

Yet it is my contention that we are not simply dealing with a historical hoax. More precisely, it's a stage performance, if you will—more on that in a moment. Mass deception is quite easy to implement, mainly because mankind hungers endlessly for it. The heart is deceitful above all else and desperately wicked (Jeremiah 17:9). We need only hold that obese portrait of the United States from 2012 in a line-up of other CG "Blue Marble" Earth images, and the obedient patriot of Scientism will stomp his feet and clinch his teeth. Perhaps this will only be committed intellectually. But it will likely be done, either in the darkness of his skull or physically in person. He will not stand for our admission to his religious error.

Again, my entire point being, this programming is all by design.

2

THE TWO WITNESSES NEED NO INTRODUCTION to the lifelong deliberator and considerate connoisseur of eschatology. Our church fathers Tertullian, Hippolytus, and Bellarmine have long fingered Enoch and Elijah as our missing suspects. Even Irenaeus, who was the disciple of Polycarp, who in turn was the disciple of the Apostle John, confirmed this aboriginal Christian belief. The Book of Enoch, which was wildly important to the writings of the Apostles, is quoted from its very opening: "The words of the blessing of Enoch, with which he blessed the elect and righteous, who will be living in the day of tribulation, when all the wicked and godless people are to be removed from the Earth (Enoch 1:1)."

I believe we are to take Enoch's opening remarks to mean: the prophet's ministry—his written words in the very least, if not his physical person—is directed specifically toward the last generation. My reader will also likely concur. All signs point to the times in which we live. We are that last generation. It is a rather bizarre turn of events, but it appears as though his ministry is only *now* beginning. And may I be so bold as to proclaim; those of us who pick up his banner of Flat Earth in these perilous last days, exposing the great and dreadful delusional lie to anyone with ears to hear and eyes to see—should we do so for God's glory, and not our own—we are preparing the way for Enoch's soon arriving ministry. Enoch's removal from canon is no mistake.

At any rate, if the Spirit counsels us then we shall know them when they arrive, whatever names they go by. I wholly expect the two prophets to be not so dissimilar in function from Moses and Aaron, who found particular disfavor with Pharaoh's sorcerers and conjurers. It's rather ironic in a way, and well regarded by anyone in the know, that so much of this grand deception—I am speaking about the globe and everything that is associated with the beast government, which rules over the globe—finds its identity in Hermeticism and the occultist Mystery Schools of ancient Greece and Babylon and Egypt. I guess what I'm trying to say is, the wizards of Pharaoh's government, who once shackled the better discretion of their subjects, are very much alive and functioning today. The spells are cast, and the blinders very much still in place.

I feel well within my comfort zone to conclude—and perhaps even announce to the newcomer—that NASA's entire space catalogue, which includes not only the Apollo moon landings but the day-to-day operations of the International Space Station, are important components of the spell.

Do you believe in Magik? I do. I've looked into the abyss. The darkness has eyes. For a moment I saw them. Make no mistake—the abyss turned its gaze upon me. And there have been times, when looking into these matters—I could hear whispers lifting from its damnable depths. Even the walls seemed to breathe.

Pharaoh's school of conjurers, being the proprietors and custodians of Globe Earth, still lead the main stream media's narrative through the many stage performances of our day. We need only look to the December 14, 2012 shooting massacre at Sandy Hook Elementary School in Newtown, Connecticut, to expose a plethora of others. Super Bowl XLVII is no accident. That the "slain" children were paraded in front of us almost two months later, to 111-million worldwide viewers, as part of the Sandy Hook choir, was not *an oopsy-daisy*. That President Obama was able to raise the dead by hugging a "slain" Newtown girl only days after the shooting, and in view of the press—this meeting was publicized—was not a lapse in judgement. Sandy Hook's mortally wounded principal, who is said to be loved by many, suddenly emerged some four months later, only she was a victim of the Boston bombing. And then there's Adam Lanza, the man who is reported to have murdered 20 children and 6 adult workers at Sandy Hook. His former classmate, going by the name of Alex Israel, later emerged as Katie Foley, sister of James Foley, who was supposedly beheaded by ISIS on camera. And let's not overlook actor David Wheeler, playing two roles in one movie—a responding SWAT officer and mourning "dad" of a little child. We were all given the opportunity to observe such glaring contradictions and willfully choose our part in the denial.

These crisis drills, as well as everything NASA has to offer us, are designed to look fabricated for a reason. This is subconscious human conditioning; psychological warfare on a subliminal level—or rather, the masterful art of deception perfected. In order to buy into this filth, we are expected to swim upstream against what our own God given gift of common sense speaks against, all so that the trauma and the belief which our denial demands binds our hearts to a degree of irreconcilable wickedness. Look no further than "Performance Witchcraft." I'll say this again. Pharaoh's virtuosos of the spiritual realm are alive and well. And this is where witchcraft essentially musters its muscle—the performance. When capturing the audience's attention, by getting them to admit belief, the spell is enacted—even from the television screen. And one of its sickening side-effects is the tepid sort of person who prefers spiritual sleepiness.

Let me be clear on this. Sandy Hook and the Boston bombing, 9-11 alongside an entire fleet of admitted false flag and "staged" attacks, as well as the 2016 Miami gay nightclub shooting, not overlooking our most recent 2017 shooting massacre in Las Vegas, ultimately have little to do with gun control. Everything points to the MARK of the Beast. The spell is cast. And many, who choose not to break themselves of it—Cold Turkey, as drug culture would say—are in critical danger. Their spiritual discernment has been compromised. Even worse, they've already shown themselves to be of such ignoble character, even when presented with the bold-faced deception, as to happily embrace the lie.

We must shake the tree. Violently if need be. With all of our God-given might we must grasp the tree by its trunk, pray: "Lord, help me," and sway its branches side to side—all in hopes that an apple or two may fall. The days when evil might be openly exposed, our conspirators threatened with the end of a rope, are forever gone—until our LORD returns, that is—if indeed there ever was such a time. This will not be seen as an act of love by many—particularly the apostate church. They will see to it that their worldliness is insured, in the incident that our efforts shaking at the base of the tree should, as a side effect, make damaged goods of their worldly possessions. But what is a soul worth when weighed against the indebtedness of their emotional comforts? The sleeping soul shall grind his teeth and claw at his bed posts in a desperate effort to keep his lukewarm posture preserved. He would rather flex endlessly between a fervent declared love of God and manic worship of the world. And we shall be slapped for sure. Indeed, breaking the spell will not be taken as an act of love by anyone involved.

So too must the coming Prophets conduct their ministry in such manner. There will be no monuments or postage stamps named in their honor. We are told: "And when they shall have finished their testimony, the beast that ascendeth out of the bottomless pit shall make war against them, and shall overcome them, and kill them. And their bodies shall lie in the street (Revelation 11:7-8)." We are further informed, the nations of the world "that dwell upon the earth shall rejoice over them, and make merry, and shall send gifts one to another; because these two prophets tormented them that dwelt on the earth (Revelation 11:10)."

Pharaoh's administrators of the dark arts were exposed with Aaron's rod. So too will God's two chosen Prophets shatter this present illusion. They will overturn Satan's entire bag of tricks with the most easygoing flap of their sackcloth and whisk of their beard. They will most certainly expose Global Warming and the weather manipulation which has inflicted so many with a simple prayer. Specifically, they will "have the power to shut heaven, that it rain not in the days of their prophecy; and have the power over waters to turn them to blood, and to smite the earth with all plagues, as often as they will (Revelation 6:11)." And should anyone attempt to hurt them, should the enemies of truth deem such exposure unloving and intolerant towards the comforts of their chosen illusion, it is said according to John that fire will proceed from their mouth. Anyone who stands in their way will be immediately devoured.

That is all we can do in preparation for their arrival. We need only shake the tree to see which apples fall. And pray. Pray that the spell might be lifted from our brothers and sisters in the faith. Pray that they will choose Aaron's rod, which devoured Pharaoh's serpents and the Prophet's sackcloth over every fabricated illusion which Satan binds us to—including Globe Earth.

"And Moses and Aaron went in unto Pharaoh, and they did so as the LORD had commanded: and Aaron cast down his rod before Pharaoh….. (Exodus 7:10)."

"Or Else the Silver Cord Be Loosed..." THE ASTRAL PROJECTION OF A SPACE WALK (& the ISS Is Its Temple)

"THE SILVER CORD" IS THE LANGUAGE OF MYSTICS, for we see that it is a link between two bodies, the astral and physical. During astral projection—the act of separating one's consciousness from their physical self—the cord grants assurance to its projector that he will not wander so far from his body as to lose sight of it. Should he do so, wander inconsolably that is, the silver chord will most assuredly act as a rubber band and retract him right back into the body. It is the spirit body's lifeline to the physical body the same way that our umbilical cord is our lifeline to our mother's body during gestation. To separate from the silver cord is to die. If the cord breaks, then the separation is irreversible. In such an event, a "permanent astral projection" cannot be undone.

So too, in a likewise manner, must the astronaut wear his silver cord, for "space" is also the language of mystics.

My reader will assuredly understand by this point that when I speak of "space," I am referring to two things. Firstly, the deception, for the Bible makes no mention of space, nothing more than the firmament, which separates us from a celestial body of water, and most gloriously of all, the heaven of heavens. It is ironic indeed that the space-walk takes place in a tank of water, where bubbles frequently rise, and can even be seen doing so on camera. It is in outer space, or low earth orbit, we are expected to believe, where astronauts Luca Parmitano and Tim Kopra, having left the "underwater" ISS on two separate occasions for spacewalks of their own, almost drowned. We are rest assured by NASA that this will never happen again, as astronauts are now thoroughly equipped with snorkel gear when venturing out into the inhospitable vacuum, where puddles of water are waiting to pounce upon and ultimately strangle them.

Secondly, and this is perhaps the most important truth, the reader should invariably understand my position by now, that NASA is and has

447

been from its very conception far more than a deception of Science. It is nothing more than a taxpayer funding for the occult, whereas the worship of Satan may be played out by his Masonic disciples. The gullible citizens of its sponsoring country and throughout the world are invited to participate in the televised worship service. By watching the witchcraft played out, and simply by believing in it, they are most certainly adding validity to the performance.

Astral projection is essentially a back-alley expression of witchcraft—the Yogic tradition of transcendental meditation also embraces it—whereas the astral traveler can choose to explore this world while leaving his body behind or in a like manner, explore worlds beyond our own. How many of these worlds there are throughout the occults various branches of thought is a matter of great debate, but it seems clear that there is at least a plane that overlaps the physical world consisting of the energetic or subtle bodies of all that exists in this world. Secondly there is an underworld, where chthonic spirits reside alongside the spirits of the dead. And lastly, there is an overworld, or plane of light, which is inhabited by "The Shining Ones"—gods, angels, and other etheric beings.

The astronaut's career is focused upon transcendence into the overworld so that he might perhaps live out the promises of The Shining Ones. As he leaves his transport behind, just as in astral projection, the silver cord allows his astral person to wander only so far that his leash can aid him in finding his way back home to his physical person.

So too we are told that the devotee to the act of astral projection will build unto himself a temple on his or her frequented astral plane. He may wish, we are told, to create a place where he might relax, worship his gods, cast spells, and perform divination or simply entertain guests.

The ISS is that temple. And it functions in all of these manners.

Once again we are presented with the bold-faced allegory of the mystics, being man's transcendence from death, and most assuredly by his own free will, through the exploration and conquest of space. This is the author's contention, anyhow. I am quite certain many of my readers will agree—but certainly not all.

The oldest known reference to "the silver cord" can be found with Solomon. He says it like this:

"Or ever the silver cord be loosed, or the golden bowl be broken, or the pitcher be broken at the fountain, or the wheel

448

broken at the cistern. 7 Then shall the dust return to the earth as it was: and the spirit shall return unto God who gave it."

(Ecclesiastes 12:6-7)

The silver cord and bowl spoken of in Ecclesiastes promise certain death, but not in the manner which every other religion or government institution under the governing reins of Satan would have it. Most likely the bowl was used as an oil lamp for light, suspended by the chord. Dying is compared to the breaking of the chord, whereas the bowl violently falls and shatters. The flame is extinguished. Never will it light the room again. Similarly, if the pitcher and the pulley which lets it down into the well should break, no longer can water be drawn. The functionality of life has ended. Death has conquered. Man returns to dust, his Spirit unto God who gave it. There is no hope of Salvation or eternity apart from a second birth, which is the soul united with a resurrected body—an act which Jesus referred to as being born again.

Martin Luther said it like this:

"And ye, in putting them [the departed souls] in heaven, hell and purgatory, destroy the arguments wherewith Christ and Paul prove the resurrection... And again, if the souls be in heaven, tell me why they be not in as good a case as the angels be? And then what cause is there of the resurrection?"

The invitation remains for the soul who has yet to give his life to the Lord. I shall present it now and have little doubt as to my intention in presenting it later. The Bible makes this truth abundantly clear. He who refuses the free gift of Salvation through Jesus Christ, but rather attempts it on his own, this is the closest to heaven or the furthermost reaches of space he'll ever be—in a NASA pool. There is no one who has ascended to our Father in heaven but Jesus our Lord.

He alone holds the keys to life and death. When conquering death, our Lord was born again into an eternal and glorious resurrection. By this we can know with full assurance that His atoning sacrifice was sufficient to the Father and that we too who bind Him closely in our hearts will rise at His second coming.

He is most certainly returning soon to reclaim His creation. Mystics and occultists and astronauts be warned.

"*I Sing the Body Electric!*" THE KUNDALINI FORCE IS STRONG WITH NASA ASTRONAUT EDGAR MITCHELL

APOLLO 11 ASTRONAUT NEIL ARMSTRONG NEVER WITNESSED a single star. Not from the moon. Not from the space between the Earth and the moon. Not anywhere beyond our own atmosphere. In a 1970 interview with the BBC, Armstrong reported to *The Sky at Night* host Patrick Moore: "The sky is a deep black when viewed from the moon, as it is when viewed from cis-lunar space, the space between the earth and the moon. The earth is the only visible object other than the sun that can be seen, although there have been reports of seeing planets. I myself did not see planets from the surface, but I suspect they might be visible."

Contrarily, Apollo 14 Astronaut Ed Mitchell beheld stars. An entire smorgasbord of heavenly delights opened up before him, each luminary dilating and shining "ten times brighter" than anything he's ever experienced on Earth. During an October 1993 interview with *Hinduism Today*, Mitchell recalled the euphoric effect of his 480,000 mile roundtrip journey to the moon and back was such that: "I suddenly experienced the universe as intelligent, loving... harmonious." What he gazed into was "the primordial energy of the universe, the primal and subtlest energies." The vast canvas of outer space wasn't *just* his crowning mountaintop affair. No, no. What Mitchell experienced, he assured *Hinduism Today*, was "the kundalini force."

Accordingly, the Kundalini force is the dormant power, or primal sexual energy, lying present in every human being, and a key concept in Dharma, which touches upon a multitude of Indian religions — Hinduism, Buddhism, Sikhism and Jainism. Practically speaking, yoga heavily relies upon kundalini, which is said to reside at the base of our spine and may be invoked through a series of breathing exercises, among other activities. The word means '*coiled one,*' and if kundalini immediately invokes images of the serpent in the garden for my Christian reader, it's because such a mystic practitioner believes the

450

wise-one is tragically *mistaken* by each and every one of us. As the representative of our Divine Mother, the serpent *awakens* the truly spiritual human—apparently. And yet it remains coiled for most of us—*we* the unenlightened—biding its time through ages past, waiting on the moment when each individual's eyes are awakened and, through a combination of physical, astral, and mental methods, the soul begins to take charge of its "rightful domain."

Ed Mitchell was raised in the fundamentalist Christian faith. Those two ways of thinking, however—Christianity and Science, he says, "are not compatible." Mitchell is a true apostate. Regarding the discrepancy between Biblical Inerrancy and the Scientific Method, he further explains, "I now describe our universe a little differently; as evolutionary, intelligent, participatory and continuing to learn….What we call God is the mind of the universe, and what we experience as physical reality is the body of the universe, if you want to anthropomorphize. The creative force behind the universe is the same creative force we experience within ourselves. The atman and Brahman aspects of consciousness have to be put together in order to *create* reality."

A Christian with only a *smidgeon* of discernment should still be able to separate what Ed Mitchell is implying with what the Bible tells us of reality. Assuredly, Mitchell is correct; the Science behind this Copernican Delusion and Christianity are *not* compatible. God is not His own creation and therefore the universe is *most-assuredly* not self-aware. We are furthermore not divine atomic cells within an ever-expanding brain, which Science has a mind to prove—excuse the pun. Rather, the Psalmist assures us, "*The heavens declare the glory of God, and the sky above proclaims His handiwork. (Psalm 19:1)*"

Just this last week I was at a museum with my family in Montreal, and there was a somewhat daffy exhibit where they displayed two comparative photos, the first showing the milk and mammary glands within a woman's breast and the next a fake satellite image of *deep* space. It was kind of like, *which is space and which is the woman's inner breast?* The entire point of this "Science" presentation was to discreetly tutor us—my wife and our kids, if only in a subconscious whisper—that space itself is God. And we're His organisms. I guess in this case, if we're being technical, God is a woman—scientifically speaking.

"In the beginning you laid the foundations of the earth, and the heavens are the work of your hands" (Psalm 102:25)

In the *Book of the Law* (1904), Occultist Aleister Crowly speaks affectionately of the Egyptian sky goddess Nuit. She is traditionally portrayed in Egyptian hieroglyphics in the naked form, likewise arched over the Earth in a sexual manner (exactly where Moses would place the firmament) and dressed only with the heavenly constellations. In later writings Crowley himself identified Nuit with the Kundalini force. But namely in *"Book of the Law"* he writes, "Heaven is not a place where God lives. Nuit is Heaven itself."

Mitchell is resolved knowing, should the world's leading politicians be exposed to this therapeutic stimulus—"space" and "the kundalini force," that is—a unification process might ensue, aiding the world peace process. Actually, he clumsily straddles the fragile balance beam which might expose this end-times space deception for what it is, particularly our intended "perception of reality," when he candidly tells *Hinduism Today*. "I define God as the intelligent function. The soul would be that residual aspect of self that is eternal. I believe that the purpose of the universe is to organize itself and to experience physical reality, of which we're a part of in creating that."

To this day and now more than ever, the Apollo moon missions are riddled with surmounting contradictions and inconsistencies. NASA investigator David Orbell, hoping to come to a clearer understanding of Apollo's *"stars, no-stars"* enigma, was able to sit in on one of Mitchell's paid talks at the Hilton Metropole Hotel in Birmingham, England during its October 2012 *Autographica* program. Concerning the first man to *supposedly* walk on the moon, Orbell writes: "Neil Armstrong is credited as the astronaut with the greatest interest in observing the heavens. He had flown jet fighters at 40,000 feet to observe the clarity of the universe at that rarefied altitude."

In what Orbell describes as a venomous exchange (on Mitchell's part) between he and the sixth man to walk on the moon, which "stunned the large audience—many whom were filming," the once-astronaut sharply exclaimed, "'He [Neil Armstrong] didn't know what he was talking about!'"

Immediately following their irritable crossfire (Mitchell had returned talking about a subject which apparently excited him—our inevitable alien visitors), Orbell approached retired Air Force Brigadier General Charles Duke, actively signing autographs just down the hall.

Duke served as Lunar Module pilot on Apollo 16 and was "officially" the tenth man to walk on the Moon in 1972. Notably, Edgar Mitchell was his counterpart on Apollo 14 in 1971.

Orbell asked.

Duke replied, "No we couldn't see the stars anytime on the voyage. It was too bright!"

"The Earth was Formless and Void..."
ENSNARED IN THE CANOPY OF THE GNOSTIC SPACEMEN: "GAP THEORY" MYSTICS

WELL BEYOND PLUTO'S ORBIT, WHERE THE HELIOPAUSE kisses the boundaries of interstellar space, solar winds howled *goodbye* to Voyager 1, which suddenly had the distinction of becoming the first craft to leave the suns dominion behind. Meanwhile, here on Earth, the embers of Plato's dreams glowed ashy-red. In a rather symbolic gesture, the spiritual aspirations of the ancient Mysteries had finally been realized. The date was August 25, 2012. First launched 35 years earlier—in September of 1977—the twin satellites *Voyager 1* and *2* had accomplished what they initially set out to do. There's was an anthropologic mission peering in on the closeted behaviors of the wandering luminaries, and on the day of Voyager's final ascension, one thing seemed certain. The planets—Mars, Jupiter, Saturn, Uranus, Neptune, and Pluto; including their moons—each gave witness to the scars of a galaxy torn apart by the lusts of war. Edward Stone, chief scientist of the Voyager program, declared of the heavens: "It was Voyager that focused our attention on the importance of collisions." He added, "The cosmic crashes were potent sculptors of the Solar System." The stories they told *seemed*Gnostic in origin.

Decades earlier, the man who founded the Institute for Creation Research in 1970, served as its president, functioned as a vigorous proponent of young-Earth geology and key figure in the re-emergence of creation science, began his career as a "Gap Theorist." His name was Henry Morris, and the amateur missteps which at first guided his reading of Scripture shouldn't come as a surprise. If it was Thomas Chalmers who convinced ecclesiastics that gap-pseudoscience was a worthwhile pursuit in the years leading up to Charles Darwin, it was the work of G. H. Pember and his 1884 publication of *Earth's Earliest Ages* which canonized it. In a 1954 scholarly appraisal of creationist theories, Evangelical Bernard Ramm wrote: "The gap theory has become the standard interpretation throughout hyper-orthodoxy, appearing in an endless stream of books, booklets, Bible studies, and periodical articles. In fact, it has become so sacrosanct with some that to question it is equivalent to tampering with Sacred Scripture or to manifest modernistic leanings."

Morris' first book, *That You Might Believe*—published in 1946 when he was only twenty-eight—advocated the Gap Theory of his time. But no worries, that was only its first edition. More would follow.

This was the world in which Henry Morris was born and nurtured at the breast in. His was a gigantic spinning space rock, billions of untold years in age, hurdling through an infinite universe at breakneck speeds around an insignificant main-sequence star which reportedly converts 620 million metric tons of hydrogen each second into helium via an extremely hot core and nuclear fusion, and is also made up of carbon, nitrogen, and oxygen, and small traces of neon, iron, silicon, magnesium, and sulfur. The sun-star of Morris' upbringing was an unfathomably large ball of hot plasma rocketing around the Milky Way at 480,000 miles per hour while here on Earth he and his contemporaries were expected to stare up at the stars and believe they were penetrating through the fabric of time into prehistory, because the closest star is reportedly 25 trillion miles away—meaning its light left the nuclear reactor of its origin four years earlier. There is of course a star in Cassiopeia, which is actually 97,848,000,000,000,000, or roughly 98 trillion miles away—the light of which began its lonely journey to Earth some 16,308 years before penetrating our skulls. In that time the Earth has traveled 2.2 million miles per hour. That would be 314,287,776,000,000 miles, or 314 trillion miles. The viewer is left to wonder if the light from that distant star traveled alongside his celestial path all along.

Henry Morris changed all of that.

Well, not quite. He kept to the entire narrative reported by Copernican astronomers, as described above, but tossed out the billions of years.

For the second edition of his premiere book, Morris made a few unorthodox changes—*out with the old, in with the new*, scientifically speaking. Conclusively, the gap simply wasn't Biblical. Though Morris initially defied the law of the land by clinging to a literal six day span of creation from "In the beginning" onward, he and his fellow pseudoscientists would later write the law for Evangelicalism. Within twenty years of Ramm's proclamation, Arthur C. Custance published

455

what many believe to be the greatest defense for Gap Theory in its two-hundred year history. *Without Form and Void* was its Magnum Opus. And yet perhaps unbeknownst at the time, it would become the Gaps final stand. Only six years later, 1976 to be exact, Weston Fields published a stunning counter-strike with *Unformed and Unfilled.* Through the contributions of Henry Morris and company, a new generation of Creationist was born, one which promised to upkeep and tend-to the natural revelation of astronomy—namely, NASA and the Copernican Revolution—while dismissing any and all obvious attempts to sterilize the Bible's authenticity throughout the geological and biological realm. In one swift stroke, the Gap Theory was buried in the strata of its origin. While lecturing to audiences, the newly reformed Morris was known to remark that the first edition of his premiere book was "blessedly unavailable."

Coming to NASA's defense without being accused of wrangling Scripture—a crime Gap Theorists were accused of committing—would prove problematic. For starters, Biblical descriptions of the "waters above the firmament" haunted his ministry. If the Apollo missions were not to fall continually suspect under the scrutiny of Biblical Literalist and Flat Earthists like Samuel Shenton (who gave the press enough material to drench entire columns with the ink of mockery throughout the 1960's until his death in 1971), Morris had little choice but to uphold the canopy theory first proposed by astronomer Isaac Vail in his 1886 book, *The Waters above the Firmament: Or the Earth's Annular System.* Vail's theory was based in part on ancient Sumerian mythology and advertised a crystalline canopy formed millions of years ago as the earth evolved from a molten state. While observing the grandeur of the Grand Canyon, the seven layers or firmaments of Vail's imagination—and which seemed to be on rather friendly terms with the seven luminaries of the Mystery religion—was construed. Accordingly, at the end of each creation "day-age," the lowermost layer collapsed upon the Earth—all six of them—until the final *seventh* firmament of Genesis 1:6 rained upon Noah's ark.

Morris clearly preferred irony; for he was borrowing from the very catastrophist views—of imaginative and occultist origin, *mind you*—which he claimed to husk from his pseudoscience practices. This newly rebranded—and rather short lived—canopy of Morris' generation constituted a vast blanket of water above the troposphere, and possibly even beyond the stratosphere, in the high-temperature region now known as the ionosphere, and extending even further into space. Unlike

Shenton, Morris and his young-earth advocates negligently turned a blind eye to Scriptural observations which affirmed the sun and the moon as existing *below* the firmament. Perhaps just as importantly, the 148th Psalmist and the Apostle Peter's own declarations—that the waters above are still present and accounted for—were impolitely shoehorned from their theory.

"Praise him, ye heavens of heavens, and ye waters that be above the heavens (Psalm 148:4)."

Regardless of the obligatory compromises needed to secure the globes *whirling, spinning* foothold in Scripture, the gap theory was finally dead and buried in Charles Lyell's geologic column. So too is the canopy theory. Today the Creationist has no clear explanation. But where the Gap Theory is concerned, not everyone received the memo. Old-time Pentecostal preacher Jimmy Swaggart preferred the lavish storytelling which only the Gap could offer. So too has Kenneth Hagin and Benny Hinn. Corruption of the material world—warring angels—cosmic battlefields—Yahweh's intervention—the true spiritual self rather than the fleshly temple—the Gap Theory has long been a favorite illustration for the epic *good* vs. *evil* which the Charismatic preacher supposedly mirrors in his daily tongue-babbling, spirit-filled prayer life and ministry. In reality, with the release of *Star Wars* in May of 1977 and the launch of Voyagers 1 and 2 only a few months later, the cat was out of the bag. In hindsight it's clear. Keeping in step with the Manichean doctrine of old, which insisted upon the interference of Satan and his demons in the process of creation, the Gap Theorist prefers his origins story glazed with an extra helping of Gnosticism.

With his book, *Beyond Star Wars: Ancient Cosmic Conflicts in the Space-Time Continuum*, first published in 1978, author William F. Dankenbring would have us believe the explosive aboriginal chapter of the Bible should mirror as an opening crawl in outer space. Perhaps, we might suspect, *Star Wars* creator George Lucas even plagiarized a history which God didn't bother to publish in His Word while the ever-observant Sumerians lapped it up. It might even be titled, *HEAVEN WARS: Episode 4: A New Hope*—or something to that effect, with the scroll reading: "And the Earth was formless and void…"

"*Star Wars* really happened! Long ago great battles raged in the universe. A great war caused vast destruction throughout the cosmos and upon the earth. Super beings battled for control of the universe, space, and time."

For space age Gap Theorists like Dankenbring, the chasm spanning Genesis 1:1 and 1:2 is an untold war in which the asteroids between Mars and Jupiter form the cosmic debris of an ancient planet torn asunder in some primordial celestial cataclysm. The surface of Mars, riddled with massive craters, is best compared to an ancient battlefield—Venus too. The rings of Saturn "bespeak evidence of ancient catastrophism." Even our very own moon received a paralyzing bombardment from space. "The far side of the moon, photographs from space and Apollo space shots show, was hammered so violently by meteors that the entire original crust was shattered and torn apart... The blasts of crashing asteroids and meteors released huge volcanic eruptions covering vast sections of the moon with flowing lava" and "huge lava seas."

Then of course there's Niburu... Planet X. We shan't forget that.

Dankenbring further writes: "This *war in heaven* must have been catastrophic in nature. It must have been the greatest battle of all time! Armies of angels clashing with each other! The entire cosmos must have been shaken. The fantastic truth of what happened eons ago makes the *Star Wars* movies pale into nothingness by comparison!" A little later Dankenbring reminds us (never forsaking the opportunity for a well-placed exclamation mark): "...the original STAR WARS broke out! The thrilling story is more than merely hinted at in the opening verses of Genesis–*in the beginning.*"

Even canopy theorists like Carl Theodore Schwarze developed a taste for the Manichean cataclysm. First publishing *The Harmony of Science and the Bible* in 1942, followed up with *The Marvel of Earth's Canopies: A Fascinating Book on the Harmony of True Science and the Bible* in 1957, Schwarze chose to avoid the obvious conclusion—that God Himself created "the firmament of His power (Psalm 150:1)." Schwarze re-imagined Vail's volcanoes with atomic explosions—research which Satan had apparently been dabbling in long before Adamic times. In such a scenario, the Psalmist might have been a little clearer and referred, rather devilishly, to Satan's "firmament of power" rather than the Lord's. But Schwarze was not even satisfied leaving the highly debated pre-flood "greenhouse effect" to God. Oh-no—that *also* can be blamed on the aftermath resulting from Satan's research in atomic warfare. Manichean cataclysms and Gnosticism abounds. This ancient blast was the event described by less scientific minds in Genesis 1:2, with a future destruction to come outlined in 2 Peter 3:10.

Whereas Schwarze found his "scientific" vision in Hiroshima and the resulting Cold War, William F. Dankenbring organized his Natural Revelation—aside from an obvious curtain call at Grauman's Chinese Theater—with the Voyager mission. The data which NASA collected from its ascending satellite, drifting ever closer to the gateway of interstellar space, was *proof* of a galaxy torn apart by the lusts of war.

In *Genesis Revisited: Is Modern Science Catching Up With Ancient Knowledge?* Ancient astronaut theorist and author Zecharia Sitchin contrasts Voyager's discoveries with Sumerian texts of antiquity. Rather strange that God would expect a Christian to look to Babylonian literature in order to better understand the revelation He forsook in Holy Scripture. At any rate, Sitchin writes: "The Sumerians made clear, 6,000 years ago, the very same fact. Central to their cosmogony, worldview, and religion was a cataclysmic event that they called the Celestial Battle. It was an event to which references were made in miscellaneous Sumerian texts, hymns, and proverbs—just as we find in the Bible's books of Psalms, Proverbs, Job, and various others. But the Sumerians also described the event in detail, step by step, in a long text that required seven tablets." He adds: "The (surviving) text deals with the formation of the Solar System prior to the Celestial Battle and even more so with the nature, causes, and results of that awe-some collision. And, with a single cosmogonic premise, it explains puzzles that still baffle our astronomers and astrophysicists. "

Even more important, "whenever these modern scientists have come upon a satisfactory answer—it fits and corroborates the Sumerian one!"

Sitchin further points out that "until the Voyager discoveries, the prevailing scientific view-point considered the Solar System as we see it today as the way it had taken shape soon after its beginning, formed by immutable laws of celestial motion and the force of gravity. There have been oddballs, to be sure—meteorites that come from somewhere and collide with the stable members of the Solar System, pock-marking them with craters, and comets that zoom about in greatly elongated orbits, appearing from somewhere and disappearing, it seems, to nowhere. But these examples of cosmic debris, it has been assumed, go back to the very beginning of the Solar System, some 4.5 billion years ago, and are pieces of planetary matter that failed to be incorporated into the planets or their moons and rings. A little more baffling has been the asteroid belt, a band of rocks that forms an orbiting chain between Mars and Jupiter. According to Bode's law, an empirical rule that explains why the planets formed where they did, there should have been a planet, at least twice the size of Earth, between Mars and Jupiter."

After Voyager's flyby of Uranus in 1986, "the realization that there had to be one or more major collisions that changed the Solar System from its initial form became inescapable," commands Sitchin's pen, "as Dr. Stone has admitted." Uranus was shown to not only be tilted on its side, but it was not formed that way from the very beginning. It rings— pitch-black "blacker than coal dust," are "warped, tilted, and bizarrely elliptical..." an "obvious conclusion was that the rings and moonlets were formed from the debris of a violent event in Uranus' past."

Voyager 2 also found that Neptune's two moons Nereid and Triton "were knocked into their peculiar orbits by some large body or planet." Bradley Schaefer, a professor of astronomy and astrophysics at Louisiana State University noted, "Imagine that at one time Neptune had an ordinary satellite system like that of Jupiter or Saturn; then some massive body comes into the system and perturbs things a lot."

Uh oh. Planet X.

Unlike most Gap Theorists of centuries past, who were not afforded the thrilling exploits of science fiction to captivate their better senses, Dankenbring and other space age theologians like him extended the ruined civilizations existing before Genesis 1:2 all the way to the red planet. "Mars—unlike the other planets of the solar system—has a day almost equal to the earth's day," Dankenbring wrote. "The time of axial rotation of Mars is 24 hours, 37 minutes and 23 seconds; the earth's day is 23 hours, 56 minutes, 4 seconds. No other two planets are so alike in the duration of their day. Another striking resemblance between the two planets is the inclination of their axis of rotation. The equator of Mars is inclined 24 degrees to the plane of its orbit, whereas the equator of the earth is inclined 23 1/2 degrees to the plane of its ecliptic. Such a similarity is unequalled among all the other planets of the solar system."

Dankenbring's gullibility is most striking when he pauses to consider the mystery of Phobos and Deimos, two Mars moons which apparently shook astronomical circles when Asaph Hall announced their discovery in 1877. Why?—Novelist Jonathan Swift, who published *Gulliver's Travels* in 1726, 150 years before Asaph Hall glimpsed the two moons of Mars through his telescope, "actually wrote of them in his book!" Here Dankenbring salivates: "Swift actually described the distance of these two satellites from Mars in terms of Mars' diameter implying measurement and calculation. The Laputans, according to Swift, said Phobos was three Mars' diameters from the planet (12,420 miles). Modern instruments reveal it is actually 7,897 miles away. The Laputans said Phobos orbited Mars every 10 hours. Modern measurements show the actual time is 7 hours 39 minutes. The Laputans put the diameter of Deimos' orbit as five Mars diameters (20,700 miles). It is actually 16,670 miles. They put the revolution of Deimos at 21 1/2 hours. It is actually 30 hours 18 minutes. These figures are simply dumbfounding if Swift invented the whole story out of thin air – the crevices of his own vivid imagination! It's simply uncanny."

We must ask ourselves how novelist Jonathan Swift knew about Mars' two moons. Isaac Asimov called Swift's calculations of orbits and their periods of revolution "an amazing coincidence." He added, "However, his guess that Phobos would rise in the west and set in the east because of its speed of revolution is uncanny. It is undoubtedly the luckiest guess in literature."

For Dankenbring, the moons of Mars, as first described by Swift, is indeed proof that ancient peoples knew of the cosmic *Star Wars* long before George Lucas thought to pen a first draft.

On November 28, 2017, the thrusters aboard the Voyager 1 spacecraft did what everybody thought was impossible. Having been dormant since November of 1980—one month before I was born—they *thrusted* again. In a statement on its official website, NASA said: "The Voyager team assembled a group of propulsion experts at NASA's Jet Propulsion Laboratory, Pasadena, California, to study the problem." After 37 years of inactivity and wandering 13 billion miles from Earth, "they agreed on an unusual solution: Try giving the job of orientation to a set of thrusters that had been asleep for 37 years." The Voyager flight team dug up decades-old data and examined the software that was coded in an outdated assembler language. It *still* worked. Voyager 1's mission has been extended into the throws of interstellar space until 2025.

1970's technology is truly amazing.

There is a kind of circular logic which naturally accommodates geological thinking. In 1884 G.H. Pember reminded Christians that God had not revealed to humans how geology should be interpreted. For this he insisted upon a geologist's reliance in interpreting Scripture. Furthermore, if the Earth was "without form and void," we come to another conclusion entirely. Satan had already rebelled and destroyed a former world created by God before Genesis 1:3. In *Earth's Earliest Ages*, he writes:

"It is thus clear that the second verse of Genesis describes the earth as a ruin; but there is no hint of the time which elapsed between creation and this ruin. Age after age may have rolled away, and it was probably during their course that the strata of the earth's crust were gradually developed. Hence we see that geological attacks upon the Scriptures are altogether wide of the mark, are a mere beating of the air. There is room for any length of time between the first and second verses of the Bible. And again; since we have no inspired account of the geological formations, we are at liberty to believe that they were developed just in the order in which we find them. The whole process took place in preadamite times, in connection, perhaps, with another race of beings, and, consequently, does not at present concern us."

With Voyager, we are asked to take this same circular reasoning even further. Forty years earlier, when the Voyager twins first launched beyond the Earth's atmosphere, *Star Wars* wet the imaginative appetite for an entire generation of Biblical Gnostics in waiting. In December of 2017—less than one month after JPL managed the impossible—fans of the ongoing saga lamented over the release of *Star Wars: The Last Jedi*, the chronological eighth in the series. For many, it was the worst *Star Wars* movie of all time. The internet is practically foaming at the mouth with testimonies of stark raving men. Some are even sobbing. Once again, *Star Wars* has managed to shatter the memories of many fragile childhoods. If only they knew about Voyager 1 and 2 in light the Bible.

If only they knew that space was fake…

SCIENCE, PSEUDOSCIENCE, & THE ANTICHRIST SPIRIT—CARL SAGAN'S PERSONAL VOYAGE

CARL SAGAN IS METICULOUSLY SELECTIVE IN HIS CHOICE WORDING when he says, "Science is more than a body of knowledge; it is a way of thinking." Such an assumption is not only regarded as favorable by his contemporaries, they also concur when Sagan assures us that most individuals have "heard virtually nothing of modern science." Much of mankind has "had a natural appetite for the wonders of the Universe. He wanted to know about science. It's just that all the science had gotten filtered out before it reached him." What mankind is left with—or rather, *where* he often begins and therefore ends, is with a set of superstitious beliefs which Sagan only seems to sigh regretfully when referring to. If it isn't Science, it's relegated to the compost pile of pseudoscience. Science, the institution of Science, cannot be built upon it.

In his 1995 book, *The Demon-Haunted World: Science as a Candle in the Dark*, Sagan writes: "Pseudoscience is embraced, it might be argued, in exact proportion as real science is misunderstood—except that the language breaks down here. If you've never heard of science (to say nothing of how it works), you can hardly be aware you're embracing pseudoscience. You're simply thinking in one of the ways that humans always have. Religions are often the state-protected nurseries of pseudoscience—although there's no reason why religions have to play that role."

I can't help but wonder what Sagan ultimately implies when he holds a promised dining reservation for the religious fellow at the table of Scientism, should he strictly adhere to its guidelines—or specifically, *way of thinking*, because the naughty-no-no list of pseudoscience is quite extensive. The very inclusion of angels, demons, prayer, prophecy, miracles, healing, creationism, and particularly in my case, FLAT EARTH, on that list disqualifies any participation in the Scientific Method by *true* Christianity. Even with the fat removed, one might argue, the atoning sacrifice, resurrection of Christ, and His ascension to heaven is *bare bones* Christianity. Without these historical events, we have no hope of our own resurrection. For the scientific mind, these truths *must* be cast down in order to pursue a man-made standard of humanism which is "...based on experiment, on a willingness to challenge old dogma, on an openness to see the universe as it really is."

If the Christian finds his identity among such phrases as, "*In the beginning, God*'—if he focuses the vision of his faith upon a God enthroned above the firmament (Ezekiel 1:26), one who has set His very thoughts and even His physical positioning so specifically upon us—we who are dwelling within the confines of His created order—that He employs the Earth alone as a footstool (Isaiah 66:1), then he would be hard pressed to engage with any counter-system of logic which would lean upon, and ultimately lead to, the institutions natural conclusions. Such obvious end-roads are presented when Sagan proudly lifts the dogmatic banner of Scientism and proclaims: "Who are we? We find that we live on an insignificant planet of a humdrum star lost in a galaxy tucked away in some forgotten corner of a universe in which there are far more galaxies than people."

I am regularly accused by my beloved brethren, almost always with their nostrils raised, that I am being "*unscientific*" in my beliefs, and therefore an embarrassment to their cause—as if my feelings are somehow supposed to be hurt by all the sticks and stones which academia can throw at me. Contrarily, they are accusations which suite me well. I always smile with a bit of relief and thank them for the observation, for they are indeed correct when acknowledging Science opposes the Bible at every perceivable twist and turn. A faithful adherent to the testimonies of Holy Scripture can at best by definition set his aspirations upon the practice of pseudoscience. By forcefully raping Holy Scripture with HTD's, the Copernican and the Darwinist, both of whom infiltrate almost every conceivable rank and position of our church, uphold the only conflicting beliefs which are, by no mere coincidence, accepted by the halls of Scientism.

Sagan gleefully sweeps the three-fold horizons of the Darwinist, atheist, and Copernican when he dialogues as the spokesman for each of them. "To discover that the Universe is some 8 to 15 billion and not 6 to 12 thousand years old improves our appreciation of its sweep and grandeur; to entertain the notion that we are a particularly complex arrangement of atoms, and not some breath of divinity, at the very least enhances our respect for atoms; to discover, as now seems probable, that our planet is one of billions of other worlds in the Milky Way galaxy and that our galaxy is one of billions more, majestically expands the arena of what is possible; to find that our ancestors were also the ancestors of apes ties us to the rest of life and makes possible important—if occasionally rueful—reflections on human nature."

Had Jesus our Lord been a scientist rather than a carpenter, He would most certainly be a man of pseudoscience. Because He first and foremost upheld the written Words of Moses, psalmists, scribes and Prophets—being not of this world—He brought with Him a collection of beliefs or practices which "one might *mistakenly* regard as being based on scientific method." As Sagan emphasizes by his own admission, Science takes the Lord's place, "Because science carries us toward an understanding of how the world is, rather than how we would wish it to be, its findings may not in all cases be immediately comprehensible or satisfying."

Rarely is a finger lifted by the Christian—if ever, which would dare investigate the claims of Science should it threaten or give the slightest hint as one containing the spirit of antichrist and which, as the Apostle John warned, *"whereof ye have heard that is should come; and even now already is it in the world (1 John 4:3)."* The Christian should understand and acknowledge that God alone is his source of knowledge. He, the Christian, *first* believes in God in order to define his own existence. From there and only in this plotted position can truth illuminate his method of thinking. He is to be a temple, an empty vessel always and only in need of God for filling. If the Christian and Sagan's Science are to mutually agree, he must turn away from God's Testimony and seek a counter-way of thinking, which will no doubt in turn fill him with counter-knowledge. The road to science, no matter how much the Christian flails his hands like a chicken attempting flight and demands it so, does not lead its faithful adherer back to God, so long as the Bible's many declarations found in pseudoscience are stripped from him, and never will.

Actually, if Science has done its work on the soul, it will turn him into such a humanist that "absolute-certainty," except the darkened perversities which he can accept and imagine in his own sinful mind, will be altogether dropped and abandoned from his own methodical approach. Again, Sagan declares, "Humans may crave absolute certainty; they may aspire to it; they may pretend, as partisans of certain religions do, to have attained it. But the history of science—by far the most successful claim to knowledge accessible to humans—teaches that the most we can hope for is successive improvement in our understanding, learning from our mistakes, an asymptotic approach to the Universe, but with the proviso that absolute certainty will always elude us."

Sagan no doubt speaks for the religion of Babylon and the Mystery schools which naturally flowed from them. He has dutifully filled himself with the spirit of antichrist—as has any Christian who upholds Science over the truth of Scripture (though at least Sagan is rigidly honest about it)—when he critiques the fulfillment of past, present, and future Biblical prophecy. "Yet has there ever been a religion with the prophetic accuracy and reliability of science? There isn't a religion on the planet that doesn't long for a comparable ability—precise, and repeatedly demonstrated before committed skeptics—to foretell future events. No other human institution comes close."

"The fact that so little of the findings of modern science," Sagan concludes, "is prefigured in Scripture to my mind casts further doubt on its divine inspiration."

Though Sagan, I can only imagine, being true to his own man-made religious worldviews—holding a total lack of certainty in all things—likely smirks as he adds, "But of course I might be wrong."

THE TRUEST STATEMENT NASA EVER MADE WAS A DEATHBED CONFESSION

MY PERSONAL CONDOLENCES GO OUT TO THE SORRY JANITOR who is apparently responsible for throwing the only existing NASA blueprints of the entire Apollo space program into the trashcan. You know what they say, "Don't put all your eggs into one basket."

Veteran NASA astronaut and provocateur Don Pettit only recently admitted what we believers of the Bible's full unbroken Revelation already knows—that the US Government couldn't return to the moon even if they wanted to. "I'd go to the moon in a nanosecond," said Pettit, "The problem is we don't have the technology to do that anymore. We used to but we destroyed that technology and it's a painful process to build it back again."

Say that again—*we've regressed in technology since 1969*?

I think what Pettit meant to say was, "We couldn't fake another moon landing if we wanted to." There are simply too many "space critics" in on the movie-making process. But no matter how much they make attempts at it, telling the truth that is—and believe me, Pettit has come too close for comfort on a number of occasions—NASA can't seem to fess up, aside from the random grease off the brain. Telling lies, even professional ones, is a slippery business.

Apparently, NASA Control in Houston hasn't heard the joyous news. That tin can in which they slingshot those three Masonic boys some fifty years ago through the Van Allen belt is retrieved from televised obscurity and currently hangs on display at the Smithsonian Institute in Washington. The Apollo 11 Command Module Columbia, I believe it's called. NASA, would you like me to call them up, set an appointment to take a *looksy-loo*, have your space engineers see how our granddaddy's built it?

On a side note, I would like to ask Pettit if the janitor who threw out the Apollo program blueprints is the same sad individual who recorded over the original moon landing footage, which NASA confesses no

467

longer exists. President Richard M. Nixon, once remarking, "The American people don't believe anything until they see it on television," similarly called the televised moon landing hoax, "the greatest week in the history of the world since the creation." It's a darn shame how that original footage simply disappeared. It probably had something to do with all those "space critics" who know a thing or two about the movie-making business. I hope it was worth it, recording the Super Bowl half-time show over the most important documentation in the history of the world. Washington, you'd better not loan NASA the Declaration of Independence. They'll likely use it as a dinner napkin.

Astro-not Don Pettit adds, "The only limit to human future is in our own imaginations."

See, another attempt at honesty. If trips to Disney World have taught me anything, it's that imagination is a powerful thing—so powerful in fact, NASA has the capabilities to land on, say—Mars, as in the Mars Rover. They also apparently have their imaginations fixed on the moon Europa, now that they've penetrated the rings of Saturn. And let's not overlook the fact that only recently they announced their latest mission—to the sun. Yes, the sun. 95 million miles away, is it? Hot as hell, isn't it? And we're sending a probe there. But the moon, we've simply lost the technology.

Wernher von Braun wasn't only a rocket engineer under the pay of Adolf Hitler in Nazi Germany; he later became the father of "space science" in the United States, being accredited for developing the Saturn V. But his was another time, when NASA was more "advanced" in their technological know-how. And when it comes to honesty, since we're on the subject, there's nothing so grand as a deathbed confession. Only his is engraved in stone—a tombstone, to be exact.

If it agrees with what we who faithfully subscribe to the full unbroken Revelation of God believes—we call this the joyous cosmology—it's because *his* confesses what God Himself has testified to be true. And nobody, not even NASA, will alter that reality—aside from the whimsical world of television, that is.

And it reads:

"The heavens declare the glory of God; and the firmament sheweth his handywork." Psalm 19:1

WOW, THE SPECIAL EFFECTS IN SPACE ARE GETTING AMAZING! WHO NEEDS CLAYMATION?

A GOOD STORY LINE IS ALL I'M EVER REALLY AFTER. You know, character development, drama, a splice of romance thrown in just to raise the stakes. Special effects don't matter much to me—they actually tend to get in the way of meaty dialogue. And yet that's what we seem to get in a movie nowadays, all effects, no plot. Take a recent live feed from the European Space Agency in the ISS, when the film crew decided to impossibly beam a stuffed anime-character or fuzzy alien, whatever it was supposed to be—teddy bear in space, I guess—into the hands of an astronaut, as if this were an episode of *Star Trek* or something. You do realize we have yet to "invent" the know-how to beam teddy bears into space, right? Oh, I know, that sort of space fiction wows the young folks, but where's the substance? When it came to the Apollo missions, NASA really knew how to reel the emotions in. But that was fifty years ago! So when viewing reruns of the classics, I don't really care about special effects—I can easily look past all the technical glitches of old—if the story is good.

If you're a fan of NASA, particularly the vintage Cold War stuff, then you likely know what I'm talking about. Satellites dangling visibly on strings, stage crews accidentally showing up behind their toy rocket models and in the background of "outer space" no less, conflicting shadows originating from multiple "cosmic" light sources, electric-lit Earth globes with odd-shaped continents and clouds painted on by the prop man, which looks nothing like the globes they show today both in size and character—not overlooking bubbles rising during "space walks," that sort of thing. Once in a while I might even catch a scuba-diver scrambling by, desperately swimming to clear the shot after a stage-hand yells, "Action!" But it's to be expected in any Hollywood film of old, the stage crew sometimes shows up in a scene by accident. Besides, those astronauts preform all of their own stunts. They need lifeguards standing by, because nobody wants to see a good astronaut drown.

One of my favorite NASA movies is highly underrated, and apparently rarely watched. It's from the 1965 Gemini 4 mission, and involves this tense scene where co-pilot Ed White becomes a figure of Claymation in order to preform history's first-ever spacewalk. I especially love the part where he impossibly turns his helmet (we all realize they're locked on air-tight, right?) just to salute his "fourth-wall" and the viewing audience behind it.

See, that's just the thing about the 1960's. They appreciated good Claymation when they saw it on television. You know, Claymation—as in *Gumby*, or Christmas specials like *Rudolph the Red-Nosed Reindeer*. Perhaps American audiences were simply filled with more imagination back then. And there was a Cold War to win. It wasn't exactly a stretch of story-time logic to assume when astronauts slide into the vacuum of space that the whole of them, skin tissue, bones, DNA, *everything* becomes a figurine of Claymation. Today's audience apparently has too much sophistication and a total lack of imagination where effects are concerned to buy into such a stretch of logic. Oh well, their loss.

Kids these days—they won't sit down for any of the classics. Maybe we just need NASA to put some money into special-editions, kind of like George Lucas did for *Star Wars*. Are there any Baby-boomers out there who remember seeing *Star Wars* in 1977 and thinking, "*Wow*, these special effects look so real, I feel like I'm actually in space!" and then reviewing the film two-decades later and thinking, "Yeah, *um*, that doesn't look nearly so good as I once recall." It's kind of like that. Only now we have CG to fill in the pot-holes!

It's just the little things you need to correct, NASA. Like, when you show those vintage 24-hour time lapse videos of Earth, make sure the clouds move. Russia still has that exact same problem with their satellite footage today—the clouds never seem to move day-after-day-after-day-after-day, so you may want to talk with them about it. Isn't China getting involved? *Uh-oh.* Stuff like that is important to some people. Not me though. I mean, I'm okay with it—the outdated special effects, because I know none of this is real—so long as the plot is good.

That's just the thing. It's simply not interesting anymore. Why isn't anyone turning out scripts that hearken back to the gut-wrenching dramas of the *Apollo 13* mission? Oh, that's right, the Cold War's over. We've got terrorists as boogie men now. No actual conflicts to win this time, just civilian freedoms to steal—particularly where the internet is concerned—-which is why the government's moved on to other genres, from science-fiction to pure fantasy. The false flag attacks like Sandy Hook, the Miami Gay Night Club shooting, or that Ariana Grande London explosion hoax are continual. It's just one after the other now. And I nearly forgot the biggest Blockbuster of our time, September 11th. Does anybody still believe it *wasn't* an inside job? Those murders were sacrificial. Look at me—I'm getting off track again. That's an entirely different topic for another rant.

But you know, getting back to space and Hollywood—I have to admit, I'm somewhat a fan of Stanley Kubrick, and if there is an *Apollo 11* moon landing Director's Cut with his name attached to it, produced of course by Walt Disney Studios, then I'd love to get my hands on a copy.

Until that happens, I have to raise my kids in a world—and I never imagined such a day would come or that I'd even be talking about this—where I'll explain to them, whenever the television is on, that what they're watching isn't real, even if the majority of our sleepy population claims it is.

How does a parent introduce human life into the world by explaining to them how this is just one massively-budgeted, delusional, and seemingly unending stage production of the late, great, *planet* Earth? How does one convince his dear brethren in the faith that performance witchcraft is real, and that everyone is expected to enact the spell?

"The Wrong Side of History..." WAR CRIMINALS PREFER FLAT EARTH MAPS

FORMER U.S. PRESIDENT BARACK OBAMA once famously stated, "We don't have time for a meeting of the Flat Earth Society!" Perhaps that's because Barack Hussein Obama was too busy plotting war crimes against people. And killing people he did.

Despite candidate Obama's pledge to sweep away Bush's entanglement in Iraq and Afghanistan, no other US President fulfilled the unexpected legacy of two full terms at war. He is the very definition of a wartime president, and unlike his predecessor, Obama's killing rampage was spread worldwide. During his final year in office alone, a stunning grand finale of 26,171 bombs were dropped—that would be 72 per day—and US special operations were active in 70% of the world's nations, totaling 138 countries—a 130% increase over the Bush administration.

While filling in the breadth of two bloody-terms, thousands of innocent civilians were murdered, a total number which will likely forever remain unknown, and nearly 3 million people were deported from US shores. Where was the liberal outrage then? Even the Nobel Secretary regrets Obama's peace prize. Indeed, the man who promised peace set the world ablaze. The Iran nuclear deal and the opening of diplomatic relations with Cuba stand alone as President Obama's successful uses of diplomacy over hostility. Even Iran is criticized as a terrible farce. And history—*true* history, if permitted to be written—will alone be the judge as to his and Senator John McCain's full participation in the formation and further strengthening of ISIS, unlike what we are currently led to believe among the gatekeepers of our media.

To the liberal, Barack Hussein Obama was painted as a reluctant warrior—a dove of peace; when in fact he was an iron-clad eagle of war with both talons spread.

Obama's embrace of drones has led to a preference for killing rather than capturing terrorists. And killing, such machines are certainly proficient at. Not only have women and children been slaughtered as part of its collateral damage package, but young men of military age who the Obama administration preemptively counts as combatants—they too became acceptable moving targets in his worldwide hunting grounds. After condemning Bush for detaining terrorists in Guantanamo, he upped the ante by not only keeping the prison open, but terminating people worldwide without trial.

I suppose if you're going to run an Empire, you're going to commit war crimes. Certainly not an excuse, but it's impossible not to, seeing as how America is an Empire on par with Rome, unless your Calvin Coolidge and you like to sleep by the fishing pole. Barack Hussein Obama liked golf nearly so much as he salivated over the thought of dropping bombs, and he liked to hit his targets. Perhaps that's why, when it came to committing the *deed*, the White House Situation Room employed the use of a polar azimuthal equidistant map.

That would be a Flat Earth map.

According to the United States Geological Survey (USGS), a polar azimuthal equidistant map is accurate in displaying continents and oceans. Globe maps, oddly enough, *are not*—particularly where air and aquatic navigation is concerned. To this day the equidistant Flat Earth map is employed for such purposes—air and sea perfection; or in the case of the Obama administration, for dropping bombs. And yet the USGS enforces a disclaimer that the equidistant map is only reliable for measuring a precise distance from the North Pole to any other longitude-latitude line on the map. Contrarily, many seafarers—braving the Southern Hemisphere—have been tormented, delayed, and even pronounced unexplainably off course for grossly miscalculating Antarctica's size, and the distance between outstretched continents in that hemisphere, when calculating their course on globe maps. As many Flat Earth proponents know, the equidistant map is entirely reliable. And the government, despite filling every classroom with a globe—which is completely useless for any sort of navigational purpose except to fill the child's mind with superstition regarding a plight from Earth, which will never happen—knows this too.

It is difficult for most people to understand the layout of FLAT EARTH, and are largely incapable of committing themselves to further research on the subject, because since they days of the diaper they have opened up their mouths and said, "*Ahhhhh!*" for the magic *choo-choo* as

Plato's globe was spoon-fed into them. Those who are incapable of getting off the magic *choo-choo* at the next stop will find themselves laughing right along with Scientism's prominent enforcer and children's actor Bill Nye the Science Guy, who uses his apparent scientific prestige to deceive globe proponents with psy-op fabricated falsities by mockingly telling Flat Earthists to "drive to the edge and take pictures" as proof.

It is a shame that Bill Nye the Science Guy, during his White House visits, never once asked President Obama if he could visit the Situation Room, just so that he could see for himself and come to understand what a true and accurate Earth map looked like—sufficient at least for deploying troops and dropping bombs.

Among his unprecedented wars and killing sprees, I am reminded that Obama spoke of being on *the right side* or *wrong side* of history more than any other U.S. President. "History will end up recording that at *every juncture*," Obama claimed regarding his administrative actions in the Middle-East, "we were on the right side of history." Did you hear that—at every juncture? It seems Obama is a moral man. He knows much about it—*future* history, that is; who is on the right and who is on the wrong side.

Those whom he appoints as terrorists, unknowingly and without trial for example, are on the wrong side of history—as are Flat Earthists. Former Secretary of State John Kerry, when speaking at his usual Climate Talks, said: "Members of the Flat Earth Society are on the wrong side of history."

You know, that really hurts, Mr. Secretary. But I guess I can't take it too personal, kind of like when he accused 'climate change' skeptics of believing that with "the melting of the ice and the rise of sea level, all that extra water is just going to spill over the sides of a flat Earth."

I can't take it too personal, because he also would know something about that, wouldn't he—those who are on his *wrong side* of history— particularly since he would be intimately familiar with the equidistant map in the Situation Room, having set his mind upon it repeatedly, and undoubtedly sat in on some of the killings.

"CLIMATE CHAOS" DOES NO EXIST IN A TERRARIUM

MY READERS WILL BY THEIR OWN RESEARCH CONCLUDE that a terrarium is self-sufficient for the needs of its ecosystem. That is my contention, anyhow. Had I known about the joyous cosmology at an earlier time—that we are as the Bible claims living "*in the Earth*"—then I would have taken up this pressing matter long ago. that is, I would have wrestled against the "climate chaos" crowd within my own camp, and doing so simply by adhering to what the Holy Ghosts testifies as true, rather than sitting idly by in the back row watching my gullible brothers and sisters in the faith volunteer to be scammed by Elite they so eagerly salute. No matter, I take an issue with it now.

I think about David Latimer of Cranleigh, England, somewhere just north of 80 years-old at the moment of this writing, and last he recalls watering his favorite house plant, Richard Nixon was the sitting US President. It's still thriving. Since that time—for the record, 1972—Latimer's hardy spiderworts plant has grown to comfortably fill the 10-gallon bottle he first seeded on Easter Sunday, 1960, by surviving entirely on recycled air, nutrients, and water, with an added dosage of sunlight through the nearest window some 6-feet away—in short, photosynthesis. What we know of an enclosed garden system, as David Latimer's experiment and countless others will most certainly attest to, is that such an eco-system is self-sustaining.

More importantly to this discussion, they and Mr. Latimer's 10-gallon house-plant, as well as the self-enclosed terrarium the Bible describes us as living in, are in no need of government assistance or the taxpayer money demanded—all with the backing threat of a prison sentence, if we do not agree to the thievery—to line the pockets of its lawmakers with, all for their very existence and well-being. This will likely imply one thing for global warming, or *climate change*, or *climate chaos*, whatever the interchangeable title is today—it's as I've already suggested and what so many of us know to be true in the Spirit; a complete hoax, and a scam, and likely even the greatest hustle among the present age of man.

Climate chaos apologists will likely look at the collected data presented to them and call anyone who should oppose their overlords, on the basis of finding conflicting data, a "science denier." I myself am no stranger to the term, and warmly welcome such a time-honored badge if Moses also should find inclusion in the conflict. My brethren will surely agree that the so-called denier of Scientism rejects it on the basis that he conducts his own research or analyzes all the data afforded to him, even the purposefully overlooked data, such as the healthy build-up of Arctic sea ice and the "cooked-book" data from Global Warmings own generals, where-as warming trends cannot be proven without it, and has the common sense to recognize a lie for what it is. An apologist however will eagerly accept an invite to the multi-million dollar beachfront property of climate spokesman Al Gore, should the handshake be extended, while the so-called denier will try to keep the amusement contained within him at the very prospect that Gore only recently purchased multi-million dollar beachfront property when, according to his flawless research, should have been buried underwater over a decade ago.

There at least 60 times that I can find whereas the Bible refers to God's creation as "in the Earth." It suffices me to know there are a number of readers out there who will inevitably stumble upon this exhibiting necks well balanced on their shoulders and a head screwed on just sight, so that they may be able to visualize what the Holy Ghosts seeks to incur upon the reader when He pens the phrase. Knowing that we live below a solid firmament, specifically "*in the Earth*," and that the sun and the moon move about us, *not* mind you above the firmament where God resides, but underneath it, and that the very ground below my feet is the celestial floor by which I may observe the chandelier of our self-enclosed system with, I can then listen to what my Scientism overlords say concerning the sudden emergence of "climate chaos" in their fantastical billions of years of evolutionary timetable scenario, and compare it to the Bible's well-documented history, including the beginning of all things, where much change has occured. This I do not deny; the change from our creation week to the days we find ourselves in now, much as I do not deny the flood of Noah's day. The Earth, specifically everything *in the Earth*, has always has a spectacular way of correcting itself.

Amazing how our overlords talk and they talk and they talk, and how my fellow Christians praise them with the Greeks for their talk, and how when I hold the truth of the Word as a filter for my ears, I only see the animation of motor-mouths, for the most part. Anyhow, their continuous talk looks tiresome!

A needy person, when his attention is demanded of others, does not exhibit a desirable trait. And yet this is exactly what our government is, always in need of us—always in need to fight their wars and expand their personal interests and purchase their drugs and accept their vaccinations and line their gluttonous pockets with money, all which must coincide with a strict obedience to their evolutionary Sciences and most recently, the total disbanding of families.

We can begin to see why the *global* New World Order should have no desire to recognize the Bible as true in their endless talk, especially the joyous cosmology with its talk of a terrarium, because they are in need of us far more than we of them. And who should fill the needs of anyone who submits to the Bible but God alone? It is clear that they do not want this of us, depending on the Lord for nourishment that is, rather than their governing body, nor do they wish the health of this terrarium, which is most certainly *not* in need of them either, when their most recent crowning achievement, the Paris Climate Agreement, promises an endless supply of pockets to fill.

The politician arrives among the waving of flags, sometimes even placing his hand on the Bible, and with stars-and-stripes bleeding through the eyes of his onlookers, one or two of them is sure to turn to somebody like me, just before the continual march towards the cliff commences, and protest: "Why aren't you contributing to the program?"

"I'm sorry," is my response to that person, "I wasn't able to hear anything that politician just said. I was using my Bible as a filter."

AH, THE MEMORIES—WHEN THE U.S. LANDED SATAN ON THE MOON!

A CHRISTIAN WILL UNDOUBTEDLY OPEN UP HIS BIBLE TO READ of Satan, Belial, Baal, Beelzebub, Lucifer, Abaddon, and Apollyon, easily concluding they are all one and the same person, that crafty serpent of old, and then, having thoroughly closed its binding, put no second thought to standing back and admiring Walter Conkite's finest hour—NASA's Apollo missions, that is—as if somehow he also, the deity Apollo, is not one of his other names, the same divine being who is given the key to the bottomless pit. The Great Delusion is right here before us, as definitively as wet sticks to the rain, and the only Christian incapable of seeing it isn't the one who cannot, but the one who will not—and there's a difference.

One must almost be pressed to feel sorrow for the entire Apollo 11 crew during their moon landing press conference—all three of them, Neil Armstrong, Michael Collins and Edwin "Buzz" Aldrin. Just looking at that video footage, one might easily conclude they are the embodiment of a country song. Somebody stole their wife, flooded their house, shot their dog, and told them they were adopted before cruelly turning the cameras on. I wonder if it has anything to do with President Obama saying we've never left earth orbit. *Perhaps*….Or maybe we've had it wrong all along, inasmuch as the moon landing wasn't simply a hoax of Scientism, as the claim rightfully goes, but a far more sinister deception of the spiritual nature.

The masterful crafting of public perception is in how carefully NASA's occultist underbelly has remained concealed from its admirers for so long. The Germans who took part in the founding of the U.S. space program through Operation Paperclip, Nazi's such as Wernher von Braun, saw to it that the seedy-side remained in the furthest harvesting field from public viewing. Symbolism is important in witchcraft. The NASA logo displays a forked tongue of the serpent to symbolize it is under the control of Satan. It is nothing short of significant that the NASA moon missions were named Apollo. The sun god is often depicted riding a horse-drawn chariot with the sun shining behind him, so it should be no surprise that the Apollo 13 emblem appears to show the sun god's horses pulling the globe, which is Satan's fingerprint, rather than him.

> [3]But if our gospel be hid, it is hid to them that are lost: [4]In whom the god of this world hath blinded the minds of them which believe not, lest the light of the glorious gospel of Christ, who is the image of God, should shine unto them.

(2 Corinthians 4:3-4)

Everybody's favorite Freemason and Confederate Brigadier-General Albert Pike, in *Morals and Dogma*, stated, "Masonry is the search for light. That leads us directly back, as you see, to the Kabbalah." He furthermore went on to claim, "Lucifer, the Light-Bearer! Strange and mysterious name to give to the Spirit of Darkness! Lucifer, the Son of the Morning! It is he who bears the light, and with its splendors intolerable blinds feeble, sensual or selfish souls? Doubt it not!"

Almost everything NASA does is deluded with magic and alchemy. Kabbalah and astronomy are intertwined, as is Kabbalah with Freemasonry. And Kabbalah, being unapologetic witchcraft through-and-through, contains embedded rivers of occultist mysticism which seek to invoke the powers of devils, is a construct of Judaism. Freemasonry and NASA of course are blood-brothers—my reader will be satisfied conducting his own research on the matter—and the goal of Freemasonry is to masquerade Zionist victory everywhere in the world until the New World Order is established. So here we have before us a process which involves the creation of satanic ritual magic enabling the jubgs if tge eartg to acquire their coveted power even as the mind-controlled and manipulated masses are directed into the Alpha-state, or ever increasing states of altered consciousness.

This tangled-web weaved may seem over-complicated at first, but it all simply belongs to the same spider. It is the End Times deception we've all been wondering about, which is purposed, through the Zionists New World Order, to give rise to their Anti-Christ.

And through his shrewdness

He will cause deceit to succeed by his influence;

And he will magnify *himself* in his heart,

And he will destroy many while *they are* at ease.

He will even oppose the Prince of princes,

But he will be broken without human agency.

Daniel 8:25

It is perplexing indeed to take note of the Christian who sat around his television screen on July 20, 1969, making exemption of Satan's moon landing, if only because he preferred the bewitching wonder of it all over the Bible's account of creation, which is considered by most mundane. The joyous cosmology however, as my reader will likely note, is wholly satisfactual to this author. We know that the moon cannot be landed upon, except perhaps to slap it across the thigh, if it is indeed possible to do so and the man is braver than most or stupid. Had the Christian not made such an exemption to Satan 11's successful Hollywood broadcasting or turned a blind-eye to the Masonic lodge down his street, an undeniable sponsor of their beloved NASA, which by its very prayerful inclusion of all gods, thereby providing the embodiment of true enlightenment, we see mankind's most damnable transgression—his refusal to condone sin. Just look at the mess we're in!

When my Christian brethren takes a moment to ponder the conclusive fact that these things must happen, the deception must continue, Zionism must conquer creation through the dreaded New World Order, and the greatest alchemist in history, the Anti-Christ, must be crowned; this must all happen before the Lord may establish His eternal throne, then in light of these things we must also consider how very few of our fellow man will be saved and removed from the inheritance they crave in the Lake of Fire, where the Beast and the whore of Babylon and their confederation of conspirators are promised to be thrown, if indeed the lie is to continue to its fullest measure.

So we recklessly cast the seeds of God's Testimony concerning Himself, the Gospel, whereas this and so much more—in fact, the whole Testimony—is brought to light because of it; into the rocky and thorny soil, as well as the soft, hoping to save whom God wills. We also must equally recognize in all humility that we are not here to conquer any cause, as the affairs of the world are concerned, because soon after the internet is done with us—once our voices are silenced to the beast— those of us who proclaim the truth in these perilous times, choosing rightness where the government is wrong, may very likely give our lives to the cause.

If it is not for Jesus and His atoning sacrifice on the cross, then it is no worthwhile cause at all.

IT'S ONLY A PAPER MOON, AND NO MARVEL—A LUNAR ROCK IS A PAPER WEIGHT, ACCORDINGLY

THERE ARE NO TREES ON THE MOON. The Dutch government has come to this satisfactory conclusion, having tested their very own "moon rock" and finding contradictory results from what one might expect of its U.S. endorsed title. The rock in question was first gifted to Willem Drees, a former Dutch leader, and presented to him during a global tour by the Apollo 11 astronauts Neil Armstrong, Michael Collins, and Edwin "Buzz" Aldrin. When the Dutch wisely thought to have it sent to the lab, knowing after all that they were dealing with the Cold War propaganda of Americans, the results revealed in no uncertain terms that their present from NASA was a paper weight at best—petrified wood, actually.

Frank Beunk, a geologist involved with its investigation, summed it up accordingly: "It's a nondescript, pretty-much worthless stone."

Of the 270 Apollo 11 moon rocks and Apollo 17 "Goodwill" moon rocks that were gifted to the nations of the world by its participating astronauts and the Richard M. Nixon Administration, approximately 180 are currently unaccounted for, some being "accidently" disposed of along the way, such as unfortunate mix-ups with landfills. Of the remainders known whereabouts, many have been locked away in storage for decades, cleverly removed from the public eye. And it should come as little to no surprise among my readers that the missing moon rocks which happen to "turn up" on the black market, they're proven fakes *every* time.

The selling of "fake" moon rocks became such a recognized *problem* in the years following the Apollo moon missions that, at the turn of the last century, the United States federal government created a special undercover task force in hopes of apprehending them before they became a public issue. These sting operations, known as Operation Lunar Eclipse, were first headed up Senior Special Agent Joseph Gutheinz of NASA's Office of Inspector General (NASA OIG), posing

482

as Tony Coriasso, and Inspector Bob Cregger of the United States Postal Inspection Service, posing as John Marta. Agents from the United States Customs Service would later get involved, and rather than demanding that the media narrative be upheld, one which claims the highest levels of the U.S. Government simply and truly cares about the poor elderly space enthusiasts who are being swindled by con-artists, let us consider the next point.

Federal prosecution would ultimately expand to include the criminalization of selling any "moon rock," whether provably gifted by NASA or otherwise found to be fictitious. Such was the case with Joann Davis, a 75 year-old woman who was in 2011 interrogated for hours by six armed federal agents in front of a California Denny's restaurant, pants soaked in urine, simply for attempting to sell a legally obtained moon rock the size of a grain of rice, which was intended, she said, to pay for her son's medical care. Most notably, the pebble was gifted to her late husband by Neil Armstrong, and as such, she had the perfect right to barter it off for nickels in a garage sale. NASA however considers the moon and anything retrieved from the moon to be government property, even if it was at one time *gifted*.

The Holland moon rock wasn't exactly an easy mix-up either, as if a random stone would find its way into Michael Collins gym bag on the way from the airport—and mind you, not just any chunk of pavement from the side of the highway either. As part of their criminal investigation, the Dutch preformed a thorough background check, and finding no such petrified tree having ever existed in Europe, Asia, or the America's, determined its origins to have stemmed from the furthest reaches of the Earth—Antarctica.

It just goes to show, Satan can do nothing but masquerade Himself into something which he is not. In short, he is a loser. We know this to be true because he is ill equipped to create *anything*—not even the simplest of Earthly pleasures has he invented---except to distort what is good and true of his Creator, *our* Creator, so as to pass it off as his own. And this is exactly what he does—he *plagiarizes* in the most-wicked fashion. It has already been well-established by this point that Satan warped our understanding of God's created order—and in the case of the moon, convincing the world and the church entrusted with the truth of God's Word that a transport named in his honor, *Apollo*, had landed upon it. Yet not even the devil has the ability to venture to the surface of that luminary in our steed, it seems, if such action would succeed in

483

retrieving the simplest of souvenirs (should that transparent disk, which gives forth her own light, contain a single stone), because even the moon rocks which were purported by its conspirators to have originated form its lunar surface are proven forgeries.

> And no marvel; for Satan himself is transformed into an angel of light (2 Corinthians 11:14).

The secret must not get out. It *cannot* get out. The moon is not landable upon, and should the simplest grain of rice be placed on the market, having once been purported by Collins, Aldrin, Armstrong, or Nixon to originate from its lunar surface, prosecutions must be carried out! The Earth is provably stationary by every honest and measurable scientific experiment, as the Bible rightly claims, which makes everything about this current beast government, with their pathetic attempt at swapping moon rocks with petrified trees, *illegitimate*.

Our governing authorities certainly are illegitimate in every sense of the word. And if the moon rocks are fake—*that* they most certainly are—it's because the kings of the earth who conspired against the Lord by agreeing to collect them in the furthest outer-rim of our circular FLAT EARTH had already sold their souls to the very slave master who cannot create anything unless it prove a forgery. Everything about him is illegitimate, as is anyone who sells their soul to him for the power they so desperately crave. Indeed, Satan is a looser, and as many a-reader will note, his time is coming to an abrupt end.

THE CHRISTIAN YOGIC MASTER AND THE SPIRIT OF ANTICHRIST [*Demons Have a Way of Following You Home….*]

MY WIFE'S WORST FEAR HAD FINALLY COME TRUE. She married a Neanderthal. And everybody knew it. We'd taken up yoga classes together—this was several years ago now. It was Southern California and yoga—alongside avocados on toast, coconut water, homemade pizza parties, micro-breweries, bicycle rides to nowhere, and crepes for dinner—was simply the latest trend to *do*. Our church friends were participating in the current spiritual fashion, but this east-meets-west breathing concept never sat quite right with my spirit. Perhaps it was the fact that I could never master its dozen sun salutations, including the *downward dog*. I can still recall my instructor—on *every* occasion too—stopping our breathing exercises to clasp her fingers around my thighs, with all eyes firmly pressed upon me, and forcibly regulating how flat my abs should be in arrant contrast to how high my gluteus maximus should sail. Only moments earlier it was my imbalanced *crescent lunge* which needed adjustment. In short, I was the class example of what not to do.

We owe a debt of gratitude to the Episcopal Reverend Nancy Roth. This current Christian-yoga craze is perhaps best traced back to her book, "*An Invitation to Christian Yoga*"—first published in 1989. Children's books followed. In 2005 *Time* magazine described the trend as "a fast-growing movement that seeks to retool the 5,000-year-old practice of yoga to fit Christ's teachings." Reverend Roth refers to herself as a resource person—or more specifically, "an ecumenical minister in the area of spirituality." Essentially, matters of spiritual truth are not simply restrained to the Word of God. You might say we are free to dip our toes in other deified waters. Here Roth clarifies: "While my own journey has been greatly enriched by the wisdom of other traditions, most notably the mystical traditions of the east such as the one in which yoga was born, my particular way is the Christian way."

Let the discerning spirit recognize that God, as revealed in the pages of Holy Writ, will *not* extend His favor between one religion and another. There is only one path to the Father, and that is through Jesus Christ—who resides on the straight and narrow. Roth's critics will certainly not be satisfied by her complimentary enrichment in the wisdom of the mystics, and rightly so—but I suspect it is not her critics whom she is addressing when Roth further explains:

> "The period of relaxation and visualization at the end of class became for me a doorway into prayer. It did not matter that we had chanted 'Om' or that the exercises had Hindu names….The One I encountered, as I lay on the gym floor with my body relaxed and my mind and spirit attentive, was the God I knew in Christ Jesus." Conclusively for Roth, "there needed to be a new Christian asceticism that respected the integration of body and mind and reflected both the newest research in psychology and physiology and the wisdom of other, even more ancient spiritual traditions."

Nancy Roth is certainly not the first yogic apostate. Born in 1857, Ida Craddock also dedicated herself to the Hindu discipline. Having left the Quakers of her upbringing, she committed herself to the Unitarians—a people who deny the Trinity and believe Jesus was simply inspired by God in his moral teachings, and though he is a savior, was as normal a human being as you and me. But it was her academic interest in the occult—mainly the Theosophical Society, by which she became a member—that seeded her religious eroticism. For example, she contended in *Sex Worship (Continued)* that the cross of Christ is fundamentally a symbol of sexual union. Such sexual-yogic unions amounted to a "purity of heart," in which its practitioners might furthermore "see God." Craddock offered counseling to couples desiring their own mystical sexual experiences. In *The Wedding Night* (1902), Craddock describes a woman's orgasm—and is the first to do so in western literature. This orgasmic experience, however, is one in which the practitioner might embrace nonduality—or rather, a fundamental intrinsic oneness with divine Nature. To this effect she writes:

> "Keep self-controlled, serene, tranquil, and aspire to the highest. Pray to God, if you believe in God and in prayer: if not, think steadily and quietly what a beautiful thing it is to be at that moment in harmony with Nature in her inmost workings, and rejoice that you and your husband are a part of Nature, pulsating with her, and according to her law. Rejoice that Nature at that moment feels through you also, and through your

486

husband. Feel love—love—love, not only for your husband, but for the whole universe at that moment."

Occultist Aleister Crowley reviewed *Heavenly Bridegrooms*—one of her many publications, in the pages of his journal *The Equinox*. For Crowley, it was a rare endorsement; "...one of the most remarkable human documents ever produced, and it should certainly find a regular publisher in book form. The authoress of the MS. claims that she was the wife of an angel. She expounds at the greatest length the philosophy connected with this thesis. Her learning is enormous."

Crowley further writes:

"I am very far from agreeing with all that this most talented woman sets forth in her paper, but she certainly obtained initiated knowledge of extraordinary depth. She seems to have had access to certain most concealed sanctuaries.... She has put down statements in plain English which are positively staggering. This book is of incalculable value to every student of occult matters. No Magick library is complete without it."

In 1902, facing incarceration for charges of obscenity, Ida Craddock—at the age of 45—took her own life.

Contemporary Erin Roca is a self-declared magical sex coach. In a *Bad Witches* article titled: "*5 Ways You're Using Magic If You Do Yoga,*" Roca claims the following: "Your body is a magic wand, which directs energy and makes your intentions manifest into the world....As you move your body and focus on your breath, you recognize that what happens in your body is going to happen outside your body. By the same token, you may be recognizing that what is happening outside of you is a reflection of what's going on inside. Conversely, you may see how external factors were influencing you as well, except now you have a tool that lets you dissipate or mitigate those consequences." Furthermore, Magic is the *hidden revealed*. She adds: "Every single body movement is a part of the ritual—your opening meditation, your mantras. It's saying to the Universe and the magical fields and the spirits around you, '*We interrupt the normal course of the day to bring you this special time. This is something that contains a lot of power and I honor you with my presence.*'"

The ultimate goal of yoga, according to Roca, is cultivating a ritual or ceremony which "enables you to take yoga off the mat into your life, and take magic from the sacred spell out into the world."

I myself confess to having participated in yoga instruction, but nothing beyond three or four classes. My spirit was in conflict with the spirit of *another* nature—and though I couldn't make sense of it all then, I retired the yoga mat out of obedience to the Lord. His calling was clear. My wife followed soon after. We have *both* repented. To stay committed would be to dismiss the Holy Spirit and invite the Kundalini Spirit into our lives. This we were simply not willing to do. Attempting to persuade other so-called Christians away from this magical practice—especially our loved ones—is not entirely easy either. Yoga is advertised as a means for health, "weight loss, mental clarity, physical fitness, and a harmless path to inner peace and harmony" to the point that speaking out against yoga is to speak against our own health.

The excuse, I have found, is almost always the same. That so-called Christian, proficient at twisting Scripture at every possibly opportunity, will refer to their bodies as a temple. A Yogic temple is a humanist temple. To him I invoke the authority of the Apostle Paul, who rightly instructed Timothy: "For bodily exercise profiteth little: but godliness is profitable unto all things, having promise of the life that now is, and of that which is to come (1 Timothy 4:8)."

The term yoga comes from one of two roots "ruj" meaning *yoked together*, and "yuja," meaning *concentration.* Yoga focuses on a harmony between mind and body, a metaphysical philosophy which derives from Hinduism. The message is simple. Man and nature are one with divinity. You are god, but on an evolutionary scale—which I shall turn to in a moment. Why must I open up my mind to something which hopes to transform me from a follower of Christ to a disciple of Krishna or Buddha? Every yoga pose is a posture of worship to various Hindu gods. Thank the Lord I was terrible at posturing myself!

And another thing, Christian-yogic practitioners are rather adept with homonyms. Surya Namaskar, or "Sun Salutation" in English, is cleverly renamed "Son Salutation"—which I assume is intended to imply Jesus. How adorable. And they are most clever with *paradoxes*. In Yoga, learning to master the impulses of the world within is of the utmost importance. Attention to the inmost-self, particularly one's breath, is self-love directed at the inner-divine. The word spirit in Hebrew is *breath*. So Udgeeth pranayama, which is a chant of the mantra *"Om"*—as Nancy Roth earlier mentioned—murmured repeatedly while consciously breathing, must therefore imply the presence of the Holy Spirit. Yet the Kundalini Spirit is nothing less than the very Satanic power which the occultists have long been in touch with—or at least try to be. Practitioners beware! Beware of the pastor—or the pastor's wife—who leads their congregation down this path!

I believe Solomon might speak these words to us:

"There is a way which seemeth right unto a man, but the end thereof are the ways of death (Proverbs 14:12)."

Consider Gopi Krishna. In his 1967 classic, *Kundalini: The Evolutionary Energy in Man*, the Kundalini Spirit is "the evolutionary energy in man," or the secret "mechanism of evolution"—a "super intelligent energy" of Indian yogic lore, or "living electricity" that intends to "transform our very flesh until we become gods on earth." There is an Ocean of Mind, Krishna writes, which is "a boundless world of knowledge, embracing the present, past, and future, commanding all the sciences, philosophies, and arts ever known or that will be known in the ages to come…a formless, measureless ocean of wisdom from which, drop by drop, knowledge has filtered and will continue to filter into the human brain."

Or consider Sir John Woodroffe. *The Serpent Power*, first published in 1918, accurately describes the Kundalini—or Coiled One—as "a sleeping serpent coiled up at the base of the spine. Once aroused, the serpent power spirals up from the anal and genital centers through the stomach, heart, and throat regions into the "third eye" and core of the brain, the *brahmarandhra* or "portal of cosmic being," and then explodes out the top of the skull through the "crown chakra," through which the mystic realizes his or her true nature as an immortal energetic super consciousness (Kripal)."

Did Paul not warn us of this in yet another wise warning given to Timothy? In 1 Timothy 4:1 the Apostle writes:

"Now the Spirit speaketh expressly, that in the latter times some shall depart from the faith, giving heed to seducing spirits, and doctrines of devils…"

Yoga is demonic. Yoga is witchcraft. Yoga is a Hindu philosophy which teaches that man and nature are one with divinity. The Kundalini Spirit is a counterfeit Holy Ghost. It aims to transform our body and mind, while a Christian renews his mind through the Word of God. It is as the 19th Psalmist wrote: "Let the words of my mouth, and the meditation of my heart, be acceptable in thy sight, O Lord, my strength, and my redeemer." And yet the so-called Christian, who obstinately wishes to participate in occult practice, will simply not hear of it, despite the fact that Christianity and yoga are clearly—*clearly* incompatible. Albert

Mohler, president of the Southern Baptist Theological Seminary, presents a very convincing case. The Christian-yogic practitioner—if he is indeed *born again*—struggles with a severity of cognitive dissonance. "When Christians practice yoga they must either deny the reality of what yoga represents or fail to see the contradictions between their Christian commitments and their embrace of yoga. The contradictions are not few, nor are they peripheral."

Demons have a way of following you home.

The devil has beguiled us once again. He has somehow persuaded the Lord's congregation to avoid the séance and the Ouija board. He has even instructed us to tip-toe around the tarot card reader with a spiritual arms-length of discretion. Above all else, we are to avoid New Ageism at all cost, according to Satan—as we carry our yoga mat on the way to the studio. The devil takes personal pleasure in exposing one of his clever deceptions—in fact, many of them—while turning our heads, beguiling us completely to another.

He says:

"You will meet the Holy Spirit there."

"You will meet the Holy Spirit there."

THE CANNABIS CONSCIOUSNESS: PRIESTS AND PRIESTESSES OF APOLLO

I AM PREPARED FOR A PELTING OF PROTESTS by my peer review. You shall find no arguments for *or* against, nor endorsements for the health benefits of cannabis here. Enough has been written on that already. I will be reprimanded for sure. Rest assured, Cannabidiol (CBD), a compound derived from marijuana, and useful in treating epilepsy, anxiety, or Alzheimer's, is *excluded* from this conversation. Rather, the hypothetical promise that I might live ten or twenty years longer without the side-effects of pain by the considerate inhaling of a joint—or that I might attain a wealth of knowledge—or that I might merely experience the sunset years of a happier man by indulging in its recreational pleasures—and God forbid, that my Bible studies might become spiritually augmented, I hereby decline. The history of Occult practice is my concern—mainly, witchcraft. Is it no coincidence, the resurgence of witchcraft among this maddening shuffle of feet towards the marijuana leaf? Aptly applied with the pungent aroma fertilizing the inner-crevices of our skull, they are both one and the same.

Let us *not* conjure up the three Wayward Sisters of Macbeth and one of the most famous lines in English literature, "Double, double toil and trouble, fire burn and cauldron bubble," when speaking of the witch. What I find particularly odd about Broom Hilda, the Gingerbread hag from Hansel and Gretel, and the witches emanating from Victorian mythology as a whole—among their boiling cauldrons of cabbages, fingernails, eyeballs, and carrots; their pointy hats and broomsticks—is the very fact that they are a most convenient fabrication, for the most part. There is a major ingredient missing. The Apostles John and Paul both refer to witchcraft as *pharmakia* in Greek. The word appears a total of five times in the New Testament (Gal 5:20, Rev 9:21, 18:23, 21:8, and 22:15) and literally means *drugs*. It is one of the terrible and intricate working wheels of the great Babylon deception—that is, its sorcery. And all who practice the art will be thrown into the Lake of Fire.

In the meantime, we who are diminishing in number by *refusing* to partake in the deception behind all Earthly deceptions must shine a little while longer in Babylon—as the light from a candle. And in its streets, our saintly voices must contend with the demonic enlightenments complimenting this barbed-bouquet of necromancy—but only a little longer. We have far superior health benefits to attend to. Our wedding day fast approaches. The Bridegroom is coming for His bride. Concerning the great city of Babylon, there is coming a time when "the light of a candle shall shine no more at all in thee," and "the voice of the bridegroom and of the bride shall be heard no more at all in thee: for thy merchants were the great men of the earth; for by thy sorceries (*pharmakia*) were all nations deceived" (Revelation 18:23)."

If paganism has forsaken the old growth forest, it's because the light of the church has dimmed and our city upon the hill is darkened. Alex Mar, author of *Witches of America*—published in 2015—estimates there are, at a minimal, one million practitioners of witchcraft in the United States today. She writes: "I started to feel that you could toss a pebble in this country and hit a witch." Says Maura Dillon, a Chicago witch who brings meditation practice into schools: "A witch is a woman who worships herself as her own god. She is the creator of her own life, the healer of herself." And according to Carolyn Grace Elliot, writing for *Witch* magazine, this isn't a mere passing trend. "We are in the midst of a beautiful, occult, witch renaissance."

In her article, *Dank Magic: How Witches Use Weed in Their Craft*, Sarah Lyons writes:

> "Modern witches are continuing to use marijuana in their practices, most often in solitary meditation or to help them access the spirit realm. Elizabeth DeCoursey, owner of Antidote Apothecary and Tea Bar in Brooklyn, says she typically uses weed as a meditative aid. 'When I want to thin the veil and access ancient knowledge and the collective consciousness of water, the total, deep, and cellular calm I can achieve with an edible in deep trance is pretty profound,' she tells Broadly. There's a reason weed has historical ties to magic: Having a safe, reliable way to enter altered states of consciousness can be an amazing tool in witchcraft."

The very word *magic* originates with the Persian Magi. These mystics were a most exclusive and world renowned Mystery School of the ancient Far East; priests and astrologers mainly—Zoroastrians, whose chief religious sacrament was cannabis. Pliny the Elder wrote: "Magic had its origins in medicine and came from the East, and was 'the most fraudulent of all arts, and the most universal; the magi used herbs, herbae mirabilis, [miraculous herbs] to invoke the gods and ….to expel evil spirits from the sick." He furthermore refers to "the wonderful powers ascribed to plants by the Magi." According to Pliny, they possessed a certain miraculous plant that they would use "when they wish to call up the Gods." The Magi who journeyed to Bethlehem to meet our young Messiah would have also believed—as a tenant of their Satanic Mystery religion—that they themselves were more than mere mortal flesh and blood. They had partaken in the holiest of humanist sacraments—their eyes were opened—and were themselves *divine*.

For centuries, the Oracle of Delphi served as the priestess of Apollo—diviner of the future. So renowned, she would receive visitors from all over the known world. So significant, kings would consult with her over the tides of war. Apollo would *enter* into—or rather possess— each Oracle, including her successors, and enable. More acutely, the priestess would sit upon a tripod above a hole in the floor by which vapors arose, and these vapors would *induce* her visions within the spirit realm. Here Lyons writes:

"Though many researchers believe the vapors contained "a variety of potentially toxic natural gases" emanating from the ground, some hypothesize that hallucinogenic plants were burned beneath the temple and vented up towards the smoke-shrouded seer, or that the priestesses would smoke or eat hallucinogens in addition to inhaling the fumes from the earth. While many scholars theorize the Oracle burned bay leaves, since they were sacred to Apollo, others have taken it a step farther. Dr. DCA Hillman, a bacteriologist and classicist who has written about drug use in the ancient world, argues that there is evidence cannabis was traditionally burned to induce the Oracle's trance state since bay leaves are not known to have psychoactive properties, and marijuana was already introduced to Greece from central Asian tribes who knew of the herb's potent psychotropic powers."

In the furthest East we come upon the Vedas, or sacred Hindu text— writings which may have been compiled as early as 1400 or 2000 BC. Accordingly, cannabis was one of five sacred plants, and in rather provocative terms, a guardian angel inhabited its leaves. The god Shiva is associated with cannabis. In India the god Kali, who predates Shiva, is depicted with a girdle of human arms and a necklace of skulls. Ceremonies to Kali involve cannabis ingestion matched with ritual sex, all of which hopes to erect the kundalini spirit from the base of their spine to the brain.

I will spare us with details concerning the worldwide anthropological habits of cannabis—in China and the Himalayas to Russia and beyond. However, Mesopotamia—where the aroma of cannabis was advertised as "pleasing to the gods"—holds my interest. It is there where Kali's *godly* doppelganger is aptly coupled. So allow me to introduce to you the moon-goddess Asherah, consort of Baal, the sun-god—both of whom the Canaanites worshiped. The religion of Asherah—or Ashtaroth in our Bibles—included wild orgies and ritual prostitution. Its priests and priestesses practiced divination and fortune-telling. She even held such honorary titles as 'the goddess of the tree of life,' 'the divine lady of Eden,' and 'the lady of the serpent,' which may account for the fact that she stood in religious centers as a tree or pole. Icons dedicated to Asher also depict a sacred tree—the tree of life. In fact, she was often depicted holding a serpent—or serpents—in her hands, just in case her allegiances were in question. The Canaanites apparently had their very own—though little discussed—Mysteries. But there is, like all ancient Mystery Schools, another ingredient missing. We should not be surprised to find that her cult centered on the pungent aroma of cannabis. Even the Prophet Jeremiah rebuked Israel for her evil doings. Her women "burned incense to the queen of heaven (Jeremiah 44:19)."

Polytheism plagued Israel for most of its existence. Joshua's generation, which conquered the land promised to them under God's mighty arm, was short lived in its universal devotion to the Lord. They did not cleanse the land as they ought. They condoned and they comprised what they ought not. One generation tolerated. The next embraced. The sun and the moon gods soon ruled upon them. In Judges we read:

> "And the children of Israel did evil in the sight of the LORD, and served Baalim: And they forsook the LORD God of their fathers, which brought them out of the land of Egypt, and followed other gods, of the gods of the people that were around about them, and bowed themselves unto them, and provoked the LORD to anger. And thy forsook the LORD, and served Baal and Ashtaroth (Judges 2:11-12)."

"And the children of Israel did evil in the sight of the Lord, and forgat the Lord their God, and served Baalim and the (Asherahs) groves (Judges 3:7)."

Generations of judges came and went, and yet devotion to Asherah obstinately remained. Gideon went to war with Israel's self-appointed *goddess of heaven* when he was commanded of God, "throw down the altar of Baal that thy father hath, and cut down the [Asherah] grove that is by it (Judges 6:25)." And yet once again we tragically read:

"And the children of Israel did evil again in the sight of the Lord, and served Baalim, and Ashtaroth, and the gods of Syria, and the gods of Zidon, and the gods of Moab, and the gods of the children of Ammon, and the gods of the Philistines, and forsook the Lord, and served not him (Judges 10:6)."

Even Manasseh, who was twelve years old when he became king, "did that which was evil in the sight of the LORD, after the abominations of the heathen, whom the LORD cast out before the children of Israel." Much like the Mysteries which surrounded the boy king, Manasseh was seduced into a delusional religion contained within the stars rather than the LORD of heaven and earth, who had fixed His throne upon the firmament above them. "He built up again the high places which Hezekiah his father had destroyed; and he reared up altars for Baal, and made a grove, as did Ahab king of Israel; and worshipped all the host of heaven, and served them (2 Kings 21:2-3)."

We may catch a glimpse of this Canaanite Mystery religion with the Elysian Mysteries festival in Athens—occurring just across Mediterranean waters—where neophytes ate hallucinogenic and became one with the Mother Goddess Demeter. Women, much like the Oracle of Delphi, officiated as priestesses, and the worship was designed to induce a consciousness open to divine or mystical truths—mainly about themselves.

We must put up with this deception a little longer, and worse, we endure, though certainly not tolerate those who advertise their *pharmakia* exploration as "God sanctioned"—more precisely, Biblical, religious, and *priestly*. If Sula Benet is to be believed, the Word of God has not been preserved as Jesus assured us when He said: "it is easier for heaven and earth to pass, than one tittle of the law to fail (Luke 16:17)." In his 1936 book, *Tracing One Word Through Different Languages,* Benet apparently demonstrated that the ancient Hebrew word *kanah bosm,* which the King James later translated as calamus, was

495

in actuality "cannabis." To this effect he writes: "The sacred character of hemp in Biblical times is evident from Exodus 30:23, where Moses was instructed by God to anoint the meeting tent and all of its furnishings with specially prepared oil, containing *hemp*."

Administrators of Sula Benet's logic surround us today. Indeed, they are passively militant. Chris Bennett is an author, researcher, and spokesman for the historic role of cannabis in magic and religion—and as some delusionals have claimed, an "advocate of Christianity." In a *Cannabis Culture* article, *Cannabis and the Christ: Jesus Used Marijuana*, Bennett writes:

> "....the rediscovery of the Nag Hamadi Library marks the resurrection of a more historical Jesus, an ecstatic rebel sage who preached enlightenments through rituals involving magical plants, and who is more analogous to the Indian Shiva, or the Greek Dionysus, than the pious ascentic that has come down to us through the Bible's New Testament."

Bennett must first look to the Occult to make his case. For Bennett, Jesus' miracles can be attributed to the healing powers of cannabis. Why, because the Gnostics assure us of this. By connecting the delusional dots, the baptism of our Lord in the hands of the prophet John is a description of an intense psychological experience, "more than one would receive from a simple submersion in water." He further adds the Bible is a way in which "....the ancients interpreted the effects of cannabis and other entheogens. What we perceive as being 'high' or 'stoned' the ancients called 'possessed by the Spirit of the Lord.'"

Bennett and his kind are double-headed snakes speaking out of two forked tongues. As it is with human nature today, Bennett's brethren would have done well among God's own chosen and apostate people, who mismanaged the Law of Moses by willingly perverting it. Among Israel's darker polygamous hours, we very may well conclude that Ashera—much like her other doppelganger in Egypt, Ishtar—was even worshiped as Yahweh's consort. In his book, *"Did God Have a Wife? Archaeology and Folk Religion in Ancient Israel,"* author William G. Dever presents archeological evidence supporting this view. If men like Chris Bennett are to be believed—it is certainly a conviction which he is eager to place upon us—the God of Israel and our Savior Jesus are partnered with the Apollo and his Oracle, Shiva and Kali, Asherah and Baal, and the occulting Mystery Schools in their various forms.

If we are to burn as a light in Babylon a little while longer before its streets are desolate and inhabited no more, we must willfully forsake these wicked lusts of the flesh, which has deceived all nations and people. Let us call it what it is—sorcery, witchcraft, and every spiritual enlightenment which may be attributed to marijuana and drug use—flesh work. We must strive to bare the only fruit which our Creator deems *good*. The flesh lusteth *against* the fruit and the Spirit of God, as the Apostle would say—the only spirit worth having. In Galatians 5:16-23 Paul writes:

> "This I say then, walk in the Spirit, and ye shall not fulfill the lust of the flesh. For the flesh lusteth against the Spirit, and the Spirit against the flesh: and these are contrary the one to the other: so that ye cannot do the things that ye would. But if ye be led of the Spirit, ye are not under the law. Now the works of the flesh are manifest, which are [these]; Adultery, fornication, uncleanness, lasciviousness, Idolatry, witchcraft ("pharmakia" or drug use), hatred, variance, emulations, wrath, strife, seditions, heresies, Envyings, murders, drunkenness, revellings, and such like: of the which I tell you before, as I have also told [you] in time past, that they which do such things shall not inherit the kingdom of God. But the fruit of the Spirit is love, joy, peace, longsuffering, gentleness, goodness, faith, Meekness, temperance (self-control): against such there is no law."

THE ULTIMATE TRIP... [HOW TO TALK LIKE A HYPER DIMENSIONAL COSMONAUT AND GET AWAY WITH IT]

THE SPACE AGE OFFICIALLY COMMENCED ON OCTOBER 4, 1957. Such evidence was well-regarded by spectator sportsmen who beheld *Sputnik 1* streaking across a starlit American sky with their own eyes. No surprise, thinking back on it all. It was only a matter of time and technological know-how before the occulting mysteries, in their various interwoven and self-enlightened forms, might conjure up a scenario in which mankind *returns* to the boundlessness of outer space, particularly to the stardust of our divine origin. While the whole of esoteric history has dismissed any such Biblical notion that we derive from the *dust of the ground* in favor of the cosmic god-self, it wasn't until the twentieth century when penetration of the firmament became a rich allegorical resource for the final frontier—more importantly, the journey into "inner-space." Science-fiction is a cerebral drama of self-discovery. Indeed, space has become the cosmic center stage of existence. For science-fiction writers such as Arthur C. Clarke, Carl Sagan, and Gene Rodenberry, outer space was the theater they needed for the evolutionary advancement, not merely of technology, but the human condition.

Psychedelics and the ancient occulting Mysteries are indistinguishable from the other. This fact has already been established, and I stand by it. So one shouldn't be taken aback then when stopping to consider the frenzied resurgence of esoteric spirituality under the influence of LSD and other narcotics, all of which seemed to conveniently fall in perfect synchronicity with the political Cold War hysterics bolstering the space race, particularly the implications we might find resulting from chemist and psychiatrist Stephen Szara's pioneering research into the space-time effects of DMT. It was April of 1956, well over a year before the Soviet Union outplayed the United States bid to launch into "low Earth orbit," and his landmark bioassay quite ironically documented the very language which NASA astronauts would later employ in the decade to come—but more on that in a

498

moment. Dr. Szara initially began preforming a series of tests on animals. Take your average pessimistic cat, for example. At first frightened, Szara took note of his subject: "...when I injected the drug it became quiet and very friendly. This behavior lasted maybe for half an hour or so and then he started to be afraid and ran away." Szara wasn't content. He needed human recruits.

It is well-known by now, what keen interest the architects of Project MKUltra had in the war on psychological manipulation, particularly where the study of DMT is involved. A brainchild of the Central Intelligence Agency and coordinated with the Special Operations Division of the U.S. Army's Chemical Corps., Project MKUltra is the code name given to a program of experiments on human subjects, often illegal due to the fact that many of them were unwittingly victimized. How many Manchurian Candidates were offered to the MSM as brainwashed graduates of the American government's curriculum will never be known, especially considering the program was "officially" disbanded in 1973 and CIA Director Richard Helms ordered the termination of all documents. That's the official story, at any rate. But make no mistake—Project MKUltra is still very much alive, and it has enveloped much of the entertainment industry today.

"With a healthy budget and top-level directives to secure state interests, the CIA bought the cooperation of doctors and scientists from across the United States and Canada, many among them champions of the psychotomimetic paradigm. Often working independently from one another and oblivious to CIA designs, this well-oiled research network gathered intelligence, often using unethical methods, on the effects of a veritable pharmacopoeia on human subjects (Graham St. John, *Mystery School in Hyperspace*)." Szara more than likely made a name for himself among these shadow operatives, and for anyone paying attention, made LSD look like a cheap beer in the process. He and his colleagues initially recruited thirty volunteers to receive doses of DMT at the Central State Institute for Nervous and Mental Diseases, Budapest. While under the influence of the psychedelic, one volunteer is documented as quoting:

> "The whole world is brilliant...The whole room is filled with spirits. It makes me dizzy...Now it is too much! I feel exactly as if I were flying...I have the feeling this is above everything, above the earth." And as the effects wore off: "It is comforting to know I am back on earth again...Everything has a spiritual tinge to it, but it is so real...I feel that I have landed."

Pay attention. Some thirteen years later, Neil Armstrong would take *one small step* from the Sea of Tranquility, the highest point of his trip, quoting: "Houston, Tranquility Base here. The Eagle has landed."

Upon returning to Earth, Mission Control Center in Houston would message the Apollo 11 crew: "Roger, Tranquility. We copy you on the ground. You've got a bunch of guys about to turn blue. We're breathing again.

In his book *Mystery School in Hyperspace*, author Graham St John compares these striking similarities between the exploration of inner and outer space. "Over the next decade, the sequence of events from launch into space > orbit > return to Earth were analogous to the sequence involved in a psychedelic trip (i.e., intake > high > landing), which explains why, during this period, space programs, the activities of astronauts and cosmonauts, and NASA radio dialogue, in particular, provided immediate allegorical resources for those undergoing psychoactivated rites of passage."

Director Stanley Kubrick's contribution to the inner *and* outer space race is somewhat perplexing, should a connection between Project MKUltra, psychedelics, and the Scientism deception not be established. There is good reason to suspect Kubrick as the actual Apollo 11 moon landing "stage director." That was July 20, 1969. However, the most "acknowledged" film of his entire career was released only one year prior. *2001: A Space Odyssey* still stands as one of cinema's greatest monuments to "*the ultimate trip.*" It was even promoted as such at the time. In its mystifying and, some might argue, *incomprehensible* conclusion, astronaut Dave Bowman passes through the very mysterious black monolith which seems to show up throughout pivotal moments in evolutionary history and is propelled on a space-time "trip" through the furthest passages of trans-human existence. Author Dennis McKenna, brother of DMT enthusiast Terence McKenna, has commented on the film.

> "...the 'light show' at the climax, as David Bowman's module is sucked into the hyperspatial portal, is close enough to the DMT 'light show' that many of us assumed the film sequence had been modeled after it...Like Bowman's hyperspatial plunge into the monolith/portal, DMT brings with it a sense of rapid acceleration, of diving head-long into an overwhelmingly bizarre abyss, freighted with portentousness and hints of insect-like metamorphosis."

The "supernatural" had been criticized, challenged, and outright ignored by modernist of science and industry-age thinkers for an entire century before Kubrick and writer Arthur C. Clarke's cinematic vision came to be. Occultists needed a hidden pocket, if you will, not only for their hieroglyphic goddesses and spiritualist specters, but for the transcendence of their mind. The fourth-dimension gave them all the creative space they'd ever need. We can thank imaginative reality-tinkers like Russian theosophist Petr Ouspensky and occultist Helena Blavatsky for the fourth's initial success. Matched by its associations with geometry and all the mathematical equations that could be thrown at it, hyperspace philosophy has since flourished. Such concepts have been nested with science-fiction authors like Gene Roddenberry and Arthur C. Clarke because now they could circumnavigate the prohibition beyond third dimension space-time with the acroamatic laws of "warp drive," as it is sometimes known among fans of science-fiction—a logic which depends on the metaphysics of higher, though unprovable and scientifically untestable, dimensions as its logical crutch. Here, in the technological advancements of hyperspace, evolutionary transcendence could finally hold its legitimate scientific merit.

"Hyperspace became a powerful literary device—the source of energetic powers and capabilities that enhance and transform normal human abilities (Graham St John)." Consider Luke Skywalker and the plight of his newfound droid friends in the original *Star Wars*. Here on a binary-sun scorched planet we find a simple farm boy, having never traveled beyond his own dust-cropping homestead, which happens to lie in the furthest rim of the galaxy. He's taken up the old wizard's invitation to become like his father before him and learn the mystical magic of an all-penetrating force. He's an insider now—as esoteric knowledge goes. And quite suddenly, when a tyrannical Empire bears down upon him, Luke finds himself sputtering forward through hyperspace in order to escape what would otherwise prove his certain doom. Skywalker has ascended spiritually above the capabilities of our own human experience—and though the movie is far from over, already we can conclude that his life will never be the same.

There is a common experience with DMT and space-time. "Those who partake sense they are '*away*'longer than the duration measured on the clock," says Graham St. John. Dr. Rick Strassman, author of *DMT: The Spirit Molecule*, conducted studies with DMT among five-dozen subjects at the University of New Mexico. One of his volunteers, Sara, a member of the Wiccan community, described her own hyperspace experience while on the drug.

> "There was a sound, like a hum that turned into a whoosh, and then I was blasted out of my body at such speed, with such force, as if it were the speed of light. The colors were aggressive, terrifying; I felt as if they would consume me, as if I were on a warp-speed conveyer belt heading straight into the cosmic psychedelic buzzsaw. I was terrified. I felt abandoned. I'm completely and totally lost. I have never been so alone. How can you describe what it feels like to be the only entity in the universe?"

I don't think it's possible that the 1960's could have been "the SIXTIES" without the involvement of its high-priest, Timothy Leary and his band of Merry Pranksters. Writing the foreword to Alan W. Watts *the Joyous Cosmology*, Leary asks us to ponder this question. "What are these substances, medicines or drugs or sacramental foods? It is easier to say what they are not. They are not narcotics, nor intoxicants, nor energizers, nor anesthetics, nor tranquilizers. They are, rather, biochemical keys which unlock experiences shatteringly new to most Westerners."

By *most westerners*, I take it, the High Priest of sacramental metabolism is referring to Christendom. And when he speaks of *experiences*, I naturally conclude he is referencing the very forbidden fruit which our founding parents once partook of and which equally instituted the Mysteries to come, let alone heaved all of their descendants into an eternal separation from God. With the space race, so too the occultists had their coveted and long-prophesied sigh of relief. Their ancient religion "*from a more civilized age*" had manifested a new creed in the very acreage where heaven once dogmatically stood, and most importantly, they had the gullible Christian to go along with their schemes.

In a way, the Mysteries are no more. It is not the tree of knowledge which the occultists are after. That sacrament is available to all—to anyone who wishes to partake of it. The psychological pathologies which Christians have long held to be the damnable sinful nature of man are now suddenly reckoned to be conditions which might be improved upon through a technological evolution—to anyone who's paying attention. The LORD placed angels with flaming swords in the garden for a guarded purpose. We know where this space race has set its sights.

It is the tree of life—*immortality*—they're after.

THE MOLECULAR PATH TO SHAMANISM | FRANCIS CRICK AND THE DOUBLE-HELIX DELUSION

GENETISIST JAMES WATSON AND FRANCIS CRICK, a molecular biologist, biophysicist, and neuroscientist by trade, conducted no DNA experiments of their own, according to the U.S. National Library of Medicine. And yet in 1953 they *discovered* the DNA molecule known as the Double Helix by "drawing upon the experimental results of others" and relying on "brilliant intuition, persistence, and luck." But there is a missing ingredient here. As the story goes, Francis Crick burst through the front door of his Cambridge home spouting barely-legible gibberish to his wife about "two spirals twisting in opposite directions from one another." Being herself somewhat of an artist, she put *vision* to paper. And like Walt Disney with Mickey Mouse, the coiling double helix was promptly born. To celebrate, the couple met up with research partner James Watson, and the trio drunk themselves silly at a local pub. It should be noted that Crick was a devoted fan of author Aldous Huxley. He famously threw nude parties throughout the 1950's and 60's. But most importantly of all, Crick was a devoted connoisseur of LSD.

What Francis Crick essentially *discovered*, ironically enough, is the caduceus—the staff carried by Hermes Trismegistus throughout ancient Greek mythology. One might immediately recognize the caduceus should he have observed a pair of two intertwined snakes imprinted on ambulances and medical buildings across the world. Though one needn't only look there. The twin serpents of the double helix seem to slither frequently throughout the annals of science, from the subatomic scale to the motions of celestial mechanics and even the coils of entire galaxies. There's simply no escaping the ancient Serpent.

In *Mutants & Mystics*: *Science Fiction, Superhero Comics, and the Paranormal*, Author Jeffrey J. Kripal doesn't mince his words when writing on the oversaturation of the caduceus: "It is at once the double-helix scepter of the DNA molecule, the phallic serpent who brought sex and death into the world in the myth of the Garden of Eden, and a sign of the kundalini, the two-spiraled currents of energy that are likened to a serpent as they spark and spike up, down, and around the central channel of the spinal column in Tantric yoga. Most of all, though, the caduceus is the staff of Hermes, the ancient Greek god of language and, later, occult philosophy, alchemy, and Western magic."

The staff of Hermes has been a favorite for British comic book writer Alan Moore, who openly advertises the arts in its many varying forms to be deeply rooted in occultism. His comic book series *Promethea* (1999-2005) was a cauldron for occult philosophy, Jewish mysticism, the Tarot, Tantric yoga, psychedelia, sex magic, and infamous "spheres" of the Kabbalah. Regarding his use of the caduceus, Moore explains: "Magic, after all, is ruled by Hermes, his symbol, this caduceus, its double-helix serpents representing mankind's evolution. They wind apart, and then recombine, progressing towards their ultimate synthesis—towards winged blazing Godhead."

Yet Crick's double-helix discovery ventures even further back than the Olympian who supplied Hermeticism to western civilization. To this the snake-worshiping Chaldeans deserve due-credit. Writes A.L. Frothingham in *Babylonian Origin of Hermes the Snake-God, and of the Caduceus* (1916): "The proto-Hermes was always a snake-god, and before the era of complete anthropomorphism he was thought of in snake form. But it is an essential element of his function that he was not a single snake—for the great single Earth Snake was the Mother goddess—but the double snake, male and female, the most prolific form of copulation in the animal kingdom."

But let's not forget, the Egyptians also had a part in Crick's discovery. Did Pharaoh not wear a cobra on his crown as a symbol of the divine word and third eye—the pineal gland—by which true hidden knowledge might be discovered to the initiate? In his book, *The Secret in the Bible*, author Tony Bushby suggests the capstone of the Great Pyramid was once a clear crystal or glass that produced a visible beacon of light from its apex. He writes: "Whenever a light is shone down into a glass pyramid in exact scale or proportion as the Great Pyramid, a 'Rainbow Serpent' is created. The light provides a type of force or energy that, in turn, creates the vertical spiral of light, a serpent upraised, invisible in rock, but visible in a clear substance. That is what the Ancient Egyptian Priesthood meant when they said, *'A serpent lies coiled in the Great Pyramid.'*" Bushby's conclusion is as you might now suspect. The Rainbow Serpent, directly referenced by the priesthood, was non-other than Francis Crick's strand of DNA.

Every continent seems to have a role in ancient serpent worship. Claude Lévi-Strauss writes of the Aztecs: "In Aztec, the word *coatl* means both 'serpent' and 'twin.' The name *Quetzalcoatl* can thus be interpreted either as 'Plumed serpent' or 'Magnificent twin.'" Throughout shamanic religions, from Australia to Tibet and eastern Asia, back into Egypt again, throughout Africa, and finally North and South America, visions of "spiral ladders" or "braided ropes" cannot be overlooked either. Authors Mircea Eliade, Willard R. Trask, and Wendy Doniger write in Shamanism: Archaic Techniques of Ecstasy, "the symbolism of the rope, like that of the ladder, necessarily implies communication between sky and earth. It is by means of a rope or a ladder (as, too, by a vine, a bridge, a chain of arnyaw, etc.) that the gods descend to earth and men go up to the sky."

In 1961, anthropologist Michael Harner journeyed to the Peruvian Amazon rainforest to study the shamanistic religion of the Conibo Indians. Here he encountered a world of hallucination. Upon finally ingesting the hallucinogenic substance, and according to his own account, "giant reptilian creatures" resting "at the lowest depths of his brain" began to project a series of scenes and images before his eyes. Says Harner: "First they showed me the planet Earth as it was eons ago, before there was any life on it. I saw an ocean, barren land, and a bright blue sky. Then black specks dropped from the sky by the hundreds and landed in front of me on the barren landscape. I could see the 'specks' were actually large, shiny, black creatures with stubby pterodactyl-like wings and huge whale-like bodies....They explained to me in a kind of thought language that they were fleeing from something out in space. They had come to the planet Earth to escape their enemy. The creatures then showed me how they had created life on the planet in order to hide within the multitudinous forms and thus disguise their presence. Before me, the magnificence of plant and animal creation and speciation – hundreds of millions of years of activity – took place on a scale and with a vividness impossible to describe. I learned that the dragon-like creatures were thus inside all forms of life, including man." Here comes the crucial part of Harner's testimony to the drug. "In retrospect one could say they were almost like DNA, although at that time, 1961, I knew nothing of DNA."

Author Jeremy Narby also testifies to this bizarre Double-Helix knowledge among the shamans of the Peruvian rainforest when he writes: "By ritually ingesting mind-altering plant mixtures, Peruvian Amazon shamans take their consciousness down to the molecular level and gain access to biomolecular information." Elsewhere he states: "The first [plant] contains a hallucinogenic substance, dimethyltryptamine, which also seems to be secreted by the human brain; but this hallucinogen has no effect when swallowed, because a stomach enzyme called monoamine oxidase blocks it. The second plant, however, contains several substances that inactivate this precise stomach enzyme, allowing the hallucinogen to reach the brain. So here are people without electron microscopes who choose, among some 80,000 Amazonian plant species, the leaves of a bush containing a hallucinogenic brain hormone, which they combine with a vine containing substances that inactivate an enzyme of the digestive tract, which would otherwise block the hallucinogenic effect. And they do this to modify their consciousness. It is as if they knew about the molecular properties of plants and the art of combining them, and when one asks them how they know these things, they say their knowledge comes directly from hallucinogenic plants....Most remarkably, what they gain access to is the DNA strand itself, which appears to be conscious and capable of bestowing real knowledge about botany, medicine, culture, and life itself. Nature is minded. Hence the ladders and snakes seen in the shamanic visions and the cosmic serpent creation myths found around the world."

See, this is what irks me about modern scientists—their shameless denial. When I had the opportunity to sit down for breakfast with the resident astronomer at "Answers in Genesis," Professor Danny Faulkner—a butting of heads which I am grateful for and will fondly remember—I brought up the role Hermeticism and the Mystery Schools had in the shaping of western philosophy and the sciences, he immediately quipped: "No! No! No! You have it backwards. Science came first and then the occult twisted and contorted it!"

And yet, in light of what I've written—and so much more which has been left out!—I can only conclude the U.S. National Library of Medicine is mocking us when it writes: "The double helix has not only reshaped biology, it has become a cultural icon, represented in sculpture, visual art, jewelry, and toys."

The double-snake helix, wherever it is found—from the staff of Hermes to the capstone of Egypt's Great Pyramid, and not to be overlooked, India's kundalini—is a "conscious entity," if the occult has a say in it. And yet I cannot deny much has been accomplished through genetic studies. Just consider this. NASA has accomplished much as well. Many technological advances have been pushed through their pipeline and sold to the highest bidder, yet they will not show us a real

506

photo of Earth. Like NASA's "planet," why do we have so many CG photos of the double-helix? Have doctors believed Crick and his contemporaries on blind faith or have countless others observed a 3-D double-helix through the microscope? The simplest web search delivers smoke and mirrors.

CG...CG....CG.....and more CG.

Until only a few years ago, we never once had an "actual photo" of Crick's double-helix, and if one pays attention, the two pillars they've "photographed" looks stunningly Masonic. Ladder, coiling twin snakes, two pillars. Why couldn't they photograph Crick's discovery back in any other decade of the twentieth century? Then again, perhaps we really do have a coiling double-helix. Maybe it's all part of the enmity between the serpent and the woman. But one thing my studies into the blind faith demanded of Scientism has taught me, if it originates with esoteric learning, the occult, or the Mysteries, then I'm probably gazing through the smoke and mirror of wishful thinking.

Let us not forget, and thanks for reminding me; Francis Crick was *not* a fan of the Serpent's great competitor, the religion of Christianity. Being ever so disdainful towards the Gospel which promised to crush the head of the Beguiler, he once quoted: "I do not respect Christian beliefs. I think they are ridiculous. If we could get rid of them we could more easily get down to the serious problem of trying to find out what the world is all about."

Crick later joked, "Christianity may be OK between consenting adults in private but should not be taught to young children."

The man who most certainly explored the doors of perception with LSD and other narcotics would rather indoctrinate our children. Crick was pushing occultism and Freemasonry for the uninitiated.

THE DOUBLE-HELIX DRUG OF CHOICE | UNSEEN WORLDS & CLOSE ENCOUNTERES OF THE MOLECULAR KIND IN INNER + OUTER SPACE

THE TRAGIC HISTORY OF HUMANITY IS BEST TOLD in shadow as often as it is rehearsed in light. I have made my position known. Jesus is the light. There is no other illuminating truth on Earth but the Word of God alone, and I shall neither bend to the left nor the right of such acknowledgement. And yet *wars and rumors of wars*—the endless current of evil which fills entire volumes of books (and keeps filling them before the ink has chanced to dry), are too often employed as smoke screens in order to hide the true untold darkness which has governed this world since the beginning. The use of plants and mushrooms is a surmounting evidence for which historians have long since suppressed. Yet the proof behind all counterfeit religions is staggering. The civilization of *Cain*—everything that was contained within the cities of Cain—were likely initiated by such psychedelics. Only recently have the books been opened. And finally the great and delusional deception of Globe Earth and everything that is contained within the globe as dictated by the ancient Mysteries are held to the light for anyone who wishes to expose them.

Among the "sixty" of Dr. Rick Strassman's critical New Mexico study into the religious effects of DMT, even further evidence of the double-helix's residency throughout "inner-space" can be found—as well as the occultist reality behind "outer-space" itself. Karl was Straussman's first volunteer. Within two minutes of receiving his first low dose of N,N-dimethyltryptamine, he is said to have reported: "There were spirals of what looked like DNA, red and green." Strassman found that his subjects were prone to get entranced, perhaps even paralyzed, by the initial display of tie-dye colors. To this he states, "If they can go through the curtain that the colors seem to represent, there often is more information and feeling than just the colors themselves." Upon receiving a high dose of DMT, Karl would accomplish that very task. His first volunteer passed the cosmic curtain and entered the mystical land of machine elves once famously traversed by psychonaut Terence McKenna.

Of these elves Karl reports:

"There were a lot of elves. They were prankish, ornery; maybe four of them appeared at the side of a stretch of interstate highway I traveled regularly. They commanded the scene, it was their terrain! They were about my height. They held up placards, showing me these incredibly beautiful, complex, swirling geometric scenes in them. One of them made it impossible for me to move. There was no issue of control; they were totally in control. They wanted me to look! I heard a giggling sound—the elves laughing or talking at high-speed volume, chattering, twittering."

Cleo was forty years-old and legally blind due to a genetic eye disorder when she volunteered for Dr. Rick Strassman's study. Though born into a Jewish family, Cleo later turned to the Wiccan religion, and once while on LSD claimed having visions of a "past-life" experience where she burned at the stake for her participation in witchcraft. Recent experiments with mushrooms also presented otherwise forgotten memories of her father sexually molesting her as a child.

At any rate, she too met up with visions of the double-helix. "There was a spiral DNA-type thing made out of incredibly bright cubes," she said. "I *felt* the boxes at the same time that my consciousness shifted." Cleo reported going into every cell in her body. "It was amazing. It wasn't just my body....themselves...themselves...it's all connected." At the 30 minute mark, she could feel the DMT burning in her veins. She also began to speak, as Straussman reports, with more clarity. Then the patterns began. "I said to myself, *Let me go through you.*" Unlike Karl, Cleo journeyed into outer space.

"At that point it opened, and I was very much somewhere else. I believe it was at that point that I went out, into the universe— being, dancing with, a star system. I asked myself, 'Why am I doing this to myself?' And then there was, 'This is what you've always been searching for. This is what all of you has always been searching for.' There was a moment of color. The colors were words. I heard what the colors were saying to me. I was trying to look out, but they were saying, 'Go in.' I was looking for God outside. They said, 'God is in every sell of

509

your body'…..The colors kept telling me things, but they were telling me things so I not only heard what I was seeing, but also felt it in my cells. I say felt, but it was like no other felt, more like a knowingthat was happening in my cells. That God is in everything and that we are all connected, and that God dances in every cell of life, and that every cell of life dances in God."

Yet another of Strassman's "sixty" reported seeing the familiar double-helix pattern. Philip states: "The visuals were dropping back into tubes, like protozoa, like the inside of a cell, seeing the DNA twirling and spiraling. They looked gelatin-like—like tubes, inside which were cellular activities. It was like a microscopic view of them."

And then there's Sara, forty-two years old when she volunteered for Strassman's New Mexico study. She claimed an "angel" had visited her once when she was stricken with a high fever as a child, and now reported "spirit guides" with whom she communicated with for advice and support. As part of Strassman's "sixty," Sara also claimed an excursion with the double-helix. "I felt the DMT release my soul's energy and push it through the DNA. It's what happened when I lost my body. There were spirals that reminded me of things I've seen at Chaco Canyon. Maybe that was DNA. Maybe the ancients knew that. The DNA is backed into the universe like space travel. One needs to travel without one's body. It's ridiculous to think about space travel in little ships."

Strassman writes of her low-dose experience being somewhat typical—"pleasant, relaxing, with a sense of more to come." Actually, what began with "lots of spinning colors," also included clowns—lots of animated clowns, which Strassman insists is a common experience for DMT travelers. On her second of four trips, Sara passed through the curtain of "the aggressive spinning colors" which were "almost familiar" by this point. She reported seeing "a pulsating entity (which) appeared in the patterns," looking somewhat "Tinkerbell-like," and which coaxed her to go with it. Though she did want to go with it, the drug had begun to wear off, "and I wasn't high enough to follow it. I told it, *I can't go with you now. See, they want me back.* It didn't seem to be offended and, in fact, followed me back until I sensed it had reached its boundary. I felt like it was saying goody-bye. Reentry was slow…."

While she agreed that "the most intense part of each trip was spent tangled up in these colors," on her third trip she "quickly blasted through to the other side. I was in a void of darkness. Suddenly, beings appeared. They were cloaked, like silhouettes. They were glad to see me. They indicated that they had had contact with me as an individual before. They seemed pleased that we had discovered this technology. I felt like a spiritual seeker who had gotten too far off course and, instead of encountering the spirit world, overshot my destination and ended up on another planet. They wanted to learn more about our physical bodies. They told me humans exist on many levels. I needed to reconnect with my body in time for the blood pressure check and blood sampling. It was as if they, rather than Laura, were collecting the information and they appreciated my doing it for them. Somehow we had something in common. They told me to *embrace peace.*"

Sara's fourth and final DMT trip is perhaps the most interesting:

"I went directly into deep space. They knew I was coming back and they were ready for me. They told me there were many things they could share with us when we learn ow to make more extended contact. Again, they wanted something from me, not just physical information. They were interested in emotions and feelings. I told them: We have something we can give you: spirituality. I guess what I really meant was Love. I tried to figure out how to do this. I felt a tremendous energy, brilliant pink light with white edges, building on my left side. I knew it was spiritual energy and Love. They were on my right, so I reached out my hands across the universe and prepared to be a bridge. I let this energy pass through me to them, I said something like, See, there I did it for you. You have it. They were grateful. I was coming down off the DMT, losing altitude. I would have to go back."

Sara didn't feel comfortable in her role as an earthly spiritual emissary. To this she concluded: "I thought that the only way to encounter them is with bright lights and flying saucers in outer space. It never occurred to me to actually encounter them in our own inner space. I thought the only things we could encounter were things in our own personal sphere of archetypes and mythology. I expected spirit guides and angels, not alien life-forms."

"A World of Pure Imagination" | WHY THE OCCULT SO DESPERATELY NEEDS BOTH SIDES OF OUR BRAIN

AT THE THREAT OF BEING LABELED A "POSTMODERNIST," I'll admit to it forthright. I believe all roads lead to the SAME RELIGION. Well, sort of—but more on that in a moment. First, let's address pre-Christian Gaelic Ireland and their tales of the *Tuatha De' Denann*. In ancient times the *Tuatha De' Denann* were gods and goddesses, having either come from islands in the north of the world or the sky. We refer to these spirit beings today as fairies. The modern materialist-critic, likely being a cultivated and civilized city man, will not fall for the trap of looking over his shoulder in hopes of seeing Ireland's little people on command quite so easily as believing you when told that his zipper is down or his shoe is untied. For the well-minded skeptic, the fairies extinction is proof enough. They are fanciful fabrications stemming from the overtly zealot minds of glamorized superstition. Come to think of it, the entire world is wrought with historical contradictions, where mythology is concerned—but only to the untrained eye.

Just so you know this isn't *really* about fairies. It is about the Titans and the Olympians; Scandinavian elves and the hammer-wielding Thor of Norse mythology; the domovoi and kikimora spirits of pre-Christian Slavic superstition—and so much more. Though I shall only name most of them in passing. Before poets or composers in ancient Greece began their projects, they would *invoke* the Muses for help. They were the sister goddesses, and not only inspired the liberal arts, but even "the sciences." Though their conception is attributed to Zeus—yet another rapturous affair with a young woman—they were raised by Apollo, who personally tutored them in the sciences and arts—each to their own specialty. And as proof that not all past mythologies are extinct, might I point you in the direction of the nearest museum—if you are indeed a cultivated and civilized man of the city. The very word *museum* means "seat" or "institution of the Muses." But you probably knew that already.

Then again, this *is* about fairies, because author W.Y. Evans-Wentz believes in them. In his book, *The Fairy Faith* (1911), he writes:

"There seems never to have been an uncivilized tribe, a race, or nation of civilized men who have not had some form of belief in an unseen world, peopled by unseen beings. In religions, mythologies, and the Fairy-Faith too, we behold the attempts which have been made by different peoples in different ages to explain in terms of human experience this unseen world, its inhabitants, its laws, and man's relation to it."

I therefore ask you to consider the possibility of ONE RELIGIOUS TRUTH. Most importantly, there's Jesus Christ, who is "the same yesterday, and to-day, and forever," as Paul would say (Hebrews 13:8). But my serial reader should already know this about me, including the follow-up—because there is Jesus, our only way unto the Father, and then there are the counterfeits. *They* of course, our every mythology and religion, are run under the same terrible management. His name was Apollo in Greek times, though John called him Apollyon, and Paul might preferably call him in passing, "the prince of the power of the air" (Ephesians 2:2).

King James, also believing as I do in one truth, identified fairies for what they *truly* were. In his dissertation *Daemonologie*, the little people of Ireland were exposed as nothing more than demonic entities with the ability to prophesy, consort with, and aide those whom they served. There is little difference between the Celtic fairies, the medieval hobgoblin and gnome, and the demons of the four Gospels—which Jesus had no trouble in casting out; just as it is with the specters of a table-knocking séance in Victorian times and the little green men of saucer mythology today. Jesus holds power over all of them. None can hear His name without their own knees knocking.

If my critic can entertain the thought of fairies and goblins, the Titans and the Olympians and Muses, then let's complicate matters, because not so long ago a comic book writer—and somewhat of an occult connoisseur in his own right—Doug Moench, was visited by a black-hooded gorilla named Brutus. Well, sort of. In his book, *Mutants & Mystics: Science Fiction, Superhero Comics, and the Paranormal*, author Jeffrey J. Kripal describes a first-hand story told to him while interviewing prolific comic book writer Doug Moench. Kripal writes:

"Moench had just finished writing a scene for a Planet of the Apes comic book about a black-hooded gorilla named Brutus.

The scene involved Brutus invading the human hero's home, where he grabbed the man's mate by the neck and held a gun to her head in order to manipulate the hero. Just as Doug finished the scene, he heard his wife call for him in an odd sort of way from the living room across the house. He got up, walked the length of the house, and entered the living room only to encounter a man in a black hood with one arm around his wife's neck and the other holding a gun to her head: 'It was exactly what I had written…it was so, so immediate in relation to the writing and such an exact duplicate of what I had written, that it became an instant altered state. The air in the room congealed, became almost like fog, and yet, paradoxically, I could see with greater clarity. I could see the individual threads of his black hood…..It really does make you wonder. Are you seeing the future? Are you creating a reality? Should you give up writing forever after something like that happens? I don't know.'"

Maybe Moench and the power of graphic novels are *too much* for the cultivated and civilized city man. Perhaps we should reel the imaginative possibilities and potential realities back several paces, returning again to the ancient mythologies. Still the material-critic will likely shake his head at the untidy entanglements of religions and mythologies laid out before him. There are two options I would ask of him to consider. Firstly, the "Naturalistic Theory" states that the gods, spirits, and fairies of ancient times and in all human cultures can best be explained or rationalized by *natural phenomenon*. To this W.Y. Evans-Wentz writes: "For example, amid beautiful low-lying green hills and gentle dells of Connemara (Ireland), the 'good people' are just as beautiful, just as gentle…." He further states: "Without an object to act upon, environment can accomplish nothing." If this is true, then *Twilight Zone* writer Rod Serling, who once quipped—and I quote: "There is nothing in the dark that isn't there when the lights are on," is full of it. They *arrive* where the mood best suites them.

But secondly, and just as importantly, we come to the Druids—or what W.Y. Evans-Wentz quite simply calls the "Druid Theory." In *The Secret Teachings of All Ages* (1928), occultist Manley P. Hall reminds us of their close-connection with all of Satan's counterfeit religions, albeit the Mysteries, when he writes: "the Druids were initiates of a secret school that existed in their midst. This school, which closely resembled the Bacchic and Eleusinian Mysteries of Greece or the Egyptian rites of

Isis and Osiris, is justly designated the Druidic Mysteries." For Evans-Wentz, the "Druid Theory" is easily explained.

The Druidic Mysteries *alone* brought the fairies into existence.

Today, some 2.5% of the US population reports having some personal, intimate experience with an alien abduction. These are staggering numbers, and it all began not so long ago with Barney and Betty Hill. On the night of September 19, 1961, having been followed by a bright light on a rural highway, the Hill's became the first alien abductees in recorded history. Their story—which they told first to a psychiatrist, then in a book and TV movie—secured the many more abductions to follow. It is an American phenomenon. Whether or not the claimed-victims who fill the 2.5% have deceived themselves into an abduction-scenario or not, if they can so easily match their collective experiences down to the fine print, it's likely because the constituents of an "alien abduction" are boldly bred into mainstream entertainment. We can thank Barney and Betty Hill—and the prince of the power of the air—and television—and the occult which manages it—for that.

The occult needs pop-culture. They need movies; they need comic books; they need toys and merchandise items; they need natural phenomenon and the Druid Theory; they need everything they can throw at us in order for the aliens to land and the specters to creep in our shadow—specifically, for their agents to materialize in our mind's eye. Or as Kripal states: "The truth needs the trick, the fact the fantasy. It's almost as if the left brain will not let the right brain speak (which it can't anyway, since language is generally a left—brain function), so the right brain turns to image and story, to say what it has to say (without saying it)." In other words, the alien needs the science-fiction writer just as the fairy needed the Druid.

The prince of the power of the air demands his fantastical stories; his hieroglyphs; his esoteric texts and hidden wisdom; and all the artillery of books, movie reels, and media that he can throw at us in order to be heard—and also, if you're catching my drift, for his agents to *materialize* through the curtain. But is it any surprise?

God uses His Word to speak with us.

Why should we give the fullest attention of our day to the gods of this world? The occult is not lacking. And it needs us. Oh, it so desperately needs us to live and to breathe.

And to *eat*.

And besides, God has never spoken to me through Shakespeare, Homer, Mark Twain, or Stephen King. They have found their inspiration among the muses. Must they inspire us too?

Let the man who wishes to hear from God pick up his Bible and read.

"You Will Be Like God...." | EVE OPENS THE DOORS OF PERCEPTION TO THE HEAVENLY SIDE OF SCHIZOPHRENIA

1

THE MOTHER OF ALL HUMANITY HAD ALREADY BITTEN into the forbidden fruit and, aside from its pleasing allure, little to no fanfare or parade route of existential enlightenment came of it. Eve had grudgingly agreed to partake in the sacrament, perhaps out of a growing sense of peeping curiosity; though she'd convinced herself while chewing on it that her momentary lapse of discretion was for no other purpose than to prove her Father right and the Serpent wrong. *The body of god* is what *he* called it. The Serpent, who proudly referred to himself as 'the Enlightened One,' couldn't possibly have known what he was talking about,' she thought to herself. If only he'd known her Father, as she had—having walked and talked with Him in the cool of the day. Despite letting him know of his wrongness, she was never-the-less perplexed when nothing happened, and truth be told, somewhat disappointed. Because, if indeed her confession was of honest quality, she had deep down inside hoped that something—*anything* of esoteric knowledge spoken of by the Serpent, could be so easily accessed, as he had promised.

> "And when the woman saw that the tree was good for food, and that it was pleasant to the eyes, and a tree to be desired to make one wise, she took of the fruit thereof, and did eat...." (Genesis 3:6)

"Give it more time," the Serpent gave consideration to his breathing, and proceeded to lay his head upon the knoll; for he too had partaken in the ceremonious sacrament. It wasn't his first helping to the tree either. Given the proper dosage, one truly would *"be like God."* This he knew as fact. Eve would *eat* her words.

WHAT YOU ARE ABOUT TO READ, INDEED, what you have been reading—if you've made it thus far—is a work of assumption, nothing more. The assumption is that our queen mother's civil act of disobedience against Yahweh was anything resembling the Mystery religions enveloping the breadth of human history, and even more specifically, as described by American author Aldous Huxley, who wrote of his first experiment with peyote in *The Doors of Perception*, first published in 1954. Please understand—*this* is the great mystery behind all Mysteries; that one may approach the Tree of Knowledge and partake in its sacrament. That person may eat "the body of God," and in doing so, he may acquire the insider's knowledge that defies all other textbook perceptions of worldwide paganism. In actuality, he has *become* god.

Huxley himself participated in the reawakened occultism emanating the great Mysteries of old, which was only then opened to public understanding, and like the ancient mystics themselves—as it is among their religious adherents today—his concept of the Tree of Knowledge was terribly skewed, for he "was seeing what Adam had seen on the morning of his creation—the miracle, moment by moment, of naked existence," according to his report. Nothing however worth remembering happened to Huxley for half an hour after swallowing his pill, and so for all practical purposes, let us assume the same allotted time had passed since Eve agreed to ingest the fruit.

"...it was pleasant to the eyes..." (Genesis 3:6)

So too at that half-hour mark did Eve, according to Huxley's own experience, become "aware of a slow dance of golden lights." Closing her eyes, there would be other anomalies, such as "a complex of gray structures, within which pale bluish spheres kept emerging into intense solidity and, having emerged, would slide noiselessly upwards, out of sight."

"Is it agreeable?" The Serpent asked.

"Neither agreeable nor disagreeable," Huxley answered his handler, and so likewise must Eve answer her Enlightener, "It just *is*."

Soon her body would dislocate from itself. More specifically, Eve would dissociate herself from what she now realized was her former being. *Isolation* is the only word she could come up with to describe it— a cruel and intolerable solitude. Next arrived a sense of vibrant perception; colorful absorption, deep and penetrating. The thing is—it wasn't just the world around her. The 'Enlightened One' called this otherwise-unfathomable vision her "third eye." Up until now, it had ceased to be *truly* woken. Yes, she had seen her Father. She had walked with Him, talked with Him, and her 'third eye' had acted as a sort of receiver to her soul. But now waves of color washed over and about her; which then in turn flowed into her very being and, having done its work, returned outward from whence it came, as though Being itself were a kaleidoscope and she were the sponge.

Nobody else in all the Earth, not even her husband Adam, could have "seen a bunch of flowers shining with their own inner light and all but quivering under the pressure of the significance with which they were charged...the divine essence of all existence."

Walt Whitman would later give poetic life to this mystery:

"I celebrate myself, and sing myself,
And what I assume you shall assume,
For every atom belonging to me as good belongs to you."

"This is how one ought to see," Huxley repeated to himself as he looked down at the cosmic Universe contained within the fabric of his trousers. They were flannel, by the way. Perhaps for Eve—knowing nothing of clothing for the entirety of her care-free being—it was the hairs on her arm which captured her gaze. Here, we might consider, she found the deeper penetration of all that was or ever could be flowing in and out of her, consecrating and connecting everything into one Being. Formerly, her Father was advertised as something other than His creation, and His creation was certainly not to be confused with Him. But how could that be so, now that her eyes were truly opened, and she had become herself *a god*—like one of the elohim? "If one always saw like this," Huxley would recall of his trousers, "one would never want to do anything else. Just looking, just being the divine Not-self of flower, of book, of chair, of flannel."

Up until that very hour she was an uninspired dabbler in *names* and *pronunciations*—intellectual arrangements. There were the animals of course, which her husband had been granted authority over. He named them. With each naming came "articulation." Then there were the plants and the trees, rivers and streams, realms of the botanical and geographical. All she had ever known were places and distances. Such concepts and restrictive duties ceased to be of interest. If only she could have known in her complacency of *intensity* and *significance* that everything glowed about her with a living light. Certainly, there were some items of interest which glowed more majestically and with more brilliance than others. But time and space had lost its predominance in her life. Up until now, she never even perceived measurements or marked locations to be a category. *This* however was a higher dimension of the self, the other side of paradise—a celestial plane of cleansed perceptions. Huxley warmly called it the heavenly side of schizophrenia.

She had been baptized into a new life by the Enlightened One, so to speak. Eve understood that now.

See, all she had ever known of contemplation was its mere elementary pursuits—all excursions into mediocrity really. If only Adam had such intimate experience before he'd chanced to name each living thing. How would he describe them now? If only he could perceive a world as Huxley described it, "where everything shone with the Inner Light, and was infinite in its significance."

Eve spent several minutes thinking about that—or was it an entire century—and what of time? She of course had looked up at the positioning of the sun and had judged by the length of its shadows what hour of the day it was, but *that*, she already knew, was another existence—the Universe of Plato's shadows. See, had the queen mother been around millennia's later to hear of Plato teaching on "chair-ness," she and a multitude of others who partook in the occultist Mysteries would have immediately understood what the philosopher meant by it— being *in the know*. She understood such esoteric logic to be true simply by gazing down at the hairs on her arm. All she'd ever seen were forms—imitations, as one who saw only shadows in caves. The Chair-ness on her flesh wasn't an ordinary perception. What she saw now was the real thing. At any rate, it was a Universe in which she had ascended from only moments prior and which she might gaze upon now as a goddess, like the many gods of the pantheons to come—completely indifferent to its course of events, whether she chose to observe them or not. Was her indifference really a bad thing?

I can even imagine the Serpent, still thoroughly enjoying the trip from the grassy knoll which he had chosen as his pillow, explaining for Eve what Cambridge philosopher Dr. C.D. Broad many millennia's later would call "Mind at Large."

"Each person is at each moment capable of remembering all that has ever happened to him and of perceiving everything that is happening everywhere in the universe. The function of the brain and nervous system is to protect us from being overwhelmed and confused by this mass of largely useless and irrelevant knowledge, by shutting out most of what we should otherwise perceive or remember at any moment, and leaving only that very small and special selection which is likely to be practically useful."

Evolution, Eve might now consider, as dictated by her Father in heaven, had indiscriminately slowed her intake of knowledge down, and for what reason than His own godly pleasure? All she had ever known of contemplation was in its more elementary forms. They were drafty at best, now that she thought about it. She was a vessel studying the great works of art that her heavenly Father had laid out before her as one might politely attempt in a museum—though failing miserably to comprehend; or a daft pupil of music and poetry, always waiting—tirelessly latching on to each note or word of insight for the right sort of inspiration to spring upon her. Her Father was a great painter, she thought, a master architect. And yet, all He had left for her were confusing hieroglyphs, unfathomable mysteries of purer being, were it not for the sacrament. How could she go on gazing at art, as simpler minds might, even if it was His art, when He had hidden from her its true forms?

Her husband had belonged to the world which the fruit had delivered her from. Eve realized she was purposely avoiding him. But it wasn't for reasons of shame. Not yet, at least. Huxley would describe his own deliberate evasion of eye-contact from his wife, for she "belonged to the world from which, for the moment, mescaline had delivered me." For relief Eve turned back to the hairs on her harm just as Huxley "turned back to the folds on [his] trousers," because, "these are the sort of things one ought to look at. Things without pretensions, satisfied to be merely themselves, sufficient in their Suchness, not acting a part, not trying insanely, to go it alone, in isolation from the Dharma-Body, in Luciferian defiance of the grace of God." Yes, that is what it was—everything in the garden surrounding her, from the largest trees to the tiniest insects. An unknown haiku poet would later write of *roses*: "The flowers are easy to paint—the leaves difficult." That God was Himself Divine and separate from His creation was a bit of paradox considering this "unspeakable" and yet self-evident truth—that what she saw in every living thing and on every leaf and fig was a complexity beyond measure and the freshwater source of all that is divine.

Indeed, the Serpent had proven without a shadow of a doubt—she could see it now—that the life her Father had intended for her was a vision both monotonous and dry. And yet, hadn't God given her the *urge* to escape, the longing to transcend, to ascend to the heights and wear the stars as her crown? This, the Serpent had accurately prescribed, was the entire point for the appetite of her being which, if she were truly being honest, she felt from time to time in her soul. And what would God mind of this, seeing as how, after all, she was merely minding her own business, keeping to the affairs of her own personal estate. What wrong could possibly come of that?

The thing is, "when we feel ourselves to be sole heirs of the universe," as Huxley quipped, "when the sea flows in our veins....and the stars are our jewels, when all things are perceived as infinite and holy, what motive can we have for covetousness or self-assertion, for the pursuit of power or the drearier forms of pleasure? Contemplatives are not likely to become gamblers, or procurers, or drunkards; they do not as a rule preach intolerance, or make war." And so she read over the list in her head concerning all her moral deeds, being a "contemplative" now by nature. She was a Not-Self. Her husband still knew only his self, all lowercase. All circumstances withstanding, she *felt* for him.

And another thing the Enlightened One had proven; her refusal to partake in the sacrament up until that very hour had been an act of defiance against god. Her Father in heaven would most certainly be displeased. But this nagging thought she could compartmentalize for the time being, because all she'd ever been was an apple. How dreadful a thought, that she, the great goddess womb-mother would always be painted and hung in museums as the boring strokes of an apple bitter! And then the even more terrible thought occurred to her! How might history (or her husband, for that matter) judge her if they could not grasp the true enlightened understanding of sin—that is, should they not perceive all of manifested consciousness as infinite and holy? How dreadful, wishing to paint her in the unflattering frame of an apple connoisseur, should they themselves not feel or understand their part as sole inheritors of the Dharma-Body Universe or comprehend the Serpent in any shade other than the great Maestro of the Inner Light?

For a moment, the woman even gazed into a nightmarish vision of the future. She foresaw her children in coming generations, a countless multitude of them, wondering as hungry sheep yet never fed by the religions and institutions which provided them pasture. She saw them listening to daft sermons, gazing foggy-eyed at great works of art, trying desperately to hinge upon each note of music, as she once had, bleeding into one mute ear and out the other, while their *thirst* always remained. And so they were doomed to cover their nakedness with vain philosophies and damnable distractions. "What wonder, then, if human beings in their search for the divine," added Huxley, "preferred to look within?"

To her critics, those who refused to recognize the divine within—Eve was certain of this—she would only go down as an apple-bitter.

Eve looked to her husband with a swaddling deluge of sympathy. He was still an animal in his thinking—unevolved; always obsessed with words and ideals without ever partaking in the sacrament that might enlarge his mind; to perceive God from *within* rather than simply remaining complacent walking *alongside* of Him. Adam also likely saw her as just another apple biter. Oh, the drudgery! In other words, what he perceived as foreign to him need not impress him deeply. And now that she thought about it, the man who had once aroused her inner and outer being had suddenly become boring, pre-occupied with the upkeep rather than coming to a deeper knowledge of the hieroglyphs which he tended to. That's all they really were, the flora and the fauna; hieroglyphs which, when properly deciphered, unveil the true meaning of Wisdom and Mystery, conjurations beyond words. Adam was an intellectual, not a contemplator. Or as Huxley said, compared to the Inner Light, all mortal intellectual concepts were "chaff in the wind."

My Christian reader knows how the remaining story goes. Eve told her husband of everything that she had tasted of and seen, and Adam, also being of a curious mind, he too partook in the sacrament. *"And the eyes of them both were opened."* Yet coming down from her *cleansing* experience with the forbidden fruit, having realized in her sobriety the extent of her deception; a death in two parts—first the spirit and then the soul; one which tragically cast generations of her unborn children into a separation from God rather than the union which the Mystery sacrament claimed to offer—Eve would report of the Serpent, "He has *beguiled* me!"

If only Aldous Huxley had the same fall-out with the Serpent as our first mother and father so wisely chose. They admitted to their nakedness and came clean with the Creator. Moses, being an initiate himself to the Egyptian Mysteries, and likely partaking in such sacrament—in which his eyes would have been opened—but having later repented of them, made the right conclusion when He attested to the true facts of history in the Spirit.

> "...and they knew that they were naked; and they sewed fig leaves together, and made themselves aprons. And they heard the voice of the LORD God walking in the garden in the cool of the day: and Adam and his wife hid themselves from the presence of the LORD God amongst the trees of the garden. (Genesis 3: 7-8)"

Among the many graduates of the Mysteries, having followed in Eve's footsteps and, by their own free will, ingested the tree of knowledge—history is expected to have taken another turn of events entirely. According to Huxley's conclusion:

> "For Angels of a lower order and with better prospects of longevity, there must be a return to the straw. But the man who comes back through the Door in the Wall will never be quite the same as the man who went out. He will be wiser but less cocksure, happier but less self-satisfied, humbler in acknowledging his ignorance yet better equipped to understand the relationship of words to things, of systematic reasoning to the unfathomable Mystery which it tries, forever vainly, to comprehend."

Of course we know this—as do our parents Adam and Eve, quite conclusively—to be the most fallacious and erroneous of errors.

CAN THE PINEAL GLAND BE TRUSTED? OUR SPIRITUAL "THIRD EYE" IN CONFLICT WITH THE GUIDING LIGHT OF GOD'S WORD

CAN THE PINEAL GLAND BE TRUSTED, or does our "third-eye" beguile us with a most peculiar yet enchanting entrapment? That we should play the game of *peek-a-boo* beyond the cosmic curtain, complete with spectacular visions or voices of otherworldly inhabitants, is expected of us, at one time or another—even if we refuse to volunteer for the part. It is no surprise then that we find a smorgasbord of religions laid out before us. They are certainly confusing and seemingly contradictory around their hand-hewn edges, when viewed as a whole. Yet each mythology is easily outed as the same damnable confederation of spiritual entanglements which has vowed to enlighten the whole of human history *apart* from God's anointed one, Jesus. The Word of God exposes them. Even many of the claimed spiritual experiences and prophetic words arousing from my own Christian brethren give me reason for pause.

Adam and Eve *walking with God in the cool of the day* is a thought which I have often pondered. I confess—their very ability to visually observe the manifested presence of our Creator in the temporal body peaks my curiosity. For the Bible believer, these experiences are no more. Such exercises ceased the moment after God confronted them of their sin and cut a cloth of animal skin, or perhaps even *before*. How Adam and Eve *perceived* their Father's presence after they hid themselves in shame is not made immediately clear. But at any rate, God is holy and sinful man is not. A physical separation was necessary. Or as Paul writes: "For the wages of sin is death." *This* I hope we can agree upon. If anything, we deserve to be cast out of God's eternal presence, which makes the punishment two-fold. But let us not overlook another result of sin. Even our biological *being* was tampered with. Thank God for the atoning sacrifice of our Lord and Savior, Jesus Christ, but at present, our biological "tampering-with" remains. What if our inability to properly *perceive* the LORD—from the moment of the forbidden fruit onward—played a part in His decision to physically excuse Himself from our lives? This brings me back to the pineal gland.

I know—I know. I'll immediately be reprimanded by my fellow Christian, "What does the….."

"Pineal gland," I'll say.

"Yes…. *pineal gland*. What does that have to do with *my walk* with God?"

Let me get to that in a moment.

See, the human pineal gland, which is roughly the size of a fingernail and accurately resembles a pine cone, is not actually part of the brain. Rather, it develops from special tissues in the roof of the fetal mouth. From there it migrates to the center of the brain, and as Dr. Rick Strassman has pointedly exclaimed, "has the best seat in the house." Humanist philosopher Rene Descartes of "*I think therefore I am*" fame believed the pineal gland was the seat of the soul, the intermediary between the spiritual and physical—or the stream of consciousness, if you will. Although commonly attributed to Descartes, the notion that our pineal gland was the interfacing organ where the spirit of man gained access and animated the human body *supposedly* originated with a Greek physician named Herophilus. As a contemporary of Alexander the Great, and living three centuries before Christ, Herophilus specialized in dissecting corpses, mainly reproductive organs and the brain. This is all *official* history, by the way. I shall also be reprimanded for not mentioning the mainstream narrative. So there you have it. But truth be told, neither he nor Descartes were solitary in their knowledge.

That pine cone symbol, completely independent from the reckoning of official establishment history, was openly hewn in ancient stone by the very conglomerate of self-enlightening faith-systems which seemingly contradict each other in their outward perceptions yet arguably blend together with spiritual ease. One needn't look far to unearth a pine cone. The Indonesians, Babylonians, Egyptians, Greeks and Romans, Gnostics, the theosophists, Freemasonry, the whole of esoteric knowledge and the occult, and not to be overlooked, the Vatican, all give reliable testimony to its supernatural appeal. The Sumerian god Marduk can be viewed holding a pine cone. The Egyptian god Osiris was equipped with a pine cone staff, as was the Greek god Dionysus and Bacchus, his Roman counterpart. Even the temple ruins of Angkor Watt in Cambodia are filled with pine cone symbolism, including its magnificent stone steeples, which keep their magical upwards gaze towards the heavens. I could go on with honorable mentions.

The pine cone however holds the same meaning for all. It is nothing less but the secret vestigial organ which we were all endowed with—our third eye.

For Dr. Rick Strassman, particularly in light of the "sixty" who volunteered for his New Mexico study on the effects of DMT—the similarities between those undergoing near-death, spiritual, and mystical states with or without the drug should not merely be considered a coincidental occurrence. The resemblance between encounters of non-material beings with everyday people and his "sixty" is also undeniable. By all appearances, Room 531—where he conducted his study; and the outside world are bound at the hip. DMT, Strassman is quick to note, is naturally produced in the body and therefore *commonplace* to our human experience. "The most general hypothesis," he writes, "is that the pineal gland produces psychedelic amounts of DMT at extraordinary times in our lives. Pineal DMT production is the physical representation of non-material, or energetic, processes. It provides us with the vehicle to consciously experience the movement of our life-force in its most extreme manifestations."

Accordingly, the pineal releases a flow of DMT at birth. We were *born* with spiritual experiences. Throughout our lives, pineal DMT is successively secreted, therefore producing further spiritual and religious insights—possibly even at pivotal moments until finally, as we breathe our last, another flood of DMT in the pineal produces near-death and other religious experiences.

Psychedelia is everywhere. Alchemist Alexander Shulgin writes: "DMT is....in this flower here, in that tree over there, and in yonder animal. It is, most simply, almost everywhere you choose to look." Strassman would only add to this, "Indeed, it is getting to the point where one should report where DMT is *not* found, rather than where it is."

Is it *possible* that in a perfectly created order, without the damnable stain of sin (and I only stress the *possibility*), natural dosages of DMT was the method employed by our Creator in which we, beautifully crafted within our temporal bodies, might perceive Him? I will be reprimanded for sure.

"Most of us," writes Strassman, "including the most hard-nosed neuroscientists and non-materialistic mystics, accept that the brain is a machine, the instrument of consciousness. It is a bodily organ made up of cells and tissues, proteins, fats, and carbohydrates. It processes raw sensory data delivered by the sense organs using electricity and chemicals."

Strassman asks that we consider the function of our brains as "receivers of reality." By visualizing our brain as a television, "it's possible to think of how altered states of consciousness, including psychedelic ones brought about by DMT, relates to the brain as a sophisticated receiver." The subjects of Room 531 exhibited the same sensations, feelings, and memories as the rest of us, but when DMT was enacted, the television antennae became adjusted for *better* clarity. And besides, "the euphoria brought on by DMT helped volunteers more unflinchingly look at their lives and conflicts." Practically speaking, a man or a woman under the added influence of DMT would understand the reality behind past actions and the consequences resulting from them.

I return now to my question. Should my reader cling to the Word as his or her *only* trusted Testimony of truth, where God is concerned—and I most certainly do—then what of the pineal gland is to be trusted? It most certainly has a purpose. Or rather, it did at one time. And even now, I willingly confess, the LORD speaks to us through it. This I cannot deny. He speaks to me. He speaks to us, as a Father to His child, but only if we are confiding in His written Word, and certainly not if our grandest of otherworldly voices should tutor us to oppose it. Even in the church we are barraged with an endless feather-flapping line-up of self-appointed prophets, ear-tickling benefactors of visions, tongue-babblers, and bedtime dream interpreters. Eclipses can be accurately determined down to their very moment, and centuries in advance, yet our third-eye provocateurs are almost always wrong in the simplest of details. And that's being kind. They are not held accountable. Why must we put up with them?

The 119th Psalmist must have felt—or rather concluded—that the world was a terribly dark place to be if he should pen the phrase, *"Thy word is a lamp unto my feet and a light unto my path"* (Psalm 119:105). Everything around him—and us, including our own perceptions—is darkness. It would be especially difficult to reckon this passage in any other scenario, whereas foolishly letting go of the God's Word—even if it is to grasp for and rely on some visionary or self-illuminating peephole in our skull—is eternally fumbling around for a light switch in the dark.

We will see visions, alright, if we seek them out. God doesn't hold back His graces, and neither does Satan his lusts. Indeed, the coveted days when God walked alongside Adam and Eve through the cool of the day is no more. Satan will walk alongside of us if we ask him to, and he will be willing to do it on a sun-scorched afternoon. The Creator meanwhile will not be found outside of His Word. Even His Spirit, who favorably rests upon His children, relies on Holy Writ to instruct us. We cannot veer an inch from the left or the right of it. As the writer of Hebrews would remind us, the Word *is alive*.

> "For the word of God is quick, and powerful, and sharper than any two-edged sword, piercing even to the dividing asunder of soul and spirit, and of the joints and marrow, and is a discerner of the thoughts and intents of the heart." (Hebrews 4:12)

The man who employs the Word as his firm foundation needs only a carefree glimpse into Strassman's research and others like him. The esoteric, occultist, and shamanistic traditions as a whole all seem to agree upon one thing. The God of the Bible will not be found among them. That man may return to his studies in the pages of Holy Writ with ease, knowing there is truth in part to Strassman's conclusions—knowing there is truth in part to all of them; be they damnable ones at best, when he incites our spiritual taste buds with the beckoning call of an age-old Mystery School Psychonaut: "What happens when the spirit molecule pulls and pushes us beyond the physical and emotional levels of awareness? We enter into invisible realms, ones we cannot normally sense and whose presence we can scarcely imagine. Even more surprising, these realms appear to be inhabited."

"...And the Inhabitants Thereof Are as Grasshoppers..." WALT DISNEY WORLD, EPCOT, & THE THEATER OF DECEPTION

1

THE MEDIA-MAKER IS a PERSISTENT VIOLATOR of the need to include a globe portrait within their passing narrative—why? They are incestuously bluffing their way through a make-believe vantage point—the video camera held so far back as to capture the whole of our *supposed* blue marble as it wanders *aimlessly* through the sackcloth of space. The documentary genre holds much blame. I have often observed that such glimpses of "the heathen's globe" predictably beds with the shot I am about to describe. We quickly cut in to the habitual routine of people—all of whom issue from a hodgepodge of cultures—navigating the current of their commuter belt. Both shots are worthy of comparison, as they and the globe are on their way to a feckless job. With such incautious glances at creation from the ceiling of space the media-maker most certainly errs. And yet in light of the Copernican Revolution, particularly the augmented reality which entitles us to a belief in it, this is how our tutors wish that we perceive ourselves—from an ascendancy of which only God has granted Himself permission.

But *once* or *twice* in the Bible's unfolding narrative is the breadth of the Earth revealed from above. Here as always it is presumably delivered, as we might deduce, from the perspective of God's throne. Isaiah 40:22 informs us:

> "It is He that sitteth upon the circle of the earth, and the inhabitants thereof are as grasshoppers; that stretcheth out the heavens as a curtain, and spreadeth them out as a tent to dwell in."

My serial reader will likely understand—and willingly *accept*—the wondrous picture which is framed here. Nowhere does the Bible recognize an infinite abyss of *blacker than black* space, as some astronauts have described their own "Isaiah 40:22" experience. The wishful reasoning for the *circle of the Earth* representing a "ball" rather than a circle has been so thoroughly reputed as to expose the self-deceived and despairing heart which obstinately refuses it. Regardless, they prefer the astronauts "Isaiah 40:22" account over the Lord's own eye-witness statement. That is their loss. They would rather expound on the human experience by indulging in the esoteric fantasies of deep space beyond our own line of vision, which the Bible outright rejects but augmented reality affords. My serial reader will concur, heaven stretched out "as a curtain" or the roof of a tent is a poor description of space, yet admittedly it accommodates everything we know of "Hebrew cosmology."

Before the Copernican Revolution—we shall also not accommodate Occult wisdom as a consideration—were there ever such attempts to gaze perversely down upon the Earth when discussing the *nature of human being*, let alone imagined? I think not. If we are to navigate through the treacherous avenues of augmented reality, then we must do so with brave and veracious conviction. The media is a wet sponge dripping with subliminal messaging which hopes to knock upon the Gnostic heart within each of us and light the "divine spark."

2

WALT DISNEY WORLD RECEIVES OVER 52-MILLION VISITORS per year. The Disney theme parks—which includes Disneyland in Anaheim, California—currently dominates any and all of the worlds most photographed places, beating out the Golden Gate Bridge, Yosemite National Park, New York and Paris landmarks. Then the massively impressive geodesic sphere which serves as a symbolic structure for EPCOT needs very little introduction. We know it as *Spaceship Earth*. Its story-line was conceived by eminent science-fiction author Ray Bradbury, one in which we are promised to "take a journey through time unlike any every experienced or imagined." Spiraling gently upward into the geosphere through the strata of ages past, Time Machine vehicles carry its guests to the very beginning of communication—not *God spoke*, as the Bible records, but rather to a Cro-Magnon cave where early man first began documenting events on his wall. *Thousands of years* soon pass to the Kingdom of Egypt, where we witness papyrus invented, thereby making the Cro-Magnon's "wall" portable. The Phoenicians will invent the alphabet.

According to *Walt Disney World* (1986), a time traveler within Spaceship Earth will observe the movable type press invented, in which "the evolution of communication gathers speed. With the Age of Invention, new communication technologies develop at an incredibly swift pace.... To this point, the Time Machines have been ascending into the dome of Spaceship Earth. Before beginning their descent, the vehicles turn, and we see the blue and white oasis of Earth against the dark and mysterious star-sprinkled galaxies. For the first time, we see our planet as it really is—a traveling spaceship. This is the Spaceship Earth experience—a voyage that fills its travelers with an insight into man's evolution, from the dawn of our yesterday to the sunrise of our tomorrow."

Anyone who has ridden Spaceship Earth may recall the narrator's parting words—spoken now by Judi Dench—which neatly sums up the challenge of a future set apart from God's promises. Having gazed upon creation as only our God has a right to—ironically *here* a counterfeit creation—the rider begins his descent to Earth like the stardust of our evolutionary origin, and hears: "Tomorrow's world approaches, so let us listen and learn, let us explore and question and understand. Let us go forth and discover the wisdom to guide great Spaceship Earth through the uncharted seas of the future. **Let us dare to fulfill our destiny.**"

With his journey through the evolution of communication finally complete, the guest is returned to the gateway of EPCOT, where the future of *Planet* Earth awaits and, just beyond the Lagoon, the *world itself* invokes exploration. With the Copernican Revolution employed as his filter, the guest may choose his experience—tomorrow's dreams in Future World or the various ethnic countries which make up *Planet* Earth's bludgeoning centralized governance in World Showcase. But whatever his outcome, EPCOT's globular geosphere almost always looms upon his horizon. It is brilliant indoctrination.

I have a confession to make. *Spaceship Earth* is my favorite ride at Walt Disney World—perhaps because history is my strong suit. But there's more. Throughout our marriage—nearing two decades now—Mrs. Hadley and I have managed to become closeted Disney theme park addicts; though *closeted* no longer. Living most of our lives in Southern California, we probably made a dozen pilgrimages to the Magic Kingdom. And that was *before* we succumbed to annual passes. The amusements which could be found there—not only in Walt Disney World's four theme parks, two water parks, and its dozens of creature-comfort resorts, but the choicest medley of fine dining experiences—

certified the fact that no two trips in any given year were exactly alike. In fact, Mrs. Hadley and I were annual pass holders when we succumbed to the reality of Flat Earth over a spirited dinner conversation. The Disney World experience would never be the same—and that is a *good thing*.

Mrs. Hadley and I were pushing our twin sons in their stroller—mouse ears pronounced upon both toddler heads—and the "world apart from the real" which Disney World bases its very cornerstone upon was suddenly stripped away with unsettling clarity. It was more of a revelation—a bittersweet aftertaste tugging at her heart and mind. With widened eyes she said: "Spaceship Earth is a globe. They want you to *think* the Earth is a globe. And yet the countries of World Showcase are as flat as Florida!"

The whole illusion came toppling down.

We let our subscription expire, and we have yet to renew them. The addiction however remains. I *confess* it hasn't been easy. We've only recently talked about going. I even picked up the phone to make reservation. I can't help it. **I want more of the Mouse.**

Anticipating the children which God would one day bless us with was in itself a maze of disappointments. How we waited! How we waited! And we waited! And we fed our Disney addiction—in part because we dreamed of one day filling the imaginations of our children in its clean swept gutters—as we waited. And now that we have children of our own the Lord has asked us to surrender the Disney theme park experience—*all of it*. We almost went anyways. But this is not about my twitching fingertips, because the Disney theme park experience is an *affront* to the holiness of the Lord.

In *The Magic Kingdom* (1986), Disney paints its prized Florida destination as "a world apart from the *real*." If we are to accept Disney's premise, then we must also detach ourselves from the moral paraphernalia which clothes the otherwise naked Christian faith. For example, Disney has described the Haunted Mansion as "a poltergeist's paradise." By merely participating in Madame Leota's conjuring of "familiar spirits," we are willingly engaging in a complete subversion of Leviticus 19:31; 20:27; and Deuteronomy 18:10-13. Necromancy is a damnable offense—worthy of death. Disney makes a joke of it and expects us to laugh along, particularly when Hitchhiking ghosts follow us home.

"And the soul that turneth after such as have familiar spirits, and after wizards, to go a whoring after them, I will even set my face against that soul, and will cut him off from among his people (Leviticus 20:6)."

Next we find ourselves at *Pirates of the Caribbean*, a boat guided tour which outlines "the capture, pillaging, and burning of a seacoast town by a crew of swashbucklers who would shiver the timbers of Blackbeard." And yet, "while their victims may fret just a bit, they seem to be having as much fun as the buccaneers."

Here the 11th Psalmist confronts us:

"The Lord tests the righteous, but his soul hates the wicked and the one who loves violence. (Psalm 11:5)"

Disney's *Animal Kingdom* devotes an entire land to teaching children about dinosaurs and the hundred-plus million years their evolutionary narrative demands. Its E-Ticket attraction, aptly named *Dinosaur*—a fast-moving chiropractic-inducing dark ride which is described as "a turbulent journey through the Cretaceous period"—takes scissors to the opening chapters of Genesis. If one is to sit back and enjoy the ride, he *must*forsake the eye-witness Testimony of his Creator, and comply. *Dinosaur's* Disneyland counterpart is *Indiana Jones Adventure: Temple of the Forbidden Eye*—same exact ride system and track, different story—in which the demon Mara offers his visitor one of three choices: earthly riches, eternal youth, or visions of the future.

With *Pandora – The Land of Avatar*, a massive themed area based on James Cameron's series of films, we are challenged to another philosophical quandary. What makes us uniquely human? Some transhumanists, so-called "uploaders," hold to the idea that technology will eventually allow us to separate mind from body and enjoy immaterial eternal life, either in the heavens or cyberspace. *Avatar* accepts this premise but tacks on animalism. In such a construct, souls or spirits exist not only in men and fauna but in flora, in rocks, even in natural phenomena such as mountains, rivers and streams. If consciousness can be transferred to another body at will—today male, tomorrow female, an entirely new sexual organ the day thereafter—then the very fact that we are created in God's image has been arrested, tried, and disproved. *Avatar* would have us know that the Bible is an ill-conceived lie. The *true* Christian will have no part in this.

Eat… Sleep… Disney… Say, *"Psychodrama…"*

Walt Disney World is a nothing less than a psychodrama. Often employed within psychotherapy, the willing participant uses spontaneous dramatization and role playing, all under the guise of self-presentation, in order to investigate and gain insight into his life. As a therapy model, it is a means of altering one's values, and works particularly well in molding the morality of children contrary to their parents. Psychodrama is arguably the most common form of magic practiced, and likely the sole discipline of magic which all occultists seem to agree upon. It *is* magic—*real* magic. Not the pointy hat and broom stick magic which Disney parades for cheering audiences—though the large 25-story "magic wand" held by a representation of Mickey Mouse's hand which was constructed upon *Spaceship Earth's* sphere should still turn heads. Unfortunately, it *didn't* mine. Psychodrama was how Anton LaVey described magical ritual in *The Satanic Bible*. His position was that the ritual was cathartic; a purification and purgation of emotions—particularly pity and fear—through art or any extreme change in emotion that results in renewal and restoration, and proved psychological benefits regardless of whether or not the practice directly influenced the outside world. When aptly applied, Psychodrama includes elements of theater, often conducted on a stage, or a space that serves as a stage area, where props can be used. The fellow addict will likely concur—Disney refers to all guest accessible areas of the parks as "on-stage."

In *The Theatre and It's Double*, first published in 1938, French *surrealist* Antoni Artaud writes: "Aside from trifling witchcraft of country sorcerers, there are tricks of global hoodoo in which all alerted consciousnesses participate periodically... That is how strange forces are aroused and transported to the astral vault, to that dark dome which is composed above all of... the poisonous adhesiveness of the evil minds of most people...the formidable tentacular oppression of a kind of civic magic which will soon appear undisguised."

Psychodrama is performance witchcraft. *Global* voodoo, civic magic, public sorcery... Consider the demon "Tinker Bell" zipping alongside the simultaneous swing of a spotlight to announce an incoming display of fireworks... or Mickey Mouse commanding Satan—rather ironically—with his mighty white glove and wand while over the loudspeaker we hear the coo of a child: "Believe!" By garnishing the audiences' willful participation—like an entire nation glued to the television screen during Apollo 11's moon landing and Apollo 13's *malfunction*—the spell is cast. This is the Occult's masterful hand at play—*performance witchcraft*. Knowing then that Disney is a cesspool of falsehoods, the Apostle John would implore of us not to love and practice falsehood. In Revelation 22:15 he writes concerning an eternity in heaven:

> "Outside are the dogs and sorcerers and the sexually immoral and murderers and idolaters, and everyone who loves and practices falsehood."

On a much larger stage, the media has become not only a persistent violator of "Isaiah 4:22," but a cult of drama and violence. The 9/11 false flag event, as well as dozens of theater, nightclub, school, church, and concert shootings—none of which will be outright mentioned here—are arguably all psycho-dramatic exercises. They are orchestrated in advance and executed. Let him who has the eyes to see—*see*. We have been conditioned to psycho-dramatic exercises for decades. Mrs. Hadley and I were born into this norm. So were *you*, likely. In *Secret Societies and Psychological Warfare* (2001), Michael A. Hoffman II reminds us of the rituals gleaming ambition. "This theater of death began as a ritual of the cult members themselves and ended as a giant magical ceremony for the processing of the entire nation... This is the alchemical psychodrama for the transformation of humanity. We are processing just by reading or watching *the news*." And yet there is a defining difference between the worldwide stage; this unholy union of *this present* reality—the media narrative wedded with "a world apart from the real"—and what I have been exclusively describing. My reader cannot control which tower the Occult wishes to collapse; which schools or nightclubs or entertainment venues they consecrate with the tears of crisis actors; nor can I. But with due discipline and diligence, we can manage our jurisdiction in the stage of another kind.

To say we are in love with the Lord and yet willingly lust for the flesh of a man or a woman is adultery and rebellion against our Creator. Thus sayeth Jesus. As the Apostle John would claim, "If we say that we have fellowship with Him, and walk in darkness, we lie, and do not the truth... (1 John 1:6)." In the same vain—can we lust towards a mastery of abracadabra or play the game of peek-a-boo into necromancy, or simply covet violence—even as entertainment would provide it—not forgetting a thirst for the possibilities which transhumanism offers our handicaps, insecurities, and sensuality, and still love the Lord? With Walt Disney World, I could go on... The willing participant in the ongoing performance wears an RF chip so that his every footstep may be tracked. He is even photographed unaware. He delivers his very being over to an almost omnipotent power from the moment he arrives—power to manipulate his exocentric reality with the esoteric; to manipulate his subconscious with apostate desire; in short, to manipulate him and the values of his children.

> "For if we sin wilfully after that we have received the knowledge of the truth, there remaineth no more sacrifice for sins.. (Hebrews 10:26)."

Magic is all around us. Determination results in magic. Imagination is a key for magic. And practice makes *better* magic. To this cause we *must not* apply.

Over the loudspeaker we hear the voice of a child softly cooing: "*Believe.*"

MARY POPPINS: *Part Time Nanny, Full Time Witch* | P.L. TRAVERS AND THE OCCULT

1

IN THE LATE SUMMER OF 1926 AUTHOR P.L. TRAVERS stood on the doorstep of poet and Irish senator William Butler Yeats Dublin home soaked and disheveled—her arms bundled with the branches and berries she'd collected from the island of Innisfree. In return Yeats showed the 27 year-old the egg his canary had just laid. By Hollywood standards, Travers was no great beauty. Her dreams of achieving stage and silent screen stardom had sailed, and she'd only recently moved from Sydney to London in order that she might earn a wage reporting on the very theatrical world which was otherwise determined to reject her. Adding insult to injury, the boatman whom she had hired to charter her to and from Innisfree in the pouring rain had identified her landmark as Rats Island. But in truth, the Avalon of Yeats imagination didn't actually exist. Yeats knew it and Travers knew it. For this reason, some say *Mary Poppins*, the fictional nanny from her book series, was born that day. Travers desired the unseen realm, and quite ironically, the branches and berries she'd collected in a torrential downpour attested to her devotion. Her preference was for witchery.

2

WILLIAM BUTLER YEATS MEMBERSHIP WITH THE THEOSOPHICAL Society is no secret. But where Occult authors like L. Frank Baum found much satisfaction in Madame Helena Blavatsky and her society of experimental mystics, the Irish poet ultimately found little. When compared with a man of Yeats intellect and ambition, her members simply lacked the appetite and discipline for *true* Occultism. Though to be fair, it was Madame Blavatsky who manipulated the mystic Mohini Mohun Chatterji into leaving India for the United Kingdom. Chatterji would have a profound lifelong impact on both Yeats and Irish poet George Russell. In *Yeats and Theosophy*, author Ken Monteith suggested that Chatterji was "the source of his theosophical interests."

Almost from the beginning Theosophy was beset by rows and splits. In 1890 Yeats would prove no exception. With the Theosophists behind him, Yeats became a First Order initiate of the Hermetic Society of the Golden Dawn, a brotherhood founded only two years earlier in England, with many of its members passing first through Theosophy—and likely already deprived of its inadequacies. In *W.B. Yeats: A Life*, author R.F. Foster affirms that the Golden Dawn's mission was to reach even higher than Blavatsky's already-lofty ambitions and "follow through the interest in ritual magic and study prescribed by Esoteric Theosophists." Members of the Golden Dawn concentrated their teachings with the practicality of discipline by applying ritual magic, particularly the Kabbalah, to all things. His great love Maud Gonne was a member, as was the actress Florence Farr, Welsh author Arthur Machen and English authors Evelyn Underhill and Aleister Crowley whom, even in his own day, was world renowned and recognized as the wickedest man alive. As a First Order member, Yeats would have familiarized himself first with the Hebrew alphabet, understanding Hebrew Scripture with the mystically-perverse Kabbalah as its guide, meditation and divination practices of the tarot (a prized possession of his), and perhaps most importantly, *intimate* knowledge of the Tree of Life. Yeats later confessed in a letter that "the mystical life is the centre of all that I do and all that I think and all that I write."

It was Utopia he was after.

And much like Theosophy, the First Order simply couldn't quill his insatiable appetite for the self-appointed divine. Yeats set his ambitions upon the Second Order of the Golden Dawn, a closed inner-circle scarcely populated with advanced practitioners of magic. Very few ascended into its upper ranks. Yeats however did. This was 1890—an important year for Yeats, because with his initiation into the First Order, so too was one of his greatest poems released.

For Genevieve Pettijohn, the poet's 1890 publication of *The Lake Isle of Innisfree* is dripping wet with "Kabbalism, numerology, and tarot cards to which these societies looked for inspiration in their occult practices" to such a degree as to demonstrate "mastery over the Golden Dawn's basic tenants." Pettijohn further elaborates:

> "Yeats further showcased his magical abilities in Innisfree by describing the sights and sounds on the island itself. Several

personal accounts confirm that Yeats had special powers transcending the natural realm. Maud Gonne, the object of Yeats' unrequited love, asserted in her Memoirs that Yeats was able to call upon spirits to communicate symbolic images to her; during one such session, she cried, 'I see a figure holding out its hand with a skull in it,' and the two knew they were spiritually compatible. Indeed, soon after joining the Golden Dawn, Yeats bragged that he could make 'the visible world completely vanish and another world summoned by the symbol would take its place'"

From this mystical island of his mind, completely uninhibited by Christianity, the poet-Occultist could prove himself a conjurer of Magic capable of becoming one with the natural world, far away from the industrial society in which he resided. So one day in the late summer of 1926 a bedridden P.L. Travers arrived on his doorstep, arms bundled with branches and berries in a symbolic but astonishingly disciplined gesture which stated that she had brought his mystical island to him—or perhaps more importantly, she too had been there.

3

POETRY HAD BROUGHT THEM TOGETHER—and the Occult. But *mostly* the Occult. The paintings of Theosophist George William Russell often depicted fairies, angels, and saintly beings imbued with mystical dreamlike qualities. He was deeply involved in crafting one such composition when he heard *something* whisper into his ear.

The speaker said: *"Aeon."*

Aeon was a term of Gnosticism and Manichaeism for the first created being and one of the orders of spirits that emanated from the Godhead. Russell took the whisper to be a sign—*that* and the open-faced book he came across in a library, in which the very word caught his eye. Russell began using Aeon to sign his manuscripts. Among his devoted readership, the founding member of the Theosophical Society of Ireland and editor of the *Irish Statesman*, leading literary journal of the nascent Irish Free State, was simply known as a symbol—Æ.

Australian P.L. Travers was one such devotee, and as fate would have it, she sent him a poem.

The 57 year-old editor of the *Irish Statesman* returned her stamped envelope with a check and an accompanying letter. In short, Russell loved her work. And perhaps more importantly, W.B. Yeats did too. Yeats thought she had "poetic merit," Russell wrote, and "that means a good deal from him." *Oh*, and another thing. If she was ever in Dublin, he said, stop by his home or office and say *hello*. Her poem was straightaway published.

Travers took him up on that offer.

The Australian author would involve herself in many liaisons with members of both sexes, but only from Æ would she receive a collection of endearing letters, often coated with colorful sketches, in which she was intimately referred to as "*my angel.*" In time Russell would come to believe that he and Travers had met in a former life. Their friendship would be devoted to such conviction until the end of his life in 1935, when Travers bid him farewell on his deathbed.

4

IF HICCUPS COMPLICATED THE AUSTRALIAN AUTHOR and Æ's reincarnated love affair, it was likely due to the fact that Travers was a womanizer. *This* according to Valerie Lawson, her own biographer. Though her circles of friends was gradually introduced and expounded upon through their liaison together, many of whom likely had a hand in typecasting *Mary Poppins*, the Australian author preferred the company of women. And yet after Æ, her subsequent love life was disastrous. There was "Francis Macnamara and then three women—Madge Burnand, Jessie Orage and an artist called Gertrude Hermes," writes Valerie Lawson in *Mary Poppins, She Wrote*. "There was a lot of angst, a lot of intimacy. After that she turned her eye to the gurus." Like Freemasonry, Theosophy was a fashionable—though perhaps *closeted*—pursuit for power-hungry socialites. As a leading Theosophist, her male lover had a phone book of connections. One of Russell's own correspondences was with American Theosophist Henry A. Wallace, who would come to serve as 33rd Vice-President of the United States in the Franklin Delano Roosevelt White House. Soon after her arrival in Europe, Travers would become familiarize herself with Occultist George Gurdjieff.

As a central tenant of Gurdjieff's teachings, mankind cannot perceive reality because man does not possess a unified consciousness. Rather, he lives in a hypnotic state of *waking sleep*. "Man lives his life in sleep, and in sleep he dies," Gurdjieff said. For Gurdjieff, humanities ambition should be a conscious and collective mission of *waking*, because as things now stand, each individual soul is an island of subjective perspective. But if a soul could be *woken*, he would become a different sort of human altogether. The light at the end of his tunnel was Utopia.

Gurdjieff's star pupil however was the Russian esotericist Pyotr Demianovich Ouspensky, whose lectures in London were attended by such literary figures as Aldous Huxley, T. S. Eliot, and Gerald Heard. A researcher would tire himself out connecting the dots through this close-knit circle of literary and scientific acquaintances, so let me be brief. Aldous Huxley had been initiated into the mysteries of peyote through W.B. Yeats' bitter rival, Aleister Crowley. Crowley found inspiration in Madame Blavatsky, who in turn studied under Nikolai Fedorov and Tsiolkovsky—Russian cosmists and fathers of the space race. On the American front, it was Crowley who mentored Occultist Jack Parsons, founder of JPL and father of American rocketry. This is interesting to note, since it is said that Crowley also initiated famed science fiction writer H.G. Wells into the mysteries of hashish. Not only was the famed science-fiction writer one of Darwin's chief apostles, his own mentor was none other than Huxley's paternal grandfather, Thomas Huxley. By tenaciously devoting his life to the human-ape relationship, Huxley was both revered and disdained by many as Darwin's Bulldog. Through fantasy authors like Wells, Occult studies could be successfully blended and packaged to the public masses by indiscreetly promoting a fanatical faith in science as a cure-all to human misery.

With his own first published work, *The Fourth Dimension*, Ouspensky further explored the evolutionary ideas of Charles H. Hinton. For Hinton, an untenured mathematics instructor at Princeton, the fourth dimension was a mathematical concept represented by the cube, which essentially entailed our higher and immortal self. The fourth dimension is essentially just a walk-in closet for the hoarder of esotericism. In his book, *Mystery School in Hyperspace*, author Graham St. John writes of the Occultist:

> "Hinton developed his views on the mystical and evolutionary significance of four-dimensional space. The fourth dimension was perceived to be the source of alternative modes of

consciousness like those experienced by mystics, psychics, mediums, and others with evolved means of perception. For Hinton, the fourth dimension was not a mathematical abstraction, but a mode of perception integral to the development of human consciousness."

While bedding with Æ, the literary character who *became* Mary Poppins would be welcomed and massaged into being through Gurdjieff and Ouspensky's influences. It is reasonable beyond doubt that the Occult fostered her. But where the British nanny's forward thinking sexuality is explicitly concerned, it is Gurdjieff who garnishes the gaze of today's lesbian scholars. In spite of his professed advocacy of rigid gender roles, the Russian mystic created a rather odd and inclusive woman's-only group in the 1920's known as *The Rope*, whose members were billed as strong and successful professionals. In other words, none subscribed to traditional gender roles. But more specifically, all members happened to be lesbian.

Travis joined the group.

One of these women, Jessie Orage, scandalized the Gurdjieff community by wearing men's trousers and smoking cigarettes. She and Travers also became lovers.

For this reason Travers never married. That Travers was not a nun is also safe to conclude. The author found herself writing "saucy erotica inviting readers to imagine taking off her undergarments" for orgasmic purposes, none of which brought her fame, but likely served among her inner-circle contemporaries as a coveted recipe in ritual magic. It was her ten year live-in relationship with Madge Burnand, daughter of the editor for *Punch* Magazine, and which her "hyper-discreet biographer begrudgingly described as *intense*," that she wrote *Mary Poppins*. In her book, the British nanny was described as being 27 years of age.

It is likely no coincidence that Travers was herself 27 years of age when she stood on the doorstep of poet W.B. Yeats Dublin home soaked and disheveled—her arms bundled with the branches and berries she'd collected from the island of *Innisfree*.

5

THERE IS A REFERENCE IN MADAME H.P. BLAVATSKY'S *The Voice of the Silence*, a treatise derived from the eastern-mystic *The Book of the Golden Precepts*, which deserves our attention. Blavatsky would in effect first introduce the Theosophist to *Mary Poppins* decades before Travers initiated the public into a willful participation with witchcraft. The ascendancy spoken of here is perhaps the most coveted degree of the ancient Mystery Religion. We read:

> "Then from the heart that Power shall rise into the sixth, the middle region, the place between thine eyes, when it becomes the breath of the ONE-SOUL, the voice which filleth all, they Master's voice. 'Tis only then thou canst become a "**walker of the sky**," who treads the winds above the waves, whose step touches not the waters."

Blavatsky relished in the Yogi, "formed of the wind; as a cloud from which limbs have sprouted out." The *sky-walker*, she called him, is a transcendent master so benevolently evolved as to behold "the things beyond the sea and stars; he hears the language of the Devas and comprehends it, and perceives what is passing in the mind of the ant." From the physical plane his "astral body is organized as a vehicle," and he can even "travel through the pure akasha from globe to globe" and to any number of astral planes—or as she would aptly describe in other writings, "there are millions and millions of worlds and firmaments visible to us" by which we can travel, but "there are still greater numbers beyond those visible to the telescopes, and many of the latter kind do not belong to our objective sphere of existence."

Travers would even refer to Poppins in her books as the "Great Exception." In Theosophical terms, this means that "she has gone beyond the evolution of humanity and her life now stands in contrast to those who have not yet reached this stage." Writing for Theosophical Society's *Quest Magazine*, Helene Vacht further described Poppins as one who "resembles a guardian angel, demon, or cosmic being who comes from time to time to visit Earth." For the guardian of *hidden knowledge* in Mesopotamian epics, Poppins is apkallu.

In Enochian terms, Poppins is a *Watcher*.

So begins the Mary Poppins series. Poppins first appears as an unidentified alien shape, "tossed and bent under the wind," like the coming cloud of Theosophy. Jane and Michael Banks notice that the shape is carried by the east wind and flung at the gate, then lifted by the wind and carried to the front door.

Upon accepting the position as nanny, Michael Banks asks, "You'll never leave us, will you?"

To this Poppins replies, "I'll stay till the wind changes."

Vacht adds: "She never settles with the Banks family for very long, but while she is there, she teaches the family, primarily the children, about the deeper meaning of life. She does this through magical outings with the children during the day or at night when the children dream or wake up and seem to leave their room."

In one such episode, Jane and Michael are invited to *walk the sky* and participate in a celestial circus, which is quite opposite from an earthly circus, mind you. Here the constellations become living animals that perform a dance of the Wheeling Sky, and in the great Mystery tradition, the circus master is the sun. This is all in honor of Mary Poppins, of course—their Ascended Master. Though Michael is given the moon to hold, it soon shrinks away. The sun then schools the two children on the nature of reality. The read is asked to ponder: was Michael truly holding the moon and—just as importantly, while considering their ritual magic—is any of their experiences in the heavens *real*? One might further ask, have they truly ascended into the heavens to begin with?

"Then," said Jane wonderingly, "is it true that we are here tonight or do we only think we are?"

The Sun smiled again, a little sadly. "Child," he said, "seek no further! From the beginning of the world all men have asked that question. And I, who am Lord of the Sky—even I do not know the answer!"

Poppins appetite is for the reality *behind* this illusion—Maya; an exacting discipline which cultivates a complete manipulation of the natural world, where garden parties may be attended under the sea and tea-time might be celebrated from the ceiling. For Poppins, contact with our own shadow—and on Halloween of all nights—is a rhythmic dance with the unconscious, or in Jungian psychology, welcoming the part of ourselves that is unknown. Poppins can even master the reality *beyond* by visiting other planets. Nature itself might also be *summoned*, such as a star named Maia from the Pleiades cluster of the Taurus constellation, who accompanies them while Christmas shopping. Though Poppins world is completely unexpected, it is only so because of the ceremonious.

When a disembodied voice calls Jane and Michael to the zoo late at night, they come to learn that animals run the zoo after hours while the people are thrust into cages. Though the lion believes he is the king of the animals—as many of us would likewise conclude—it is a huge hooded snake that truly runs the show. In a rather familiar—and dare I say *predictable*—Occultist twist, Poppins calls him "cousin." Her identity has been further given away. Though an Ascended Master, she is in ultimate allegiance to the worldwide worship of the Serpent, and is indeed—to some degree—of his kind. She will later wear the skin he has shed as a belt buckle.

Lesbian playwright Carolyn Gage writes: "Mary Poppins has become what one writer calls 'untouchable and distant,' but I would use the word *'exalted.'* She is morphing into archetypal forms. Æ suggested the goddess of destruction and empowerment, Kali—and Travers did not disagree." She further adds: "I believe what we are dealing with here is a lesbian butch. A guardian/warrior archetype who combines military discipline with a Gurdjieffian mysticism that enables her to ascend to the stars and commune with the animals."

Poppins possessed such uncanny ability and divine-like nature as to meddle with the affairs and aftermath of Titanomachy, or the War of the Titans, which ended in victory for the Olympian gods—according to Greek mythology, anyway. By invoking a statue of Neleus to come alive in the park—thereby redirecting the Nephilim spirit back to this side of consciousness—one might wonder if Mary were revoking Poseidon's decision to blackball his son.

"What is your father's name? Where is he?" Jane was almost bursting with curiosity.

"Far away. In the Isles of Greece. He is called the King of the Sea." As he spoke, the marble eyes of Neleus brimmed slowly up with sadness.

Among the endless cycles of moon magic and the nanny's constant comings and goings, all of which occurs over the course of several books, the Occultists personal devotion to the study of—and perhaps even mastery *over*—reincarnation plays a heavy hand. Once more we turn to the image of a bedridden Travers on the doorstep of Occultist W.B. Yeats for inspiration. Writes C. Nicholas Serra in *To Never See Death: Yeats, Reincarnation, and Resolving the Antinomies of the Body-Soul Dilemma*:

"...scattered among hundreds of poems, twenty-six plays, and dozens of essays, Yeats's vision encompasses time before time and worlds before creation, a thousand myriads of worlds ultimately extending outward into unutterable realms of Negative Existence and no-thing-ness. He attempted to chart the psychology of incarnation, the interplay of the individual soul and the World Soul, the Anima Mundi and the Divine, the immanent divinity and the transcendent and Absolute—of which the metaphysical calculus *surrounding his theories of reincarnation are only one fraction.*"

Travers was certainly not shy in introducing Yeats lifelong devotion to her children audience. When a starling visits the nursery at Cherry Tree Lane, the wise bird is able to commune with Mary Poppins and the babies, John and Barbara. What's more, the reader becomes aware that everyone involved, including the toddler twins, perfectly understand the language of the wind, the stars, and the sunlight. After the starling laments that the children will soon forget everything concerning the knowledge and whereabouts of their transmigration, the children protest. Never the less, they soon forget. And so it goes. One might wonder *why* Poppins possesses intimate knowledge of the hidden realms once described in Plato's *Phaedo* and *The Republic* while the children were destined to forget. But that is not to say that she herself has not once forgotten. It is up to the Banks children now to relearn through a lifetime of devotion in Occult studies all that is hidden from human knowledge—that is, if they should hope to model themselves after their beloved teacher.

In *Mary Poppins Comes Back*, published the year of Æ's death in 1935, a new baby is born to the Banks household. This completes five children, Jane and Michael, the toddler twins John and Barbara, as well as the new baby girl Annabel. Once more, the wise starling returns. Annabel's birth is a indeed a pronouncement of glad tidings. The starling asks the newborn soul to tell the fledgling accompanying him where she came from. the newborn Annabel's response is nothing short of *haunting*, for we read:

"I am earth and air and fire and water," she said softly. "I come from the Dark where all things have their beginnings. I come from the sea and its tides, I come from the sky and its stars, I come from the sun and its brightness—and I come from the forest of earth. Slowly, I moved at first always sleeping and dreaming. I remembered all I had been and I thought of all I shall be. And when I had dreamed my dream I awoke and came

547

swiftly. I heard the stars singing as I came and I felt warm wings about me. I passed the beasts of the jungle and came through the dark, deep waters."

"It was a long journey! A long journey indeed!" said the starling softly, lifting his head from his breast. "And ah, so soon forgotten!"

Once again, as any Occultist would come to expect, the soul of every newborn, including that of Annabel, soon forgets.

With Mary Poppins, "she turned that mystical conception into a domestic one, and actually made it more compelling," writes Edward Rothstein at the *New York Times*. "Poppins regularly opens a door into dimensions outside ordinary space and time for the benefit of her charges: a star from the Pleiades constellation comes to Earth in the form of a girl, a statue of a Greek god comes to life to play with Jane and Michael, an ancient crone grows fingers made of barley-sugar. Mary Poppins herself seems a creature of the heavens temporarily brought to Earth."

Rothstein concludes, "Eventually the children learn that *'Appearances are Deceptive.'* They learn, that is, that there is a split between the inner life and outward appearance, between the magic of Mary Poppins and her thoroughly adult facade. This is not a reflection of hypocrisy. Both realms are necessary. Authority, order, precision— mocked in the film and on Broadway—are intertwined with her magic."

For Travers, childhood contains a powerfully penetrating, seemingly contradictory double vision of the adult—a melding of two realms. With a domesticated nanny for their guru, Jane and Michael and their younger three siblings could observe authoritarian order and rigid precision crowned with the wild-eyed realization of magical freedom. Poppins is a caricature of the self-effacing master of discipline and self-knowledge which Gurdjieff demanded of his disciples. She is in essence a woman of her own design and, as a well-noted promoter of liberated sexuality, a *true* graduate of The Rope. She contains within her *being* the multi-dimensional awareness of Ouspensky and Hinton and the manipulative prowess of Yeats, particularly the esoteric evolution necessary to conjure *Innisfree* for the undisciplined child. Poppins comes to us not from any ordinary coven of witchery. She is an ascended Master, having undergone the spiritual transformations of initiation. Much like her male counterpart *Superman,* who was developed in precisely the same decade, Poppins is an Occult Messiah.

HER BELOVED FRIEND FROM ANOTHER LIFETIME was dead. In 1939, just four years after she bid Æ farewell in bed, Travers adopted the grandson of his publisher—one of them, anyways. This connection between Æ and the opportune child is often noted, as is the sobering fact that he was also a twin. Hard pressed on which of the two she should take, the author turned her attention between both boys lying in separate beds, but couldn't make up her mind.

The children's grandfather said: "Take two, they are only small."

Travers consulted her astrologer. Together they agreed upon Camillus. Only Anthony remained behind in bed. Camillus was raised believing he was the *only* son of a wealthy sugar baron, and that his father had died about the time of his birth. That lie was almost exposed when Anthony appeared at their home in Chelsea at 17 years of age. Travers wouldn't have it. She promptly threw the boy out.

According to the twins' biological older brother, Joseph Hone, Travers' decision to separate the boys and then concoct a false reality surrounding his origin brought both lives to ruin. "Pamela Travers saw herself as Mary Poppins and thought she could play Poppins with poor little Camillus," Joseph Hone told the *Mail*. When Walt Disney finally coaxed the intransigent author to Hollywood in order that she might become an instant millionaire overnight, her son was incarcerated in England for drunk driving without a license. Camillus Hone had become a boozer.

One fateful day he had met his twin brother in a bar and realized he'd been lied to about everything.

7

TO SAY PAMELA TRAVERS DISFAVORED Walt Disney's 1964 production of her title character is an understatement. As the decades passed—while Travers watched Poppins endlessly promoted with the glop of nostalgia; crowned with the royalty of a beloved classic—the bitterness inside of her curdled. Travers would come to hate Disneyland's counterfeit. Disney's script had turned the tables on her narrative and centered on bad parenting. The strong and successful women of Gurdjieff's *Rope* were now demoted to suffragettes so silly they'd be hacked to bits with Carrie Amelia Nation's hatchet and immediately swept up by the parading brooms of the temperance movement. Disney was sloppy with Theosophy. His magic boiled down to parrot-knobed umbrellas and over-sized mouse gloves. His alchemy was the proper antidote of sugar matched with astral-laughter and his esoteric end-game was the rediscovered *gnosis* of childish irresponsibility in every kite flying mother and father. And besides, Julie Andrews was too beautiful and sang too sweet a tune. Or as lesbian playwright Carolyn Gage put it—Disney's Poppins simply wasn't *butch* enough.

It's a shame really—the *Satanic Panic,* which swept through the church like hellfire in the closing decades of the 20th century, never thought to peek in on 17 Cherry Tree Lane.

SATAN TEMPTED JESUS WITH THE KINGDOMS OF THE WORLD *(and E.T. Visited the UN)* | NOW COMMENCE WITH THE "SATANIC PANIC"

1

BY DAY, JACK PARSONS LAUNCHED THE COLD WAR. By night, the founder of NASA's Jet Propulsion Laboratory emerged from a coffin to perform the Enochian magic first began by Englishman John Dee. His own esoteric works were often mixed with his scientific experiments, and it has been reported that Parsons attempted to invoke spirits while working with rocket fuel. His mentor Aleister Crowley had espoused science with the practice of sex magic, Kabbalism, rites taken from Freemasonry and medieval grimoires—a quest which Parsons could stand behind. Parsons used his own salary to conduct occult experiments in hopes of ushering in a new age of magical freedom. In the Mojave Desert, he and Church of Scientology founder L. Ron Hubbard were attempting to invoke the power of a goddess. This divine being—identified by Crowley as both the Biblical whore of Babylon and the goddess Ishtar—would bring the end to an age of repressive Christian morality. It was 1946. They dubbed the project "the Babalon Working." And on the 18th of January, only two weeks into their fusion of sex-magic, Parsons announced to Hubbard, "It is done."

2

THE LOS ALTOS DRIVE-IN THEATER, once located at 2800 N. Bellflower Boulevard in Long Beach, California, where I watched such classics as *Raiders of the Lost Ark, Back to the Future* and—in its final hours before closing—*Jurassic Park*, is now a typical shopping mall, complete with the *ho-hum-drum* of a Papa John's Pizza and K-Mart.

Upon its wide release on June 11, 1982, *E.T.* invaded every American city and suburb. Within two weeks, Reese's Pieces sales tripled. *Variety's* McCarthy critiqued *E.T.* as "the best Disney film Disney never made." Mrs. Hadley would have been only a few blocks away and just as many *weeks* old when I participated in my own screening of the film from the front seat of the family wagon, and I can distinctly recall walking around the church parsonage in Hawthorne, California endlessly rehearsing: "E.T. phone home! E.T. phone home!" This is likely due to the fact that my parents documented those persistent words on cassette tape, and for years thereafter I wore out the ribbon by rewinding and playing my performance on the very Japanese-made Panasonic that had earlier recorded it.

But I wasn't the only one. Neil Diamond wrote a hit song, *Heartlight*, based on the film's central tropes. Michael Jackson not only purchased one of the working puppets used in the film but—in a somewhat more masterful performance than my own—can be heard crying at *E.T.'s* death during his own special LP-length recording. At President Reagan's request, Spielberg held a private screening in the White House. The First Lady cried during the films third act. Then again, so did The Gipper. Spielberg told *Twilight Zone*Magazine, the leader of the free world could not withhold "a little moisture in his eyes. I view that as a very positive sign."

On the 17th of September, E.T. made an unprecedented appearance at United Nations headquarters in New York City. *Twilight Zone* Magazine writer David Shifren was on hand to witness the event and interview its director. He wrote: *E.T.'s* "United Nations debut came before a standing room only crowd of foreign dignitaries, consulate members, and UN staffers who saw the young director received the UN's Medal of Peace, the first time the prestigious award has ever gone to a filmmaker. They then watched a special showing of Spielberg's blockbuster hit, *E.T.*" Shifren adds: "Despite the event's formal setting—the UN's spacious Trusteeship Council Chamber, where almost every seat bears an official placard naming a member country—the audience was completely swept up by the film." They applauded enthusiastically during the closing credits, particularly for Spielberg's name, and cheered during the more exciting scenes.

The "UN and E.T. are one and the same," Spielberg said in his acceptance speech. "They both have the desire and the need to communicate, to care, and to love. This film is dedicated to all children of all ages." Further voicing approval for the UN, Spielberg concluded:

"The United Nations represents everything that *E.T.* stands for—*love* and *communication*."

E.T.'s arrival at the UN did nothing to massage the nerves of right-wing evangelicals. Eschatological-minded Christians had long been suspicious of the UN's potential to fulfill the prophecies of the Apostle John. By making this the case in *The Late Great Planet Earth*, Christian Zionist and dispensationalist author Hal Lindsey prompted an entire baby-boomer generation to gaze up at the clouds for the Lord's return. While science-fiction writer Arthur C. Clarke had already called out the aliens bluff, detailing them as your run of the mill Biblical devil and then being so bold and perverse to glory at their destined arrival in *Childhood's End* (1953), the books of Christian author Frank Peretti would be instrumental in cementing the alien-demon connection. The blood of American radio host and televangelist Bob Larson simply boiled over the connections he made between rock music and Satanism. His book, *Satanism: the Seduction of America's Youth* persuaded countless parents that forces were influencing America's youth through "ghoulish games, horror films, black metal music, and drugs, as well as the occult enticements" in hopes of selling their souls to Satan. *Dungeons & Dragons* was criminalized in the church. And as most online reviews by a grown and apparently *bitter* millennial will show, Phil Phillips book, *Turmoil in the Toy Box* (1986), pillaged and plundered the playtime carpets of countless childhoods by convincing their parents that *He-Man, G.I. Joe, Star Wars, My Little Pony*, and *Smurfs* were laced with occult ties.

I remember it well.

"It was something we didn't realize at the time, but now, it looks like a low-scale version of the McCarthy-era paranoia around communism," said Peter Bebergal, author of *Season of the Witch: How the Occult Saved Rock and Roll*, in an interview with *io9*. "The devil worshippers could be anywhere. They could be your next-door neighbor. They could be your child's caregiver." He furthermore added: "A lot of it was having a spiritual vacuum, created by the fact that the 1960s promise of this cosmic, spiritual consciousness didn't really pan out. Then you had this 1970s uptick of paranormal investigations, ESP, an interest in UFOs, really climaxing with Close Encounters of the Third Kind. But the aliens never actually landed, you know? I think it led to a cynicism that led to kind of a cultural paranoia: there is no meaning. There was already an uptick in fundamentalist Christianity. The Reagan Right had begun to dominate politics. And it was the beginning of a cultural war; that's when the Parents Music Resource Center started to put labels on album covers to warn against profanity or even references to the occult. It was a perfectly ripe stew for *Satanic Panic*. In a way, believing that Satan is running the world is still offering a kind of order to things, in a world that can feel very disorderly."

And yet the *Satanic Panic* which once sent the baby-boomer generation into a tailspin is no more. More precisely, it is but a *whimper*—already doomed to messy back-filing in the annals of discomforted minds. Somewhere along the way the Christian dusted his devil-worshiping Led Zeppelin album off and returned it straightway to their turntable, callously shrugging as he did so. Despite Jimmy Page's lifelong devotion to Aleister Crowley, I can only deduce that songs like *Highway to Heaven*—particularly Page's clear pronunciation of "Hail Satan!" when played backwards—means little but theatrics to the haphazard person who deceives himself into claiming a love for the Lord while singing along. The devils music has become family entertainment. For many—and dare I say *most*—the Spirit is thoroughly quenched. Looking back on it all, there is a tragically missed opportunity in Christian musician Keith Green's 1977 song, *Nobody Believes in Me Anymore,* which was written from Satan's perspective and played as an anthem for the *Satanic Panic* generation.

Most seem to paint the Satanist with shades of Shakespeare rather than the *real thing*—the "double, double, toil and trouble, fire burn and cauldron bubble," of the Three Witches of Macbeth, or Wayward Sisters—one of the most famous lines in English literature. Rumors of poisoned Halloween candy and Druid-like childcare workers abounded, in part thanks to daytime television. Mention of the Kabbalists, the alchemists, or the mystics of Science were altogether muted. In the end, the *Satanic Panic* crowd based much of its content on broad-sweeping theatrical generalizations, chasing after wind-swept caricatures and the elongated shadows of gnats rather than *real magic*—the kind which saturates our very cognition through the alpha waves of television and with the potency to program—the kind of magic which sends men to the moon and, in the most delusional of indoctrination power, changes the shape of the earth.

Phil Phillips is clearly a man of God. After publishing *Trouble in the Toy Box* and its follow-up, *Saturday Morning Mind Control*—authoring 15 books in total and selling 1.3 million copies—and succumbing to a stool and dunce cap of ridicule, he has become the president of *God Loves Kids,* a missions organization caring for almost 4000 children and which currently builds orphanages in Nepal. As a Christian, Phillips is the real deal. He came to warn us. Most didn't listen. The thing is, much like the *Satanic Panic* movement which prompted him to action, many of his ideas seem ill-considered. For example, when warning parents of the Occult's almost-omnipresence in *E.T.*, he seems to get some details wrong in the investigation, such as the children "playing *Dungeons & Dragons* in the opening scene," which makes one wonder if he actually saw the movie to begin with. And according to Phillips, E.T. "tells Elliott that he'll always be with him in his *heart*." For someone playing the part of town squire, he tragically mismanages an important detail—assuming he took the time to see the movie at all.

E.T. doesn't tell Elliott he'll "be with him in his heart." What E.T. actually accomplishes to get away with is far more frightening, and precisely why the Satanic Panic crowd seemed to be grasping at straws rather than spiritual discretion. The movement perished for lack of knowledge. With a glowing fingertip E.T. points to the boy's forehead and assures him, "I'll be right here." By turning our attention to Elliott's third-eye, E.T. has just given himself away. He is not *truly* a cosmic traveler. He is as old as the angels, which according to Enoch, conspired to take human wives on Mount Hermon—I shall explain *why* in a moment—and likely accommodated them. And his method of *waking up* is older. With his long, glowing finger reaching out like the hand of God in Michelangelo's famous painting—an image used for the film's promotion and which seemingly went unchallenged—E.T. is Elliott's astral-guide.

Even Neil Diamond seemed to get the memo. With *Heartlight* he wrote:

> "Turn on your heartlight
>
> In the middle of a young boy's dream
>
> Don't wake me up too soon
>
> Gonna take a ride across the moon
>
> You and me."

Further generalizations and unsubstantiated rumors only make Phillips claims ill-considered when he reports a recent "conversation with one screenwriter of E.T., a man deeply troubled at his involvement with the movie. He told me about the visual subliminals the screenwriters wove into the movie, many of which were specifically designed to enhance the reputation of and change the nation's thinking about the homosexual community." This is as far as Phillips dares to go—perhaps because he did not actually have the capacity to recognize subliminal homosexuality while keeping on the lookout for them. He could have mentioned the shed where Elliott first meets E.T., or the Reese's which he cleverly coaxed him to his bedroom with, or the woman's clothing which Gertie dresses him in—or the fact that E.T. was never conclusively identified as male or female. In fact Spielberg confessed to writing E.T. as an asexual creature, which only complicates the films budding pubescent sexuality. Consider E.T. getting drunk with an indiscriminate portion of beer. Telepathically—which is an Occult practice, by the way—Elliott also succumbs to drunkenness at school. When E.T. watches John Wayne kiss Maureen O'Hara in a televised broadcast of John Ford's *The Quiet Man*, we are left to ponder whether E.T. was sexually stimulated by Wayne or O'Hara. And when it comes to subliminal messaging, let's not overlook the rainbow which clearly breaks God's own laws of natural science to paint a starry sky at E.T.'s departing.

One thing is certain—those who *refuse* to acknowledge the *work* of Satan in the world were immediately capable of critiquing the film's underbelly to America, and with remarkable acuteness. As the 1980's dawned, conservative familialism was maintained under the protection of patriarchal culture and sought to vilify unconventional families—such as gays and lesbians as well as single parents. It actually mirrored the *Satanic Panic* with its widespread fear that a battle of good versus evil was raging just below the surface of American culture. In the face of soaring divorce rates—which more than doubled between 1970 and 1980—and widespread invocations to sustain marriages at all costs, E.T. simply spun that around and gave us a look at the alternative. Actually, that alternative brought America to tears. Whatever the outcome of Elliott's blossoming sexuality may prove to be, one thing remained certain. His father had run off to Mexico with another woman and his mother was on the verge of emotional collapse. And yet the child of divorce could not only survive, but also thrive. In short, the family would get along just fine. After its premiers at the Cannes Film Festival, film critic Pauline Kael wrote in *The New Yorker*: "It is bathed in warmth and seems to clear all the bad thoughts out of your head." Film critic Marina Heung maintained that "the enduring appeal of E.T. inheres in the dissolution of the nuclear heterosexual family over the latter half of the twentieth century and the concomitant threat posed by this disintegration to many believers in the nuclear heterosexual family's powerful, and presumably positive, effect on child development (*Making E.T. Perfectly Queer,* Brooke M. Beloso)." It is an "odd little love story between an

556

alien and a child," wrote Thomson of The Guardian, which clears those "bad thoughts."

In the *E.T. Storybook*, based in part on Melissa Mathison's screenplay and released with the movie's premiere, author William Kotzwinkle describes the *alienated* alien with all the zig and zag lines of a modern Renaissance Man—the artist, inventor, healer. His race is described with "misshapen heads, their drooping arms and roly-poly, sawed off torsos" One might mistake him for a goblin, with his "enormous bulbous eyes" and "webbed feet coming almost directly out of his low-hanging belly and his long hands trailing along ape-fashion behind it." What particularly strikes my interest is the mystical woods, still untouched by the bulldozer and which rises high above Elliott suburban home, where we first meet him. Bunched together amongst the flora, one might mistake them for "little old elves caring for their misty, moonlit gardens," which would "make one think of elfland, and the tenderness they showed the plants might add to this impression." E.T. and his crew of botanists were very old, for they had "collected everything that grew or had grown on Earth throughout its existence," including what only remains now "in fossil form, imprinted in coal." The botanist has had "millions of years' experience" on Earth, Kotzwinkle assures us. E.T. is the perfect description of the Watchers who, for thousands of years, have invigorated the Mystery Religion and cultivated the wisdom as well as Sciences of Eastern and Western civilization. "He loved Earth, especially its plant life, but he liked humanity too, and always, when his heart-light glowed, he wanted to teach them, guide them, give them the stored intelligence of millions of years."

Space itself is the grand illusion. Being first and foremost a botanist, we find E.T.'s meaning in the Pagan religion from which he originated from—animism and pantheism. The little garden gnome not only watched over the physical preservation of Earth's vegetation, but their *souls*. Wandering off the fire road into Elliott's backyard—a path which carried him down like a god from the mountain—Kotzwinkle further elaborates on his extraordinary gifting: "Something in the yard was sending soft signals. He turned and saw the vegetable garden. He crept toward it, embraced an artichoke, and asked the vegetables what he should do. Their advice, to go and look in the kitchen window, was not welcome....The artichoke insisted, grunting softly, and the extraterrestrial crept off obediently." And then, when the pizza delivery person arrived, E.T. panicked. "*There's nothing to fear,* said a tomato plant. *It's only the Pizza Wagon.*" When E.T. dove into the shed to protect himself, he found tools, particularly a diffing fork with which to defend himself. "Don't stab yourself in the foot, said a little potted ivy." E.T. could feel the life of the orange diminish as it was plucked from a tree. Like a true fairy of Theosophy, E.T.'s spirit seemed interlocked with a common house plant. When E.T. died, so did the geranium.

There is another ingredient to E.T.'s role as a Watcher of old. He was *conjured*.

Elliott's mother Mary—only recently divorced and in dire need of excitement in her life—we are told by Kotzwinkle, looks strangely upon her two sons and their friends as they play *Dungeons & Dragons* with "their six-sided cube" in her kitchen, a "rubble of a ruined city of Crush bottles, potato chip bags, books papers, calculators." She tries to make sense of their talk.

One voice says, "So you get to the edge of the forest, but you make a truly stupid mistake, so I'm calling in the Wandering Monsters."

And then another, "Can I get Wandering Monsters called out for just befriending a goblin?"

"Steve's Dungeon Master," that would be her son Michael, "He's got Absolute Power."

Absolute Power, Mary sighs. *But she couldn't even get them to dry a dish.*

And then Elliott—she recognizes the voice of her second-born—shouts: "I run down the road. They're after me. Just when they're about to get me and they're really mad, I throw down my portable hole. I climb in and pull the lid closed. Presto. Disappeared into thin air."

'*Portable hole? If only I had one to disappear into,*' Mary thought.

What she doesn't realize—what none of them do—is that an actual demon is being *conjured* through the ritual. In fact, Elliott has rather arrogantly laid out a precise plan of action for his astral-guide in the days to come. Within moments the two will meet under the light of a waxing moon like something from Aleister Crowley's *Moonchild*. We should recognize some semiotics at play—it is rather Kabbalistic in nature—because the letters "E" and "T" begin and end with the protagonist, Elliott, therefore foreshadowing the mystical connection that the two will share. That said, the feminine moon, with her wealth of esoteric potency, is a major player in the unfolding drama—despite not being listed in the closing credits. E.T. and Elliott's soaring flight on a bicycle *made for two* will bypass the light of the moon at its fullest. This will occur on Halloween night, which is also the ancient druidic festival of Samhain; a dreadfully important moment in the pagan and occult ritual calendar. Samhain is the night when the gates and doors to the "otherworld" are opened, and the spirits of the dead enter our realm. It is also the very night in which E.T. sets up his computer to call upon them.

This is precisely the significance of the shadow government scientist played by real-life Marxist Peter Coyote, but whom we only know as Keys. For most of the movie we never see Coyote's face, only the keys jingling from his belt. On the esoteric level his flashlight reminds us of the hidden knowledge which pierces the darkness. However we need also reference the *Key of Solomon*, an Occultist text of the Italian Renaissance—typical of Renaissance Occult-Science—which is inaccurately ascribed to King Solomon but deals with conjurations, invocations and curses to summon and constrain spirits of the dead and demons in order to compel them to do the operator's will. Aleister Crowley translated one version of it. With E.T., the Scientists of the shadow government are non-other than wizards attempting to summon a botanical gnome—*not* spacemen. Considering all this and what we know of Aleister Crowley, Jack Parsons, and Jet Propulsion Laboratory, which created the American space program, the fact that government esotericists arrive up to apprehend E.T. dressed as NASA astronauts lends further credence to this movie representing one massive ceremony.

Imagery stylized after a Kubrick move seems to fill every frame. Remember when an intoxicated E.T. watches John Wayne kiss Maureen O'Hara on the television? While this transpires, we cut to Elliott's classroom, where three distinct posters depict Voyager, Jupiter, and Io. Voyager was the mission that sent probes to Jupiter and Saturn in the late 1970's—all thanks in to Jet Propulsion Laboratory.

In *Magia Sexualis*, author Hugh Urban described Crowley's use of sex magic as a powerful means to shatter the limited rational mind and finite human ego. "However, the ultimate goal that Crowley sought through his sexual magic went far beyond the mundane desire for material wealth or mortal power. In his most exalted moments, Crowley believed that he could achieve a supreme spiritual power–the power to conceive a divine child, a godlike being, who would transcend the moral failings of the body born of mere woman. This goal of creating a divine fetus, Crowley suggests, lies at the heart of many esoteric traditions, from ancient Mesopotamia to India to the Arab world: 'This is the great idea of magicians in all times–To obtain a Messiah by some adaptation of the sexual process. In Assyria they tried incest....Greeks and Syrians mostly bestiality.... The Mohammedans tried homosexuality; medieval ph ilosophers tried to produce homunculi by making chemical experiments with semen. But the root idea is that any form of procreation other than normal is likely to produce results of a magical character.' Sex magic, particularly in its transgressive, non-reproductive forms, can thus unleash the supreme creative power: the power to create not an ordinary fetus, but a magical child of messianic potential."

Even the movie itself was filmed in a pomp in ceremonious fashion. If one watches the DVD commentary, Drew Barrymore reminisces that E.T. was like a "guardian angel for them," insisting that he was almost *real*. We can surmise that E.T. is a type of reptilian creature, which is best hinted at when he telepathically commands Elliott to free the frogs moments after scriptwriter Melissa Mathison's husband Harrison Ford tells his class: "the frogs won't feel a thing." E.T. has Kundalini energy about him—a serpent presence—or what the Occultists would gladly call, "the light bearer." E.T. fills each shoe nicely. Steven Spielberg once told *The Best of Starlog*: "There was a severe reverence on the set shown by everybody, even the guys who swept the floors, toward E.T. Severe reverence... The kids believed in E.T. the way we believe in Santa Claus... or should believe in Santa Claus. Everybody had such a belief in E.T. as a living, breathing, organism that no one would dare go up to him and make fun of his appearance or make fun of his awkwardness. He really did seem to have a life of his own."

"Elliott, your friend is a rare and valuable creature," Keys tells Elliott in Kotzwinkle's *Storybook*, "We want to know him. If we can get to know him, we can learn so many things about the universe and about life."

Keys fictional words line-up with Spielberg's. He told *Twilight Zone* Magazine: "I think that, in the presence of an extraterrestrial, the United States government or any government of the world would want knowledge, not conflict or hostility. I believe that we will solve all our own problems—but I would be nice to know that there's somebody up there who likes us. It helps."

Dare I call E.T. Satanic? But I will—I *must*. There is hardly a worse cause for mockery than to call anything for what it is. To call Rock music Satanic in a serious way or to accuse Hollywood of the same damnable falsehood is cause for a burlesque rebuttal. That is because hardly anyone—and I include much of the *Satanic Panic* generation in this—seems to grasp the implications of Jesus' pacifism when He answered in John 18:36:

> "My kingdom is not of this world: if my kingdom were of this world, then would my servants fight, that I should not be delivered to the Jews: but now is my kingdom not from hence."

The Devil had already taken Jesus to "an exceedingly high mountain, and showed Him all the kingdoms of the world and their glory," as Matthew records. And he, being the Devil, said to Him, "All these things I will give You if You will fall down and worship me (Mathew 4:8-9)."

Jesus did not dispute the Devil. He certainly didn't call him a liar. It is indeed an eye-opening moment to shed the pounds of cognitive dissonance and come to the awareness that Satan fully manages and operate the kingdoms of the world—all of them. I hope I am not being cavalier. I certainly didn't stumble upon this realization—or rather, the scales which had likely been placed over my eyes the very year I was born were not shed—until I *discovered* what the Bible said, and what's more, *believed* what the Bible declares as true regarding the shape of the Earth. Surely, we are being lied to—by *everyone*. Every kingdom, including North Korea—Iran—China—Russia—Israel—and our very own, the United States of America—are operated and managed by Satan. The Bible does not disagree. NASA is most certainly operated and managed by Satan. It exists as an entity of the Executive branch of government. But then let us not forget the Democrats. And the Republicans. Hollywood is Satan's dominion. Nashville is Satan's dominion. The Boy Scouts of America probably is too. There are 192 nations currently under the UN, by my count. They *also* are operated and managed by Satan—every one of them.

Our Lord Jesus wouldn't bend a knee for a single claim to fame from any of them. He did not defeat Satan by running for government. He crushed his head on the cross, and by His blood he has snatched us away from the kingdom of darkness. His kingdom is not of this world—*yet.* So why must ours? Where is the outrage? Where is the—dare I say it—*Satanic Panic*? Get out of Babylon!

Spielberg's highest ambition for the movie, he told TZ: "I would hope the film would encourage interests from off the planet to come visit us someday. That would be nice—and very rewarding." But knowing what we do of the little garden gnome and his kind, we're already being tended to. *He touched Elliott's forehead*, writes Kotzwinkle. "I'll be right here," *he said, fingertip glowing.* The last line of Kotzwinkle's narrative reads:

He went into the misty light, with his geranium.

"Strangers In the Night..." | ERIC DUBAY'S FLAT EARTH MYSTERY SCHOOL & MY FIRST MEETING WITH ASTRONOMER DANNY FAULKNER

FIRST THE CITIES OF CAIN—ATLATNIS WE MAY EVEN WISH to include among them—then the Great Deluge, and naturally, as regurgitated human behavior predictably proves, Babylon followed. Egypt, Persia, Greece, and Rome—in that order, most of us are familiar with. How much of western society, I wonder, has been built upon the foundations—even nursed at the bosom—of the occult? *Much* is my reply. When I sat down with "Answers in Genesis" astronomer Danny Faulkner at the first Flat Earth International Conference in Raleigh, North Carolina last November, I asked him this very question. Let us open up our Bible's and ponder: *which came first?* The answer, as one might suspect of Ken Ham's employees, was undeniably in disharmony with my position.

Dr. Faulkner was an absolute pleasure to speak with, and dare I say, the highlight of my conference experience. He was certainly not a presenter, was never announced as attending, and being an astronomer, we can easily deduce that he is yet another *delusion denier*—a Copernican, like the "Answers in Genesis" staff he represents. I am however quite familiar—and just as often *agitated*—with his body of work, and therefore immediately recognized my cosmological foe from across the hotel lobby. I was half-expecting the cute and lovable though somewhat arrogant teddy-bear persona which I've observed of him in words and video presentation dozens of times over. I was pleasantly surprised however to find that he has all the cerebral talons of a well-oiled educator in person.

In an article titled: *What I Learned at the First Flat Earth International Conference*, Dr. Faulkner mentions our friendly meeting. He writes:

"Getting a good night's sleep helped, for when I awoke the next day, I decided that I was going to be more engaging with people on the second day of the conference. That prepared me for the next person who recognized me, Noel Hadley. Noel approached me at breakfast in the hotel where the conference was held, and I invited him to join me. We talked probably for an hour. Noel had grown up with materials from Answers in Genesis, as well as the Institute for Creation Research, so he was familiar with my work. This also included my criticism of flat-earth, something that he came to embrace in recent years. He expressed astonishment that I was at the conference, so he had to ask why I was there, which I was happy to explain. Our discussion was very pleasant, even though he confessed that he had, in his words, "blasted" me in a blog, as well as in a recent book he had published. I searched on the internet for some of what he had written about me, but I wasn't offended by what I found. So, relax, Noel."

Among his pressing criticisms of the Flat Earth movement—what he *presumed* was a Christian one—is none other than its apparent founder, Eric Dubay. Dubay certainly takes credit for the myth. And it would be a point well taken, *if* that were in any way true. God has always had his loyal servants. Dubay is *not* one of them. There is a long succession of geocentrists since well before Moses, with the late Marshall Hall (1931–2013) volunteering for the part of an exiled Biblical literalist and cosmological educator. Dubay is no Hall—far from it. Dubay is a point-blank New Ager and devoted blasphemer. He insists Jesus never existed. And in an article titled, *I Am That I Am*, our enlightened Flat Earth guru deliriously advocates that he is the "I Am." You know that lie which the Serpent told Eve in the garden? Dubay has also partaken of the forbidden esoteric fruit, and unlike our aboriginal parents, he's unashamed of it. Eric Dubay isn't only promoting Flat Earth, he's essentially a neophyte—opening the doors to the Lower Occulting Mystery Schools; and anyone who responds to his invite must be wise enough to navigate around them—or foolish enough to fall right back into the deception from whence they've only just arrived.

It is the mistake of any historian to gaze upon the pyramids of Egypt, Peru, and the Yucatan, Stonehenge England, forgotten Scotland and Gaul, or the ruins of Assyria and Babylonia as some forgotten splendor. The Mysteries, like the pre-flood cities of Cain and the great visible markers that thereafter accentuated his unrepentant civilization, are very much alive and well—perhaps even healthier than ever before. Quite contrary, they are certainly not fixed upon coordinates on a map. In her book, *The Mystery Schools*, author Grace F. Knoche writes: "The precise locations of these schools are indiscoverable except by the worthy. Never-the-less, the Mystery Schools are perhaps more numerous today than they have been at any other time in human history." Even Theosophist H.P. Blavatsky wrote: "The Secret Association is still alive and as active as ever."

And what is the ultimate purpose, one might ask, of a Mystery School? In the most abstract manner, author Grace F. Knoche defines them as "a university of the soul, a school for the study of the mysteries of the inner nature of man and of surrounding nature. By understanding these mysteries, the student perceives his intimate relationship with divinity, and strives through self-discipline and devotion to become at one with his inner god."

The Greeks have a word for this. *Theophany*, meaning: "divine appearance" or "showing forth of a divinity." Such a notion is the manifestation of man's own higher self to himself. Finally—ultimately— man knows himself, not merely as the offspring spiritually of his own inner god, but as that inner god itself, in his essential being."

Dubay promotes the wisdom of Egypt in his writings, among other esoteric Mysteries, like the Roman cult of Mithras, when advocating astral-projection matched with the ingestion of mushrooms and natural psychotics. NASA's hidden purpose in faking the heliocentric model is to misdirect humanity from his "I AM" spirituality—*this* according to Dubay. They are in effect attempting to draw us away from Lucifer's damnable lie, the divine spark within—as promised to Eve in the garden—by committing the ignorant masses to a false materialistic science of outer space inhabited by extraterrestrial beings, lest we rediscover our true connection to the astral beings of Egypt lore, and essentially a higher state of consciousness, which the Elite fear most— our oneness with Brahma. Dubay has much to say on the subject—astral projection, and the true intent of astral projection, that is. Allow me to quote just a taste of Dubay's delusion:

> "There's military craft that look like flying saucers from the bottom but look like a plane from the top, yet thousands of years ago up until today there are also people in the Amazon who drink ayahuasca or take peyote and other natural substances and they also talk about things very similar to aliens

and UFOs and they paint pictures of them and they show flying saucers and beings getting out of them and interacting with them and giving them advanced knowledge of the plants and other things of things that will happen and all this. But these are known to be interdimensional creatures, interdimensional phenomenon happening when you interact with these entheogens, these psychedelic plants. And the most powerful psychedelic on earth is produced naturally in our pineal gland in our third eyes and it comes out when we sleep, and so dreams are actually a product of this and so when people are asleep and they're abducted by aliens and they have this experience that's so real to them and so unfamiliar. It very well could be an endogenous DMT burst causing these same kinds of ayahuasca visions that the ayahuasca in Peru are seeing and know to be interdimensional beings. But if we've been fed this new propaganda that there's extraterrestrial aliens and UFO physical UFOs, then we start to think that this phenomena that's been known and talked about for thousands of years of these star beings, these astral beings—and astral travel that we're able to do—turns into physical space travel and Star Trek type stuff that they're trying to get us to believe in, many people thousands of years ago believed in so-called aliens or big star beings but and they say that they traveled to the stars like the ancient Mithras cults...."

Dr. Faulkner will certainly smirk at this—our dialogue skimmed over *the Book of Enoch* in passing—but Enoch, as attributed by the book which bears his name and which curiously inspired the New Testament immensely, was a cosmological Flat Earther. No, Dr. Faulkner, it's not *poetry*. Unlike Dubay, Enoch—our Flat Earth movement's first inspired leader—walked with God. Moses testifies to this much. Enoch refused compromise with Cain's lineage. For this very reason, we might easily deduce, he was not so easily fooled by the darkness which mankind victoriously proclaimed as a saving light. It is likely the Watchers of Enoch's own lifetime, fallen angels who found the daughters of men fare and begot hideous giants with them, which the occultists and the shamans and our very own Eric Dubay so fondly gaze upon.

In her book, *The Mystery Schools*, author Grace F. Knoche rather poetically writes: "Like a stream of brilliance across the horizon of time, divine beings, manasaputras, sons of mind, descended among the sleeping humans, and with the flame of intellectual solar fire lighted the wick of latent mind, and lo! the thinker stirred." These are the woken sons of the cities of Cain—or Atlantis, as the Occultists nostalgically gaze back upon. Theosophist H.P. Blavatsky writes of this coveted pastime: "In the darkness of human history, humanity was an infant. Mankind was lost to its ego. Recognition of the ego slept." But with the arrival of the Brotherhood, she adds: "Truth was freely given and freely accepted in that golden age."

For their heinous crime, the lustful angels of Enoch's generation "who kept not their first estate"—Jude, the brother of Jesus, has assured us of it—were imprisoned in darkness and everlasting chains until the day of judgement, and it is why, I presume, the Watchers have not manifested themselves in likewise manner today. But make no mistake of it, there are Watchers still watching over us. Our modern Occultists have a name for them. They are the Brotherhood of Light. In her book, *9 Life Altering Lessons: Secrets of the Mystery Schools Unveiled*, Kala Ambrose writes: "The Brotherhood is a group of ascended Masters who exist in a spiritual hierarchy on the other planes. These souls, male and female, work together in service to help humanity advance further along the path and advance into each age. As students' progress, they first meet their spirit guides on the other side who assist them with their learning. Students who progress further, eventually work with the Brotherhood, often times in dream states and in meditation and other ways, both on the earth plane and the spiritual planes."

Ambrose describes the dream state experience to her students as "attending Night School." Here she adds: "One would view the Brotherhood as a university in the other dimensions, whose mission is to educate, inspire and serve, in love for all humanity. Many of these advanced beings are souls who once walked the earth and are considered to be master teachers including Jesus, Buddha, Mary/Isis, Kwan Yin, Confucius, Krishna and many others."

This *right here* is a very important point. Contemplate it. And I hope Dr. Faulkner, as well as Ken Ham and his "Answers in Genesis" associates can understand what is, or rather *has been* happening since the dawn of human civilization—what the Bible tells us began with the cities and civilization of Cain and continued right on after Noah's flood. Western Civilization is not only fostered by, but is a *result of* hidden knowledge. The Occult came *first*. To this effect, Grace F. Knoche writes in two parts. First: "There is the esoteric form commonly known as the Lesser Mysteries, open to all sincere and honorable candidates for deeper learning; and the esoteric form, or the Greater Mysteries, whose doors open but to the few and whose initiation into adeptship is the reward of those whose interior nobility enables them to undergo the solar rite."

Some will ask the practicality behind all of this, as world history concerns us. Secondly, writes Knoche: "Gradually as knowledge of divine things became abused by those strong in will but weak in morality, truth was increasingly veiled. The planetary watcher now felt the need of selecting a brand of co-workers to act as bodyguard and protector of the ancient wisdom" Essentially, these Watchers—or the Brotherhood—drives an Elitist society. ".....the periodic appearance of world teachers, the inspiers of what later became the great religious and philosophical schools, messengers from the lodge who came forth at cyclic periods to strike anew the 'keynote of Truth.' Hence every great religion, every noble philosophy, every fundamental scientific insight was born from the Sanctuary, to become a 'new' religion, a 'new' philosophy, a 'new' science: fresh and new for the age and the people, but ancient beyond time because nurtured in the womb of esoteric antiquity."

If Dr. Faulkner wants to investigate Christianity—or rather, the Christians of Flat Earth—then drop Eric Dubay. Dubay is an Occultist. He is filled with some half-truths, as puzzle-pieces are concerned. But mostly he is *the lie*. As a God-fearing Christian and Biblical literalist, the comparison with Flat Earth's self-declared guru is an insult. It's a shame that Dr. Faulkner labors so feverishly as a gatekeeper for his profession—and indeed, I have earnestly begun to like him—that he insists God's Testimony regarding Himself and His Creation in the Bible presents no cosmology at all.

Perhaps that's because God's Word obstinately snubs the Copernican faith completely—and rightly so. Or as the Apostle Paul once put it: *Let God be true, and every man a liar.*

RED PILL INDOCTRINATION: "THE MATRIX" AND THE NEOPHYTE'S SEVEN DEGREES INTO THE GREATER MYSTERIES

IN 1999 WE CHOSE THE RED PILL. The turn of the century moviegoer might recall eagerly partaking in the holiest of humanist sacraments, despite the fact that Morpheus had offered us an alternate exit option. By digesting the blue pill "the story ends, you wake up in your bed and believe whatever you want to believe." But no, the red pill—we wanted to stay in Wonderland and see how deep the rabbit hole really goes. The movie in question was *the Matrix*. It spawned an entire trilogy, and by the first entries closing credits—just as it was for Neo— our choice poison would have us wake up to our own *divine* potential.

I ditched class with a friend to see it on opening day—it was our senior year of high school. That very month I skipped another day of public school instruction for *Star Wars: Episode I*—much to our disappointment—but that's another story. In the ensuing years *the Matrix* became a point of fixation for esoteric study. The message behind its dystopian depiction of Plato's cave became an instant anthem for my generation. We discussed its deeper encodings in church circles. It practically became a Bible study. We were gullible enough to believe— or rather, deceive ourselves into thinking—that Morpheus was a representation of *our* John the Baptist and Neo *our* blessed Lord. But we were delirious, because Hollywood is a gangrenous hot tub propagating humanist transmitted diseases—or HTD's for short. Neo wasn't the Jesus who saves us by the atoning sacrifice of His blood alone—quite contrary, in fact. Neo is the Jesus of esoteric lore who shines the sort of light which might aide and abed us in *saving ourselves*. The script, which was written *then* by Laurence and Andrew Wachowski, aka the Wachowski brothers—both of whom have now completed gender transitions and are known as Lana and Lilly Wachowski, aka the Wachowski sisters—might as well have been written by the sun gods Mithras or Apollo. Perhaps it *was*, because—should I have followed the Matrix through to its natural conclusions—I would have been indoctrinated into the occulting Mysteries.

Let's not overlook other natural perversities of Platonic thinking. The Matrix offered legs to the Simulation Theory too, and worse, revived the Gnostic Demiurge—in this case the evil Architect—who apparently designed the programmed world which we unenlightened call reality. We Christians know Him as our beloved Jehovah, though for the Gnostic our God is the wicked enslaver of humanity. Much has been written on *the Matrix*, very little of which I will cover here, and yet knowledge of the Mysteries is scarce. So I ask this question: Why do the two complement each other as a looking-glass of sorts with exceptionally broad and rather bold strokes? Why, for example, does the Oracle, an intermediary between god and man—whom we shall come to learn in a later installment conspires with the Architect—smoke cigarettes, just as the Oracle of Delphi gained her insight from Apollo with the pungent aroma of cannabis? Most conspicuously, the very name Neo—our *Matrix Trilogy*protagonist—is short for Neophyte. In her how-to book, *9 Life Altering Lessons: Secrets of the Mystery Schools Unveiled*, author and self-described wisdom teacher Kala Ambrose writes: "In the esoteric definition, a Neophyte is a student who has just become aware that they may be more than what they previously considered themselves to be."

Traditionally there are seven steps which the Neophyte must maneuver—all of which rank among the ascending seven heavens emanating from Plato's globe and which, by no coincidence, *the Matrix* skillfully masters. For the Mystery School of Mithraism, when the heliocentric model was a religion rather than *simply* a science, the first degree neophyte was called *Corax*, or "raven" in English. Such an inductee exhibits the dawning light of wisdom without having yet peeled back the ever-growing onion peels of his "woken" competence. Just as Neo committed himself to the red pill, Grace F. Knoche explains of the *Corax* inductee: "It signified likewise a servant: one who gives of his heart totally before receiving admission into the second degree."

I can still recall as a moviegoer being enveloped by the red pill—mainly, being slayed with wonder by the worldly wizardry which Morpheus illustrated for his *Corax* student, revealing—in no uncertain terms—how easy it was for a master to manipulate the supposed reality of the everyday uninitiated. Such is the very first lesson given to the most ancient neophyte. Writes Ambrose:

"We Live in a Magical Universe,

which means that,

The Possibilities of What We Can Create Are Infinite!"

Ambrose is quick to affirm: "…we do live in a magical universe, which listens to every thought we have, every word we say and every action we take and it responds accordingly, like a genie following our commands." Should my reader question the Mystery School's pledge of allegiance, she furthermore describes this magical-alliance as follows: "When we activate our consciousness, the all seeing eye of the universe then becomes aware of us and looks back at us! Its practitioner has become a conscious creator—essentially the I AM working from a higher level and from higher bodies within ourselves." She is talking about Satan. Additionally, as we would come to find with Neo's own breakthroughs, "As the All Seeing Eye or Universal Energy becomes aware that you are aware, its energy quickens and vibrates more excitedly with yours….It has no problem keeping up with you, as quickly as you are willing to progress."

Neo didn't exactly take to his newfound discoveries at first either— a magical reality which is, much like the very world we live in, indistinguishable from technology. Futurist Arthur C Clarke, who once "imagined" and cleverly patented the satellite, also compared sufficiently advanced technology as indistinguishable from magic, and C.S. Lewis referred to it as "the magician's twin." If I recall, Neo initially *wanted out* with such feverish ferocity, having regretted swallowing the red pill, that he panicked and altogether pulled himself from the simulation theory "Construct," which he was expected to bend and shape to his will, only to end up vomiting on the floor—and then passing out. When waking up in the bunk of a dystopian nightmare he kindly asks his mentor, "I can't go back, can I?"

To this Morpheus replies: "No."

But as movie-goers we needn't worry too much. Despite his initial reaction we come to find that Neo couldn't have been discovered at all if he were not first searching—or perhaps more specifically, had he not been *ready*. Kala Ambrose adds: "As this begins to sink in, your world is turned upside down. Everything you have been taught by society, by your families and your schools, you have just been told that it is not so, not as it appears. At first, you disbelieve and perhaps react with shock and return back to your "normal" life, thinking that this has all been a ridiculous discussion. However, for many of you, as the old saying goes, *When the student is ready, the teacher appears.*"

There are two particular features which mark the Minor Mysteries, both of which surround the first two acts and final climax of *the Matrix*. In her book, *The Mystery Schools*, author Grace F. Knoche describes the two successively as: "(a) instruction in the deeper sciences of the cosmos," which I shall briefly cover, "and (b) dramatic rites portraying that which the initiate must go through without outside help in the Greater Mysteries." The second and third degrees are termed *Cryphius*, or "occult," and *Miles*, or "soldier." With each degree Neo is first accepted as a disciple of esoteric lore and then "receives sufficient training and purification to become a worker for good"—in that order. In fact, the magic of *the Matrix* best functions with the technological downloads which Neo or any other fellow neophyte might instantaneously receive from their occultist brotherhood via transhumanism. For many such technological advancements—should we revel or find our very identities in them rather than the Savior—we need only thank the Occult. The Mahatma Letter, Letter XXIVB, states:

> *"Many braches of the arts and sciences were taught in the Lesser Mysteries, notably geography, astronomy, chemistry, physiology, psychology, geology, meteorology, as well as music, the "most divine and spiritual of arts."*

Perhaps more specifically—and this is important: "In Greece and Rome, nearly all the great men of historic note were initiates of one or more degrees of the Lesser Mysteries." So our techno-punk hackers of *the Matrix*—Morpheus and Neo—must also glaze humanity with their greatness. Explicitly, their Luciferian servitude is best enacted in the hopes of *saving* us through disciplined *self-saving* instructions. "Thus did these early civilizations ripen in spiritual things under the guidance of initiated philosophers and statesmen, artists, and musicians."

Knoche describes the fourth degree as "the turning or deciding point where those who underwent the discipline and training of the preliminary stages are put to the test of actual experience in self-identification." This is the passing from the Lower Mysteries into the Higher. In fact, very few reach such heights of enlightenment, I am told, for lack of discipline. She further adds, "Of these higher degrees scarcely anything is known to us. This is natural, and indeed appropriate; for how could words describe that which can be understood only by the initiate?" For the fourth-degree initiate and beyond—termed *Leo* the lion among the Mithrian Mysteries—no quarter is given. In fact *many* do not survive. "In the Greater Mysteries the passage into the underworld ceases to be a mere ritual of the Lesser Mysteries in which the candidate participates. He must now approach *'the confines of death'* with full knowledge and in the garment of soul-consciousness pass beyond the veil of visible nature into the arena of worlds invisible."

Such a meeting with "the confines of death" is certainly not *mere ritual* for our protagonist either, because if I'm not mistaken, Neo dies. Here we likely find ourselves in or somewhere bordering the fifth-degree. Neo and his fellow occultists form a rescue party to save their teacher Morpheus from the simulated-agents of the Demiurge Architect. This degree was called by the Greeks *theophany*, meaning "divine appearance" or "showing forth of a divinity." It is, writes Knoche, "the appearance or manifestation of man's own higher self to himself." Like any fifth-degree Mystery Occultist, Neo and his fellow Gnostics become divine "for a short time." In *Fundamentals of the Esoteric Philosophy,* G. de Purucker writes: "And while in the average candidate this sublime moment of intellectual ecstasies and high vision lasted but a short time, with further spiritual progress of the candidate, the theophanic communion became more enduring and lasting, until finally, ultimately, man knew himself, not merely as the offspring spiritually of his own inner god, but as that inner god itself, in the essential being."

In Neo's case, he defies reason by remaining the *inner-god*. Despite being killed by an agent of that simulated world's magazine spray of bullets—his name, for the record, is Agent Smith—Neo's lover and fellow Gnostic—her name would be Trinity—raises him from the dead. "Neo," says she to our antichrist savior, "I'm not afraid anymore. The Oracle told me that I would fall in love and that that man... the man that I loved would be the One. So you see, you can't be dead—you can't be—because I love you. You hear me? I love you." This of course is followed by the sort of kiss which might raise the dead to life, whereas Neo likely enters the sixth-degree.

When our protagonist, who we know now with cinematic certainty as the Chosen One, stands courageously before his killer, Agent Smith, he observes not the hallway surrounding him as an unenlightened person might; he sees the various coded numbers and otherwise illegible messages which make up the Matrix's simulated construct. Furthermore, when Neo breathes, so does the Matrix surrounding him. This sixth initiation was called *theopneusty* by the Greeks—a word literally signifying "god-breathing" or "divine inspiration." Here the master of wisdom would feel "the inbreathing from his own inner god and became, thus, inspired, the very word inspiration meaning *inbreathing* (Knoche)."

In the seventh but certainly not last degree, which is called *theopathy*—a Greek word meaning "god-suffering" or "divine enduring," the neophyte passes the portals of the sun. Specifically, Neo flies away. Roll end credits. For de Purucker, such an esoteric master "becomes the Wondrous Watcher himself." This is no doubt referring to the shadowy Brotherhood of astral-projection, but more precisely the Watchers of Enoch's own time. Of this covetous rank de Purucker adds, it is the "most enduring mystery of all... The initiate, the candidate, suffered himself to become, abandoned himself fully to be, a truly selfless channel of communication of his own inner god, his own higher self; he became lost as it were in the greater self of his own higher self." For the next two *Matrix* films to follow, Neo, Morpheus, and Trinity continue their service to humanity as Watchers, servants as we know to them to be—of Satan himself. Their goal, of course, is to aid and encourage us in the hope of *saving ourselves*.

There is of course an eighth, ninth, and tenth degree of initiation—*supposedly*. Writes Knoche: "While seven were the degrees usually enumerated in the Mysteries, hints have been given of three higher degrees than the seventh. But so esoteric would these be that only the most spiritualized of humanity could comprehend and hence undertake these divine initiations. Rare indeed are those who become avatara-like; rarer still, '*as rare as are the flowers of the Udumbara-tree*' are the Buddha's." Perhaps these final three degrees might be visited in *the Matrix's* two remaining installments. But Knoche warns of any such bystander vision: "As for the tenth and last—such has been left unmarred by description."

It is no secret that "Truthers" love *the Matrix,* in part because of its techno-punk *meets* anime visuals, mind-bending bullet sequencing effects, and keyboard warrior mentality, but also because—and this is important—it lends personal muscle to their creeds of a humanism without accountability to the Creator—specifically the Lord, and substitutes Him with the sparkplugs of the inner-divine. Can my reader please understand that it is not the Elite—the Agent Smiths of our world—who are trying to keep us from enlightenment? No—no! The Enlightened and the Elite are in bed together! Our world is managed and operated by the Light Bearer and his enlightened. The Watchers still instruct the chosen sons of Cain!

Agent Smith, by the way, is only a strawman.

Jesus—the *real* Jesus—the very Word which brought all things into being, instructed Adam and Eve to partake of the blue pill. But Adam and Eve wanted to see how deep the rabbit hole really goes.

In short, they chose the red.

AUTHORS OF CONFUSION + BABBLINGS OF BABEL = ORACLES OF LIGHT | "TONGUE-SPEA" AS THE LANGUAGE OF THE INNER DIVINE

THE PRACTITIONER OF "TONGUE-SPEAK" SHALL SURELY FIND, having *left* the Charismatic faith behind him—that his gift *remains*. That is, *if* he wishes his emotional babblings to continue. Upon closer investigation, he may stumble upon the Buddhist and Shinto priests in East Asia or the Sufis of Islamic mysticism—even the Zulu in South Africa—all of whom maintain his *gifting*. Yet supposing he cannot travel far, the shamans of *every* continent on Earth can accommodate him. He may even risk a voodoo lounge. If however these tongues are too exotic for his taste buds—or socially impractical—he may find that the Church of Jesus Christ of Latter-day Saints engages in his practice. But Paganism and local cults are only the beginning. There is an entire experiential catalog for the Tongues-speaker to discover. No surprise, the New Age religion is featured in its centerfold.

1

CURIOSITY KILLED THE CAT. But that was three decades ago. Back then Yvonne Perry was a devoted Charismatic. Only problem—she had yet to experience the *Spirit baptism* that her church made a regular habit of advertising. After a prayer partner left her home, Perry closed the door to her bedroom so that her kids wouldn't overhear what she expected might—and very will *did*—occur. "Very timidly," she writes of her experience, "I began to intone and move my lips asking that the Holy Spirit…help me *stir up* this ability and bring it forth as a prayer tool." Within minutes Perry found herself pronouncing the phrase: "*porta-reek-may-co-con-tay-go.*" The babbles sounded almost *alien*. She desperately needed an interpreter. There were none to be found. But no matter—the gift was *born*. Perry is no longer a practicing Charismatic. This is important to note, because the gift *remains*.

Now-a-days, Yvonne Perry is a metaphysical author and self-described *Light Language* practitioner. The babbling mantra which first came upon her that fateful hour, by the way, was finally interpreted.

"You have asked and received."

And as for the Holy Spirit which once delivered the message—Perry now recognizes *her* as "the Divine Mother."

Some call it the tongues of angels, others the language of the soul. For Yvonne Perry, the act of praying, speaking, or uttering in *unknown* tongues "is also known as light language, galactic language, star language," and "cosmic language." Altering only slightly in outlook from her Charismatic origins, this language of light "is meant to override the conditioning and programming of the logical mind and allow one to commune directly with Source."

For everyone involved, Charismatic or none, "Tongue-speak" sources its origin in the divine. More precisely, it is a "powerful sacred gift that gives purposeful expression of love from Creator." Perry affirms the language of light is a "sacred geometry produced by vibration," and believes it contains the code of creation which correlates not only with our DNA, but atoms, crystals, mandalas, hieroglyphs, and pyramids. Light language allows the New Age practitioner to access information from realms beyond what is commonly accessed. In true pantheistic fashion, the language of light can be borrowed from animals, plants, elementals, crystals, minerals, even fairies—spirits which cannot easily advocate for themselves.

"The very fiber of our physical biology holds information from everything on Earth and beyond," she says. "These are woven together to form an interconnected network or pathway of communication. Humans have been conditioned to believe that they are separate and superior. We have a mixture of DNA from our many star families. Their languages or signals are embedded into our knowing, and as we awaken to our full potential, the codes for these vibrations are activated. This is why light language sounds so familiar to us or touches us on a deep level in our emotional body."

Some reference their astral-guides. Perry calls them galactic ambassadors, who travel throughout the universe or perhaps through other dimensions speaking multiple DNA languages in order to communicate with us. Whatever the case, Perry can rest assured: "Earth is a foreign country to star-seeds. Hearing the language of home is a comforting sound."

2

LIGHT LANGUAGE IS AN ANCIENT TEACHING that was passed down from the Shamans of Vera Cruz, Mexico, and rooted in the Mayan culture. In other words, the Mayans were light years ahead of Pentecostal Father Charles Fox Parham.

Homaya Amar felt as though God were setting her on His lap, saying (translated from Tongue-Speak): "You have done a great job till now. I am going to teach you a bit more of how I work."

3

SHERRI-LEE LAVENDER DESCRIBES HERSELF as a "Cosmic Frequency Transceiver," and like metaphysical author and self-described light language practitioner Yvonne Perry, she too was tutored in tongue-speak among the clutches of Charismatics. She writes: "I pressed and pressed again to tap into this 'stream of the Holy Spirit," but could only sound a single syllable, *ah*. "Yet being the stubborn and driven bitch that I am, I persisted." Sherri-Lee soon made out the utterance *Abba*—the Hebrew word for father—and began singing "in this mysterious cadence of nonsensical '*words*' and felt as though my spirit soured, free and happy beyond the trappings of the human dullness."

Becoming a New Age mystic wasn't exactly an overnight decision. For the following fifteen years Sherri-Lee "walked through the experiences of judgement rife within Christian church culture related to the *appropriate* use of Tongues in the congregation." For this reason the Cosmic Frequency Transceiver will not capitalize letters for nouns such as "pentecostal," "christian," and "god"—"simply because I do not believe they deserve the deference." When her belief matrix, as she calls it, of organized religion finally collapsed around her, "many crazy-ass things happened." In other slightly less poetic terms, the floodgates opened, and the "language of unknown origin erupted in a sometimes violent cascade of crashing frequencies."

While a Charismatic, Sherri-Lee employed the Holy Spirit as a transceiver. What she came to realize however—among her spoken animal sounds, the clicks and pulses, varying tones and songs that were emitted by Mother Nature and which formed her spoken dialects—she was ultimately picking up information from *realms beyond*. Actually, what Sherri-Lee discovered is "Tongue-speaks" natural and ultimate conclusion—Gnosticism. "The Earth human was initially intended as a more fluid home for the Spirit Essence, one which could be moved in and out" of this material existence without the forceful prompting of a near-death experience. At some point in antiquity, "the body systems were limited....wherein once a spirit essence entered, it could not leave." Gnosticism indeed...

Why now?—I mean, *why* has Tongues swept across the Earth like a wind-swept forest fire? To this questions Sherri-Lee contends: "The remembrance of Light Language seems to appear for some having a kundalini awakening or after being attuned with Reiki or some form of shamanic healing. The frequencies of light language bring in intense energies that help with spiritual activation, processing shifts in consciousness, facilitating light body restructuring, and getting information/guidance needed. It connects us to higher realms where we have a better understanding of our *multi-dimensional* experiences."

Simply stated, evolution has *accelerated.*

Though the archaeologist has failed to take his planting rake and digging trowel to the lost city of Atlantis, there is very little adrift from that continent. The Watchers of that once-great Mystery Religion are still capable of guiding those who seek them. Says Sherri-Lee: "We may have used this form of communication in other lifetimes or dimensions such as during the Golden Age of Lemuria. Some of the star-seed languages are the channeled voices of galactic beings of light who are assisting us in healing ourselves and others." Because the frequencies accessed by the employment of light language can affect our DNA, Sherri-Lee is happy to conclude: we are thus reconnected "with the blueprint and template upgrades for the divine human."

4

THE MEDIEVAL PHILOSOPHER AND OCCULTIST POET Rumi (1207-1273), a Sufi-mystic and favorite for the New Age Tongue-Speak practitioner, taught that the chief end of man was to emancipate himself from human thoughts and wishes, including the outward impressions of the senses, so that he may become a mere mirror for the Deity.

He wrote: "The soul has been given its own ears to hear things the mind does not understand."

5

KIKI CINZA RECENTLY CONFESSED OF HER latest Tongue-Speak experience: "It was almost as if my ancestors—my spirit guides— my *spiritual pose*, if you will, kind of came through me and argued it out for me and I was almost like a witness to it, because I remember as I was speaking I was looking over in a different direction almost watching it happen; the sounds almost manifested themselves into beings arguing out everything I was feeling. When I was done speaking I just felt so much relief and I felt better and I knew right away—I was like, *oh my gosh*, you took care of this for me. And I was so appreciative and thankful."

Her higher consciousness was being worked out for her simply by allowing the language to come through. It is, as Kiki described it, a dam of information bursting through in a free and clear way.

Kiki ends, as Charismatics often do: "but that was my own personal experience."

6

A WOMAN IDENTIFYING HERSELF to Light Language guru Kiki Cinza as a former Charismatic—though she grew up Baptist and Lutheran—began speaking in tongues because her church elders had convinced her it was proof of the Holy Ghost. In order to secure her Spirit baptism, church mothers coached her into it by the laying on of prayerful hands. Now days she begins each tongues session by chanting:

"I am immortal. I am a messenger of the Almighty Absolute Everything…"

And then:

"*Ah-na-ho-you—tobata-eee.   Yea-he-ne—yama-no-co-ha-na. Ay.*"

During an online homework assignment, Kiki Cinza asked her students to record their Light Language Tongue-Speak and then jot down a possible interpretation.

Her student responded: "The whole process usually lasts only a few minutes, and it takes me longer to 'come down.' Sometimes I dance while speaking in tongues, as if I'm in a powwow. I am taken away, as the power surges through my body. I get the impression that my indigenous ancestors are talking through me. My only hesitation is in attempting to put these sacred sounds into English, but here goes: 'Ah; means, *yes*. ;Na-ho-yo' means, *I know you*. 'Tobata-eee' means, *we are here to help*. 'Yea-he-ne' means, *it is good*. 'Yama-no-co-ha-na' means, *beloved, here am I*. 'Ay' means, *always*.

7

BABETTE IS A SELF-DESCRIBED MEDICAL PRACTITIONER who understands perfectly well what is meant when Tongue-Speak is referred to as *directed energy*. To this she says: "It came to me that speaking in tongues or *glossolalia*is the language of energy. While thinking about this it dawned on me that this would be perfect to use for spell work, invocation or basically directing my intentions. In the past I have often been challenged with writing or speaking, using English, to state my intentions for spell work, invocations or magic. Immediately I'd begin to think that perhaps what I stated was not good enough or sufficient, I don't have this problem now. By creating/allowing the feeling of my intention I can speak in tongues and know that my intention/energy is flowing unhampered by my programmed mental gymnastics. I'm speaking in tongues purposely now and have incorporated into my developing practices."

8

L. RAYNOR GREW UP BAPTIST AND LATER learned to speak Tongues in Charismatic churches. She recently told Kiki: "Speaking in tongues seems to me that it's our ancestral past trying to remind us that it's still alive and well and if we are willing, guidance will come... it enables puzzle pieces to become complete, helps us know that universally we are one and our individual selves are pieces trying to find the greater whole. To me "Language" is just one of the barriers we must fight through—it kind of doesn't exist. When we tap in with who we are and who we should synch with, the language will be universal…"

In order to speak in tongues, she begins by rehearsing a variation of the Hermetic Axiom: "*You shall be All, All shall be You.*" By instigating mantras, sigils are created. *Tongues*, Raynor insists, is a powerful magical tools beyond the confines of the English language.

9

ANOTHER STUDENT OF KIKI CINZA refers to herself as *Sipher*. She says: "I believe that speaking in tongues is accessing your God being… If the eyes are the windows to the soul, then I think the mouth is the door and the tongue is the key. What if speaking in tongues is a password and the key to the end of division? What if there is a whole culture emerging that speaks only in tongues and if you are still trying to enforce rudimentary languages constructed by man, then you may have difficulty communicating?"

Tongue-Speak is the outbreak of a new religion—one which as reversed the curse yoked upon mankind at the Tower of Babel. Sipher concludes: "It will force everyone to evolve."

10

I HAVE NO REASON TO DOUBT THE MULTITUDE of witnesses, whether Charismatic or New Age, who all seem to agree: Tongue-Speak bathes them abundantly with the feelings of ecstasy and Divine love. While fellow Light Language practitioner Lalama agrees with Kiki Cinza that Tongues is about channeling truth from another dimension or possibly another past life, or allowing a spirit guide to speak through her, she seems to digress into the very illogical emotional-based slump which enthusiastically drives every Tongue-Speaker when she advocates its universal message:

"You just keep doing what you're doing, be a good person and everything will be ok."

Trust yourself in what you're doing. The subconscious mind is the catch-all for everything. It is the crown chakra absorbing and relaying

582

messages either for you or for God or the benefit of those listening. Tongues are an ancient language—a universal language. There's a collective understanding in this. Don't think.

Just let go…

A Charismatic may be easily spotted. They are likely to confess such things as "God showed me" rather than "Scripture says." Christians entering these movements are generally concerned with having an experience, not digging at the truth of God's Word. For this very reason—because of its emphasis on feelings rather than intellect—it may seem an impossible task to talk rationally to those intimately involved in a futile practice. If Charismatic congregations rarely publish statements of faith, its because few of those entering its ranks would bother reading them. We must shake the tree anyhow—forcefully if need be—in hopes that an apple or two may fall.

In *The Aquarian Conspiracy*, New Ager Merilyn Ferguson writes: "Paradoxically, if we give up the need for certainty in terms of control and fixed answers, we are compensated by a different kind of certainty—a direction, not a fact. We begin to trust intuition, whole-brain knowing…as we become attuned to the inner signals, they seem stronger."

GENE RODDENBERRY AND STAR TREK'S IMPOSSIBLE FIVE-YEAR MISSION: *"To Boldly Go Where No Man Is Ever Capable of Going"*

HE ENVISIONED A FUTURE WITHOUT RELIGION. To this end Gene Roddenberry found cause for celebration, and a dedicated weekly audience to join in. The entire platform for *Star Trek* built its foundation upon such principles, one in which Moses, Jesus, and the Prophets were condemned in their efforts, not only for uttering blasphemous falsities against the institution of Scientism, but according to Roddenberry, for committing a far worse crime against generations of humanity—taking away the power of rational decision and draining people of their free will. To this he added, "Religions vary in their degree of idiocy, but I reject them all. For most people, religion is nothing more than a substitute for a malfunctioning brain. If people need religion, ignore them and maybe they will ignore you, and you can go on with your life."

When Roddenberry began developing *Star Trek*, it was brought to his attention that he would need a chaplain on board the Enterprise.

To them he replied, "No, we *don't*."

One day in 1975, half a decade after *Star Trek* had been canceled, actor William Shatner, aka Captain James T. Kirk, decided to walk around the old abandoned stage on the Paramount Studios lot, where the series had been filmed, when he suddenly heard the clapping of a typewriter. Shatner recalls, "That was the strangest thing, because these offices were deserted. So I followed the sound, till I came to the entrance of this building. And the sound was getting louder as I went into the building. I went down a hallway, where the offices for *Star Trek* were … I opened the door and there was Gene Roddenberry. He was sitting in a corner, typing. I hadn't seen him in five years. I said, '*Gene, the series has been canceled!*'"

Roddenberry was writing a script for what would eventually become *Star Trek: The Motion Picture*. And yet the movie which arrived in theaters was not his vision. True to his disdain for Christianity and the Doctrine of Infallibility, Roddenberry was busy fleshing out a story-line where the God of the Bible was revealed to be nothing more than an alien entity in which ancient man had mistakenly believed to be divine. In its climactic conclusion, Captain James T. Kirk was to delve into a fist-fight with the shape-shifting alien of religious superstition on the bridge of the USS Enterprise. After several shape-shifting transitions; always asking the Captain if he knew *who* he was—Kirk did not—the alien entity finally revealed his most worshiped earth identify. He was Christ the Carpenter.

He was to say, "Do you know me?"

In which Kirk was to reply, "Oh, *now* I know who you are."

Thus, the fistfight was to commence.

Concerning his vision for the script, Roddenberry is quoted, "But I also wanted to suggest that it might have been as much the devil as it was God. After all, what kind of god would throw humans out of Paradise for eating the fruit of the Tree of Knowledge? One of the Vulcan's on board, in a very logical way, says, 'If this is your God, he's not very impressive. He's got so many psychological problems. He's so insecure. He demands worship every seven days. He goes out and creates faulty humans and then blames them for his own mistakes. He's a pretty poor excuse for a supreme being."

A Christian displays symptoms of cognitive dissonance when expressing *surprise* at NASA's proclamation that the name of Jesus may not be uttered within its ranks. And yet mankind's self-proclaimed manifest destiny in space, which includes the moon landing, is not of God. The Christian must recognize this stark contrast between what he and the humanist are expected to believe. Heaven and all that is in the heavens are not for the taking. *This* is a truth made pointedly clear in the opening chapter of the Bible. God has not gifted the dominion of heaven to mortal man. All that is within the Earth is ours to subdue and have dominion over, says the Lord (Genesis 1:27-30). But the heavens, not a single passage in the entire wingspan of Holy Writ can be found where the realm of the luminaries is permitted by God as an infinite expanse in which we might have interface with, a fence to climb over and explore, let alone conquer or subdue with a religious, philosophical or even scientific attitude. For the trans-humanist, this is Moses and Prophets' arrest-able offense.

"So God created man in his own image, in the image of God created he him; male and female created he them. And God blessed them, and God said unto them, Be fruitful, and multiply, and replenish the earth, and subdue it: and have dominion over the fish of the sea, and over the fowl of the air, and over every living thing that moveth upon the earth. And God said, Behold, I have given you every herb bearing seed, which is upon the face of all the earth, and every tree, in the which is the fruit of a tree yielding seed; to you it shall be for meat. And to every beast of the earth, and to every fowl of the air, and to everything that creepeth upon the earth, wherein there is life, I have given every green herb for meat: and it was so (Genesis 1:27-30)."

To this proclamation, Roddenberry defiantly states, "Earth is the nest, the cradle, and we'll move out of it."

A Christian would never dream that he or she is professing to have faith in two contradictory systems, especially of the religious nature, and which if understood could not be held together in a reasonable mind. But to the believer in Christ, this is what is so important about the doctrine of the shape of the earth. It's not simply a debate over the lack of curvature. If this were so, I wouldn't be writing about it tirelessly (to the frustration of many), and globular Christians would not become so heated, infuriated even, at the mere consideration that their devotion to NASA—the very organization which forbids the mention of Jesus' name—is somehow not of God. And yet I urge you, brothers and sisters, to scour through the Holy Scriptures and find God's commissioning that we should dominate and subdue the heavens, let alone have deeper knowledge of it in *addition* to the Earth. To claim this chronic pursuit into the heavens is somehow a commissioning which aligns itself with man's stated purpose is a belief I myself can no longer stand behind.

"We must question the story logic of having an all-knowing all-powerful God," said Roddenberry, no doubt reflecting upon his own *story logic*, "who creates faulty humans and then blames them for his own mistakes."

Roddenberry exhibits the very mocking antichrist spirit which Peter warned us against in the last days. Most of our science-fiction writers do. In fact, I doubt we would have such a genre without it. He said: "*For this they willingly are ignorant of, that by the word of God the heavens were of old, and the earth standing out of the water and in the water* (2 Peter 2:5)."

If God went out of His way to let us know He spread a solid firmament over the Earth, a boundary marker which He called heaven, with waters which once drowned the whole world still contained and stored in-plenty, as the Psalmist and the Apostle Peter both attest to, the conclusion should be immediately clear to any God-fearing individual. We have no business going beyond a barrier by which God in the very least claimed to have constructed—or to even make an attempt at it. The exploration of space is wishful thinking for the rebellious sort.

"*Childhood's End*"—ARTHUR C. CLARKE'S 'THREE LAWS' IN LIGHT OF THE SCIENCE DELUSION

THE UNITED STATES AND RUSSIA ARE BOTH ENGAGED WITH THE DAWNING DAYS of the space race. It is still the late 20th century, and the only obstacle which can hinder either opposing party from *physically* manning space, by no small coincidence, does in fact occur. Monster alien spacecrafts peacefully intercept their planned flights, hovering over every major metropolis in the world. It is by the will and to the satisfaction of the majority of the human race that their "Overlords," as they're soon known by all, have secured a true Utopia on Earth, through UN participation no less, and with a centralized one world government to show for it. An entire fifty years will pass before these Overlords fulfill a promise first made at their arrival. They reveal their *true* forms. Indeed, they are the devils of the Bible.

We are living in a science-fiction novel. Author Arthur C. Clarke— he and his genre contemporaries, saw to that. If any of the above plot sounds familiar, or should it accredit merit as the slightest possible outcome in our future, it's because Clarke gave creative license to it. Science-fiction is little more than an imaginative set of ideas which begin in the head, and though they have yet to exist, *soon* will—not in a book or projector, but in our very *perception* of reality. I am summarizing Ray Bradbury. "It is always the art of the possible, never the impossible," he said. So if anyone should ask which came first, the chicken or the egg, you can answer them, "Science-fiction."

The novel in question is called "*Childhood's End.*" It is considered by many to be Arthur C. Clarke's finest work. The big reveal, by the way, is hardly its climax. The connection between devilish entities and the Utopia they seek to gift mankind with should arouse suspicion in the most casual of readers, as should the mysterious "Overmind," never seen but is sufficiently powerful enough to make permanent servants of the Overlords. Even Ouija boards are used by humans to assimilate knowledge of them. It is furthermore no surprise that society should decompose in light of their influence, first through boredom for lack of want, and then conclusively spirals into moral depravity.

The Overlords most stunning realization is in why they were sent to Earth. After deceiving all of humanity with gifts of want for well-over half a century, the deception is finally peeled away by the narratives handful of *truthers*. The Overmind, that powerful being of thought and energy talked about but never seen—except once as an avatar—wishes to assimilate the race of humanity into its own collective ever-expansive consciousness, specifically through its children. This act is described by the Overlords as the next phase of evolution, and "beautiful." Ironically, this is a step in which the Overlords have never been able to make and may never be able to. Knowledge of technology equals power—specifically of the psychological nature, but even knowledge and technology has its limitations. It *must* co-exist with the supernatural in order for its full intended purpose to be fulfilled, and this can only come through transcendence with the Overmind.

At last we see Earth deserted. Most of humanity has committed suicide. Only its three-hundred million strange children remain to be rounded up and collected. They have grown immensely in mystical power, and yet their personal individual identities have vanished. When the Overmind finally arrives to collectively absorb them, they in turn consume the world's energy, and everything, including the Earth itself, is destroyed. The last generation of humans has finally transcended. The End.

It is difficult to conclude such a story can derive from anything less than a spiritually-influenced and deranged, though admittedly brilliant, mind. And yet I only bring this up because Childhood's End *eerily*—and I stress eerily—describes Scientism's own claim to our fast approaching future. Which came first, the chicken or the egg? Make no mistake, we will transcend. Or rather, those who agree to it—transhumanism, that is; they *will* be promised assimilation into eternity. *That*, as we Christians know, is nothing but a disgusting lie. More precisely, it is the final damnation. All who take the mark will be eternally damned. And yet it will be perceived, or at least advertised by its administrators, as "beautiful."

We as a people are in desperate need of a good deception. We crave a savory lie like carnal knowledge and chocolate, and have thus made a sport of it. We will pay admission to sit in a dark room in front of a grand screen and grow giddy at the knowledge that they will gladly spoon-feed the lie to us, no questions asked. A Christian, I have found, would rather hear of a toddler pulled from its mother's breast than have his entertainment threatened. I am told, according to his tiresome foot-stomping rebuttal, that he has a God-given right to the wandering imagination of our ever-progressing narrative—the road to transcendence. For our current Scientism Overlords, we make it too easy. The lie is everywhere.

I expect Clarke's three laws need little to no introduction here, being familiar with the most common reader. If I rehearse them now, it's only because I employ them in an entirely new light, now that I've woken up from the deception. Read, memorize, and know them well. An apologist for Scientism will likely discern all three and nod his head in agreement, muttering, "Of course."

Then again, so will the person who now recognizes the Science Delusion for what it truly is. Clarke's three laws, he may suddenly come to realize, is either diagnosed with the masterful strokes of its genius author, or else a Dissociative Identity Disorder. He too will read Clarke's three great laws, only with a pronounced smirk and a raised-eyebrow, as though he's only ever glossed right over them until this very moment, exclaiming: "Of course!"

They are as follows:

1 When a distinguished but elderly scientist states that something is possible, he is almost certainly right. When he states that something is impossible, he is very probably wrong.

2 The only way of discovering the limits of the possible is to venture a little way past them into the impossible.

3 Any sufficiently advanced technology is indistinguishable from magic.

Do you see it too? Read it again, *if not*. Reflect on it. Memorize the script. The Science Delusion *as a set of rules* was right in front of our faces the entire time, for anyone paying attention. It came in part from the spiritually-driven imaginations of its science-fiction taskmasters, and we are asked today to partake in it—CERN and NASA and their ultimate damnable destinations—as gospel truth, even if only in the ill-advised succulence of the free-ranging mind.

590

"*Peace! Peace! They Say, Where There Is No Peace…*" DR. STRANGE, MARVEL COMICS & THE RELIGION OF HAIGHT-ASHBURY IN DEFIANCE OF THE SECOND COMING OF CHRIST

EVIDENCE OF A HIGH-RANKING CONSPIRACY against our LORD's return is conspicuous to the Christian who carefully examines the Apostle John, particularly when he writes: "*And I saw the beast, and the kings of the earth, and their armies, gathered together to make war against him that sat on the horse, and against his army* (Revelation 19:19)." The one event which ultimately promises to unite the entire world into a singular rank of battle, the United States alongside the Russian Federation, backed by their assortments of allied and axis friends in the UN, is not an invasion of fictional Hollywood aliens, but the imposing crowning ceremony of our LORD, Jesus Christ.

As we near this certain event it will be required of us—we who long to stand behind the ranks of He who sits upon the horse and His angels—that we endure surmounting hostility. Our very path shall be a gauntlet of malicious tidings, with malnourished eyes always pressed upon us. The conscious of sinful man will surely demand social insubordination against such cause, perhaps even passing into law hopes of craftily defying it, particularly the mere recognition of any promised appearance of the risen Son of Man. And the church, which has lost the culture war against western civilization and now flails its wings like a flightless chicken in dire hopes of garnishing favor with the very world which rejects its tenets, will predictably shake its head at those of us who fervently seek His face among the clouds. "A loving god would not— No, he could not, interfere in the pluralistic affairs of our good natured world." With these words our counterfeit church will castrate us. "Our prosperity must endure without His mingling!" Simply put, we will be an embarrassment to the *Days of Noah* apostates in power.

In the face of apostasy the church has done little to nothing to stop the humanist parade, a centuries-old line-up of festivities which has obstinately exchanged its address from a FLAT to globular earth, except to join in with the trends rather than to arrest them. The church in essence, by contextualizing its message of discipleship and daily living, has become the culture it once attempted to convict. Ironically, the apostates have converted us. The church's abandonment first of the Bible's cosmogony in favor of Hellenization has cheapened our faith— even retarded it so that a typical mainstream worship service, with its colorful displays of lights and irreverent bray of guitars, deviates only slightly from the Haight-Ashbury religion it willingly derives from. A Christian is only able to live out the worldview he has been taught, and for the most part we have become what Jesus once warned against, *saltiness without flavor.*

No wonder youth pastors induct their teenage youth into the cult of Hollywood, allowing for frequented "church outings" to the public arena of entertainment in hopes that the message of Jesus can be found in the illusion of a large-screened digital projection rather than in the understanding of their own spiritual heritage. As part of Disney's masterfully maneuvered stronghold over the ticketholder, its cinematic universe of Marvel has fused together a cosmogony as tightly wound as its comic counterparts. Among the superheroes of Marvel Comics, evolution abounds. Furthermore, the transhumanist implementation of mortal man accelerates a better understanding of one's self. In short, the Marvel universe is not Christian, nor will Jesus be found in its age-old deception. He is not Iron Man, neither the patriotic Captain America, nor the pagan-god Thor.

Contrarily, Marvel's current and ongoing cinematic storyline in *Avengers*, which details the coming threat of an evil sentient being, namely the character Thanos, and who is bent on enslaving humanity to his rule upon arrival, is difficult to be seen as an allegory for Satan. The Prince of the power of the air already rules the Earth. But Jesus, who is not a celebrated figure in Hollywood, is soon returning. This we can be certain of. Perhaps the imposing threat of an intergalactic menace throughout the greater interwoven narrative of Hollywood hits closer to the doorstep of Revelation 19:19—the kings who assemble for battle against the King of Kings—than the Christian, in his warped pagan education, is willing to give credit for. And when it comes to Marvel, it is up to the Nephilim, *"the mighty men who were of old, the men of renowned* (Genesis 6:4)," or *the sons of God*, to stop Him.

It could be said that Steve Ditko and Stan Lee's original *Dr. Strange* comics were a considerable contributor, though a mostly-unacknowledged back-seat driver at best, behind the developing hippie counterculture. Throughout the 1960's university students took drugs and discussed humanist philosophy among a cauldron of blended religions, particularly Eastern mysticism, all in an effort to "expand their minds." The pages of a typical Dr. Strange comic would drip with the Great Deception: flavors of Salvador Dali, mysticism, black magic, the occult, astral projection, alternate realities and dimensions, Egyptian and Sumerian mythology, and the study of dreams, all of which enhanced their own psychedelia.

Science-fiction writer Ross Rocklynne was staying with his two sons in the Haight-Ashbury district during November of 1966, one of whom was attending San Francisco State at the time, and admittedly based his short story *"Chez Witch"* off his experiences in what he referred to as a semi-hippie apartment, with the like-minded sort always coming and going. Concerning the 12-page narrative that he clapped on a typewriter there, he said, "The older son handed me a stack of Marvel comics and remarked, incredibly, that Stan Lee and what he was saying was part of the religion of the Berkeley Haight-Ashbury scene. I was entranced with The Hulk, with Prince Namor of Atlantis, with The Fantastic Four, with Doctor Strange, the Mighty Thor, and others. I lay on the bed face closed to the floor and read and glutted myself in leisure."

In his 1968 biographical narrative, *"The Electric Kool-Aid Acid Test,"* author Tom Wolfe gave similar credit to drug enthusiast Ken Kasey, who in turn had authored *"One Flew over the Cuckoo's Nest"* in 1962. Kasey and his Merry Pranksters held LSD gatherings around San Francisco's bay area, including Haight-Ashbury, and according to Wolfe, he would often accommodate his trips with the latest issue of *Dr. Strange.*

If a Christian utilizes a crucifixion device as a symbol for his salvation, notably as it relates to Jesus' atoning sacrifice by becoming sin for us and taking our place on the cross, then the symbol of the counterculture peace-loving hippie has much to say of its followers, particularly the cross which it openly opposes.

To the Nazi it is called a "todesune," or death rune. For the Saracen of the middle-ages it represents a broken cross, a raven's claw, and a witch's foot, all calling cards of Satan. For the Hindu, the downward "V" is a mystical character for "*Aum*," a sacred word which, once pronounced in repetition, is said to awaken the power of Brahma at the base of the spine. Pagan sorcerers, especially in Germanic tribes, included it in their ceremonies. For Anton LaVey, founder of the Church of Satan, it is the background of his altar. Emperor Nero, regularly employing the downward fork to represent a broken cross or broken Jew, crucified the Apostle Peter on one. As such church history, conscious of these matters, has referred to it as a "Neronic cross."

I am speaking of the hippie's protest *friendly* "peace sign," which lives on even today in our intellectual language. For author Rudolph Koch, in "*The Book of Signs*," the downward pointing fork implies "the death of man," while the circle surrounding it indicates "the total death of all people." And while Gerald Holtom's modern day re-creation of the age-old symbol is well documented, intended to represent hand-held flag symbols (or semaphores) of an N and D, representative of "nuclear disarmament," (I see no reason why Gerald Holtom should not receive the benefit of the doubt,) Bertrand Russell is without excuse. As one well informed of its occultist lifespan, and furthermore being an open supporter of communism, the man who first brought it to America proclaimed its message with clarity. For Russell it reads: *peace without God*.

In light of this, when one digs five decades back beyond the historical revisionism of the mythological carefree hippie portrayed in the media, and the comic book culture which helped to create it, the words of the Prophet Jeremiah should be made immediately clear.

> They have healed also the hurt of the daughter of my people slightly, saying, Peace, peace; when there is no peace. Were they ashamed when they had committed abomination? Nay, they were not at all ashamed, neither could they blush: therefore they shall fall among them that fall: at the time that I visit them they shall be cast down, saith the LORD.

(Jeremiah 6:14-15)

The true Christian knows full-well that peace, effectual and lasting peace, can only be embedded within the hearts of every man, woman, and child when our King of Kings arrives in the clouds. He is a deathly threat to the Haight-Ashbury and materialist globe religion. The new age man believes sin is simply the ignorance of one's personal divinity. He believes the major problem of mankind is in his ignorance, specifically the Christian belief which has sought to inform and convince him otherwise—that if truth be told, we are all indeed divine. Jesus is nothing more than an avatar, one of many gods who've come and gone with the breeze, perhaps to remind us of our ultimate potential, and therefore completely understood by his own disciples who wrote of Him. According to the New Age man, salvation involves personal enlightenment, not the cross, mainly release from the darkness of our own ignorance, which the upside-down fork can apparently help to deliver. Jesus threatens all of this. He threatens to topple the self-declared evolution of man. Yes, the New Age man, whose eyes are firmly fixed on the crowning achievement of evolution, his own immortality and the resurrection of all mankind through the technological craftsmanship of transhumanism; Jesus' upheaval among future human events not only threatens his own impossible awakening, but most importantly, he threatens to cut short the arrival of Satan's long-promised Age of Aquarius and its shining capitol city, Mystery Babylon, when mankind will attain their ultimate absorption into the impersonal godhead—or so the New Age belief goes.

In one of *Dr. Strange's* earliest and most inspirational counterculture-shaping storylines, Stephen Strange essentially meets God, aka Sise-Neg, a 31st-century sorcerer of sorts who travels back through time in order to enhance and solidify his god-status. While he does succeed in ultimately destroying the Universe (once arriving at the beginning of time); rather than creating a new one in his own image, as was Sise-Neg's original plan, thanks to Dr. Strange he is convinced to create the exact same evolutionary Universe again, just not in God's image. Dr. Strange will then witness the Big Bang's commencement. During one memorable segment, Strange acts as one of the three angels of Genesis who travels into Sodom alongside the villainous god-figure, Sise-Neg, in hopes that he might stop him from destroying both cities, the other being Gomorrah. In this attempt our hero fails. Sodom and Gomorrah are destroyed, as the God of the Bible would have it, and here, through Stephen Strange's eyes, we are expected to witness the Christian God as our Marvel superheroes perceive Him. To them, the Judeo-Christian God is evil.

If such a possibility were true, that Hollywood wasn't just a highly-budgeted monument celebrating the wishful thinking of godless humanism and its storylines were somehow manifested as true, then it shouldn't be too hard for the Christian, unless cognitive dissonance and decades of apostate indoctrination has the better of him (which certainly may be the case), to envision his plight of safety behind the ranks of our

Master Shepherd, while our superheroes of the Haight-Ashbury religion—Thor, The Hulk, Iron Man, The Fantastic Four, The X-Men, Captain America, and not forgetting Dr. Strange—stands in defense, with the kings of the Earth to back them.

Indeed, their threat has finally arrived. And they are in opposition of Him.

"*Mutants, Know that You Exist!*" | DARWIN'S SCHOOL FOR GIFTED YOUNGSTERS & THE ART OF WAR

IMAGINE IF YOU WILL A SPINNING BALL hurdling through an uncharted infinity of outer space—a *supposed* reality where people walk upside down and are held in place, among entire cities and bodies of water, by an unexplained magical force called "gravity." Then turn your attention to two antipodal residents needing little to no introduction. The first is Charles Darwin, bestselling author, naturalist, and biologist. Next is Albert Einstein who—among his various displays of mathematical wizardry—demonstrated that matter, including the matter of the human body, is really frozen energy. There is a third and fourth antipodal worth noting—Francis Crick and James Watson, discoverers of the double-helix structure of DNA. Throw in the purported blasts of an atomic bomb over the island of Japan and, since we're on the subject, a comic book creator named Stan Lee. The narrative before us unfolds quite naturally under the shadow of two familiar San Franciscan sign-posts—the street corners of Haight and Ashbury. Understand it's not the 1960's. It's the SIXTIES, and *anything* is possible.

Specifically, it's January of 1967, and those kids down on the Haight have a message for you and me, should we set our cup of coffee down and crack open the *San Francisco Oracle*. It's called a *Manifesto for Mutants*, and boldly reads:

"Mutants! Know now that you exist!

They have hid you in cities

And clothed you in fools clothes

Know now that you are free."

This is what we might call a falling domino—one in a succession of many. If Darwin, Einstein, Robert Oppenheimer, Watson and Crick, Stan Lee, and now these self-declared "mutants," better known in subsequent years as *hippies*, fit into the same equation—and I most certainly believe they do—then the conclusion is mandatory. Mutation *happens*. It *must* happen. More like a pipe dream, really, because I stand on the shoulders of men like Sir Ernst Boris Chain. The German-born British biochemist, and a 1945 co-recipient of the Nobel Prize, Physiology or Medicine, for his work on penicillin, once claimed: "Nine-tenths of the talk of evolutionists is sheer nonsense, not founded on observation and wholly unsupported by facts. This museum is full of proofs of the utter falsity of their views. In all-this great museum, there is not a particle of evidence of the transmutation of species."

No-no! Life *is* transhuman. Mutation *must* happen! The narrative demands as much, in one way or another—that is, according to the counterfeit religion of Scientism. The underlining message behind *The Origin of Species* is unavoidable, particularly on the corners of Haight and Ashbury. Darwin's prototype human is only a transitional phenomenon on its way to something else. Basically, what they're saying over at the *Oracle* is this: "We're all mutants—or should *hope to be*, if we are to remain one step ahead of the Atom bomb." Hold on, everyone. Hippies are *proving* evolution.

It's a shame really; because rumor has it Hiroshima and Nagasaki were not *really* destroyed by atomic bombs—*or*, flashes lasting less than a second and instantaneously massacring 360,000 persons. Can nuclear fission truly occur *outside* of a laboratory or nuclear power plant, and without moderated conditions? As criminal line-ups are concerned, napalm carpet-fire bombings seem a far better culprit for the climatic conclusion to a terrible world at war. The Japanese built their houses of straw and sticks—and by the way, most survived to tell of it.

Regardless, some of those kids down on the Haight are old enough to recall Hiroshima, perhaps only faintly, but old enough to have participated in the *Duck and Cover Drills* which dominated the memory of many baby boomer Americans. And if this "Mutant talk" is familiar to any of them, it's because they likely passed the newspaper stand several years earlier, 1962, for the record, and picked up a copy of Marvel's *X-Men* #1—Stan Lee's latest Occultist offering for children.

Indoctrination runs deep.

With its premiere issue, the mutants' wheelchair bound schoolmaster, Professor Xavier, connects the dots between Oppenheimer's radiation and Darwin's mutation. He not only informs his new recruits exactly *how* he himself became a mutant; he lays it out for everyone. His parents had worked on the very first atomic bomb.

Specifically, they had been active participants in the Manhattan Project. Silly, I suppose—but not really. The Atom bomb was *exactly* what the counterfeit religion of Scientism needed. And besides, there was a bloody conflict to be won. Military deception and political propaganda runs deep. This is the art of war. Successively, Francis Crick and James Watson's discovery couldn't have come at a more perfect time.

In 1968 some of those mutants down on the Haight will sit in a darkened theater watching an overtly silly film about three astronauts who crash land upon the *Planet of the Apes*. There's the unforgettable ending—forgive me if I'm ruining it for you—in which Charlton Heston discovers the Statue of Liberty buried in the sand and, quite understandably, laments: "I'm back. I'm home. All the time, it was…we finally really did it. You Maniacs! You blew it up!"

Why are weapons of mass destruction so important to the Occultist narrative? That is, why do we so desperately need them—because we will obliterate ourselves if we don't get this right…if we don't….*mutate*? The real kicker; the sheer irony; arrived with its 1970 follow-up, *Beneath the Planet of the Apes*. Charlton Heston—weary of the madness; the apes; the mystical super-human mutants; the small-mindedness of un-evolved religion (an offensive cycle which even the apes drew upon)—finally commits himself to an unthinkable task, which no other evil dictator in the history of Planet Earth has ever had the gull to do. In an explosive *Bridge on the River Kwai* moment, it is the astronaut who pushes the button and instantaneously destroys the very planet which he once vowed to be a representative of. Charlton Heston, like the self-destructive humanity he represents, chose to end it all rather than to go on evolving.

If the narrative *must* persist, then men like Dr. Robert Etheridge are to be ignored. As a world famous paleontologist—or rather, fossilologist—of the British Museum, he spoke with authority when claiming: "…the educated public continues to believe that Darwin has provided all the relevant answers by the magic formula of random mutation plus natural selection—quite unaware of the fact that random mutations turned out to be irrelevant and natural selection a tautology."

Oh well.

Francis Crick, co-discoverer of the double-helix DNA molecule in 1953, was clearly a priest of the counterfeit religion. In 1973 he co-published a paper with chemist Leslie Orgel on something called "directed panspermia," the theory that organisms were deliberately transmitted to the earth by intelligent beings from another planet. Crick and Orgel wrote: "Darwin and a number of other biologists concluded that life must have evolved here long ago when conditions were more favorable. A number of scientists, however, drew a quite different conclusion. They supposed that if life does not evolve from terrestrial non-living, matter nowadays, it may never have done so. Hence, they argued, life reached the earth as an "infection" from another planet." More specifically, Crick and Orgel added: "Gold (1960) has suggested that we might have evolved from the micro-organisms inadvertently left behind by some previous visitors from another planet (for example, in their garbage)." Apparently, the saucer from space narrative doesn't only occupy Hollywood. "Could life have started on Earth as a result of infection by microorganisms sent here deliberately by a technological society on another planet, by means of a special long range unmanned spaceship?"

Aside from atomic age mystics, those self-declared mutants down on Haight-Ashbury had other influences, like the micro-organisms of Ken Kesey, to keep them company. The man who authored *One Flew over the Cuckoo's Nest,* and who was himself nurtured by Theodore Sturgeon's *More than Human,* might as well have been Crick and Orgel's alien. Kesey was a driving force for San Francisco's acid-rock scene, and ultimately America's booming counterculture. It started *here* and mainly with *him.* On his psychedelic bus trips across America, Kesey's Merry Pranksters could feel the mutations resulting from their LSD-fueled diets. They were, like their fictional *X-Men* counterparts, "acquiring strange powers." Beatnik Poet Neal Cassady, who often acted as the buses driver, discovered that he could focus in on several thoughts at once. More precisely, he could *read minds,* specifically the minds of those in his passenger seats. The Merry Pranksters began to believe that their separate psyches were fusing into a single-collective consciousness, matched with superhuman strength. Telepathy, psychokinesis, and precognition were among its ingredients, and astral projection filled their hours. What began with their psychedelic bus, and friends like Jack Kerouac and Allen Ginsberg, whom they met along the way, could soon, they believed, envelope the entire world.

Apparently, the SIXTIES counterculture had a fetish for mutants. Timothy Leary once proclaimed: "I declare that The Beatles are mutants. Prototypes of evolutionary agents sent by God, endowed with a mysterious power to create a new human species, a young race of laughing freemen."

At any rate, our next stage of evolution will be a spiritual one, says Stan Lee and Jack Kirby, Ken Kesey and the Merry Pranksters, those writers down at the *Oracle*, an entire counterculture of baby-boomers who were inspired by them, and Alfred Russel Wallace—but I'll get to him in a moment. Or so help us if a Heston-type egomaniac has a bad day and pushes the button first.

It would be a mistake, however, to regard Marvel comics as the sole proprietor of the mystical and superhuman powers which define the mutant myth apostasy. Indeed, the *X-Men* were not merely a creation of Stan Lee and Jack Kirby. The spiritually-driven mutant myth has flourished among the intellectual, the philosopher, and the scientist since the late nineteenth century. Professor X's telepathy can be traced back across the Atlantic Ocean to the London Society of Psychical Research and that of Fredric Myers, the Church of England clergyman and apostate who founded it. The British Society of Psychical Research, or S.P.R., passed the Occultists flickering torch from esoteric halls to post-Newtonian Science, where spiritualism, apparitions, haunts, and psychic abilities could be openly explored and expanded into mainstream consciousness. At the first official meeting in 1882 was none other than Alfred Russel Wallace, co-originator of the theory of evolution with Charles Darwin. Wallace cared little for the orthodoxies of religion and science.

Writes author Jeffrey J. Kripal: "He attended séances, performed mesmeric experiments on his students, asserted the postmortem survival of our mental and spiritual nature, and speculated with his S.P.R. colleagues that 'there yet seems to be evidence of a Power which has guided the action of those (evolutionary) laws in definite directions and for special ends.'" The cat is out of the bag. Professor Xavier's school for gifted youngsters is the Occult.

Here Kripal adds:

"The first thirty issues, written by Stan Lee and Roy Thomas, read like a veritable glossary of technical terms taken directly from these academic traditions (it is Professor X, after all). These technical terms include: telepathy (coined, again, by Myers in 1882), telekinesis, teleportations (coined by Fort in 1931), levitation, extrasensory perception of ESP (coined by Rudolf Tischner but popularized by Rhine at Duke), the sixth sense, counter-ego (what was called a 'double personality' in the nineteenth-century literature), trance, and perhaps most obvious of all, magnetism (from the earlier 'animal magnetism'). Indeed, in one delightful X-Men panel, Jean is even seen telekinetically pulling some books on "telekinetic research" off the shelves of Professor Xavier's library in order to borrow them so that she can 'continue to study ways to utilize my mutant power' (XM 555). Here the debt is openly acknowledged."

When Roy Thomas took over the *X-Men* comics from Stan Lee in 1966, each member of the team—not just Professor X this time—was immediately added to the roster of those who were parented by the Manhattan Project. Hippies were comic book readers. By December of 1975, the *X-Men* would be officially referred to as: "Children of the atom, students of Charles Xavier, MUTANTS." The series devoted readers would become intimately familiar with *that*, and more—so much more. It is perhaps not a coincidence that the counter-cultural sexual revolution simply caught up with Stan Lee and Jack Kirby's atomic bomb mutations, including Harvey Milk's political-activism in 1970's San Francisco and the LGBT movement, both of which played the part of a broom and swept America. X-Men is an overtly *out of the closet* tale. But that is the way it goes. The Occult comes first in all of its legible and hieroglyphic art forms. And culture, being a willing though perhaps arguably *unconscious* recipient, flows out from it.

Certainly, not everyone will agree.

For example, I had a pastor once tell me: "It's *just* a story."

This was in response to my protest over the current narrative making its way into the church—propaganda and indoctrination films like *X-Men*. His wife delivered her signature pendulum eyes, designating the disgust of her disapproval, where inquiry was concerned, which naturally encouraged his follow-up question:

"What are you saying about entertainment?"

I opened my mouth to speak—almost said, "Pornography is also entertainment," but clamped my teeth shut instead. It was no use. He'd already sold the Word of God for a lesser authority—the counterfeit religion.

That pastor was a Darwinist.

Those poor-poor mutant hippies down on the Haight—imagine the sickness of our beastly world governance. That is to say, should the *rumors* be true and the destruction of Hiroshima proves yet another elaborate staging of War Art. First the US acquires the bomb. Then Russia acquires it—then the UK—then China—then India—then Israel. And finally the *Planet of the Apes* acquires one, in which Heston dubiously does us in. The sickness; the grotesque child abuse; entire generations of children forcibly molested into the indoctrination of Planet Earth through an endless barrage of *Duck and Cover* drills. Perhaps we have all the evidence we need of Mr. Darwin's disastrous error. Proof that Evolution is fictitious as its comic book counterparts is the fact that the hippies—self-declared mutants of the bomb—never evolved at all. Let the *San Francisco Oracle* stand as evidence for the court, with Sir Chain as witness. Mutation is never advantageous. Proof is in the pudding—or should I say *primordial soup*. If we've mutated in any way, it's because humanity has regressed away from a faith in God, specifically His own Testimony.

Planet Earth—you've probably heard of it.

And if you have, the macro-mutation involving millions of undiscovered missing links over a fictitious span of billions of years needs no introduction. They've already emptied your pockets for tax dollars indoctrinating you with it. That math can *prove* Occultist theory—or perhaps more precisely, chalk board equations which *disprove* the observable science laid out before us—needs none either. Or that Francis Crick and James Watson *discovered* a DNA double-helix molecule which in no way corresponds with the coiling snake of DMT-induced shaman visions and, even further back within the annals of human history, the Mysteries. There is no need to imagine that Copernicus laid a foundation—that Darwin built his mansion upon it—or that Albert Einstein, Oppenheimer, Crick, and Lee, among thousands of other contributors, added the decor. They are only the antipodal occupants of a spinning planet, hurdling hundreds-of-thousands of miles-per-hour through uncharted infinity, who happened to set their Bibles down and *stumble* upon these truths.

Or don't believe any of it. Pin my name to the wall of Science-deniers, right next to Moses and the Prophets and the Word of God. Blame those misguided kids down on the Haight. Couldn't they simply go about evolving in a civilized manner?

Just keep reminding yourself that none of this could possibly be a deception—because there are too many parts to make the wheels turn.

Look into the mirror when you wake each morning and tell yourself as comfort before you enter the terrifying Darwinist world:

"The late, great *Planet* Earth is simply too big of a lie."

"*Are You Experienced?*" | OUR GREATEST SONGWRITERS OF ROCK N' ROLL ARE AS ANCIENT AS THE MYSTERY SCHOOLS THEY DERIVE FROM

SIR PAUL MCCARTNEY OF THE BEATLES CANNOT READ or write music. '*Yesterday,*' he told Larry King, simply came to him in a dream. And I know what you're likely already thinking. As one of history's greatest hit-makers, McCartney was simply being modest. Let us then consider John Lennon's interview with *Playboy* Magazine. Concerning the construct of his own music, he admitted: "It's like being possessed, like a psychic or a medium." To this Yoko Ono would add of her late husband's band: "They were like mediums. They weren't conscious of all they were saying, but it was coming through them." If there's any doubt as to what John and Paul were channeling, Lennon put an end to that when he confessed: "I felt like a hollow temple filled with many spirits, each one passing through me, each inhabiting me for a little time and then leaving to be replaced by another. (*People* Magazine)" If the Beatles weren't writing their own music, then who was?

Little Richard was somewhat more forthcoming about the secret ingredient behind his musical potency, and as we shall soon come to find, is only one straightforward witness among a multitude of others. In *The Life and Times of Little Richard*, Charles White quotes of Richard:

> "I was directed and commanded by another power. The power of darkness ... that a lot of people don't believe exists. The power of the Devil—Satan"

That Rock N' Roll is the soundtrack to Satan's homecoming parade is an obvious conclusion to make. Such a claim has been openly advertised among its muses for decades. It shouldn't come as a surprise then to learn that Apollo isn't only the Sun, giver of all animal and plant life; he is also the god of music. In *The Secret History of Rock 'N' Roll*, Christopher Knowles writes: "Apollo was himself the ultimate rock god. *The Homeric Hymn to Pythian Apollo* depicts him as ancient cross between Hendrix and Bowie, 'clad in divine, perfumed garments…at the touch of the golden key his lyre sings sweet.' When Apollo did his act for the Olympians, 'the undying gods think only of the lyre and song.'"

David Bowie would agree. He told *Rolling Stone*, "Rock has always been the devil's music; you can't convince me that it isn't. I honestly believe everything I've said—I believe rock and roll is dangerous. … I feel that we're only heralding something even darker than ourselves." Perhaps more importantly, Jim Morrison of The Doors made the connection between ancient and modern times. To this he said:

> "I like to think of the history of rock & roll like the origin of Greek drama. That started out on the threshing floors during the crucial seasons, and was originally a band of acolytes dancing and singing. Then, one day, a possessed person jumped out of the crowd and started imitating a god."

Morrison was referring to rocks true origins—the ancient Mystery Schools. And here's the age-old secret recipe regarding the Mysteries. They can best be summed up with a Greek word; *Entheogen*, meaning, *"Creating the God within."* Just know this, the mystery religions, despite being highly disciplined in their art forms, weren't about dogma—they were about experience, as Hendrix would say. Everything one might hope for in a rock concert was accounted for in Greece, Egypt, and Babylon: drink, sex—sometimes even orgies—ear-numbing musical throbbing, rowdy pyrotechnics, confrontations with police, spiritual transcendence, and on the wildly-lit stage, often elevated, was an encounter with "god" himself. But the greatest mystery behind the Mysteries was drugs. More specifically—mushrooms. Or as R. Gordon Wasson wrote in *The Road to Eleusis*, mushrooms "leap forth seedless and rootless, a mystery from the beginning…They express religion in its purest essence, without intellectual content. Aristotle said of the Eleusinian Mysteries precisely the same."

Psychonaut Terence McKenna, author of *Food of the Gods: The Search for the Original Tree of Knowledge*, advocated what he called the "stoned ape theory," in which hallucinogens were the primary catalyst in the evolutionary development of all human intelligence. Essentially summing up the Serpents temptation with Adam and Eve (Genesis 3) and every Elitist Mystery cult which has followed, McKenna concluded this of his studies in psychedelic drugs, plant-based entheogens, shamanism, metaphysics, and alchemy: "You are a divine being. You matter, you count. You come from realms of unimaginable power and light, and you will return to those realms."

So secretive were these Mystery festivals, which ironically birthed the philosophies, religions, music and arts of worldwide civilization as we know it—all the comforts and damnable distractions which we furnish our lives with today—that we have very little insight into the actual logistics of what went on behind closed doors. We do have a few glimpses, however, scraps of papyrus that survived the sands of time. There was Egypt's Festival of Bast. Greek historian Herodotus once observed this Isis cult on the Nile, claiming the young women on boats would make a noise with rattles and mock the women of the place by standing and lifting their skirts, while others danced and got into mischief—not quite unlike Mardi Gras today. Elsewhere across the Mediterranean, in one of ancient Greece's most famous plays, Euripides' *The Bacchae*, a messenger spy reports on the festival of Dionysus (we mostly know him as Bacchus—another counterpart of Apollo), and the wild Bacchant women—housewives mainly—who would be whipped up into a drunken frenzy whenever god came around. The messenger reports, "The entire mountain and its wild animals were in one Bacchic ecstasy. As these women moved, they made all things dance."

There were of course the Maenads, who would consume their drug-laced "wine" and "preform sexual, or violent, or sometimes violently sexual rituals to the thrashing of drums and flutes. Rumor had it that the Maenads used such extreme methods as cutting and flagellation in their initiations, and even that wooden or clay phalli (worn on belts) played some unspeakable role." Not overlooking the Korybantes, "the noise-crazed madmen of the ancient Mysteries....literally screaming their songs until their throats were raw (Christopher Knowles, *The Secret History of Rock 'N' Roll*)." But whatever the particulars, historian Walter Burkert had this insight: "Mystery festivals should be unforgettable events casting their shadows over the whole of one's future life, creating experiences that transform existence."

The Mystery of Mithras is of particular interest. Its cult members, always secretly hiding from their Christian contemporaries in tomb-like bathhouses, would douse their naked bodies in the blood of a bull while huddled together in a dark underground cavern and, taking communion—the body of "god" being a mushroom mixed with other psychedelics—they would chant the nonsensical lyrics that can be found in the 4th-century Egyptian Mithraic liturgy:

"I invoke the immortal names, living and honored which never pass into mortal nature and are not declared in articulate speech by human tongue or mortal speech or mortal sound: EEO OEEO IOO OE EEO EEO OE EO IOO OEEE OEE OOE IE EO OO OE IEO!"

What follows for Mithras initiates, according to the liturgy: "you will see yourself being lifted up and ascending to the height, so that you seem to be in midair....You will hear nothing either of man or of any other living thing, nor in that hour will you see anything of mortal affairs on earth, but rather you will see immortal things." Most importantly, should the Mithrian disciple achieve the highest degree, he will encounter Mithras himself. The sun god, Apollo—Satan, is once again described as a youthful god, beautiful in appearance, dressed in a white tunic and a scarlet cloak, with fiery red hair, lightning bolts for eyes, stars issuing forth from his body, and wearing a fiery crown.

Irrefutable evidence connects Rock 'N' Roll with the Mysteries. Christopher Knowles makes this observation: "Mystery cult centers were the ancient equivalents of today's clubs and concert halls, which may be why so many of the old pagan place-names are still in use—the Orpheum, the Apollo, the Academy, the Palladium...." And where the Mithrian Mystery is concerned, let us not forget an ancient Roman Mithraeum in Liverpool, England, which was in the 1950's converted into a nightclub. It was conveniently called the Cavern Club. And the Beatles made their name there.

So, getting back to Jim Morrison—in his biography, *No One Here Gets out Alive*, authors Jerry Hopkins and Danny Sugarman cite Doors keyboardist Ray Manzarek as having said:

"When the Siberian shaman gets ready to go into his trance, all the villagers get together... and play whatever instruments they have to send him off [into trance and possession]. ... It was the same way with The Doors when we played in concert... I think that our drug experience let us get into it... [the trance state] quicker.... It was like Jim was an electric shaman and we were the electric shaman's band, pounding away behind him. Sometimes he wouldn't feel like getting into the state, but the band would keep on pounding and pounding, and little by little it would take him over. God, I could send an electric shock through him with the organ. John could do it with his drumbeats."

Michael Jackson referred to this shaman spirit while speaking with *Teen Beat* in 1984. "When I hit the stage it's all of a sudden a 'magic' from somewhere that comes and the spirit just hits you, and you just lose control of yourself." Stevie Nicks of Fleetwood Mac did too. On April 14, 1971 she told *Circus*: "It's amazing, cause sometimes when we're on stage, I feel like somebody's just moving the pieces. ... I'm just going, 'God, we don't have any control over this.' And that's magic."

Ginger Baker was drummer to Eric Clapton's band, *Cream*. He said: "It happens to us quite often–it feels as though I'm not playing my instrument, something else is playing it and that same thing is playing all three of our instruments. That's what I mean when I say it's frightening sometimes. Maybe we'll all play the same phrase out of nowhere. It happens very often with us"

But it goes beyond the stage, as the Lennon and McCartney have attested to. Never to be outmatched by the Beatles, Keith Richards of the Rolling Stones told *Rolling Stone* Magazine in 1977, "We receive our songs by inspiration, like at a séance."

Robert Plant and Jimmy Page of Led Zeppelin are in equal agreement; they don't know who wrote their most popular song, *Stairway to Heaven*. Davin Seay, author of *Stairway to Heaven*, quotes Plant as having testified:

"Pagey had written the chords and played them for me. I was holding the paper and pencil, and for some reason, I was in a very bad mood. Then all of a sudden my hand was writing out words. ... I just sat there and looked at the words and then I almost leaped out of my seat."

Elvis Presley believed he had a twin that communicated with him spiritually. Strangely, it was when he was high on drugs that Gospel music most *inspired* him. Folk singer Joni Mitchell even enlisted the help of a male spirit to write her music. This she confided to the press in 1974. Time Magazine reports: "Joni Mitchell credits her creative powers to a 'male muse' she identifies as Art. He has taken so much control of not only her music, but her life, that she feels married to him, and often roams naked with him on her 40-acre estate. His hold over her is so strong that she will excuse herself from parties and forsake lovers whenever he *calls*."

The gods of Rock 'N' Roll aren't simply prototype memes of distant pagan cultures. They are, in many ways, gods of old incarnate—avatars, if you will. Mythology once more realized. And for every ancient Mystery School surrounding the fertile crescent of the Mediterranean, with their various social outlooks and disciplinary styles, there are, quite eerily, modern day rock stars and musicians to fill them. The gods are alive. They speak. It's as Led Zeppelin once sang, "Let the music be your master, won't you heed the master's call? Oh Satan!"

I don't know about you, but I'm done listening to music crafted from the twisted minds of angels and demons—translated to us, both on stage and in the studio, through spiritual shamans. I've devoted too much of my life to spiritual duality. I confess to claiming a love of the LORD while filling in the bulk of my hours celebrating the processions and festivals of the Mysteries in all its musical forms and which sought nothing else than to promote the damnable lie of the Serpent. *We too can be like God.* Perhaps I have never tasted of the tree of the knowledge of good and evil and experienced what it is to be like god by partaking of his body. But I too have been indiscreet with the words of my Master, having once drawn a line in the sand: "No man can serve two masters: for either he will hate the one, and love the other; or else he will hold to the one, and despise the other. Ye cannot serve God and mammon (Matthew 6:24)." I am guilty of juggling the two, God and the master musician, Apollo—but no more.

Get out of the Mystery Schools while you can—the entire heliocentric religion of Apollo. Or as Bon Jovi would call his religion, the *Homebound Train*—because anyone who's willingly riding upon it is going:

"Down, down, down, down, down."

"It's a Bird! It's a Plane! It's……." THE OCCULT ORIGINS OF SUPERMAN (OR AS FRIEDRICH NIETZSCHE WOULD SAY: *"God Is Dead"*)

SUPERMAN'S CREATORS WEREN'T EXACTLY YOUR AVERAGE RUN of the mill science-fiction aficionados. Writer Jerome Siegel and artist Joseph Shuster dabbled in esoteric knowledge. Their earlier creation, albeit an unsuccessful one at the time, was *"Dr. Mystic: The Occult Detective."* As one might logically deduce from the title alone, Dr. Mystic preformed sleuth-work for the occult. Aside from having an identical face and build of Clark Kent, mild-mannered reporter for *The Daily Planet*, he was also the comic books first flying caped-figure. More specifically, he flew "faster than the speed of light" through the spirit world, by way of astral projection. Such forthright directness, particularly for a depression-era audience, was subtly suppressed until Siegel and Shuster could retrace their steps in a more coded *hieroglyphic* language. It paid off. From the moment Superman crash landed onto *Planet* Earth in 1938 he was an immediate runaway success. *Action Comics #1* promptly sold out of its initial run—a printing of 200,000 copies. Within months DC Comics predecessor, National Allied Publications, would be emptying newsstands of a million Superman titles per month.

It is no secret that Siegel and Shuster's inspiration came from German philosopher Friedrich Nietzsche. The first English translation of *"Thus Spoke Zarathustra"* was published in 1896, only then Nietzsche's champion-figure—*Ubermensch* in German—was known as "Beyond-Man." It wasn't until another 1909 translation by Thomas Common that *Ubermensch* became Superman, and the name stuck.

The very suggestion that Jesus was "not of this world," ironically enough, did not sit well with the German philosopher. Nietzsche was disquieted by the Christian's hope of salvation through its divine Messiah, mainly His promise of a spiritual rebirth beyond physical death into His Father's heavenly kingdom, which might come through faith in

611

Jesus' blood and righteousness alone. Quite contrarily, Nietzsche's Zarathustra admonished those who would promise other-worldly hopes in order to draw them away from the Earth. This turning away, we come to learn, results from the Christian's dissatisfaction with the human condition, a resentment which causes its wishful-thinker "to create another world in which those who made one unhappy in this life are tormented."

Nietzsche's most popular suggestion, and oftly regurgitated slogan, should be immediately recognized. "GOD IS DEAD." If this is true—if God truly is dead, then the Bible can no longer provide moral values as a guiding compass for humanity—glories by which we are to measure our life as a standard with and, if our reading comprehension is up to par, always fall short of. Finally, the humanist may sigh with relief. For the reprobate, Moses has been defeated with one driving stake to God's heart. But if the critic is concerned about our future moral state of affairs in an infinitely expanding universe without a value-system *written in stone* then fear not, because according to Nietzsche, Superman is coming to fill in the vacuum of nihilism. Whereas Christianity is a reaction against the fallen human state; mainly Adam and Eve's partaking in the tree of knowledge and the sin—with its damnable wages—which has resulted from it; Superman is motivated by a love of this world and utmost concern for life. Superman *is* the meaning of the Earth. More precisely, Superman is the anti-Christ.

For Nietzsche's Zarathustra, Superman should be a set goal for civilizations eventual graduation beyond its own present state. Accordingly, humanity can find ultimate meaning, not in friendship with its Creator, but by its own advancement into a new generation of advanced beings. Says Zarathustra: "I teach you the Superman. Man is something that shall be surpassed. What, to man, is the ape? A joke or a shame. Man shall be the same to the Superman: a joke or shame....Man is a bridge connecting ape and Superman (*Thus Spoke Zarathustra*)." Or as Nietzsche would later write: "Man is a rope stretched between the animal and the Superman—a rope over an abyss."

In *Thoughts and Aphorisms* (1913), Indian yogi and philosopher Sri Aurobindo would sum up Nietzsche's contempt for the Christian soul: "Evolution is not finished; reason is not the last word, nor the reasoning animal the supreme figure of Nature. As man emerged out of the animal, so out of man the superman emerges."

No wonder Siegel and Shuster introduced their comic book sensation as "the Man of Tomorrow." Superman best functions when perceived as a prototype for the future evolution of all humankind. In this existence, *God is dead*, and man's only hope, should he conclusively understand his place in the Copernican Universe, is relied upon the individual who has mastered transcendence. He must look to the superhero. In a letter to *Buck Rogers* artist Russell Keaton, dated June 12, 1934, Siegel described the infant Clark Kent as having escaped the end of the world after being placed in a time-capsule by the last man on Earth, naturally his father, and then promptly jettisoned back to a more primitive decade—the year 1935 specifically, only seconds before giant cataclysms destroy the entire planet. Despite Superman's origins taking a slight narrative diversion from a distant millennia to another distant planet, the concept remains the same. On the very first page of *Action Comics #1* we read: orphanage attendants were unaware that "the child's physical structure was millions of years advanced of their own."

Siegel and Shuster's Man of Tomorrow wasn't only a mirror reflection of Nietzsche's Superman; he quickly became the prototype standard and launching pad for an entire superhero phenomena to come. The Copernican deception was now indoctrinating children with sledgehammer force. No longer were they led away from Biblical cosmology, with its rich and fulfilling theological conclusions, by the lies of the government-endorsed classroom alone. They were willingly investing their own dime to be entertained by it. *Action Comics #1* only recently sold on Ebay for $3.2 million dollars and some change. But at any rate, western society was ripe for the deception. Writes Jeffrey J. Kripal in *Mutants & Mystics*: "The cosmos was now so unspeakably vast, its physics so utterly mind-bending, that individuals were simply no longer capable of processing everything. A few elite astronomers and astrophysicists may have understood a portion of the math, but no one, *no one*, could now fathom the total vision, much less what it all meant. Hence the famous quip of J.B.S. Haldane that '*the universe is not only queerer than we suppose, but queerer than we can suppose.*'"

Siegel and Shuster wouldn't forget their occult fascinations either. On January 16, 1939, only half a year after his premiere, the planet which the infant Superman arrived from was promptly named. Krypton translates from the Greek—and Greek it is—as the *Hidden* or the *Occult*. In other words, the Man of Tomorrow has come to us from the Occult. If he is an alien living among us, it's because we have yet to become like him. It's actually the perfect allegory. "The last son of Krypton" is perhaps a play on words. The people of Superman's home world had crumbled and decayed into what Nietzsche most feared of a Christian-led civilization. They had collectively corroded as a society in order to attain laziness, comfort, and complacency, having nothing left to offer but their own disillusionment with the state of things. And because of *this* sin, they promptly perished. Superman's parents however were of the enlightened nature. Because of their hidden knowledge, he has arrived on Earth to spare us of the same misfortune. Let us not forget, the only thing that can truly hurt or impair Superman, thereby threatening the very existence of humanity's own guided evolution, is a substance from his place of birth, Kryptonite. So too is the Christian religion, with its declarations of God, a threat to Nietzsche's Superman.

There is an even greater esoteric mystery to be uncovered in all of this. That which is expected to descend upon the world, thereby allowing us to realize our own evolutionary and divine strength, is a basic teaching throughout Eastern religions, including some yogic traditions. Siegel and Shuster however, like many of the mover and shaker founding-architects of the comic book industry, were Jewish. I'm certainly not the first comic book *reader* to see Clark Kent in the phone booth and undress him for what he is truly intended to be. Understand it like this. After world harmony is achieved through a worldwide dispensing of political and religious Zionism to the masses, specifically through the guiding blueprint of the Kabbalah, the *Messiah* will come.

Nietzsche put it like this, "I love those who do not first seek a reason beyond the stars for going down and being sacrifices, but sacrifice themselves to the earth that the earth of the Superman may hereafter arrive."

FOUR WORDS: *"Have Them Fight God"* | STAN LEE & THE GNOSTIC REALITY BEHIND MARVEL COMICS

IN OUTER SPACE ANYTHING IS POSSIBLE. Eight years before Armstrong and Aldrin's fictitious walk on the moon, having passed twice through the Van Allen belt without consequence, a handful of hypothetical cosmonauts collided with yet another radiation in outer space, only they became the super group known as "The Fantastic Four." For the record, that would be November of 1961, when Mister Fantastic, the Invisible Woman, the Human Torch, and the Thing came into our lives. For most they need no introduction. The fact is the average person knows more of occult philosophy and its imaginative storytelling—in both cases; comic books and moon landings—than they do of the Bible. It is yet another tragic turn of events, where the history of the church is concerned. And I hold the leaders of our congregations responsible.

Fast forward to August 31, 2009; the Walt Disney Co. announced a deal to acquire Marvel Entertainment for 4.24 billion dollars. Just three years later, in 2012, Disney purchased Lucasfilm for an additional 4 billion, adding the legendary *Star Wars* franchise to its recognizable roster of theme park characters. Disney's complete acquisition of Marvel characters would be completed in 2017, when the company acquired the majority of 21st Century Fox for an a somewhat unimaginable 52.4 billion dollars. Finally Spiderman and the X-Men could wear the coveted mouse ears right alongside their other Marvel contemporaries. With this merger, Disney is provably accomplishing one of the most ambitious, awe-inspiring, and wholly successful franchises in the history of western civilization. The ancient Mysteries have become a corporate empire. And they even have complementary theme parks.

The *Avengers* films, which focuses upon a conglomerate of individual superheroes paired up into one centralized team, is of particular interest. What began by *Fantastic Four* creators Stan Lee and Jack Kirby over fifty years ago is now re-surging on the big screen. Earth's greatest threat is coming again, and we *must* put a stop to him. It was 1966. Lee and Kirby were outlining what would become Fantastic Four #48-50, and Lee spoke to Kirby these four landmark words: "Have them fight God."

Kirby's response: "I went to the Bible, and I came up with Galactus."

"The Galactus Trilogy" is a profoundly Gnostic tale. For anyone out of the cultural loop, Galactus is a cosmic being who feeds off the life energies of entire planets. That's bad news for the Copernican. The rest of us need not concern ourselves—for nothing gets in or out of the firmament. Of no coincidence, it is in this very series where the Silver Surfer is first premiered. He's basically a cosmic scout for the hungry deity. But there's a catch. The Silver Surfer doesn't go along with his master's plan. Rather, he warns humanity of *who* is coming. And for this treacherous crime against the evil Galactus, the great enlightener cannot be forgiven.

"In any case," writes Jeffrey J. Kripal in his book, *Mutants and Mystics: Science Fiction, Superhero Comics, and the Paranormal,* "fighting God and being a Gnostic are more or less the same thing. What the Gnostic is really fighting, of course, is a lower god pretending to be the real God. What he seeks is the God beyond god, the cosmic truth of things beyond all the religious bullshit."

Who is this adversary of the superhero Gnostic; this clerical poppycock; this "lower god pretending to be the real God?" His name is Yahweh.

Ask your local Gnostic. It is this very demiurge who's responsible for the placement of Adam and Eve in the garden. It is he who created the fleshly bodies to entrap their spirit—or rather, supernatural abilities. It is he who dictated Adam's spell of ignorance—who caused him to fall into a terrible slumber—and convinced our first forefather, along with Moses and the Prophets and the rest, that there was no other god but him. It is the demiurge who wishes to keep all of humanity forever ignorant, always worshiping him alone rather than the far nobler gods. The Gnostic needs only thank the semi-divine cosmic scout; the fallen angel who is trapped on Earth as a punishment for refusing to do the creators ill-will. It is the Serpent who opened their eyes to *true knowledge.* The forbidden fruit has been consumed, and the spell of ignorance is therefore broken—should the "truther" wish to break free of his enslavement and pursue his mind's enlightenment. Conclusively, don't blame Satan or sin. The "True God," whoever he or she or it turns out to be, is not the creator of this evil imperfect world.

The Apostle John once warned about the kings of the Earth who will gather with Satan for battle. They will do so, quite arrogantly, in vain hopes of striking the Lord Jesus down upon His return. To this coming event he wrote: "And I saw the beast, and the kings of the earth, and their armies, gathered together to make war against him that sat on the horse, and against his army (Revelation 19:19)." In the meantime, we have the Silver Surfer to enlighten us of what is soon approaching. And better yet, we have Iron Man, Spiderman, Thor, Black Widow, Ant-Man, Doctor Strange, and the Hulk—among a mishmash of others, to take up the challenge in our defense.

I have personally observed pastors eagerly lining up their youth for the next Marvel installment. The culture war is lost. Sadly, they've surrendered. Esoteric entertainment has become cause for a church picnic. And yet the Gnosticism presented here is not confused. Stan Lee's utter disdain for God is not hidden from us. So I must ask this question: are our shepherds confused? Let me rephrase that. Are they leading their flock—or rather, indulging in occult entertainment with darkened eyes? Or do they simply not care either way? Jesus will not be gawked at in such manner. He will not be spoken to in this way. And let's be clear of one thing.

If our pastors are not pointing out the wolves, then we must turn to the next grim reality. They themselves are the wolves.

TEENAGERS—AN AMERICAN INVENTION | *"When I Was a Child…"* I WAS A PRISONER TO THE VACUUM TUBE OF NOSTALGIA

1

IF THERE WAS ANY QUESTION AS TO WHY the silent screen actor Rudolph Valentino had earned himself the nickname "Latin Lover," the unbridled screams of 10,000 women, who invaded his funeral in 1926—having died at the pre-mature age of 31—should erase any doubt. After Frank Sinatra's legendary opening at the New York Paramount Theater in 1947 some two decades later, the clean-up crew found that the seats were still wet from the bobby soxers in attendance. Sweaty, throbbing, mind-pulsating young girls, contaminated with an almost alien case of *hormones*, were simply unable to compose themselves among the shock-and-awe swooning from the man who was later referred to as Chairman of the Board. In America, *something* was happening. One might think Bacchus, yet another counterpart of Apollo, and the wild Bacchant women arising within the Dionysian Mysteries—housewives mainly—who would be whipped up into a drunken frenzy whenever their favorite god came around for a forest romp, had returned.

Across the Atlantic pond the Brits were seemingly immune to the burgeoning howls of western sexuality. For a time they could only watch film reels manufactured by the very Americans who had recently helped to rescue them from nightly bombardment of Nazi Germany and which depicted youthful boys in lettermen jackets paired with girls in poodle-skirts, bobbing their pony-tails while guzzling Coca-Cola, milk shakes and hamburgers to the spells of a jukebox—attempting to make sense of it all. Liverpool's John Lennon understood the difference between the youth of Britain and America. Some years later, after invading America with his mop-top quartet, the Beatle remarked: "America had teenagers. Everywhere else just had people."

In *John Lennon: the Life*, author Philip Norman reports of the British, they "had regarded the process of growing up as perfectly straightforward. The system was that children went on being children until puberty was well advanced. Then, virtually overnight, they turned into grown-ups, wearing the same kind of clothes as their parents, aspiring to the same values, and seeking the same amusements. The effect of rioting hormones on immature and impressionable minds had yet to be studied in any depth by scientists or sociologists."

When Elvis first shook his hips on a censured television screen in the spring of 1956, not even Lennon could resist. *"He gave release to the tension that had built up in young men with no more global conflict to burn off than testosterone,"* writes Norman. The very opening words of Presley's first hit, *Heartbreak Hotel*, said it all. *Well, since my baby left me...* Elvis goes on to speak of a bellhop whose "tears keep flowing" and a "desk clerk dressed in black." We learn of "broken hearted lovers" who end up "down at the end of Lonely Street." Unlike the adult themes emanating from rhythm and blues, a musical genre which *Heartbreak Hotel* heavily borrowed from, Presley had—for the first time—channeled into and defined the teenage experience. According to Norman, it "reached directly to the primary adolescent emotion" and "melodramatic self-pity."

We should stop and consider the absurdity of every parent's worst nightmare—the sexual alienation of their one-time innocent child—and question why it is that we consider the teenager as *gifted* to the human experience by our Creator when psychologists have only recently materialized and grafted him into existence. But perhaps far more importantly, so have the capitalists. America, it seems, invented the teenager.

2

THEN AGAIN, FOR THE BULK OF HUMAN HISTORY, children as we know them today did *not* exist. Allow me to clarify. Antiquity will show they were dressed with the adult clothes of their social class in the months following one's departure from the cradle. While the British may have succumbed to the revived Dionysian Mysteries in America's music scene—partly due to the Beatles—in turn we may extend our stateside gaze across the Atlantic pond to witness the intellectual manufacturing of another modern upbringing. With the invention of the middle class, so too was the child developed as a sort of social etiquette to accommodate the Victorian era. And yet up until this time, one might imagine the grubby-cheeked, moist-eyed child of a Charles Dickens novel, without any protection from the hardships of the furnaces and the coal pits and the smoke stacks of the industrial revolution. "They were treated as short adults with responsibilities and with productivity demanded to the limits of their physical capabilities," writes Carolyn L. Burke and Joby G. Copenhaver in *Animals as People in Children's Literature*. Here Burke and Copenhaver further add:

> "As a middle or merchant class developed, every person was no longer needed to work at providing the family income. With leisure came the opportunity to recreate the place of children in society. The emerging view declared that children needed extended time to develop before they would be able to take on the full responsibilities of adulthood. They needed guidance and instruction to maintain their safety and to allow them to grow into full membership in society. Play came to be viewed as child's work during which they were discovering and practicing lessons, and pleasure came to be seen as an enticement in this process."

There is a rather strange *spiritual* phenomenon which came into being through the advent of the Victorian child. Animals with human characteristics began to appear in children's literature. For this, we may thank Mr. Charles Darwin. Before the theory of evolution and *On the Origin of Species*, first published in 1859, we are hard pressed to find animals which take on a coat and trousers and a thankless job— essentially a *soul*. With Darwin's ape unexpectedly showing up at the family reunion of man, the Bible's eye-witness account that we are "created in the image of God" was so thoroughly shaken that the very promise was also extended to nature. Once again, the parent embraced pantheism for his child—long thought dormant—and if literature soon had its way, the wood just beyond the garden wall was dripping with fairies and pagan spirits in the dew.

In the immediate aftermath—within six years of Darwin's publication—three significant texts were delivered unto the newly developed Victorian child. Margaret Gatty's *Parables from Nature* and Charles Kingsley's *The Water-Babies* attempted to educate the reader with their own responses to the Darwinian controversy, with Lewis Carroll's *Alice's Adventures in Wonderland* delving even further into the magnum opus of literary nonsense. As a biologist, Gatty sought to challenge the arrogance and materialism she saw in the Darwinian Theory. Her rebuttal however was an odd choice. After campaigning Sir

Thomas Browne's quip that "there are two book from whence" he collected his "divinity;" the first being the "written one of God, another his servant, Nature—that universal and public manuscript that lies expanded unto the eyes of all: those that never saw Him in the one have discovered Him in the other," Gatty writes from a narrative in which animals and plants are valorized above their arrogant male doubters, thereby subverting the overt didactic message of her evangelical text. If she were attempting to re-direct the child's attention to the Bible's promise that we are created in God's image, and therefore *not* evolved, then she failed miserably.

Quite contrarily to Gatty's oppositions, Kingsley had been one of the first to praise Darwin. He even received an advanced copy. On the 18th of November, 1859, four days before *On the Origin of Species* hit store shelves, Kingsley wrote that he had "long since, from watching the crossing of domesticated animals and plants, learnt to disbelieve the dogma of the permanence of species," and had "gradually learnt to see that it is just as noble a conception of Deity, to believe that He created primal forms capable of self-development into all forms needful pro tempore and pro loco, as to believe that He required a fresh act of intervention to supply the lacunas which He Himself had made," asking "whether the former be not the loftier thought." Kingsley took his love of evolution to the child, and by doing so once more redefined him—once believed to have been created in God's image—as recapitulative. Kingsley preferred fantasy as provisions for a new myth, one which dangerously integrated the Christian faith with Darwinian evolution—and so much more. For example, in *The Water-Babies,* Kingsley argues that no person is qualified to say that something never seen—whether a human soul or a water baby—does not exist. To this effect he writes:

> "How do you know that? Have you been there to see? And if you had been there to see, and had seen none, that would not prove that there were none … And no one has a right to say that no water babies exist till they have seen no water babies existing, which is quite a different thing, mind, from not seeing water babies."

Nearly a century later, Christian academic and medievalist C.S. Lewis would successfully wed the pantheism of pagan religion with the faith he was accredited of being a spokesperson for through the publication of *The Lion, the Witch, and the Wardrobe* in 1950. The church bought it—for the most part. One might wonder if the spirit of anthropomorphism, which apparently possessed his childhood imaginations, were first developed under the pupilage of Beatrix Potter.

With *The Tale of Peter Rabbit*, published in 1902, the rabbits are first shown as normal, realistic animals in the woods. The next scene depicts Peter and his three sisters as being dressed by their mother and handed baskets for collecting produce. And yet, after meddling in human affairs—specifically, Mr. McGregor's garden—Peter's jacket causes him to be trapped in a net, and his shoes slow down his running. From beginning to end, Potter's first offering is a brilliant page-turner. Despite its natural English setting, "this beautiful, idealized place," writes Margaret Blount, suddenly "made the fantasy more real and the pleasure more possible, the animals' humanity…more natural."

We are presented with a rather strange opportunity. Parents would happily deliver their children to animals for tutoring privileges in reading, math, and any number of developing social skills—basically what it is to be created in God's image. I know I have. As I write these words, my children in the other room watching the Muppets of Sesame Street. It just goes to show that today we are no better off than our spiritual forefathers—morally speaking. We have succumbed to the seemingly living, breathing, animated and god-like idol of Babylon we call television in order that the spirit of anthropomorphism which possesses it may help in the process of raising them. We let animals teach our children. How forward thinking and evolutionary of us! In the bulk of Judeo-Christian history, I can't help but wonder—would the church stand for this; would they see us as lukewarm; would they even call our Easy-Believism in the ways of the world *moral*? Most will disagree. I will surely find myself outnumbered. Psychologists are gifted at convincing us of its benefits.

3

IT IS NO SECRET THAT JESUS BROKE WITH HUMAN TRADITION. He laid hands on children and blessed them, and is recorded in three separate Gospels as having asked His disciples that they "suffer little children, and forbid them *not*, to come unto Me (Matthew 19:14)." Such a thought, that a rabbi would contend with children, was repulsive. And yet, because a young child is destitute of ambition, pride, contemptuousness, and hypocrisy, he or she is therefore *teachable*.

Jesus had a way of flipping the tables, not only in His Father's house, but with the uncountable Luciferian institutions of the mind. In His Father's kingdom—we shall come to learn—the only way to ascend *up* into heaven is to first go *down*. James the brother of Jesus phrased it like this: "Humble yourselves in the sight of the Lord, and he shall lift you up (James 4:10)."

Children must depend upon their parents for food and clothing, proper discipline, spiritual training, and even a roof over their heads. They are highly receptive and seemingly incapable of producing good works to merit heaven. Like *these* we are to become, open to His provisions and not depending upon our own presumed goodness. This is to contrast the rich young man who thereafter approached Jesus and asked of Him, "Good Master, what good thing shall I do, that I may have eternal life?" We are told he "went away sorrowful: for he had great possessions (Matthew 19:22)."

Today we have teenagers to contend with. Mrs. Hadley and I will have two of them in as little as several years. Fact is childhood has been extended *dramatically* from the few years it was originally intended until the individual person feels good and ready. There was a time not so long ago that the child grew up when the parent was good and ready. If they worked around the house, it's because the home was a business. The Luciferian governments of our world have certainly taken advantage of this *increase*—they likely even had a hand behind it—and those of us inhabiting this joyous cosmology shouldn't be surprised to find the public school system developing as a rib partner with the advent of modern childhood. It is just like our ruling authorities to convince us we need an ever-expanding universe of time within the mind of each young person for nurturing apart from the morals of his parent.

Thirty is the new twenty—I am told. Some will say technology is to blame, others the economy—or perhaps both. The thing is, our current gauntlet of Hollywood blockbusters are movies which were once intended for children and are geared now towards a certain standard of thinking—drained of the intellectual meat which might have filled the pages of scripts in past decades. The various Comic Cons across the United States, a tradition which began in San Diego, are attracting upwards of 200,000 attenders—mostly adults. And the Walt Disney World resort rakes in 50 million visitors per year. While not all attenders are traveling with children, even Disney adopts a certain standard of thinking.

When prompting us to suffer little children, and forbid them not, to come unto Him, Jesus did not promote the artlessness of a child's own indiscretion, a feeble mind which is easily drawn to myths and fantasies. Jesus was not promoting that ever-widening gorge in a man's life which the psychologist and the capitalist and the government may plug into and steal from. While I am in no way promoting other human institutions, particularly the excesses and cruelty of child labor; the predominant view before Victorian times—that we leave the crib and the milk of our mother and digest the meat of Godly maturity, backed with sound Biblical doctrine, and wielding our very being with the morality of our spiritual forefathers—is most certainly a Biblical attitude. Childhood is a state of mind, which Holy Writ only thinks to speak of in passing.

To this effect, the Apostle Paul writes in 1 Corinthians 13:11:

"When I was a child, I spake as a child, I understood as a child, I thought as a child: but when I became a man, I put away childish things."

As if creating the teenager was not enough, nostalgia has become an entire industry in and of itself. Adult human souls are monetized and expected to relive childhood memories through an ever deepening well of the mind in which—if correctly executed—we are never expected to climb out of.

REVISITING THE MANDELA EFFECT (*aka* Rants & Ravings from the Check-Out Aisle of the Piggly Wiggly)

1

ODYSSEUS PLUGGED THE EARS OF HIS SAILORS with a healthy helping of beeswax, ordering that he remain bound to the mast while they rowed closer to shore. This was all done so that he alone could digest the song of the Sirens. Otherwise, he might bray contradictory orders in a weakened state, which would surely shipwreck his crew if followed. And so, reader, I ask the same of you. Make no mistake about it. The Mandela Effect is a bewitching siren, if ever I've heard one. Even now, as I write these words, I am inclined to gaze once more upon the Effect with a sense of prying curiosity and wonder, despite my escape to reason—wanting nothing further to do with it. No, I *rebuke* her sorcery. And yet my mind is junked. I have had a meeting with madness. I therefore invoke the strongest and bravest of men to tie me to the mast as I recall—or rather re-investigate for the reader—my *former* wrecking upon the rocks; imploring that you maintain our predesignated course into the perfectly preserved Word of God, no matter what is uttered, and row—row—row.

If you cannot agree to this, then turn the page *now*.

2

BRAVO! YOU HAD ME FOOLED, FIONA BROOME. Can you hear my hands slow-clapping? Bravo! They're slow clapping for you. Do you know how many times I've wanted to hold a Kit Kat bar over my head in the check-out aisle of the Piggly Wiggly and shout at the grocery clerk like a crazy mad man: "IT'S CHANGED AGAIN! IT'S CHANGED AGAIN!"

But that is the way with it—the Mandela Effect. I fell for it. Your witchcraft actually had me convinced that shared false memories

625

really *do* exist; that realities are changing all around us; that it's due to a so-called *glitch in the matrix*; that the *glitch* in question points to Austrian physicist Erwin Schrodinger's cat and the tiresome ramblings of a multiverse resulting from his slaphappy thought experiment, and to the simulation theory deception, and all that dribbles from the fairy-tale tinkerers in quantum mechanics. You had me believing that Nelson Mandela died in prison, Fiona Broome—but that he didn't die at all, according to *this* present reality. You had me believing *that* and so much more. You had my mind rewired to recall long forgotten childhood memories—seemingly real memories—whereas the Berenstain Bears were really spelled the Berenstein Bears. And here in the check-out aisle of the Piggly Wiggly you had me believing that Kit Kat, as the spelling of candy bar logos go, might flip back and forth between Kit Kat, without a dash, and Kit-Kat with a dash—all in real time and in a maddening game of sanity ping pong.

Of course, had I informed the grocery clerk to the *truth* of the matter, that reality had indeed changed from a dash to no dash and that we were all living within an alternate reality or time traveling paradox— albeit from CERN or super quantum computers—she'd only look at me with a crooked face and say something to the effect: "So what? A candy company can change their logo from a dash to no dash if they want to."

Would I...could I have looked at her with the wide eyes of a completely sane person and responded: "AH-HA! That's where YOU ARE WRONG! It's because this is yet another example of the MANDELA EFFECT, and it's very R-EEEEE-AAAAA-L!"

And that's just the thing. The magic behind it was so *authentic*. I'd stand in the check-out aisle of the Piggly Wiggly and see Kit-Kat spelled with a dash, when in fact the week before it was spelled without a dash. This I was certain of. My own eyes certified the line-up. And what would the all-knowing wisdom of Google tell me—soon as I returned home? That it's always been spelled *with* a dash. Of course, there would be some person in a chat room asking the same question: *Did anyone see Kit Kat become Kit-Kat again?*—in which dozens, perhaps even hundreds of other spellbound contributors—including myself, would be like, "Um, yeah, it happened for me too, and I just let the grocery clerk in on it."

THIS ALL HAPPENED DURING THE SUMMER OF 2016. JFK's 1961 Lincoln Continental limousine, which he rode through Dallas on that cruel November day, formerly had two bench seats by my count—now suddenly had three. There was *that* to contend with and the Smithsonian *Institute* becoming the Smithsonian Institution and now the Ron Howard movie, *Apollo 13*. I was fourteen with its original release—when Tom Hanks spoke his famous line. Repeating it was a regurgitated teenage joke, given the right circumstance in or out of the classroom, and could garnish a dozen laughs. But in my Mandela Effect summer Tom Hanks no longer spoke his landmark line as I'd so long remembered: "Houston, we have a problem."

According to every VHS tape, digital copy, and even AFI's 100 Greatest Film Quotes—anything in existence, Tom Hanks now said: "Houston, *we've had* a problem."

Thousands of others affected by the Mandela Effect agreed. The line, though arguably a *small offense*—had changed. And this is where it really begins to get strange. See, in the actual Apollo 13 mission, astronaut Jack Swigert told NASA control: "Okay, Houston, we've had a problem here"—in which Jim Lovell, played by Hanks in the movie, added: "Uh, Houston, we've had a problem." Their argument was—the Mandela Effect deniers and detractors, that is—since Jim Lovell always said, "*we've had*," then the movie naturally would have followed suite, and therefore all of our memories were clearly wrong. But this is the strange part. I woke up one morning—this being the summer of 2016—with the news from ME observers that Howard's *Apollo 13* had been diagnosed with a case of the Ping Pong. Once again, Tom Hanks clearly quoted the line as we all remembered it.

"Houston, *we have* a problem."

This goes for every known digital and hard copy of the film, including VHS, the American Film Institute, and practically all online discussions regarding the previous changes. The Mandela Effect decided it liked the original line best. Evidence erased. And do you know what the detractors had to say about it? "Oh, you crazies are just confusing '*we have*' and '*we've had*' with the actual Apollo 13 space mission. In the movie, Tom Hanks *never* said that."

The Mandela Effect was *madness*.

Funny thing is, I watched Kit Kat ping-pong back and forth between a dash and without its dash so often and for so long that I could no longer recall, in the wreckage of my mind, whether it originally had a dash or no dash at all.

4

SHAME ON YOU, FIONA BROOME, shame on you, *witch*. Be gone! You and your disciples had me thoroughly convinced that God's Word had changed. In Isaiah 11:6, the lion once lay with the lamb, but now—because of CERN, apparently—the wolf dwelt with the lamb. But worse—in my delusional mind, I tried to convince Christians of it. By enacting the spell upon others, I played the part of the demon. That's the point of the Effect, isn't it? That God's Word was written by men and is therefore prone to error. All Mandela Effects ultimately point to Holy Writ. There are dozens, *no—hundreds* of Mandela Effect changes to the Bible, aren't there Broome? Your demon-disciples continue with their diggings. More Scriptural changes must be found!

Lord, forgive my maladjustment. I had succumbed to the entrapping's of humanism by turning against the only lamp which might guide my feet through the darkness (Psalm 119:105). As an advocate of the Mandela Effect, I claimed to know better than God Almighty. Jesus Himself prophesied of His Word: "Heaven and earth shall pass away: but my words shall not pass away (Mark 13:31)" Our Master also said: "And it is easier for heaven and earth to pass, than one tittle (or small mark in Hebrew lettering) of the law to fail." By gazing into the Mandela Effect, I was calling my Master Shepherd a liar.

Take this as a warning, dear reader, and I pray that you continue rowing on course (for the tug of the Siren song is, as I write these words, undeniably strong)—the Mandela Effect was and still is a damnable abyss. It is the sort of landscape where shadows curve against the natural angles of the sun and claw as a sinus in the back of one's skull. I myself gazed into it—the abyss, that is. And the abyss had eyes—in fact, *many*. One might say the Mandela Effect was conscious of its existence, because for the first time in my life, the darkness gazed back.

Its evil became incarnate.

Dare I describe it? Cosmetically he was an alien gray—my nighttime visitor—standing about four feet high. I know... I know...

Despite the aura of reprobate dripping from his black-as-death eyes—malice, hatred, jealousy, and covetous rage—nothing about his physicality spoke of emotion. Actually, he seemed incapable of moving his lips to speak, though what message he had (and he most certainly had one—though I dare not repeat it) was spoken as the Occultists would have it—*telepathically*.

For all of his rabbit-hat tricks, I find it particularly interesting—now as well as then—that this demonic entity was never allowed entry into our house, despite my sleep paralysis. The Spirit of the Lord protects his servants. Rather, he stood by the dock behind our home, glimmering under the pale light of the moon, looking up through our warmly lit windows. That's where I saw him, down alongside the water. It's where he spoke to me—where he made his presence known.

As the nights progressed I would lie in bed *feeling* what was determined to come inside. I'd have these vivid dreams where one of my toddler twin sons carried a voodoo doll fashioned in the likeness of the very demon inhabiting the night, just beyond the window. And then I'd awaken *in reality* to the violent blood-curdling screams of my son in the other room. I'd rush upon him to cradle his quivering body and pray. The demon was taunting me. And though the crying would soon refrain, no quick prayer would dispel this spirit for long. He or *it* was persistent, tag-teaming tactics between haunting me and then tormenting my son. Rinse and repeat. Only Jesus had the power to remove him.

Meanwhile, back at the Piggly Wiggly again, one of my twin sons pointed towards a box of *Froot* Loops. So I threw the box of Froot Loops in the grocery cart, remembering when Froot Loops was spelled *Fruit* Loops—and before that, when it was Froot Loops—and still before that, in a maddening game of paradoxical ping pong, when it was *Fruit* Loops again. Should I have also let the grocery clerk in on the fact that Febreze was spelled Febreeze—with a second "e," and Chick-Fil-A was once Chic-Fil-A, without the "K?" Perhaps she was not the eternally gullible child, and the far more likely scenario is that it was I who had been implanted—and willingly—with the power of suggestion.

But far more importantly, the Mandela Effect had pressed its eyes upon me. That is the reality behind it. Necromancy. By admitting my guilt as a practitioner in Broome's divination, I invited the alien gray into my life—into the life of my family. Shame on me—shame—shame—for asking others to do the same.

5

HOW IRONIC IS IT THAT A MOVIE BASED ON TIME TRAVEL would become the mugging victim of an alternate reality or paradox prank? In *Back to the Future*, the Libyan terrorist who guns down Doc Brown at the Twin Pines Mall didn't always do so in a VW Bus. No, if my memory suffices—at one time I was certain of it—they chased Marty McFly's DeLorean in a 1984 Toyota Van.

Perhaps no other movie alteration bothered me with more teeth grinding severity than Roger Moore's take as James Bond in *Moonraker*. This particular film came out in 1978 as a response to the success of *Star Wars*, and if you'll recall the notable villain wasn't one-time bad guy Hugo Drax, but the repeat performance from a guy named Jaws. You know, Jaws—the 7-foot tall strongman with metal teeth that could clamp through electrified rebar or chew on broken glass for cereal. If so, then you'll likely also recall the most memorable moment in the entire film, when Jaws met a buxom blond named Dolly and the two fell instantly in love. What makes their meeting so memorable is the chain of events. Mainly, Jaws smiles down upon Dolly with those gruesome metal teeth of his. Rather than feeling frightened, Dolly smiles back. Only she too is wearing braces—I mean pearly whites. *Wait, huh?* Didn't Dolly smile back at Jaws with braces? No, apparently not.

There is no shortage of Mandela Effects. Yet I won't recall them all, and for your sake, I pray that you've continued rowing as you ought. I have written about dozens of Effects in my recent past, but they are removed from public observance (as wax in the ears for the ill-prepared and weak-minded), and at the Lord's prompting. It is a relief. Not too long ago I was in the Outer Banks, North Carolina, wholly convicted as to my willing participation in Broome's devilry. I was pumping diesel into my truck, and pulling my wallet from my pants pocket I noticed something new in the realm of *peculiar*. The VISA logo was not as I'd once remembered it. Indeed, as the internet would confirm, I had stumbled upon another Mandela Effect. It was the *last* Mandela Effect of which I'd ever commit myself to writing about—because you know what thought came to mind?

So what if it's changed?

Jesus Christ once asked concerning a Roman coin:

"Whose is this image and superscription? They say unto him, Caesar's. Then saith He unto them, Render therefore unto Caesar the things which are Caesar's; and unto God the things that are God's. When they had heard these words, they marveled, and left Him, and went their way (Matthew 22:20-22)."

This world is Caesar's. Perhaps more specifically, Caesar's throne is Satan's throne, and all that denies or supplements God's goodness is his. VISA belongs to Satan. *Star Wars*, *Back to the Future*, James Bond, let us throw Kit Kat and Froot Loops into the recipe, and dare I say the Berenstain Bears—they all belong to Satan. In slightly better terms, they are under his management. He may press his thumb upon his kingdoms merchandise and do to them as he pleases, should God grant him the know-how and abracadabra. Tied presently to the mast, I confess to having heard things—indeed, relished in things—which I ought not. My mind, once shipwrecked upon the rocks, is confused. That is the cold, logistical reality behind the spirit of deception. It is so very *convincing*. But this I know for certain, duplicity or no duplicity, he cannot have the Bible—not one single lettering of the Hebrew or Greek.

Neither can you, Fiona Broome.

Thank God, there is no such incantation. The Gospel must *first* be preached to all nations (Mark 13:10), and for this cause, it *must* be preserved. Heaven and Earth will pass, but God's Word is eternal. Despite all your seductions, your nagging questions, your promises of enlightenment—I've shut that door. Be gone! There is a spiritual battle for the mind and the soul just waiting for the gullible saint on the other side, and you cannot have either one of them. To you, Broome, I invoke the name of Jesus Christ, and cast your demons from the room.

SIMULATION THEORY + NEW MATHEMATICS = (SAME TIRESOME DAMNABLE LIE)

PLATO NEVER OWNED AN APPLE COMPUTER. Suffice to say, had Steve Jobs been around to dialogue with Socrates in 5th Century Athens, Plato likely would have subscribed to the Simulation Theory. Is it not quite unlike Plato's "Allegory of the Cave" in his philosophy of *Forms*? For Plato, *Forms* (or ideas) represent the most accurate reality. Forms are the essence of various objects. So too the Simulation Theory invokes ghostly images and projections from a level of reality so far above our own that reality itself is currently unobtainable by mortal man. *True* reality, accordingly, rises beyond space and time.

University of London physicist David Bohm, a protégé of Einstein's and one of the world's most respected quantum physicists, worked in the field of plasma physics during the 1950's. He first noted that in plasmas (ionized gases) the particles stopped acting as individuals and began behaving as though they were part of a larger and interconnected whole. Continuing the demolition of reality, which Einstein's *theory of relativity* had already taken a sledgehammer to, Bohm was instrumental in teaching that the tangible reality of our everyday lives is really only an illusion, like one massively interconnected holographic image. At the subquantum level, location ceases to exist. Physicists call this property "nonlocality." Because all points in space become equal to all other points in space, it is therefore pointless to speak of anything as being separate from anything else. Everything is interconnected—*and* an illusion.

Philosopher Nick Bostrom first popularized Simulation Theory with his 2003 paper, *"Are You Living in a Computer Simulation?"* In it he suggests members of an advanced post-human society with vast computing power beyond our own may be running simulations of their ancestors. That would be us. Either we are the simulations, or we shall soon simulate ourselves—which we may *still do* but also may have already done. Say that again and let your head spin.

632

So, has human society already run its course and are we living in a simulation? SpaceX co-founder Elon Musk seems to think so. In fact, an entire swath of technologists and physicists, many emanating from California's Silicon Valley, believe their sim theory will be proved. "There's a billion to one chance," Musk says, "we're living in base reality."

For Plato, *Forms* (or ideas) represent the most accurate reality. Forms are the essence of various objects. For instance, there are countless tables and chairs in the world. But the Form of *table-ness* and *chair-ness* is at the core of every table and chair in the world. The higher world of Forms is the essence of all of them, transcended to our own existence—we are the world of substances—and also the essential basis for all reality. One might understand it in this light. There is nothing which exists in our perceived reality, not a chair, not a table, nor a computer, had it not first been passed down from the highest mountaintop of reality.

Or one might consider it like this. If mankind is able to design a computer program, it's only because a greater and far superior computer program has already been designed. Every existing computer program, both past and future, is but a shadow of the real thing—the higher Form. If the computer advances in our reality, so too has the advancement have *already* been made. Therefore, if we are able to simulate, it is proof enough that a simulation has already been designed, perhaps even billions of them, and there is a chance that we ourselves are simulated.

"Forty years ago we had Pong–two rectangles and a dot. That's where we were. Now forty years later, we have photorealistic, 3D simulations with millions of people playing simultaneously and it's getting better every year. And soon we'll have virtual reality, we'll have augmented reality," said Musk. "If you assume any rate of improvement at all, then the games will become indistinguishable from reality."

Rich Terrile of NASA's Jet Propulsion Laboratory says, "Soon there will be nothing technical standing in the way of making machines that have their own consciousness....If one progresses at the current rate of technology a few decades into the future, very quickly we will be a society where there are artificial entities living in simulations that are much more abundant than human beings."

And given Nick Bostrom's other possibility—human civilizations inevitable ceiling of technology—Musk says we'd better hope that we're *already* a simulation. "Either we're going to create simulations that are indistinguishable from reality, or civilization will to cease to exist. Those are the two options."

While one might suspect Bostrom's inspiration derives from a recent viewing of *The Matrix* movies, we need only look a little ways beyond that to Russian cosmist and mystic Nikolai Fyodorovich Fyodorov (1829–1903). As a founding father of the space race, he was an orthodox Christian apostate who advocated the perfection of the human race through transhumanism and space colonization, all of which would include not only physical immortality, but the resurrection of the dead—as in our ancestors—using scientific methods.

Pay attention to what dribble Hollywood is pushing out—they're all over this like gravy on potatoes—and then let us consider if this is something that we as Christians should align with. The lie is everywhere. Hollywood endorses it—Simulation Theory, that is, and I'm *out*. So often a Christian believes it is in his job description to act as an intellectual cowboy of sorts. He attempts to sight God in pagan creativity, including the Hollywood narrative. He will lasso the wild indiscreet imaginations of the humanist mind in order to neatly "Christianize" his views within the boundaries of a church chorale, all so that it may be discussed and dissected among his peers, or perhaps simply harnessed for his own personal and justifiable amusement. A Christian needs only hold up his Bible to discern the most common of themes. In the end it's all the same—slightly different spin on reality, *perhaps*, but the lie is ever-present and far-reaching as always. So why is Dr. Chuck Missler getting involved with the holographic universe?

Quite similar to Plato's *Forms* (or ideas), which represent the most accurate reality over the lesser physical, quantum physicist David Bohm referred to this deeper level of reality as the "implicate" (enfolded) order, with our level of existence being the "explicate" (or unfolded) order. Dr. Chuck Missler seems to think this view is not entirely inconsistent with the Biblical presentation of the physical world being a subordinate to the spiritual. Everything, according to Missler, is relative, because the dimension of space is nothing more than a hologram.

No, Dr. Chuck Missler, this is not Biblical. It reeks of Gnostic thought. The spirit is not superior to the flesh. We are not in dire need of departing from these corrupted bones in order to transcend to some greater reality, nor is the physical world a subordinate. That is not the Biblical narrative by any means. God will dwell with us. Heaven will be here on Earth with us. Everything we can see and touch and smell is to be redeemed. We're not going anywhere.

The Christian always seeks to "Christianize" the pagan belief—including mathematics and Science—as if declaring God is behind each *discovered* perversion he will somehow convince the humanist of his wrongness without having to dismiss the very perversion which pulled him away from God's truth in the first place—as if the Bible was *right* in explaining it. Nick Bostrom and his many humanist colleagues, including the well-financed horsepower behind Hollywood, have already let us in on who is behind it. Bostrom states: "It (Sim Theory) suggests naturalistic analogies to certain traditional religious conceptions." Another words, there is a higher being, but it is not the Christian God. It is some version of us.

Scientism's official enforcer for Globe Earth, Neil deGrasse Tyson, has stated not only his belief in Simulation Theory but, with his usual air of religious mockery, that its architect is probably some middle-aged man in his mom's basement.

If a Christian truly believes we are living in a holographic universe, as Dr. Chuck Missler claims, one must wonder why creation matters. What does the shape of the Earth matter? This includes Evolutionary Globe-Earth proponents as well. Why fight for the globe or even Flat Earth if measurement itself is as collapsible as the tiniest atom? What does religion matter? What is consciousness and morality and who is to say our many video game creations within our own personal video game is not their own reality? What if history doesn't actually exist and we are the only generation who ever lived, confined forever to some Samsara recycling program doomed to reboot and repeat over and over again?

If all we are is coding—*pixilation* rather than dust in the wind, as the atheist once claimed—does anything truly matter? A proponent of Simulation Theory will ultimately conclude everything he can see and touch and smell around him is nothing more than base rules for *perceived* reality—which he is free, in the very least, to disobey and attempt to break free of. Who is he accountable to—the architect? Even now, according to Musk, there are billionaires engaged in breaking us out of the simulation.

Where this is heading, I cannot say. But one thing I am confident of, fellow Christian. If this indeed should climax with the *days of Noah*, one thing I can be absolutely certain of, and you should be too; "the architect" who will be revealed behind this grand show of force in the religion of Scientism will be anyone but God.

WHEN *NOT* TO SPEAK THY MIND—BRAIN COMPUTER INTERFACE & THE MARK OF THE BEAST HAS GOT NOTHING ON THE AMISH

CRITICISM HAS OVERSHADOWED OUR SHARED PORTRAIT of the Amish for generations. The Great Commission commands us to go throughout the entire world preaching the Gospel. This, their Christian neighbor demands, the Amish have willingly failed at—*as if* the bulk of Christianity has made better use of the call. And yet it can be argued that the Amish didn't forsake us. Rather, they held fast to certain *ideals*, and by their own consent, the world moved on without them. For this transgression against man's self-declared renaissance in Science, literature, and the arts they are rarely forgiven. It should be promptly noted that the Amish, originating from the Swiss Anabaptists and, being the very last vestige of the Great Reformation—in a way; historically hold to the *literal* promises of God's Testimony. Ask an Amish gentleman about the shape of creation and, historically speaking, he'll likely tell you the earth is flat. The Swiss Anabaptists were notorious soul sleepers too.

It is a strange expectation that the Amish should exchange the very lifestyle which has satisfied mankind since the beginning of history for a technological imprisonment overshadowed by the beast government of John's Revelation, thereby causing them by association to be indebted to it. And it lies. Concerning the shape of the Earth, our government lies to each and every one of us. This is no secret to the Amish. They have every reason to separate the authority of their church from the state, but none to doubt God's Testimony, or His enduring goodness. Yet they are criticized to no end for dismissing any notion that our current technological renaissance is a "gift from God," while their Christian accusers rarely exhibit the slightest understanding as to why they choose simplistic sovereignty over a complex spider web of technological enslavement. People everywhere have allowed the beast to convince them that unpractical scientific theory outweighs their better sensory judgement and they live on a ball in a vacuum of space. The Amish know better.

Like discarded fashion, for those of us who have attempted to keep up with the trending spin of Plato's globe, there is seemingly always a new technological era to be dressed in. The Amish decided over a century ago against electrical housewares, though now we, not quite unlike the Amish before us, find ourselves having to face another unparalleled decision in human history. Will we speak our mind and plug our brain into the machine?

If Elon Musk, chief executive of Tesla and SpaceX, has it his way, we are expected to do just that. His latest start-up company, Neuralink, is centered on creating brain-computer interface and neuro lace devices that can be implanted within our skull—inserted, he says, through the jugular vein—all in an effort to merge humans with the rapid advancement of artificial intelligence.

Such an endeavor is being advertised as our next stage of evolution. And if we don't do it—if we choose not to evolve beyond the image which God has created us in, then artificial intelligence promises to sail right past us on the food chain. To this notion Musk says, "I don't love the idea of being a house cat, but what's the solution? I think one of the solutions that seems maybe the best is to add an AI layer, a third digital layer that could work well and symbiotically with the rest of your body."

"We are currently bandwidth limited," he adds. "We have a digital, tertiary-self in the form of our e-mail capabilities like computers, phones, applications—we are effectively superhuman, but we are extremely bandwidth constrained in that interface between the cortex and the tertiary digital form of yourself."

In other words, "If we can create a high-bandwidth neural interface with your digital self, then you're no longer a house cat."

The ability to hack the brain has been a subject of futurism and cyberpunk science-fiction for decades, including "*Ghost in the Shell*" and "*The Matrix*." Entrepreneur Bryan Johnson, founder of the online payments company *Braintree*, which he sold to PayPal in 2013 for $800 million, invested $100 million from that sell-off into a startup company called *Kernel*, all in hopes of bringing film fiction to reality. With his team of committed neuroscientists and software engineers, Johnson plans to "enhance human cognition" through direct interface with computing devices by upgrading our brains. Think faster, smarter, and hardwired.

The dominoes are falling. Facebook has announced its own "brain mouse" for augmented reality. With social media, our brain will function much as our hands would when controlling cursers. Regina Gugan, head of Facebook's Building 8 control group, said, "What if you could type directly from your brain... with the speed and flexibility of voice and the privacy of text?" In only a few short years, apparently, people will be writing everything from text messages to novels by thoughts alone—and probably ordering food too. Then again, computers will soon be preforming those tasks anyways—writing bestsellers and ordering our food, that is. As of this writing, developers at Facebook's Artificial Intelligence Research have already completed A.I. "chat box" robots which have reportedly conversed in human language and negotiated human trade among each other.

Even DARPA spent $60 million in 2016 developing an implantable neural interface. The project, which is part of former president Barack Obama's "BRAIN INITIATIVE," wants a device that can read 1 million neurons simultaneously and stimulate at least 100,000 neurons in the brain. Its implant is expected to be wireless, the size of a nickel, and ready for deployment in only a few years.

The chip is coming at us full speed. Businesses are already requiring it of their employees. It's being implanted in the hand, just as the Apostle John said it would (Revelation 13:16). And we have very little idea how far this is going to go—how many months, years, or even decades we and our children have left, thirsting and hungering for relief against this coming trans-humanist nightmare, perhaps even succumbing to starvation in the streets, before God finally puts a stop to it. I don't know about you, but guys like me are going the way of the caveman—and *willingly*, because I'm not choosing to co-evolve my inner-skull with the computer. I've already made that decision. Nothing of technological value is getting implanted within my flesh. Not in my head, not in my hands, not even in my rectum. It ends here.

People are going to be lining up for a brain-computer interface, smart dust, neural lace, and whatever other chip invention they're rolling out on the belt. Masayoshi Son, the second richest man in Japan, is investing $100 billion to build a computer chip with an IQ of 10,000. Expect college degrees to be worthless currency for those of us who forsake such a god-like IQ. Neural chips are even being designed to store memories for us. This godless generation will undress their mind, exchanging the most cherished endowment of privacy for worldly comfort. Unfortunately, as these things often go, technological

639

advancements only begin on a volunteer basis. And we Christians know where it's ending.

The finish line of this sprint is the Mark of the Beast.

Because the Amish made their decision long ago, they have a sleek advantage over us late arrivals—for now. As a society, they are self-sufficient. We are not. They don't need a chip implant. We do. When the cash flow stops, the only way the beast government is forcing them into submission is by bulldozing their farms down. Perhaps that will happen. In the end, once society has evolved beyond their own claim at humanity, they too will have to make a decision, if only to keep their heads from rolling. But make no mistake about it; the day of decision is coming. For me, the boundary marker is set.

Certainly, when we pronounce, *"Enough is enough!"* and unplug from this Matrix, our impact on society—our ability to carry out the Great Commission—will be severely handicapped, if not made completely impotent. It is why, in that day, we should remember the Amish. They have been fulfilling the Great Commission all along, if only in the best way they know how. By *"keeping themselves unspotted by the world* (James 1:27)," as James the brother of Jesus requires, their testimony is made known, and their light goes out to the entire world.

ACCEPT JESUS CHRIST AS YOUR LORD AND SAVIOR OR "BANG! BANG! GO TO HELL!"

JESUS WAS BORN UNDER MARTIAL LAW. He also died under martial law. Conclusively, Jesus knew not a day of His earthly ministry, let alone His upbringing, when He was not under the tyrannical thumb of martial law. Yet today we are faced with the Jesus follower of another sort. The *western* gun-toting Christian, stars and stripes bleeding from his eyes, can think of no worse nightmare than martial law. The Blue Helmets, he assures us, are coming to a doorstep near you. *Lock and load*. If his own ambitions are to be believed, he is more likely to shoot bullets from the hip than he is to throw Scripture at his enemy. He has perhaps forgotten what pierces even to the dividing asunder of soul and spirit. Assuredly, he would not do so well in Christendom's finest hours—when the followers of Jesus *fled* the bloodhounds of Rome or died in the attempt. More precisely, our spiritual fathers would not even think to call him a Christian. Let it be known to every Lexington revolutionary in waiting, that time is once more coming—and is perhaps soon upon us. When they arrive for my Bible, even my very life, it will be the decisive hour for me—for all believers—to pick up our crosses.

We must follow the path of our Master.

Today we are faced with a great tragedy, should the gun-toting Christian "survivalist" be believed. So many martyrs spanning two millenniums of history, one million in the last ten years alone, are simply *stupid*. No, *immoral*. That is the argument, at least. "By not stocking up on ammunition to defend our family, we are living in sin." Willful martyrdom, I am told, is sin. Not possessing one of the 300-million guns in America is sin. However, if the well-endowed revolution of a violent nature occurred in the decades after Jesus' resurrection, I have not been made aware. The First Jewish–Roman War of 66-73 AD I know of. It ended with the siege of Masada. Jerusalem was destroyed. But the Great Christian-Roman War (had there been one, *hypothetically*), such revolutionaries were apparently not worth remembering or recording. I am of course being facetious, because Christians were not a part of them.

Let us simply consider the Apostles, who made application of our Lord's teachings for each successive generation to follow. Bartholomew was skinned alive. Matthias was burned alive. Thomas was run through with a spear, Matthew a sword. James was stoned. Paul was beheaded. Andrew was crucified—Peter upside-down. Though John escaped execution, he died in prison. And for centuries thereafter millions of Christians were tortured and martyred for His namesake.

There is rarely a greater sin in western Christendom than asking a follower of Christ to even *consider* disarming for the sake of the Gospel. Assuredly, when the Blue Helmets come for our Bible—even our very life—there will be some among our ranks who will *live by the sword and die by the sword*, as Jesus would say. The New World Order will certainly have them to contend with, and it stands to reason that Satan's kingdom will indulge in one final laugh while singing right along with them. "*....the rockets' red glare, the bombs bursting in air, gave proof through the night....*" Yet there is no satanic power on earth so strong that can overcome the blood of martyrdom—even as it flows in the gutter, and more importantly, under the heavenly alter. There is nothing, I am convinced—no nothing, which advances God's kingdom quite like the willful back-ache of a splintered cross. At the mere sight of them, our beloved Savior cracks his knuckles and raises his shepherd's crook. His sheep will not be slaughtered in vain. With the cross—not the sword, but *the cross*—the church advances.

More precisely, it *explodes*.

The ending of this story has already been written so that there should not be too many surprises, as plot twists are concerned. The Lord is returning. And *that*—even in our darkest hour—we must never forget to rejoice over. The Lord is returning. We *must* prepare. The Lord is returning. Even so, Satan and his occult—which still remains hidden from the untrained eye, as of this writing—must also be exposed. They will play their final hand. That hour is assuredly coming. Jesus said it would be a time unlike any other. Specifically, if the days were not cut short, sayeth our Master, no one would survive them. So we should not be surprised to find ourselves—if we are indeed a servant of the living Christ—rounded up into camps. Surely, the guillotine awaits us.

What command is given that we are to spill the blood of our persecutors? We are called to pray for them (Matthew 5:43-48). We are described—if Christ is our Shepherd—as lambs going to the slaughter (Romans 8:35-39; 1 Peter 2:21-23). We are promised persecution (2 Timothy 3:12). We are to repay no evil for evil (Romans 12:17-21). All who live by the sword will die by the sword (Matthew 26:51-54). Because we are not of the world, the world will hate us (John 15:18-20). We are to rejoice in suffering for His namesake (1 Peter 4:12-14). Our Master Himself set the example when He said: "Greater love has no one than this: to lay down one's life for one's friends" (John 15:13). Or consider this, only those who suffer with Jesus will reign with Him (Romans 8:16-18, Revelation 3:21). Great is their reward in heaven (Matthew 5:10-12). And something else to consider—nothing will separate us from the love of God, not even the sword (Romans 8:35-37).

The great *rounding up* does not concern me—not that I won't try my very best to defend my family and flee. I need no weapon in my defense, *except* prayer. We Christians must carry prayer and the Word of God as a weapon everywhere we go—a shield and drawn sword always in hand, never sheathed. Our Shepherd Himself warned us: "Do not fear what you are about to suffer. Behold, the devil is about to throw some of you into prison, that you may be tested, and for ten days you will have tribulation. Be faithful unto death, and I will give you the crown of life (Revelation 2:10)." The Lord is our avenger. And besides, a time is coming when Michael—the highest and mighty of the archangels—shall stand up in our defense.

What good will it do us then—our endless conspiracy theories—if we crowd around our fellow prisoners (having endlessly tired our friends and family with dire warnings of chemtrails, vaccines, 9-11, the Federal Reserve, Agenda 21, the health benefits of drinking our own pee, and important to our coming circumstances, FEMA camps)—but cannot quote a single Word of Scripture? They have stripped our Bibles from us. We are in a famine of hearing the Word and awaiting the guillotine. What use will our wild theories serve if we have not *hidden Thy Word in our hearts that we may not sing against thee*, as the 119th Psalmist would say? Are we equipped, while we dig ditches before our executioners, to lead our fellow Christians in songs of praise and worship? Can we even lead our Blue Helmet captors to salvation? What good will our conspiracy theories do us then?

They will do not*h*ing for us.

No—absolutely nothing.

COME MONDAY MORNING... I'LL FINALLY WALK AWAY FROM IT ALL *(Flat Earth & the Truther Movement)*

THERE'S A SAYING AMONG THE PREACHERS OF OLD. Come Monday morning—or rather, come *every* Monday morning, they begin writing their resignation letter.

Not too long ago I had this alluring, lucid dream. I dreamt I cut the umbilical cord that kept me attached to the computerized world—this media saturated augmented false-reality which we are ceremoniously indoctrinated into believing—and then dove into a pool. From underneath the shadow of swaying palms I gazed up at the sunlit world, listening to the aroma of music as it penetrated, like the muffle from a seashell, into the chlorine blue—pretending like all of this...my bizarre interim with the *Truther* Movement in its variant of patterns...never happened. Come Monday morning, *every* Monday morning, I sit and relish in that dream. I often contemplate what that moment will be like, after I pull the plug, after I dive head-first in the pool, and then float within the watery underworld watching the bubbles rise past my eyes—just holding my breath, numbering the bubbles, feeling the sensational touch of water as it shrouds every arching curve of my body, and waiting to be *left behind* from the times I find myself in the world above.

Come Monday morning, I think about that moment when I finally climb out of the pool and the sun kisses my skin.

But that's only the first part of my dream.

When I finally decided to come out in support of Hebrew cosmology some years ago, the burlesque rebuttals were almost immediate. I was making a mockery of the Gospel, they said. I had become reprobate, they said. I'd never experienced anything like that before. I'd never experienced so many eyes pressed against me—brothers and sisters in the faith whom I had thought were dear friends, whom I'd broken bread with, and prayed with, gnashing their intellectual teeth and salivating. The fallout was ugly. There are people whom I will likely never speak with again.

There was a senior pastor and his wife—they run a rather large church in central California—the two of them followed me around on social media simply to hate-watch. I don't know if they were sitting on the couch together, thumbing at their phones, or sitting in separate rooms clapping away on their computers, but they would simultaneously track me down hoping to publicly shame what I was hoping to point people to in the Bible. I'll never forget, he actually told me, and I quote, "tears are flowing from Yah's throne because of me."

Excuse my description, because I don't know what else to call their behavior other than psychological self-flagellation. They were pleasuring themselves. It was just sick and disgusting, and slimy, coming from their spiritual pay grade.

Coming out, and publicly writing about it, day after day—that was a difficult time.

My best friend—we attended the same high school together (as did my wife); we joined the army at the same time; we served and led ministries together. He was my best friend. I loved him dearly. We did almost everything together. We were practically attached at the hip—he and I. We would sit around smoking cigars and sipping Scotch late into the night discussing anything on the table, from conspiracy talk to theology. You know—the furthest pastures of Biblical inquiry. We weren't afraid to go there and look into it. So he also looked into it, Flat Earth that is—soon after I threw my weight behind it. It certainly interested him. He was intrigued. I had actually hoped, I really believed for a time that he'd come on-board—that we could take this venture together. And for specific reasons he couldn't, or rather, he chose not to follow along with me. He just couldn't take that path. And so I started along on my own. About that time the fallout happened. Please understand, there never was an argument between us, though I'm certain I said some hurtful words, but I think it became abundantly clear that he could no longer be associated with me because of my views.

I think we all understand that this isn't really a debate about the shape of the earth, but where we see ourselves in the world, and more importantly, how we view the world—the shape of humanity. All things considered, I think our continued friendship became an insurance issue.

Fact of the matter is I miss him.

There's such a void in my life—recalling all the faces lost. It feels like I left a trail of breadcrumbs, hoping they might catch up, but in reality those crumbs were bits and pieces of me. I think of the fallout—people whom I once broke bread, the meaty discussions we held over God's Word, and then the venomous reaction after my coming out about Hebrew Cosmology.

I don't hold it against them.

I'm on this pilgrimage journey now—my wife and I together—desperately seeking out the Celestial City, like a narrative from *Pilgrim's Progress*, and should any one of them race to our side again, I will most certainly embrace them.

I guess I forgot to tell you about the second part of my dream.

Essentially, it goes something like this. I climb out of the pool, and then turn on the television. Perhaps it's not an actual television—but far more likely the furniture which fills the memories of my mind But it's all there on the flickering screen—the alpha waves which serves as the witch doctor's potion, and the grand-scaled psycho-drama which drowns the whole world in the spells of their electronic programming.

I see a demolition of towers while Isis looks on. I see a field and a pentagon-shaped building without plane wreckage. I see the death camps. I see murdered children who sing before millions of televised audiences, crisis actors who have a habit of getting cast in various mass shooting events. I see trails of chemicals vandalizing the skies over *the bread and circuses* of sporting arenas to mock the very citizens who never care to look up. I see people lining the pharmacy aisles to receive their annual poison. I see our worshiped celebrities and the very world leaders we vote for and place our confidence in throw up their allegiance to Satan before our very eyes. I see astronauts on wires, the green screen of space, moon props, flat horizons, motionless skies—I see an entire earth covered by the surface of water. I see the wave of the hand—the pigeon in the sleeve. I see the stage, the performance, and the script. I see my friends and loved ones mourning for phantoms. I see the Zionist conquest of the world. I see the Mystery religion as a corpse exhumed. I see the damnable lie of the ages fleshed out in our conversation. I see Protestants shaking hands with Jesuits; pastors spoon-feeding a gospel of lawlessness; generations of men forsaking Sabbath worship; entire congregations openly worshiping a counterfeit spirit; the filth of Platonism bleeding from our doctrine; and the signposts ahead suggest we're closer to Rome than ever.

I see what so many of you see.

And I'm tired. I'm sick of it. I am weary of the satanic media's groundbreaking news story being that I am fake news. And yet, there are things I've seen—what so many of us have seen—that simply cannot be forgotten.

I gaze into the pages of God's Word, like so many of you do, and come every Monday morning see what very few are *willing* to see. And yet, it's all there. Mystery Babylon surrounds us.

It's a Tuesday morning, and I sit in the office of the senior pastor— yet another church my family has been visiting. It has become routine for me to schedule a private meeting with the pastor rather early on. Before investing our time in any congregation, I feel it's best to expound upon my beliefs and let the things I've *seen* be known, just so that there are no surprises—let the pastor kick us out early, if need be. And so I told him some of what I've seen—only short clips and frames, really. But where do you really begin—where is the starting line? Do we tell them about the 9-11 demolition or the moon landing lie? Or do we go much further back, thousands of years even, to the very first lie—do we go to the garden and begin from scratch?

He had already looked me up online. He knew all about me. Come Monday morning, I had contemplated pulling the name Noel J Hadley offline. I considered sending in my resignation letter to the world. He looked me up on a Monday, and *refused* to believe any of it.

The senior pastor examined me square in the eyes and asked: if I was to continue in his congregation, could I set that part of me aside. He wanted to know if I could divide my soul. When I dress myself in a tie and coat come Sunday morning, could I could leave the part of me who wishes to help people *see* the great delusion in the closet. Could I not be weird about the world around me, he said. Could I be—normal?

He looked at me, unblinking, as I considered his offer of friendship.

I thought about my dream of the pool. I remembered the saying among preachers of old. I thought about the Prophet Jeremiah, who warned Judah of the Babylonians; who pleaded with them to cast out their idols; whose entire ministry was defined by tears. I thought about Jeremiah after he was taken into custody, a prison cell which was, rather ironically, adjacent to the Temple in Jerusalem.

It must have been Monday morning in prison, because the Prophet wrote:

I have become a laughingstock all day long;

Everyone mocks me.

For each time I speak, I cry aloud;

I proclaim violence and destruction,

Because for me the word of the Lord has resulted

In reproach and derision all day long.

(Jeremiah 20:7-8)

It must have been Monday morning, because the Prophet sent in his resignation. To this effect he wrote: "Then I said, 'I will not make mention of Him, nor speak any more of His Name.'" But then Monday evening rolled around, as it *often* does, and after careful, though tormented contemplation, the lonely man of God concluded:

Then in my heart it becomes like a burning fire

Shut up in my bones;

And I am weary of holding it in,

And I cannot endure it.

The senior pastor seemed to stand outside of time as he stared me down, unblinking—waiting upon my answer.

I thought about my friends, whom I broke bread with—who snarled their self-righteous teeth. I don't hold it against them. I miss them dearly.

I had hoped to hide the weariness, the unending loneliness in a world numbed by the spell of grand wizards, and I considered my beautiful dream of the pool, but this was a Tuesday morning, after I had declined sending in the resignation letter, and so I said: "What I have seen, what I have heard, and what I have read about the reality of the days we live in is something I simply cannot look away from. Its wardrobe is as much a part of me as His words are planted in my heart."

"*We Took Sweet Counsel Together...*" THE GOSPEL OF JESUS CHRIST ACCORDING TO JUDAS ISCARIOT

HIS NAME MEANS "JEHOVAH LEADS" IN HEBREW. But for Judas Iscariot, there is a rich irony here, because no other individual was more clearly led by Satan than he. Supposing a man returned to our present day by way of Einsteinian equations and mind-bending bewitchments of science—basically, employing the use of a time machine—having successfully beheaded Judas Iscariot with the blade of a Saracen before he could fulfill the prophesy of the Prophet Zechariah, I believe he would have a surprise or two waiting for him. I am convinced there's nothing especially unique about the son of perdition—nothing at all. He is as they say a dime a dozen. Regarding the "familiar friend, in whom I trusted, which did eat of my own bread," whom King David wrote of in Psalm 41:9; the time traveling assassin will no doubt have already discovered him replaced in the pages of history by another *nobody* as soon as he should return. And worse—after another successive roundtrip mission to the past and back, and yet another, and another, and still another, he will not only see Iscariot replaced again and again and again and then again, but will even begin to identify the many faces that make up Satan's servant here in the present.

In a generation of morally outraged social activists, keyboard warrior movement pushers, self-proclaiming do-gooders, and ego-sensitive narcissists who appear solid as a prison turret on the outside yet frail and wisp-like as a-snot drenched tissue on the inside, our science-fiction protagonist will begin seeing the face of Iscariot *everywhere*. Particularly—and this is important—among his social media friends.

To be fair, the twelve disciples were not necessarily spiritually motivated—at first. Judas' contemporaries likely thought of Jesus as an oriental monarch who would rid Israel of all that gave intellectual muscle to Rome—pagan occupation, Occult Science, and even Plato's globe, which a successive line of Caesar's enforced through the Mithraic

Mystery religion—after the establishment of the Davidic kingdom. And yet they embraced, and would come to love, the *true* Messiah, yet whom—in the face of this reality—Judas would subconsciously hate. Knowing the identities of those "who should betray Him (John 6:64)," Jesus warned that there were some in rank who believed not. He furthermore claimed: "Therefore said I unto you, that no man can come unto me, except it were given unto him of my Father." We read that "many of His disciples went back, and walked no more with Him (John 6:66)." The irony—and *true* treachery—is that Judas remained loyal to Jesus while others deserted him. But quite like those who openly deserted him, he never gave the Creator his heart. When Jesus taught about the spiritual dimensions of His kingdom, they became eager partakers, and if Judas felt abandoned, it's because he remained loyal to the only kingdom he'd ever truly known or loved—his own. Essentially, the Apostles became sons of God while Iscariot tragically succumbed to a paradox. His was the sort of spiritual upbringing which can only be nurtured in the very kingdom of darkness which he zealously sought to suppress.

Why shouldn't Judas have taken the money? Jesus was doing *nothing* to expand upon His own potential. Like most *woken* men, Judas wanted spiritual Utopia for the All of self. He wanted human freedom. He wanted the establishment to crumble—the Luciferian kings and their armies and their occult sciences and their monetary system, which secured the kingdom of darkness, to be exposed and overthrown. He was sick of the propaganda, sick of the lies and the deception. The glorious Gospel which the Spirit laid down for the age to come was simply not enough. When Roman law required a Jewish native to carry his equipment for an entire mile, should he be conscripted to do so, Jesus instructed his followers to go *beyond* the requirements of the law another mile. He even ordered them to pick up their cross and follow Him. The sort of change which the Gospel of Jesus Christ advocated spoke *nothing* of human rights. Judas had only one life to live, and like Joel Osteen's book, he wanted his best life now. Servitude under the lordship of Jesus, as it turned out, stole his career, his success, his potential, and worst of all, his very life. Under Jesus and the workings of the Spirit which accompanied Him, true potential was suppressed—immorally so.

Let us not forget, publicly speaking, Judas was the ethical sort. Actually, he had a way of pointing out his own morality with enough dexterity as to deceive even the other eleven. John 12 records that Mary took "a pound of ointment of spikenard, very costly, and anointed the feet of Jesus, and wiped his feet with her hair: and the house was filled with the odour of the ointment (John 12:3)." It was Judas Iscariot, Simon's son, who interjected with the sublimity of principled protest. "Why was not this ointment sold for three hundred pence, and given to the poor?"

This he said, the Apostle John is quick to add as commentary, "not that he cared for the poor..." And we shouldn't be surprised of this, because in modern terms, while exhibiting the smug illusion of preening kosher superiority, Judas Iscariot's feigned concern for the orphans, the widows, the diseased, crippled, and oppressed, was nothing more or less than *virtue signaling*.

Today, were he updating his Christian pupilage for his online friends and followers on Facebook, Twitter, or YouTube, he might display pictures depicting all the right spiritual poses, or vent at the ever-shifting media-sponsored morality of the hour, even challenge his social networkers with the latest-greatest trending hashtags. He might masterfully exemplify a self-aggrandizement cloaked in humility. While his was a message of false-humility, employing lazy tools to condemn the political and religious opponents across the aisles as woolly thinkers and naïve, posturing himself in so many words: "I'm no big deal," he would cleverly spin it with, "I'm the last decent person left in the world." There is no call to repentance of the self. If there were, his mission in which everyone might gather on his side of the line, which has likely been drawn for him in the sand, would not be a success. He has no choice but to succumb to winning the approval of his friends by pandering to their lesser senses. Essentially, Judas mocked others with moral superiority.

And the Savior rebuked him for it.

Yes, I am most convinced, Judas would do exceptionally well today in a world saturated with social media, and would even surround himself with many like-minded friends, those of whom desire a menu beyond the ingredients of the Gospel. By advertising a kingdom of little flocks, Jesus *foolishly* dismissed mega-churches. And though it may be true that Judas wanted his own personal Jesus for himself and for others—for his children, grandchildren, and his grandchildren's-children—he also wanted a movement.

In today's terms, he likely dreamt up star-studded conferences, book deals, media exposure, all the Facebook *likes* and YouTube *subscribers* his quirky and crowd-pleasing posts or monetized videos could muster. Even here in the "Truther" community, the spirit of Iscariot exemplifies the ongoing and unquenchable religion of Babel, which seeks men in every avenue and discipline of life throughout all generations to gather together in order that they might "make a name for themselves." When the hammer falls on Plato's globe and Mystery Babylon which sponsors it—whether taking turns at the podium or interlocking arms together on the street or through the ecumenical Jacuzzi found in chat rooms—his kindred most certainly hopes to find themselves at the head of the table. And the best part is they can accomplish all of this with a select few verses while bolstering them in Jesus' name.

I cannot think of a more dreadful phrase than to stand before the Lord, having mustered a lifetime of prosperous words, and hear: "I never knew you; depart from Me, you who practice lawlessness!" (Matthew 7:23) This thought alone should bring us pause. It is a warning for the ages. Take it to heart. Let us kneel before our Lord in all humility—far from the ears and the eyes of social media—and exhibit an honest and true fear of God. Let us interrogate ourselves, with the Holy Spirit as our confidence, and ask the Lord to correct our false actions. And where Flat Earth is concerned, may it be peopled by the penitent sort, brothers and sisters in Christ who undress its lack of curvature far beyond the skin-depth of Eratosthenes sticks and Pythagorean Theorems. Rather than lazily shifting the blame on easy targets for the covetous applauds of our contemporaries, let us not hide under false pretenses in order to justify our misguided actions. Flat Earth is not a *movement* of God.

For the Judas Iscariot of all ages and every shape of the Earth, Jesus is *his* ends-means.

"Accepting Christ..." THE ETERNAL ELIXIR OF EASY BELIEVISM (AKA THE HOLE IN THE BRIDGE WHERE MILLIONS FALL THROUGH)

ACCEPTING CHRIST...HERE IS "THE HOLE IN THE BRIDGE where millions fall through," warned A.W. Tozer. To the astonishment of a great many people, *"accepting* Christ" as a choice of wording cannot be found anywhere in the Bible—nor can the *"heart* invitation" which has captivated audiences. Those who wish to gamble their souls will not be bothered by this. Such a person treats the salvation prayer from decades past with the same air of assurance as a Catholic would his infant baptism. And yet it is this very doctrine—which asks us to invite Jesus into our heart—that has captured the evangelical's attention over the last century and likewise has swept a great many untold and unsuspecting bystanders into the pit of eternal damnation. From this they happily conclude the Reformers cry of *"sola fide!"* or *faith alone*, grants the subscriber a license to sin without submitting to the Lordship of Christ as evidence of their salvation. The Reformers would most assuredly consider this a gruesome perversion. True faith in Christ will always lead to a changed life.

The *good news* is not necessarily hidden from us. But we shan't see it as some leisurely stroll through a public garden or—quite similarly—a neighborly terrace enclosed behind a stone divider, which the common pedestrian must dreamily peer at through a locked iron gate, wishing, hoping, and praying to get in. Rather, the Gospel is a wide open, seemingly barren field. And though it is visible and known by all, perhaps even a bearer of heavy foot traffic—it is rarely dug into. Jesus told it like this.

> "Again, the kingdom of heaven is like unto treasure hid
> in a field; the which when a man hath found, he hideth,
> and for joy thereof goeth and selleth all that he hath, and
> buyeth that field (Matthew 13:44)."

We can only imagine the frenzied state of his mind as the man who discovered the treasure breathlessly scrambled home empty handed—in hopes of maintaining a calm demeanor, no less—and in such a way as to not tip off Satan, lest his plans be foiled. Learning of the empty lot—and observing that he'd husked the worldliness from his life in order to invest in it—his family and neighbors must have thought his final trip to the Escrow officer an incredibly rash and foolish mistake. If the devil showed up at his garage sale dressed for the part of a snake oil peddler, complete with the dubious credentials that no doubt foiled many, he could not shake off the persistent landowners nagging determination. Why should he think little of the kingdom he'd invested a lifetime building for his self? He dared to dig into the Gospel—that why. What he tasted there was a recipe of the delectable. With one final scoop of the trowel, he discovered the man *behind* the name. For the first time in his life, he pronounced *Jesus* with intimacy.

Maybe Christianity in America is dying because the field on the edge of town is boring everyone to death. The Easy-Believism of our day and age no longer instructs us to have *reverence* for the field, an *obedience* to visit it often, a *duty* to tell others about it. We are not expected from the moment we wake each morning to have our thoughts *ravished* by the treasure we once discovered below the dust and weeds. The field itself is socially obsolete, outworn fashion, sacred no more. We have replaced words like *holy* and *sin* or the mere mention of *eternal punishment* for such phrases as "friendship" and "tolerance" and "help" in hopes that the cross of Christ not inconvenience anyone. We are instructed to needlessly chase after the wind of "cultural relevance," plagued with riddles as to why a ministry sometimes grows exponentially in number—at least by the count of heads—and yet miserably fails entire generations of hell-bound souls. Evangelicalism has dressed up the field with a new blueprint—the temple of the humanist mind—and therefore has only succeeded in burying the land with layer upon layer of fudge icing and sprinkles, a cherry and whipped cream and two-scoops of mint chocolate-chip ice cream, all in the vanity of capturing the apathy of mankind. Here on the once-empty field, the disease has become the remedy. Rather than show them the Gospel and *only* the Gospel, they have attempted to compete with the trending wisdom of this world and by doing so have criminally succeeded. They are stealing lost souls from the only truth which can save them.

Perhaps we might better frame the undeveloped anchorage of land not as a plot on the outskirts of town but as one surrounded on all sides by a modern Metropolis of gadgets and augmented wonders which commits itself to doing one thing only *but* doing it exceptionally well—filling every imaginable craving of the flesh. We have before us a land of billboards and fashion boutiques and a media-driven reality which delights in substitutions and the cult of violence amplified by product placement and cleverly timed commercials, each entitling us to the only *real* vacuum of space which is the American dream. Surrounding the lot we might further find the latest-greatest condominiums for bicycle riding hipsters conveniently located among strip malls and entertainment complexes, relaxation denominations and old warehouses converted into breweries and sushi bars and menus with overpriced crepes, not to overlook institutes of higher learning, Science-endorsed museums, and any number of monuments devoted to wealth and green-colored greed, "*In God we trust*," and Thomas Jefferson's pursuit of happiness.

How many sad-sap souls pass the sidewalks surrounding that empty lot, where fleshly magazine covers once ornamented newspaper stands, staring down at the far craftier diversion we currently call *phones*—begging for *likes* and followers on social media? How many will categorize themselves as Christian if asked—and may even seek to debate the issue once *offended*—because they've been fooled into the lifestyle which best exemplifies the damnable doctrine of Easy Believism?

They too perchance once committed the deed of "*accepting*" Jesus, or they are content "*believing*" in Him, and have bothered to embrace Him only so much as a casual fan might a popular sporting team come playoffs. He will most certainly wear his intellectual jersey when the calendar suggests he do so, and may have even convinced himself that Jesus loves gay marriage and transgenderism and abortion and any manner of social awareness issues sweeping the national media-driven consciousness—that His true morality was simply mistaken or suppressed by generations of bigoted zealots until the currents of this modern decade have held them to the light of clarity. Maybe he is a "Truther" and his eyes have simply done what Satan asked of Eve and *woken*. Every artifact—unless it guides him as an arrow through the road construction to the eye-sore he callously passes—is at best a beguilement which gladly reminds him he is now free now to remain in his vices.

Most will slight the Gospel because they only look upon the surface of the field and judge alone by its rocky dust and weeds in contrast to the magnificent city of Cain towering overhead. For most, there is no excellency in the institution of Christ above the philosophers of our world. And yet we must have no part in the run-around, nor should we attempt to dress up the works which the Holy Spirit has perfected.

"Where is the wise? Where is the scribe? Where is the disputer of this world? Hath not God made foolish the wisdom of this world? For after that in the wisdom of God the world by wisdom knew not God, it pleased God by the foolishness of preaching to save them that believe (1 Corinthians 1:20-21)."

We cannot simply ask each pedestrian: "Have you *accepted* Jesus as your Lord and Savior?"

Or: "Did you say the prayer—did you invite Him into your heart?"

At the risk of offending, we must hand them a Bible as an X on the map, tell of the treasure which might be dug up, discovered and delighted in there and—soberly knowing that hell awaits them—fundamentally demand: "Dig, man!"

"DIG!!!"

This will prove offensive to most.

But worse, we will be labeled *legalistic*. They cannot fathom in their minds how the man in the field could possibly discover a love so *unordinary* that his knees simply buckled—so passionately engrossing as to jostle him home in a rabid fever—so breathlessly jealous that he would dismantle the kingdom he built for himself in order to possess a treasure so small—so inconceivably precious—that *it*, or rather *He* (being the treasure) once quivered and cried helplessly for the milk of His mother while lying in a feeding trough, and yet is somehow so eternally large at present as to envelope the beginning and the end of all eternity and creation, who holds the keys of Hades, and even now sits at the right hand of God.

The calloused pedestrians have sold themselves to the sort of faith which demands little to nothing of repentance; a faith which exemplifies a state of lifelong carnality without so much as batting an eye. They fail to see what the man in the field suddenly realizes of himself—that he was prompted as one whom God foreknew without deserving the courtesy (Romans 8:9). He understood in a moment of jubilation that—though being a wretched sinner—his salvation is freely delivered by the gift of *Sola Gratia* (grace alone), through *Sola Fide* (faith alone), in *Solus Christus* (Christ alone), to *Soli Deo Gloria* (to the glory of God alone), all of which can only arise through the field he invested his time

656

in—*Sola Scriptura* (Scripture alone). It is a faith which "cometh by hearing. and hearing by the word of God (Romans 10:17)." Essentially, the essence of his Lordship Salvation doctrine derives from Ephesians 2:8-9, which states:

"For by grace are you saved, through faith, and that not of yourselves. It is the gift of God, not of works, lest any man should boast."

We can safely conclude of the man whom Jesus spoke a parable concerning that—by forsaking his worldly riches—he has turned in an about-face direction from his previous life of carnality (Acts 3:19; Luke 24:47), a self-ownership which consists not of human work but a divinely bestowed grace (Acts 11:18; 2 Timothy 2:25), imbued by the genuine sort of repentance which secures a recognizable change of behavior (Luke 3:8; Acts 26:18-20). Those who truly *believe* will love Christ (1 Peter 1:8-9; Romans 8:28-30; 1 Corinthians 16:22), and will therefore long to obey Him (John 14:15, 23), since obedience is evidence of one's faith (1 John 2:3).

Never the less, the Easy Believists will wildly dispute these facts in favor of their almost-alchemical "faith" formula—their *eternal elixir*, if you will. The story of Passover would have been comfortable, and dare I say sufficient enough for them, had the Israelite's painted their door posts with the blood of the lamb but remained thereafter in Egypt without ever demonstrating the active faith which crossed them from one end of the red sea to the other. Having already warned of the "hole in the bridge where millions fall through," A.W. Tozer redressed Jesus' Parable of the Prodigal Son in order to better accommodate the obstinate evangelist of Easy-Believism. He quotes the following:

"That prodigal son, look at him. A certain man had two sons and one of them said unto his father, "Give me the goods that falleth to me and he divided unto them, the two of them, the boys, his living. And after a few days the boy left – the younger – and went into a far country and there he spent his substance in riotous living. And when he became hungry and had nothing to eat he went and attached himself to a swineherd and he fed swine. And he was there in the swine-pen and he got hungry because his wages wouldn't buy enough to eat. And it was a humbling thing for a Jew to feed swine. And one day a man appears – and here I depart from the Scriptures. One day a young man appears and this young man says to this boy who had gone away from home and was feeding swine – he had a bundle of tracts, this young feller, he was just out of Bible school – and he had been taught how to win souls in nine easy lessons.

And he goes up to this prodigal son lying among the swine and he says, "I have good news for you!" And he looks up and says, "Thank God, I need it. I need good news. What is it?" "Your father is ready to forgive you!" "Well," the boy says, "thank the Lord!" "Your father is ready to forgive you; do you believe it?" And the boy says, "Yes, I believe it." "All right now, thank God now, let's bow our heads and you thank the Lord you're saved. You believe the father forgives you. Yes, well, Amen! Now, we'll thank the dear Lord that you're saved. And now goodbye! Don't forget to witness, and sometime I'll be around again."

So this swineherd stays right there in the far country and he gets zealous and missionary and he goes out and he starts to make converts among the other swineherds and pretty soon he has them all believing that the father forgives, and they all do, and say, "I thank God the father forgives." Alright, and then they build a little tabernacle call it the First Tabernacle of the Converted Swineherds. And they all stay right there in the far country; nobody goes home. And that boy is still ragged and dirty and smelly and the people — the respectable people of the neighborhood – when they pass by elevate their nose and hurry by. And they say, "So persecuted they the prophets which were before us. It is the result of our holy living that they are giving us the cold shoulder."

Then one day while they are singing choruses in this First Church of the Converted Swineherds in the far country a young fellow comes along and asks permission to speak and he rises and says to them, "Put away your sins, ye wicked! Put away your sins! Learn to do good; cease to do evil, be righteous and follow the Lord and do good and you'll be saved." And they pick him up and throw him out and say, "He's a legalist!" and that he 'doesn't believe in grace.' "Why, we're saved by accepting the doctrine." But this young fellow wanders off and time goes on and the fatted calf gets old and dies and the father passes away and the boy stays on in the far country.

Now that's evangelism as it is preached a good deal today in America! It is, "Believe on Christ. Accept Christ and stay where you are!" Now that is excused and explained by a hundred different learned ways but it leaves the sinner in his sins! And the man in his sins will be damned as certainly as the sun rises in the east and goes down in the west!"

We must not be so gullible as to think the Gospel of Jesus Christ, often delivered to the so-called Christian, cannot go in one ear and out the other. The man who finds the *true*treasure—buried in the most undeveloped of human institutions—he will *forever* be a changed man. If this is *you*, then those of us who have discovered and conclusively accepted the free gift of salvation through the blood of Jesus must not stray so far from the field that those who pass with their hands slung in pockets and eyes hung lazily upon their shoes cannot hear the collective roar of our tearful pleas:

"Dig! Dig! Dig!"

RUB-A-DUB-DUB, THREE SINNERS IN A TUB | THE MEAT, THE MILK & SAINT PETER'S BROTHER (*Flat Earth & the House It Darkened*)

MRS. HADLEY AND THE KIDS WERE ALREADY IN BED for the night, so we stripped down of everything but our bathing suites and yielded to the potency of a bubbling cauldron. I was almost immediately pressed to a conversation among strangers that I'd hoped to retreat from and which they likely wouldn't be letting their families in on—once returning home to Melbourne. But I was terrible at hiding. The Ozzies had found me out and learned what I did for a living. My attempt at steering them away from my research into *Flat Earth* towards an intimate knowledge of Jesus was not a success. And so in the Salinas Valley, halfway between Monterey and Santa Cruz, the glimmering of gold within the embankment of a rolling mist—which seemed to materialize whenever high beams danced sporadically among lanes of eucalyptus—gave way to devilish delight, intellectual grinning, and the stench of gratifying self-flagellation.

It is a conversation—like many others held across North America—which still haunts me. They needed to know they were sinners in desperate need of Jesus, and all they wanted to do was meet a Flat Earthist while on Sabbatical so that they might poke sticks through the firmament of His power. And worse, they had made the connection between a cosmological artifact exhumed from antiquity with the superstitious shibboleth of dusty hymnbooks and stained-glass windows. The first gave way to an interconnected rejection of the other. They were toothless babes requiring the milk of Jesus before they could chew on the spiritual meat of the creation which is revealed in His Word. And I made the mistake of spoon-feeding it to them in reverse order.

2

FLIES MIGHT AS WELL HAVE EATEN GORDON'S EYES while we spoke under the shadows of grand oak and the sun-splashed Spanish moss which hung from their intertwined avenue of branches. My neighbor was dying, but he never let anyone in on it. He seemed healthy enough. Yet according to his own testimony he was already dead inside—this much I was certain of. I have never spoken about Gordon before. But now that we're back in our adopted hometown of Charleston, South Carolina, having traveled across the United States and Canada for years in our fifth-wheel—a journey which first began from Long Beach, California—I think about him more often than not. Gordon was a sweet old man. And though he wore the kindred spirit of a southern gentleman, his true identity was no different than the back porch majority of sinful humanity. Gordon was a dead man walking.

The old rice plantation where I first met Gordon is a mostly-forgotten, happily overlooked microcosm of American culture populated of oaks, cypress trees, bald eagles, owls, fireflies, and an endless parade of alligators. The Native Americans once named this place *Yeshoe*, meaning: "Green Water." The nearby overpass, which replaced the tired coach and buggy bridge, and the train which still whistles through the night from beyond the pale moonlit trees beyond our bedroom windows, both served as vital supply routes for the doomed Confederacy. Here among the bayou, starving adolescents and shoe-less old men in gray uniform once fled the ashes of Atlanta for shelter, and with Sherman's final northward march from Savannah, they attempted one of their final stands. My neighbor appreciated history as much as I. We talked about the land I've come to love—and *more*.

But if I gaze back at Gordon and sorrowfully shake my head, it's because I recall my *meaty* pronunciations which sought to dominate our conversations. I had only just discovered the *truth* of Flat Earth. This awakening was an intimate one, but only because it enhanced the joy of my salvation. It was what I likened to a pre-wedding present from the bridegroom. I finally understood what Satan meant when he offered Jesus the kingdoms of this world if He bowed and worshiped him—and Jesus also, when declaring He was not of this world. It changed everything for me. The straight and narrow suddenly became straighter and narrower. But even more harrowing than my pilgrim's journey to the Celestial City—in John Bunyan terms—a thorough retrospective of my own life inquired if I'd even departed from the City of Destruction to begin with, as I once thought. Conclusively, Flat Earth is a second chance; a joyous journey of discovery which I desperately desired for others—and *still* do. Yet whenever Gordon comes to mind, I recollect my insistence that we currently stood upon a flat, stationary Earth—just as the Bible declares—and *wince*.

I was contending that he meet the Creator in a *reverse* order. Gordon wasn't even a babe in Christ yet. A babe in Christ does not have the teeth to chew and digest a spiritual meat. Before they can mature beyond the squashed vegetables which adorn the bib—before they can let go of the coffee table and hobble across the rug—before they can pull up their big boy pants—they must be held to the breast and nurtured. Gordon wasn't even *born again* yet. There were of course the moments between our conversations when the Lord prompted me to put my fascinations aside and speak *truth* with Gordon. No, He didn't want me to prove the old rice plantation surrounding us was inhabited by *flat*—albeit green—water. Gordon needed to hear about Jesus. He needed to dip his hands in the cool life giving water and refresh his lips. Gordon needed the only truth which would cause him to thirst no more.

He needed the milk which Paul wrote about in 1 Corinthians 3:1-3, and which very few Christians can apparently ween off of:

"And I, brethren, could not speak unto you as unto spiritual, but as unto carnal, even as unto babes in Christ. I have fed you with milk, and not with meat: for hitherto ye were not able to bear it, neither yet now are ye able. For ye are yet carnal: for whereas there is among you envying, and strife, and divisions, are ye not carnal, and walk as men?"

There is a clear defining difference between the Creator and his conspiracy-plagued creation, despite the fact that I'd convinced myself otherwise. Truth be known, I was only interested in throwing a precious soul down the rabbit hole of humanism and perverse inquiry in hopes that he'd come out alright in the end. I wanted Gordon to inhabit my very Wonderland of the conspirator, a realm populated of roaming goats—an unseen crumb on the map with no *x marks the spot* or delivery address for the inquirer—where its endless abstractions may be found among the naked mannequins, dusty boxes, and blanketed display cases one floor above the department stores highest *advertised* elevator button. For the conspirator, it is the crowning virtue of his existence, a dimly-lit rectitude of breaker boxes and cobwebs which often leads to a worse condition of cognition than the multitudes of sheep he gawks at roaming the city streets below him. I was only interested in leading Gordon towards a Flat Earth movement which is populated by wolves, with hirelings for shepherds. I was enlisting him as a malnourished sheep and insuring that he'd be ripped to pieces.

Truly, I *cringe*.

One afternoon I recall Gordon was on my mind, and for once the prerogative to creation was clear. He needed an introduction to its Creator. With the squeaks and the clamber of my sons little red tricycles following uncomfortable close to my heels, and having already discredited the aptitude of my mind, I walked towards Gordon's porch, wiped the sweat from my brow, loosened the top buttoned of my shirt, and gulped.

3

ANDREW MUST HAVE FELT LIKE A STRANGER in a very strange land. So the giddy-up to his gut only felt like a natural knee-jerk reaction when the Baptist declared from the banks of the Jordan, "Behold, the Lamb of God!" The person approaching was exactly the sort of stranger he was looking for.

The man who had distinct privilege of becoming the very first disciple called upon by Jesus (John 1:35-40)—much like the three Ozzies—had taken a sabbatical. His destination was not a Jacuzzi in the Salinas Valley, but the Jordan River, where the Baptist was preaching a message of repentance in anticipation of the Messiah. We know Andrew as an Apostle, though if we think about him *little*, it's likely because his domineering brother came along. Of the four leading disciples, which include his brother Peter and the quarrelsome siblings James and John, Andrew is the least known. When asked, most people wouldn't even realize *the rock* which Jesus built His church upon (Matthew 16:18) had a brother, despite the fact that among his nine humble mentions in the New Testament—some of which simply lists him as a member of the group—he is pointedly referred to as "Peter's brother." Actually, before Simon was even introduced to the reader, a name which means: "Hot-tempered, volatile, and violent," John referred to the first disciple as "Simon Peter's brother."

His recognized identity, being the *lesser half*, is a long held tradition. Archaeologists have discovered the house which Andrew and

Peter occupied in Capernaum, as first indicated in Mark 1:29, where they operated a fishing business, perhaps in league with Zebedee, the father of James and John (Matthew 4:21). They have only thought to name their discovery "Peter's house," perhaps in part because three Gospels record Jesus as having healed Peter's mother-in-law of a fever there. The message seems clear. Nobody cares to be Andrew. And perhaps just as importantly, nobody wants to stand next to him.

There is an uncomfortable truth here. Despite the fact that his name will be forever adorned on one of the twelve gates in New Jerusalem, Andrew exemplified a close relationship with Christ which very few care to have. His is most evident in the fact that he was often the means by which others encountered Him. It was Andrew who brought the young boy with the five barley loaves and two small fish to Jesus while the other disciples seemed clueless (John 6:9). Andrew was so thorough at telling others about Jesus, when Greeks sought out the Messiah through Philip (John 12:20-22), Philip corralled Peter's brother. If Andrew knew how to set up an introduction with the life giver, it's only because he understood—maybe better than anyone—that Jesus wanted to meet *everyone* who desired to meet Him (John 6:37).

Knowing full well his brother's tendency to dominate, Andrew did not hold Peter back from salvation, even though he could have convinced himself otherwise, in hopes that he might have Jesus all to himself, perhaps even rise to a position of coveted applause after His kingdom was ushered in. Peter was so brash he even dominated the twelve disciples. Introducing Peter to the Messiah meant slipping back into the shadows—losing his prime seat at the ministry table—laboring in obscurity. And yet he personally led *the rock* to Jesus (John 1:41-42). It was his very first recorded action. One thing seems certain, Andrew did not seek to be the center of attention, nor resent those who did. The Bible never once corrects Andrew for his missteps nor thinks to document them. He was slow to speak, careful in what he said, and he is only recording as saying the right thing. The same cannot be said of Peter and John.

In time, Andrew would be martyred like the rest of them. But it wasn't for *stirring* the masses against the Science paradigm of his day. We read of no account in Scripture where any Christian was persecuted for befriending contemporaries of other religions in order to challenge the seat of philosophers, all of whom ascribed to a Science *falsely so-called*, nor beat men over the head with a book inscribing 200 Scripture proofs promising to refute Plato's globe. He was ultimately crucified in

Greece, near Athens, for delivering milk—*saving milk*. His only crime: leading "one soul" to Christ. Never concerned about those who would overshadow him in this present kingdom or the one to come, nor demanding credit from the stage for his accomplishments, Andrew led the provincial Roman governor's wife to the Lord.

Upon learning of her introduction to Jesus through the Apostle, the governor demanded that his first lady recant. But how could she? She had dug up the hidden treasure in the open field (Matthew 13:44) and had found the only reason for living. Digging up further truths recorded in His Word was certain, and would likely enhance the joy of her salvation. Perhaps she may have even been led to denounce Plato's globe in time. The Bible abounds with unexpected revelations which threaten our everyday *experiences,* so long as we are willing to cast our self-professed wisdom, religious entanglements, and *science falsely so-called* aside, and mature—even if it means calling every man a liar in order to agree with the Lord. Naturally, she *refused.* In turn, Andrew met the same fate as Peter.

"Peter's brother" was crucified.

I recall reading some time ago how, in the years leading up to the Second World War, archaeologists began to uncover within the hushed halls beneath Saint Peter's Basilica a necropolis containing the sepulchers of wealthy Roman families dating back to the first and second centuries. The frescoed mausoleums displayed colorful paintings, etchings, and mosaics illustrating the stories of the deceased, but there was one stunning feature which overshadowed the entire lot of them. Early Christian graffiti seemed to focus toward one crypt in particular. In fact, as one moved closer, the otherworldly expression of joy seemed increasingly dramatized by relatives of the deceased for affording the opportunity to bury their loved ones so close to the celebrated Saint. As digging parties finally came upon an adjacent wall to the tropaion, graffiti marked the spot: *Petros eni.* Or "Peter is within."

Some people want to be the bride at every wedding and the corpse at every funeral. And where Peter is concerned, even in death others wanted to be buried *next* to him.

4

THE OLD HOUSE, WITH ITS OVERGROWN GARDEN, sits empty, silent, and secret, hinged together only by the afterthought of darkness. He died while we were away on travel—particularly when I was writing my first Flat Earth book in Canada, *Avoid Science Falsely So-Called*. Gordon didn't need to know about the Jesuit plot against Christendom or the Zionist takeover of the world. He didn't need to know space is fake—how it all began with the Mystery religion, or how the Science deception, having claimed succession from the Occult after the alchemists and Isaac Newton bowed out, is bleeding right back into the genetic strand which created it. He needed the only cure for his disease. He needed Jesus.

And I never even made it so far as to ring his doorbell.

If the Lord did not send another evangelist to his door while I was away seeing the world—that is, after my failing to do so—and Gordon did not wash his garments white in the blood of the lamb, then the Bible is clear on his coming fate. It is a bitter truth to swallow. My action—or rather, lack thereof—is nothing short of criminal.

While I was dreaming up the generous possibilities; screeching megaphones, ever-broadening platforms and Pentecost-sized crowds which this Flat Earth movement seemed to promise its chiefest-rankers; and reserving my seat at the *after party*, once Plato's globe was finally done away with—Gordon desperately needed Peter's brother to make an introduction to Jesus. But I was too occupied with being Peter. And quite unlike Andrew, I never saw the potential in Gordon.

If Andrew were here, he might have seen Gordon as the next Peter.

THE PROSTITUTE NEXT DOOR | MY LIFE & TIMES WITH THE WOMAN AT THE WELL

MOST PEOPLE DON'T KNOW THIS ABOUT ME, but for nearly a decade of my adult life I was a nationwide "renowned" wedding photographer. I rarely talk about it anymore. History has moved on without me. It is by my own decision and design—and I am gratefully forgotten. Based out of Long Beach, California, I was "commuting" to work almost every weekend through the portals of an airport terminal—not forgetting thousands of additional miles logged by rental car. New York, Washington DC, and Boston, Puerto Rico, Hawaii, Alaska, Maine, Boulder, Colorado, and everywhere in-between. Even Mexico. I probably photographed this great continent of ours dozens of times over. The earth from 30,000 feet up filled in countless hours of philosophical or religious inquiry. Why I was rarely hired in my hometown of Los Angeles is a mystery which is left for God alone to explain.

Strange being a homeowner with my wife, and yet I spent most of those years feeling somewhat homeless. In order to save money, it wasn't uncommon to spend a night under a chair at the airport or in the trunk of my rental car; a couple of times on the rain drenched sidewalk of a tropical or island paradise, forsaking sleep in order to keep my photography gear dry. I even have the rather fond and mostly non-eventful memory of making the pee-infested NYC subway my bed, riding the #2 red line from Brooklyn across the East River to Manhattan and on up to the Bronx before returning back again, holding conversation with a transvestite for some of it. Rinse and repeat until sunrise.

Most of the motels I stayed at were mired with adultery. You know, couples who parked in separate cars, met for about thirty minutes during the workday lunch hour (one would slink into their room with such suspicion that I might have concluded they were married to the FBI, with their partner falling in line maybe five minutes later). They were rooms that could be split between the two, $20 cash from their lunch money, no questions asked back home. I guess I'd know, since I chose bed-bug infested budget motels for $40 a night. If there was any question as to what they were up to, the pulsating paper-thin wall, which even managed to slap my own bed board across the back of my head, often seemed to answer. And it wasn't terribly uncommon to hear porn videos being filmed for several straight hours.

I distinctly recall this one prostitute somewhere in Pennsylvania, where the smoke stacks blended with the corn fields and late-night train whistles could have doubled for the chilling cry of a ghost. In-between the comings-and-goings of her clientele—it was nearing the midnight hour—I caught sight of a cigarette glowing in-front of my balcony window, and so stepped outside to strike a conversation. Life had not been kind to her. There was a distinct scar upon her nose, and though she had no doubt adorned herself with the natural grace of beauty only a few years earlier, she already wore the disfigured burden of her lifestyle, steeped no doubt in drugs, which was striking when one considers the fragile decade of her youth had not yet transpired.

But it was her eyes, mainly. Deep, impenetrable, and black—as though there was no spark of life left in the pupils which had no doubt once kindled the spiritual fire of every little hopeful girl, filled with dreams. Prostitutes have always fascinated me—to some degree. That they could offer their entire "self" to a man for one or two-hundred dollars, often less, and yet hide the very soul which God intends when a man and woman are united together (in the binds of marriage no less), burying it so far down into their catacomb of bone and marrow that it is entirely impenetrable, not only from the man who pays for her, but likely from herself.

I take it most will agree that she and others like her are not so dissimilar from the "woman at the well," which Jesus spoke with in John chapter 4. I have tried to strike many loving God-centered conversations with prostitutes on my journeys across America, but to no avail. To convince them that God the Son has the water of life to offer, which will cause them never to thirst again, is not so easily done. They have given themselves to men—endlessly. They have granted them everything they want—and in doing so, they hate them for it.

I'll never forget that hotel in Washington DC. The Capitol building was a block or two away, with Pennsylvania Avenue rounding the next street, and perhaps three or four prostitutes worked the corner 24-hours a day. I witnessed several "unmarked" cars slow down, with a hand of some mysterious Washington worker rising from a crack in the back window to signal one or two of them to climb in.

It was raining one night and, after three days of grueling work photographing a Sikh wedding (with another wedding the next morning in Williamsburg, Virginia—busy schedule) I swooped into the last available open slot, which just so happened to be managed by two of those prostitutes huddling under a single umbrella. I apparently parked, as my wife later explained, in their "drive-thru" window, because the following morning my tires were slashed.

Let's just say they were standing by and they weren't willing to strike up a friendly conversation with me later. Contrast all of this with the bride and groom on their wedding day.

In my current neighborhood there is a "massage parlor" within a short walking distance of my house, convenient for the home owners in this rather well-to-do neighborhood, a former South Carolina rice plantation. It's run by a white woman who fits all the same striking resemblances to any other woman at the well. Likely stunning to behold at one time, her career and life choices have disfigured the flesh which men thoughtlessly crave for their own—disposable as the cigarette she smokes, I suppose—and which she kindly offers. But it's mostly her eyes. I catch sight of them often as she's smoking out front between clientele. Deep, dark, and impenetrable—they must not crave her soul. And what remains is impoverished.

Her car is nice though. It's a convertible.

I used to pray that my God Yahweh would shut her business down while on my walks. But I was wrong. I was terribly wrong—dead wrong—in praying that. Men crave sex without the unification and rib-partnership which God designed it for, and they'll have their meaningless depraved sex, always hopelessly starving for fleeting moments of intimacy. And they'll do it to anything that moves or beeps or expands with air until the end of time. Shut down one whorehouse and another will rise in its place. There will always be prostitutes giving men exactly what they want—and all the while they'll hate them for it.

No, no—I walk now past that "massage parlor" praying that she'll find the light of Christ. I long that she'll drink from the water which will cause her never to thirst again, that it will rejuvenate her spirit and make her the beautiful woman which God intended her for, first from within.

Time is short.

I can't seem to keep track of the seasons anymore. The summer heat swelters and then the sky grows crisp and the leaves litter the dew.

Presently they're budding again. And meanwhile, our bridegroom's wedding day approaches.

It doesn't matter what she or anyone else has done. The water of life is a free gift for anyone who wishes to drink of it. Jesus is that well. And His water is a delight. Blessed is he or she who searches for and finds it. Jesus turned the water into wine, and I can only imagine there will be an endless supply in His coming kingdom—each serving brimming-over with joy.

All He asks is that we confess our sins and repent of them. Turn from this wicked world. Make Jesus the shepherd of our life. That is my prayer for the woman down the street from where I live. My heart longs to see her delight in Jesus. I long to see her become beautiful again.

I long to call her a sister in Christ.

THE JOYOUS COSMOLOGY | MY MEETING WITH DR. DANNY FAULKNER AND "ANSWERS IN GENESIS"

THE RUMOR THAT I WAS TO RIDE UPON A WHITE HORSE—shirtless and glistening with massage oils like Schwarzenegger or Russian Prime Minister Vladimir Putin before a mob of swooning schoolgirls—by victoriously planting the Flat Earth flag on the "Answers in Genesis" headquarters, was not started by me. Suffice to say some of my Geocentric brethren were tossed into confusion when observing that nobody on staff—Bodie Hodge, Dr. Georgia Purdom, Buddy Davis, nor founder and CEO Ken Ham—were wearing burlap shirts and sackcloth pants, mournfully pouring hot ashes upon themselves for their decades of Biblical oversight, after I left the building. Conclusively, Flat Earth did not reclaim Christendom. Not yet, at least.

I certainly did not arrive at AiG to challenge them to a duel of superior logic—with a glove and bumblebee sting of a slap across each cheek to match; nor to overturn their Copernican-sponsored tables and whip them into a buttered-cream of frenzy. I went as a gentleman guest of Dr. Danny Faulkner and a representative—I hope—of my brothers and sisters in Christ (on either side of the aisle). I'm rather clumsy with speech—in person, that is—and would be of no more effect before Pharaoh as Moses would without Aaron to back him. And yet the Lord called me out to Kentucky without my counterpart, *whoever* he may be. I am terrible at oral exams. Regardless, I went obediently, if only to sit in front of Professor Faulkner's desk—who has no doubt given many frightful exams to failing students—fumbling over my own poor pronunciations and *tip of the tongue* forgetfulness, and extend an olive branch.

A snowstorm delayed my planned arrival by almost three hours, which likely scrambled Dr. Faulkner's own schedule. Regardless, he was most generous with his time—an entire day, in fact. There are those within my ranks who will remind me that Dr. Faulkner is simply using my supposed gullibility as a tool for his research *against* the

671

movement—perhaps so. I am not concerned. There is likely never a time in history—since Moses first sat down to write the Torah—that Biblical cosmology was not scoffed at for its lack of scientific credibility. Not forgetting the oftly-stated quotation of old: "Keep your friends close and your enemies closer." In case my reader is wondering, I paid either thought no mind. I went at the Lord's prompting, and by Faulkner's charitable invitation—whatever the outcome.

Then again, Dr. Faulkner's and my relationship—albeit a recent one—hasn't exactly been exempt of dysfunction. He has openly mocked a Biblical belief which I affectionately cling to—a personal conviction described by Faulkner only one week before my arrival as a movement which "preys upon the ignorance of people." I have had my unkind words in return—or as Faulkner thoughtfully told me: "Christians don't have a habit of getting along." But *get along* we most certainly did—we were determined to—with Dr. Faulkner personally assigning himself the role as my very-own museum guide. He also saw to it that every staff member, including Ken Ham's secretary, greeted me. There was the museum itself to comb through, but Faulkner was so thorough in his diplomatic duties that even Ham's *behind the scenes* operation was altogether explored, including the copper sink in the basement.

We spoke of many things; my breaking of fellowship with the Flat Earth movement *as a whole*; the hope that my fellow Flat Earth brothers and sisters in Christ will recognize *our* calling to not be unequally yoked with unbelievers and do the same; that we would not hold hands with blasphemers, heretics, Gnostics, apostates, and perverse humanists—most of whom dominate this "Truther" movement—when presenting our demands for *Scripture Alo*ne to the church, nor share the stage with those who obstinately oppose Jesus in our Geocentric proclamations; and as an important component to our unyoking with unbelievers, that we would actually take the Bible literally, as we claim to—despite the fact, quite ironically, that our fellow brothers and sisters who reject the Lord's geocentric account of creation often take the Bible far more literally in its applications than *most* of us in this movement do. Hypocrisy abounds. We spoke about these behemoth issues and more. We spoke about dinosaurs too.

We discussed our differences throughout the day and, just as chiefly, our commonalities. Whenever a joke presented itself, we laughed together. I rather enjoyed Faulkner's self-degradating old-man humor, particularly a photo of him standing below a sign in the road which read DIP. We both had a good laugh about that. Hours before our day had ended Dr. Faulkner called me "friend." Hearing that from Dr. Faulkner—or Professor Faulkner, as he prefers to be called—was incredibly moving, and I most certainly hope it to be true. Indeed, I extended an olive branch to him and him to me, but not necessarily in that order. And that is how we parted.

We spoke about stars and their relationship with angels. We spoke of *planets*, specifically the wandering stars "who kept not their first estate, but left their own habitation (Jude 1:6)," thereby making this entire Copernican deception possible. Their habitual departure is a crime so great, we are told by the brother of Jesus, as to be compared to the sins of Sodom and Gomorrah—angels which "hath reserved in everlasting chains under darkness unto the judgment of the great day." Indeed, the Copernican deception, like its Darwinist counterpart, has sent many to hell. There was a moment when Professor Faulkner, with his feet upon the desk, gazed off into some distant corner of his office, and in a rather cold and pensive tone, though to be fair, perhaps nostalgically warm—I know not which—he spoke of high-powered telescopes and the heavenly realm. With mesmerized eyes he said, still fixed upon the distant heavens in the whereabouts of his bookshelf: "Saturn is one of the most beautiful things I've ever beheld."

I thought about that for a time—the intrinsic beauty of a planet which kept not its own estate. There was often a lull between us; sporadic intervals of serenity intermingling with sentences—the comfortable calming sort of silence allotted for friends. And while I couldn't recall everything that was spoken between those thoughtful pauses—*if* I were asked to give full account of our meeting, one particular break vividly remains with me. Dr. Faulkner looked into my eyes and, rather melancholy again, asked: "Do you think I'm *deceived?*"

My response did not come without first reminding him of his credentials and the wealth of scientific knowledge which he can demonstrate with the flex of his intellect. I shan't publicly debate him. But that is the nature of a deception. It is so oftly convincing. *Science*, I had the opportunity to tell him, *is the Great Delusion.* In short, I looked across his desk and answered: "Yes, according to the Bible, and despite your wealth of education, I believe *you are.*"

I wonder if Dr. Faulkner detected the threat of an imposing tear. That would be *my* tear. Suffice to say I found no satisfaction in calling him *deceived.* But he asked, and I answered. And he didn't run me out of his office for the honesty.

In one AiG exhibit, two paleontologists are digging up a dinosaur fossil. The first admits to being a young earth Creationist; the other a Darwinist. The point being that the Darwinist looks at the fossil and undresses a narrative spanning millions of years, where-as the Christian, because he is working with the Bible as his framework, he can see a narrative—clear as day—spanning a few thousand. This I can most certainly relate to as a former Copernican. After all, I was at one time a punching bag for AiG. I recall countless evolutionists—an endless line-up of them—dumbfounded by my outright rejection of their Darwinian error when the deception itself—the darkness by which they weighed their reality apart from God—complimented their intelligence. But I too was in error. I too am guilty of force-feeding a "natural revelation" into a text which clearly doesn't belong. The entire Bible functions better without the Copernican revolution and Plato's globe to dampen its narrative—*far better*. Quite contrarily, it flourishes.

There is yet another inspiring exhibit, in the Ark Encounter, actually—I took my wife and twin boys there on the following day—in which the entire wall of a room is filled with various children's books and bathtub toys resembling cartoonish depictions of Noah's Ark. It captured my twin son's interest—*naturally*. And the message is straightforward. "Answers in Genesis" acknowledges a widespread conspiracy against the Bible's flood account. Noah's Ark is made to look silly—irreparably childish—and therefore perceived as a practical impossibility from the moment a child first enters the crib. I wish Dr. Faulkner and Answers in Genesis could comprehend the same line-of-logic with the globe which they so obediently advocate. The very Luciferian system which delivers unto the baby and the toddler a silly bubble-bath rendition of Noah's Ark is also handing that child a rather sophisticated globe—in both counts to mock God's own narrative of creation *and* judgement, but more importantly, to undermine their prospects of a future saving grace.

I so desperately want Danny Faulkner and Ken Ham and his staff at AiG to see what I see—what so many of us in this latter-day downpour of the Holy Spirit see. When we throw the Copernican apostasy out from God's Word, the joyous cosmology is finally found! There is a *true* complimentary and observable science in which we can finally perceive the reality of creation, if only we allow Holy Writ to inform and function as our framework. Believe me when I tell you, it is a Joyous Cosmology. I want them to see that. And just as they so desperately crave approval from a Luciferian agency of Science which opposes the

Lord—attempting to convince them, as they ought, that the Bible's non-Darwinian approach to science is a true and worthwhile practice—why do they, the Copernican Christians, then in-turn mock us, just as the unbelieving world so devilishly mocks them, simply for struggling a notch below them on the food chain?

If only Answers in Genesis—and this is my one demand, should our relationship continue as it ought in Christ—if only they would hold as their standard of presentation, a belief which we the Geocentric Christians actually believe. Listen carefully. I am not demanding that Dr. Faulkner or anyone else on Ken Ham's payroll *become* one of us. I did not go to Kentucky to convert them, and I will certainly not hold my breath waiting—though even the Apostle Paul had a surprise on the road to Damascus. An open discussion is welcome. Feel free to debunk us, *if* they can. I am not worried in the least. But I ask—I kindly ask with all seriousness that they represent us without the stench of deception. There is, quite unfortunately, a stench. While attempting to pull the cloth out from under the table and strip us bare, they must let their readers know *what* we believe and *why* we believe it. I implore of them—if they are an honest group of men and women—to show an illustration of Hebrew cosmology in their hopes of debunking us. Just show them. Why won't they? Are they concerned—and they most certainly should be—that the Spirit of God will open the eyes of our opponents, just as He did for me—and many of us?

I think so.

There is at present another tragedy. Among the shots fired back and forth between Answers in Genesis and my fellow brothers and sisters in Christ inhabiting the Joyous Cosmology, only two individuals have bothered to call Dr. Faulkner up at all to express concern or attempt in the slightest the beginnings of a healthy discussion. One might go so far as to say that the Flat Earth movement has *rejected* Answers in Genesis rather than the other way around.

"Robbie Davidson," I said when naming the first.

Dr. Faulkner nodded.

And then there would be myself—the other caller.

"The thing is," Dr. Faulkner sighed, "it's not like I'm unlisted."

RAISING THE "FORBES BROWN DIRT ALLOSAUR..." PUTTING EBENEZER TO REST (*Joe Taylor and Answers in Genesis*)

JOE SAID, "IF YOU'RE GOING TO DO A WRITE-UP on that Allosaur they got in Ken Ham's museum, do me a favor."

"What's that?" I spoke into my end of the phone.

"Call him by his real name."

If I spoke anything, aside from a stutter, static likely filled dead air, so Joe explained: "It's not Ebenezer."

Clearly, further explanation was needed.

"It says Ebenezer on the plaque. But no—that ain't right. Call him by his real name. Dana Forbes discovered him. It's only right that he retain the name *he gave*."

It was *Answers in Genesis* astronomer Danny Faulkner who first introduced me to the Allosaur, and the inevitable story to follow, while giving me a personal tour of Ken Ham's Creation Museum in Petersburg Kentucky. Her discovery, I'd quickly come to learn, is a story of greed, of theft, of betrayal, of grievous error, and above all else—which is perhaps not surprising, all things considered—the 2004 presidential election. But if I were in any way moved to gaze upon her fossilized remains, and I most certainly was, it's because Taylor himself was involved. Paleontologist Joe Taylor and I met at the first annual Flat Earth International Conference in Raleigh, North Carolina. We actually had dinner together, and though he is no proponent of a geocentric flat earth, our conversation was never-the-less invigorating. Taylor is a real-life giant hunter. Nephilim is his game. Though Taylor is also passionate about dinosaurs, and in the case of an Allosaur named *Ebenezer*, the exhumed spirits of Nephilim, which I suspect have a credible part to play in her own life-cycle narrative, nearly destroyed him.

Dr. Faulkner knew one of my nagging questions centered on the historicity of dinosaurs—mainly, did they exist at all, even as dragons?

676

In light of this cosmological revelation, I do find such a proposal *worth* considering. Once the Copernican's heliocentric-universe is disregarded, evolution is just as thoroughly done away with—and rightly so. Can the championed protagonists of the Darwinian narrative, and perhaps their most regurgitated tool of propaganda, still fit within a young-earth creation model? The creationists at *Answers in Genesis*, despite obstinately clinging to a Copernican belief which cannot be supported with the Bible, would most certainly say *yes*. The reality is, many within the Flat Earth movement no longer believe in the existence of dinosaurs, and there is social pressure from *within* to throw the baby out with the bathwater, despite the fact that fossils are actively being dug up around the world and, perhaps far more notably, are provably fossilized as the result of a swift and sudden deluge.

Says *Answers in Genesis* founder Ken Ham on the issue: "While evolutionists use dinosaurs more than anything to promote their worldview, especially to young students, our museum uses dinosaurs to help tell the account of history according to the Bible."

My own Flat Earthist contemporary Eric Dubay has stated: "…just like the many supposed Ape-Man species, all dinosaur reconstructions are 100% fictional fabrications created by invested and inventive evolutionists." In his same article, *Dinosaurs Never Existed*, Dubay further notes: "All the museum displays, models, mannequins, cartoons, and movies of prehistoric monsters you have ever seen are all imaginative reconstructions based on incomplete skeletons arranged in a manner paleontologists believe to be most realistic. Furthermore, the skeletons exhibited in museums are all admittedly intricate fabrications made of plaster, fiberglass, various epoxies, and other animal bones, not original fossils."

Similarly, in his article, *The Dinosaurs Never Existed*, Robbin Koefoed writes:

> "Most people believe that dinosaur skeletons displayed in museums consist of real dinosaur bones. This is not the case. The real bones are incarcerated in thick vaults to which only a select few highly placed researchers hold a key, which means that NO independent researcher has ever handled a tyrannosaurus rex bone."

On the day in which I visited Ken Ham's Creation Museum I did not have a tyrannosaurus rex at my disposal, but I was standing before a slightly lesser theropod—or the representation of one, for that matter—

677

and wanted to engage with the proper questions. So I asked Dr. Faulkner: "Is there any possibility that I might see the *real bones* in the back?"

He was at first confused by this inquiry, perhaps because, as I'd come to learn, there were no bones in the back. In fact, I had to reword my line of questioning two or three times before any and all confusion could be erased.

Dr. Faulkner replied, "You're looking at them."

I said: "The real bones?"

"Well, yes—*what* bones were recovered…"

Ebenezer was a healthy specimen, nicely filling in the measurements of the average allosaur—10 feet tall and about 30 feet long, for the record—and his skeletal remains are more completed than most. It is rare to dig up a dinosaur skeleton beyond 50% completion, but 56% of Ebenezer remains intact with 139 bones recovered from a possible 250. While Dr. Faulkner could not speak for any other museum in the world, he assured me the theropod on display at Ken Ham's Creation Museum is in-fact *real*. Even its supplement bones, to fill in the remaining 111 still missing, are clearly marked so as to avoid confusion. But let us not overlook the icing on the cake. There is also the skull to consider.

Here Dr. Faulkner adds:

"…the allosaurus skull is 97% complete…and the missing 3% is entirely teeth. The CT scan showed teeth underneath developing. Apparently dinosaurs and extant reptiles with teeth are like sharks—they replaced teeth continually as they were lost. Therefore, it is likely that 100% of the skull that Ebenezer died with was preserved. We even have the small bone that the tongue connected to. That's a very rare find."

In October of 2000 landowner Dana Forbes detected bones protruding from the ground of his Skull Creek Basin property in northwest Colorado. Word spread among the creationist community. Carl Baugh of the Creation Evidence Museum in Glen Rose, Texas visited with Forbes on May 20, 2001. Baugh recommended that he employ a professional dinosaur paleontologist—specifically, Taylor, and others from his Mt. Blanco team. The two were currently working at a site a few miles away. While Baugh and Taylor had been digging there together annually since 1995, they had been in a working relationship since 1986. And though the species of animal was not then known, it was immediately evident, upon arrival the following day, what Taylor was gazing at.

678

Dana Forbes produced several dinosaur bones for Taylor to examine. What he had before him was the fossilized remains of an allosaur—that, and so much more.

Taylor was soon thereafter contractually assigned as "Chief Excavator" for all work on the Forbes' property. Actually, from the hill above, Taylor not only identified the bones of an allosaurus protruding from the flat strata of brown dirt which had buried it, but two sauropods. The first was positioned roughly 20-feet above the Allosaur, with the second—what Joe believes to be a brachiosaurs—roughly 1500 feet below. There were other sauropod bones on the site, as well as a second allosaurus off to the west—though Taylor assures me very little remained of it. Later a large tooth was found of a probable saurophaganax, Taylor says, which is a genus of the allosaurid-kind.

Floodwater was clearly the culprit behind the flat strata which buried this ancient dragon. Is there any exception? "Its neck was recurved back in the death position, indicating drowning," Taylor said. "Due to massive upheavals of the strata, the once flat layer was tilted at a 30-degree angle." Furthermore, the bones were stained brown because of iron in the sediments and also because it "lay on a bed of brown plant material," whereas "most bones turn black in the area." Staining of this nature can happen fast—even within 100 years of fossilization. In the Mt. Blanco Fossil Museum, Taylor has several alligator skulls and bones "replaced by minerals of various colors that have replaced the bone with minerals that are purple, red, brown, black, white, blue, green, mauve, cream, and one which is almost transparent."

To the dinosaur doubter, Joe Taylor delivers this plea:

"Today we have birds with short arms. T-Rex was a lizard with short arms. Today, some humming birds have teeth; some juvenile ostriches have claws on their wings. Why would this make dinosaurs any stranger than birds? Are they extinct? Nobody but God knows if anything is extinct.... Sharp teeth don't necessarily mean they were vicious meat eaters. There are deer with long fangs. There were huge camels 20 feet tall with fangs as big as bananas. There were rhinos with saber-toothed fangs. None of them were meat eaters. Pigs have teeth very similar to humans. We are alike, omnivores but our teeth don't look like meat-eaters. All animals were designed by God to eat vegetation. Even today, crocodiles and large snakes have been seen eating leaves. Bears love grass and coyotes would live on cantaloupe if they could get them. Evolutionists have told us T-Rex and this Allosaur were killing machines. Yes, they did eat meat and bones, but originally they may have eaten that giant fruit that tastes like chicken."

The allosaur was without a doubt a magnificent find, and Pete DeRosa, who later advertised himself as "a veteran archaeologist and paleontologist," yet had never taken part in a dinosaur dig before, according to Taylor and other sources, wanted a piece of the action.

"DeRosa pleaded," Taylor sighs at the memory.

Regardless, Taylor agreed.

Excavation assistance would now be provided in part by Pete DeRosa's *Creation Expeditions,* based in Crystal River, Florida, comprised of himself and his two sons Pete Jr. and Mark DeRosa, and *Vision Forum* president Doug Phillips, along with thirty homeschoolers. Phillips quickly announced further intentions. He would produce a video documentary on their three-day excursion into the Colorado wilderness. A script was written. He then hired a film crew to stage the event, with his own agenda filling in the narrative. Joe Taylor was written out of the story. And here the honeymoon ended.

> COLORADO, May 20 — A dinosaur fossil expedition for home educators sponsored by Vision Forum and Creation Expeditions has excavated a rare, large, intact Allosaurus measuring more than 22 feet in length, 10 feet in height, with a complete skull more than a yard long. Allosaurs are believed to be a close relative of the Tyrannosaurus rex, and differ from the T. rex primarily in size and cranial capacity.
>
> Under the leadership of Vision Forum president Doug Phillips, an adjunct professor of apologetics with the Institute for Creation Research, and Peter DeRosa, a veteran archaeologist and paleontologist with Creation Expeditions, the team of thirty home educators spent a week hunting for and excavating fossils in a privately owned location in the Skull Creek Basin of Northwest Colorado.
>
> *Vision Forum News Release, May 20, 2002*

In his article, *Raising the Allosaur, A Doug Phillips Fraudumentary*, T.W. Eston writes:

"Doug Phillips' news release was replete with half-truths, lies, fabrications, and stealing credit from the men who had actually been responsible. Even the claim that they'd 'spent a week hunting for and excavating" was a lie. In reality they had only spent three days on site excavating.' On November 15, 2002, Doug Phillips and *Vision Forum* released its very first feature documentary film, '*Raising the Allosaur: The True Story of a Rare Dinosaur and the Home Schoolers Who Found It*, which would run at 60-minutes in length. Eston adds: "It's ironic but not surprising that Phillips selected a title that included the word *True*, for there is very little truth to it."

In fact, the 2003 Vision Forum Catalog stated:

"Consider that our dinosaur site was completely excavated by home educators. The paleontologists were home educators. The team doing the restoration was made up of home educators."

Upon its release, the film immediately found itself treading for survival in a deluge of controversy. The sauropod which Taylor had accurately classified on site was then misidentified by the DeRosa boys and Doug Phillips as a stegosaur. How embarrassing for DeRosa, being a self-declared "veteran archaeologist and paleontologist." But there were other allegations, "the most notable of which was the failure to give any credit for the excavation to the directing paleontologist Joe Taylor."

The film was an instant success—and a lucrative one at that—among the home schooling market. Regardless, it was quietly pulled in October of 2004, only a month before it was expected to show at the San Antonio Independent Christian Film Festival. According to Eston, who had already completed his own investigation, Phillips refused to return phone calls.

By 2003 the DeRosas had taken possession of Ebenezer against Taylor's will, which was estimated now at a value of one million dollars, housing it in Doug Phillip's Vision Forum building in San Antonio, Texas for safekeeping. The following year Joe Taylor prepped for Christian mediation with the DeRosas and Doug Phillips. Phillips however did not attend. Taylor and his Mt. Blanco team lost the custody battle. The DeRosas agreed to pay Taylor $129,399 to own the Allosaur. And this is where it gets interesting. The money to pay Taylor was said to have come from one-time presidential candidate Michael Peroutka, who ran the following year in 2004 on the Constitution Party ticket.

Taylor however was never paid.

Michael Peroutka says of his fossil, it "is a testimony to the creative power of God and also lends evidence to the truth of a worldwide catastrophic flooding of the earth about 4,500 years ago as described in the Bible."

Filed on March 24, 2010: TEXAS COURT OF APPEALS, THIRD DISTRICT, AT AUSTIN: Joe Taylor vs. Pete DeRosa, Peter DeRosa, Linda DeRosa, Mark DeRosa, and *Creation Expeditions*: Joe Taylor "awarded" the DeRosas $129,399.64 for damages and attorney's fees. Taylor's two appeals were overruled.

Taylor was not only robbed, but he had to pay the robbers for their time *and* labor. The robbers apparently made out with more than one payment because, according to Ken Ham's Creation Museum, "the Elizabeth Streb Peroutka Foundation bought the specimen and housed it." Peroutka then "donated the Allosaur known as Ebenezer to Ken Ham's Creation Museum in Kentucky on the condition," Taylor informed me, that he personally "volunteered to restore the Allosaur, but the job went to an un-named preparer who mounted what was left of the skeleton with a cast of another Allosaur."

Once again, the man who raised Ebenezer was dismissed.

Answers in Genesis thanked the DeRosas instead. AiG publicly states: "thousands of hours later, the bones of this magnificent fossil are almost completely cleaned and restored thanks to the DeRosa family of *Creation Expeditions*."

Ken Ham says of Ebenezer, that it "fulfills a dream I've had for quite some time. For decades I've walked through many leading secular museums, like the Smithsonian in Washington, D.C., and have seen their impressive dinosaur skeletons, but they were used for evolution. Now we have one of that class for our museum."

Ebenezer fulfilled Ham's dreams. And pockets were filled. But it practically ruined the man who excavated him. It ruined his creation ministry too. Successively, his Mt. Blanco museum locked its doors several times over. His excavation and restoration team, one of the best in the country, was disbanded. The museum's fossil news magazine and DVD series halted. And numerous opportunities for new excavations and research, Taylor insists, were forever lost. Almost two decades later and Taylor has yet to recover.

Dinosaurs, though once buried by God—and might I suggest for good reason—have the power to fill pockets and dreams. They have the skill-set to do *that*—but just as it once was, when "all flesh was corrupted" (as Genesis 6:12 informs us), they still have the potency to incite the spirit of Nephilim in the corruptible sort who conspires to raise them from the earth. In short, dinosaurs still devour and destroy, even the innocent offender.

"So what is his name then?" I asked Taylor over the phone.

"His name," said Taylor, "is the Forbes Brown Dirt Allosaur."

THE SHAPE OF THE EARTH IN THE AGE TO COME—SATAN'S FINAL GLOBE DECEPTION

FIRST LET US DISPENSE WITH THE BAD NEWS. Satan is to be released from the prison of the Watchers. *This*—after he is gladly disposed of and the key is thrown; but the sainthood needn't worry about that for at least another thousand years. There is of course the good news. The accuser is to be defeated once and for all. Revelation chapter 20 informs us of these still distant but coming events; that the great deception by which he currently birdbrains the entire Earth into believing—it is indeed a long laundry list of foolery—will serve only as a fading memory. Upon receiving parole he will desperately need a new carrot-like boondoggle to dangle before the ever-curious humanist mind. A thousand years is ample time to coordinate and strategize, I suppose. There's no better place for a man to be alone with his own thoughts than a cell—or in Satan's case, a bottomless pit.

At any rate, what this new deception will look like—fashionably speaking—is impossible to tell, but repeating Copernicus and Kepler's "New Astronomy" all over again would certainly be asinine. The globe— like evolution and a thousand other lies of the Occult—will prove no better than a broken egg shell; quite unrepairable. The general's war diary, if you will, shall be published and available for grade school reading—theoretically, of course—and "Globe Earth" will be forever deflated. *Amen*.

For example, it is by no means a stretch of the imagination to conclude that every resident within God's holy city and beyond will understand very basic and elementary concepts and principles, such as: "water always remains level." Its surface cannot arch nor conform to the imaginary core-mantle below it.

Perhaps the Holy Spirit is trying to clue us in to the fact that Satan's final rampage is prophetic in more literal ways than we have previously come to consider when he spoke through John: "And they [Satan and his sad-sap army of deceived souls] went up on the breadth of the earth, and compassed the camp of the saints about, and the beloved city (Revelation 20:9)."

See, in the Greek, the actual word used for breadth is "platos." Think *plateau* in French. We might therefore translate this as: "And they came up on the broad (or flat) plane of the earth."

This leads me to conclude that mankind's new and final deception will not be of the Copernican nature. That the inhabitants of this coming age will shake their heads at the delusional minds of our own brothers and sisters today is also imaginable. As Satan approaches to "compass the camp of the saints....and the beloved city (Revelation 20:9)," he will have no choice but to go about his business with the understood logic by all involved that he is traveling across a created order which resembles a plane.

I am not worried about it—the *shape* of this coming deception. And you shouldn't be either, if you keep to the unshakable rule of "Scripture interprets Scripture"—as opposed to the longstanding and mostly unspoken exemption to the rule, which every Globular Christian defiantly clings to. "Scripture interprets Scripture...except when 'Science' interprets it."

Wait, what—*huh*?

The Holy Ghost will not have us fall for the deception of "Globe Earth" or any other shape of the Earth—an oblate spheroid or pear perhaps—should we obey His Testimony and consider Him trustworthy and true. Currently in the age of grace we have His Word to cling to. But in the City of God we shall have Jesus Christ in the flesh to rest upon. He is our Word. By Him all things were spoken into being. So worry not. We will have the Creator of heaven and earth easily accessible when Satan makes his last great wizardly attempt at damnable deceptions. Put it in another way, we shall not fall for Satan's cunning mastery of the cosmological hustle so long as we exemplify the rule which drinking from the water of life will fundamentally require: "Jesus Christ interprets Jesus Christ."

It is unfortunate that a great many sad souls will be deceived—but that is the nature of things—those who live not by the rule but the exemption: "Jesus Yeshua interprets Jesus Yeshua....except for when 'Science' interprets Him."

Let's not be presumptuous. Perhaps Satan will not call the Great Delusion of man 'Science' a thousand years from now. Still, I have little doubt it will be the same cunning lie. Has it really changed since the garden? "God didn't really mean that...." Next time, just as it was with the first, we can expect that line, only presented with the laces and the bows and the trim of a slightly different-sized package and glitter of parcel paper. In the meantime, let's call it what it is—the antichrist religion; or as we specifically know it today, Scientism.

> "And when the thousand years are expired, Satan shall be loosed out of his prison, And shall go out to deceive the nations which are in the four corners of the earth, Gog, and Magog, to gather them together to battle: the number of whom is as the sand of the sea. And they went up on the breadth of the earth, and compassed the camp of the saints about, and the beloved city: and fire came down from God out of heaven, and devoured them."

(Revelation 20: 7-9)

THE NEW CITY OF JERUSALEM WILL ONLY EXIST ON A FLAT EARTH

NIMROD'S TOWER WHICH HE AND THE ARCHITECTS of Babel once wickedly endeavored to build, God has promised to accomplish, but this time on His own terms. And yet still to this day the "self-enlightened" humanist desires the complete overthrow of the LORD's throne, either by soliciting access to heaven through his own fabricated merit or altogether imagining an eternal dwelling where God will not so much as lift a finger or sigh if it should bother his perversions. Quite contrarily, the good news of the Word is not our ascent to heaven. Rather, it is God's descent to Earth, where the meek and the righteous humbly await Him. So shall it be according to John's vision of the New Jerusalem (Revelation 21). The many rooms in our Fathers House, prepared by Jesus Christ Himself, are unmistakably observed descending down from Heaven to Earth. And so shall our free access to Him remain forevermore. Amen.

Accordingly, John describes the Holy City as one gigantic cube, measuring 1500 miles at its base, with an equal distance of 1500 miles to its ceiling, and right away the so-called Christian who cares only for what can be explained by his own humanist self-enlightenment and the institutes of academia—particularly as he fractures Scripture to keep with the apostasy of Copernicus and Kepler's "New Astronomy" rather than relying wholly on the literal intent of Holy Writ—has a problem. He will be faced with a terrible dilemma while simply attempting to explain this away as a carefree "prophetic metaphor," because John makes it absolutely clear that the rod is being stretched with the measurements of man.

NASA tells us the Kármán line, which is the unofficial boundary marker of "cosmic infinity," begins only 62 miles above our head, some 90 kilometers, which places almost the entire city of New Jerusalem in a non-gravitational vacuum of outer space. It is here where the temperature abruptly increases, rising at stunning rates for another 62 miles, 124 miles in total height, whereby it begins to level off—speculatively;

although other sources claim it continually rises. While temperatures may vary, the thermosphere can reach as high as 2500 degrees Celsius, or 4532 degrees Fahrenheit!

Let us compare. The oven in your kitchen may reach somewhere around 464°F. A ceramic laboratory oven for jewelers and dentists, which is intended for the melting of gold, can reach just over 2000°F. Temperatures in a blast furnace for melting iron can climb as high as 4000°F. And yet Apollo astronauts were able to slingshot themselves in a tin can around Earth's gravitational pull and catapult through a radiation belt reaching 4532°F and land safely on the moon fifty years ago. NASA has openly admitted that they no longer have the technology to pass the radioactive Van Allen belt. And yet the International Space Station, we are expected to believe, along with a cosmic junkyard of satellites, makes its happy home in the thermosphere.

A globular belief raises further issues. For the Copernican, he must take into consideration the sun, whose employment is no longer required. He is furthermore obliged to acknowledge prophetically what is to come—that being a complete abandonment of Newton's gravity. There are of course other complications, such as the amount of flat surface needed for a foundation of Biblical proportions. If, in his gluttonous embrace of cognitive dissonance—it is a working of his own design—the reality behind such an undertaking does not bend or break him, he shall need to explain how, when he assumes that Earth's ground level is unmeasurably spinning at a thousand miles per hour, with a further revolution of 67,000 miles per hour around the sun as it hooks us into the snares of its gravitational pull, the penthouse inhabitants of New Jerusalem could withstand the thrill of being spun through the vacuum of the thermosphere at an additional several thousand miles per hour!

New Jerusalem is going to be a behemoth Metropolis. Standing directly underneath the city's outer wall, it will likely be impossible to see the very top floor. Even viewing it from 5,000 miles away, the city will appear 130 times larger than our current moon. To appear as the actual size of the moon—this according to NASA's estimates—a citizen of God's coming kingdom would have to stand 160,427 miles away! Of course we simply know this to be impossible, since we currently live on a flat plane, and always will. Space does not exist. I hope the reader will understand, should he shed the skin of his Satanic indoctrination; there will be nowhere on Earth where the New Jerusalem cannot be seen. It is most probable that the city will reach such heights that it towers even above our current glass ceiling—the firmament. Let the spiritual implications of this begin to sink in.

I shall no doubt need to find pause here. In my mind, I can already hear the angry rebuttals. The Copernican will obstinately stomp his feet, grind his teeth, and dutifully proclaim: "This will be a new Heaven and a new Earth! The rule of Newton and the Copernicans does not apply here as it always has before us and even now exists!"

With yet another delirious stomp of the foot and feverish sweat of the brow, the Darwinist also insists on exceptions to the rule of the ape. If he were being honest, he would know the righteous will not senselessly wait around for billions of years while God evolves the new Heaven and Earth into being. By the Spirits own Testimony concerning Himself, creation is instantaneous. The Word speaks, and it is so. And yet he will dutifully proclaim: "This will be a new Heaven and a new Earth! The rule of Darwin does not apply here as it always has before us and even now exists!"

They have neglected their studies—mainly, that the new Earth will be a restoration of what was and currently is, not a completely different creation. The same rules still apply. In Koine Greek, two separate words are translated as new in our English Bible; *neos* and *kainos*. Neos implies "new in time," whereas here, according to John's vision, kainos directs our attention to an Earth which is "new in nature."

The Apostle Paul, when employing kainos to describe a new creation, would have us believe, and rightly so—there is continuity between the old person and the new. We are not two separate individuals, nor are we the dreaded clones of godless Scientism. Rather, we are renovated. God is not fond of discarding that which He has made. He wishes nothing more than to save, not obliterate. This is most evident when Paul wrote:

> "Therefore if any man be in Christ, he is a new [kainos] creature: old things are passed away; behold, all things are become new (2 Corinthians 5:17)."

Similarly, the Apostle Peter would have us believe, and rightly so—that the whole of the Bible, where the breadth of the created order is concerned, directs our faith and hope to one of renovation; same house foundation but new bathroom and kitchen. When speaking before the temple in Jerusalem, Peter advised:

"Repent ye therefore, and be converted, that your sins may be blotted out, when the times of refreshing shall come from the presence of the Lord. And he shall send Jesus Christ, which before was preached unto you: Whom the heaven must receive until the times of restitution of all things, which God hath spoken by the mouth of all his holy prophets since the world began (Acts 3:19-21)."

If I take any further pause, it will be as an end of this discussion. I wish to let the spiritual truths sink in. We will need no further use for the sun because Jesus Christ will be the light of this world, just as it was in the beginning—that being the first four days of creation (Genesis 1). John makes this fact abundantly clear when he writes:

> "And the city had no need of the sun, neither of the
> moon, to shine in it: for the glory of God did lighten it,
> and the Lamb is the light thereof (Revelation 21:23)."

The so-called Christian who wishes to remain a delusional Copernican during his eternal residency on the renovated Earth can only hope that he is not assigned property on the other side of his "globe," which his costly education paid for and which will assuredly always remain in the dark—if his illusion is to remain functional. But I myself am not worried, particularly if my assignment sees me traveling to the furthest ends of the Earth. For the world, you see, is stationary, unmovable on its foundations, as the Bible rightly prescribes, and undeniably flat. Wherever my adventures guide me, even to the outer Antarctic rim of the Earth, I can never be lost. No curvature shall blind my path. The New Jerusalem will always be visible, just as the glorious light of our reigning King, who has relieved the sun of its duty, will forever illuminate the whole of Creation from it.

"Vain Jangling…" THE APOSTLE PAUL CAUGHT UP TO THIRD HEAVEN & HOW TIMOTHY DEALT WITH FIRST-CENTURY "TRUTHERS"

THERE CAN BE NO DOUBT THE APOSTLE PAUL spoke of himself when ascending to the *third* heaven and—knowing what we do now of the Apostle, having run his race in full—we can conclude with full confidence that God chose the right man for the celestial journey. Paul did not think to publish a book about his rapturous crossing, nor quench our tireless and thankless appetites with what he saw and encountered. If Paul were alive today, there would be no attempts at marketing his story to a larger audience; rubbing elbows for a bigger platform; hiring scriptwriters or delivering to Hollywood a special effects heavy narrative and which was sold in theatrical previews as being "based on a true story." And yet, the Apostle described more of heaven than almost anyone gives him credit for—or most care to know. It is the *true* heaven which he himself tasted, and which was penned down in his numerous epistles for the praise or the contempt of the nations. He was handed the glorious doctrine of Christ there, and we should stop to consider how the very foundations of the church have been laid down upon it. Paul's knowledge of divine matters—including our own, if we place our hope and faith in them—comes directly from heaven.

> "I knew a man in Christ above fourteen years ago, (whether in the body, I cannot tell; or whether out of the body, I cannot tell: God knoweth;) such an one caught up to the third heaven." (2 Corinthians 12:2)

The celestial spheres of Plato or Aristotle's geocentric cosmology—and soon thereafter Ptolemy's—which had already griped the entire Scientific world in delusion, was not an option of debate when he spoke of the third heaven *in passing*. Neither was Hipparchus of Nicaea, the father of trigonometry, who had declared the heavenly bodies as infinitely distant some two-centuries earlier. Paul was naturally

691

hearkening us back to Moses; and a few centuries earlier to the Prophet Isaiah, whereas: "I saw also the Lord sitting upon a throne, high and lifted up, and His train filled the temple (Isaiah 6:1)." By declaring the presence of God in the *third*, rather than the seventh or the eighth, which formulated the opposing belief-system of *occult* Science, he spoke unashamedly of Hebrew cosmology.

It is a good thing—at the risk of being marked a "Science denier" by brighter minds—that the Apostle who visited heaven contended for the faith of his fathers. Plato, Aristotle, Ptolemy, and the lot of them were later dismembered by the Copernican Revolution—though Hipparchus, who may be ranked among the greatest scientist that ever lived, also was the product of gross error. In his book, *King's Dethroned* (1922), author Gerrard Hickson writes of Hipparchus and his trigonometry which administered the intellectual minds of Paul's day ("and which is the basis of all the methods of measuring distance which are in modern astronomy today"):

> "The times in which he lived did not provide the conveniences which were necessary for his undertaking, the conditions were altogether impossible, and so it is not at all surprising that he failed to get any triangulation to the stars. As a result, he came to the conclusion that they must be too far off to be measured, and said: '*The heavenly bodies are infinitely distant.*'

> Such was the extraordinary conclusion arrived at by Hipparchus, and that statement of his lies at the root of astronomy, and has led its advocates into an amazing series of blunders from that day to this. The whole future of the science of astronomy was affected by Hipparchus when he said, '*the heavenly bodies are infinitely distant.....*'"

No quarter to the infinitely distant places of Hipparchus-lore and space-mythology was given by the 6th-century Prophet Ezekiel when he wrote of his own vision: "And above the firmament that was over their heads was the likeness of a throne....." (Ezekiel 1:26). *Third* heaven is not merely a spiritual realm. It is fixed upon the *second* heaven—the firmament—and is therefore *physical*. Holding true to the Scripture writers before him was only a natural thing to do, since Paul himself—whether in or out of the body—experienced the very same realm and reality as Isaiah and Ezekiel. Should Paul have concurred with the philosophers of his own day—dismissing this written revelation of the Spirit, in order to do so—he would have derailed his own reputation as a "profane and vain babbler." We need only look at his instructions towards Timothy to find false teachers—perhaps disciples of Plato, Aristotle, Hipparchus, and Eratosthenes—who were attempting to bleed into Christian theology when he wrote to Timothy:

> "Oh, Timothy, keep thou which is committed to thy trust, avoiding profane and vain babblings and oppositions of sciences, falsely so called which some professing have urged concerning the faith (1 Timothy 6:20)."

The Science which these false teachers boasted, wrote the English Baptist minister John Gill, "was not true, solid, spiritual, and saving; it was not an experimental knowledge of the Gospel; it was not the excellent knowledge of Christ, which has eternal life connected with it; it was merely notional and speculative; it was idle, empty, and useless, mere Pagan philosophy, and vain deceit, upon which they formed antitheses, or oppositions and objections to the truths of the Gospel; and even opposed themselves, and the word of God, as well as the faithful ministers of it." We must also be dutiful in recognizing the fact that Paul merely thought to mention *third* heaven in passing. Just as it was with Ezekiel, the Apostle spoke of heaven's cosmology as a footnote to the *true message* which heaven unashamedly declares and which Paul had been dutifully commissioned to affirm. Had Paul fumbled heaven's only saving Gospel and focused his various epistles merely on combating the deceptions of Greek philosophy, or perhaps the *shape* of the Earth, he himself would have become the very "vain babbler" that he adamantly wrote against. We also are not exempt from haughty drivel.

We are warned.

Let me now introduce to you Hymenaeus and Philetus—a contemptible pairing of first-century "Christ followers." As "Truthers" in their own time, they would no doubt be popular on social media today. They even proclaimed Jesus, as so many whimsical provocateurs often do, but with all the added theological baggage of their own artistic licenses. By theorizing that the resurrection of the saints had already happened—perhaps noting eye-witnesses and those who awoke from their tombs at the resurrection of Christ—they doubted the accepted account of a promised future resurrection. They had woken up to the abracadabra of themselves, and had fallen into gross error. Worse, they needed everyone else in the church to wake up to the open-sesame of truth falsely so-called. According to Paul, they were a contagious canker.

"Shun profane and vain babblings for they will increase unto more ungodliness and their word will eat as the canker of whom is Hymenaeus and Philetus who concerning the truth have erred saying that the Resurrection is past already and overthrow the faith of some." (2 Timothy 2:16)

Worse, Hymenaeus had settled into blasphemy. Satan awaited him.

"...of whom is Hymenaeus and Alexander; whom I have delivered unto Satan, that they may learn not to blaspheme." (1 Timothy 1:20)

We are not an Apostle. It is not within our jurisdiction to deliver anyone into Satan's hands, as Gill writes concerning Paul's prerogative, "for the destruction of the flesh; that is, that his body might be shook, buffeted, afflicted, and tortured in a terrible manner; that by this means he might be brought to a sense of his sin, to repentance for it, and make an humble acknowledgment of it: that the spirit may be saved in the day of the Lord Jesus...." But some of us residing here on the furthest outpost of the Lord's church—that is, Flat Earth—may very well feel like Timothy. As Paul's disciple, and later his constant companion and co-worker in preaching, Timothy no doubt wished to carry on with his spiritual father but was besought to "abide still at Ephesus" while the Apostle carried on to Macedonia, "that thou mightest charge some that they teach no other doctrine, neither give heed to fables and endless genealogies, which minister questions, rather than godly edifying which is in faith: so do" (1 Timothy 1:3-4).

We also have been assigned a rather inconvenient task. We must hold fast to sound Biblical doctrine in a land inhabited with habitual conjurers of the awakened self. There is no end to it—the unprofitable talk. We are stranded here on the remotest end of Hadrian's Wall, strangers in a remarkably strange land, where new theological theories abound as a rule of fashion. We labor until the Lord returns while the likes of Hymenaeus and Philetus and Alexander's surround us. The movement which bares this cosmological name is perverse with contagious canker-sores. We must not share the same drinking glass. For the sake of the Gospel, the total abandonment of vain and unprofitable talk is necessary.

If I have failed you—if I have made the most deplorable of errors, bedazzling men with this cosmological knowledge and urging them to make an idol of it, or worse, sculpt it into their *very* gospel—it would be better that a millstone be hanged about my neck, as Jesus would say, and cast into the sea, than that I or anyone should "offend one of these little ones (Matthew 17:1-2)." There is only one *true* Gospel, but there are millions of counterfeits, whatever the shape of the Earth.

Hebrew cosmology is not the Gospel. If we speak of it, we do so *in passing*—*always* in passing. Rather than argue the properties of Earth in proportion to heaven, I implore of you, let us keep to its vocabulary as the Prophets and the Apostle did—always in passing—and rather, tell them *of* heaven.

THANK YOU, OUTHOUSE! (Psalm 91, the KJV, and the Joyous Cosmology)

AN OUTHOUSE IS A USEFUL TOOL FOR THE PROPER DISPOSAL of human waste when no plumbing is made available, but an abominable place to become confidentially affectionate with—or dare I say *fond of.* I can't help but wonder if that little shack atop of the grassy knoll; the initials W.C. for a name; complete with a squatting stool and dreadfully small hole for late-night aiming—both of which were generally caked with several shades and textures of fecal batter, as a rule—still stands. From its hill I could gaze immediately east over the thorny caps of yellow-fever trees, which giraffes often congregated under—often dozens at a time—and to Lake Naivasha, with its legion of hippos, perhaps half a kilometer beyond.

This scene unfolded in the Rift Valley of Kenya, and I can still smell, even now while recounting W.C. two decades later, the nauseating fumes which would arise from its hellish hole in the ground as I lay over it heaving with an inconsolable sickness and trembling from the cold. At 16 years of age and 135 pounds, I was told I had begun to resemble a skeleton. And yet, after ejecting 30-pounds of body weight—there had been at least nine weeks of vomiting, always under the crystalline night sky—the muscle spasms didn't agonize anymore as they had probably intended. I felt no pain. Truth be known, I looked forward to my nights—particularly the intervening moments between vomiting, when I could lie upon the grass gazing up at the glorious girdle of stars.

On a cloudless night there was no hiding from the Milky Way. Its brilliance was simply incommunicable to a teenager who had only familiarized himself with trampling upon sidewalks glazed with stars, all of which blazed for a moment in time and then fell under the shadow of the Hollywood sign. Beyond the hill where W.C. stood, the ghost-like glow of hyena eyes, matched with their whooping-wails, haunted the agonizing yip of zebras they preyed upon. A warthog occasionally bullied a nearby bush. There were occasions when I was unable to leave my tent behind—even to vomit—due to a hippo which might toddle up the hill from Lake Naivasha to idle between myself and the outhouse. And dare I overlook those hunted zebras, which violently stampeded my tent. But the stars! What could I do but worship my Lord who fancied them as blueprints in His mind before the beginning of time? There was this one moment, after the steady current of vomit had steadied, that I listened in to the gruesome gnashing of hippo fangs between two competitors in the nearby lagoon and lifted my eyes to the heavens.

I verbally praised Him for the distant suns nestled within an infinite universe quadrillions of miles away and the plurality of hidden worlds which must have surrounded them. God was guiding me—this I know—so much so that, as I lay there lifting up my voice, God stopped me.

"No, that's not true," He said.

The scolding hurt. What had I said wrong?

Recollections of my childhood returned to me. *This* present girdle of African stars was nothing like my five year-old counterpart admiring the three pale luminaries which Orion's belt offered through the smoggy canopy of Hawthorne, California, a suburb of Los Angeles International Airport. But at least *then* I also heard the Lord's guiding instructions. I recall climbing out of our Plymouth Voyager—the very same model they've got on display now in the Smithsonian—when I recognized God's unexpected yet wholly welcome voice. What I was looking at, if I understood Him right, was something like a sheet or the canvas of a tent pulled over us, and the stars were its chandeliers. Heaven, I was quite convinced in my budding years, was just on the other side of that canvas. If the moon looked as though it simply *hung* there with the grin of a Cheshire cat, it's because little of what I was being otherwise taught was true. All God had to do was peel that covering in the sky—and there would be no more need for a sun.

How do I know it was the Lord instructing me—or in the case of Kenya, disciplining my misguided praise? It's because His guidance corresponded with the written Word. Oh no—*not* the New International Version kept next to my sleeping bag. Naturally, I was rather confused by the contradictions. Why wouldn't the Lord welcome my praise regarding an unseen deluge of galaxies? Problem was I hadn't thought to consider astronomy with the King James Version as my cherished guide—that is, the Textus Receptus, or *Received Text*—and wouldn't for many years to come. I knew nothing concerning the occult pairing of Westcott and Hort and their Vatican approved Codex Sinaiticus and Codex Vaticanus texts, by which all other translations come into being. I knew not the Hebrew, despite a vague familiarity with the word *firmament*. But it did not win the part in my Bible translations.

The New International Version has this to say of Psalm 19:1:

"The heavens declare the glory of God; the **skies** proclaim the work of his hands."

The New Living Translation also pronounced "*skies*," while the ESV declares "*sky above*," and both the NASB and ISV claim "*their expanse*."

The authorized King James Version gets it right. The KJV says "*firmament*."

"The heavens declare the glory of God; and the **firmament** sheweth his handywork (Psalm 19:1 KJV)."

We can thank the translators of the New International Version for altering Scripture itself. Their antagonism towards God's geocentric creation is most evident in Isaiah 38:8, where-as "sunlight" is falsely described as having traveled back ten steps on a "stairway" rather than what actually occurred—the sun *itself* returned ten degrees in the sky.

The King James Bible correctly tells:

"Behold, I will bring again the shadow of the degrees, which is gone down in the sun dial of Ahaz, ten degrees backward. **So the sun returned ten degrees, by which degrees it was gone down** (Isaiah 38:8)."

The New International Version is a product of the Copernican Universe:

"I will **make the shadow cast by the sun go back the ten steps** it has gone down on the stairway of Ahaz. So the **sunlight went back the ten steps** it had gone down (Isaiah 38:8 NIV)."

The NASB also unashamedly states:

"So the sun's shadow went back ten steps...."

In *The Greatest Lie on Earth: Proof That Our World Is Not a Moving Globe*, author Edward Hendrie writes regarding the NIV translators, they "have removed the miracle of the event entirely by stating that the shadow went back ten steps on a stairway, rather than ten degrees on a sundial. A shadow cast by a pillar can go up and then back down steps due to the ordinary travel of the sun across the sky, however, the shadow cast upon a sundial cannot move backwards unless the sun moves backwards."

"No, that's not true," God stopped my prayer in Kenya.

The stars were *not* distant suns nestled within an infinite universe quadrillions of miles away. The three stars of Orion's belt, piercing through the electric glow and smog of Hawthorne, California sprung to mind.

"I'm right *here*."

To the west of the hill where W.C. stood, a handsome Masai, though rather short for his east African ethnicity, operated a dutiful fire. Daniel was his name. The local Masai village, maintained with mud, manure, and a convenient brier-patch, couldn't have been more than two or three kilometers away. Daniel, he never bothered me. But he conscientiously kept watch over the fire—and *me*. I never recall him intervening in my habitual sickness except to gesture with a hand if I felt up to joining his crackling orb of light—wiping whatever bile remained on my lips as I approached—and its ashy glow illuminated a face equally as kind. Even then my guardian rarely spoke unless I initiated conversation. Usually we were content just sitting and listening—star gazing. His English was good—he never brought up the vomit, which must have plagued him with concern—but I preferred listening to his Swahili tongue, if he offered it. There were our adventures during the day to consider. They could be practically comedic at times—chasing down a tribe of baboons who'd run off with cans of food from the storage shed. And then at night he'd captivate me with stories—like the lion he'd killed with only a sharpened stick.

There was of course the *other* lion, which he only thought to mention on the morning *after* it had walked right past W.C. and the tent—paw prints for proof. That lion, by the way, was hunted later in the day. It's crime—eating human.

The stories I could tell.

I can't help but wonder if Daniel entered the ministry—if he this very moment pastors an east African church, as he confessed aspiring to do. His dutiful service to me; managing that little fire near the outhouse on the hill while the Lord guided me in deconstructing the Copernican Universe; is not even quantifiable except by heavenly standards. Actually, I put little thought into those glorious Rift Valley skies until years later—two decades, actually—when the missing pieces of the puzzle finally came together and the *truth* no longer needed to be suppressed. Fact is, the universe became an uncomfortable back-pocket subject. I simply wouldn't—No, I couldn't—give God praise for something so indescribably delightful but which the Lord also rebuked me for doing. God is so good and loving—and patient—that He would think to correct me in error, even over a great chasm of time. By His providence alone I finally opened up a King James Bible and discovered the joyous cosmology.

It read:

"The heavens declare the glory of God....."

Even now I can close my eyes and recognize Daniel's kind face flushed with the heat of ember. A spear adorns his arm. The whooping-wails of hyenas still advertise the hunt. And if I look up, it is the firmament of His power which garnishes my gaze.